An Introduction to the Intel Family of Microprocessors

A HANDS-ON APPROACH UTILIZING THE 8088 MICROPROCESSOR

An Introduction to the Intel Family of Microprocessors

A HANDS-ON APPROACH UTILIZING THE 8088 MICROPROCESSOR

JAMES L. ANTONAKOS
Broome Community College

Merrill, an imprint of
Macmillan Publishing Company
New York

Maxwell Macmillan Canada
Toronto

Maxwell Macmillan International
New York Oxford Singapore Sydney

This one is for Heather and Jeff,
with all my love.

Cover photo: Phillip A. Harrington/Fran Heyl Associates
Editor: Dave Garza
Production Editor: Sharon Rudd
Art Coordinator: Lorraine Woost
Cover Designer: Robert Vega
Production Buyer: Patricia A. Tonneman
Illustrations: Academy ArtWorks, Inc.

Intel 386™ is a trademark of Intel Corporation.

This book was set in Century Schoolbook by York Graphic Services, Inc. and was printed and bound by R.R. Donnelley & Sons Company. The cover was printed by Phoenix Color Corp.

Macmillan Publishing Company
866 Third Avenue
New York, NY 10022

Macmillan Publishing Company is part of the
Maxwell Communication Group of Companies.

Maxwell Macmillan Canada, Inc.
1200 Eglinton Avenue East, Suite 200
Don Mills, Ontario M3C 3N1

Library of Congress Cataloging-in-Publication Data

Antonakos, James.
    An introduction to the Intel family of microprocessors : a hands-on approach
utilizing the 8088 microprocessor / James L. Antonakos.
        p.   cm.
    Includes index.
    ISBN 0-675-22173-0
    1. Intel 8088 (Microprocessor)   I. Title.
QA76.8.I2924A58   1992
004.165—dc20
                                                                    92-19845
                                                                    CIP

Printing: 1   2   3   4   5   6   7   8   9   Year: 3   4   5   6   7

MERRILL'S INTERNATIONAL SERIES IN ENGINEERING TECHNOLOGY

INTRODUCTION TO ENGINEERING TECHNOLOGY

Pond, *Introduction to Engineering Technology, 2nd Edition,* 0-02-396031-0

ELECTRONICS TECHNOLOGY

Electronics Reference

Adamson, *The Electronics Dictionary for Technicians,* 0-02-300820-2
Berlin, *The Illustrated Electronics Dictionary,* 0-675-20451-8
Reis, *Becoming an Electronics Technician: Securing Your High-Tech Future,* 0-02-399231-X

DC/AC Circuits

Boylestad, *DC/AC: The Basics,* 0-675-20918-8
Boylestad, *Introductory Circuit Analysis, 6th Edition,* 0-675-21181-6
Ciccarelli, *Circuit Modeling: Exercises and Software, 2nd Edition,* 0-02-322455-X
Floyd, *Electric Circuits Fundamentals, 2nd Edition,* 0-675-21408-4
Floyd, *Electronics Fundamentals: Circuits, Devices, and Applications, 2nd Edition,* 0-675-21310-X
Floyd, *Principles of Electric Circuits, 4th Edition,* 0-02-338501-4
Floyd, *Principles of Electric Circuits: Electron Flow Version, 3rd Edition,* 0-02-338531-6
Keown, *PSpice and Circuit Analysis,* 0-675-22135-8
Monssen, *PSpice with Circuit Analysis* 0-675-21376-2
Tocci, *Introduction to Electric Circuit Analysis, 2nd Edition,* 0-675-20002-4

Devices and Linear Circuits

Berlin & Getz, *Fundamentals of Operational Amplifiers and Linear Integrated Circuits,* 0-675-21002-X
Berube, *Electronic Devices and Circuits Using MICRO-CAP II,* 0-02-309160-6
Berube, *Electronic Devices and Circuits Using MICRO-CAP III,* 0-02-309151-7
Bogart, *Electronic Devices and Circuits, 3rd Edition,* 0-02-311701-X
Tocci, *Electronic Devices: Conventional Flow Version, 3rd Edition,* 0-675-21150-6
Floyd, *Electronic Devices, 3rd Edition,* 0-675-22170-6
Floyd, *Electronic Devices: Electron Flow Version,* 0-02-338540-5
Floyd, *Fundamentals of Linear Circuits,* 0-02-338481-6
Schwartz, *Survey of Electronics, 3rd Edition,* 0-675-20162-4
Stanley, *Operational Amplifiers with Linear Integrated Circuits, 2nd Edition,* 0-675-20660-X
Tocci & Oliver, *Fundamentals of Electronic Devices, 4th Edition,* 0-675-21259-6

Digital Electronics

Floyd, *Digital Fundamentals, 4th Edition,* 0-675-21217-0
McCalla, *Digital Logic and Computer Design,* 0-675-21170-0
Reis, *Digital Electronics through Project Analysis* 0-675-21141-7
Tocci, *Fundamentals of Pulse and Digital Circuits, 3rd Edition,* 0-675-20033-4

Microprocessor Technology

Antonakos, *The 68000 Microprocessor: Hardware and Software Principles and Applications, 2nd Edition,* 0-02-303603-6
Antonakos, *The 8088 Microprocessor,* 0-675-22173-0
Brey, *The Advanced Intel Microprocessors,* 0-02-314245-6
Brey, *The Intel Microprocessors: 8086/8088, 80186, 80286, 80386, and 80486: Architecture, Programming, and Interfacing, 2nd Edition,* 0-675-21309-6
Brey, *Microprocessors and Peripherals: Hardware, Software, Interfacing, and Applications, 2nd Edition,* 0-675-20884-X
Gaonkar, *Microprocessor Architecture, Programming, and Applications with the 8085/8080A, 2nd Edition,* 0-675-20675-6
Gaonkar, *The Z80 Microprocessor: Architecture, Interfacing, Programming, and Design, 2nd Edition,* 0-02-340484-1
Goody, *Programming and Interfacing the 8086/8088 Microprocessor: A Product- Development Laboratory Process,* 0-675-21312-6
MacKenzie, *The 8051 Microcontroller,* 0-02-373650-X
Miller, *The 68000 Family of Microprocessors: Architecture, Programming, and Applications, 2nd Edition,* 0-02-381560-4
Quinn, *The 6800 Microprocessor,* 0-675-20515-8
Subbarao, *16/32 Bit Microprocessors: 68000/68010/68020 Software, Hardware, and Design Applications,* 0-675-21119-0

Electronic Communications

Monaco, *Introduction to Microwave Technology,* 0-675-21030-5
Monaco, *Preparing for the FCC Radio-Telephone Operator's License Examination,* 0-675-21313-4
Schoenbeck, *Electronic Communications: Modulation and Transmission, 2nd Edition,* 0-675-21311-8
Young, *Electronic Communication Techniques, 2nd Edition,* 0-675-21045-3
Zanger & Zanger, *Fiber Optics: Communication and Other Applications,* 0-675-20944-7

Microcomputer Servicing

Adamson, *Microcomputer Repair,* 0-02-300825-3
Asser, Stigliano, & Bahrenburg, *Microcomputer Servicing: Practical Systems and Troubleshooting, 2nd Edition,* 0-02-304241-9
Asser, Stigliano, & Bahrenburg, *Microcomputer Theory and Servicing, 2nd Edition,* 0-02-304231-1

Programming

Adamson, *Applied Pascal for Technology*,
0-675-20771-1
Adamson, *Structured BASIC Applied to Technology, 2nd
Edition*, 0-02-300827-X
Adamson, *Structured C for Technology*, 0-675-20993-5
Adamson, *Structured C for Technology (with disk)*,
0-675-21289-8
Nashelsky & Boylestad, *BASIC Applied to Circuit
Analysis*, 0-675-20161-6

Instrumentation and Measurement

Berlin & Getz, *Principles of Electronic Instrumentation
and Measurement*, 0-675-20449-6
Buchla & McLachlan, *Applied Electronic Instrumentation
and Measurement*, 0-675-21162-X
Gillies, *Instrumentation and Measurements for Electronic
Technicians, 2nd Edition*, 0-02-343051-6

Transform Analysis

Kulathinal, *Transform Analysis and Electronic Networks
with Applications*, 0-675-20765-7

Biomedical Equipment Technology

Aston, *Principles of Biomedical Instrumentation and
Measurement*, 0-675-20943-9

Mathematics

Monaco, *Essential Mathematics for Electronics
Technicians*, 0-675-21172-7
Davis, *Technical Mathematics*, 0-675-20338-4
Davis, *Technical Mathematics with Calculus*,
0-675-20965-X

INDUSTRIAL ELECTRONICS/
INDUSTRIAL TECHNOLOGY

Bateson, *Introduction to Control System Technology, 4th
Edition*, 0-02-306463-3
Fuller, *Robotics: Introduction, Programming, and Projects*,
0-675-21078-X
Goetsch, *Industrial Safety: In the Age of High Technology*,
0-02-344207-7
Goetsch, *Industrial Supervision: In the Age of High
Technology*, 0-675-22137-4
Horath, *Computer Numerical Control Programming of
Machines*, 0-02-357201-9
Hubert, *Electric Machines: Theory, Operation, Applications,
Adjustment, and Control*, 0-675-20765-7
Humphries, *Motors and Controls*, 0-675-20235-3
Hutchins, *Introduction to Quality: Management, Assurance,
and Control*, 0-675-20896-3
Laviana, *Basic Computer Numerical Control Programming*
0-675-21298-7

Reis, *Electronic Project Design and Fabrication, 2nd Edition*,
0-02-399230-1
Rosenblatt & Friedman, *Direct and Alternating Current
Machinery, 2nd Edition*, 0-675-20160-8
Smith, *Statistical Process Control and Quality Improvement*,
0-675-21160-3
Webb, *Programmable Logic Controllers: Principles and
Applications, 2nd Edition*, 0-02-424970-X
Webb & Greshock, *Industrial Control Electronics, 2nd Edition*,
0-02-424864-9

MECHANICAL/CIVIL TECHNOLOGY

Keyser, *Materials Science in Engineering, 4th Edition*,
0-675-20401-1
Kraut, *Fluid Mechanics for Technicians*, 0-675-21330-4
Mott, *Applied Fluid Mechanics, 3rd Edition*, 0-675-21026-7
Mott, *Machine Elements in Mechanical Design, 2nd Edition*,
0-675-22289-3
Rolle, *Thermodynamics and Heat Power, 3rd Edition*,
0-675-21016-X
Spiegel & Limbrunner, *Applied Statics and Strength of
Materials*, 0-675-21123-9
Wolansky & Akers, *Modern Hydraulics: The Basics at Work*,
0-675-20987-0
Wolf, *Statics and Strength of Materials: A Parallel Approach to
Understanding Structures*, 0-675-20622-7

DRAFTING TECHNOLOGY

Cooper, *Introduction to VersaCAD*, 0-675-21164-6
Goetsch & Rickman, *Computer-Aided Drafting with AutoCAD*,
0-675-20915-3
Kirkpatrick & Kirkpatrick, *AutoCAD for Interior Design and
Space Planning*, 0-02-364455-9
Kirkpatrick, *The AutoCAD Book: Drawing, Modeling, and
Applications, 2nd Edition*, 0-675-22288-5
Lamit and Lloyd, *Drafting for Electronics, 2nd Edition*,
0-02-367342-7
Lamit and Paige, *Computer-Aided Design and Drafting*,
0-675-20475-5
Maruggi, *Technical Graphics: Electronics Worktext, 2nd
Edition*, 0-675-21378-9
Maruggi, *The Technology of Drafting*, 0-675-20762-2
Sell, *Basic Technical Drawing*, 0-675-21001-1

TECHNICAL WRITING

Croft, *Getting a Job: Resume Writing, Job Application Letters,
and Interview Strategies*, 0-675-20917-X
Panares, *A Handbook of English for Technical Students*,
0-675-20650-2
Pfeiffer, *Proposal Writing: The Art of Friendly Persuasion*,
0-675-20988-9
Pfeiffer, *Technical Writing: A Practical Approach*,
0-675-21221-9
Roze, *Technical Communications: The Practical Craft*,
0-675-20641-3
Weisman, *Basic Technical Writing, 6th Edition*, 0-675-21256-1

PREFACE

The rapid advancement of microprocessors into our everyday affairs has both simplified and complicated our lives. Whether we use a computer in our everyday job, or come in contact with one elsewhere, most of us have used a computer at one time or another. Most people know that a microprocessor is lurking somewhere inside the machinery, but what a microprocessor is, and what it does, remains a mystery.

PURPOSES OF THE BOOK

This book is intended to help remove the mystery concerning the 8088 microprocessor, through detailed coverage of its hardware and software and examples of many different applications. Some of the more elaborate applications are visible to us. A large collection of personal computers (IBM, Zenith, Compaq, and others) utilize 8088-based architecture, as do some popular commercial video games, electronic engravers, and speech recognition systems. Industry and the government have also adopted the 8088 for many commercial and military applications as well.

The book is intended for 2- or 4-year electrical engineering, engineering technology, and computer science students. Professional people, such as engineers and technicians, will also find it a handy reference. The material is intended for a one-semester course in microprocessors. Prior knowledge of digital electronics, including combinational and sequential logic, decoders, memories, Boolean algebra, and operations on binary numbers, is required. This presumes knowledge of standard computer related terms, such as RAM, EPROM, TTL, and so forth. Some prior experience with microprocessors is helpful, but not necessary.

OUTLINE OF COVERAGE

For those individuals who have no prior knowledge of microprocessors, Chapter 1, Microprocessor-Based Systems, is a good introduction to the microprocessor, how it functions internally and how it is used in a small system. Chapter 1 is a study of the overall operation of a microprocessor-based system, and includes a section on integrated circuits commonly found in such systems. For historical curiosity, Appendix D is included as a review—or an introduction—to the 8085 CPU, the 8-bit forerunner of the 8088. Some programming examples are included to familiarize you with the 8085.

Chapter 2, An Introduction to the 8088, highlights the main features of the 8088. Data types, addressing modes, and instructions are surveyed. Other processors in the 8088 family are examined as well.

Chapter 3, Software Details of the 8088, provides the foundation for all programming in the remaining chapters. The 8088's instruction set and addressing modes are covered in detail, with over 50 examples provided to help the student grasp the material. A number of simple programming applications are also presented, to lay the groundwork for additional programming in Chapters 5, 6, 10, and 11.

Chapter 4 covers interrupt processing. The basic sequence of an interrupt is covered, as are multiple interrupts, special interrupts, and interrupt service routines. The instructor may choose to cover this chapter after Chapter 6 in order to get right to the programming examples.

Chapter 5, Running Machine Language Programs on a Personal Computer, shows the reader how to create new, executable .EXE and .COM programs, how to single-step through them with the DEBUG facility, and in general explains the basic operation of DOS on the personal computer. Some examples are provided for those who wish to experiment with their own 8088-based computers.

The first real programming efforts are found in Chapter 6, An Introduction to Programming the 8088. Numerous programming examples are included, showing how the 8088 performs routine functions involving binary and BCD mathematics, string operations, data table manipulation, and control applications. Instruction timing is also covered. Each program is written in such a way that its operation may be grasped quickly. Most examples, however, leave much room for improvement. The improvements are deliberately left for the student. The end-of-chapter problems require modifications or additions to existing routines, and the creation of new ones. Chapter 6 was written in this way to challenge the student into writing his or her own code.

The hardware operation of the 8088 is covered in Chapter 7, Hardware Details of the 8088. All CPU pins are discussed, as are timing diagrams, the difference between minmode and maxmode operation, the Personal Computer Bus Standard, and two chips that are essential to 8088-based systems: the 8284 clock generator and the 8288 bus controller.

Chapter 8, Memory System Design, covers the details needed to design an operational RAM and EPROM-based memory system for the 8088. Static and dynamic RAMs, EPROMs, DMA, and full and partial address decoding are covered.

The I/O system is covered in Chapter 9, I/O System Design. In this chapter the difference between the processor's memory space and port space is covered, as are the techniques needed to design port address decoders. Two 8085-based peripherals are covered: the 8255 parallel interface adapter and the 8251 UART, with 8088 interfacing and programming examples provided.

Programming with 8088 Peripherals is the subject of Chapter 10. In this chapter, three peripherals designed to interface with the 8088 are examined. These peripherals implement interval timing, interrupt control, and floating-point operations. Programming and interfacing is discussed for each peripheral, with specific examples.

Many textbooks rarely cover hardware and software with an equal amount of detail. This book was written to give equal treatment to both, culminating in a practical exercise: *building and programming your own single-board computer!* Chapter 11, Building a Working 8088 System, is included to give students a chance to design, build, and program their own 8088-based computers. The system contains 8KB of EPROM, 8KB of RAM, a serial I/O device, a parallel I/O device, and 8-bit D/A and A/D converters. Future memory expansion is built in. The hardware is designed first, followed by design of the software monitor program.

Some books choose to explain the operation of a commercial system, such as the SDK-86. This approach is certainly worthwhile, but does not give the student the added advantage of knowing *why* certain designs were used. The hardware and software designs in Chapter 11 are sprinkled with many questions, which are used to guide the design towards its final goal.

The single-board computer presented in Chapter 11 can be easily wire-wrapped in a short period of time (some students have constructed a working computer in seven days), directly from the schematics provided in the chapter. It is reasonable to say that most students can build a working system in one semester.

USES OF THE BOOK

Due to the information presented, some chapters are much longer than others. Even so, it is possible to cover certain sections of selected chapters out of sequence, or to pick and choose sections from various chapters. Chapter 3 could be covered in this way, with emphasis placed on additional addressing modes, or groups of instructions, at a rate deemed appropriate by the instructor. Also, some sections in Chapter 10 may be skipped over, depending on the instructor's preference for peripherals. Some instructors may wish to cover hardware (Chapters 7 through 9) before programming (Chapters 3 through 6). There is no reason this cannot be done.

To aid the instructor, answers to the end-of-chapter study questions are not included in the text, but are provided in a detailed solutions manual. The solutions manual is designed in such a way that solutions to all odd-numbered questions are grouped together, followed by solutions to all even-numbered questions. This allows the instructor to release selected odd-only or even-only answers to students, while retaining others for testing purposes. Leaving the answers out of the text encourages students to make a real attempt to solve the study questions, without being able to work backwards from the supplied answers.

The appendix to this text is used to present a full list of 8088 instructions, their allowed addressing modes, flag usage, and instruction times. In addition, the appendix contains data sheets for three 8088-based peripherals, the 8259 interrupt controller, the 8254 interval timer, and the 8087 floating point coprocessor. This avoids the need for second references. Also included is a historical review of the 8085 microprocessor.

In summary, over 170 illustrations and 30 different applications are used to give the student sufficient exposure to the 8088. The added benefit of Chapter 11, where a working system is developed, makes this book an ideal choice for a student wishing to learn about microprocessors. The old saying, "8-bit machines are easier to learn on," is out-dated now. The instruction sets of the newer 16-bit machines, though more complex, are easier to learn and code with. Furthermore, even though this book deals only with the 8088 family, the serious microprocessor student should also be exposed to other CPUs as well. But to try to cover two or more different microprocessors in one text does not do either justice. For this reason, all attention is paid to the 8088 family, and not to other CPUs.

ACKNOWLEDGMENTS

I would like to thank everyone at Macmillan, especially my editor, Dave Garza, his assistant, Suzanne Murchland, and my production supervisor, Sharon Rudd.

The following individuals contributed many helpful comments during the writing, and I am grateful for their advice: Michael J. Horn, Ward Technical College; Douglas Hunter, Texas State Technical Institute; Charles Javens, Haywood Community College; Robert Laquerre, New England Institute of Technology at Palm Beach; Lyle McCurdy, California State Polytechnic University; Yusaf Motiwala, Prairie View A & M; Richard Rouse, DeVry Institute of Technology; and Roger Rowe, Ferris State University.

CONTENTS

CHAPTER

1

Microprocessor-Based Systems

Objectives

In this chapter you will learn about:

- The block diagram of a microprocessor-based system and the function of each section

- The processing cycle of a microprocessor

- The way software is used to initialize hardware and peripherals

- The history of the microprocessor and of the different generations of computers

- Some of the integrated circuits used in microprocessor-based systems

1.1   INTRODUCTION

The invention of the microprocessor has had a profound impact on many aspects of our lives, since today even the most mundane chores are being accomplished under its supervision—something that allows us more time for other productive endeavors. Even a short list of the devices utilizing the microprocessor shows how dependent we have become on it:

1. Pocket calculators
2. Digital watches (some with calculators built in)
3. Automatic tellers (at banks and food stores)
4. Smart telephones
5. Compact disk players
6. Home security and control devices
7. Realistic video games

8. Talking dolls and other toys

9. VCRs

10. Home computers

The purpose of this chapter is to show how the microprocessor is used as a master controller in a small system. While no specific hardware or software will be presented, we will see what types of hardware functions are most desirable to include in a small system and what jobs must be performed by the software to control the hardware. Section 1.2 covers the block diagram of a microprocessor-based system and explains each functional unit. Section 1.3 reviews the basic operation of a microprocessor. Section 1.4 discusses the hardware and software requirements of a small microprocessor control system. Section 1.5 shows how the microprocessor has evolved over time, from the initial 4-bit machines to today's 16- and 32-bit processors. Finally, Section 1.6 presents a number of special logic gates well suited for use in a microprocessor-based system.

1.2   SYSTEM BLOCK DIAGRAM

Any microprocessor-based system must of necessity have some standard elements such as memory, timing, and input/output (I/O). Depending on the application, other exotic circuitry may be necessary as well. Analog-to-digital (A/D) converters and their counterpart, digital-to-analog (D/A) converters, interval timers, math coprocessors, complex interrupt circuitry, speech synthesizers, and video display controllers are just a few of the special sections that may also be required. Figure 1.1 depicts a block diagram of a system containing some standard circuitry and functions normally used.

As the figure shows, all components communicate via the **system bus.** The system bus is composed of the processor address, data, and control signals. The **central processing unit (CPU)** is the heart of the system, the master controller of all operations that can be performed. The CPU executes instructions that

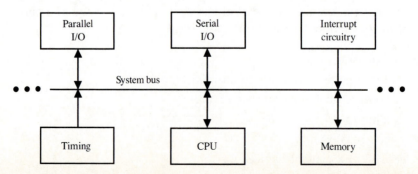

FIGURE 1.1   Standard block diagram of a microprocessor-based system

are stored in the **memory** section. For the sake of future expansion, the system bus is commonly made available to the outside world (through a special connector). Devices may then be added easily as the need arises. Commercial systems have predefined buses that accomplish this. All devices on the system bus must communicate with the processor, usually within a tightly controlled period of time. The **timing** section governs all system timing and thus is really responsible for the proper operation of all system hardware. The timing section usually consists of a crystal oscillator and timing circuitry (counters designed to produce the desired frequencies) set up to operate the processor at its specified clock rate. Using a high-frequency crystal oscillator and dividing it down to a lower frequency provides for greater stability. Figure 1.2 shows the distribution of timing signals throughout the microprocessor-based system. The timing section supplies timing signals for a number of different sections.

The CPU section consists of a microprocessor and the associated logic circuitry required to enable the CPU to communicate with the system bus. These logic elements may consist of data and address bus drivers, a bus controller to generate the correct control signals, and possibly a math coprocessor. **Coprocessors** are actually microprocessors themselves; their instruction set consists mainly of simple instructions for transferring data and complex instructions for performing a large variety of mathematical operations. Coprocessors perform these operations at very high clock speeds with a great deal of precision (80-bit results are common). In addition to the basic add/subtract/multiply/divide operations, coprocessors are capable of finding square roots, logarithms, a host of trigonometric functions, and more.

The actual microprocessor used depends on the complexity of the task that will be controlled or performed by the system. Simple tasks require nothing more complicated than an 8-bit CPU. A computerized cash register would be a good example of this kind of system. Nothing more complicated than binary coded decimal (BCD) addition and subtraction—and possibly some record keeping—is needed. But for something as complex as a flight control computer for an aircraft or a digital guidance system for a missile, a more powerful 16- or 32-bit microprocessor must be used.

The **memory** section usually has two components: **read-only memory (ROM)** and **random access memory (RAM).** Some systems may be able to

FIGURE 1.2   Distribution of timing signals in a small system

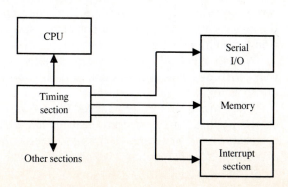

work properly without RAM, but all require at least a small amount of ROM. The ROM is included to provide the system with its intelligence, which is ordinarily needed at start-up (power-on) to configure or initialize the peripherals, and sometimes to help recover from a catastrophic system failure (such as an unexpected power failure). Some systems use the ROM program to download the main program into RAM from a larger, external system, such as a personal computer (PC) or a mainframe computer. In any event, provisions are usually made for adding additional ROM as the need arises.

There are three types of RAM. For small systems that do not process a great deal of data, the choice is static RAM. Static RAM is fast and easy to interface but comes in small sizes of 32 kilobytes (KB) or less as of this writing. Larger memory requirements are usually met by using dynamic RAM, a different form of memory that has high density (256K bits per chip or more) but that unfortunately requires numerous refreshing cycles to retain the stored data. Even so, dynamic RAM is the choice when large amounts of data must be stored, as in a system gathering seismic data at a volcano or in one receiving digitized video images from a satellite.

Both static and dynamic RAM lose their information when power is turned off, which may cause a problem in certain situations. Previous solutions involved adding battery backup circuitry to the system to keep the RAMs supplied with power during an outage. But batteries can fail, so a better method was needed. Thus came the invention of **nonvolatile memory (NVM),** which is memory that retains its information even when power is turned off. NVM comes in small sizes and therefore is used to store only the most important system variables in the event of a power outage.

We will not consider other storage media such as disks or tape, since they require complex hardware and software to operate and are not required in most control applications.

With a microprocessor used in control application there will be times when the system must respond to special external circumstances. For example, a power failure on a computer-controlled assembly line requires immediate attention by the system, which must contain software designed to handle the unexpected event. The event actually *interrupts* the processor from its normal program execution in order to service the unexpected event. The system software is designed to handle the power-fail interrupt in a certain way and then return to the main program. An interrupt, then, is a useful way to grab the processor's attention, get it to perform a special task, and then resume execution from the point where it left off.

Not all types of interrupts are unexpected. Many are used to provide systems with useful features, such as real-time clocks, multitasking capability, and fast input/output operations.

The interrupt circuitry needed from system to system will vary depending on the application. A system used for keeping time only has to use a single interrupt line connected to a timing source. A more complex system, such as an assembly line controller, which may need to monitor multiple sensors, switches, and other items, may require many different prioritized interrupts and would therefore need more complex interrupt circuitry.

Some systems may require serial I/O for communication with an operator's console or with a host computer. In Figure 1.3 we see how a small system might communicate with other devices or systems via serial communication. While this type of communication is slow, it has the advantage of simplicity: Only two wires (for receive and transmit) plus a ground are needed. Serial communication is easily adapted for use in fiber-optic cables. Parallel I/O, on the other hand, requires more lines (at least eight) but has the advantage of being very fast. A special parallel operation called **direct memory access (DMA)** is used to transfer data from a hard disk to a microcomputer's memory. Other uses for parallel I/O involve reading switch information, controlling indicator lights, and transferring data to A/D and D/A converters and other types of parallel devices.

All of these sections have their uses in a microprocessor-based system. Whether or not they are actually utilized depends on the designer and the application.

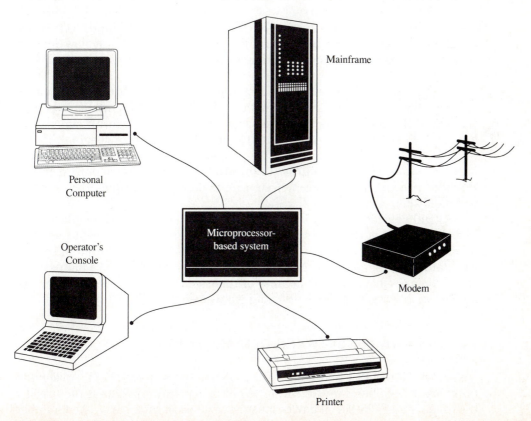

FIGURE 1.3   Serial communication possibilities in a small system

1.3 MICROPROCESSOR OPERATION

No matter how complex microprocessors become, they will still follow the same pattern of operations during program execution: endless fetch, decode, and execute cycles. During the fetch cycle the processor loads an instruction from memory into its internal instruction register. Some advanced microprocessors load more than one instruction into a special buffer to decrease program execution time. The idea is that while the microprocessor is decoding the current instruction, other instructions can be read from memory into the instruction **cache,** a special type of internal high-speed memory. In this fashion the microprocessor performs two jobs at once, thus saving time.

During the decode cycle the microprocessor determines what type of instruction has been fetched. Information from this cycle is then passed to the execute cycle. To complete the instruction, the execute cycle may need to read more data from memory or write results to memory.

While these cycles are proceeding, the microprocessor is also paying attention to other details. If an interrupt signal arrives during execution of an instruction, the processor usually latches onto the request, holding off on interrupt processing until the current instruction finishes execution. The processor also monitors other signals such as WAIT, HOLD, or READY inputs. These are usually included in the architecture of the microprocessor so that slow devices, such as memories, can communicate with the faster processor without loss of data.

Most microprocessors also include a set of control signals that allow external circuitry to take over the system bus. In a system where multiple processors share the same memory and devices, these types of control signals are necessary to resolve **bus contention** (two or more processors needing the system bus at the same time). Multiple-processor systems are becoming more popular now as we continue to strive toward faster execution of our programs. **Parallel processing** is a term often used to describe multiple-processor systems and their associated software.

Special devices called **microcontrollers** are often used in simple control systems because of their many features. Microcontrollers are actually souped-up microprocessors with built-in features such as RAM, ROM, interval timers, parallel I/O ports, and even A/D converters. Microcontrollers are not used for really big systems, however, because of their small instruction sets. Unfortunately, we have yet to get everything we want on a single chip!

1.4 HARDWARE/SOFTWARE REQUIREMENTS

We saw earlier that it is necessary to have at least some ROM in a system to take care of peripheral initialization. What type of initialization is required by the peripherals? The serial device must have its baud rate, parity, and number of data and stop bits programmed. Parallel devices must be configured because most allow the direction (input or output) of their I/O lines to be programmed in many different ways. It is then necessary to set the direction of these I/O lines when power is first applied. For a system containing a digital-to-analog converter it may be important to output an initial value required by the external hardware. Since we can never assume that correct conditions exist at power-on, the microprocessor is responsible for establishing them.

Suppose a certain system contains a video display controller. Start-up software must select the proper screen format and initialize the video memory so that an intelligent picture (possibly a menu) is generated on the screen of the display. If the system uses light-emitting diode (LED) displays or alphanumeric displays for output, they must be properly set as well. High-reliability systems may require that memory be tested at power-on. While this adds to the complexity of the start-up software and the time required for initialization, it is a good practice to follow. Bad memory devices will certainly cause a great deal of trouble if they are not identified.

Other systems may employ a special circuit called a **watchdog monitor.** The circuit operates like this: During normal program execution the watchdog monitor is disabled. Should the program veer from its proper course, the monitor will automatically reset the system. A simple way to make a watchdog monitor is to use a binary counter, clocked by a known frequency. If the counter is allowed to increment up to a certain value, the processor is automatically reset. The software's job, if it is working correctly, is to make sure that the counter never reaches this count. A few simple logic gates can be used to clear the counter under microprocessor control, possibly whenever the CPU examines a certain memory location.

For flexibility, the system may have been designed to download its main program from a host system. If this is the case, the system software will be responsible for knowing how to communicate with the host and place the new program into the proper memory locations. To guarantee that the correct program is loaded, the software should also perform a running test on the incoming data, requesting the host to retransmit portions of the data whenever it detects an error.

Sometimes preparing for a power-down is as important as doing the start-up initialization. A power supply will quite often supply voltage in the correct operating range for a few milliseconds after the loss of AC. It is during these few milliseconds that the processor must execute the shutdown code, saving important system data in nonvolatile RAM or doing whatever is necessary for a proper shutdown. If the system data can be preserved, it may be possible to continue normal execution when power is restored.

For systems that will be expanded in the future, the system bus must be made available to the outside world. To protect the internal system hardware, all signals must be properly buffered. This involves using tristate buffers or similar devices to isolate the internal system bus from the bus available to the external devices. Sometimes optoisolators are used to completely separate the internal system signals from the external ones. The only connection in optoisolators is a beam of light, which makes them ideal when electrical isolation is required.

Figure 1.4 sums up all of these concepts with an expanded block diagram of a microprocessor-based control system. Notice once again that all devices in the system communicate with the CPU via the system bus.

1.5 EVOLUTION OF MICROPROCESSORS

We have come a long way since the early days of computers, when ENIAC (for Electronic Numerical Integrator and Computer) was state of the art and occupied thousands of feet of floor space. Constructed largely of vacuum tubes, it was slow, prone to breakdown, and performed a limited number of instructions. Even so, ENIAC ushered in what was known as the **first generation** of computers.

Today, thanks to advances in technology, we have complete computers that fit on a piece of silicon no larger than your fingernail and that far outperform ENIAC.

When the transistor was invented, computers shrank in size and increased in power, leading to the **second generation** of computers. **Third-generation** computers came about with the invention of the integrated circuit, which allowed hundreds of transistors to be packed on a small piece of silicon. The transistors were connected to form logic elements, the basic building blocks of digital computers. With third-generation computers we again saw a decrease in size and increase in computing power. Machines like the 4004 and 8008 by Intel found some application in simple calculators, but they were limited in power and addressing capability. When improvements in integrated circuit technology enabled us to place *thousands* of transistors on the same piece of silicon, computers really began to increase in power. This new technology, called large-scale integration (LSI), is even faster than the previous medium- and small-scale integration (MSI and SSI) technologies, which dealt with only tens or hundreds of transistors on a chip. LSI technology has created the **fourth generation** of computers that we use today. An advanced form of LSI technology, VLSI, meaning very-large-scale integration, is also being used to increase processing power.

The first microprocessors that became available with third-generation computers had limited instruction sets and thus restricted computing abilities. Although they were suitable for use in electronic calculators, they simply did not have the power needed to operate more complex systems, such as guidance systems or scientific applications. Even some of the early fourth-generation microprocessors had limited capabilities because of the lack of addressing modes and instruction types. Eight-bit machines like the 8080, Z80, and 6800 were indeed more advanced than previous microprocessors, but they still did not possess multiply and divide instructions. How frustrating and time consuming to have to write a program to do these operations when needed!

Within the last decade microprocessor technology has improved tremendously. Sixteen-bit processors can now multiply and divide, operate on many different data types (4-, 8-, 16-, and 32-bit numbers), and address *millions* of

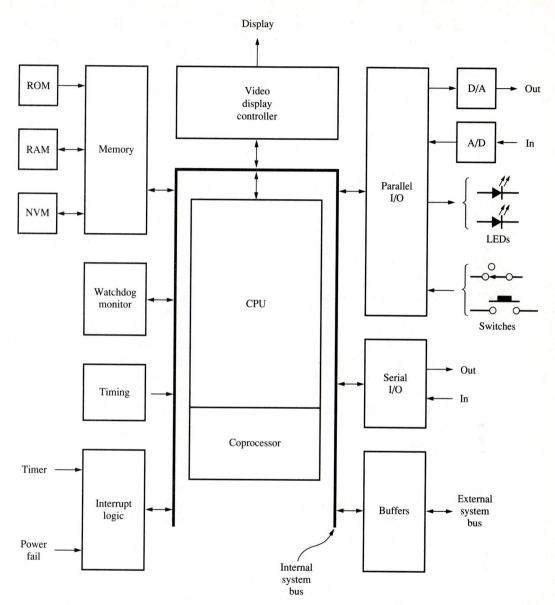

FIGURE 1.4 Expanded block diagram of a microprocessor-based system

bytes of information. Processors of the 1970s were limited to 64KB, a small amount of memory by today's standards.

Each new microprocessor to hit the market boasts a fancier instruction set and faster clock speed, and indeed our needs for faster and better processors keep growing. A new technology called RISC (for reduced instruction set computer) has recently gained acceptance. This technology is based on the fact that most microprocessors utilize only a small portion of their entire instruction set. By designing a machine that uses only the more common types of instructions, processing speed can be increased without the need for a significant advance in integrated circuit technology.

Why the need for superfast machines? Consider a microprocessor dedicated to displaying three-dimensional color images on a video screen. Rotating the three-dimensional image around an imaginary axis in real time (in only a few seconds or less) may require millions or even billions of calculations. A slow microprocessor would not be able to do the job.

Eventually we will see fifth-generation computers. The whole artificial intelligence movement is pushing toward that goal, with the desired outcome being the production of a machine that can think. Until then we will have to make the best use of the technology we have available.

1.6   SPECIAL GATES FOR MICROCOMPUTER USE

Unfortunately, we cannot simply throw a CPU, memory chips, and a handful of peripherals together and come up with a working computer. Other chips are needed to control the system timing and support communication between the peripherals and the processor. In this section we will examine some of the most common integrated circuits used in the design of a microprocessor-based system. Since most of the available microprocessors are designed for TTL (transistor transistor logic) compatibility, we will examine TTL integrated circuits only. You are encouraged to keep a TTL data book handy as you read this section.

The Octal Buffer

Figure 1.5 shows the schematic diagram of a commercial 74LS244 octal buffer. This chip is very useful in many ways. It can be used to buffer address lines and control the flow of information onto a data bus. When a system is designed with multiple memory devices, all of which require address and data lines, the

FIGURE 1.5   The 74LS244 octal buffer

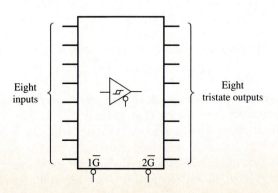

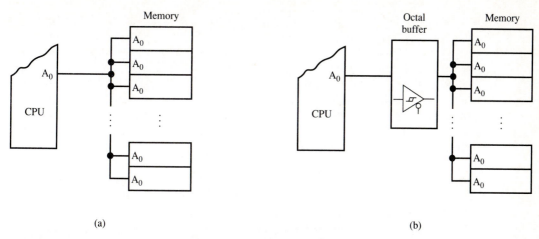

FIGURE 1.6 Microprocessor address line: (a) cannot drive required number of memory devices; (b) drives all memory devices via octal buffer

fan-out of the microprocessor's output lines can easily be exceeded. Having a CPU address line drive three or four inputs is not unreasonable, but trying to drive twenty or twenty-five inputs with an unbuffered output will certainly not work. This is because of the output current limitation of the processor's signal lines; most CPUs cannot supply more than a few mA. The 74LS244 is designed to correct this problem. Each of its outputs is able to sink 24 mA, more than enough to satisfy our design needs.

The octal buffer is placed *between* the CPU and the memory chips (or peripherals), as we can see in Figure 1.6. This design actually serves two purposes. It not only provides the necessary drive capability to the CPU address lines, but also serves to isolate the CPU from the system bus. If we consider a system that will have other devices (or processors) using its system bus, the host CPU can be easily disconnected by tristating its octal buffers.

The Octal Bus Transceiver

The 74LS245 is an octal bus transceiver. Figure 1.7 shows that this device is used to buffer signals in two directions, making it suitable for use in buffering a bidirectional data bus. The transceiver is controlled by two inputs: $\overline{EN}$* (enable) and DIR (direction). If $\overline{EN}$ is high, the transceiver is tristated in both directions and will not pass data either way. When $\overline{EN}$ is low, data is passed in the direction specified by DIR.

Normally the CPU's R/$\overline{W}$ line is used to control the direction of data through the transceiver. When R/$\overline{W}$ is high, the 74LS245 passes data into the processor. When R/$\overline{W}$ is low, data is output from the processor.

---

*The overbar in $\overline{EN}$ is used to show that the asserted (active) state of this signal is low. EN would be an active high signal.

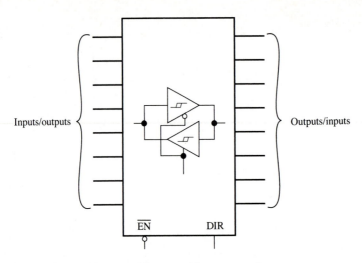

FIGURE 1.7   The 74LS245 octal bus transceiver

The 74LS245's 24-mA drive capability on each output makes it ideal for driving the CPU's bidirectional data bus.

The Octal D-Type Flip-Flop

Figure 1.8 shows the schematic of a 74LS273 octal D-type flip-flop. This device is very useful when constructing 8-bit output ports (or 16-bit ports by using two devices). All eight flip-flops share a common clock and clear line. This makes it easy to either capture a byte of data or clear all outputs at the same time. When only 8 bits must be latched, the 74LS273 is a perfect choice, being cheaper and easier to use than a full-blown parallel device.

FIGURE 1.8   The 74LS273 octal D-type flip-flop

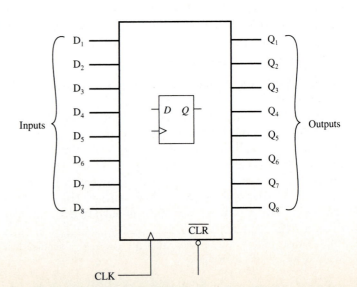

FIGURE 1.9   The 74LS138 3- to
8-line decoder

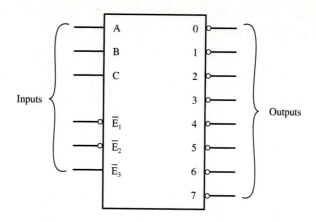

The 3- to 8-Line Decoder

The 74LS138 3- to 8-line decoder is very useful when designing memory circuitry. Figure 1.9 shows the schematic for this device, which activates one of
its outputs at a time, depending on the binary code present at the inputs. When
used in a memory circuit, the A, B, and C inputs will be connected to three
upper address lines (with the lower address lines going directly to the ROM
and RAM chips). The outputs will be connected to the $\overline{CE}$ inputs of the memory
chips. This will cause different memory devices—or maybe none—to be enabled, depending on the condition of the upper address lines.

The Priority Encoder

The 74LS148 8- to 3-line priority encoder, pictured in Figure 1.10, finds application in interrupt circuitry. Quite often a system will be presented with a
number of interrupt signals. What should the processor do when more than one
interrupt signal is active at the same time? The 74LS148 solves the problem by
prioritizing the interrupts. Normally a single input will go to the low state,
causing the A_0 through A_2 outputs to represent the binary code of the input

FIGURE 1.10   The 74LS148
priority encoder

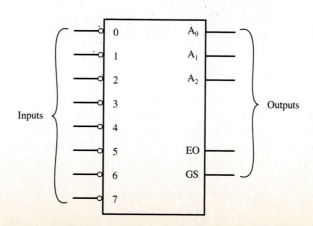

FIGURE 1.11   The 74LS180
parity generator/checker

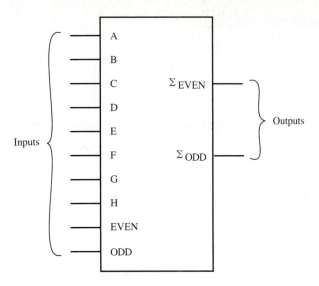

that became active. If two or more inputs go low at the same time, the outputs
will represent the number of the highest active input (for example, this would
be input 5, if 5, 4, and 2 are all active).

The Parity Generator/Checker

Figure 1.11 shows the schematic diagram of the 74LS180 even/odd parity gen-
erator/checker. This device is most useful in memory circuitry that requires
high reliability. Instead of storing just 8-bit values in each memory location,
9 bits are used, with one dedicated to the parity of the stored data. When the
CPU writes data to a memory location, the 74LS180 generates the parity bit
for the data, which is then stored. When the processor reads the same location,
the parity of the 8 data bits is recomputed by the 74LS180 and compared with
the parity bit that was stored. A **parity error** results when the two bits fail to
match. This type of memory failure is usually catastrophic because there is no
way to recover the good data.

Parity generators/checkers are also used in serial transmission circuitry,
and are usually contained within the transmitter/receiver sections.

1.7   SUMMARY

In this chapter we have examined the operation of microprocessor-based systems. We saw that the complexity of the hardware, and thus of the software, is
a function of the type of application. Through the use of many different types of
peripherals, such as parallel and serial devices, analog-to-digital converters,
and others, a system can be tailored to perform almost any job. We also re-
viewed the basic fetch, decode, and execute cycle of a microprocessor, and ex-

amined the other duties the CPU performs, one of which was interrupt handling.

We also covered the initialization requirements of peripherals used in a microprocessor-based system, and why it is necessary to perform initialization in the first place. Other types of hardware and software requirements were also examined, such as the use of a watchdog monitor and a nonvolatile memory.

Four different generations of computers were presented and their differences highlighted. Current computing trends dealing with parallel processing and artificial intelligence were also introduced.

Finally, we looked at a number of different TTL gates that for various reasons find their way into many microcomputer designs.

STUDY QUESTIONS

1. Make a list of 10 additional products containing microprocessors that we use everyday.
2. Why would an oscillator circuit utilizing a resistor-capacitor network to control its frequency be unstable and unsuitable for use in a microprocessor-based system?
3. Speculate on the uses for timing signals in the serial I/O, memory, and interrupt sections.
4. Why do coprocessors enhance the capabilities of an ordinary CPU?
5. Draw a block diagram for a computerized cash register. The hardware should include a numerical display, a keyboard, and a compact printer.
6. What kind of initialization software would be required for the cash register of Question 5?
7. What would be the difference in system RAM requirements for two different cash registers, one without record keeping and one with?
8. What type of information should be stored in NVM during a power failure in a system designed to control navigation in an aircraft?
9. What types of interrupts may be required in a control system designed to monitor all doors, windows, and elevators in an office complex?
10. Name some advantages of downloading the main program into a microprocessor-based system. Are there any disadvantages?
11. Suppose that a number of robots making up a portion of an automobile assembly line are connected to a master factory computer. What kinds of information might be passed between the factory computer and the microprocessors controlling each robot?
12. A certain hard disk transfers data at the rate of 8 million bits per second. Explain why the CPU would not be able to perform the transfer itself, thus requiring the use of a DMA controller.
13. What kinds of problems arise if two devices attempt to use the system bus at the same time?
14. Explain how two microprocessors might be connected so that they share the same memory and peripherals.
15. Suppose that three microprocessors are used in the design of a new video game containing color graphics and complex sounds. How might each microprocessor function?

16. Why did processing speed increase with each new generation of computers?
17. List five different applications that might need the fast computing power of a RISC-based machine.
18. One reason 16-bit processors are faster than 8-bit machines is because they operate on twice as many data bits at the same time. Why doesn't everyone using an 8-bit machine just switch over to a 16-bit processor?
19. An upward-compatible microprocessor is one that can execute instructions from earlier models. How would a designer of the new CPU implement upward compatibility?
20. Explain how an octal buffer may be used to load information from a set of switches onto the CPU data bus.
21. Show how an octal latch could be used to control a 7-segment display (including the decimal point).
22. Why use a 74LS244 instead of a 74LS245 to buffer a CPU's address lines?
23. How can two groups of three different signals each be connected to a priority encoder, so that one group has a priority of 6 and the other a priority of 3?
24. Why would a parity checker only recognize single, or odd-numbered, bit errors?
25. What advantages does a microcontroller have over a microprocessor? What disadvantages does it have?

2

An Introduction to the 8088 Microprocessor

Objectives

In this chapter you will learn about:

* The register set of the 8088

* The addressing capabilities and data types that may be used

* The different addressing modes and instruction types available

* The usefulness of interrupts

* Some of the hardware and software advantages of the 8088

* Some of the differences between the 8088 and the 8086/186/286/386 microprocessors

2.1 INTRODUCTION

The introduction of the 8088 into the arena of microprocessors came at a time when we were reaching the limits of what an 8-bit machine could do. With their restricted instruction sets and addressing capabilities, it was obvious that something more powerful was needed. The 8088 contains instructions previously unheard of in 8-bit machines, a very large address space, many different addressing modes, and an architecture that easily lends itself to multiprocessing or multitasking (running many programs simultaneously).

In this chapter we will examine the features of the 8088 microprocessor and its cousins, the 8086, 80186, 80286, and 80386™. Only basic material will be covered, leaving the hardware and software details for upcoming chapters. From reading this chapter you should become aware that the 8088 is a machine with many possibilities.

Section 2.2 covers the software model of the 8088. Section 2.3 provides a brief functional description of the processor. Section 2.4 introduces the numerous registers contained within the 8088, followed by a brief discussion of data organization, instruction types, and addressing modes in Sections 2.5, 2.6, and 2.7. Interrupts are the subject of Section 2.8, followed by a summary of the advantages of the 8088 in Section 2.9. The remaining sections, 2.10 through 2.13, deal with the upward-compatible architectures found in the 8086, 80186, 80286, and 80386.

2.2 THE SOFTWARE MODEL OF THE 8088

The 8088 microprocessor contains four data registers, referred to as AX, BX, CX, and DX. All are 16 bits wide, and may be split up into two halves of 8 bits each. Figure 2.1 shows how each half is referred to by the programmer. Five other 16-bit registers are available for use as pointer or index registers. These registers are the *stack pointer* (SP), *base pointer* (BP), *source index* (SI), *destination index* (DI), and *instruction pointer* (IP). None of the five may be divided up in a manner similar to the data registers.

A major difference between the 8088 and many other CPUs on the market has to do with the next group of registers, the *segment registers*. Four segment registers are used by the processor to control all accesses to memory and I/O, and must be maintained by the programmer. The *code segment* (CS) is used during instruction fetches, the *data segment* (DS) is most often used by default

FIGURE 2.1 Software model of the 8088

	15	8 7	0	
AX	AH	AL		Accumulator
BX	BH	BL		Base
CX	CH	CL		Count
DX	DH	DL		Data

	15	0
SP	Stack pointer	
BP	Base pointer	
S I	Source index	
D I	Destination index	
I P	Instruction pointer	

	15	0
CS	Code segment	
DS	Data segment	
S S	Stack segment	
ES	Extra segment	

15	0
Flags	

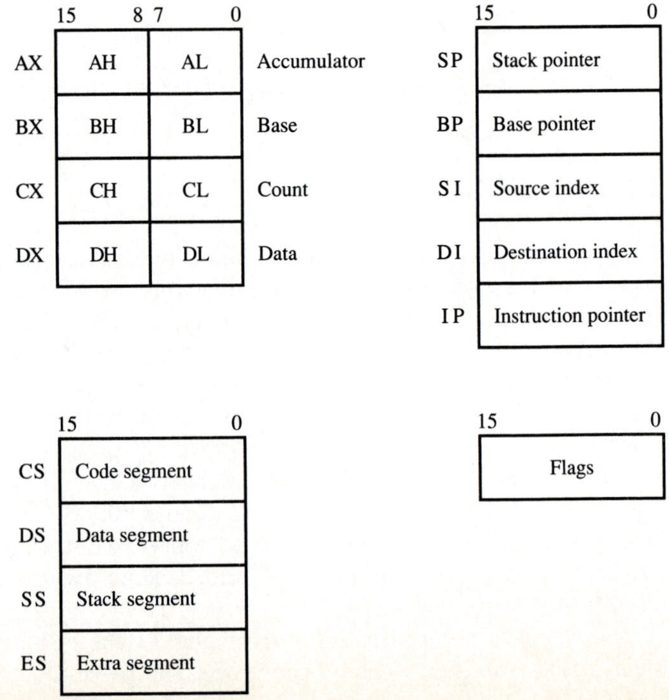

when reading or writing data, the *stack segment* (SS) is used during stack operations such as subroutine calls and returns, and the *extra segment* (ES) is used for anything the programmer wishes. All segment registers are 16 bits long. Section 2.4 explains in more detail how the segment registers are used by the 8088.

Lastly, a 16-bit *flag register* is used to indicate the results of arithmetic and logical instructions. Included are zero, parity, sign, and carry flags, plus a few others. Together, these fourteen registers make an impressive set!

2.3 A FUNCTIONAL DESCRIPTION OF THE 8088

The 8088 microprocessor incorporates some interesting architectural features that deserve mentioning. As Figure 2.2 shows, the processor is internally divided into two functional units, the *execution unit* and the *bus interface unit*. This division of operations had never been handled in such a way in a microprocessor before; it was designed to reduce execution time.

FIGURE 2.2 Block diagram of the 8088 CPU architecture

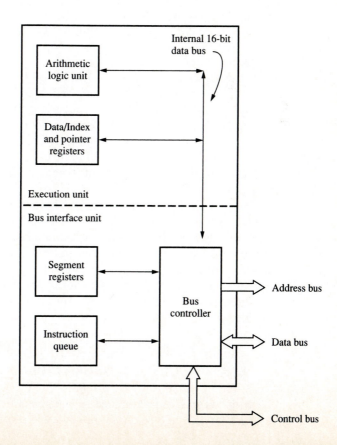

The Execution Unit

The execution unit (EU) houses the *arithmetic logic unit* (ALU), which is responsible for executing program instructions provided to it by the bus interface unit (BIU), which has fetched the instructions from memory. Communication is provided by an internal 16-bit data bus. The ALU also maintains the processor flag register. All data, index, and pointer registers are also contained in the execution unit. All instructions and data arrive at the execution unit via the BIU. Notice from Figure 2.2 that the EU has no external connections.

The Bus Interface Unit

In order to increase program efficiency, it is necessary to first understand the inefficiency that goes along with most single-processor systems. In these systems, endless fetch, decode, and execute cycles are performed. The processor fetches an instruction from memory, decodes it, and then executes it. While the processor is busy with this fetch-decode-execute cycle, the address and data busses remain idle. Only when an instruction calls for a memory or I/O access do the busses leave their inactive state. Thus, we have **idle** address and data busses, even during full-speed operation of the system. The 8088 eliminates a good deal of this idle time by utilizing a bus interface unit. The bus interface unit is responsible for performing all memory and I/O accesses. During an instruction fetch, the BIU will pass the instruction on to the execution unit, and then **prefetch** more instructions! An internal queue (buffer) called an instruction queue is designed to hold the next four bytes of code in memory following the current instruction. When the execution unit is ready for the next byte (data or instruction), it pulls it from the instruction queue. The BIU then prefetches the next byte from memory and places it in the instruction queue so that the queue is always full. This internal cooperation between the execution and bus interface units results in increased execution efficiency, since the processor is capable of executing and fetching instructions at the same time.

The only time this scheme does not work is when the current instruction is a jump, subroutine call, or return instruction. In such cases the instructions prefetched by the BIU are incorrect and are discarded. The next instruction is then fetched from the new address and the queue reloaded. Also, whenever the current instruction needs to use the bus (for a memory or I/O access), the BIU completes any prefetching it was doing and handles the bus request from the EU. Overall, however, efficiency is improved by the instruction queue and bus interface unit.

2.4   8088 PROCESSOR REGISTERS

The 16-bit registers introduced in Section 2.2 are combined in an interesting way to form the necessary 20-bit address required by memory. If you recall, there were no 20-bit registers shown in the software model. How then does the 8088 generate 20-bit addresses?

Segment Registers

The four segment registers, CS, DS, SS, and ES, are all 16-bit registers that are controlled by the programmer. A segment, as defined by Intel, is a 64K-byte block of memory, starting on any 16-byte boundary. Thus, 00000, 00010, 00020, 20000, 8CE90, and E0840 are all examples of valid segment addresses. The information contained in a segment register is combined with the address contained in another 16-bit register to form the required 20-bit address. Figure 2.3 shows how this is accomplished. In this example, the code segment register contains A000 and the instruction pointer contains 5F00. The 8088 forms the 20-bit address A5F00 in the following way: first, the data in the code segment register is shifted four bits to the left. This has the effect of turning A000 into A0000. Then the contents of the instruction pointer are added, giving A5F00. All external addresses are formed in a similar manner, with one of the four segment registers used in each case. As we will see in Chapter 3, each segment register has a default usage. The 8088 knows which segment register to use to form an address for a particular application (instruction fetch, stack operation, and so on). The 8088 also allows the programmer to specify a different segment register when generating some addresses.

General Purpose Registers

The seven general purpose registers available to the programmer can be used in many different ways, and they also have some specific roles assigned to them. For instance, the accumulator (AX) is used in multiply and divide operations and also in instructions that access I/O ports. The count register (CX) is used as a counter in loop operations, providing up to 65536 passes through a loop before termination. The lower half of CX, the 8-bit CL register, is also used as a counter in shift/rotate operations. Data register DX is used in multiply and divide operations and also as a pointer when accessing I/O ports. The last two registers are the source index and destination index (referred to as SI and DI). These registers are used as pointers in string operations.

FIGURE 2.3   Generating a 20-bit address in the 8088

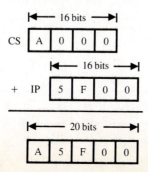

Even though these registers have specific uses, they may be used in many other ways simply as general purpose registers, allowing for many different 16-bit operations.

Flag Register

Figure 2.4 shows the nine flag assignments within the 16-bit flag register. The flags are divided into two groups: **control** flags and **status** flags. The control flags are IF (*interrupt enable flag*), DF (*direction flag*), and TF (*trap flag*). The status flags are CF (*carry flag*), PF (*parity flag*), AF (*auxiliary carry flag*), ZF (*zero flag*), SF (*sign flag*), and OF (*overflow flag*). Most of the instructions that require the use of the ALU affect the flags. Remember that the flags allow ALU instructions to be followed by conditional instructions.

2.5   8088 DATA ORGANIZATION

One of the differences between the Intel line of microprocessors and those made by other manufacturers is Intel's way of storing 16-bit numbers in memory. A method that began with the 8080 and has been used on all upgrades, from the 8085 to the 80386, is a technique called **byte-swapping.** This technique is sometimes confusing for those unfamiliar with it, but becomes clear after a little exposure. When a 16-bit number must be written into the system's byte-wide memory, the low-order eight bits are written into the first memory location and the high-order eight bits are written into the second location. Figure 2.5 shows how the two bytes that make up the 16-bit hexadecimal number 2055 are written into locations 18000 and 18001, with the low-order eight bits (55) going into the first location (18000). This is what is known as byte-swapping. The lower byte is always written first, followed by the high byte. Byte-swapping is one of the most significant differences between Intel processors and other machines, such as Motorola's 68000 (which does not swap bytes).

Reading the 16-bit number out of memory is performed automatically by the processor with the aid of certain instructions. The 8088 knows that it is reading the lower byte first and puts it in the correct place. Programmers that manipulate data in memory must remember to use the proper practice of byte-swapping or discover that their programs do not give the correct, or expected, results.

15   0

-	-	-	-	OF	DF	IF	TF	SF	ZF	-	AF	-	PF	-	CF

FIGURE 2.4   8088 flag register

FIGURE 2.5 Word storage using
Intel byte-swapping

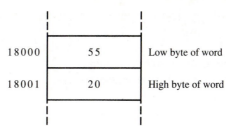

2.6 8088 INSTRUCTION TYPES

The 8088's instruction set is composed of six main groups of instructions. A discussion of instruction specifics will be postponed until Chapter 3. Examining the instructions briefly here, however, will give a good overall picture of the capabilities of the processor.

Data Transfer Instructions

Fourteen data transfer instructions are used to move data between registers, memory, and the outside world. Also, some instructions directly manipulate the stack, while others may be used to alter the flags.

The data transfer instructions are:

MOV	Move byte or word (two bytes) to register/memory
PUSH	Push word onto stack
POP	Pop word off stack
XCHG	Exchange byte or word
XLAT	Translate byte
IN	Input byte or word from port
OUT	Output byte or word to port
LEA	Load effective address
LDS	Load pointer using data segment
LES	Load pointer using extra segment
LAHF	Load AH from flags
SAHF	Store AH into flags
PUSHF	Push flags onto stack
POPF	Pop flags off stack

Arithmetic Instructions

Twenty instructions make up the arithmetic group. Byte and word operations are available on almost all instructions. A nice addition are the instructions that multiply and divide. Previous microprocessors did not include these instructions, forcing the programmer to write subroutines to perform multiplication and division when needed. Addition and subtraction of both binary and BCD operands is also allowed.

The arithmetic instructions are:

ADD	Add byte or word
ADC	Add byte or word plus carry
INC	Increment byte or word by one
AAA	ASCII adjust for addition
DAA	Decimal adjust for addition
SUB	Subtract byte or word
SBB	Subtract byte or word and carry
DEC	Decrement byte or word by one
NEG	Negate byte or word
CMP	Compare byte or word
AAS	ASCII adjust for subtraction
DAS	Decimal adjust for subtraction
MUL	Multiply byte or word (unsigned)
IMUL	Integer multiply byte or word
AAM	ASCII adjust for multiply
DIV	Divide byte or word (unsigned)
IDIV	Integer divide byte or word
AAD	ASCII adjust for division
CBW	Convert byte to word
CWD	Convert word to doubleword

Bit Manipulation Instructions

Thirteen instructions capable of performing logical, shift, and rotate operations are contained in this group. Many common Boolean operations (AND, OR, NOT) are available in the logical instructions. These, as well as the shift and rotate instructions, operate on bytes or words. No single-bit operations are available.

The bit manipulation instructions are:

NOT	Logical NOT of byte or word
AND	Logical AND of byte or word
OR	Logical OR of byte or word
XOR	Logical Exclusive-OR of byte or word

TEST	Test byte or word
SHL	Logical shift left byte or word
SAL	Arithmetic shift left byte or word
SHR	Logical shift right byte or word
SAR	Arithmetic shift right byte or word
ROL	Rotate left byte or word
ROR	Rotate right byte or word
RCL	Rotate left through carry byte or word
RCR	Rotate right through carry byte or word

String Instructions

Nine instructions are included to specifically deal with string operations. String operations simplify programming whenever a program must interact with a user. User commands and responses are usually saved as ASCII strings of characters, which may be processed by the proper choice of string instruction.

The string instructions are:

REP	Repeat
REPE (REPZ)	Repeat while equal (zero)
REPNE (REPNZ)	Repeat while not equal (not zero)
MOVS	Move byte or word string
MOVSB (MOVSW)	Move byte string (word string)
CMPS	Compare byte or word string
SCAS	Scan byte or word string
LODS	Load byte or word string
STOS	Store byte or word string

Program Transfer Instructions

This group of instructions contains all jumps, loops, and subroutine (called **procedure**) and interrupt operations. The great majority of jumps are **conditional,** testing the processor flags before execution.

The program transfer instructions are:

CALL	Call procedure (subroutine)
RET	Return from procedure (subroutine)
JMP	Unconditional jump
JA (JNBE)	Jump if above (not below nor equal)
JAE (JNB)	Jump if above or equal (not below)

JB (JNAE)	Jump if below (not above nor equal)
JBE (JNA)	Jump if below or equal (not above)
JC	Jump if carry set
JE (JZ)	Jump if equal (zero)
JG (JNLE)	Jump if greater (not less nor equal)
JGE (JNL)	Jump if greater or equal (not less)
JL (JNGE)	Jump if less (not greater nor equal)
JLE (JNG)	Jump if less or equal (not greater)
JNC	Jump if no carry
JNE (JNZ)	Jump if not equal (not zero)
JNO	Jump if no overflow
JNP (JPO)	Jump if no parity (parity odd)
JNS	Jump if no sign
JO	Jump if overflow
JP (JPE)	Jump if parity (parity even)
JS	Jump if sign
LOOP	Loop unconditional
LOOPE (LOOPZ)	Loop if equal (zero)
LOOPNE (LOOPNZ)	Loop if not equal (not zero)
JCXZ	Jump if CX equals zero
INT	Interrupt
INTO	Interrupt if overflow
IRET	Return from interrupt

Processor Control Instructions

This last group of instructions perform small tasks that sometimes have profound effects on the operation of the processor. Many of the instructions manipulate the flags.

The processor control instructions are:

STC	Set carry flag
CLC	Clear carry flag
CMC	Complement carry flag
STD	Set direction flag
CLD	Clear direction flag
STI	Set interrupt enable flag
CLI	Clear interrupt enable flag
HLT	Halt processor

WAIT   Wait for $\overline{\text{TEST}}$ pin activity

ESC   Escape to external processor

LOCK   Lock bus during next instruction

NOP   No operation

In Chapter 3 we will examine each of the 8088's instructions in detail, and see many examples of how they are used.

2.7   8088 ADDRESSING MODES

The 8088 offers the programmer a wide number of choices when referring to a memory location. Many believe that the number of **addressing modes** contained in a microprocessor is a measure of its power. If that is so, the 8088 should be counted among the most powerful processors. Many of the addressing modes are used to generate a **physical address** in memory. Recall from Figure 2.3 that a 20-bit address is formed by the sum of two 16-bit address registers. One of the four segment registers will always supply the first 16-bit address. The second 16-bit address is formed by a specific addressing mode operation. We will see that there are a number of different ways the second part of the address may be generated.

Addressing Space

All addressing modes eventually create a physical address that resides somewhere in the 00000 to FFFFF addressing space of the processor. Figure 2.6 shows a brief memory map of the 8088's addressing space, which is broken up into 16 blocks of 64K bytes each. Each 64KB block is called a **segment.** A segment contains all the memory locations that can be reached when a particular segment register is used. For example, if the data segment contains 0000, then addresses 00000 through 0FFFF can be generated when using the data segment. If, instead, register DS had contained 1800, then the range of addresses becomes 18000 through 27FFF. It is important to see that a segment can begin on *any* 16-byte boundary. So, 00000, 00010, 00020, 035A0, 10800, and CCE90 are all acceptable starting addresses for a segment.

Altogether, 1,048,576 bytes can be accessed by the processor. This is commonly referred to as one **megabyte.** Small areas of the addressing space are reserved for special operations. At the very high end of memory, locations FFFF0 through FFFFF are assigned the role of storing the initial instruction used after a RESET operation. At the low end of memory, locations 00000 through 003FF are used to store the addresses for all 256 interrupts (though not all are commonly used in actual practice). This dedication of addressing space is common among processor manufacturers, and may force designers to conform to specific methods or techniques when building systems around the 8088. For instance, EPROM is usually mapped into high memory, so that the starting execution instructions will always be there at power-on.

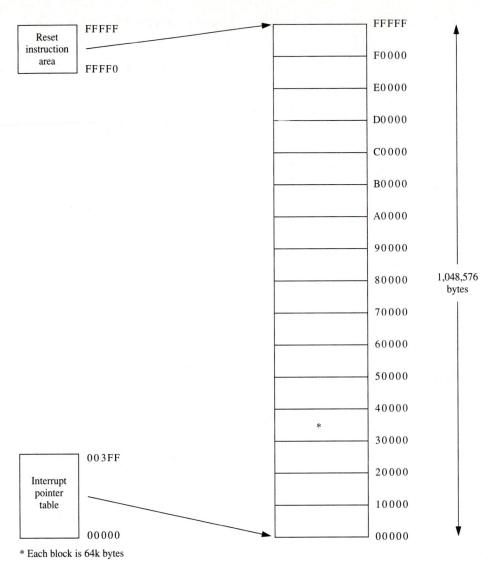

FIGURE 2.6   Addressing space of the 8088

Addressing Modes

The simplest addressing mode is known as **immediate.** Data needed by the processor is actually included in the instruction. For example:

```
MOV  CX,1024
```

contains the immediate data value 1024. This value is converted into binary and included in the code of the instruction.

When data must be moved between registers, **register** addressing is used. This form of addressing is very fast, since the processor does not have to access external memory (except for the instruction fetch). An example of register addressing is:

        ADD   AL,BL

where the contents of registers AL and BL are added together, with the result stored in register AL. Notice that both operands are names of internal 8088 registers.

   The programmer may refer to a memory location by its specific address by using **direct** addressing. Two examples of direct addressing are:

        MOV   AX,[3000]

and

        MOV   BL,COUNTER

In each case, the contents of memory are loaded into the specified registers. The first instruction uses square brackets to indicate that a memory address is being supplied. Thus, 3000 and [3000] are allowed to have two different meanings. The second instruction uses the symbol name COUNTER to refer to memory. COUNTER must be defined somewhere else in the program for it to be used this way.

   When a register is used within the square brackets, the processor utilizes **register indirect** addressing. For example:

        MOV   BX,[SI]

instructs the processor to use the 16-bit quantity stored in the SI (source index) register as a memory address. A slight variation produces **indexed** addressing, which allows a small offset value to be included in the memory operand. Consider this example:

        MOV   BX,[SI + 10]

The location accessed by the instruction is the sum of the SI register and the offset value 10.

   When the register used is the base pointer (BP), **based** addressing is employed. This addressing mode is especially useful when manipulating data in large tables or arrays. An example of based addressing is:

        MOV   CL,[BP + 4]

Including an index register (SI or DI) in the operand produces **based-indexed** addressing. The address is now the sum of the base pointer and the index register. An example might be:

        MOV   [BP + DI],AX

When an offset value is also included in the operand, the processor uses **based-indexed with displacement** addressing. An example is:

```
MOV  DL,[BP + SI + 2]
```

It is easily seen that the 8088 intends the base pointer to be used in many different ways.

Other addressing modes are used when string operations must be performed.

The processor is designed to access I/O ports, as well as memory locations. When **port** addressing is used, the address bus contains the address of an I/O port, instead of a memory location. I/O ports may be accessed two different ways. The port may be specified in the operand field, as in:

```
IN  AL,80H
```

or indirectly, via the address contained in register DX:

```
OUT  DX,AL
```

Using DX allows a port range from 0000 to FFFF, or 65,536 individual I/O port locations. Only 256 (00 to FF) are allowed when the port address is included as an immediate operand.

All of these addressing modes will be covered again in detail in Chapter 3.

2.8 8088 INTERRUPTS

The 8088 microprocessor is capable of responding to 256 different types of interrupts. These interrupts are generated in a number of different ways. External hardware interrupts are caused by activating the processors NMI and INTR signals. NMI is a **nonmaskable interrupt** and cannot be ignored by the CPU. INTR is a maskable interrupt which the processor may choose to ignore depending on the state of an internal interrupt enable flag.

Internal interrupts are caused by execution of an INT instruction. INT is followed by an interrupt number from 0 to 255, giving the programmer the option of generating any number of specific interrupts during program execution. We will see later that machines based on the 8088 that contain a software disk operating system (DOS) have very specific functions assigned to certain interrupts (INT 21H for example) that allow the user to read the keyboard, write text to the screen, control disk drives, and so forth.

Some interrupts are generated internally by the processor itself. *Divide error* is one example. This interrupt is caused when division by zero is detected in the execution unit (during execution of the IDIV or DIV instructions). The processor can also generate single step interrupts at the end of every instruction if a certain flag called the trap flag is set. Another internal interrupt is INTO (interrupt on overflow).

All interrupts utilize a dedicated table in memory for storage of their interrupt service routine (ISR) addresses. The table is called an **interrupt pointer table,** and is 1024 bytes long, enough storage space for 256 4-byte entries. Since an ISR address occupies four bytes of storage, the table holds addresses for all 256 interrupts. Each ISR address is composed of a 2-byte CS value and a 2-byte instruction pointer address. Thus, if the table entry for a type-0 interrupt (divide error) was CS:0100 and IP:0400, the divide error ISR code would have to be located at physical address 01400.

Interrupt processing will be covered in detail in Chapter 4.

2.9 ADVANTAGES OF THE 8088

It is useful to compare the characteristics of one microprocessor with another to determine any advantages or disadvantages that may exist between them. The comparison may lead to a choice of one CPU over the other at the beginning of the design of a new system. In this section we will compare the 8088 to the 8085 microprocessor covered in Appendix D. Since the 8088 is a 16-bit machine we expect it to outperform the 8-bit 8085.

The 8085 has seven internal registers (A, B, C, D, E, H, and L), each of which is 8 bits wide. The 8088 also has seven internal registers (AX, BX, CX, DX, BP, SI, and DI), all of which are 16 bits wide. Though these registers have specific uses assigned to them for different instructions, they can all be used for general purpose operations as well. Both processors have stack pointers and program counters too, but only the 8088 has four segment registers that assist in accessing memory. The larger size of the 8088's registers provides additional flexibility for the programmer.

When we compare the addressing space of each processor, we see that the 8085 operates within a 64KB range via its 16-bit address bus. The 20-bit address bus of the 8088 can access *sixteen* 64KB blocks of memory (over one million bytes). This allows the 8088 to execute larger programs much more efficiently than the 8085. In addition, the 8088 contains a bus interface unit capable of pre-fetching instructions, further increasing efficiency.

Though the 8085 contains more external hardware interrupt signals, the 8088 is actually capable of handling a much larger number of interrupts. In addition, the 8088 contains a more powerful instruction set, runs at a faster clock speed, and is designed to easily interface with a mathematical coprocessor, the 8087.

One final point deserves mention. The 8085 is commonly referred to as an *accumulator-based* machine, where the results of all arithmetic and logical operations are placed in the accumulator (register A). The 8088 is a *register-based* machine, where any register can store the results of an ALU operation (i.e., can act like an accumulator).

Overall, the 8088 has many advantages over the 8085. This is not to say that the 8088 should always be used, for there are many applications that do not require the power of the 8088 and are very well suited for the 8085 microprocessor. A system designed to monitor and maintain temperature in an environmental chamber can be easily controlled by the 8085. Can you think of other examples where one CPU would be a better choice than the other?

2.10 THE 8086: A COMPATIBLE 16-BIT MACHINE

Our examination so far of the 8088 has shown that it is a 16-bit microprocessor that communicates with the outside world over an 8-bit data bus. Since the data that is processed (instruction fetches, word-wide memory accesses) can only come into the 8088 eight bits at a time, the processor is always performing two memory accesses for each 16-bit chunk. This slightly increases the time required to execute a program, but is not a terrible disadvantage. Many designers are very comfortable working with 8-bit data busses and architectures (and less expensive peripherals). The 8086, on the other hand, really is a true 16-bit machine, equipped with a full 16-bit-wide data bus. Figure 2.7 compares the pin assignments of the 8088 with those of the 8086. As you can see, the majority of pins are the same for both processors. Differences exist on address lines A_8 through A_{15}. On the 8088, these lines are merely address lines. On the 8086, these are **multiplexed address/data** lines AD_8 through AD_{15}. This is where the other half of the 16-bit data bus comes in. The 8086 is capable of reading or writing 16-bits of data at once and for that reason has a slight speed advantage over the 8088.

Internally, both processors are almost identical. Any program written for the 8088 will run without change on the 8086, and vice versa. This means that the instruction sets of both machines are identical. The 8-bit version is a popular choice among manufacturers of personal computers and is therefore featured in this text, but keep in mind that much of what will be said about the 8088 also applies to the 8086.

Both processors have the capability of operating in **minimum mode** or **maximum mode.** Both modes have different ways of dealing with the external busses; thus we see (again in Figure 2.7) that some pins on the processors have two functions. For example, pin 29 on both machines is $\overline{WR}$ in minimum mode, and $\overline{LOCK}$ in maximum mode. The use of maximum mode requires some additional hardware outside the CPU to generate bus control signals.

It is useful to understand that the 8088 and 8086 are not two entirely different microprocessors. You may wish to think of the 8088 as an 8086 on the inside, with an 8-bit data bus on the outside.

2.11 A SUMMARY OF THE 80186

Intel made great efforts to make future processors compatible with the 8086 while at the same time offering additional enhancements and features. The 80186 High-Integration 16-bit Microprocessor can be thought of as a super 8086. Its instruction set is upward compatible with the 8086, which allows programs written for the 8086 to run on the 80186. Ten additional instructions are included, some of which control the additional 80186 hardware features.

Unlike the 8086, which comes in a 40-pin Dual In-line Package (DIP), the 80186 contains 68 pins and comes housed in a variety of different packages.

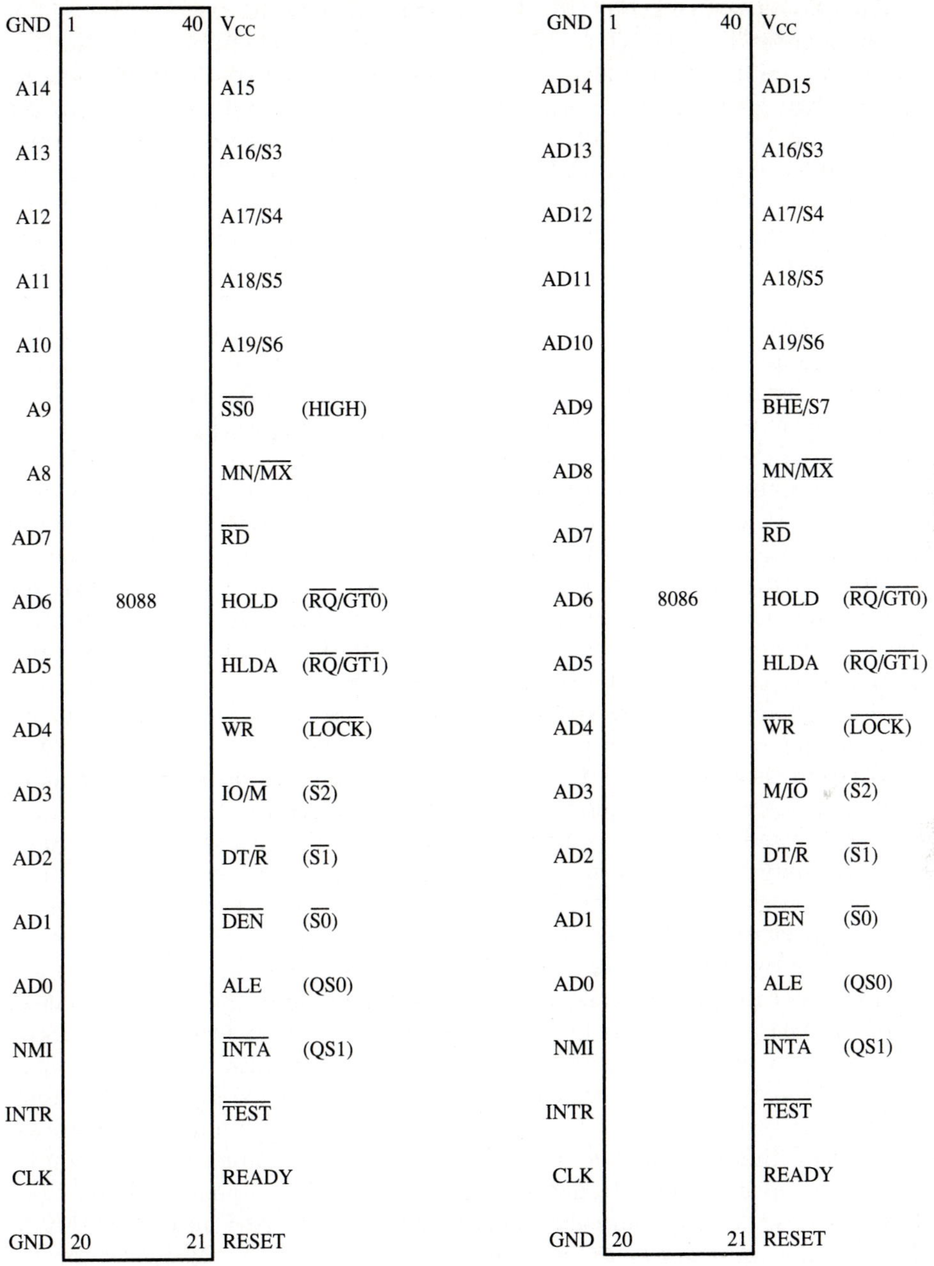

GND	1		40	V_{CC}			GND	1		40	V_{CC}	
A14				A15			AD14				AD15	
A13				A16/S3			AD13				A16/S3	
A12				A17/S4			AD12				A17/S4	
A11				A18/S5			AD11				A18/S5	
A10				A19/S6			AD10				A19/S6	
A9				$\overline{SS0}$	(HIGH)		AD9				$\overline{BHE}$/S7	
A8				MN/$\overline{MX}$			AD8				MN/$\overline{MX}$	
AD7				$\overline{RD}$			AD7				$\overline{RD}$	
AD6		8088		HOLD	($\overline{RQ}$/$\overline{GT0}$)		AD6		8086		HOLD	($\overline{RQ}$/$\overline{GT0}$)
AD5				HLDA	($\overline{RQ}$/$\overline{GT1}$)		AD5				HLDA	($\overline{RQ}$/$\overline{GT1}$)
AD4				$\overline{WR}$	($\overline{LOCK}$)		AD4				$\overline{WR}$	($\overline{LOCK}$)
AD3				IO/$\overline{M}$	($\overline{S2}$)		AD3				M/$\overline{IO}$	($\overline{S2}$)
AD2				DT/$\overline{R}$	($\overline{S1}$)		AD2				DT/$\overline{R}$	($\overline{S1}$)
AD1				$\overline{DEN}$	($\overline{S0}$)		AD1				$\overline{DEN}$	($\overline{S0}$)
AD0				ALE	(QS0)		AD0				ALE	(QS0)
NMI				$\overline{INTA}$	(QS1)		NMI				$\overline{INTA}$	(QS1)
INTR				$\overline{TEST}$			INTR				$\overline{TEST}$	
CLK				READY			CLK				READY	
GND	20		21	RESET			GND	20		21	RESET	

Note: ( ) denotes a MAX mode signal

FIGURE 2.7   8088 and 8086 pin assignments

Plastic Leaded Chip Carrier (PLCC), Ceramic Pin Grid Array (PGA), and Ceramic Leadless Chip Carrier (LCC) are the three types of packages that the 80186 may be found in. Both the PLCC and LCC packages have 17 pins on each of their four sides. The pins on the PGA come out of the bottom of the package. These new types of packages occupy less space on printed circuit boards and are thus very popular with designers.

Many of the additional pins are needed for signals used and generated by the new hardware features of the 80186. A **programmable interrupt controller** has been added, which supervises the operation of five hardware interrupt lines, including a nonmaskable interrupt signal. These interrupt lines can be programmed for different modes of operation. In *fully nested* mode, the four maskable interrupts are used to generate internal interrupt vectors on a prioritized basis. In *cascade* mode the four interrupt lines become handshaking signals for an external interrupt controller, greatly increasing the interrupt capability of the processor.

Three 16-bit **programmable timers** have also been added. Two of the timers interface with the outside world and can be programmed for many different operations, such as counting and timing external events and generating waveforms (such as square waves and pulses). The third timer is used for internal operations. The timers can be programmed to cause an interrupt when a certain count (called a terminal count) is reached. All timers are clocked at a frequency equal to one-quarter of the CPU's internal clock.

A **programmable DMA unit** connected to the internal processor bus allows two independent DMA channels to operate under processor control. The DMA channels are especially useful when transferring large blocks of data between the processor, memory, and I/O devices. Both 8-bit and 16-bit transfers are allowed, and may be transferred as fast as 2.5 megabytes per second. Priorities may be assigned to the two DMA channels in two ways: with one channel having a higher priority than the other, or with both channels having the same priority. Each channel can be programmed to interrupt the processor when it has completed its data transfer.

The **bus interface unit** is similar to the one found in the 8086, with additional signals providing the use of synchronous and asynchronous bus transfers. Finally, a **clip-select unit** has been added, which contains programmable outputs that can be used to select banks of memory or I/O devices. This task was previously accomplished by additional chip-select logic outside the processor. Putting this logic inside, and making it programmable, further reduces the amount of hardware needed to operate the microcomputer system. Wait states can also be programmed to be automatically inserted into bus cycles, to allow for slow memory or I/O devices.

From a software standpoint, the 80186 is compatible with the 8086, utilizing the familiar register set we saw in Section 2.4. Many additional hardware registers have been added for the purpose of controlling the new services provided by the 80186. These registers are contained in a dedicated area called the **peripheral control block.** The PCB is automatically placed at the top of the processor's I/O space (port addresses FF00H to FFFFH) whenever the CPU is reset, but can be moved to a different location by changing the contents of the processor's **relocation register.** The PCB contains interrupt control registers, timer control registers for all three timers, chip-select control registers, and DMA descriptors for both channels. Programming all of the internal hardware enhancements is done through these registers.

A number of new instructions have also been added. PUSHA and POPA deal with the stack and are used to push or pop *all* of the 80186's registers (AX, BX, CX, etc.). The integer multiply instruction IMUL has been enhanced to allow immediate data as an operand. Also enhanced are the shift and rotate instructions, which now allow a count value to be included in the instruction. For I/O operations, two new instructions allow 8-bit and 16-bit data to be input or output between an I/O device and a memory location (instead of the usual use of the accumulator). These instructions are INS and OUTS. For byte operations INSB and OUTSB are used, and INSW and OUTSW for word operations. A special form of the instruction allows a **string** of bytes or words to be transferred. Two other instructions are used to manipulate the stack area (with the help of the BP register). These instructions are ENTER and LEAVE, and have been included to assist in the implementation of procedure calls in high-level languages. Finally, the BOUND instruction is included to help in the partitioning of memory for multiuser environments. BOUND checks the contents of a specified register against an allowable range and generates an interrupt if the register is "out of bounds."

All in all, the 80186 offers many significant improvements over the 8086, while still being upwardly compatible. For those designers still determined to use an 8-bit data bus, Intel offers the 80188. This processor is an exact internal copy of the 80186, but differs in its use of an external 8-bit data bus.

2.12   A SUMMARY OF THE 80286

The next improvement in Intel's line of microprocessors was the 80286 High Performance Microprocessor with Memory Management and Protection. Unlike the 80186, the 80286 does not contain the internal DMA controllers, timers, and other enhancements. Instead, the 80286 concentrates on the features needed to implement **multitasking,** an operating system environment that allows many programs or tasks to run seemingly simultaneously. In fact, the 80286 was designed with this goal in mind. A 24-bit address bus gives the processor the capability of accessing 16 megabytes of storage. The internal memory management feature increases the storage space to one **gigabyte** of virtual address space. That's over one billion locations of virtual memory! Virtual addressing is a concept that has gained much popularity in the computing industry. Virtual memory allows a large program to execute in a smaller physical memory. For example, if a system utilizing the 80286 contained 8 megabytes of RAM, memory management and virtual addressing permits the system to run a program containing 12 megabytes of code and data, or even multiple programs in a multitasking environment, *all of which* may be larger than 8 megabytes.

To implement the complicated addressing functions required by virtual addressing, the 80286 has an entire functional unit dedicated to address generation. This unit is called the address unit. It provides two modes of addressing: 8086 real address mode and protected virtual address mode. The 8086 real address mode is utilized whenever an 8086 program executes on the 80286. The one megabyte addressing space of the 8086 is simulated on the 80286 by the use of the lower 20 address lines. Processor registers and instructions are totally upward compatible with the 8086.

Protected virtual address mode utilizes the full power of the 80286, providing memory management, additional instructions, and protection features while at the same time retaining the ability to execute 8086 code. The processor switches from 8086 real address mode to protected mode when a special instruction sets the protection enable bit in the machine's status word. Addressing is more complicated in protected mode, and is accomplished through the use of **segment descriptors** stored in memory. The segment descriptor is the device that really makes it possible for an operating system to control and protect memory. Certain bits within the segment descriptor are used to grant or deny access to memory in certain ways. A section of memory may be write protected, or made execute-only, by the setting of proper bits in the access rights byte of the descriptor. Other bits are used to control how the segment is mapped into virtual memory space and whether the descriptor is for a code segment or a data segment. Special descriptors called **gate descriptors** are used for other functions. Four types of gate descriptors are call gates, task gates, interrupt gates, and trap gates. They are used to change privilege levels (there are four), switch tasks, and specify interrupt service routines.

The instruction set of the 80286 is identical to that of the 80186, with an additional sixteen instructions thrown in to handle the new features. Many of the instructions are used to load and store the different types of descriptors found in the 80286. Others are used to manipulate task registers, change privilege levels, adjust the machine status word, and verify read/write accesses. Clearly, the 80286 differs greatly from the 80186 in the services it offers, while at the same time filling a great need for designers of operating systems.

2.13   A SUMMARY OF THE 80386

Intel continued its upward compatible trend with the introduction of the 386 High Performance 32-bit CHMOS Microprocessor with Integrated Memory Management. Software written for the 8088, 8086, 80186, 80188, and 80286 will also run on the 386. A 132-pin Grid Array package houses the 386, which offers a full 32-bit data bus and 32-bit address bus. The address bus is capable of accessing over 4 gigabytes of physical memory. Virtual addressing pushes this to over 64 *trillion* bytes of storage.

The register set of the 386 is compatible with earlier models, including all eight general purpose registers, plus the four segment registers. Though the general purpose registers are 16 bits wide on all earlier machines, they can be extended to 32 bits on the 386. Their new names are EAX, EBX, ECX, and so on. Two additional 16-bit data segment registers are included, FS and GS. Like the 80286, the 386 has two modes of operation: real mode and protected mode. When in real mode, segments have a maximum size of 64KB. When in protected mode, a segment may be as large as the entire physical addressing space of 4 gigabytes. The new extended flags register contains status information concerning privilege levels, virtual mode operation, and other flags concerned with protected mode. The 386 also contains three 32-bit control registers. The first, machine control register, contains the machine status word and additional bits dealing with the coprocessor, paging, and protected mode. The second, page fault linear address, is used to store the 32-bit address that caused the last page fault. In a virtual memory environment, physical memory is divided up into a number of fixed size **pages.** Each page will at some time be loaded with a portion of an executing program or other type of data. When the processor determines that a page it needs to use has not been loaded into memory, a **page fault** is generated. The page fault instructs the processor to load the missing page into memory. Ideally, a low page-fault rate is desired.

The third control register, page directory base address, stores the physical memory address of the beginning of the page directory table. This table is up to 4KB in length and may contain up to 1024 page directory entries, each of which points to another page table area, whose information is used to generate a physical address.

The segment descriptors used in the 80286 are also used in the 386, as are the gate descriptors and the four levels of privilege. Thus, the 386 functions much the same as the 80286, except for the increase in physical memory space and the enhancements involving page handling in the virtual environment.

The computing power of each of the processors that have been presented can be augmented with the addition of a floating point coprocessor. All sorts of mathematical operations can be performed with the coprocessors, with 80-bit binary precision. The 8087 coprocessor is designed for use with the 8088 and 8086, the 80287 with the 80286, and the 80387 with the 386.

2.14   SUMMARY

This chapter has taken an introductory look at the 8088 microprocessor and its related family of upward compatible microprocessors. The software model of the 8088 was examined first, showing all the 16-bit general purpose registers (AX, BX, CX, DX, SI, DI, BP, and SP) and the four 16-bit segment registers (CS, DS, SS, and ES). We then examined the operation of the execution unit and the bus interface unit. To improve execution speed, the bus execution unit is capable of prefetching the next four bytes of code from memory.

Though the 8088 contains only 16-bit registers, its architecture allows the generation of 20-bit physical addresses, giving the processor a one megabyte addressing space. One of the four segment registers is always involved in a memory access. The general purpose registers were shown to have specific tasks assigned to them by default, such as the use of AX in multiply and divide operations.

A technique called Intel byte-swapping was also introduced, which accounts for the way a 16-bit number is stored in memory (low byte first). This technique, along with the use of a multiplexed address and data bus, is rarely seen on other microprocessors.

The entire instruction set was presented to give you a feel for the type of operations the 8088 is capable of performing. This discussion was followed by a brief discussion of what a segment is, and what addressing modes are available. Some examples were shown to illustrate the use of different addressing modes. This was followed by an explanation of the 8088's interrupt structure.

When the 8088 was compared to the 8085, it was clear that a 16-bit machine has many advantages over an 8-bit machine. Some of these advantages include additional instructions, increased memory space, and larger registers. The comparisons continued upward through the entire 8086 family, highlighting new features along the way, and continually stressing that programs written for the 8088 execute properly on all of the newer machines.

In the next chapter we will take a detailed look at the software operation of the 8088.

STUDY QUESTIONS

1. Name all of the 8088's general purpose registers and some of their special functions.
2. How are the segment registers used to form a 20-bit address?
3. If CS contains 03E0H and IP contains 1F20H, from what address is the next instruction fetched?
4. If SS contains 0400H and SP contains 3FFEH, where is the top of the stack located?
5. Explain how the bus interface unit increases execution efficiency.
6. Why does the instruction queue have to be cleared and reloaded after a jump?
7. What is a segment?
8. Two memory locations, beginning at address 3000H, contain the bytes 34H and 12H. What is the word stored at location 3000H?
9. What is Intel byte swapping?
10. Count the number of different instructions available on the 8088. How many are there?
11. How many addressing modes does the 8088 provide?
12. What is a physical address?
13. Why is register addressing so fast?
14. What do square brackets mean when they appear in an operand (e.g., MOV   AX,[3000])?
15. What is the difference between MOV   AX,1000H and MOV   AX,[1000H]?

16. How does port addressing differ from memory addressing?

17. What is a nonmaskable interrupt? Which 8088 interrupt is nonmaskable?

18. Name one instruction that can cause an interrupt.

19. List three differences between the 8085 and the 8088.

20. How do minimum mode and maximum mode differ?

21. List the important features of the 80186.

22. What is one advantage of virtual memory?

23. What is a page fault?

24. Compare two 386 systems, one containing 512KB of RAM, the second containing 4 megabytes. How would the number of page faults compare when:

   a) a 220KB application is executed on both machines?

   b) a 6 megabyte application is executed on both machines?

25. Which has the greater effect on the number of page faults, physical memory size or the size of the program being executed?

26. Why would we resist building a complete physical memory for the 386? Does the reason apply to the 8086?

27. Why would anyone possibly need 4.3 billion bytes for a program? Can you think of any applications that may require this much memory?

28. List three differences between the 80286 and the 386.

Software Details of the 8088

Objectives

In this chapter you will learn about:

*   The style of source files written in 8088 assembly language

*   The different addressing modes of the 8088

*   The various groups of instructions available

*   The special properties of relocatable code

*   How an assembler generates machine code

3.1 INTRODUCTION

This chapter is intended to introduce you to the instruction set of the 8088 microprocessor, and the ways that different addressing modes and data types can be used to make the instructions do the most work for you. The 8088 contains instructions not previously available with other processors (especially the earlier 8-bit machines), instructions that perform multiplication and division, others that manipulate strings, and special types of interrupts. The combination of instructions and addressing modes found in the 8088 makes the job of writing code much easier and more efficient than before. Programming examples will be shown to demonstrate the use of different addressing modes and instructions. Specific programming examples will not be covered until after we study interrupt processing in Chapter 4.

Section 3.2 introduces the conventions followed when writing 8088 assembly language source code. Section 3.3 explains the different instruction types available; this is followed by coverage of the 8088's addressing modes in Section 3.4. The entire instruction set is covered in Section 3.5 (including an explanation of the processor flags). The internal operation of an assembler is described in Section 3.6, followed by a number of simple programming examples in Section 3.7. Finally, Section 3.8 shows the reasons why relocatable code provides programming flexibility and efficiency.

3.2   ASSEMBLY LANGUAGE PROGRAMMING

Program execution in any microprocessor system consists of fetching binary information from memory and decoding that information to determine the instruction represented. The information in memory may have been programmed into an EPROM, or downloaded from a separate system. But where did the program come from and how was it written? As humans, we have trouble handling many pieces of information simultaneously and thus have difficulty writing programs directly in **machine code,** the binary language understood by the microprocessor. It is much easier for us to remember the mnemonic SUB   AX,AX than the corresponding machine code 2BC0. For this reason, we write **source files** containing all the instruction mnemonics needed to execute a program. The source file is converted into an **object file** containing the actual binary information the machine will understand by a special program called an **assembler.** Some assemblers allow the entire source file to be written and assembled at one time. Other assemblers, called **single-line assemblers,** work with one source line at a time and are restricted in operation. These kinds of assemblers are usually found on small microprocessor-based systems that do not have disk storage and text-editing capability.

The assembler discussed here is not a single-line assembler but a **cross-assembler.** Cross-assemblers are programs written in one language, such as FORTRAN or Pascal, that translate source statements into a second language: the machine code of the desired processor. Figure 3.1 shows this translation process. The source file in the example, TOTAL.ASM, is presented as input to the assembler. The assembler will convert all source statements into the correct binary codes and place these into the object file TOTAL.OBJ. Usually the object file contains additional information concerning program relocation and external references, and thus is not yet ready to be loaded into memory and

FIGURE 3.1   Source program assembly

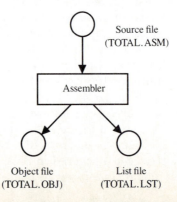

Source file
(TOTAL.ASM)

Assembler

Object file   List file
(TOTAL.OBJ)   (TOTAL.LST)

executed. A second file created by the assembler is the **list file,** TOTAL.LST, which contains all the original source file text plus the additional code generated by the assembler.

Let us look at a sample source file, a subroutine designed to find the sum of 16 bytes stored in memory. It is not important at this time that you understand what each instruction does. We are simply trying to get a feel for what a source file might look like and what conventions to follow when we write our own programs.

```
        ORG   8000H
TOTAL:  MOV   AX,7000H    ;load address of data area
        MOV   DS,AX       ;init data segment register
        MOV   AL,0        ;clear result
        MOV   BL,16       ;init loop counter
        MOV   SI,0        ;init data pointer
ADDUP:  ADD   AL,[SI]     ;add data value to result
        INC   SI          ;increment data pointer
        DEC   BL          ;decrement loop counter
        JNZ   ADDUP       ;jump if counter not zero
        MOV   [SI],AL     ;save sum
        RET               ;and return
        END
```

The first line of source code contains a command that instructs the assembler to load its program counter with 8000H. The ORG (for origin) command is known as an assembler **pseudo-opcode,** a fancy name for a mnemonic that is understood by the assembler but not by the microprocessor. ORG does not generate any source code; it merely sets the value of the assembler's program counter. This is important when a section of code must be loaded at a particular place in memory. The ORG statement is a good way to generate instructions that will access the proper memory locations when the program is loaded into memory.

Hexadecimal numbers are followed by the letter H to distinguish them from decimal numbers. This is necessary since 8000 decimal and 8000 hexadecimal differ greatly in magnitude. For the assembler to tell them apart, we need a symbol that shows the difference. Some assemblers use $8000; others use &H8000. It is really a matter of whose software you purchase. All examples in this book will use the 8000H form.

The second source line contains the major components normally used in a source statement. The label TOTAL is used to point to the address of the first instruction in the subroutine. ADDUP is also a label. Single-line assemblers do not allow the use of labels.

The opcode is represented by MOV and the operand field by AX,7000H. So far we have three fields: label, opcode, and operand. The fourth field, if it is used, usually contains a comment explaining what the instruction is doing. Comments are preceded by a semicolon (;) to separate them from the operand field. In writing source code, you should follow the four-column approach. This will result in a more understandable source file.

The final pseudo-opcode in most source files is END. The END statement informs the assembler that it has reached the end of the source file. This is important, since many assemblers usually perform two passes over the source file. The first pass is used to determine the lengths of all instructions and data areas, and to assign values to all symbols (labels) encountered. The second pass completes the assembly process by generating the machine code for all instructions, usually with the help of the symbol table created in the first pass. The second pass also creates and writes information to the list and object files. The list file for our example subroutine looks like this:

```
 1   8000                      ORG    8000H
 2   8000  B8  0070  TOTAL:    MOV    AX,7000H
 3   8003  8E  D8              MOV    DS,AX
 4   8005  B0  00              MOV    AL,0
 5   8007  B3  10              MOV    BL,16
 6   8009  BE  0000            MOV    SI,0
 7   800C  02  04    ADDUP:    ADD    AL,[SI]
 8   800E  46                  INC    SI
 9   800F  FE  CB              DEC    BL
10   8011  75  F9              JNZ    ADDUP
11   8013  88  04              MOV    [SI],AL
12   8015  CB                  RET
13                             END
```

Normally the comments would follow the instructions, but they have been removed for the purposes of this discussion.

The first column of numbers represents the original source line number.

The second column of numbers represents the memory addresses of each instruction. Notice that the first address matches the one specified by the ORG statement. Also notice that the ORG statement does not generate any code.

The third column of numbers are the machine codes generated by the assembler. The machine codes are intermixed with data and address values. For example, B8 00 70 in line 2 represents the instruction MOV   AX,7000H, with the MOV instruction coded as B8 and the immediate word 7000H coded in byte-swapped form as 00 70. In line 3 the machine codes 8E D8 represent MOV   DS,AX. Neither of these two bytes are data or address values, as there were in line 2. Look for other data values in the instructions on lines 4 through 6. Line 5 makes an important point: The assembler will convert decimal numbers into hexadecimal (the 16 in the operand field has been converted into 10 in the machine code column).

Finally, another look at the list file shows that there are one-, two-, and three-byte instructions present in the machine code. When an address or data value is used in an instruction, chances are good that you will end up with a two- or three-byte instruction (or possibly even more).

Following the code on each line is the text of the original source line. Having all of this information available is very helpful during the debugging process.

The actual form of an 8088 source file is much more complicated than the simple example we have just examined. When writing 8088 source files, we separate code areas from data areas. We may even have a separate area reserved for the stack. The new source file for TOTAL, which includes separate

areas called **segments,** contains many new pseudocodes to help the assembler
generate the correct machine code for the object file.

```
DATA        SEGMENT PARA 'DATA'
            ORG     7000H
POINTS      DB      16 DUP(?)       ;save room for 16 data bytes
SUM         DB      ?               ;save room for result
DATA        ENDS

CODE        SEGMENT PARA 'CODE'
            ASSUME CS:CODE,DS:DATA
MAIN        PROC FAR
            ORG     8000H
TOTAL:      MOV     AX,DATA         ;load address of data segment
            MOV     DS,AX           ;init data segment register
            MOV     AL,0            ;clear result
            MOV     BL,16           ;init loop counter
            LEA     SI,POINTS       ;init data pointer
ADDUP:      ADD     AL,[SI]         ;add data value to result
            INC     SI              ;increment data pointer
            DEC     BL              ;decrement loop counter
            JNZ     ADDUP           ;jump if counter not zero
            MOV     SUM,AL          ;save sum
            RET                     ;and return
MAIN        ENDP
CODE        ENDS
            END     TOTAL
```

In this new source file we use a DATA segment and a CODE segment. These
areas are defined by the **SEGMENT** pseudocode and terminated by **ENDS** (for
end segment). The TOTAL subroutine is now defined by the **PROC FAR** (for
far procedure) and **ENDP** (for end procedure) assembler directives. In the
DATA segment, 16 bytes of storage are reserved with the DB   16 DUP(?)
instruction. DB stands for define byte, and DUP for duplicate. The ? means we
do not know what value to put into memory and is a way of telling the assembler that we do not care what byte values are used in the reserved data area.
We could easily use DB   16 DUP(0) to place 16 zero's into the reserved area.
Words can also be defined/reserved in a similar fashion, using, for example,
DW   8 DUP(0) or DW   8 DUP(?). The ORG   7000H statement tells the assembler where to put the data areas. It is not necessary for this ORG value to
be smaller than the ORG of the subroutine. ORG   87C0H would have also
worked in place of ORG   7000H. It is all a function of where RAM exists in
your system.

   The addition of the TOTAL label in the END statement informs the assembler that TOTAL, not SUM, is the starting execution address. This information
is also included in the object file. When a large program must be written by a
team of people, each will be assigned a few subroutines to write. They must all
assemble and test their individual sections to ensure the code executes correctly. When all portions of the program (called **modules,** after a technique
called modular programming) are assembled and tested, their object files are
combined into one large object file via a program called a **linker.** Figure 3.2
represents this process. The linker examines each object file, determining its

FIGURE 3.2   Linking multiple
object files together

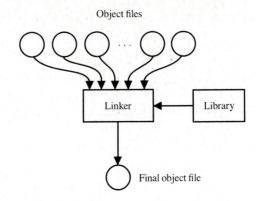

length in bytes, its proper place in the final object file, and what modifications should be made to it.

In addition, a special collection of object files is sometimes available in a **library** file. The library may contain often-used subroutines, or patches of code. Instead of continuously reproducing these code segments in a source file, a special pseudocode is used to instruct the assembler that the code must be brought in at a later time (by the linker). This helps keep the size of the source file down, and promotes quicker writing of programs.

When the linker is through, the final code is written to a file called the **load** module. Another program called a **loader** takes care of loading the program into memory. Usually the linker and loader are combined into a single program called a **link-loader**.

So, writing the source file is actually only the first step in a long process. But even before a source file can be written, the programmer must obtain an understanding of the instructions that will be used in the source file. The remaining sections will cover this important topic.

3.3   8088 INSTRUCTION TYPES

For purposes of discussion in this section, the instruction set of the 8088 microprocessor is divided into seven different groups:

1. Data transfer
2. Arithmetic
3. Bit manipulation
4. Strings
5. Loops and jumps
6. Subroutine and interrupt
7. Processor control

The data transfer group contains instructions that transfer data from memory to register, register to register, and register to memory. Instructions that perform I/O are also included in this group. Data may be 8 or 16 bits in length, and all of the 8088's registers may be used (including the stack pointer and flag register).

The arithmetic group provides addition and subtraction of 8- and 16-bit values, signed and unsigned multiplication and division of 8-, 16-, and 32-bit numbers, and special instructions for working with BCD and ASCII data.

The bit manipulation group is used to perform AND, OR, XOR (Exclusive OR), and NOT (1's complement) operations on 8- and 16-bit data contained in registers or memory. Shift and rotate operations on bytes and words are also included, with single or multi-bit shifts or rotates possible.

The next group deals with strings. A string is simply a collection of bytes stored sequentially in memory, whose length can be up to 64KB. Instructions are included in this group to move, scan, and compare strings.

Loops and jumps are contained in the next group. Many different forms of instructions are available, with each one testing a different condition based on the state of the processor's flags. The loop instructions are designed to repeat automatically, terminating when certain conditions are met.

The subroutine and interrupt group contains instructions required to call and return from subroutines and handle interrupts. The processor stack can be manipulated by a special form of the return instruction, and two classes of subroutines, called near and far procedures, are handled by these instructions.

The final group of instructions are used to directly control the state of some of the flags, enable/disable the 8088's interrupt mechanism, and synchronize the processor with external peripherals (such as the 8087 coprocessor).

Many different addressing modes can be used with most instructions, and in the next section we will examine these addressing modes in detail.

3.4   8088 ADDRESSING MODES

The power of any instruction set is a function of both the types of instructions implemented and the number of addressing modes available. Suppose that a microprocessor could not directly manipulate data in a memory location. The data would have to be loaded into a processor register, manipulated, and written back into memory. If an addressing mode were available that could directly operate on data in memory, the task could be done more effectively. In this section we will examine the many different addressing modes available in the 8088, and see how each is used. The examples presented make use of the MOV instruction, which has the following syntax: MOV ⟨destination⟩,⟨source⟩. It will be obvious in the examples what is being accomplished with each MOV instruction, so a detailed description is not included here. Also, whenever the contents of a memory location or an address or data register is referred to, assume that the value or address is hexadecimal.

Creating an Effective Address

Chapter 2 introduced the concept of segmented memory, where a segment is a 64KB block of memory accessed with the aid of one of the four segment registers. Whenever *any* address is generated by the 8088, the 20-bit value that appears on the processor's address bus is formed by some combination of segment register and an additional numerical offset. This address is referred to as the **effective address.** Many of the data transfer instructions use the data segment register by default when forming an effective address. As we saw in Chapter 2, instruction fetches generate effective addresses via the addition of the code segment register and the instruction pointer. Stack operations automatically use the stack segment register and the stack pointer. Thus, from a programming standpoint, almost all instructions require proper initialization of a segment register for correct execution and generation of effective addresses.

One way to initialize a segment register is to first place the desired segment address into the AX register and then copy the contents of AX into the corresponding segment register. For example, to initialize the data segment register to 1000H, we would use the following instructions:

```
MOV   AX,1000H
MOV   DS,AX
```

Remember that the direction of data transfer in the operand field is from right to left, so 1000H is MOVed into AX, and then the contents of AX are MOVed into DS, as you can see in Figure 3.3. (Unfortunately, MOV   DS,1000H is an illegal instruction. We are *not allowed* to move a numerical value directly into a segment register!)

All of the examples used to explain the processor's addressing modes assume that the corresponding segment register has already been initialized.

FIGURE 3.3   Initializing the data segment register

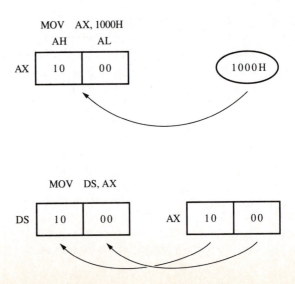

Immediate Addressing

We often use **immediate data** in the operand field of an instruction. Immediate data represents a constant that we wish to place somewhere, by MOVing it into a register or a memory location. In MOV   AX,1000H, we are placing the immediate value 1000H into register AX. Immediate data is represented by 8- or 16-bit numbers that are coded directly into the instruction. For example, MOV   AX,1000H is coded as B8 00 10, and MOV   AL,7 is coded as B0 07. Notice in the first instruction that the 16-bit value 1000H has its lower byte (00) and its upper byte (10) reversed in the actual machine code. As we saw in Chapter 2, this technique is commonly referred to as *Intel byte-swapping,* and it is the way all 16-bit numbers are stored.

An important question at this time is "How did the assembler know that the 7 in MOV   AL,7 should be coded as the single byte value 07, and not the 2-byte value 07 00 (in byte-swapped form)?" The answer is that the assembler looked at the size of the other operand in the instruction (AL). Since AL is the lower half of the AX register, the assembler knows that it may only contain 8 bits of data. Knowing this, do you see why MOV   AL,9C8H would be an illegal instruction? If you cannot answer this question, think about how many bits are needed to represent the hexadecimal number 9C8. Since 12 bits are needed, we cannot possibly store 9C8H in the 8-bit AL register.

Let's apply what we have just seen in an example.

Example 3.1:   What is the result of MOV   CX,7?

Solution: Since register CX is specified, the immediate value 7 is coded as the 2-byte number 00 07. Figure 3.4 shows how this 2-byte number is placed into CX.

The machine code for MOV   CX,7 is B9 07 00.

FIGURE 3.4   An example of immediate addressing

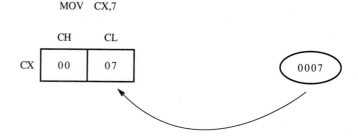

Register Addressing

The operand field of an instruction in many cases will contain one or more of the 8088's internal registers. Register addressing is the name we use to refer to operands that contain one of these registers. The MOV   DS,AX instruction from the previous section is an example of register addressing, as we are only using processor registers in the operand field. Instructions of this form often execute very quickly, since they do not require any memory accesses beyond the initial instruction fetch cycles. The machine code corresponding to MOV DS,AX is 8E D8, a 2-byte instruction containing all the information necessary for the 8088 to perform the desired operation. DEC   DX (decrement the DX register) is another example of register addressing, and has 4A as its corresponding machine code.

Example 3.2:   If register AX contains the value 1000H and register BL contains 80H, what is the result of MOV   AL,BL?

Solution: The contents of the BL register are copied into the AL register, leaving AH undisturbed. The final value in AX is 1080H. Notice that the contents are *copied* during the MOV. MOV can also be interpreted as "make a copy of." So, when we move data from one place to another, we actually are just making a second copy of the source data.
   The machine code for MOV   AL,BL is 88 D8.

It is important to note that only the code segment register is needed to execute the instructions used in Examples 3.1 and 3.2.

Direct Addressing

In this addressing mode the effective address is formed by the addition of a segment register and a displacement value that is coded directly into the instruction. The displacement is usually the address of a memory location *within a specific segment*. One way to refer to a memory location in the operand field is to surround the memory address with square brackets. The instruction MOV   [7000H],AX illustrates this concept. The 7000H is not thought of as immediate data here, but rather as address 7000H within the segment pointed to by the DS register. DS is the segment register used by the 8088 whenever brackets ([ ]) are used in the operand field (unless we override the use of DS by specifying a different segment register). A detailed example should serve to explain this addressing mode more clearly.

Example 3.3:   What is the result of MOV   [7000H],AX? Assume that the DS register contains 1000H, and AX contains 1234H.

Solution: Examine Figure 3.5 very carefully. Remember that when the 8088 uses a segment register to form an effective address, it shifts the segment register 4 bits to the left (turning 1000H into 10000H) and then adds the specified 16-bit displacement (or offset). Thus, the effective address generated by the processor is 17000H. Since register AX is used in the operand field, two bytes will be written into memory, with the lower byte (34) going into the first location (17000H) and the upper byte (12) going into the second location (17001H). Once again we can see that the processor has byte-swapped the data as it was written into memory.

The machine code for MOV   [7000H],AX is A3 00 70.

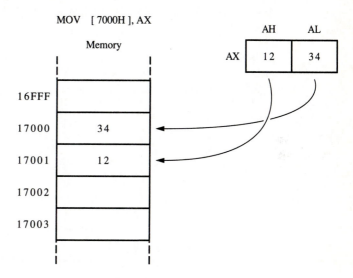

FIGURE 3.5   An example of direct addressing

Another form of direct addressing requires the use of a label in the operand field. The sample program TOTAL that we examined in Section 3.2 used direct addressing in the MOV   SUM,AL instruction. Another look at the TOTAL source file should convince you that the SUM label represents a displacement value within the segment pointed to by the DS register.

The automatic use of the DS register for memory accesses can be overridden by the programmer by specifying a different segment register within the operand field. If we wish to use the extra segment register in the instruction of Example 3.3, we would write MOV   ES:[7000H],AX. The machine code required to allow the use of the ES register in this instruction is 26 A3 00 70. Note the similarity to the machine code in Example 3.3.

Register Indirect Addressing

In this addressing mode we have a choice of four registers to use within the square brackets to specify a memory location. The four registers to choose from are the two base registers (BX and BP) and the two index registers (SI and DI). The 16-bit contents of the specified register are added to the DS register in the usual fashion.

Example 3.4: What is the effective address generated by the instruction MOV   DL,[SI], if register SI contains 2000H, and the DS register contains 800H?

Solution: Shifting the DS register four bits to the left and adding the contents of register SI produces an effective address of 0A000H. Figure 3.6 illustrates this process.
   The machine code for MOV   DL,[SI] is 8A 14.

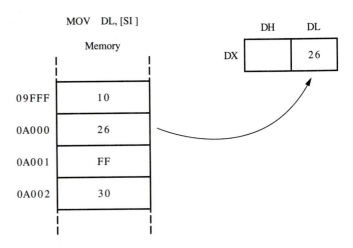

FIGURE 3.6   An example of register indirect addressing

MOV   DL, [SI]

Memory

DS: 0800 _
+ SI: 2000
0A000

Using a register in the operand field to point to a memory location is a very common programming technique. It has the advantage of being able to generate any address within a specific segment, simply by changing the value of the specified register.

Based Addressing

This addressing mode uses one of the two base registers (BX or BP) as the pointer to the desired memory location. It is very similar to register indirect addressing, the difference being that an 8- or 16-bit displacement may be included in the operand field. This displacement is also added to the appropriate segment register, along with the base register, to generate the effective address. The displacement is interpreted as a signed, 2's complement number. The 8-bit displacement gives a range of −128 to +127. The 16-bit displacement gives a range of −32768 to 32767. So, the signed displacement allows us to point forward and backward in memory, a handy tool when accessing data tables stored in memory.

Example 3.5:   What is the effective address generated by the instruction MOV   AX,[BX+4]? Assume that the DS register contains 100H and register BX contains 600H.

Solution: Figure 3.7 shows how the DS register, the BX register, and the displacement value are added together to create the effective address 1604H. This address is then used to read the word out of locations 1604H and 1605H into the AX register.
     The machine code for MOV   AX,[BX+4] is 8B 47 04.

FIGURE 3.7   An example of based addressing

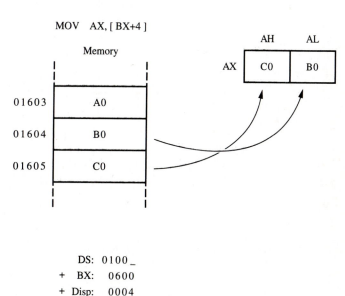

Indexed Addressing

Like based addressing, indexed addressing allows the use of a signed displacement. The difference is that one of the index registers (SI or DI) must be used in the operand field.

Example 3.6:   What is the effective address generated by the instruction MOV   [DI−8],BL? Assume that the DS register contains 200H and that register DI contains 30H.

Solution: Figure 3.8 shows how the negative displacement is combined with the DI register. Notice that although the DI register points to address 30H within the data segment, the actual location accessed is 8 bytes behind.

The machine code for MOV   [DI−8],BL is 88 5D F8. As in the previous example, the third byte in the machine code is the displacement value. In this case, the displacement of −8 is coded as F8 hexadecimal, which is the 2's complement of 8.

FIGURE 3.8   An example of indexed addressing

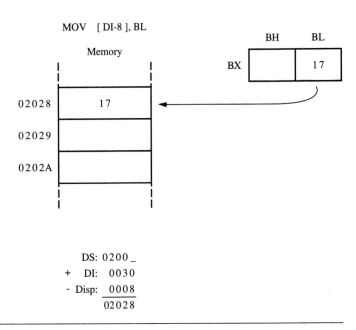

Based Indexed Addressing

This addressing mode combines the features of based and indexed addressing but does not allow the use of a displacement. Two registers must be used as the source or destination operand, one from BX/BP and the other from SI/DI. The contents of both registers are *not* interpreted as signed numbers: therefore, each register may have a range of values from 0 to 65535.

Example   3.7:   What   is   the   effective   address   generated   by   MOV [BP+SI],AH? Assume the DS register contains 2000H, register BP contains 4000H, and register SI contains 800H.

Solution: Shifting the DS register 4 bits to the left and adding the contents of BP and SI gives an effective address of 24800H. See Figure 3.9 for an illustration of this. Also note that a different form of the instruction is used in the figure. MOV   [BP][SI],AH is a different way of saying MOV   [BP+SI],AH. Both methods of specifying the operand are acceptable.

The machine code for MOV   [BP+SI],AH is 88 22.

FIGURE 3.9   An example of based indexed addressing

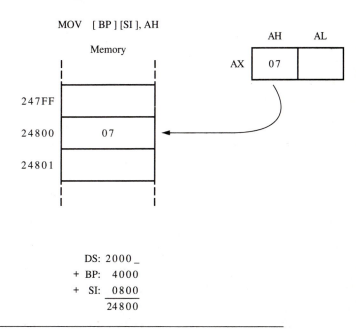

Based Indexed with Displacement Addressing

This addressing mode combines all of the features of the addressing modes we have been examining. As with all the others, it still only accesses memory locations within one 64KB segment. It does, however, give the programmer the option of using two registers to access stored information, and the addition of the signed displacement makes this addressing mode the most flexible of all.

Example   3.8:   What   memory   location   is   accessed   by   MOV CL,[BX+DI+2080H]? Assume that the DS register contains 300H, register BX contains 1000H, and register DI contains 10H.

Solution: Figure 3.10 shows how the three registers and the displacement are added to create the memory address 06090H. The byte stored at this location is copied into register CL.

The machine code for MOV   CL,[BX+DI+2080H] is 8A 89 80 20. In this case the last two bytes are the byte-swapped displacement.

FIGURE 3.10   An example of based indexed with displacement addressing

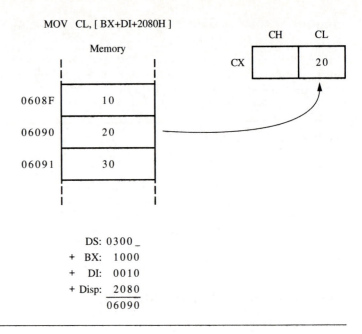

MOV CL, [BX+DI+2080H]

Memory

0608F	10
06090	20
06091	30

```
      DS: 0300_
  +  BX:  1000
  +  DI:  0010
  + Disp:  2080
          06090
```

String Addressing

The instructions that handle strings do not use the standard addressing modes covered in the previous examples. So, when we look at a string instruction we will not see any registers listed in the operand field. For example, consider the string instruction MOVSB (move byte string). No processor registers are shown in the instruction, but the 8088 knows that it should use both SI and DI during execution of the instruction. All of the string-based instructions assume that the SI register points to the first element in the source string (which might be either a byte value or a word value) and that the DI register points to the first element of the destination string. The 8088 will automatically adjust the contents of SI and DI during execution of the string instruction.

We will examine string operations in more detail in Section 3.5.

Port Addressing

The Intel brand of microprocessors differ from other processors on the market in their implementation of the use of **I/O ports** for data communication between the processor and the outside world. One way to get information into the 8088 is to read it from memory. Another way is to read an **input port.** When sending data out of the CPU, we can direct it into a memory location or send it to an **output port.** The 8088 provides the programmer with up to 65536 input and output ports (although many useful designs rarely use more than a handful of I/O ports). An I/O port is accessed in much the same way that memory is accessed, by placing the address of the I/O port onto the address bus and enabling certain control signals. The address of the I/O port can be coded directly into an instruction, as in:

```
IN   AL,40H
```

or

```
OUT  80H,AL
```

In this case, the port address must be between 00 and FFH, a total of 256 different I/O ports. Notice that the AL register is used to receive the port information. We could also use AX to receive 16 bits of data from an input port.

A second method of addressing I/O ports requires that the port address be placed into the DX register. The corresponding instructions are:

```
IN   AL,DX
```

and

```
OUT  DX,AL
```

Since we are now using register DX to store the port address, our choices range from 0000 to FFFFH, a total of 65536 I/O locations.

I/O ports are very useful for communication with peripherals connected to the 8088, such as serial and parallel I/O devices, video display chips, clock/calendar chips, and many others.

Take the time now to review the addressing modes we have just examined, since they are crucial to understanding the operation of the instructions we will now look at in Section 3.5.

3.5 THE 8088 INSTRUCTION SET

As with any microprocessor, a detailed presentation of available instructions is important. Unless you have a firm grasp of what can be accomplished with the instructions you may use, your programming will not be efficient. Indeed, you may even create problems for yourself.

Still, there is no better teacher than experience. If you have an 8088-based computer, you should experiment with these instructions and examine their results. Compare what you see with the manufacturer's data. A difficult concept often becomes clear in practice.

Each of the following sections deals with a separate group of instructions. Information about the instruction, how it works, how it is used, what its mnemonic looks like, how it affects the condition codes, and more, will be presented for each instruction. Even so, it is strongly suggested that you constantly refer to Appendix B as you read about each new instruction. Most of the material in this appendix, such as allowable addressing modes and condition code effects, is not reproduced here.

The instructional groups are organized in such a way that the more commonly used instructions are presented first, followed by less frequently used instructions. For example, in the group dealing with data movement instructions the MOV instruction is presented first, due to its wide range of applications. Though the LDS and LES instructions come first alphabetically, they have restricted functions and are not needed in many programming applications. So, they do not get to steal the spotlight from MOV by appearing first.

Hopefully, covering the instructions in this fashion will allow you to study the important instructions first (in each group), and the other instructions as the need arises.

In most cases the machine code for the instruction will be included. This is done simply to compare instruction lengths and explain new features about the 8088.

Examples will also be given for each instruction.

The Condition Codes (Flags)

The 8088 microprocessor has a number of status indicators that are referred to as *condition codes* or *flags*. Both terms convey useful information. The "condition" part of condition codes refers to information about the most recently executed instruction. Did the last DEC AL instruction produce a zero in AL? The "zero condition" is an example of a condition code. From another point of view, when we see a flag waving, we often know that some new event has just occurred. In this sense, the **zero flag** is a way for the processor to wave at the programmer when a zero condition has occurred. Figure 3.11 shows how the zero flag changes from a 0 to a 1 when the AL register is finally decremented to zero. The flag is really a single bit in the 8088's flag register. This bit can only be a zero or a one. There are many instructions that look at the zero flag and make a decision based on its contents (e.g., jump if the zero flag is not zero).

The 8088 has five main flags that are commonly tested during the execution of a program and a few others that we will examine later. The five main

FIGURE 3.11   Operation of the zero flag

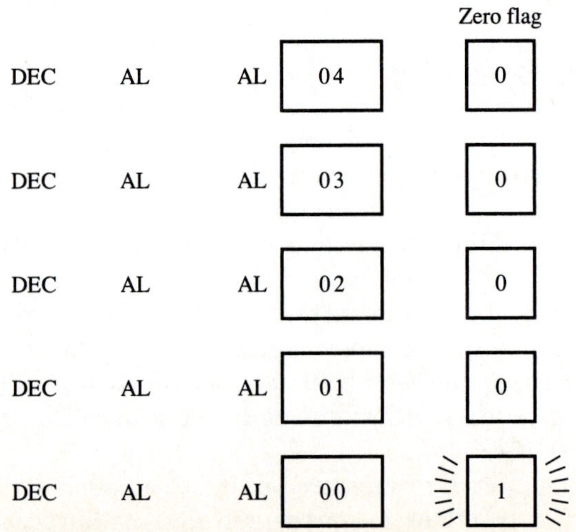

flags and their bit position within the processor's flag register are shown in Figure 3.12(a). Since there are only five flags in this half of the flag register (which is actually 16 bits long), three bit positions are undefined. The flags and their meaning are as follows:

Sign (Bit 7)   When we make use of signed binary data in a program, there are times when we wish to know if the last addition or subtraction produced a positive or negative result. Remember that when we use 2's complement format, the most significant bit in the data is used as the sign bit. This would be bit 7 for a byte value and bit 15 for a word value. The processor examines this bit and adjusts its sign flag accordingly. When the sign flag is zero, the processor is saying that the number produced by the last arithmetic or logical instruction is positive. When the sign flag is a one, the number can be interpreted as a negative number in 2's complement notation.

Zero (Bit 6)   We were briefly introduced to the zero flag in the beginning of this section. The zero flag is set (made equal to 1) or cleared (made equal to 0) after execution of many arithmetic and logical instructions. In Figure 3.11 we saw that the zero flag was set when the AL register was finally decremented to zero. The zero flag is often used in programs to determine when a match has been found in a compare operation, when a register or memory location contains zero, and when a loop should be terminated. It is not difficult to see that the zero flag is set when a "zero" is created by an instruction.

Carry (Bit 0)   Suppose that register BL contains FEH. If we increment BL we will get FFH. This represents an 8-bit number containing all ones (or 255 decimal). If we increment BL again, what do we get? The correct answer is not 100H, but 00 *with a 1 in the carry flag*. Figure 3.13 shows this concept in graphical form. Since 100H requires 9 bits for representation we cannot store 100H in register BL. We can only store the lower 8 bits, which are all low. The carry flag is used to store the ninth bit (or the 17th bit in a 16-bit operand).

FIGURE 3.12   8088 flag register

7	6	5	4	3	2	1	0
S	Z	-	A	-	P	-	C

(a) Condition code half

15	14	13	12	11	10	9	8
-	-	-	-	O	D	I	T

(b) Additional flags

FIGURE 3.13 Operation of the
carry flag

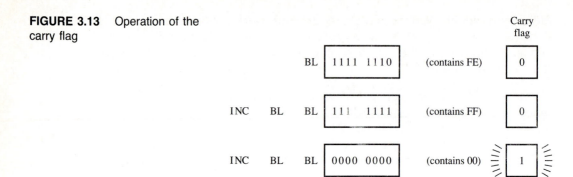

Auxiliary Carry (Bit 4) The operation of this flag is very similar to that of the carry flag except that the carry is out of bit 3 instead of bit 7 (or 15). In other words, the auxiliary carry flag indicates a carry out of the lower 4 bits. The main reason for including this flag is to aid in the execution of the 8088's decimal adjust instructions. There are no instructions that directly test the state of this flag as there are for the sign, zero, and carry flags.

Parity (Bit 2) The parity bit is used to indicate the presence of an even number of 1s in the lower 8 bits of a result. For example, if a logical instruction produced the bit pattern 11010010 in register AL, the parity flag would be set, since there are an even number of 1s (four actually) in AL. If the pattern had been 11110010, the parity flag would be cleared, since five 1s is not even.

Of the five flags just examined, the first three (sign, zero, and carry) are the most often used. It is important to be familiar with the processor flags to understand the results produced by many of the instructions we will examine in the next section.

Other Flags A number of flags are found in the upper byte of the flag register (see Figure 3.12(b) for these). The trace, direction, interrupt-enable, and overflow flags will all become important to us later. For now, simply keep in mind that they are also part of the flag register.

The flags, or condition codes, contain valuable information concerning the operation of a program, on an instruction-by-instruction basis. Thus, you should make good use of the flags when writing programs. Employ the conditional jump instructions where possible, and pay attention to how the flags are affected by all instructions in your program. Sometimes a well-written program that appears completely logical in its method will still yield incorrect results because a flag condition was overlooked.

Keep the condition codes in mind as you study the remaining sections, and be sure to use Appendix B as you examine each new instruction.

Data Transfer Instructions

This group of instructions makes it possible to move (copy) data around inside the processor and between the processor and its memory and I/O systems. Remember that the more popular instructions are covered first.

MOV *Destination,Source (Move Byte or Word Data)*   We have already seen many examples of the MOV instruction in its role of explaining the 8088's addressing modes. So, instead of repeating those examples here we will examine other aspects of the MOV instruction. When we use MOV to load immediate data into a register, the assembler will look at the size of the specified register in the operand field to determine if the immediate data is a one- or two-byte number. For example:

MOV AL,30H   and   MOV AX,30H

are two different instructions and the immediate data 30H is interpreted differently in both of them. In the first instruction the 30H is coded as a byte value because it is being MOVed into AL. In the second instruction the 30H is coded as a word value, since it is being MOVed into AX. This is clearly shown by the resulting code for both instructions. MOV   AL,30H is coded as B0 30. MOV   AX,30H is coded as B8 30 00. Note that the second 2 bytes represent the byte-swapped value 0030H.

This much we have already seen. But what happens when the assembler does not have any way of determining how large the operands should be? For example, in MOV   [SI],0 the processor does not know if the 0 should be coded as a byte value or as a word value. This instruction would then produce an error during assembly. For cases like this, include some additional information in the instruction's operand field. If you wish to MOV a byte value into memory, use MOV   byte ptr [SI],0. A word value requires MOV   word ptr [SI],0. The **byte ptr** and **word ptr** assembler directives stand for "byte pointer" and "word pointer." The corresponding code for MOV   byte ptr [SI],0 is C6 04 00. For MOV   word ptr [SI],0 it is C7 04 00. This feature of the assembler can be applied to many of the 8088's instructions.

PUSH *Source (Push Word onto Stack)*   It is often necessary to save the contents of a register so that it can be used for other purposes. The saved data may be copied into another register or written into memory. If we are only interested in saving the contents of one or two registers we could simply reserve a few memory locations and then directly MOV the contents of each register into them. This practice is limiting, however, since we cannot easily modify our program in the future (say, to save additional registers in memory) without making a significant number of changes. Instead, we will use a special area of memory called the **stack.** The stack is a collection of memory locations pointed to by the stack pointer register and the stack segment register. When we wish to write data into the stack area we use the PUSH instruction. We commonly refer to this as pushing data onto the stack. The processor will automatically adjust the stack pointer during the push in such a way that the next item pushed will not interfere with what is already there. Example 3.9 shows the operation of PUSH in more detail.

Example 3.9:   The stack segment register has been loaded with 0000 and the stack pointer register with 2000H. If register AX contains 1234H, what is the result of PUSH   AX?

Solution: The stack pointer (presently containing 2000H) points to a location referred to as the top of the stack. Whenever we push an item onto the stack, the stack pointer is decremented by two. This is necessary because all pushes involve two bytes of data. Decrementing the stack pointer during a push is a standard way of implementing stacks in hardware. Figure 3.14 shows the new contents of memory after PUSH AX has executed. The data contained in memory locations 01FFF and 01FFE is replaced by the contents of register AX. Notice that the contents have been byte-swapped during the write (34 comes before 12) and that the new stack pointer value is 1FFE. It is important to remember that the stack *builds* towards zero. As more items are pushed, the address within the stack pointer gets smaller by two each time. Also notice that the contents of register AX remain unchanged.

The machine code for PUSH AX is 50.

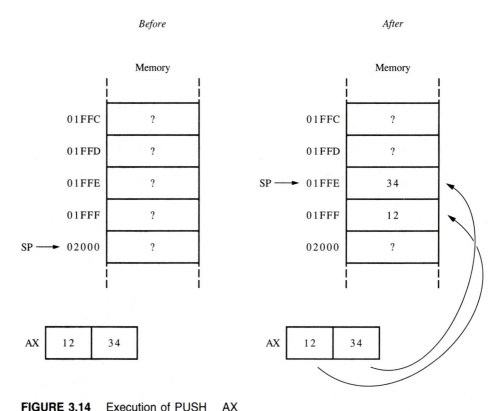

FIGURE 3.14 Execution of PUSH AX

All of the processor registers can be pushed. This means that AX, BX, CX, DX, BP, SI, DI, CS, DS, ES, and SS can all be pushed, if necessary.

POP Destination (Pop Word off Stack) The POP instruction is used to perform the reverse of a PUSH. The stack pointer is used to read two bytes of data and copy them into the location specified in the operand field. The stack pointer is automatically incremented by two.

Example 3.10: Assume the contents of the stack segment register and the stack pointer are 0000 and 2000H respectively. What is the result of POP BX?

Solution: Figure 3.15 shows a snapshot of memory contents in the stack area. The contents of location 2000 (20) are copied into the lower byte of BX. The stack pointer is incremented and the contents of location 2001 (30) are copied into the upper half of BX. The old contents of BX are lost. The stack pointer is then incremented a second time. Compare the operation of PUSH and POP and you will see that they complement one another.

The machine code for POP BX is 5B.

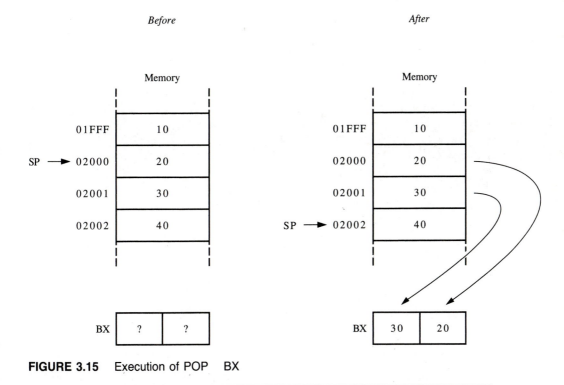

Before   *After*

FIGURE 3.15 Execution of POP BX

IN Accumulator,Port (Input Byte or Word from Port)   This is another instruction that was briefly introduced during our examination of 8088 addressing modes. The processor has an input/output space that is separate from its memory space. There are 65,536 possible I/O ports available for use by the programmer. In almost all cases a machine designed around the 8088 would use only a handful of these ports.

The input port is actually a hardware device connected to the processor's data bus. When executing the IN instruction, the processor will output the address of the input port on the address bus. The selected input port will then place its data onto the data bus, to be read by the processor. Data read from an input port *always ends up in the accumulator.*

The 8088 allows two different forms of the IN instruction. If a full 16-bit port address must be specified, the port address is loaded into register DX, and IN   AL,DX or IN   AX,DX is used to read the input port. If the port number is between 00 and FFH, a different form of IN may be used. In this case, to input from port 80H we would use IN   AL,80H or IN   AX,80H. Using AL in the operand field causes 8 bits of data to be read. Two bytes can be input by using AX in the operand field.

Example 3.11:   What is the result of IN   AL,80H if the data at input port 80 is 22?

Solution: The byte value 22 is copied into register AL.
   The machine code for IN   AL,80H is E4 80.

It may be helpful for you to remember the expression "All I/O is through the accumulator" when working with the I/O instructions. Input ports can be used to read data from keyboards, analog-to-digital converters, DIP switches, clock chips, UART's, and other peripherals that may be connected to the CPU.

OUT   Port,Accumulator (Output Byte or Word to Port)   This instruction is a complement to the IN instruction. With OUT, we can send 8 or 16 bits of data to an output port. The port address may be loaded into DX for use with OUT   DX,AL or OUT   DX,AX, or specified within the instruction, as in OUT   80H,AL or OUT   80H,AX.

Example 3.12:   What happens during execution of OUT   DX,AL if AL contains 7C and DX contains 3000?

Solution: The port address stored in register DX is output on the address bus, along with the 7C from AL on the data bus. The output port circuitry must recognize address 3000 and store the data.
   The machine code for OUT   DX,AL is EE.

We will examine the operation of input and output ports in much more detail in Chapter 9.

LEA   Destination,Source (Load Effective Address)   This instruction is used
to load the offset of a memory operand into one of the processor's registers. The
memory operand may be specified by any number of addressing modes.

Example 3.13:   What is the difference between MOV   AX,[40H] and LEA
AX,[40H]?

Solution: In MOV   AX,[40H] the processor is directed to read two bytes of
data from locations 40 and 41 and place the data into register AX. In LEA
AX,[40H] the processor simply places 40H into register AX. Modifying these
instructions slightly should help to further define the difference just presented.
Suppose that a label called TIME has been defined in a program, and has the
memory address value of 40H associated with it. Using MOV   AX,TIME will
cause the data at locations TIME and TIME+1 (40H and 41H) to be read from
memory and stored in AX. Using LEA   AX,TIME will cause the effective
address of the label (which is 40H) to be copied into AX. The memory location
TIME is never accessed in LEA   AX,TIME. All operands dealing with memory locations are assumed to be found in a 64KB block pointed to by the data
segment register.
    What does LEA   AX,[SI] do? It *does not* read the contents of the memory
locations pointed to by SI. Instead, the value of SI at execution time is loaded
into AX. We will use this instruction to load label addresses in many of our
example programs.
    The machine code for LEA   AX,[40H] is 8D 06 40 00. The machine code
for LEA   AX,[SI] is 8D 04.

PUSHF   (Push Flags onto Stack)   There are times when it is necessary to
save the state of each flag in the processor's flag register. Usually this is done
whenever the processor is interrupted. Saving the flags and restoring them at
a later time, along with the processor registers, is a proven technique for re-
suming program execution after an interrupt.

Example 3.14:   Assume that the stack segment register and the stack
pointer have been loaded with addresses 0000 and 2000H respectively, and
that the flag register contains 00C0H. What is the result of PUSHF?

Solution: PUSHF writes the contents of the flag register into stack memory.
The operation of PUSHF is similar to PUSH, as you can see in Figure 3.16. The
stack pointer is decremented by two. Then the lower byte of the flag register
(C0) is written into stack memory, followed by the upper byte (00). As usual,
we see that the 16-bit flag register has been byte-swapped as it was written
into memory.
    The machine code for PUSHF is 9C.

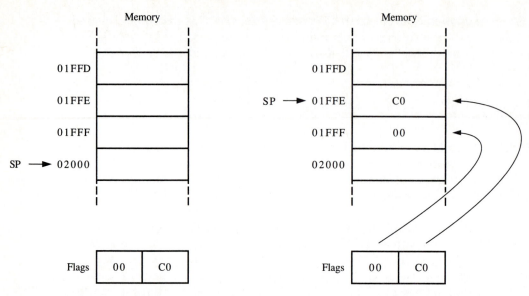

FIGURE 3.16 Operation of PUSHF

POPF (Pop Flags off Stack) This instruction reverses the operation of PUSHF, popping two bytes off the stack and storing them in the flag register. The operation is similar to POP, with the stack pointer increased by two at completion.

The machine code for POPF is 9D.

XCHG Destination,Source (Exchange Byte or Word) This instruction is used to swap the contents of two 8- or 16-bit operands. One operand must be a processor register (excluding the segment registers). The other operand may be a register or a memory location. If a memory location is used as an operand it is assumed to be within a data segment.

Example 3.15: Registers AL and BL contain 30 and 40 respectively. What is the result of XCHG   AL,BL?

Solution: After execution, AL contains 40 and BL contains 30.

The machine code for XCHG   AL,BL is 86 C3. It may be interesting to note that the machine code for XCHG   BL,AL (which performs the same operation as XCHG   AL,BL) is 86 D8.

XLAT Translate-Table (Translate Byte) Some programming applications require quick translation from one binary value to another. For example, in an image processing system, binary video information defining brightness in a gray-level image can be false colored by translating each binary pixel value into a corresponding color combination. The process is easily accomplished with the aid of a color look-up table. XLAT is one instruction that is useful for implementing such a look-up table. XLAT assumes that a 256-byte data table has been written into memory at the starting address contained in register BX. The number in register AL at the beginning of execution is used as an index into the translation table. The byte stored at the address formed by the addition of BX and AL is then copied into AL. The translation table is assumed to be in a data segment block of memory.

Example 3.16:   A translation table resides in memory with a starting address of 0800H. How does XLAT know where the table is? If register AL contains 04, what is the result of XLAT?

Solution: XLAT uses register BX as the pointer to the beginning of the translation table, so it is necessary to place the address 0800H into BX before executing XLAT (assume here that the DS register contains 0000). This can be easily done with MOV   BX,0800H. Figure 3.17 shows the result of executing XLAT with AL equal to 04. The byte at address 0804H is copied into register AL, giving it a final value of 44.

The machine code for XLAT is D7.

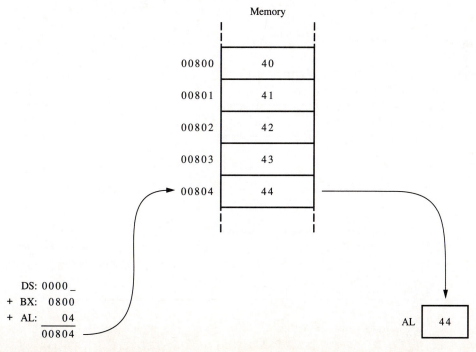

FIGURE 3.17   Execution of XLAT

A very useful application of XLAT is encryption. Suppose that the 26 letters of the alphabet are scrambled up and then written into memory at a starting address found in register BX. If register AL is restricted to numbers from 1 to 26 (1 representing A, 26 representing Z), executing XLAT will map one letter of the alphabet into a different letter. In this fashion we can encrypt text messages one character at a time. A second table would then be needed to translate the encrypted message back into correct form.

Another application involves personal computer keyboards. Since each key on a keyboard generates a unique 8-bit code, it is possible to create different keyboard "layouts," where the layout is actually a translation table that contains user defined keyboard codes. The original keyboard codes are used as addresses within the translation table to generate the correct code.

LDS ***Destination,Source (Load Pointer using DS)***   This instruction is used to load *two* 16-bit registers from a 4-byte block of memory. The first 2 bytes are copied into the register specified in the destination operand of the instruction. The second 2 bytes are copied into the DS register. This instruction will come in handy when working with source strings, which we will look at in the String Instructions section.

Example 3.17:   Assume that the DS register contains 0100 and register SI contains 0020. What is the result of LDS   DI,[SI]?

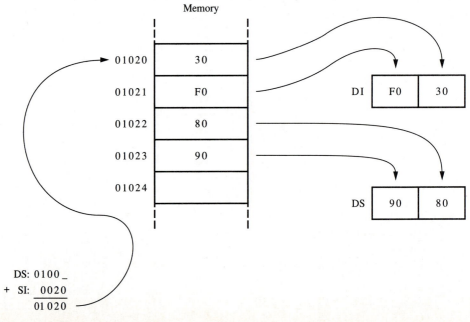

FIGURE 3.18   Execution of LDS

Solution: Figure 3.18 shows how the SI register is used to access the data that will be copied into DI and DS. Note that the addresses read out of memory are byte-swapped. After execution, the DS register contains 9080 and register DI contains F030.

The machine code for LDS   DI,[SI] is C5 3C.

LES   Destination,Source (Load Pointer Using ES)   This instruction is nearly identical to LDS. The difference is that the second address read out of memory is written into the ES register instead of the DS register. The address of a destination string can be loaded with this instruction.

LAHF   (Load AH Register from Flags)   One way to determine the state of the flags is to load a copy of them into a register. Then individual bits within the register can be manipulated or tested by the programmer. LAHF can be used to copy the lower byte of the flag register into register AH.

Example 3.18:   The lower byte of the flag register contains 81H. What is the result of LAHF and what is the state of each flag?

Solution: LAHF copies 81 into register AH. Refer to Figure 3.12 for information on the flag positions. Since the binary equivalent of 81H is 10000001, we see that the sign and carry flags are currently set, and the zero, auxiliary carry, and parity flags are cleared.

The machine code for LAHF is 9F.

SAHF   (Store AH Register into Flags)   This instruction is used to load a new set of flags into the flag register. The contents of register AH are copied into the lower byte of the flag register, giving new values to all five main processor flags.

The machine code for SAHF is 9E.

Arithmetic Instructions

This group of instructions provides the 8088 with its basic math skills. Addition, subtraction, multiplication, and division can all be performed on different sizes and types of numbers. You will need to refer to Appendix B often to fully understand the effects of each instruction on the processor's flags.

ADD   Destination,Source (Add Byte or Word)   This instruction is used to add 8- or 16-bit operands together. The sum of the two operands replaces the destination operand. All flags are affected.

Example 3.19: If AX and BX contain 1234H and 2345H, respectively, what is the result of ADD AX,BX? How would this answer compare with ADD BX,AX?

Solution: Considering ADD AX,BX, adding 1234H to 2345H gives 3579H, which replaces the contents of AX. BX still contains 2345H. ADD BX,AX generates the same sum, but the contents of BX are changed instead.
    The machine code for ADD AX,BX is 01 D8. For ADD BX,AX we get 01 C3.

It is also possible to add constants (immediate data) to registers or memory. For example, ADD CX,7 would add 7 to the number stored in register CX. The machine code for this instruction is 83 C1 07.

ADC   Destination,Source (Add Byte or Word with Carry)   The operation of ADC is similar to ADD; however, in addition to the source operand the processor also adds the contents of the carry flag. The carry flag is then updated based on the size of the result. Other flags are also affected.

Example 3.20: Using the same register values from Example 3.19, what is the result of ADC AX,BX if the carry flag is set?

FIGURE 3.19   Execution of ADC AX,BX

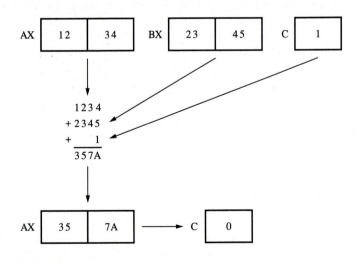

Solution: Figure 3.19 shows how AX, BX, and the carry flag are added together to get 357AH, which replaces the contents of register AX. The carry flag is then cleared, since 357AH fits into a 16-bit register.
    The machine code for ADC AX,BX is 11 D8.

INC   Destination (Increment Byte or Word by 1)   There are many times when we only need to add 1 to a register or to the contents of a memory location. We could do this using the ADD instruction, but it is simpler to use INC. Also, in many cases the use of INC generates less machine code than the corresponding ADD instruction, resulting in faster execution. All flags are affected.

Example 3.21:   The two instructions ADD   AX,1 and INC   AX both increase the value of register AX by 1. The machine code for each differs greatly, with ADD   AX,1 assembling into 3 bytes (05 01 00) and INC   AX only requiring one byte (40). Since 3 bytes take longer to fetch from memory than one byte, INC   AX executes faster than ADD   AX,1.

SUB   Destination,Source (Subtract Byte or Word)   SUB can be used to subtract 8- or 16-bit operands. If the source operand is smaller than the destination operand, the resulting borrow is indicated by setting the carry flag.

Example 3.22:   If AL contains 00 and BL contains 01, what is the result of SUB   AL,BL?

Solution: Subtracting 01 from 00 in 8-bit binary results in FFH, which is the 2's complement representation of −1. So, the contents of AL are replaced with FFH, and both the carry and sign flags are set to indicate a borrow and a negative result.

SBB   Destination,Source (Subtract Byte or Word with Borrow)   SBB executes in much the same way as SUB, except the contents of the carry flag are also subtracted from the destination operand. The contents of the carry flag are updated at completion of the instruction.

DEC   Destination (Decrement Byte or Word by 1)   DEC provides a quick way to subtract 1 from any register or the contents of any memory location. All flags are affected.

Example 3.23:   What is the result of DEC   byte ptr [200H]? Assume that the DS register contains 0500H.

Solution: Since we are decrementing the contents of a memory location, the assembler must be informed of the operand size. This is accomplished with the byte ptr directive. Figure 3.20 shows the change made to location 05200H when the instruction executes.

The machine code for DEC byte ptr [200H] is FE 0E 00 02. Notice that the last two bytes are the byte-swapped address 0200H.

FIGURE 3.20 Execution of DEC byte ptr [200H]

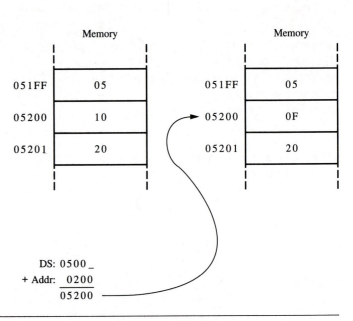

CMP Destination,Source (Compare Byte or Word) This very useful instruction allows the programmer to perform comparisons on byte and word values. Comparisons are employed in search algorithms and whenever range checking needs to be done on input data. For example, it may be beneficial to use CMP to check a register for a zero value prior to multiplication or division. The internal operation of CMP is actually a subtraction of the destination and source operands without any modification to either. The flags are updated based on the results of the subtraction. The zero flag is set after a CMP if the destination and source operands are equal, and cleared otherwise. All other flags are also affected.

Example 3.24: What CMP instruction is needed to determine if the accumulator (AX) contains the value 3B2EH?

Solution: We should use CMP AX,3B2EH to do the checking. As we will see later, we should follow the CMP instruction with some kind of conditional jump (as in JZ MATCH or JNZ NOMATCH). We could also test each half of

AX individually, using CMP   AH,3BH and CMP   AL,2EH, but this results in more code and slower execution time.

The machine code for CMP   AX,3B2EH is 3D 2E 3B.

MUL   Source (Multiply Byte or Word Unsigned)   This unsigned multiply instruction treats byte and word numbers as unsigned binary values. This gives an 8-bit number a range of 0 to 255 and a 16-bit number the range 0 to 65,535. The source operand specified in the instruction is multiplied by the accumulator. If the source is a byte, AL is used as the multiplier, with the 16-bit result replacing the contents of AX. If the source is a word, AX is used as the multiplier, and the 32-bit result is returned in registers AX and DX, with DX containing the upper 16 bits of the result. All flags are affected.

Example 3.25:   What is the result of MUL   CL if AL contains 20H and CL contains 80H? What is the result of MUL   AX if AX contains A064H?

Solution: The decimal equivalents of 20H and 80H are 32 and 128, respectively. The product of these two numbers is 4096, which is 1000H. Upon completion, AX will contain 1000H. The decimal equivalent of A064H is 41,060. MUL   AX multiplies the accumulator by itself, giving 1,685,923,600 as the result, which is 647D2710H. The upper half of this hexadecimal number (647DH) will be placed into register DX. The lower half (2710H) will replace the contents of AX.

The machine code for MUL   CL is F6 E1. The machine code for MUL AX is F7 E0.

IMUL   Source (Integer Multiply Byte or Word)   This multiply instruction is very similar to MUL except that the source operand is assumed to be a *signed* binary number. This gives byte operands a range of −128 to 127 and word operands a range of −32,768 to 32,767. Once again the operand size determines whether the result will be placed into AX or AX and DX.

Example 3.26:   What is the result of IMUL   CL if AL contains 20H and CL contains 80H?

Solution: While this example appears to be exactly like Example 3.25, it actually is not, since the 80H in register CL is interpreted as −128. The product of −128 and 32 is −4096, which is F000H in 2's complement notation. This is the value placed into AX upon completion.

The machine code for IMUL   CL is F6 E9.

DIV   Source (Divide Byte or Word Unsigned)   In this instruction the accumulator is divided by the value represented by the source operand. All numbers are interpreted as *unsigned* binary numbers. If the source is a byte, the quotient is placed into AL and the remainder into AH. If the source is a word, it is divided into the 32-bit number represented by DX and AX (with DX holding the upper 16 bits). The 16-bit quotient is placed into AX and the 16-bit remainder into DX. If division by zero is attempted, a type-0 interrupt is generated. All flags are affected.

Example 3.27:   What is the result of DIV   BL if AX contains 2710H and BL contains 32H?

Solution: The decimal equivalents of 2710H and 32H are 10,000 and 50, respectively. The quotient of these two numbers is 200, which is C8H. This is the byte placed into AL. Since the division had no remainder, AH will contain 00.

The machine code for DIV   BL is F6 F3.

IDIV   Source (Integer Divide Byte or Word)   As with MUL and IMUL, we also see similarities between DIV and IDIV. In IDIV the operands are treated as signed binary numbers. Everything else remains the same.

Example 3.28:   What is the result of IDIV   CX if AX contains 7960H, DX contains FFFEH, and CX contains 1388H?

Solution: Since a word operand is specified, the 32-bit number represented by DX and AX will be divided by CX. Combining DX and AX gives FFFE7960H, which is −100,000. CX represents 5000. Dividing −100,000 and 5000 gives −20, which is FFECH. This value is placed into AX, and 0000 is placed into DX since the division has no remainder.

The machine code for IDIV   CX is F7 F9.

NEG   Destination (Negate Byte or Word)   This instruction is used to find the signed 2's complement representation of the number in the destination. This is accomplished by subtracting the destination operand from 0. All flags are affected.

Example 3.29:   What is the result of NEG   AX if AX contains FFECH?

Solution: Subtracting FFECH from 0 gives 0014H, which is positive 20. Take another look at Example 3.28 and you will see that we have just proved the results of the IDIV instruction.

The machine code for NEG   AX is F7 D8.

CBW   (Convert Byte to Word)   This instruction is used to extend a signed 8-bit number in AL into a signed 16-bit number in AX. This is sometimes necessary before performing an IDIV or IMUL. No flags are affected.

Example 3.30:   What does AX contain after execution of CBW if AL initially contains 37H? What if AL contains B7H?

Solution: Since 37H is a positive signed number, the result in AX is 0037H. Note that the most significant bit is still a zero. B7H, however, is a negative signed number, resulting in AX becoming FFB7H. Note here that the MSB is a one, indicating a negative result.

The machine code for CBW is 98.

CWD   (Convert Word to Double-word)   This instruction extends the sign of the number stored in AX through all 16 bits of register DX. This results in a 32-bit signed number in DX and AX. CWD is useful when preparing for IMUL and IDIV. No flags are affected.

Example 3.31:   What is in DX after CWD executes with AX containing 4000H?

Solution: Since 4000H is positive (the MSB is zero), DX will contain 0000.
The machine code for CWD is 99.

DAA   (Decimal Adjust for Addition)   When a hexadecimal number contains only the digits 0–9 (as in 07H, 35H, 72H, and 98H), the number is referred to as a **packed decimal** number. So, instead of a range of 00 to FFH we get 00 to 99H. When these types of numbers are added together, they do not always produce the correct packed decimal result. Consider the addition of 15H and 25H. Straight hexadecimal addition gives 3AH as the result. Since we are interpreting our numbers as packed decimal numbers, 3AH seems to be an illegal answer. The processor is able to correct this problem with the use of DAA, which will modify the byte stored in AL so that it looks like a packed decimal number. Numbers of this type are also referred to as **binary coded decimal (BCD)** numbers.

All flags are affected.

Example 3.32:   If ADD   AL,BL is executed with AL containing 15H and BL containing 25H, what is the resulting value of AL? What does AL contain if DAA is executed next?

Solution: Adding 15H to 25H gives 3AH, as we just saw. When DAA executes it will examine AL and determine that it should be corrected to 40H to give the correct packed decimal answer. It is interesting that the processor adds 06H to AL to convert it into a packed number.
  The machine code for DAA is 27.

DAS   (Decimal Adjust for Subtraction)   This instruction performs the same function as DAA except it is used after a SUB or SBB instruction. All flags are affected.

Example 3.33:   If AL contains 10H and CL contains 02H, what is the result of SUB   AL,CL? What happens if DAS is executed next?

Solution: Subtracting 02H from 10H will result in AL containing 0EH. Following the SUB instruction with DAS will cause AL to be converted into 08H, the correct packed decimal answer.
  The machine code for DAS is 2F.

AAA   (ASCII Adjust for Addition)   Occasionally the need arises to perform addition on ASCII numbers. The ASCII codes for 0-9 are 30H through 39H. Addition of two ASCII codes unfortunately does not result in a correct ASCII or decimal answer. For example, adding 33H (the ASCII code for 3) and 39H (the ASCII code for 9) gives 6CH. Using DAA to correct this result will give 72H, which is the correct packed decimal answer but not the answer we are looking for. After all, 3 plus 9 equals 12, which must be represented by the ASCII characters 31H and 32H. AAA is used to perform this correction by using it after ADD or ADC. AAA will examine the contents of AL, adjusting the lower four bits to make the correct decimal result. Then it will clear the upper four bits, and add one to AH if the lower four bits of AL were initially greater than 9. Only the carry and auxiliary carry flags are directly affected.

Example 3.34:   Register AX is located with 0033H. Register BL is loaded with 39H. ADD AL,BL is executed, giving AL a new value of 6CH. What happens if AAA is executed next?

Solution: AAA will see the C part of 6CH and correct it to 2 (by adding 6). Next, the upper four bits of AL will be cleared. Now AL contains 02. Since the lower four bits of AL (prior to execution of AAA) were greater than 9, one will be added to AH, making its final value 01. We end up with AX containing

0102H. If we now add 30H to each byte in AX, we will get 3132H, the two ASCII digits that represent 12.

The machine code for AAA is 37.

AAS (ASCII Adjust for Subtraction) This instruction performs the same correction procedure that AAA does, except it is used after SUB or SBB to modify the results of a subtraction. Also, if the number in the lower four bits of AL is greater than nine, one will be *subtracted* from AH.

Example 3.35: AX is loaded with 0037H and BL is loaded with 32H. SUB AL,BL is executed and the processor replaces the contents of AL with 05H. What happens if AAS is now executed? What are the results if BL was initially loaded with 39H?

Solution: Since the number in the lower four bits of AL (5) is not greater than nine, AAS does not change it. The upper four bits of AL are cleared. Since no change was needed there is no need to add one to AH. The final value of AX is 0005H. Adding 30H to each byte in AX gives 3035H, the two ASCII codes for the number 05.

If BL is initially loaded with 39H the results of SUB AL,BL is FEH, which is placed in AL. When this value is examined by AAS the E in FEH will be changed to 8 (by subtracting 6) and the upper four bits will be cleared. AL now contains 08H. Note that 7 minus 9 is −8. AL now contains the 8 part of the answer. Since AL required modification, AH will be decremented. The final value of AX is FF08H. The FFH in AH indicates that a borrow occurred (and so does the carry flag). Adding 30H to AL results in the correct ASCII code for 8 (which is 38H).

The machine code for AAS is 3F.

AAM (ASCII Adjust for Multiply) This instruction is used to adjust the results of a MUL instruction so that the results can be interpreted as ASCII characters. Both the operands used in the multiplication must be less than or equal to nine (their upper four bits must be zero). This ensures that the upper byte of the result placed in AX will be 00, a necessary requirement for proper operation of AAM. AAM will convert the binary product found in AL into two separate digits. One replaces the contents of AL and the other replaces the contents of AH. Software can then be used to add 30H to each value to obtain the ASCII codes for the correct product. Only the parity, sign, and zero flags are directly affected.

Example 3.36: AL and BL are given initial values of 7 and 6 respectively. MUL BL produces 002AH in AX. Note that 7 times 6 is 42 and that 2AH is equal to 42. What are the contents of AX after AAM is executed?

Solution: Since the upper four bits of each operand used in the multiplication were zero and the lower four bits contained numbers less than or equal to nine, AAM will be able to correctly convert the product in AX. AAM converts the 2AH in AL into the digits 4 and 2 and writes them in AH and AL, respectively. The final contents of AX are 0402H. If we now add 30H to each byte in AX we get 3432H, the two ASCII codes for 42.

The machine code for AAM is D4 0A.

AAD   (ASCII Adjust for Division)   This instruction is executed *before* DIV to change an unpacked 2-digit BCD number in AX into its binary equivalent in AL. AH must be 00 after the change to produce the correct results. The number in AL can then be divided (via DIV) to get the correct binary quotient in AL. Only the parity, sign, and zero flags are directly affected.

Example 3.37: Register AX is loaded with 0600H. These two bytes correspond to the unpacked BCD number 60, not its decimal equivalent of 1536. If BL is loaded with 04H we expect that the use of AAD and DIV will produce the correct answer of 15 (which is 60 divided by 4). What are the contents of AX after AAD and after DIV BL?

Solution: AAD examines AX and finds that it contains a valid unpacked BCD number. The value 600H is converted to 003CH, the correct binary equivalent of 60. DIV BL then divides this number by 4 to produce 000FH in AX. Remember that AL contains the quotient and AH contains the remainder. The quotient 0FH equals 15 and the remainder is 0, so AAD correctly adjusted AX before the division.

The machine code for AAD is D5 0A.

Bit Manipulation Instructions

The instructions in this group are used to perform Boolean operations on binary data, and to shift and rotate data both left and right within registers or memory.

NOT   Destination ("NOT" Byte or Word)   This instruction finds the complement of the binary data stored in the destination operand. All 0's are changed to 1's, and all 1's to 0's. No flags are affected.

Example 3.38: What is the result of NOT   AL if AL contains 3EH?

Solution: The binary equivalent of 3EH is 00111110. When these bits are complemented we get 11000001, which is C1H. This is the final value in AL.

The machine code for NOT   AL is F6 D0.

FIGURE 3.21   Truth table for an
AND gate

A B	f
0 0	0
0 1	0
1 0	0
1 1	1

A ⊃— f
B

AND   Destination,Source ("AND" Byte or Word)   This instruction performs
the logical AND operation on the destination and source operands. AND is a
useful way of turning bits off (making them 0). Refer to Figure 3.21 for a
review of the truth table for a two-input AND gate. Note that it takes two 1's to
make a 1 on the output of the AND gate. The processor AND's the bits in each
operand together to produce the final result. This logical operation is very
useful for masking off unwanted bits during many types of comparison operations. All flags are affected.

Example 3.39:   What is the result of AND   AL,[345H]? Assume that the DS
register contains 2000H and that AL contains BCH.

Solution: Figure 3.22 shows how the processor accesses location 20345H and
AND's its contents (27H = 00100111) with that of the AL register (BCH =
10111100). The result is 24H, which is placed into AL.
    The machine code for AND   AL,[345H] is 22 06 45 03.

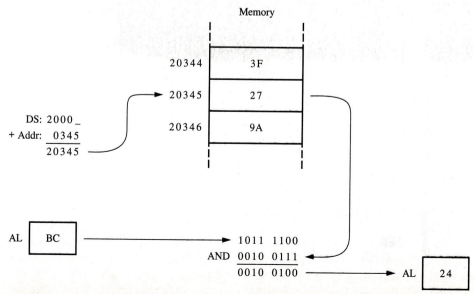

FIGURE 3.22   Operation of AND

FIGURE 3.23 Truth table for an
OR gate

A —⊐D— f
B —

A	B	f
0	0	0
0	1	1
1	0	1
1	1	1

OR   Destination,Source ("OR" Byte or Word)   This instruction performs a logical OR of each bit in the source and destination operands. OR can be used to turn bits on (make them 1). Figure 3.23 shows the truth table for a two-input OR gate. The output of the OR gate will be high if a one is present on either (or both) inputs. Respective bits in each operand are OR'd together to produce the final result. All flags are affected.

Example 3.40:   Register BX contains 2589H. What is the result of OR BX,0C77CH?

Solution: As a matter of habit, whenever we use a hexadecimal number in an instruction, we precede it with a leading zero if the first hexadecimal digit is greater than nine. So, the correct way to specify C77CH in the OR instruction is to write 0C77CH. The purpose for doing this is to prevent the assembler from thinking that C77CH is the name of a label somewhere in the program. Putting a leading zero first does not change the value of the hexadecimal number but does tell the assembler that it is working with a number and not a name.

So, in Figure 3.24 we see how the OR instruction operates on BX and the immediate data to produce the final result of E7FDH in register BX.

The machine code for OR   BX,0C77CH is 81 CB 7C C7.

FIGURE 3.24 Operation of OR

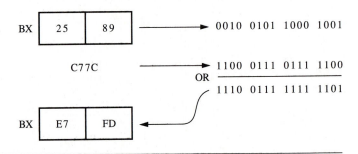

XOR   Destination,Source (Exclusive-OR Byte or Word)   XOR is a special form of OR in which the inputs *must be different* to get a 1 out of the logic gate. Figure 3.25 shows the truth table for a two-input XOR gate. Clearly, the output is high only when the inputs are different. The XOR function can be used to toggle bits to their opposite states. For example, 011 XOR'd with 010 gives 001. Note that the second bit in the first group has been changed to 0. If we XOR 001 with 010 again, we get 011. The two XOR operations simply toggled

FIGURE 3.25 Truth table for an
Exclusive-OR gate

A	B	f
0	0	0
0	1	1
1	0	1
1	1	0

the second bit back and forth. This is due to the 1 in the second group of bits. It may be interesting to note that XOR   AL,0FFH does the same job as NOT   AL. All flags are affected by XOR.

Example 3.41: What is the result of XOR   AX,CX if AX contains 1234H and CX contains 4567H?

Solution: Figure 3.26 shows how the two 16-bit binary numbers in AX and CX are XOR'd together. The result is placed in AX.
   The machine code for XOR   AX,CX is 31 C8.

FIGURE 3.26   Operation of XOR

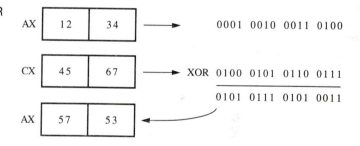

TEST   Destination,Source ("TEST" Byte or Word)   TEST can be used to examine the state of individual bits in a byte or word, or groups of bits. Internally, the processor performs an AND operation on the two operands without changing their contents. The flags are updated based on the results of the AND operation. In this way, testing individual bits is easily accomplished by putting a one in the correct bit position of one operand and examining the zero flag after TEST executes. If the bit being tested was high, the zero flag will be cleared (a *not-zero* condition). If the bit was low, the zero flag will be set.

Example 3.42: What instruction is needed to test bits 0, 1, and 13 in register DX?

Solution: We must determine the immediate data needed to perform the desired test. Figure 3.27 shows how the three 1's needed to perform the test create the required immediate word 2003H. Since immediate data cannot be used as a destination operand we end up with the instruction TEST

DX,2003H. It will be necessary to examine the flags (possibly only the zero flag) to decide what to do with the results of the test.

The machine code for TEST DX,2003H is F7 C2 03 20.

FIGURE 3.27   Operation of TEST

Bit 13   Bit 1   Bit 0

0 0 1 0 0 0 0 0 0 0 0 0 0 0 1 1

Immediate data = 2003H

SHL/SAL   Destination,Count (Shift Logical/Arithmetic Left Byte or Word)
This is the first of a number of different instructions that we will encounter that go by two names. The programmer may have personal reasons for using SHL instead of SAL, or vice versa, but to the assembler both names are identical and generate the same machine code.

The count operand indicates how many bits the destination operand is to be shifted to the left. For 1-bit shifts we simply use 1 as the source operand, as in SHL   AL,1. For multibit shifts, the count must be placed in register CL. The corresponding instruction for a multi-bit shift would then be SHL AL,CL. All bits in the destination operand are shifted left, with a zero entering the LSB each time. Bits that shift out of the MSB position are placed into the carry flag. Other flags are modified according to the final results.

FIGURE 3.28   Execution of SHL

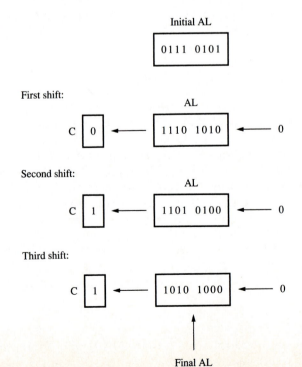

Initial AL

0111 0101

First shift:

AL

C 0 ← 1110 1010 ← 0

Second shift:

AL

C 1 ← 1101 0100 ← 0

Third shift:

C 1 ← 1010 1000 ← 0

Final AL

Example 3.43: What are the results of SHL AL,CL if AL contains 75H and CL contains 3?

Solution: Figure 3.28 shows the state of register AL after each shift is performed. A zero is shifted in from the right each time. The last bit shifted out of the MSB position is the final state of the carry flag. The final contents of AL are A8H. Could the same results be obtained by executing SHL AL,1 three times? The answer is yes, at the expense of generating more code and consuming more execution time.

This type of shift instruction is very useful for computing powers of 2, since each time a binary number is shifted left it doubles in value.

The machine code for SHL AL,CL is D2 E0. The machine code for SHL AL,1 is D0 E0.

SHR Destination,Count (Shift Logical Right Byte or Word) This instruction has the opposite effect of SHL, with bits shifting to the right in the destination operand. Zeros are shifted in from the left and the bits that fall out of the LSB position end up in the carry flag. Figure 3.29 details this operation. Keep in mind that shifting right one bit is equivalent to dividing by two.

Example 3.44: What instruction (or instructions) is needed to divide the number in BX by 32?

Solution: Since 32 equals 2 raised to the fifth power, shifting BX to the right five times is equivalent to dividing it by 32. The shift count 5 must be placed into register CL before the shift instruction SHR BX,CL is executed. An alternate solution would involve five executions of SHR BX,1.

The machine code for SHR BX,CL is D3 EB. The machine code for SHR BX,1 is D1 EB.

SAR Destination,Count (Shift Arithmetic Right Byte or Word) SAR is very similar to SHR with the important difference being that the MSB is shifted back into itself. This serves to preserve the original sign of the destination operand. When we deal with signed numbers, the MSB is used as the sign bit. If SHR is used to shift a signed negative number to the right, the zero that gets shifted into the MSB position forces the computer to then interpret the result as a positive number. SAR prevents this from happening. Negative numbers

FIGURE 3.29 Operation of SHR

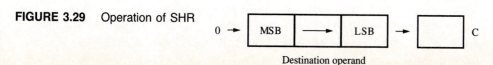

Destination operand

stay negative and positive numbers stay positive, and each gets smaller with every shift right.

Example 3.45:   What are the results of SAR   CL,1 if CL initially contains B6H?

Solution: B6H is the signed 2's complement representation of -74. Figure 3.30 shows how the contents of register CL are shifted right one bit, with the MSB coming back in from the left to preserve the negative sign. The final value in CL is DBH, which corresponds to -37, exactly one half of the original number. A zero is shifted out of the LSB into the carry flag.

The machine code for SAR   CL,1 is D0 F9.

FIGURE 3.30   Operation of SAR

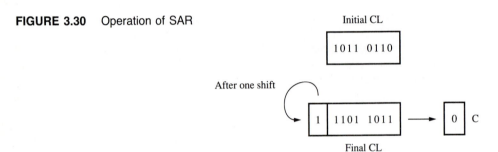

ROL   Destination,Count (Rotate Left Byte or Word)   The difference between ROL and SHL is that bits that get rotated out of the LSB position get rotated back into the MSB. Thus, data inside the destination operand is never lost, only circulated within itself. A copy of the bit that rotates out of the LSB is placed into the carry flag. The only other flag affected is the overflow flag.

Example 3.46:   What is the result of ROL   byte ptr [SI],1? Assume that the DS register contains 3C00H and that register SI contains 0020H.

Solution: In Figure 3.31 the DS and SI registers combine to form an effective address of 3C020H. The byte stored at this location is rotated one bit left, resulting in a final value of 82H. The zero rotated out of the MSB is placed in the carry flag.

The machine code for ROL   byte ptr [SI],1 is D0 04.

ROR   Destination,Count (Rotate Right Byte or Word)   This instruction has the opposite effect of ROL, with bits moving to the right within the destination operand. The bit that rotates out of the LSB goes into the carry flag and also into the MSB.

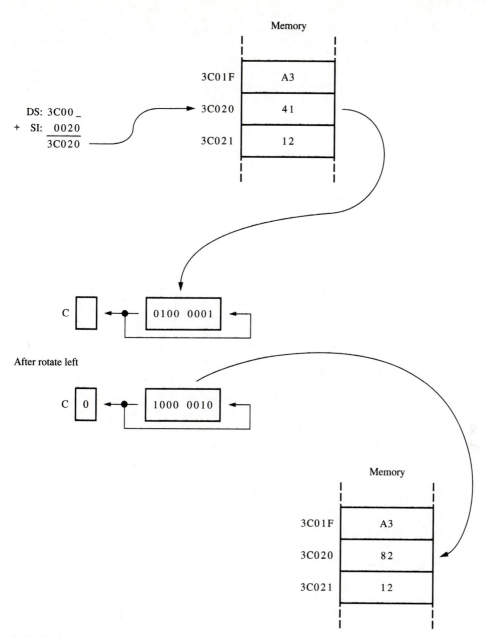

FIGURE 3.31   Operation of ROL

Example 3.47: What is the result of executing ROR   AX,1 twice? AX initially contains 3E95H.

Solution: Figure 3.32 shows the results of each rotate right operation. The final value in AX is 4FA5H. The carry flag is cleared as a result of the second shift.
    The machine code for ROL   AX,1 is D1 C8.

FIGURE 3.32   Operation of ROR

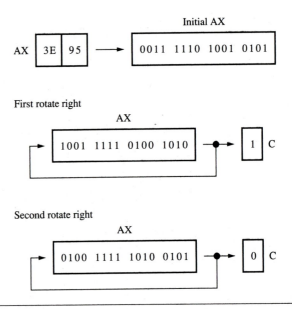

RCL Destination,Count (Rotate Left through Carry Byte or Word)   The operation of RCL is similar to ROL except for how the carry flag is used. ROL is an 8-bit or 16-bit rotate. RCL is a *9-bit* or *17-bit* rotate. The bit that gets rotated out of the MSB goes into the carry flag and the bit that was in the carry flag gets rotated into the LSB. By controlling the carry flag we can place new data into the destination operand, if that is our desire.

Example 3.48: What is the result of executing RCL   DL,1? Assume that the carry flag is initially cleared and that DL contains 93H.

Solution: The contents of DL are rotated left one bit through the carry. The zero in the carry flag rotates into the LSB of DL. The one in the MSB of DL rotates out of the register into the carry flag. This is shown in Figure 3.33. The final value in DL is 26H.
    The machine code for RCL   DL,1 is D0 D2.

FIGURE 3.33 Operation of RCL

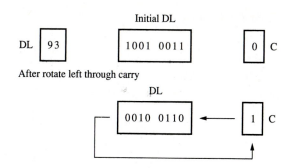

RCR **Destination,Count (Rotate Right through Carry Byte or Word)** This instruction complements the operation of RCL, rotating data bits right within the destination operand. The bit rotated out of the LSB goes into the carry flag. The bit that comes out of the carry flag goes into the MSB.

Example 3.49: What is in AX after execution of RCR AX,CL if CL contains 2 and AX contains ABCDH. The carry flag is initially cleared.

Solution: Figure 3.34 shows the result of each rotate right operation. The final value in AX is AAF3H. The carry flag is cleared after the second rotate. The machine code for RCR AX,CL is D3 D8.

FIGURE 3.34 Operation of RCR

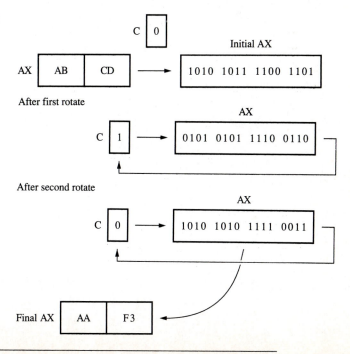

String Instructions

A particularly nice feature of the 8088 microprocessor is its ability to handle strings. A string is a collection of bytes or words that can be up to 64KB in length. An example of a string might be a sequence of ASCII character codes that constitute a password, or the ASCII codes for "YES". A string could also be the seven bytes containing your local telephone number. No matter what kind of information is stored in a string, there are a number of common operations we find useful to perform on them. During the course of executing a program, it may become necessary to make a copy of a string, compare one string with another to see if they are identical, or scan a string to see if it contains a particular byte or word. The 8088 has instructions designed to do this automatically. A special instruction called the **repeat prefix** can be used to repeat the copy, compare, or scan operations. Register CX has an assigned role in this process. It contains the repeat count necessary for the repeat prefix. CX is decremented during the string operation, which terminates when CX reaches 0. The SI and DI registers are also vital parts of all string operations. The processor assumes that the SI register points to the first element of the source string, which must be located in a data segment. The destination string is located in a similar way via the DI register and must reside in the extra segment. A special flag called the **direction flag** is used to control the way SI and DI are adjusted during a string instruction. They might be automatically incremented or decremented based on the value of the direction flag.

Figure 3.35 gives an example of two text strings stored in memory. The first string spells out SHOPPER, and is followed by a blank (20H) and a carriage return code (0DH). The second string spells out SHOPPING and is followed by only a carriage return code. Though the strings are the same length (nine bytes) they are different after the fifth character. We will be able to use these strings in our examples to understand the operation of the 8088's string instructions.

Initializing the String Pointers   Before we can use any string instruction we have to set up the SI, DS, DI, and ES registers. There are a number of ways this can be done. The source string (SHOPPER) in Figure 3.35 could be pointed to by these instructions:

```
MOV   AX,510H      ;string segment-address
MOV   DS,AX
MOV   SI,0         ;string offset within segment
```

When the contents of SI and DS are combined to form an effective address, 05100H will be the first byte accessed in the data segment. A similar technique is used to initialize the destination string (SHOPPING):

```
MOV   AX,4A8H      ;string segment-address
MOV   ES,AX
MOV   DI,0         ;string offset within segment
```

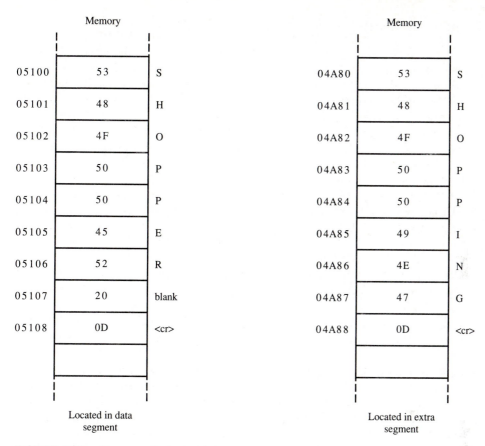

FIGURE 3.35   Two sample test strings

Remember that we cannot move immediate data directly into a segment register, hence our use of the accumulator in the first instruction.

Another way to initialize the string pointers is through the LDS and LES instructions. In this way, both strings can be initialized with only two instructions:

```
LDS  SI,STRINGA
LES  DI,STRINGB
```

where STRINGA and STRINGB are the labels of two 4-byte fields that contain the string offset and segment values. Refer to Example 3.17 for a review of LDS and LES.

REP/REPE/REPZ/REPNE/REPNZ   These five mnemonics are available for use by the programmer to control the way a string operation is repeated, if at all. REP (*repeat*), REPE (*repeat while equal*), REPZ (*repeat while zero*), REPNE (*repeat while not equal*) and REPNZ (*repeat while not zero*) are all recognized by the assembler as prefix instructions for string operations. MOVS (*move string*) and STOS (*store string*) make use of the REP prefix. When preceded by REP, these string operations repeat until CX decrements to 0. REPE and REPZ operate the same way but are used for SCAS (*scan string*) and CMPS (*compare string*). Here an additional condition is needed to continue the string operation. Each time SCAS or CMPS completes its operation the zero flag is tested and execution continues (repeats) as long as the zero flag is set. This makes sense, since a compare operation involves an internal subtraction, and the subtraction produces a zero result when both operands match. The zero flag is set in the case of matching operands and cleared for different ones.

REPNE and REPNZ also repeat as long as CX does not equal 0 but require that the zero flag be cleared to continue. So, we have three ways to repeat string operations:

1. Repeat while CX does not equal 0.
2. Repeat while CX does not equal 0 and the zero flag is set.
3. Repeat while CX does not equal 0 and the zero flag is cleared.

If necessary, combinations of string operations can be used to perform a specific kind of string function.

MOVS   Destination-String,Source-String (Move String)   This instruction is used to make a copy of the source string in the destination string. The names of the strings must be used in the operand fields so that the processor knows if they are byte strings or word strings. A byte string might be defined like this:

```
STRINGX    DB   'SHOPPER ',0DH
```

and a word string like this:

```
STRINGY    DW   1000H,2000H,3000H,4000H
```

The assembler will associate the DB or DW directive used in the source line to set the type of string being defined. Thus, the assembler will know what kind of strings it is working with when it encounters the operands in MOVS   STRINGA,STRINGB, for example.

When MOVS executes, it assumes that the strings are pointed to by DS:SI and ES:DI and if any of the REP prefixes are used that CX is initialized to the proper count. The state of the direction flag will determine which way the strings are copied. If it is cleared, SI and DI will auto-increment. If the direction flag is set, SI and DI will auto-decrement. The direction flag can be cleared with the CLD instruction and set with the STD instruction.

MOVSB/MOVSW (Move Byte or Word String)   These two mnemonics can be used in place of MOVS and cause identical execution. Since they explicitly inform the assembler of the string size there is no need to include the string operands in the instruction.

Example 3.50: What instructions are necessary to make a copy of the SHOPPER string from Figure 3.35? We want the destination string to have a starting address of 3000H, and the index registers should auto-increment during the string operation.

Solution: Since the SHOPPER string is 9 bytes long, we must initialize CX to 9. The direction flag must be cleared to get the copy performed in the correct manner, and REP must be used to copy bytes from the source string until CX is decremented to zero. One way to do all this would be:

```
B8 10 05    MOV     AX,510H     ;source string segment-address
8E D8       MOV     DS,AX
29 F6       SUB     SI,SI       ;source string offset
B8 00 03    MOV     AX,300H     ;destination string segment-address
8E C0       MOV     ES,AX
29 FF       SUB     DI,DI       ;destination string offset
FC          CLD                 ;auto increment
F3          REP                 ;repeat while CX <> 0
A4          MOVSB               ;copy string
```

Note the alternate method used to place 0000H in SI and DI. The SUB instructions require two bytes of code each. MOV   SI,0 and MOV   DI,0 would require three bytes each. The code is included for each instruction for your interest.

CMPS   Destination-String,Source-String (Compare Byte or Word String)
This instruction is used to compare two strings. The compare operation, as we have already seen, is accomplished by an internal subtraction of the destination and source operands. So, in this case, a byte or word from the destination string is subtracted from the corresponding element of the source string. If the two elements are equal the zero flag will be set. Different elements cause the zero flag to be cleared. The REPZ prefix will allow strings to be checked to see if they are identical. This is a very handy tool when writing interactive programs (programs that require a response from the user). For example, if a user enters "ZOOM IN" when asked for a command, the program can check this string against all legal command strings to see if it matches any of them. String comparisons are also employed in **spell checkers,** programs that automatically find misspelled words in a text file. (The text for this book was run through a spell checker in a relatively short period of time.)

Since the flags are adjusted during execution of CMPS, we know if the two strings matched by examining the zero flag at the end of execution. JZ   MATCH (jump to MATCH if the zero flag is set) can be used to detect matching strings.

Example 3.51: Assume that DS:SI and ES:DI have been initialized to the starting addresses of the two strings from Figure 3.35. If REPZ CMPS

STRINGA,STRINGB is executed with CX equal to 4, do the strings match? Do they match if CX equals 8? What state must the direction flag be in?

Solution: The direction flag must be cleared so that SI and DI auto-increment during the compare. When CX equals 4, the processor only compares the first four bytes of each string. Since each string begins with "SHOP" the zero flag remains set throughout the compare and we get a match. When CX equals 8, CMPS will repeat until SI and DI point to the sixth byte in each string. Then the comparison fails due to the "E" in "SHOPPER" and the "I" in "SHOP-PING." The zero flag is then cleared and the instruction terminates, even though CX has not yet decremented to 0. This indicates that the strings are different.

The machine code for CMPS is A6 for byte strings and A7 for word strings.

Some assemblers allow the use of CMPSB and CMPSW as alternate forms of the instruction. Once again no operands are needed with these instructions.

SCAS   Destination-String (Scan Byte or Word String)   This instruction is used to scan a string by comparing each string element with the value saved in AL or AX. AL is used for byte strings, AX for word strings. The string element pointed to by ES:DI is internally subtracted from the accumulator and the flags adjusted accordingly. Once again the zero flag is set if the string element matches the accumulator, and cleared otherwise. The accumulator and the string element remain unchanged. If REPNZ is used as the prefix to SCAS, the string is effectively searched for the item contained in the accumulator. Alternately, if REPZ is used, a string can be scanned until an element *differs* from the accumulator. This is especially handy when working with text strings. Suppose a text string contains a number of leading blanks (ASCII code 20H) before the actual text begins. SCAS can be used with 20H in AL and REPZ as the prefix to skip over the leading blanks. When the first nonblank (non-20H byte) character is encountered, the scan will terminate with DI pointing to the nonblank character.

Example 3.52: Suppose that the ES and DI registers are initialized to point to the starting address of the "SHOPPING" string in Figure 3.35. What is the result of REPNZ   SCAS if CX contains 9 and AL contains 4EH?

Solution: With CX set to 9 the processor will be able to scan each element of the "SHOPPING" string. However, the REPNZ prefix will allow the scan to continue only as long as the current string element does *not* match the byte stored in AL. There is no match between the accumulator until ES:DI points to address 04A86H. At that point the accumulator matches the contents of memory and the scan terminates with the zero flag set.

The machine code for SCAS is AE for a byte string and AF for a word string.

Some assemblers recognize SCASB and SCASW as alternate forms of SCAS.

LODS *Source-String (Load Byte or Word String)* This instruction is used to load the current string element into the accumulator and automatically advance the SI register to point to the next element. It is assumed that DS:SI have already been set up prior to execution of LODS. The direction flag determines whether SI is incremented or decremented.

Example 3.53: Refer to Figure 3.35 once again. Assume that DS:SI currently point to address 05105H and that the direction flag is set. What is the result of executing LODS with a byte size operand?

Solution: LODS copies the byte from the current address indicated by DS:SI (which is 45H) into AL and then *decrements* SI by 1 to point to the next element. SI is decremented because the direction flag is set. The next string element is at address 05104H.

The machine code for LODS is AC for byte strings and AD for word strings.

Some assemblers accept LODSB and LODSW as explicit uses of LODS.

STOS *Destination-String (Store Byte or Word String)* This instruction is used to write elements of a string into memory. The byte or word in AL or AX is written into memory at the address pointed to by ES:DI and then DI is adjusted accordingly depending on the state of the direction flag and the size of the string elements.

Example 3.54: We wish to modify the "SHOPPING" string of Figure 3.35 by adding the word "MALL" to it. The carriage return code 0DH will be replaced by a blank, and the character codes for "MALL" and another carriage return will be added. How should STOS be used to accomplish this modification?

Solution: Since the modification represents 6 bytes to write into memory, we will use the word version of STOS to write two codes into memory at a time. First we will write the blank code and the letter "M". Then the codes for "A" and "L", and finally the code for "L" and the carriage return. The direction flag will be cleared to allow auto-incrementing of DI, and ES:DI must be initialized to address 04A88H to begin. The necessary instructions are as follows:

```
B8 A8 04    MOV  AX,4A8H    ;destination string segment-address
8E C0       MOV  ES,AX
BF 08 00    MOV  DI,8        ;destination offset
FC          CLD              ;auto increment
B8 20 4D    MOV  AX,'M '     ;code for BLANK and 'M'
AB          STOSW
B8 41 4C    MOV  AX,'LA'     ;code for 'A' and 'L'
AB          STOSW
B8 4C 0D    MOV  AX,0D4CH    ;code for 'L' and CR
AB          STOSW
```

The first three instructions are needed to initialize ES:DI to address 04A88H. Since the 04A8H number in ES will become 4A80H when the processor forms the effective address, DI must be initialized to 0008 to get the right starting address for the modification. Since the 8088 will byte-swap the string words as they are written into memory, it is necessary to place them into AX in reverse order. For example, in MOV AX,'M ' the ASCII codes for M and blank become the word 4D20H (when the assembler looks up the ASCII codes). The lower byte of 4D20H is 20H, the first character we wish to write into string memory. The upper byte gets written into memory next, which places the code for "M" *after* the code for blank. Figure 3.36 indicates this operation. Three STOSW's are needed to write the six new string characters.

The machine code for STOS is AA for byte strings and AB for word strings.

FIGURE 3.36 Modifying a string with STOS

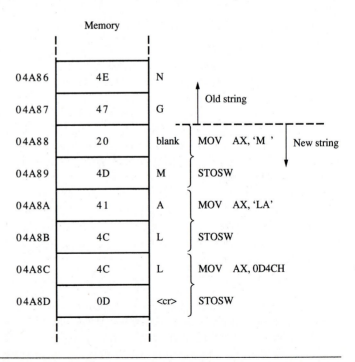

As with the other string instructions, some assemblers recognize STOSB and STOSW as explicit forms of STOS.

Loop and Jump Instructions

In Chapter 2 we saw that the 8088 fetches instructions from sequential memory locations and places them into an instruction queue. Many instructions simply perform a specific operation on one of the processor's registers or on the data contained in a memory location. There are, however, many times when the results of an instruction need to be interpreted. Did the last instruction set the zero flag? Was the result of the last subtraction negative? Did a zero rotate into bit 7 of register BL? There may be many different choices to make during execution, requiring a number of different portions of machine code to handle the choices. The program needs to be able to change its execution path to respond appropriately. For example, in a program designed to play tic-tac-toe it makes a big difference who goes first and whether you put an X in the center or not. The machine language responsible for handling these differences may need to be executed in a different order each time the game is played. For this reason we need to be able to change the path of program execution by forcing the processor to fetch its next instruction from a new location. This is commonly referred to as a **jump.** A jump alters the contents of the processor's instruction pointer (and sometimes its CS register as well). Remember that the CS and IP registers are combined to determine the address of the next instruction fetch. If we change the contents of these registers, the next instruction is fetched from a new address. The CS and IP registers define a 64KB segment of memory. Any instruction that jumps to an address within this segment performs an **intrasegment transfer.** For example, an instruction located within a code segment beginning at address 10000H can perform an intrasegment transfer to address 1C000H. But what about instructions located in other areas of the system memory? Suppose that a certain 8088-based system has 32KB of EPROM located at address 48000H. It is not possible for an instruction located in the code segment at 10000H to do an intrasegment jump to one at 48000H. In this case an **intersegment transfer** is needed. The difference between intrasegment transfers and intersegment transfers is that an intrasegment transfer only requires a change in the IP register, whereas the intersegment transfer requires both the CS and IP registers to be modified. For example, if the CS register contains 1000H, then all values of the IP from 0000 to FFFFH generate addresses 10000H to 1FFFFH. No other addresses are possible. If the CS register instead contained 4800H, then the range of reachable addresses is from 48000H to 57FFFH. Do you see why an intersegment transfer needs also to modify the CS register?

When the assembler examines a jump instruction it is often able to determine what kind of jump is required, but many times it needs specific guidance from the programmer to generate the correct code. Assembler directives **near** and **far** are used to indicate intrasegment and intersegment transfers and are included directly in the source statement. For instance, JMP FAR PTR TESTBIT indicates an intersegment transfer to the address associated with the label TESTBIT. The machine code generated for this instruction would contain information for both the CS and IP registers. JMP NEXTITEM, on the other hand, is assumed to contain a near label. NEXTITEM must be contained within the current code segment.

JMP **Target (Unconditional Jump to Target)** The word unconditional in the description of this instruction means that no condition has to be met for the processor to jump. JMP *always* causes a program transfer. The target operand may be a near or far variable and must be indicated as such for the assembler to produce machine code. In a **direct** jump the target address is given in the instruction. In an **indirect** jump the target address might be contained in a register or memory location. A special form of the direct jump, called the *short* jump, is used whenever the target address is within +127 or −128 bytes of the current IP address. Instead of specifying the actual target address within the instruction, a **relative offset** is used instead. In the case of the short jump, the relative offset is coded in a single byte which is interpreted as a signed binary number. Thus, short jumps are capable of moving forward up to 127 locations and backward up to 128 locations. When the target address is outside of this range, but still within the same segment, a near jump is used and the target address is coded as a 2-byte offset within the segment. Far jumps require 4 bytes for addresses: two for the new IP address and two for the new CS address.

No flags are affected.

Example 3.55: Let us examine the code for three different types of JMP instructions. A short jump JMP 120H is located at address 100H. The corresponding machine code is EB 1E. The EB part of the machine code means "short jump." The 1E part is the relative offset of the target address. This offset is added to the current IP value, which is 102H, the first available location following JMP 120H. If we add 1EH to 102H we get 120H, the desired target address to jump to. Now let us assume that a second short jump JMP 0C0H is located at address 102H. The machine code for this instruction is EB BC. Since the target address is smaller than the current instruction pointer address of 104H, the relative offset will be negative. The offset value BC is a negative signed number equal to the difference between C0H and 104H. In both of these instructions, the current IP value was *not* the address of the JMP instruction itself, but the address of the *next* instruction. Since JMP 120H is located at 100H and only required 2 bytes, the next instruction begins at 102H.

Now consider a near jump JMP 3000H located at address 200H. The assembler knows that it should use a near jump since the difference between the 3000H target and the current IP was greater than 127. The machine code for JMP 3000H is E9 00 30. The E9 part indicates a near jump and 00 30 is the byte-swapped target address.

A far jump JMP FAR PTR XYZ requires 5 bytes of code. The first byte is EA, which indicates a far jump. The next 2 bytes are the new IP address, and the last 2 bytes are the new CS value. Where does EA 00 10 00 20 take the processor? The new IP address from this machine code is 1000H. The new CS address is 2000H. The processor will perform a far jump to address 21000H.

Other legal forms of JMP involve using registers or the contents of memory locations to supply the target. For example, JMP   AX indicates a near jump to the address contained in register AX. If AX contains 4500H, then the processor will jump to address 4500H within the code segment. JMP   [SI] causes the processor to read the word stored in the memory locations pointed to by the SI register, and use that word as the target address. Figure 3.37 shows this instruction in more detail. The [SI] operand indicates an indirect jump and requires that the memory word pointed to by SI be read and placed into the IP register. In this fashion, JMP [SI] sets the processor up to fetch its next instruction from address 1234H within the current code segment.

The machine code for JMP   AX is FF E0. The machine code for JMP [SI] is FF 24.

Conditional Jumps   The 8088 has a large variety of conditional jumps, all of which depend on specific flag states to enable their operation. Many of these conditional jumps test only one specific flag. For example, the JC and JNC instructions examine only the state of the carry flag to determine their next step. Others, such as JA and JNA, perform a Boolean test of more than one flag. All of the conditional jump instructions are coded as short jumps, allowing them a relative range of only +127/−128 bytes from their current location. Furthermore, none of the flags are affected by the jumps. As we have previously seen, a number of 8088 instructions go by more than one name. Such is the case for the unconditional jumps. The instructions, their required flag conditions, and their interpretations are as follows:

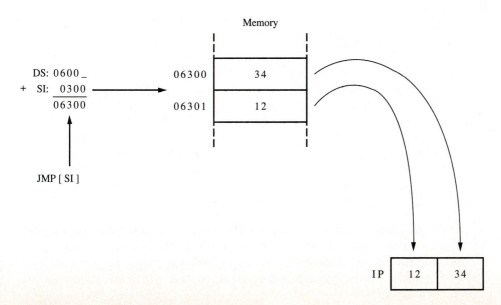

FIGURE 3.37   Operation of an indirect JMP

Instruction	Flag Tested	Explanation
JNC	CF = 0	jump if no carry
JAE	"	jump if above or equal
JNB	"	jump if not below
JC	CF = 1	jump if carry
JB	"	jump if below
JNAE	"	jump if not above nor equal
JNZ	ZF = 0	jump if not zero
JNE	"	jump if not equal
JZ	ZF = 1	jump if zero
JE	"	jump if equal
JNS	SF = 0	jump if no sign
JS	SF = 1	jump if sign
JNO	OF = 0	jump if no overflow
JO	OF = 1	jump if overflow
JNP	PF = 0	jump if no parity
JPO	"	jump if parity odd
JP	PF = 1	jump if parity
JPE	"	jump if parity even
JA	(CF or ZF) = 0	jump if above
JBNE	"	jump if not below nor equal
JBE	(CF or ZF) = 1	jump if below or equal
JNA	"	jump if not above
JGE	(SF xor OF) = 0	jump if greater or equal
JNL	"	jump if not less
JL	(SF xor OF) = 1	jump if less
JNGE	"	jump if not greater nor equal
JG	((SF xor OF) or ZF) = 0	jump if greater
JNLE	"	jump if not less nor equal
JLE	((SF xor OF) or ZF) = 1	jump if less or equal
JNG	"	jump if not greater

Note that you must supply the target address in the jump instruction. Unlike JMP, we are not allowed to use register names or other fancy addressing mode operands. The nice thing about relative jumps is that they always jump to the correct location within the code segment, no matter where the code segment appears in memory.

Example 3.56:   Is it possible to perform a conditional jump that has a target address outside of the relative range of $+127/-128$ bytes?

Solution: Yes. Two instructions are needed to synthesize a conditional jump of this type. Consider the following code:

```
                    JNZ     SKIPJMP
                    JMP     NEWPLACE
          SKIPJMP:  ---
```

Here the conditional jump JNZ is used to jump over a near JMP to NEWPLACE whenever the zero flag is cleared. When the zero flag is set, the JNZ will *not* jump to SKIPJMP, but simply continue execution with the next instruction in memory, which is the JMP   NEWPLACE instruction. So, the zero flag must be set to perform a near JMP to NEWPLACE.

LOOP   Short-Label (Loop)   This instruction will decrement register CX and perform a short jump to the target address if CX does not equal zero. LOOP is very useful for routines that need to repeat a specific number of times. CX must be loaded prior to entering the section of code terminated by LOOP.

Example 3.57:   In Figure 3.38(a) a LOOP instruction is used to execute a short section of code. The number placed into CX at the beginning of the loop (10 decimal in this case) determines how many times the loop repeats. Notice that the LOOP BACK instruction does not contain a reference to CX. The processor knows it should automatically decrement CX while executing this instruction. LOOP BACK actually performs a short jump to BACK as long as CX does not equal zero.

FIGURE 3.38   Using LOOP instructions

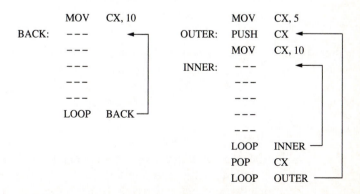

(a) A single loop   (b) A nested loop

In some cases it becomes necessary to perform a "loop within a loop," or *nested* loop as it is more commonly known. Figure 3.38(b) shows an example of a nested loop. The outer loop executes 5 times and the inner loop 10 times. Instructions in the body of the loop execute 50 times. The PUSH and POP instructions are used to preserve the contents of the outer loop counter.

A single LOOP can be repeated up to 65,535 times! How many loops are possible with a nested loop? The answer is over *4 billion*!

LOOPE/LOOPZ   Short-Label (Loop if Equal, Loop if Zero)   This instruction is similar to LOOP except for a secondary condition that must be met for the jump to take place. In addition to decrementing CX, LOOPZ also examines the state of the zero flag. If the zero flag is set and CX does not equal 0, LOOPZ will jump to the target. If CX equals zero, or if the zero flag gets cleared within the loop, the loop will terminate. As always, when a conditional instruction does not have the correct flag condition, execution continues with the next instruction. LOOPE is an alternate name for this instruction.

LOOPNE/LOOPNZ   Short-Label (Loop if not Equal, Loop if not Zero)   LOOPNZ is the opposite of LOOPZ. The zero flag must be *cleared* to allow further looping. LOOPNE has the same function.

JCXZ   Short-Label (Jump if CX = 0)   This instruction jumps to the target address if register CX contains 0. CX is not adjusted in any way. There are times when JCXZ should be used at the beginning of a section of LOOP code, to skip over the code when CX equals 0.

Example 3.58:   In Figure 3.39 a JCXZ instruction is used to skip over the AGAIN loop whenever CX equals 0. If the JCXZ instruction were absent, how many times would the loop execute?

FIGURE 3.39   Operation of JCXZ

```
DOLOOP:   JCXZ    SKIPLOOP ─┐
  AGAIN:  ADD     AX, 3  ◄─┐│
          LOOP    AGAIN ──┘│
SKIPLOOP:  ─ ─ ─         ◄──┘
```

Solution: If JCXZ is removed and the loop is entered with CX equal to 0, it will repeat 65,536 times! This is because LOOP decrements CX before it tests for zero. If CX is decremented from 0 it becomes FFFFH, which means 65,535 more decrements are needed to get back to zero. Note that the code (JCXZ included or not) works properly for every other starting value of CX.

Subroutine and Interrupt Instructions

Although subroutines and interrupts are called or generated in different ways, they share some common ground. Both require the use of the stack for proper operation. Both have a means of returning to where they came from (via information returned from the stack).

A **subroutine** is a collection of instructions that is CALLed from one or many other different locations within a program. At the end of a subroutine is an instruction that tells the processor how to RETurn (go back) to where it was called from. Figure 3.40 shows how a subroutine called ALPHA can be called from many different places within a program. The RET instruction at the end of ALPHA always causes the processor to go to the instruction immediately following the last CALL. It does this by popping a return address off the stack, which was placed there by the corresponding CALL. For example, when the first CALL is encountered, the address of the instruction immediately following the CALL is pushed onto the stack. When the RET instruction at the end of ALPHA executes, the return address is popped off the stack and placed into the IP register. Using the stack in this way guarantees that RET will go back to the right place no matter which of the three CALL instructions has been used.

Interrupts operate in a similar manner but require more use of the stack. In addition to a return address, the 8088's interrupt mechanism also pushes the processor flag register onto the stack. An interrupt is generated through software by the use of the INT or INTO instructions, which are to interrupts what CALL is to subroutines. An **interrupt service routine,** or ISR for short, is a common way of referring to the code used to handle an interrupt. Since the stack is used differently, RET is not used to return from an ISR. IRET is used instead to ensure that the stack is popped correctly. The processor has many different types of interrupts, which we will cover in detail in Chapter 4.

CALL   Procedure-Name (Call Procedure)   This instruction is used to call a subroutine. The subroutine may be located in the current code segment or in a different one. Like the intrasegment and intersegment jumps we also have

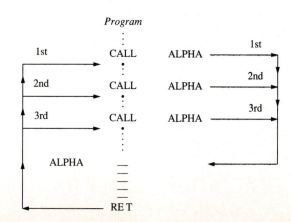

FIGURE 3.40   Calling a subroutine from many different places

intrasegment and intersegment CALLs. We think of these as calls to near or far *procedures*. A procedure is another way of referring to a subroutine and has to do with the assembler directives PROC and ENDP used in the source file. The direct and indirect types of JMPs that we have previously seen also apply to CALL. In a direct CALL the address of the procedure is specified in the instruction (usually via the label naming the procedure). In an indirect CALL the procedure address may be contained in a processor register or memory location. CALL pushes the address of the instruction immediately following itself onto the stack. In the case of a near CALL, this address is just one word of data. In the case of a far CALL, two pushes are performed: one for the instruction offset and the second for the code segment address. CALL then jumps to the address of the procedure and resumes execution.

Example 3.59: Figure 3.41 shows the contents of the stack after near and far CALLs to the same procedure. For the near call, only the offset of the next instruction is pushed. For the far call, the instruction offset and the code segment value are pushed. If both instructions were located at offset 100H within a code segment located at 5000H (e.g., CS equals 0500H), the stack will be filled with the data you see in the figure. The near call to XYZ will cause only the return address 103H to be pushed. Since the near call requires 3 bytes of machine code, address 103H is the first available instruction address.

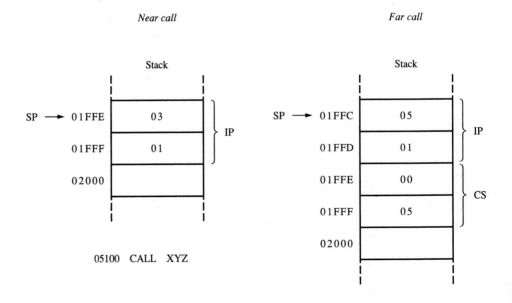

FIGURE 3.41 Stack contents during CALL

The far call is a 5-byte instruction and needs to push more information onto the stack. First the contents of the CS register are pushed (0500H). Then the instruction offset is pushed. This offset is 105H now because of the length of the far call instruction. The procedure must be careful not to modify the contents of these stack locations. It is also important to guarantee that the SP register points to the correct address before executing RET. It is OK to push items onto the stack while inside the procedure, but these items must all be popped off before returning.

RET   Optional-Pop-Value (Return from Procedure)   This instruction is used to provide an orderly exit from a procedure that has been called. It is important to understand that RET does not know *anything* about the procedure it terminates except for its type being far or near. All RET does is pop the appropriate information off the stack and place it into the assigned registers. For a near procedure, RET pops one word off the stack and writes it into the IP register. For a far procedure, RET pops 2 words. The first goes into the IP register, the second into the CS register. Once these pops are made (for either type of return), the optional-pop-value is used to pop additional words off the stack, if any at all. The optional-pop-value is added to the stack pointer, advancing it past information that was pushed before the procedure was called. This value is assumed to be zero when no pop-value is included.

Example 3.60:   The return addresses of two different subroutines are contained in the stack. The subroutine called first was a far procedure. The instruction that called it pushed the return address 0350:1C00, where 0350H is the segment address and 1C00H is the offset. The second subroutine called was a near procedure with a return address of 4080H. The second procedure was called from inside the first procedure. What are the top three items on the stack?

Solution: Figure 3.42 shows the stack created by the return addresses for each procedure. When the second procedure finishes, its near RET will pop 4080H off the stack and put it into the IP register. This gets us back into the first procedure (which called the second). The far RET in this procedure pops 1C00H off the stack, puts it into the IP register and then pops 0350H off the stack and places it into the CS register. Any number of procedure return addresses can be nested in this way, as long as the correct RETurns are always used and you do not run out of stack memory.

The machine code for a near RET is C3. The machine code for a far RET is CB. When pop-values are used, 2 additional bytes are added to the instructions. They contain the pop-value. The machine code for a near RET 2 is C2 02 00.

FIGURE 3.42 Nested return addresses

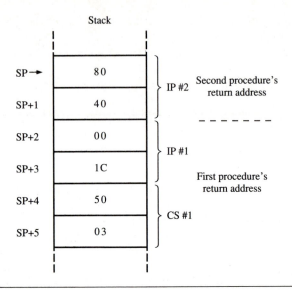

INT *Interrupt-Type (Interrupt)* The 8088 supports 256 software interrupts. While we will not go into detail on them until we get to Chapter 4, know that they initially operate in a manner similar to CALL. When INT is encountered, the processor will first push the flags onto the stack. This is an important step, since the flags tell us part of the 8088's internal state at the time it was interrupted. Then it clears two special flags called the **trace flag** and the **interrupt-enable flag.** It does this to prevent additional software interrupts from occurring while it processes the first.

Next the processor pushes the current CS register onto the stack and follows that with the contents of the IP register. The last two pushes resemble the operation of a far call. The *number* of the interrupt, rather than its address, is coded into the instruction, and is now used to find the correct place in the processor's **interrupt vector table,** a 1KB block of memory located in the beginning of the processor's address space. Its range of address is from 00000 to 003FFH. The interrupt number is called the **interrupt-type,** and is multiplied by 4 to get the address within the vector table that contains the interrupt service routine address. All ISR addresses are 4 bytes long and in the standard CS:IP format.

Once the vector address is known, the 8088 reads the ISR address out of the table, places the information into the CS and IP registers, and resumes program execution at the new location.

Example 3.61: What is the sequence of events for INT   08H if it generates a CS:IP return address of 0100:0200? The flag register contains 0081H.

Solution: The flags are pushed first. The return CS and return IP addresses are pushed next. Multiplying interrupt type 8 by 4 gives 32, which is 00020H.

The ISR address stored at this vector address (see Figure 3.43) is read into CS:IP and execution continues at address 05810H.

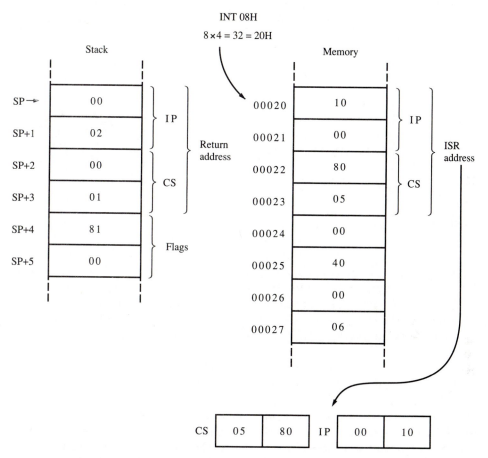

FIGURE 3.43 Operation of INT 08H

IRET (Interrupt Return) Since the operation of an interrupt requires different handling of the stack, an IRET instruction must be used at the end of an ISR. A normal RET instruction will not pop the flags off and will most likely result in incorrect program execution. IRET pops the CS and IP return addresses and then restores the flag register by popping its value too. Thus, the flags will resemble their state at the exact moment of the interrupt.

Example 3.62: What is the return address and the contents of the flag register when IRET uses the stack information from Figure 3.44?

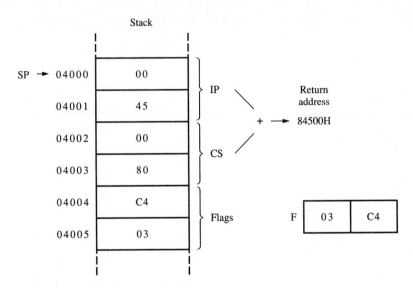

FIGURE 3.44   Operation of IRET

Solution: The word 4500H is popped into the IP register. 8000H is popped into the CS register. Together, these values indicate a return address of 84500H. Next, 03C4H is popped into the flags. The new value of the stack pointer is 04006H.

The machine code for IRET is CF.

INTO   (Interrupt on Overflow)   If the overflow flag is set when INTO is encountered, it will generate a type-4 interrupt, with all of the pushes and operations performed by INT. The interrupt vector address of INTO is 00010H. If the overflow flag is cleared when INTO executes, no interrupt is generated and execution resumes with the next instruction. This interrupt is useful for determining when the results of an arithmetic operation have gone out of bounds.

Processor Control Instructions

This last group consists of instructions used to make changes to specific bits within the flag register and to externally synchronize the processor. Also included is an instruction found on practically all microprocessors: the NOP.

CLC (Clear Carry Flag)   The instruction clears the carry flag. Its machine code is F8.

STC (Set Carry Flag)   This instruction sets the carry flag. Its machine code is F9.

CMC (Complement Carry Flag)   This instruction inverts the carry flag. Its machine code is F5. These three carry-flag instructions are useful when dealing with the rotate instructions and with multibit mathematical routines.

CLD (Clear Direction Flag)   The direction flag is cleared by this instruction. Its machine code is FC. The direction flag is used by the processor to determine if index registers should be incremented or decremented during string operations.

STD (Set Direction Flag)   The direction flag is set by this instruction. Its machine code is FD.

CLI (Clear Interrupt-Enable Flag)   This instruction clears the interrupt-enable flag. This prevents the processor from responding to a hardware INTR request. No other interrupts are affected. Its machine code is FA.

STI (Set Interrupt-Enable Flag)   Setting the interrupt-enable flag allows the processor to acknowledge an interrupt signal on the INTR input. Its machine code is FB. If a request was made to INTR while the interrupt-enable flag was cleared (which we call a *pending* interrupt), that interrupt request would be acknowledged after completion of the next instruction after STI.

HLT (Halt Until Interrupt or Reset)   This instruction terminates program execution. Its machine code is F4. It places the processor in a halt state, in which it will remain until it receives a hardware reset, or an interrupt request on NMI or INTR. If the request is on INTR, interrupts must be enabled to leave the halt state.

WAIT (Wait for TEST Pin Active)   This instruction causes the processor to enter a wait state whenever its TEST input is high. Its machine code is 9B. The processor will resume normal execution when TEST is pulled low.

NOP (No Operation)   Though this instruction does not do anything at all (no flags or registers are affected) it is still quite useful in many ways. Specifically, one application of NOP is its use within timing delay loops. There are applications that require specific time delays to be generated (for slowing down a graphics display to see the action, for example). Sometimes it is useful to throw a couple of NOP's into the timing loop, to increase the loop time. After all, it takes a few microseconds to fetch, decode, and execute NOP. It is nice to be able to use an instruction that takes up a little time but does nothing.
    Its machine code is 90.

LOCK (Lock Bus During Next Instruction)   When the 8088 is operating in maximum mode, executing LOCK causes the processor's $\overline{\text{LOCK}}$ output to go low for the duration of the next instruction. Thus, LOCK is used as a prefix to another instruction. Locking the bus is a way of giving the 8088 some privacy while it executes the subsequent instruction, which cannot be interrupted until it completes.

The prefix code for LOCK is F0.

ESC (Escape to External Processor)   When the 8088 is connected to its coprocessor, the 8087, we can include coprocessor instructions in our source files. The assembler will insert an ESC code before every coprocessor instruction it encounters. When the coprocessor sees the ESC code appear on the bus it captures some of the data that follows it. In this fashion the 8088 can send information to external processors over its bus, without affecting its own program execution.

We will shortly begin looking at some example programs. Review the entire instruction set, look at all the instruction names, think about the different groups of instructions, and use Appendix B as often as you need to.

3.6   HOW AN ASSEMBLER GENERATES MACHINE CODE

At the beginning of the chapter we looked at a sample source file and its assembled list file. During assembly, source statements are read one line at a time and examined. If they contain legal 8088 instructions, the assembler can determine the required machine code by filling in missing bits in a basic opcode format. For example, the instructions MOVSB and MOVSW both have the same basic opcode format: 1010010w, where w is a variable that takes on 0 for a byte operation and 1 for a word operation. Thus, if the assembler reads in a source statement that contains MOVSB, once it recognizes the MOVS part of the instruction, it will then look for a "B" or a "W" to determine the correct value of w. It is easy to see that MOVSB has A4 as its machine code and that MOVSW has A5 as its machine code. If the assembler does not see a "B" or a "W" after MOVS, it will generate an error message.

Other instructions are more complicated to assemble than MOVS. The multiplication instruction MUL can have two sizes of operands (byte and word), and the operands can be registers or memory locations. Clearly, the basic opcode format for MUL must be more complicated. In fact, the format is 1111011w mod 100 r/m. This strange looking string of symbols is used to specify all possible opcodes for MUL.

Consider the instruction MUL   CX. The w bit works as it did in the MOVS example. Since CX is a word-size register, w will be set to 1. *Mod* is a 2-bit variable that is set to 11 by the assembler when the operand is a processor register. The register specified in the instruction is indicated by the 3-bit variable r/m. Register CX has the code 001 associated with it. So, MUL   CX becomes 11110111 11100001, or F7 E1 in machine code. MUL   SI would be F7 E6, since SI's internal code is 110.

In our last example we encounter an instruction that has two operand fields. In XCHG   AL,BL, the operands are both byte-size registers. Each register will have its own internal code. The destination register AL is coded as 000. The source register BL is coded as 011. The basic opcode format for XCHG is 1000011w mod reg r/m. The new variable *reg* represents the 3-bit code for the destination operand. *R/m* indicates the source operand. When exchanging registers, *w* will be set to 11. Inserting these 2 bits and the 6 bits that are used to specify AL and BL, we get 10000110 11000011. This is the machine code 86 C3. Similarly, XCHG CX,DX has 87 CA for its machine code. Can you determine the 3-bit codes associated with CX and DX? (You should get 001 and 010, respectively.)

So we see that the process of assembling a program involves a great deal of time picking the right combination of bits to place into opcode patterns. Let us keep this in mind when we assemble our own programs later in the book. When the assembler indicates an error, its not because it picked the wrong bits, it is because the information supplied was incorrect, missing, or of the wrong type.

3.7 PROGRAMMING EXAMPLES

Now that we have a feel for the instruction set of the 8088, we can examine the operation of a few simple programs. These programs are designed to show how different instructions are used to perform a simple task. More complicated examples will be covered in the chapters to come.

Data Summing

Adding up elements in a data table is a nice way to use arithmetic and looping instructions together, in a simple routine. Many practical applications make use of this operation, particularly those of a statistical nature or in the algebra of signal processing. In this example, a data table called VALUES, consisting of signed words, is to be totaled, and the result stored in SUM. Then the average of all elements will be computed and saved in AVE. COUNT contains the number of entries in VALUES. Assume that the DS and CS registers have been properly initialized.

```
COUNT     DB    128          ;there are 128 words
SUM       DW    ?
AVERAGE   DW    ?
VALUES    DW    128 DUP(?)   ;data table of words
  .
  .
FINDAVE:  LEA   SI,VALUES    ;init pointer to data table
          MOV   AX,0         ;clear result
          MOV   CL,COUNT     ;init loop counter
ADDLOOP:  ADD   AX,[SI]      ;get a data word and add to result
          ADD   SI,2         ;point to next word in data table
          DEC   CL           ;decrement loop counter
          JNZ   ADDLOOP      ;repeat until done
          MOV   SUM,AX       ;save sum
```

```
        CWD                      ;convert into 32-bit result
        MOV     BX,128           ;and divide by 128 to get average
        IDIV    BX
        MOV     AVERAGE,AX       ;save average
```

There are many ways that this routine can be simplified through the use of different instructions, and you are encouraged to rewrite the routine yourself. Are there other aspects of this routine that can be improved? For instance, the largest sum of all data values is limited to a signed 16-bit value. How can the routine be rewritten so that the sum may be larger? What other changes would be made if the number of items in the table is fixed—for example, if there are always 20 items?

Searching a List

The next example illustrates how a list of items can be searched. The list consists of a series of data bytes. The last byte will have the value FF. This byte is used to indicate the end of the list, and no other bytes may have this value. The search subroutine is written in such a way that, upon entry, BX contains the starting address of the list, and the lower byte of AX, the items to be searched for. Upon exit the zero flag will indicate the success (Z = 1) or failure (Z = 0) of the search.

```
SEARCH:    CMP     AL,[BX]       ;compare AL with data byte
           JZ      FOUND         ;jump if equal
           CMP     [BX],0FFH     ;are we at the end of the table?
           JZ      FAIL          ;yes, no match found
           INC     BX            ;no, point to next data byte
           JMP     SEARCH        ;and continue search
FAIL:      LAHF                  ;get a copy of the flags
           AND     AH,0BFH       ;clear zero flag
           SAHF                  ;save new flags
FOUND:     RET
```

Since RET is used as the final instruction, SEARCH is a subroutine. A valid stack must exist before SEARCH is called, so the processor has a place to store the return address.

Study the example so that you understand why the zero flag is set automatically if the item is found. If the item is not found, the AND instruction will clear the zero flag, indicating failure.

How might this subroutine be modified to return the position of the data item within the list, for example, first element, second, thirtieth?

Block Move

It is sometimes necessary to move a block of data from one portion of memory to another. In this example, a 16K word block of memory is moved. The original data block begins at the location pointed to by SI. The destination address is contained in DI.

```
BLOCKMOVE:   MOV    CX,16384      ;init loop counter
MOVEDATA:    MOV    AX,[SI]       ;read word from memory
             MOV    [DI],AX       ;write word into new location
             ADD    SI,2          ;update pointers
             ADD    DI,2
             LOOP   MOVEDATA      ;repeat until finished
```

Raise to Power

This subroutine is used to raise the unsigned 8-bit number in DL to any power from 0 to 255. The power is passed to the subroutine in CL. The binary result is returned in AX, but may not be accurate if the power is too large for the result to fit into a 16-bit register. For example, if DL equals 10 and CL equals 3, AX will contain 1000 when PRAISE returns. But if CL contains 5 or more, AX will not be accurate, since its largest positive integer value is 65,535.

```
PRAISE:      MOV    CH,0          ;fix upper half of CX
             MOV    AX,1          ;init result
             JCXZ   DONE          ;check for CX = 0
MULDL:       MUL    DL            ;multiply by DL until CX = 0
             LOOP   MULDL
DONE:        RET
```

Note the use of JCXZ to determine the use of the zero power (which must give 1 as the result).

A Subroutine Dispatcher

In this example, a set of six subroutines are available, with each one containing a near RET instruction. The subroutines are named SUB0 through SUB5. The purpose of the dispatcher is to call the correct subroutine, depending on the number contained in AL. For example, if AL contains 0, then SUB0 is called. If AL contains 4, then SUB4 is called. A seventh routine, ERROR, is branched to whenever AL is outside the range 0 to 5.

```
SUBTAB    DW     SUB0              ;address of subroutine 0
          DW     SUB1
          DW     SUB2
          DW     SUB3
          DW     SUB4
          DW     SUB5              ;address of subroutine 5
   .
   .
   .
DISPAT:   CMP    AL,6              ;AL must be less than 6
          JNC    ERROR
          MOV    AH,0              ;fix upper half of AX
          ADD    AX,AX             ;double AX
          MOV    BX,AX             ;prepare for indexed lookup
          CALL   SUBTAB[BX]        ;call subroutine pointed to by BX
          JMP    DISPAT
```

The advantage this routine has over one that uses a loop to find the correct subroutine address is that of time. This routine takes the same amount of time to get any subroutine address, no matter what AL contains. If a loop search is used, subroutine addresses at the end of the list will take much longer to find.

3.8 THE BEAUTY OF RELOCATABLE CODE

In the early days of microprocessors few addressing modes were available. The limited ability of the early microprocessor to access its own memory required, in most cases, the generation of specific *absolute* addresses within instructions. For example, if an instruction located at address 1000H needed to examine the data in memory location 106FH, the address 106FH would have to be coded in the instruction as a 2-byte absolute address. The 8088's relative mode of addressing gets rid of the absolute address portion of the instruction and replaces it with a single byte of relative address information. Now only the offset 6FH must be saved within the instruction's machine code. You may think that saving a single byte here and there will make little difference. In short programs this is true. But in longer programs, which are more likely to access temporary values or data tables stored in memory or perform a significant number of jumps, a substantial savings in space results.

A second, more important feature of relative addressing is its built-in **relocatability.** A relocatable program is a program that can be loaded into memory at any address and then execute normally. Early microprocessors did not generate relocatable code and thus required their programs to load into memory at a specific location. For instance, a program ORGed at address 3C00H had to load into memory at address 3C00H in order to run properly. The same program loaded at 5000H, or anywhere else, would contain absolute addresses (such as the address 106FH with the example instruction at the beginning of this section) that did not look at the correct locations. For the program to run correctly, each absolute address would have to be adjusted depending on the new load address. For example, the 106FH address might be changed to 506FH. While this type of program modification is possible, programs will require additional load time when we try to execute them. Relocatable code does not have this disadvantage. An instruction that accesses the location "30 locations forward" of its own address will get the address right no matter where it is loaded. The 8088's ability to utilize relocatable code is an attractive feature.

3.9 SUMMARY

In this chapter we examined the format of an 8088 assembly language source file. We saw that there are a number of predefined fields for information on any given source line. Label, opcode, operand, and comment fields must be properly maintained so that your source file may be easily examined.

We then looked at the operation of an assembler and the types of files generated, which were list (.LST) and object (.OBJ) files. Many object files are combined into one, and executed, by a link-loader.

Most of the chapter dealt with the addressing modes and instruction set of the 8088 microprocessor. The examples presented were intended to give you ideas about writing your own instructions and how the instructions and addressing modes work.

The five programming examples given at the end of the chapter were included to give you more exposure to 8088 programming. In upcoming chapters we will explore programming applications in detail.

STUDY QUESTIONS

1. Explain the use of the ORG, DB, DW, and END assembler directives.
2. What happens when a source file is assembled?
3. What two files are created by the assembler?
4. What are the opcode, data type, and operand(s) in this instruction:

   ```
   MOV   AH,7
   ```

5. What is meant by byte-swapping?
6. Which of the assembler directives produce data: ORG, DB, DW, END?
7. What does a linker do?
8. List the seven basic instruction groups.
9. Identify the addressing mode in each of these instructions:

   a) MOV AX,BX
   b) MOV AH,7
   c) MOV [DI],AL
   d) MOV AX,[BP]
   e) MOV AL,[SI+6]
   f) JNZ XYZ
   g) CBW

10. Why are the flags so important in a control-type program?
11. What does this two-instruction sequence do?

    ```
    XCHG   AX,BX
    XCHG   BX,CX
    ```

12. What does this instruction accomplish?

    ```
    SUB   AX,AX
    ```

13. Memory locations 00490H through 00493H contain, respectively, 0A, 9C, B2, and 78. What does AX contain after each instruction? (Assume that SI contains 00490H and that BP contains 0002.)

    a) MOV AX,[SI]
    b) MOV AX,[SI+1]
    c) MOV AX,[SI][BP]

14. Registers AX, BX, CX, and DX contain, respectively, 1111H, 2222H, 3333H, and 4444H. What are the contents of each register after this sequence of instructions?

```
PUSH AX
PUSH CX
PUSH BX
POP  DX
POP  AX
POP  BX
```

15. What is the difference between LDS and LES? When should each be used?
16. If AX contains 1234H, what is the result of ADD   AL,AH?
17. What is the state of each flag after ADD   AL,AH in the previous question?
18. Memory location 2000H has the word 5000H stored in it. What does each location contain after INC byte ptr [2000H]?
19. Repeat Question 18 for DEC word ptr [2000H].
20. What is the state of the zero flag after CMP   CL,30H if CL does not contain 30H?
21. What instruction is needed to check if the upper bytes of AX and BX are equal?
22. Show the instructions needed to multiply AX by 25. Assume the results are unsigned.
23. If DX contains 00EEH and AX contains 0980, what is the result of:

```
MOV BX,0F0H
DIV BX
```

24. Repeat Question 23 for the instruction IDIV   BX.
25. What instruction is needed to find the signed 2's complement of CX?
26. What are the results of CBW if AL contains 30H? What if AL contains 98H?
27. What is the final value of AL in this series of instructions?

```
MOV AL,27H
MOV BL,37H
ADD AL,BL
DAA
```

28. If DX contains 7C9AH, what is the result of NOT   DX?
29. If AL contains 55H and BL contains AAH, what is the result of:

   a) AND AL,BL
   b) OR AL,BL
   c) XOR BL,AL

30. What does SHL   AL,1 do if AL contains 35H?
31. What is the data in BX after SHR   BX,CL if CL contains 6?
32. Memory location 1000H contains the byte 9F. What instructions are needed to rotate it one bit right?
33. Show the instructions needed to scan a 200-byte string for the byte 25H.
34. Repeat Question 33 for the word value 9A25H.
35. Redo Example 3.50 for auto-decrement copying.
36. Redo Example 3.54 by using byte operation instead.
37. Explain the difference between short and near jumps.
38. What conditional jump instruction should be used after CMP   AL,30H to jump when AL equals 30H?
39. What instruction is needed in Question 38 to jump when AL is less than 30H?

40. The lower byte of the flag register contains 95H. Which of the following instructions will actually jump?

a) JZ
b) JNC
c) JP
d) JA
e) JGE
f) JLE

41. How many times does the NOP instruction execute in the following sequence?

```
            MOV   CX,20H
      XYZ:  PUSH  CX
            MOV   CX,9
      ABC:  NOP
            LOOP  ABC
            POP   CX
            LOOP  XYZ
```

42. A near CALL generates a return IP of 1036H. What are the contents of stack memory after the call, if SP initially contains 2800H?

43. Repeat Question 42 for a far CALL located in code segment 0400H.

44. What are the final SP values in Questions 42 and 43?

45. Explain the operation of near and far RETurns.

46. What are all of the activities following an INT   16H?

47. What does INTO do in this sequence of instructions?

```
            MOV   AL,30H
            MOV   BL,0E0H
            ADD   AL,BL
            INTO
```

48. What instructions are needed to add AL, BL, and DL together, and place the result in CL. Do not destroy BL or DL.

49. What is the difference between MOV   AX,0 and SUB   AX,AX? There may be more than one difference to comment on.

50. Multiply the contents of AX by 0.125. Since fractional multiplication is not available, you must think of an alternate way to solve this problem. Assume that AX is unsigned.

51. What does this sequence of instructions do?

```
            MUL   BL
            DIV   CL
```

52. What are the largest two decimal numbers that may be multiplied by MUL? Repeat for IMUL.

53. Find the volume of a cube whose length on one side has been placed into BL. The volume should be in DX when finished.

54. Write the appropriate AND instruction to preserve bits 0, 3–9, and 13 of register BX, and clear all others.

55. What OR instruction is needed to set bits 2, 3, and 5 of AL?

56. Show how ROL can be used to rotate a 32-bit register composed of AX and BX, with AX containing the upper 16 bits.

57. Why is it important for SAL to preserve the value of the MSB?

58. Why must a subroutine contain RET as the final instruction?
59. Modify the data summing example so that bytes are added together instead of words.
60. Write a subroutine to compute the area of a right triangle whose side lengths are stored in AL and BL. Return the result in AX.
61. Write a subroutine that will compute the factorial of the number contained in DL. Store the result in word location FACTOR.
62. A data byte at location STATUS controls the calling of four subroutines. If bit 7 is set, ROUT1 is called. If bit 5 is clear, ROUT2 is called. ROUT3 is called when bits 2 and 3 are high, and ROUT4 is called if bit 0 is clear and bit 1 is set. These conditions may all exist at one time, so prioritize the routines in this way: ROUT1, ROUT3, ROUT2, and ROUT4.
63. Write a routine to swap nibbles in AL. For example, if AL contains 3E, then it will contain E3 after execution.
64. Write a subroutine that will increment the packed-decimal value stored in COUNT and reset it to 00 each time it reaches 60.

Interrupt Processing

Objectives

In this chapter you will learn about:

- The differences between hardware and software interrupts

- The differences between maskable and nonmaskable interrupts

- Interrupt processing procedures

- The vector address table

- Multiple interrupts and interrupt priorities

- Special function interrupts

- The general requirements of all interrupt handlers

4.1 INTRODUCTION

The 8088 microprocessor provides a very flexible method for recovering from what are known as *catastrophic* system faults. Through the same mechanism, external and internal interrupts may be handled and other events not normally associated with program execution may be taken care of. The method that does all of this for us is the 8088's **interrupt handler.** In this chapter we will see that there are many kinds of interrupts. Some of these deal with issues that have always plagued programmers (such as the divide-by-zero operation), while still others may be defined by the programmer. The emphasis in this chapter is on the definition of the numerous interrupts available. Actual programming examples designed to handle interrupts will be covered in the next chapter.

Section 4.2 explains the differences between hardware and software interrupts. Section 4.3 gives details on the processor's interrupt vector table. The entire process of how an interrupt is handled is presented in Section 4.4, followed by a description of multiple interrupts in Section 4.5. Section 4.6 explains the special interrupts incorporated into the 8088, such as the divide-by-zero interrupt. Examples of actual interrupt service routines in Section 4.7 complete the chapter.

4.2 HARDWARE AND SOFTWARE INTERRUPTS

An **interrupt** is an event that causes the processor to stop its current program execution and perform a specific task to service the interrupt. We are all interrupted many times during the day. A ringing telephone or doorbell, a knock on the door, or a question from a friend all indicate the need to communicate with you. The situation is much the same with the microprocessor. The interrupt is used to get the processor's attention. Interrupts may be used to inform the processor in an alarm system that a fire has started or a window has been opened. In a personal computer, interrupts are used to keep accurate time, read the keyboard, operate the disk drives, and access the power of the disk operating system.

Two kinds of interrupts are available: hardware and software interrupts. Hardware interrupts are generated by changing the logic levels on either of the processor's hardware interrupt inputs. These inputs are **NMI (nonmaskable interrupt)** and **INTR (interrupt request)**. INTR can be enabled and disabled through software with the use of the STI and CLI instructions. This means that INTR can be *masked* (disabled). NMI gets its name from the fact that its operation cannot be disabled. NMI *always* causes an interrupt sequence when it is activated. Chapter 7 shows that a rising edge is needed on NMI to trigger the interrupt mechanism, and that INTR is level sensitive, requiring a high logic level to interrupt the processor.

The processor automatically generates a type-2 interrupt when NMI is activated. This number refers to the entry in the processor's interrupt vector table that is reserved for NMI. INTR (when enabled) initiates an interrupt acknowledge cycle, which is used to read an interrupt vector number or type from the processor's data bus.

Software interrupts are generated directly by an executing program. Some instructions, like INT and INTO, initiate interrupt processing when they are executed. Other instructions are capable of generating an interrupt when a certain condition is met. DIV and IDIV, for example, cause a type-0 interrupt (divide error) whenever division by zero is attempted.

What happens when a software and hardware interrupt occur at the same time? The processor has a technique for handling this situation; it requires that the interrupts be *prioritized*. Table 4.1 shows the interrupt priority scheme used by the 8088.

Interrupts with the highest priority are divide-error, INT, and INTO. NMI and INTR have lower priorities, with single-step having the lowest. If both hardware interrupts are activated simultaneously, NMI will be serviced first,

TABLE 4.1   Interrupt priorities

Interrupt	Priority
Divide-error	Highest
INT, INTO	
NMI	
INTR	
Single-step	Lowest

with INTR **pending** until it gets its chance to be recognized by the processor. If a divide-error and NMI occur simultaneously, divide-error will be recognized first, followed by NMI.

In the next section we will examine the details of the interrupt vector table, which is accessed when any type of interrupt is initiated.

4.3   THE INTERRUPT VECTOR TABLE

All types of interrupts, whether hardware or software generated, point to a single entry in the processor's interrupt vector table. This table is a collection of 4-byte addresses (two for CS and two for IP) that indicate where the 8088 should jump to execute the associated interrupt service routine. Since 256 interrupt types are available, the interrupt vector table is 1024 bytes long. The 1KB block of memory reserved for the table is located in the address range 00000 to 003FFH. Some earlier processors automatically loaded their first instruction from address 0000 after a reset. Chapter 7 shows that the 8088 fetches its first address from location FFFF0H. This indicates that we are able to begin program execution without first having to place values into the interrupt vector table. If we plan on using any interrupts it will be necessary to initialize the required vectors within the table. This can be done easily with a few MOV instructions.

Figure 4.1 shows the organization of the interrupt vector table. Each 4-byte entry consists of a 2-byte IP register value followed by a 2-byte CS register value. This indicates that interrupt service routines are considered far routines. Notice that some of the vectors are predefined. Vector 0 has been chosen to handle division-by-zero errors. Vector 1 helps to implement single-step operation. Vector 2 is used when NMI is activated. Vector 3 (breakpoint) is normally used when troubleshooting a new program. Vector 4 is associated with the INTO instruction. Vectors 5 through 31 are reserved by Intel for use in their products. This does not mean that these interrupt vectors are unavailable to us, but that we should refrain from using them in an Intel machine unless we know how they have been assigned.

FIGURE 4.1 Interrupt vector table

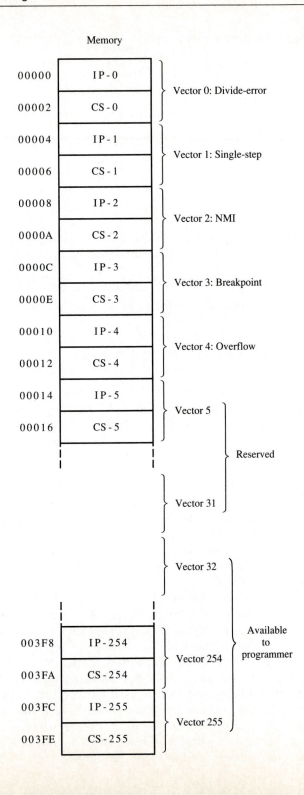

Vectors 32 through 255 are unassigned and free for us to use. To initialize an interrupt vector we must write the 4 bytes of the interrupt service routine address into the table locations reserved for the interrupt. A short example shows one way this can be done.

Example 4.1:   The interrupt service routine for a type-40 interrupt is located at address 28000H. How is the interrupt vector table set up to handle this interrupt?

Solution: An easy way to determine the address within the interrupt vector table that is used by an interrupt is to multiply the interrupt number by four. Multiplying 40 by 4 and converting into hexadecimal gives 000A0H as the starting address of the vector for INT 40. The interrupt service routine address 28000H can be generated by many different combinations of CS and IP values. If CS is loaded with 2800H and IP with 0000 we get the correct address of 28000H. Thus, it is necessary to write these two address values into memory starting at 000A0H. The short section of code shown here is one way to do this:

```
PUSH    DS                      ;save current DS address
MOV     AX,0                    ;set new DS address at 0000
MOV     DS,AX
MOV     DI,00A0H                ;offset for INT 40 vector
MOV     WORD PTR [DI],0         ;store IP address
MOV     [DI + 2],2800H          ;store CS address
POP     DS                      ;get old DS address back
```

FIGURE 4.2   ISR address for INT 40H and INT   41H

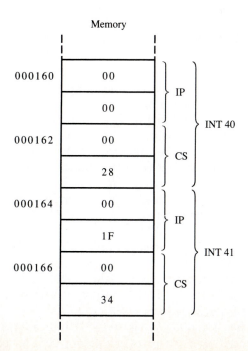

The PUSH DS instruction is used to save the current value of the DS register on the stack. Since we need to access memory in the 00000 to 003FFH range, it is convenient to load DS with 0000 and use DI as the offset into the vector table. Notice that the first word written is 0000, which goes into locations 000A0H and 000A1H. Then the CS value 2800H is written into locations 000A2H and 000A3H. Figure 4.2 provides a snapshot of memory after these instructions execute. Now, when INT   40 executes, it will cause a jump to the interrupt service routine located at address 28000H. The POP   DS instruction restores the old value of the DS register.

Figure 4.2 also shows the contents of memory for the vector associated with INT 41. What is the address of the ISR? As usual, the 2 words have been byte-swapped. The word at address 000A4H is 1F00H. The word at address 000A6H is 3400H. The effective address created by the addition of these 2 words is 35F00H, which is the address of the ISR for INT   41.

The machine code for INT   40 is CD 28 (note that 28H equals 40 decimal). The machine code for INT   41 is CD 29. All INT instructions begin with CD as their first byte and have the interrupt number as the second byte. The only exception to this rule is INT   3, *breakpoint,* which has only the byte CC as its opcode.

In the examples presented later we will see other ways in which the interrupt vector table can be initialized.

4.4   THE INTERRUPT PROCESSING SEQUENCE

In Chapter 3 we were introduced to the interrupt process in the coverage of the INT and INTO instructions. These software interrupts initiate a sequence of steps in which the flags and return address are saved prior to loading CS and IP with the ISR address. The same process is followed for hardware interrupt NMI, which automatically generates a type-2 interrupt. The sequence initiated by INTR (when interrupts are enabled) is slightly different, since the processor must first read the interrupt number from the data bus. When interrupts are enabled, INTR causes the processor to perform two **interrupt acknowledge cycles.** External devices recognize these cycles by examining the state of the 8088's $\overline{\text{INTA}}$ output, which goes low during each cycle. The first low-going pulse on $\overline{\text{INTA}}$ is used to indicate to other devices on the system bus that the processor is beginning an interrupt acknowledge cycle. In minimum mode this indicates that the processor will not acknowledge a hold request until the interrupt acknowledge cycle completes. In maximum mode the processor activates its $\overline{\text{LOCK}}$ output to prevent a system bus takeover during the interrupt acknowledge cycle.

The second low pulse on $\overline{\text{INTA}}$ indicates that the interrupt number should be placed onto the processor's data bus. A special peripheral designed to respond to the 8088's interrupt acknowledge cycle is the 8259A programmable interrupt controller, which we will cover in Chapter 10.

Once the interrupt number is read from the data bus, the processor performs all of the steps that we are familiar with. Let us review the overall process once more.

Get Vector Number

The processor obtains the interrupt number in one of three ways. First, the interrupt number may be specified directly using one of the INT instructions. Second, the processor may automatically generate the number, as it does for INTO, NMI and divide-error. Third, it may have to read the interrupt number from the data bus (after receiving INTR).

Once the interrupt number is obtained, it is used to form the location within the interrupt vector table that contains the requested ISR address.

Save Processor Information

Once the interrupt vector is known, the processor pushes the flag register onto the stack. This is done to preserve some of the 8088's internal state at the time of the interrupt (a very necessary step if we are to resume normal execution later). Once the flags are pushed, the processor clears the interrupt enable and trace flags, to disable INTR while interrupt processing is taking place. Next, the IP and CS values at the time of the interrupt are pushed onto the stack. Figure 4.3 shows how the stack is used when an interrupt occurs. The contents

FIGURE 4.3   Stack contents during an interrupt

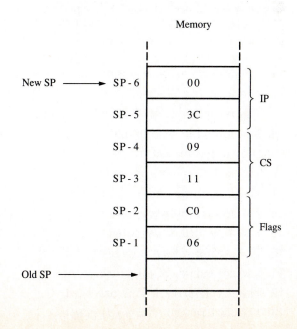

of the flag register at the time of the interrupt were 06C0H. The address of the instruction that was about to be fetched when the interrupt occurred was 1109:3C00 (in CS:IP format).

Fetch New Instruction Pointer

Once the return address has been pushed, the processor can fetch the new values of IP and CS out of the interrupt vector table and begin execution of the interrupt service routine. The address generated by the interrupt number is used to read the 2 ISR address words out of the table.

One word of caution: Since the stack contains the information needed to return to the interrupt point, we must be careful not to change the contents of stack memory or alter the stack pointer in any way that would prevent the correct information from being popped off. The processor will not remember anything about the interrupt and relies only on the data popped off the stack for a proper return.

4.5 MULTIPLE INTERRUPTS

In the course of program execution, chances are good that eventually two interrupts might request the processor's attention at the same time. For example, just as division-by-zero is attempted in an executing program, NMI is also activated. The processor needs to "break the tie" when this happens and recognize one of the two interrupts first. When we examined Table 4.1 earlier, we saw that divide-error has a higher priority than NMI. So, in our current example, divide-error will be recognized first, and the following sequence of steps will occur:

1. Divide-error is recognized.
2. The flags are pushed.
3. The return address (CS and IP) is pushed.
4. The interrupt-enable and trace flags are cleared.
5. NMI is recognized.
6. The new flags are pushed.
7. The new return address is pushed.
8. The interrupt-enable and trace flags are cleared.
9. The NMI ISR is executed.
10. The second return address is popped.
11. The second set of flags are popped.
12. The divide-error ISR is executed.
13. The first return address is popped.

14. The first set of flags are popped.

15. Execution resumes at the instruction following the one that initiated the divide-error.

It is easy to see that the stack plays an important role during this process.

A more common occurrence of a multiple interrupt is seen when the processor's trace flag is set. The trace flag, when set, puts the processor into single-step mode, where a type-1 interrupt is generated after completion of every instruction. If the current instruction is INT or INTO, you can see that two interrupts will need servicing: the INT or INTO interrupt and the single-step interrupt. Single-step has the lowest priority of all interrupts and thus gets recognized last. We will see how single stepping with the trace flag can be a useful tool when debugging a program.

4.6   SPECIAL INTERRUPTS

We will now examine the specific operation of the 8088's dedicated interrupts. Some may be very useful to implement, while others may never be needed in a program for proper operation. Even so, you are better off knowing how each one works and when to use it.

Divide-error

Figure 4.4 shows the contents of four memory locations that contain the code for these two instructions:

```
B3 00     MOV  BL,0
F6 F3     DIV  BL
```

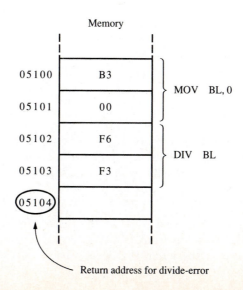

FIGURE 4.4   Instruction sequence causing a divide-error interrupt

The first instruction is located at address 05100H. The second instruction is located at address 05102H. Since DIV   BL is a 2-byte instruction, the next instruction must be located at address 05104H. This address becomes the return address when DIV BL generates a divide-error interrupt.

The interrupt service routine for divide-error can do anything the user wishes in order to recover from the error. One programmer may wish simply to load the accumulator with 0 or some other number, while another may want to display an error message on the user's display screen.

Since divide-error is a type-0 interrupt, its address vector is stored in memory locations 00000 through 00003.

Single-step

This interrupt relies on the setting of the trace flag in the flag register. When the trace flag is set, the 8088 will generate a type-1 interrupt after each instruction executes. Remember from the interrupt processing sequence that after the flags are pushed the processor clears the trace flag, disabling single stepping while it executes the trace ISR. An extremely useful debugging tool can be written and used within the trace ISR. This single-step debugger may be programmed to display the contents of each processor register, the state of the flags, and other useful information after execution of each instruction in a user program. Since the trace flag is cleared before the ISR is called, we need not worry about single stepping through the trace ISR.

You may remember from our coverage of 8088 instructions in Chapter 3 that there are no instructions available that directly affect the state of the trace flag. There are other techniques that can be used to do this. For instance, a copy of the flags can be loaded into AX by first pushing a copy of the flag register onto the stack and then popping them into AX. Then an OR instruction can be used to set the trace flag. Once this is done, the flags are restored by pushing AX back onto the stack and then popping the flags. The instructions needed to accomplish this are:

```
PUSHF
POP    AX
OR     AX,100H
PUSH   AX
POPF
```

Once this is done, the processor will enter and remain in single-step mode until the trace flag is cleared. This can be done with the same set of instructions, replacing the OR with AND   AX,0FEFFH.

Example 4.2:   Assume that the trace flag is set and that the trace ISR displays the contents of AX on the screen after each instruction executes. What do we expect to see when this group of instructions executes?

```
MOV   AX,1234H
INC   AL
DEC   AH
NOT   AX
```

Solution: Since the trace flag is set, a single-step interrupt will be generated after each of the four instructions. When the first instruction completes, the trace ISR will display AX=1234. The second instruction will increase AL to 35, causing the ISR to display AX=1235 next. The third instruction will decrease AH to 11. The trace ISR will then display AX=1135. Finally, after all bits in AX are inverted, the trace ISR will display AX=EECA. We will see that the 8088-based personal computers have built-in routines capable of displaying messages and data on the screen, so writing a trace ISR is not as complicated a task as it appears.

The ISR address vector for single-step must be stored in memory locations 00004 through 00007.

NMI

Since NMI can never be ignored by the processor, it finds useful application in events that the computer absolutely must respond to. One such event is the disastrous **power-fail.** The processor unfortunately forgets the contents of its registers and flags when power is turned off and thus has no chance of getting back to the correct place in a program if its power is interrupted. One way to prevent this from happening and provide a way for the processor to resume execution is to use NMI to interrupt the processor at the beginning of a power-fail. Since the computer's power supply will continue to supply a stable voltage for a few milliseconds after it loses AC, the processor has plenty of time to execute the necessary instructions. Suppose that a certain system contains a small amount of **nonvolatile memory.** This type of memory retains its data after it loses power and acts like RAM when power is applied. So, in the event of a power-fail, the NMI ISR should store the contents of each processor register in the NVM. These values can then be reloaded when power comes back up. In this fashion we can recover from a power-fail without loss of intelligence.

The ISR address vector for NMI is stored in memory locations 00008 through 0000BH.

Breakpoint

This interrupt is a type-3 interrupt, but is coded as a single byte for reasons of efficiency. Breakpoint aids in debugging in the following way: A program being debugged will have the first byte of one of its instructions replaced by the code for breakpoint (CC). When the processor gets to this instruction it will generate a type-3 interrupt. The ISR associated with breakpoint is similar to

FIGURE 4.5   Setting a breakpoint

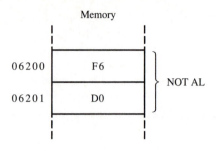

(a) Original instruction code

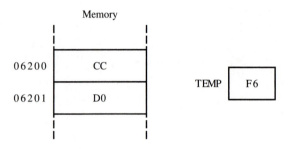

(b) First instruction byte is replaced by INT 3 (breakpoint)

the trace ISR and should be capable of displaying the processor register contents and also the address at which the breakpoint occurred. Before the ISR exits, it will replace the breakpoint byte with the original first byte of the instruction. Figure 4.5 shows how the breakpoint routine makes a copy of the first byte in the NOT AL instruction stored at location 06200H. The first byte of the instruction (F6H) is copied into a temporary location, and then replaced by the breakpoint instruction code CC. Some people like to refer to this as *setting the breakpoint*. Once the breakpoint is set, a fetch from address 06200H will initiate a breakpoint interrupt.

Clearing the breakpoint is accomplished by copying the instruction byte from the temporary location back into its original location.

Example 4.3:   A programmer wishes to find out if a conditional jump takes place or not. Where should the programmer place the breakpoint instruction? The code being tested looks like this:

```
          CMP   AL,0
          JNZ   XYZ
          NOT   AL
    XYZ:  INC   AL
```

Solution: The programmer has two choices for placement of the breakpoint instruction. It could be placed in the location occupied by NOT AL, which would cause a breakpoint when the JNZ does *not* jump to XYZ. It could also be placed in the location occupied by INC AL, activating when the JNZ *does* take place. Either way, the programmer will know the results of the CMP and JNZ instructions (by the presence or absence of a breakpoint).

The ISR address vector for breakpoint is stored in memory locations 0000CH through 0000FH.

Overflow

This type-4 interrupt is only initiated when the INTO instruction is executed with the overflow flag set. Its applications, like divide-error, tend to be of a corrective nature. You may think of overflow as the watchdog for multibit addition and subtraction operations, much like divide-error watches out for division-by-zero. If the overflow flag is cleared, INTO will not generate an interrupt.

Example 4.4: Will the following sequence of code generate an overflow interrupt?

```
MOV   AL,70H
MOV   BL,60H
ADD   AL,BL
INTO
```

Solution: Yes. Though the numbers in AL and BL can both be interpreted as positive signed numbers, the sum (D0H) looks like a negative signed number. In this case the overflow flag is set and INTO will generate an interrupt.

The ISR address vector for overflow is stored in memory locations 00010H through 00013H.

INTR

Up to now we have only discussed the basics of this hardware interrupt signal. No interrupt is generated by INTR unless the interrupt-enable flag is set. This can easily be accomplished with the STI instruction. INTR must remain high until sampled by the processor, unlike NMI which is a rising-edge triggered input. It is therefore necessary when using INTR to allow it to remain high only until an interrupt acknowledge cycle begins. The 8259A programmable interrupt controller which we will cover in Chapter 10 automatically interfaces with INTR and INTA. If the power of this peripheral is not needed, then

FIGURE 4.6 INTR conditioning circuitry

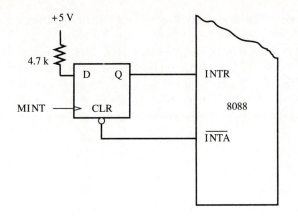

FIGURE 4.7 Circuitry needed to place an 8-bit interrupt number onto data bus

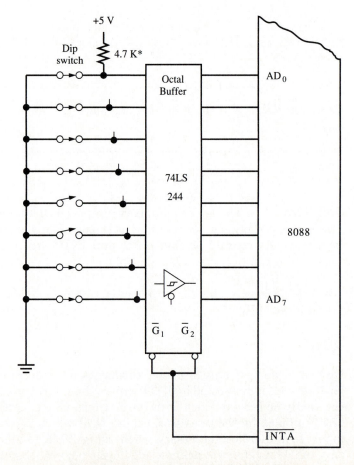

* All switches must be pulled up with individual resistors.

custom interrupt circuitry must be designed. First we need the INTR connection. The circuit shown in Figure 4.6 uses a flip-flop to condition the INTR input. A D-type flip-flop is used to convert the high-level requirement of INTR into an edge-sensitive request. A rising edge on MINT (maskable interrupt) will clock a 1 through the flip-flop, placing a high level on INTR. When the 8088 recognizes INTR and begins its interrupt acknowledge cycle, $\overline{\text{INTA}}$ will go low. This will clear the flip-flop and remove the INTR request. MINT must go low and back high again for another interrupt to be recognized.

During the second low-going pulse on $\overline{\text{INTA}}$ the processor will expect an interrupt number to be placed onto the data bus. The additional circuitry of Figure 4.7 uses a tri-state buffer to jam the 8-bit interrupt number onto the data bus when $\overline{\text{INTA}}$ goes low. You may rightly notice that the interrupt number will appear on the data bus twice, once for each low-going transition of $\overline{\text{INTA}}$. The processor will ignore the first appearance because it tristates the data bus during the first transition of $\overline{\text{INTA}}$. The 8-bit interrupt number will appear on the data bus but will be ignored by the processor until the second transition of $\overline{\text{INTA}}$. The DIP switch allows any of the 256 interrupt codes to be used. The DIP switch is currently set to produce interrupt code 30H.

For systems that require additional interrupts but still do not require the use of the 8259A, a few additional parts are needed to expand this simple interrupt circuit into a more complex one with more interrupts and a prioritization scheme. Figure 4.8 shows an interrupt circuit that allows up to eight levels of prioritized interrupts. The 74LS148 priority encoder will output a 3-bit binary number whenever any of its eight inputs go low. Also, only the highest priority input is recognized. So, if $\overline{\text{INT}}_0$ and $\overline{\text{INT}}_4$ are both low, $\overline{\text{INT}}_4$ is recognized and the output becomes 011. Note that the output is actually the inverted binary value of the input that is active. When any input is grounded, the $\overline{\text{GS}}$ output will go low. This causes a 1 to be clocked through the D-type flip-flop, signaling an INTR and latching the priority encoder's output in the 74LS374 octal flip-flop. When $\overline{\text{INTA}}$ goes low in acknowledgment of the INTR signal, the D-type flip-flop is cleared (removing the INTR request) and the output of the octal flip-flop is enabled, placing the interrupt number onto the data bus. The bit pattern stored in the octal flip-flop is 11⟨???⟩000 for any interrupt. Specifically, $\overline{\text{INT}}_0$ causes the outputs of the 74LS148 to become 111, giving us the interrupt number F8H. $\overline{\text{INT}}_1$ generates 110 at the 148's output, for an interrupt code of F0H. Take the time to find the other six interrupt numbers right now. Do you see a pattern emerge?

4.7 INTERRUPT SERVICE ROUTINES

The interrupt service routine referred to many times in this chapter is the actual section of code that takes care of processing a specific interrupt. The ISR for a divide-error is necessarily different from one designed to handle breakpoint or NMI interrupts.

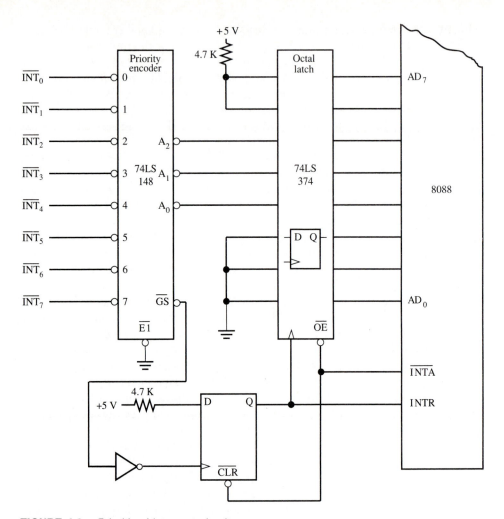

FIGURE 4.8 Prioritized interrupt circuitry

Even though these interrupt service routines are written to accomplish different goals, there are portions of each that, for the sake of good programming, look and operate the same. Recall that any time an interrupt occurs, the 8088 pushes the flags and return address onto the stack, before vectoring to the address of the ISR. Clearly, we must see that the ISR will change the data in various registers while it is processing the interrupt. Since we desire to return to the same point in our program where we left off *before* the interrupt occurred and resume processing, we insist that all prior conditions exist upon return. This means that we must return from the ISR with the state of all registers preserved. It is now the responsibility of the ISR to preserve the state of any registers that it alters. Figure 4.9 shows how this is done. In this example, DIV BL causes a divide-error interrupt. The first thing the ISR does is save the

FIGURE 4.9 Storing environment during interrupt processing

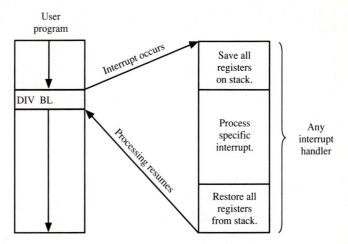

processor registers on the stack. These registers are saved with the PUSH instruction. You will need a PUSH for each register you need to save. The contents of all processor registers, including the flags, is often called the **environment** or **context** of the machine. Putting a copy of everything onto the stack saves the environment that existed at the time of the interrupt.

When the body of the ISR finishes execution, it is necessary to reload the registers that were saved at the beginning of the routine. The POP instruction is used for this purpose. POPs must be done in the reverse order of the PUSHes. An ISR that uses AX, BX, and CX would look something like this:

```
ANISR:  PUSH  AX      ;save registers
        PUSH  BX
        PUSH  CX
        ;
        ;body of ISR
        ;
        POP   CX      ;get registers back
        POP   BX
        POP   AX
        IRET          ;return from interrupt
```

Saving all registers is preferable, and will save you much heartache in the future, when you find that saving one or two registers was insufficient as the needs of the routine became more complex.

A few examples of actual interrupt service routines are now presented to prepare you for writing your own later. Try to find similarities between each routine.

An NMI Time Clock

Figure 4.10 shows a simple way to provide the 8088 with some timekeeping intelligence. In this application, the processor's NMI input is connected to a 60-Hz clock source. Thus, the 8088 gets interrupted 60 times per second. The

FIGURE 4.10   Interrupt circuit for
NMITIME

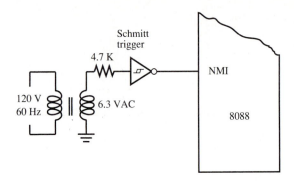

only task the NMITIME ISR needs to perform is to decrement a counter until it reaches zero, and then call the far routine ONESEC. ONESEC is then called once every second. The counter is decremented once for each NMI signal. Other code is needed to initially set the count to 60, with NMITIME resetting it automatically on each zero count.

```
NMITIME:   DEC    COUNT              ;decrement 60th's counter
           JNZ    EXIT               ;did we go to 0?
           MOV    COUNT,60           ;yes, reset counter and
           CALL   FAR PTR ONESEC     ;call ONESEC
EXIT:      IRET
```

The user program must reserve room for the COUNT location in its data segment area. COUNT DB 60 is all that is needed to reserve the byte location. Initialization software is also needed to load 60 into COUNT and place the ISR address for NMITIME into the interrupt vector table. One way to do this would be:

```
           MOV    COUNT,60       ;init 60th's counter
           PUSH   DS             ;save current DS address
           SUB    AX,AX          ;set new DS address to 0000
           MOV    AX,DS
           LEA    AX,NMITIME     ;load address of NMITIME ISR
           MOV    [8],AX         ;store IP address
           MOV    AX,CS          ;and CS address
           MOV    [0AH],AX
           POP    DS             ;get old DS address back
```

The offset of NMITIME within the code segment is stored in locations 00008 and 00009, and the CS value in locations 0000AH and 0000BH. The value of the DS register remains unchanged after execution of the initialization software.

Notice that NMITIME does not destroy a single register. In this example we can get by without having to save anything on the stack.

ONESEC can be used to do a number of things. Most likely, it will update a second set of count locations that keep track of the seconds, minutes, and hours for a 12- or 24-hour clock. Software with access to these counters will be able to utilize the passage of time in an accurate way.

A Divide-error Handler

This routine is used to handle a division-by-zero. Since the AX and DX registers may be undefined as a result of division by zero, DIVERR will load AX with 0101H and DX with 0. This guarantees that 8- or 16-bit division always ends up with a non-zero result. DIVERR also calls a special routine called DISPMSG which is used to output an ASCII text message on the display screen of the computer. The ASCII message must end with a "$" character, and the address of the first byte of the message must be loaded into the SI register prior to calling DISPMSG.

```
DIVERR:   PUSH  SI                   ;save current SI value
          MOV   AX,101H              ;load result with default
          SUB   DX,DX                ;clear DX
          LEA   SI,DIVMSG            ;init pointer to error message
          CALL  FAR PTR DISPMSG      ;output error message
          POP   SI                   ;get old SI value back
          IRET
```

PUSH and POP are used to preserve the contents of SI. The error message must be located in the program's data segment, and look similar to this:

```
DIVMSG    DB     'Division by zero attempted!$'
```

The first byte of the text message ("D") will be located in the address associated with the label DIVMSG. The last byte of the message is the required "$" character.

An ISR with Multiple Functions

This interrupt service routine will be used to perform one of four different functions when it is executed. The ISR is called with an INT 20H instruction. Register AH is examined upon entry into ISR20H to determine what should be done. If AH equals 0, AL and BL will be added together, with the result placed in AL. If AH equals 1, the registers will be subtracted. Multiplication occurs when AH equals 2, and division when AH equals 3. Any other values of AH cause ISR20H to return without changing either register. Using AH in this way lets us do more than one thing with INT 20H. This technique is commonly used when we write programs for 8088-based personal computers running a disk operating system. One interrupt might have many different functions, all of which interface with a disk drive, or display device, or printer connected to the computer. We will see specific examples of these kinds of special-function interrupts in the next chapter. The code for this ISR looks like this:

```
ISR20H:   CMP   AH,4    ;AH must be 0-3 only
          JNC   EXIT
          CMP   AH,0    ;is AH 0?
          JZ    ADDAB
          CMP   AH,1    ;is AH 1?
          JZ    SUBAB
          CMP   AH,2    ;is AH 2?
          JZ    MULAB
          DIV   BL      ;AH is 3, use divide function
```

```
EXIT:    IRET
ADDAB:   ADD   AL,BL   ;add function
         IRET
SUBAB:   SUB   AL,BL   ;subtract function
         IRET
MULAB:   MUL   BL      ;multiply function
         IRET
```

The initialization code required for ISR20H is:

```
PUSH  DS              ;save old DS address
SUB   AX,AX           ;set new DS address to 0000
MOV   DS,AX
LEA   AX,ISR20H       ;load address of ISR20H
MOV   [80H],AX        ;store IP address
MOV   AX,CS           ;and CS address
MOV   [82H],AX
POP   DS              ;get old DS address back
```

It is easy to verify that 4 times 20H is 80H, the interrupt vector table address required.

4.8 SUMMARY

We have seen that there is a fixed process used by the 8088 to implement and process an interrupt. The CPU, when interrupted, saves the flag register and program counter on the stack, clears the trace and interrupt-enable flags, and loads the interrupt service routine address from the interrupt vector table. The interrupt vector table occupies memory locations 00000 through 003FFH and contains pairs of words that represent the execution addresses for each of the 256 interrupts. These pairs correspond to IP and CS values of each ISR. The interrupt number used to access the table may be internally generated by the processor, or may be supplied by external hardware during an interrupt acknowledge cycle. The 8088 has only two hardware interrupts: NMI and INTR. NMI cannot be disabled, as INTR can.

Interrupts are caused through software, or by an external hardware request. The software interrupt may be generated intentionally by the programmer via INT and INTO, or by accident, via a run-time error such as division-by-zero. All interrupt service routines should preserve the state of any registers used to allow a proper return.

Three examples of actual interrupt service routines were also presented.

STUDY QUESTIONS

1. What is the processor's environment? Why is it important to save the environment during interrupt processing?
2. Explain the different ways interrupts are generated.
3. How is INTR disabled? How is it enabled?

4. What is the interrupt vector table address for an INT 21H?
5. The address of the ISR for INT 25H is 03C0:9AE2 (in CS:IP format). Show how this address is stored within the interrupt vector table.
6. What is the effective address of the ISR in Question 5?
7. Write the 8088 instructions necessary to place the ISR address of Question 5 into its proper place in the interrupt vector table.
8. Show the contents of stack memory after an interrupt has been initiated. Assume that the stack pointer is at address 3C00H prior to the interrupt and that CS, IP, and the flag register contain 0400H, 1890H, and 0182H, respectively.
9. What interrupt number has a vector table address range of 00280H to 00283H?
10. Which interrupt is recognized first, NMI or single-step?
11. Repeat Example 4.2 with an initial AX value of E03FH.
12. What high-priority event might require the use of NMI in a computer designed for aircraft engine control?
13. An analysis of a computer power failure showed that the computer had valid voltage levels for 2.5 milliseconds. Suppose that the microprocessor had an average instruction execution time of 2 microseconds. How many instructions can be executed during the power failure?
14. Explain why an orderly software shutdown is possible in Question 13. Assume that the shutdown involves pushing all processor registers onto a stack in NVM.
15. In Example 4.4 what is the highest AL value that will not cause an INTO interrupt?
16. Design an INTR circuit that has only two inputs: XINT and YINT. Both signals are active low. XINT should generate interrupt number 90H, and YINT, 91H.
17. What are all eight interrupt numbers for the circuit in Figure 4.8?
18. Modify the interrupt circuit of Figure 4.8 so that interrupt numbers 48H through 4FH are produced.
19. If the ONESEC procedure called by NMITIME took over 18 milliseconds to execute, would any problems arise?
20. What changes must be made to NMITIME if the frequency of the NMI clock is 1800 Hz? We still want to call ONESEC once per second.
21. What is the result of executing INT 20H with AX containing 0303H and BL containing 04? Refer to ISR20H in Section 4.7 for details.

FIGURE 4.11

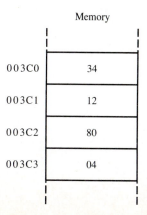

Memory	
003C0	34
003C1	12
003C2	80
003C3	04

22. Rewrite ISR20H so that four new functions are added. These functions are:

```
AH=05H : NOT AL
AH=10H : AND AL,BL
AH=20H : OR  AL,BL
AH=80H : XOR AL,BL
```

23. Figure 4.11 shows the contents of a few locations within the interrupt vector table. What will the new program counter be when the interrupt that uses these locations is processed?

24. What INT instruction is required in Question 23?

25. How is the single-step interrupt useful for examining the operation of a running program?

26. During an interrupt acknowledge cycle, 30H is placed on the data bus. Where is the ISR address fetched from?

27. The flag register contains 0344H. Will INTO generate an interrupt? Is trace enabled? Are interrupts enabled?

28. What do you imagine are some of the problems with these two interrupt service routines:

```
ISR1:   PUSH    AX          ISR2:   PUSH    AX
        PUSH    BX                  PUSH    CX
        ;                           ;
        ;body                       ;body
        ;                           ;
        POP     AX                  POP     BX
        IRET                        POP     AX
                                    RET
```

29. Write an interrupt service routine that will multiply the contents of AX by 7. If the new value of AX is greater than 8400H, call the far routine OVERSCAN. *Note:* OVERSCAN destroys AX, BX, and DI.

5

Running Machine Language
Programs on a Personal Computer

Objectives

In this chapter you will learn about:

*   The personal computer computing environment

*   How 8088 programs are assembled and linked

*   The differences between .EXE and .COM files

*   The operation and uses of DEBUG

5.1   INTRODUCTION

The topics covered so far in this text have introduced you to the hardware and software characteristics of the 8088 microprocessor. We have seen a number of different programming examples, all of a simple nature, and have also covered the operation of the processor's hardware signals. In this chapter you will learn how to utilize the power of the 8088 contained in the popular personal computer. It was only a decade ago that the first real personal computers began to hit the market. Before that, many different manufacturers sold variations of small-scale computers, equipped with parallel and serial I/O and floppy disk drives. But no standards existed due to the wide variety of microprocessors used in each model. Some manufacturers used the 8080 (an early version of the 8085), others the Z80 (another 8-bit machine that competed with the 8085). Other 8-bit processors, such as the 6502 and 6800, were also available. This wide cross section of microprocessors, each with its own instruction set, created a computer market that couldn't grow in enough directions to satisfy all its customers.

The big breakthrough came with the introduction of the 8088-based personal computer. The power of the 8088, coupled with a disk operating system more powerful than any others previously seen in small computers, soon attracted thousands of individuals and led to the quick growth of the personal computer market. It is this computer and its programming requirements that we will study here.

Section 5.2 gives an introduction to the personal computer environment. Section 5.3 explains how the DEBUG utility is used to execute 8088 programs. Sections 5.4, 5.5, and 5.6 outline the steps needed to create, assemble, and link an 8088 program. Techniques for executing .EXE and .COM programs using DEBUG are covered in Section 5.7. Lastly, Section 5.8 examines a diverse selection of programming examples, with varying degrees of complexity.

5.2   THE PERSONAL COMPUTER ENVIRONMENT

When the personal computer was first announced, it came equipped with only 256KB of memory, two 5.25-inch floppy disk drives, and a monochrome monitor. Machines on the market before this time barely contained 64KB of memory, so right away there was a significant improvement in computing power. Memory capabilities were soon upgraded to 640KB of RAM, allowing much larger programs to be executed. The machines of today boast 32-bit microprocessors buzzing along at 20- or 30-megahertz, with memory sizes measured in megabytes. High quality color graphics are now standard, and some machines have direct voice input and sound output.

For the purposes of this chapter we will concentrate on the 640K machines. It is important to note, however, that many of the features, techniques, and principles we will cover apply to the machines of today. This is due to the upward compatibility of the 8088 microprocessor with the newer, faster, and more powerful 386 and 486 microprocessors.

Memory Space

The 640K personal computer has its 640 kilobytes of RAM located in the address range 00000 to 9FFFFH, as you can see in the memory map of Figure 5.1. Some of this memory is reserved by the computer for its own functions. Three very important programs are needed to operate the computer's disk operating system. Together they represent over 64KB of reserved memory. The remainder of memory space is available for user programs.

When the personal computer is turned on, a ROM located in high memory performs initial hardware and software tests and initialization, and loads a special BIOS file into memory. BIOS, which stands for "Basic Input Output System," is a collection of routines that know how to communicate with the peripherals connected to the computer. This program uses over 16KB of memory located at the beginning of the processor's memory space (with room reserved for the interrupt vector table).

Once the BIOS program has taken care of its chores it loads the DOS program into memory. DOS requires over 28KB of RAM, and contains the

FIGURE 5.1 640K-byte memory map for personal computer

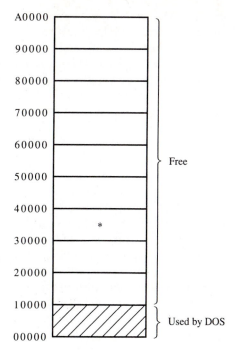

* Each block represents 64K bytes

intelligence needed to make the computer run. One important part of DOS that we will make use of is its function calls. Function calls are implemented with the 8088's INT instruction, and give the programmer access to many of the DOS routines that operate the display, disk drives, and printer, allocate memory, and read the keyboard.

The last thing DOS does is load a third program into memory called COMMAND.COM, which is the system program that interfaces with the user. All commands entered from the keyboard are interpreted by COMMAND.COM and executed by DOS. COMMAND.COM requires 23KB of RAM for itself. This entire process, which began with the application of power, is commonly called **booting up.** Once the machine has been booted up it is ready to perform tasks for the user.

The 67KB of memory used to boot up the machine are not available to the programmer. This leaves approximately 570KB of free RAM for the programmer. Note that different versions of DOS require larger or smaller amounts of reserved memory.

DOS Functions

DOS provides an easy way for programmers to tap into its routines and power through the use of DOS **function calls.** A function call is initiated with an INT instruction. Later in the chapter we will make use of a popular function call, INT 21H, to access certain DOS routines. Function calls are used to pass information to DOS and obtain information from DOS. Some DOS commands can be issued via function calls. Diskettes can be read, written, and formatted. The display screen can be modified, the keyboard read, and the computer's clock set and examined.

Most function calls require the programmer to place certain values into specific registers prior to the INT used to initiate the call. Many of these look at the value contained in register AH to determine what should be done. We were introduced to this concept in Section 4.7, where we saw how one interrupt could be used to do many different things, depending on the value passed to the routine. Other registers are used to exchange input and output data with DOS during execution of the function call. Function calls make the job of writing 8088 programs quicker and easier, since the programmer does not have to write much of the code that performs specific functions. It would be a shame if all programmers had to write the code to update the display or initialize the disk drive in their programs. DOS takes care of this for us by making the prewritten and tested code available via function calls. In Section 5.3 we will use a few simple function calls to get a feel for their operation.

Executable Files

If you made a list of all the programs you would like to run on your personal computer, it would most likely contain some of these: word processors, spreadsheets, game programs, utilities (for maintaining hard disks and fixing disk-related problems), assemblers, and programming languages such as C, BASIC, FORTRAN, or Pascal. All of these programs are saved on disk as *executable files,* and can be loaded into memory and executed simply by typing their name. For example, to run BASIC.EXE, you need only enter "BASIC" at the DOS command prompt. When DOS examines a command line, it first looks for built-in DOS commands, such as DIR, TYPE, and DEL (for delete). If none of these match, DOS will examine the current file directory for any .EXE, .COM, or .BAT files that may exist. If it finds a match (as in BASIC.EXE), it will load the selected file into memory and begin execution.

Two different types of executable files are utilized by DOS. These files must end with the extension .EXE or .COM. DOS has different ways of loading and executing these files. COM files, which are restricted to 64KB in length, always load at address 100H within any code segment. A COM file stored on disk is actually an exact copy of what will be copied into memory and executed. EXE files, on the other hand, may be much larger than 64KB. In fact, the length of some EXE files can exceed the amount of available memory in the machine! EXE files do not require a load address of 100H, but are instead loaded wherever free memory begins. This means that an EXE file may have a load address *anywhere* in free memory. One of the tasks performed by DOS when the computer is booting up is to look for a file called CONFIG.SYS, which contains commands that tell DOS how to configure itself. Some peripherals, such as the popular mouse, require special software **device driver** programs. These programs are specified in CONFIG.SYS and loaded into memory by DOS during a boot. Thus, as a result of the commands encountered in CONFIG.SYS, DOS can easily grow many thousands of bytes, reducing available free memory and changing the program load address. If DOS did not have the capability to load an EXE file anywhere in free memory, many programs could not be used when the computer is configured in a certain way. To prevent this, the EXE file contains an internal **relocation table** that indicates which parts of the file's program should be modified when it is loaded at a different address than originally intended. This relocation is done automatically by DOS and slightly increases the program's load time.

Examine the directory information for the files JLA.EXE and JLA.COM, which was obtained with the DIR JLA.* command:

```
JLA     EXE     945     7-7-91    11:44a
JLA     COM     177     7-7-91    11:45a
```

Both programs perform the same job (which involves writing a name at the top of the display screen). Why is JLA.EXE almost 800 bytes longer when stored on disk? It is because the relocation table required by DOS, along with other pieces of file information, increases the size of the file. The 177 bytes stored in JLA.COM can be directly copied into memory and executed. The 945 bytes of JLA.EXE must be examined and modified before a portion of them is loaded into memory and executed.

Before we tackle the job of writing, assembling, and linking .EXE and .COM files, let us get more familiar with the operation of DOS and a handy utility called DEBUG.

5.3   USING DEBUG TO EXECUTE AN 8088 PROGRAM

At this stage in our study of the 8088, we would be jumping the gun by attempting to write EXE or COM programs, even to do simple things. It would be much better for us to get into the programming aspects and usage of DOS with simple sections of code designed to produce clear results. The technique we will use to do this involves the use of the DEBUG.COM program that comes on the supplemental programs disk. With DEBUG, we can enter the individual 8088 instructions (or load an entire program), single step through them, and examine their results. It is best if you cover this section while sitting in front of a personal computer equipped with the DEBUG program.

What Is DEBUG?

DEBUG is a utility program that allows a user to load an 8088 program into memory, and execute it step by step. DEBUG displays the contents of all processor registers after each instruction executes, allowing the user to determine if the code is performing the desired task. In this way DEBUG is a very useful debugging tool. We will use DEBUG to step through a number of simple programs, gaining familiarity with DEBUG's commands as we do so. DEBUG contains commands that can display and modify memory, assemble 8088 instructions, disassemble code already placed into memory, trace through single or multiple instructions, load registers with data, and do much more.

DEBUG loads into memory like any other program, in the first available slot. The memory space that is utilized by DEBUG for the user program begins *after* the end of DEBUG's code. If a .EXE or .COM file was specified, DEBUG will load the program according to accepted DOS conventions.

Getting Started

The best way to get familiar with DEBUG is to work through some examples with it. The first example we will use is this three-instruction sequence:

```
MOV    AL,7
MOV    BH,2
ADD    AL,BH
```

The first instruction places the number 7 into register AL. The second instruction places 2 into register BH. These two registers are added together in the third instruction, with the results going into AL. With DEBUG we will be able to type in the instructions as they appear. DEBUG will automatically assemble them and place their respective codes into memory. We will then be able to examine the results of each instruction by tracing through the instructions one at a time.

The first step is to invoke DEBUG. This is done with a simple command, printed here in boldface. Make sure your floppy or hard disk has a copy of DEBUG.COM installed on it, and that it is in your current directory. At the DOS command prompt, enter:

```
C> debug <cr>
```

The expression <cr> indicates that you should hit the return key. Since DEBUG is a .COM file, DOS will find it in the current directory and load it into memory. DEBUG uses a minus sign as its command prompt, so you should see a "−" appear on your display.

To enter the three instructions we wish to execute, we need to use the *assemble* command. Entering the command letter "a" at the prompt should result in a display similar to this:

```
-a <cr>
1539:0100
```

This is the familiar CS:IP format that we have seen in earlier chapters. Instead of using the actual effective address, DEBUG shows us the CS value and the IP value. The 1539 address will most likely be different on your machine, since it is probably not configured like the one used to generate the DEBUG examples. The second address, 0100, should be the same. This is DEBUG telling us that it will place the first instruction into the code segment at offset 0100H. Bear in mind that DEBUG interprets *all* numbers as hexadecimal numbers.

At this point you can enter the three instructions. If you make a typing mistake, use the backspace key to correct your errors before hitting return. You should see something similar to this on your display:

```
-a <cr>
1539:0100 mov al,7 <cr>
1539:0102 mov bh,2 <cr>
1539:0104 add al,bh <cr>
1539:0106 <cr>
-
```

Notice that the IP address changes after each instruction. The fourth instruction, if there was one, would begin at address 0106. Since we are only entering three instructions, hitting a return on the fourth line will terminate the assemble command and get us back to the command prompt.

To examine the code that was generated by each instruction we use the *unassemble* command. Unassemble will show us the addresses, opcodes, and instruction mnemonics for the three instructions we have just entered. If unassemble is used without parameters it will show the next 20H bytes and their corresponding 8088 instruction equivalents. We can shorten this display by using a range parameter, like this:

```
-u 100 104<cr>
```

This command tells DEBUG to unassemble the bytes between addresses 0100 and 0104. The resulting display looks like this:

```
1539:0100 B007          MOV     AL,07
1539:0102 B702          MOV     BH,02
1539:0104 00F8          ADD     AL,BH
```

Here we can see that each instruction entered required 2 bytes of machine code.

To begin execution we should examine the contents of each register. Then we will know which registers change as we step through the program. DEBUG's *register* command can be used to display (and modify) any of the processor's registers. To display their contents, simply enter "r" and return. You should get a display similar to this:

```
AX=0000  BX=0000  CX=0000  DX=0000  SP=FFEE  BP=0000  SI=0000  DI=0000
DS=1539  ES=1539  SS=1539  CS=1539  IP=0100    NV UP EI PL NZ NA PO NC
1539:0100 B007          MOV     AL,07
```

Spend a few moments looking at the value displayed for each register. Note that all general purpose registers have been loaded with 0000. Also, the CS, DS, SS, and ES registers have all been initialized to the 1539 address we have seen earlier. IP points to address 0100, where we placed the first instruction. The end of the second line indicates the state of the flags. Table 5.1 explains the meaning of each flag code. We can see that currently there is no carry, odd parity, no auxiliary carry, not zero, and plus indicated, along with enabled

TABLE 5.1 Flag codes

Flag	Set	Clear
Overflow	OV	NV
Direction	DN	UP
Interrupt	EI	DI
Sign	NG	PL
Zero	ZR	NZ
Aux. Carry	AC	NA
Parity	PE	PO
Carry	CY	NC

interrupts, up direction (for use with string operations), and no overflow. It is sometimes important to watch the changes in flags as we step through a program.

The last line of the display shows the instruction that will be executed next. Since we have not executed any instructions yet, this is our first instruction! To execute a single instruction we use DEBUG's *trace* command, abbreviated "t," and get the following display:

```
                                -t <cr>

AX=0007  BX=0000  CX=0000  DX=0000  SP=FFEE  BP=0000  SI=0000  DI=0000
DS=1539  ES=1539  SS=1539  CS=1539  IP=0102   NV UP EI PL NZ NA PO NC
1539:0102 B702            MOV       BH,02
```

By comparing this display with the previous one, we can determine that only the lower byte of AX has been changed (it now contains 07H). No other registers except IP have been affected. No condition codes have been changed. Isn't that what MOV AL,7 should do?

Tracing through the next two instructions should look something like this:

```
                                -t <cr>

AX=0007  BX=0200  CX=0000  DX=0000  SP=FFEE  BP=0000  SI=0000  DI=0000
DS=1539  ES=1539  SS=1539  CS=1539  IP=0104   NV UP EI PL NZ NA PO NC
1539:0104 00F8            ADD       AL,BH

                                -t <cr>

AX=0009  BX=0200  CX=0000  DX=0000  SP=FFEE  BP=0000  SI=0000  DI=0000
DS=1539  ES=1539  SS=1539  CS=1539  IP=0106   NV UP EI PL NZ NA PE NC
1539:0106 8B0EDF47        MOV       CX,[47DF]
```

As expected, the final value in AL is 09H (the sum of 7 and 2). The flag display indicates that the result of the ADD instruction changed the parity flag. All other flags kept their states.

As a point of interest, look at the instruction located at address 0106. Where did it come from? We did not enter this code during any point of our exercise. Nonetheless, DEBUG thinks this is the next instruction to be executed. The reason for this is that each and every one of the computer's 640K bytes comes up in a random pattern when power is first applied. DEBUG will try to interpret these random patterns as valid 8088 instructions, as it is doing with the MOV CX instruction.

To return to DOS, exit DEBUG by entering "q" (for *quit*) at the command prompt.

To gain more experience with the DEBUG commands just used, let's work another example.

Example 5.1:   Study Question 3.27 asked for the final value in AL after this sequence of instructions executes:

```
MOV    AL,27H
MOV    BL,37H
ADD    AL,BL
DAA
```

Use DEBUG to enter these four instructions and trace their execution. What are the machine codes for each instruction? What is the final value in AL? What changes must be made when entering the instructions with the assemble command?

Solution: The purpose of this study question was to utilize the properties of the DAA instruction. When we add 27 to 37 we expect to get 64, the correct *decimal* answer. Using DEBUG to trace through the ADD instruction shows that AL contains 5EH. The next trace command executes the DAA instruction, which corrects the value in AL to 64H, the correct packed-decimal result. You should also see that the auxiliary carry flag has been set as a result of the DAA instruction.

The machine codes for each instruction are as follows:

```
B027      MOV   AL,27
B337      MOV   BL,37
00D8      ADD   AL,BL
27        DAA
```

The machine codes can be obtained in two ways. During a trace, the machine codes and mnemonics for each instruction are displayed after the register list. The unassemble command can also be used. Try **u 100 106** for this example and see what you get.

Also, notice that the "H" was left off the 27 and 37 operands, since DEBUG expects all numbers to be in hexadecimal form. If you include the "H" by accident, DEBUG will display an error message and wait for you to reenter the instruction.

Calling DOS Functions from DEBUG

Now that you have a little experience using DEBUG to execute simple sequences of instructions, we can move on to more complicated applications. We will make use of three new DEBUG commands: *enter, dump,* and *proceed*. We will also utilize a DOS function call through INT   21H. This is a very versatile DOS function, capable of performing many different operations. For our first example, we will use the display-string function of INT   21H. This function is selected by placing 9 into register AH, the register used by INT   21H to determine which of its many functions have been selected. Display-string requires that the address of the first byte of the text string be placed into DS:DX before using INT   21H. This means that the string must be contained in the data segment pointed to by DS, and have an offset equal to the value in DX. Use the assemble command of DEBUG to enter these instructions:

```
MOV    AH,9
MOV    DX,200
INT    21
```

Notice that we do not initialize the DS register. Remember that DEBUG automatically sets DS, CS, ES, and SS to the same value. This guarantees that our text string will be placed into the current data segment area. The offset value of 200H used to initialize DX is not a special value, it just happened to be a round number. Since the machine codes for the instructions are being placed into memory around address 100H, 200H seemed a good place to put the text string.

We can enter the text string two ways. First, we will make use of a new DEBUG command called *enter*. Enter allows memory to be modified on a byte-by-byte basis, beginning at the address specified in the instruction. To load the text string "Hello!$" into memory at address 200H enter **e 200** and each individual ASCII byte for every character in the text string. You will get a display similar to this:

```
-e 200 <cr>
1539:0200  66.48  6F.65  75.6C  6E.6C  64.6F  0D.21  0A.24  00.<cr>
```

The first pair of numbers are the actual address where the string is being loaded. The next number (66H) is the byte stored at location 200H. DEBUG follows it with a period and waits for you to enter the new byte value. The new value of 48H is entered, followed by the spacebar. Hitting the spacebar without entering any new value will skip over the location without changing its value. The display shows that 7 new bytes were entered. The last byte displayed (00) is not followed by anything because Return was hit to terminate the enter command. The 7 bytes entered are the ASCII values for the characters in the "Hello!$" string. The "$" character must be at the end of a text string for display-string to know where the string ends.

We can check our work with another new command: *dump*. Dump displays the bytes stored in a range of memory loacations. To verify that the text string has been properly stored, do the following:

```
-d 200 20f <cr>
1539:0200  48 65 6C 6C 6F 21 24 00-F6 38 53 79 6E 74 61 78   Hello!$..8Syntax
```

The dump command displays the starting address, followed by 16 bytes of data read from memory. The final part of each line of a dump display are the ASCII equivalent characters for each of the 16 bytes. The dump display clearly shows that we entered the string correctly.

A second technique that can be used to enter strings uses the assemble command. To place a different string at address 400H, do this:

```
-a 400 <cr>
1539:0400 db 'Try this string too...$' <cr>
1539:0417 <cr>
-
```

The "db" directive stands for *define-byte,* and causes DEBUG to look up the ASCII values of any characters surrounded by single quotes. You could easily enter numeric values with db as well. If you count all of the characters in the new string, including the blanks, you should get 23. This indicates that locations 400H through 416H will be loaded with the corresponding ASCII byte values. The next possible location to put anything in is 417H, which DEBUG is already indicating.

Getting back to the example at hand, we have placed a text string into memory at address 200H, and entered the instructions necessary to INT 21H's display-string function. Use the trace command until it gets to the INT 21 instruction. You should see that AH contains 09 and DX contains 0200. Unfortunately, there may be hundreds of instructions involved in the execution of INT   21H. It would be a waste of time to trace through each and every one of them. It would be nice if INT   21 could be treated as a single instruction by DEBUG, with all instructions of INT   21, including the final RETurn, executing by entering a single DEBUG command. Fortunately for us, DEBUG does have such a command: *proceed!* Proceed causes all INT, CALL, and REP instructions to be treated as single instructions. So, if a subroutine contains 45 instructions, using the proceed command when the CALL instruction shows up in the trace will cause DEBUG to execute all 45 instructions, and show the contents of each register *upon return from the subroutine!* We can use proceed to see what happens when we call INT   21. Your last DEBUG trace should look something like this:

```
AX=0900  BX=0000  CX=0000  DX=0200  SP=FFEE  BP=0000  SI=0000  DI=0000
DS=1539  ES=1539  SS=1539  CS=1539  IP=0105    NV UP EI PL NZ NA PO NC
1539:0105 CD21            INT    21
```

If the proceed command is now used, the resulting display becomes:

```
-p <cr>
Hello!
AX=0924  BX=0000  CX=0000  DX=0200  SP=FFEE  BP=0000  SI=0000  DI=0000
DS=1539  ES=1539  SS=1539  CS=1539  IP=0107    NV UP EI PL NZ NA PO NC
1539:0107 6C              DB     6C
```

You can see that the "Hello" string appeared on the screen in the current cursor location, and that DEBUG will get its next instruction from 1539:0107.

Obviously, INT   21H must have done its job, or the string would not have appeared. The proceed command is very useful for tracing programs that involve DOS function calls.

Example 5.2: What must be done to display the second string, which was entered with the assemble command and the db directive?

Solution: Since the string was placed at address 400H, the MOV DX,200 instruction must be changed to MOV DX,400. Then the entire sequence of instructions is executed again. DEBUG updates the IP register after each instruction executes, so it will be necessary to load IP with 100 again (if the first instruction is at 100). The register command can be used to do this. The following steps will set IP back to 100:

```
-r ip <cr>
IP 0107
:100 <cr>
-
```

The instructions for the second string can now be traced as those for the first were, with proceed used when INT   21 shows up again.

We will finish this section with one final example utilizing two more DOS function calls. INT   21H can also read the computer's time and date, if the appropriate value is placed into AH. To read the time, AH must contain 2CH. To read the date, AH must contain 2AH. The time and date are returned in various registers, as Example 5.3 shows.

Example 5.3: INT   21H requires no register setup before it is called when we are only reading the time or date. The time is returned in the following way: CH contains hours, CL contains minutes, and DH seconds. Hundredths of seconds are returned in DL. The date is returned with AL containing the day of the week, CX the year (1980 to 2099 only), DH the month, and DL the day. Can you determine the time and date from these DEBUG trace displays?

```
Time trace:
AX=2C00  BX=0000  CX=0F1C  DX=0235  SP=FFEE  BP=0000  SI=0000  DI=0000
DS=1539  ES=1539  SS=1539  CS=1539  IP=0104   NV UP EI PL NZ NA PO NC

Date trace:
AX=2A00  BX=0000  CX=07C7  DX=0707  SP=FFEE  BP=0000  SI=0000  DI=0000
DS=1539  ES=1539  SS=1539  CS=1539  IP=0108   NV UP EI PL NZ NA PO NC
```

Solution: The values contained in CX and DX in the time trace indicate that the computer's time was 15:28:02 when INT   21H was called. The values in CX and DX in the date trace show the date to be 7/7/1991. The day of the week stored in AL is 0, corresponding to Sunday. Saturday would be indicated by 6 in AL.

5.4 CREATING AN 8088 SOURCE FILE

DEBUG is a useful tool for debugging a program that is being created for the first time. But after all of the bugs have been found and the program is in sound working order we prefer it to be able to stand on its own. Execution without DEBUG will only be possible if we can turn the program into an .EXE or .COM file. The purpose of this section is to show you the format of an 8088 source file that can be assembled and linked into a working DOS program.

The source file can be created with any text editor that can save the file in ASCII format. By convention a .ASM extension is used on source file names, so NAME.ASM would be a valid name for the source file about to be described.

The source file consists of three parts: a data segment, a stack segment, and a code segment. One accepted practice is to put all data (and stack) segments first, so that any reference to a variable or label from within the code segment will already be defined. This usually leads to fewer errors during assembly. We do not want the assembler to have to guess the size or address of a label.

Take some time now to examine the following source file. Parts of it should look familiar, since it is merely a formalized version of the code that displays the "Hello!" string.

```
data       segment para 'data'
howdy      db        'Hello!$'
data       ends

stack      segment para stack 'stack'
           dw        32 dup(?)
tos        dw        ?
stack      ends

code       segment para 'code'
           assume   cs:code,ds:data,ss:stack
;initialize segment registers
start:     mov       ax,data
           mov       ds,ax
           mov       ax,stack
           mov       ss,ax
;initialize stack pointer
           lea       sp,tos
;application code begins here
;display string on screen
           mov       ah,9
           lea       dx,howdy
           int       21h
;terminate program (return to DOS)
           mov       ah,4ch
           int       21h
code       ends
           end       start
```

Note the placement of the data, stack, and code segments. The data segment contains the "Hello!" string, terminated by the "$" character as required by the display-string function of INT   21 and addressed by the label HOWDY. The stack segment is next. Here we reserve room for 32 pushes onto the stack with the DW 32 dup(?) statement. Why reserve so much room? Why reserve any room at all? We need to reserve some room for the return address when INT 21 is encountered. Also, the processor might be interrupted during execution of our program, requiring additional stack area. Reserving room for 32 pushes is more than enough to handle these events plus push every processor register onto the stack if need be.

The third segment is the code segment. This is where all of the work will be done. Whenever we use data or stack segments it is necessary to initialize the corresponding segment registers. DOS will not do this for us! The only register initialized by DOS when the program is loaded into memory is the CS register. The instructions following the START label perform the segment register initialization. Remember that we cannot directly move data into any of the segment registers, hence the use of AX for this purpose. The stack pointer must also be initialized and set to the address at the *bottom* of the reserved stack area. All of the programs that you write will require initialization of this sort. Once this is done, the code of the application can be executed. The three instructions that follow the initialization sequence are familiar to us from the previous section. They will cause the "Hello!" string to appear on the screen during program execution. When this is accomplished the program is ready to return to DOS. INT   21 can be used to do this for us automatically if we call it with 4CH in AH. This triggers INT   21's *terminate-program* function. A number of housekeeping chores must be performed by DOS, and terminate-program is the best way to ensure that they all get done properly.

A number of other points must be made about the source file. First, the file is written so that labels are in the first column, instructions in the second column, and operands in the third. A fourth column can be used for comments if you desire. Labels within the code segment must be followed by a ":"; labels in the data and stack segments need not be. Since DOS is designed to load data and code segments at even 16-byte boundaries (called **paragraphs**), we must use the PARA directive in our segment headers. For the assembler to generate proper code it must also know how the segment registers are being used. The ASSUME statement does this for us, informing the assembler that the CS register will be used with the CODE segment, and so on. Finally, the last line of the source file must contain the END directive, followed by the label associated with the instruction that should be executed first.

Take the time now to type in the program. You may wish to change the HOWDY message to something more interesting, such as:

```
howdy     db     'Hello, my name is James.',0dh,0ah
          db     '8088 programming is FUN!!!$'
```

Here we see how multiple text lines can be entered. The end of a text line must be followed with the codes for carriage return (0DH) and line feed (0AH). Without these codes, the display will look like this:

```
Hello, my name is James.8088 programming is FUN!!!
```

Once you have entered the source file, proceed to the next section where we will see how it is assembled.

5.5   ASSEMBLING AN 8088 PROGRAM

Once the source file has been created, we can assemble it with the MASM.EXE utility. Assembling the source file does not produce a program that is ready to run; that job is reserved for the linker. But assembling is the necessary second step in creating a working program. To assemble the NAME.ASM file presented in the previous section, we must execute the MASM program and input a few parameters. The process looks like this:

```
C> masm
Microsoft (R) Macro Assembler Version 4.00
Copyright  (C) Microsoft Corp 1981, 1983, 1984, 1985. All rights
reserved.

Source filename [.ASM]: name <cr>
Object filename [name.OBJ]: <cr>
Source listing  [ NUL.LST]: name <cr>
Cross-reference [NUL.CRF]: <cr>

50964 Bytes symbol space free

0 Warning Errors
0 Severe Errors
```

The assembler asks for the name of the source file, which it assumes will end with a .ASM extension. The main goal of the assembler is to produce an object file containing the code and data for the program. Since we entered **name** for the source file, the assembler automatically calls the object file NAME.OBJ, but also gives us the opportunity to call it something different. By hitting Return to the query, we tell the assembler to use the default object file name. To create a list file, we must enter a file name after the next query. List files are much longer than the original source file. As a matter of fact, the list file contains the source file in its entirety, as well as address and machine code text. Assembling with the creation of a list file generally takes more time than assembling without one. But list files are very helpful for finding assembly errors and also for seeing what the final version of the program looks like, so you may as well create it. The cross-reference file is not of much use unless you are creating a large program out of many smaller ones; it is not needed during the final linking stage.

Once these four queries are answered, the assembler opens the source file, reads it one line at a time, and creates the object and list files. If any errors are found in the source file, the assembler will output the appropriate error messages. Hopefully, you will end up with 0 Warning and 0 Severe errors. Do not go on to the linking step if you have errors!

The list file (edited for this discussion) for the NAME program looks like this:

```
1    0000                              data       segment para 'data'
2    0000    48 65 6C 6C 6F 21 24      howdy      db        'Hello!$'
3    0007                              data       ends
4
5    0000                              stack      segment para stack 'stack'
6    0000    0020[????]                           dw        32 dup(?)
7    0040    ????                      tos        dw        ?
8    0042                              stack      ends
9
10   0000                              code       segment para 'code'
11                                                assume    cs:code,ds:data,ss:stack
12                                     ;initialize segment registers
13   0000    B8 ---- R                 start:     mov       ax,data
14   0003    8E D8                                mov       ds,ax
15   0005    B8 ---- R                            mov       ax,stack
16   0008    8E D0                                mov       ss,ax
17                                     ;initialize stack pointer
18   000A    8D 26 0040 R                         lea       sp,tos
19                                     ;application code begins here
20                                     ;display string on screen
21   000E    B4 09                                mov       ah,9
22   0010    8D 16 0000 R                         lea       dx,howdy
23   0014    CD 21                                int       21h
24                                     ;terminate program (return to DOS)
25   0016    B4 4C                                mov       ah,4ch
26   0018    CD 21                                int       21h
27   001A                              code       ends
28                                                end       start
```

Many of the assembler directives (segment, assume, ends) do not generate any code, as you can see in lines 1, 3, 5, 8, 10, 11, and 27. Line 2 contains ASCII bytes generated by the db directive that represent the "Hello!" string in the data segment. No data is shown in the stack segment due to the use of the ? in the operand field of lines 6 and 7. However, the address column indicates that the TOS label is associated with address 0040H, since the first 64 locations within the stack segment are reserved for the stack area. The actual program code begins on line 13. The first instruction, B8 ---- R, requires some explanation. We are trying to load AX with the address of the DATA segment. But the assembler does not know where the data segment will be placed when DOS loads the program into memory. The actual address value is not known at assembly time, so the assembler simply reserves room for the 2-byte address (indicated by the ----). The "R" after the instruction says that this instruction is *relocatable,* meaning that the address eventually substituted in for the ---- field will be modified depending on where the program is loaded into memory. The assembler will place information into a relocation table within the object file that identifies the instruction in line 13 as one that needs to be modified during linking and loading. Other examples of this type can be found in lines 15, 18, and 22. Notice that in each of these lines the instructions contain references to labels defined in the stack and data segments.

For informational purposes, NAME.ASM contains 687 bytes, NAME.LST contains 2848 bytes, and NAME.OBJ contains 153 bytes. Not all of the bytes stored in the object file are for code and data. Remember that a relocation table is also saved in the object file, adding to its overall size. After all, there are only

26 bytes of actual code shown in the list file, plus 7 bytes of data and 66 reserved stack locations.

In our next section we will cover the final step in the creation of our 8088 program: linking.

5.6 LINKING AN 8088 PROGRAM

In this final step of the program creation process the LINK.EXE utility is used to generate a final, relocatable program. We are currently working with a single object file, NAME.OBJ, but the linker is capable of combining code and data from many different object files into one big package. This is especially useful when a team of individuals is working together on a project. Each person on the team may be responsible for one small portion of the project, be it a data table, a subroutine, or whatever. There may be a large number of source files, all separately assembled, by the time the project is ready to be combined into a single program. Each small part may communicate with the others through the use of special assembler directives that define and use **external** variables. The linker's job is to resolve all external references, if any, and combine all object files together into a single package. We will concentrate on self-contained programs for now, continuing with the creation of the NAME program. The linker is used in the following way:

```
C> link <cr>
IBM Personal Computer Linker
Version 2.30 (C) Copyright IBM Corp. 1981, 1985

Object Modules [.OBJ]: name <cr>
Run File [NAME.EXE]: <cr>
List File [NUL.MAP]: <cr>
Libraries [.LIB]: <cr>

C>
```

The linker will not give any output unless errors are discovered. We can thus assume that NAME.EXE has been successfully created, and we can execute it by entering its name at the DOS prompt:

```
C> name
Hello!
C>
```

You may be tempted to say that NAME.EXE does not do much of anything, but it actually ties together many important concepts. This simple program utilizes DOS's INT   21 function, writes text to the screen, creates its own stack, and terminates correctly. And most importantly, *it works!* In Section 5.8 we will see additional programming examples, of a slightly more complex nature. The NAME.EXE file contains 890 bytes. Compare that with the 153 used by NAME.OBJ.

Now that we are familiar with the overall procedure of program development, a few handy shortcuts are in order. First, although this is not highly recommended, you may eliminate the stack segment and associated instructions from your program if you desire. Any PUSH, POP, INT, CALL, or other stack-based instructions will use the existing DOS stack area. Though this will shorten the length of your program, it is possible to damage DOS's stack through incorrect programming and force a reboot of the computer. Linking a program that does not contain a stack segment will produce a warning message from the linker ("Warning: no stack segment"), but will not affect the creation of the .EXE file.

Second, a shorthand version of the assemble and link commands may be used. Both MASM and LINK allow file names and parameters to be included in the command line. To assemble NAME.ASM and only create NAME.OBJ (excluding the list file at this time), use:

```
C> masm name,,;
```

and the assembler will run its usual course without asking you all those questions! The same is true for linking. Use:

```
C> link name,,;
```

to create NAME.EXE without any additional prompting.

Once you have a working .EXE file you may wish to convert it into a .COM file. Many times you will be able to do this by simply using another utility program called EXE2BIN. Unfortunately, EXE2BIN cannot convert an .EXE file into a .COM file if the .EXE file contains a stack segment. So, if you wish to convert an .EXE file into a .COM file, you must do the following:

1. Remove the stack segment and associated initialization instructions from the source file
2. Remove the reference to the stack segment in the ASSUME statement
3. Add an ORG   100H statement before the START label
4. Reassemble the source file
5. Relink the object file
6. Use this DOS command: **exe2bin filename filename.com**

After all this it may still not be possible for EXE2BIN to convert the .EXE file into a .COM file. No matter—we will not be inconvenienced by having to use .EXE files instead.

5.7   RUNNING .EXE AND .COM PROGRAMS WITH DEBUG

In Section 5.3 we learned about a number of useful DEBUG commands. In this section we will examine one more command: *go*. DEBUG can automatically load an .EXE or .COM file into memory, performing all necessary relocation and initialization. The great advantage here is that we do not have to enter the program in by hand. We can also use DEBUG to execute existing programs, executing portions of them to determine how they work. Microcode exploration with DEBUG can be a tremendous learning experience.

To load a program with DEBUG, include the name of the program in the command line. For example:

```
C> debug name.exe <cr>
```

will cause DEBUG to load the NAME.EXE code into memory. Once done, we can dump, unassemble, trace, or modify the code as we see fit. If we need only to execute the program, we issue the go command, and see the following display:

```
-g <cr>
Hello!
Program terminated normally
-
```

A nice advantage of using DEBUG to execute a newly developed program in this manner is that the program exits to DEBUG, not DOS, when completed. If we desire, we can now examine the stack area, to see what values were pushed onto the stack. Or, if the program performed calculations and saved the results in the data segment, we can use dump to examine the results and verify their correctness. An example of this technique involves the data summing program from Chapter 3. It has been modified so that only 10 numbers are added and averaged. The results are then saved in the data segment (via the SUM and AVERAGE variables). The list file is included here to give an indication of what the new program looks like, and some idea as to where the results can be found.

```
0000                              data      segment para 'data'
0000    0A                        COUNT     DB        10
0001    ????                      SUM       DW        ?
0003    ????                      AVERAGE   DW        ?
0005    0064 00C8 012C 0190       VALUES    DW        100,200,300,400,500
        01F4
000F    03E8 07D0 0BB8 0FA0                 DW        1000,2000,3000,4000,5000
        1388
0019                              data      ends

0000                              code      segment para 'code'
                                            assume    cs:code,ds:data
0000    B8 ---- R       FINDAVE:  MOV       AX,DATA
0003    8E D8                     MOV       DS,AX
0005    8D 36 0005 R              LEA       SI,VALUES
0009    B8 0000                   MOV       AX,0
000C    8A 0E 0000 R              MOV       CL,COUNT
0010    03 04           ADDLOOP:  ADD       AX,[SI]
0012    83 C6 02                  ADD       SI,2
0015    FE C9                     DEC       CL
0017    75 F7                     JNZ       ADDLOOP
0019    A3 0001 R                 MOV       SUM,AX
001C    99                        CWD
001D    BB 000A                   MOV       BX,10
0020    F7 FB                     IDIV      BX
0022    A3 0003 R                 MOV       AVERAGE,AX
```

```
0025  B4 4C                    MOV    AH,4CH
0027  CD 21                    INT    21H
0029                  code     ends
                               end    findave
```

By examining the code in the data segment, we can see that the sum will be stored at address 0001 and the average at address 0003. After execution by DEBUG, we can dump these locations to view the results. We must first use the unassemble command to find out where DEBUG located the data segment.

```
C> debug findave.exe <cr>
−g <cr>

Program terminated normally
−u <cr>
1563:0000 B86115      MOV    AX,1561
1563:0003 8ED8        MOV    DS,AX
1563:0005 8D360500    LEA    SI,[0005]
1563:0009 B80000      MOV    AX,0000
1563:000C 8A0E0000    MOV    CL,[0000]
1563:0010 0304        ADD    AX,[SI]
1563:0012 83C602      ADD    SI,+02
1563:0015 FEC9        DEC    CL
1563:0017 75F7        JNZ    0010
1563:0019 A30100      MOV    [0001],AX
1563:001C 99          CWD
1563:001D BB0A00      MOV    BX,000A
−
```

The unassembly shows that the data segment begins at 1561:0000. Now we can use the dump command to examine the results.

```
−d 1561:0 0f <cr>
1561:0000  0A 74 40 72 06 64 00 C8−00 2C 01 90 01 F4 01 E8
−
```

The sum stored at address 0001 is 4074H. This equates to 16,500, the correct sum for the 10 data items included in the program. The average stored at address 0003 is 0672H, which is the proper average of 1650. Thus, we see that DEBUG can be used to verify the operation of an .EXE file and let us know if the program is working properly.

5.8 EXAMPLE PROGRAMS

A few example programs are included here to give you more exposure to 8088 programming and the use of DOS function calls. Only the source files are given for each program. Study them carefully. Do the programs have anything in common? In what ways are they different?

Heads or Tails

The first program flips an electronic coin and tells you if it came up heads or tails. The program reads the computer's clock and examines the seconds counter. If the seconds count is odd, the coin has come up heads. An even count indicates tails. The program displays one of two messages each time it is executed:

                    The coin comes up Heads!

or

                    The coin comes up Tails!

Examine the source file carefully to see how the stack and data segments are combined into one segment. When the object file is linked, a "no stack segment" warning will be issued. This is because there is no explicit naming of a stack segment within the program.

```
data      segment para 'data'
cmsg      db       'The coin comes up $'
hmsg      db       'Heads!$'
tmsg      db       'Tails!$'
          dw       32 dup(?)
tos       dw       ?
data      ends

code      segment para 'code'
          assume   cs:code,ds:data
;initialize segment registers and stack
start:    mov      ax,data
          mov      ds,ax
          mov      ss,ax
          lea      sp,tos
;output first message
          mov      ah,9
          lea      dx,cmsg
          int      21h
;read system clock
          mov      ah,2ch
          int      21h
;test for even second count
          test     dh,1
          jnz      heads
;seconds are even
;prepare for tails message
          lea      dx,tmsg
          jmp      next
;seconds are odd
;prepare for heads message
heads:    lea      dx,hmsg
;output heads or tails message
next:     mov      ah,9
          int      21h
;terminate program
          mov      ah,4ch
          int      21h
code      ends
          end      start
```

Day of the Week

This program reads the system date and displays the message "Today is" followed by the appropriate day. The date function returns the day of the week in

AL, with Sunday being 0, Monday 1, Tuesday 2, and so on. A data table containing the addresses of the day messages is accessed using based-indexed addressing. This is done by doubling the value returned in AL and adding it to the starting address of the data table. For example, if the day is Wednesday, AL will contain 3. Doubling it gives 6. The word located 6 bytes into DAYTAB is the address for the Wednesday message.

```
data      segment para 'data'
hmsg      db       'Today is $'
sun       db       'Sunday$'
mon       db       'Monday$'
tue       db       'Tuesday$'
wed       db       'Wednesday$'
thu       db       'Thursday$'
fri       db       'Friday$'
sat       db       'Saturday$'
daytab    dw       sun,mon,tue,wed,thu,fri,sat
          dw       32 dup(?)
tos       dw       ?
data      ends

code      segment para 'code'
          assume   cs:code,ds:data
;initialize segment registers and stack
start:    mov      ax,data
          mov      ds,ax
          mov      ss,ax
          lea      sp,tos
;say 'Today is'
          mov      ah,9
          lea      dx,hmsg
          int      21h
;read the date
          mov      ah,2ah
          int      21h
;create offset into daytab
          add      al,al
          cbw
          mov      si,ax
;load BP with daytab address
          lea      bp,daytab
;read day-message address
          mov      dx,[bp + si]
;display message
          mov      ah,9
          int      21h
;terminate program
          mov      ah,4ch
          int      21h
code      ends
          end      start
```

Guess the Number

This program utilizes two new DOS function calls, one that reads the keyboard and one that displays a character on the screen. The user is asked to guess a number between 1 and 5 and enter a single digit. Incorrect responses produce an error message. The computer's guess is calculated by reading the system clock and dividing the 100ths of seconds counter (DL) by 20. The result is then incremented to get a 1 to 5 range. The guess entered by the user is checked for validity. If it is acceptable, its ASCII bias of 30H is removed and the result compared with the computer's guess.

```
data      segment para 'data'
gmsg      db      'I am thinking of a number between 1 and 5.',0dh,0ah
          db      'What is your guess?$'
emsg      db      0dh,0ah,'Please enter 1 through 5 only!',0dh,0ah,'$'
rmsg      db      0dh,0ah,'You are correct!$'
wmsg      db      0dh,0ah,'Sorry, the number was $'
          dw      32 dup (?)
tos       dw      ?
data      ends

code      segment para 'code'
          assume  cs:code,ds:data
;initialize segment registers and stack
start:    mov     ax,data
          mov     ds,ax
          mov     ss,ax
          lea     sp,tos
;guess number
guess:    mov     ah,2ch
          int     21h
          mov     al,dl
          mov     ah,0
          mov     cl,20
          div     cl
          mov     bl,al
          inc     bl
;output guess message
          mov     ah,9
          lea     dx,gmsg
          int     21h
;read user response from keyboard
          mov     ah,1
          int     21h
;test for valid input
          cmp     al,'1'
          jc      error
          cmp     al,'5' + 1
          jnc     error
;input is OK, check for match
          sub     al,30h
          cmp     al,bl
          jz      right
;guess is incorrect
          lea     dx,wmsg
          mov     ah,9
          int     21h
;display computer's number
          mov     dl,bl
          add     dl,30h
          mov     ah,2
          int     21h
          jmp     exit
;input was illegal
```

```
error:   lea     dx,emsg
         mov     ah,9
         int     21h
         jmp     guess
;guess is correct
right:   lea     dx,rmsg
         mov     ah,9
         int     21h
;terminate program
exit:    mov     ah,4ch
         int     21h
code     ends
         end     start
```

5.9   SUMMARY

In this chapter you were introduced to some of the technical details of the 8088-based personal computer. We saw how memory is allocated between DOS and free storage, and how to tap the computing power of DOS through its special interrupt function calls.

The differences between .EXE and .COM files were also discussed, with .COM files limited to 64KB in length. This is not the case for .EXE files, which may be much larger, but require relocation work by DOS when they are loaded into memory. We saw the basic structure of an 8088 source file, and the commands needed to assemble and link it.

A good deal of time was spent on the DEBUG utility, which is capable of single stepping through an 8088 program one instruction at a time, with the contents of each register displayed for examination purposes. We also saw how DEBUG can be used to execute an .EXE file.

A number of different programming examples were included to give you additional programming exposure. This will prepare you for the additional programming concepts presented in Chapters 6 and 10.

STUDY QUESTIONS

1. What is meant by *booting up* the computer?
2. What are the first three programs loaded when the personal computer boots up?
3. Explain why an .EXE file may not always load at the same address.
4. How are the different functions of INT   21 selected?
5. Why is the length of an .EXE file that does the same thing as a .COM file much longer?
6. What is meant by *relocation*, and what is a relocation table used for?
7. How does the assembler indicate a relocatable instruction in the list file?
8. What files are produced by the assembler?
9. What files are produced by the linker?
10. Make a list of each DEBUG command discussed and explain its use.

11. Use DEBUG to step through this sequence of instructions:

```
MOV   AX,1234H
MOV   BL,3C
DIV   BL
```

What are the results of each instruction?

12. Use DEBUG to place the message "Time for lunch" at address 340H and then display it on the screen using the display-string function.

13. What is the difference between the trace and proceed commands?

14. Repeat Example 5.3 (time and date traces) on your own computer.

15. What are the main parts of an 8088 source file?

16. Modify the NAME.ASM program to display your name and address on the screen. The output should consist of at least three lines of text.

17. Explain how room is reserved for the stack in the source file.

18. Why is the stack needed in our example programs? Would they run properly without one?

19. What is the purpose of the linker?

20. Use DEBUG to trace through your own NAME program. At what points should you use proceed rather than trace?

21. Modify the FINDAVE program so that 15 numbers are added and averaged.

22. Modify FINDAVE so that negative numbers may also be used in the data table.

23. Modify the heads/tails program so that it flips the coin 10 times before exiting.

24. Write a program that reads the computer's date and displays the correct month (January, February, etc.) on the screen.

25. Write a program that reads the computer's date and outputs the day of the month as a two-digit ASCII number. For example, the display might read "Today is day 22."

26. Write a program that determines whether the time is AM or PM. The computer's time clock is a 24-hour clock. The display should read "It is after 5 PM," or something similar.

27. Modify the number-guessing program so that numbers in the range of 0 to 9 are allowed. Note that the technique for computing the guess must also be changed.

28. Add a second question to the number-guessing program that asks the user if he or she would like to guess again. Use the read-keyboard function to accept "y" or "n" responses.

29. Write a program to read a single digit number from the keyboard and determine if it is odd or even.

30. Write a program that counts down from 9 to 0, displaying the count on the screen, before exiting. The program should output the new count only once per second (i.e., it should take 10 seconds for the program to execute).

An Introduction to Programming the 8088

Objectives

In this chapter you will learn about:

* Breaking a large program down into small tasks

* Reading character strings from a keyboard

* Packing BCD digits into a byte

* Item search and lookup in a data table

* Comparison of data strings

* Sorting algorithms

* The use of condition flags to return results from a routine

* Binary and BCD math

* Writing a routine to perform a complex mathematical function

* Open- and closed-loop control systems (simplified theory)

* Determining program execution time and the meaning of overhead

* Simple interrupt handling

* Insertion of an item into a linked list

* The concept of multitasking

* The theory behind memory management and the need for it

6.1 INTRODUCTION

Getting the most use out of your microprocessor requires expertise, both in designing the hardware around it and in writing the code that it will execute.

The purpose of this chapter is to familiarize you with some of the standard programming principles as they apply to the 8088. We will limit ourselves to writing straight code in this chapter, using only the power of the 8088's instruction set. Hopefully you will see that many complex tasks may be performed in this way, without the use of external peripherals, which will be covered in Chapters 9 and 10.

Section 6.2 explains how large programming jobs are broken down into smaller tasks. Section 6.3 deals with the collection of various data strings. Section 6.4 gives examples of how a data table (or array) may be searched. Section 6.5 shows how an array of integers may be sorted. Section 6.6 covers mathematical routines capable of addition, subtraction, multiplication, and division, in both binary and BCD. Section 6.7 shows two examples of the 8088 in control applications. Section 6.8 discusses instruction execution times and the prediction of total execution time for a section of code. Section 6.9 explains the use of some typical interrupt handlers, such as divide-by-zero and overflow. The remaining sections, 6.10 through 6.12, deal respectively with linked lists, multitasking, and memory management—three important functions employed in major operating systems.

6.2   TACKLING A LARGE PROGRAMMING ASSIGNMENT

Writing a large, complex program from scratch is a difficult job, even for the most seasoned programmers. Even if this could be done easily, other considerations exist to complicate matters. The final program must be tested, to assure correct operation. It is a rare occurrence for a new program to work perfectly the first time.

For these reasons, a more sensible approach is to break the large program down into smaller tasks. Each task may be thought of as a subroutine, to be called, when needed, by the main program. The subroutines will each perform a single task, and thus will be easier to individually test and correct, as necessary. The technique of writing a large program in this way is often referred to as **structured programming.** We will not concern ourselves with all the details of structured programming. Instead, we will study a sample programming assignment and use the techniques previously mentioned to break the assignment down into smaller jobs.

The Assignment

The programming assignment is presented to us in the form of a **specification.** The specification describes the job that must be performed by the program. It also contains information concerning any input and output that may need to be performed, and sometimes a limit on the amount of time the program may take to execute.

Consider the following specification:

Specification: Subroutine WORDCOUNT

Purpose: To generate a data table of all different words contained in a paragraph of text, and a second data table containing the frequency of occurrence of each word.

Restrictions: Do not distinguish between uppercase and lowercase characters. Ignore punctuation, except where it defines the end of a word. No words will appear more than 255 times.

Input: A data table headed by symbol TEXT that contains the paragraph to be analyzed, represented by ASCII codes. The length of the paragraph text is undefined, but the last character in the text will always be "$". This character will not appear anywhere else in the text.

Outputs: A data table, headed by symbol WORDS, that contains a list of all different words encountered in the paragraph text. Each word ends with ".", and the entire table ends with "$". A second data table, headed by symbol COUNTS, containing the frequency counts for each entry in WORDS.

There is sufficient detail in the specification for us to determine what must be done. How to do it is another matter.

Breaking the Program Down into Modules

Once we understand what is required of the program, through information presented in the specification, the next step is to break the program down into smaller modules. This means that subroutine WORDCOUNT will actually become a main subroutine, which calls other subroutines. We must identify the other subroutines needed. This step of the process requires skill and practice. When you have given it enough thought, you might agree that these subroutines are required:

INITIALIZE   Initialize all pointers, counters, and tables needed.

GETWORD   Get the next word from the paragraph text.

LOOKUP   Search WORDS to see if it contains the present word.

INSERT   Insert new word into WORDS.

MAKECOUNT   Make a new entry in COUNTS.

INCREASE   Increase frequency count in COUNTS for a word found by LOOKUP.

There may, of course, be other required routines, depending on who is writing the code. The idea is to create a subroutine to accomplish only *one* task. None of the identified routines performs more than one task.

Once the inputs and outputs for each subroutine are identified, the code can be written for each one, and the subroutines tested.

Testing the Modules

Testing of each subroutine module is done separately, through a special program called a **driver.** The driver supplies the subroutine with sample input data, and examines the subroutine's output for correctness. It is up to the programmer to select the type and quantity of the sample data.

When all modules have been tested and verified for proper operation, they can be combined into one large module—WORDCOUNT in our example—and this module can be tested also.

Creating the Final Module

WORDCOUNT, as mentioned before, will consist of calls to the subroutines identified in the section on breaking the program down into modules. **Pseudocode,** a generic programming language, can be used to determine the structure of WORDCOUNT (and of the other subroutines as well). The following pseudocode is one way WORDCOUNT may be implemented:

```
subroutine WORDCOUNT
  INITIALIZE
  repeat
    GETWORD
    if no word found then
      return
    LOOKUP
    if word found then
      INCREASE
      else
        INSERT
        MAKECOUNT
  forever
end WORDCOUNT
```

WORDCOUNT is implemented as an infinite loop, since the length of the paragraph text is unknown. The only way out of the loop is to have GETWORD fail to find a new word in the text (that is, by reaching the "$"). This approach satisfies another requirement of structured programming: Routines should contain one entry point and one exit point. Many of the routine examples that we will study in this chapter will be written in this fashion. It is up to the programmer how the REPEAT-FOREVER and IF-THEN-ELSE statements are implemented.

The **IF-THEN** statement can be coded in many different ways. The actual structure is IF ⟨condition⟩ THEN ⟨action⟩. The *condition* must be satisfied for the *action* to take place. In the WORDCOUNT example, the first IF statement causes the subroutine to return if GETWORD did not find a new word in the paragraph text. Let us assume that GETWORD returns a 00 in AL if it did find a word, and FFH if it did not. One way to code the IF statement might look like this:

```
              CALL    GETWORD
              CMP     AL,0
              JNZ     NEXT
              RET
      NEXT:   ---
```

The CALL to GETWORD will adjust the value of AL accordingly. The CMP instruction is used to determine if AL contains 0. If it does not, a jump to NEXT is performed. This will cause execution to continue (with a CALL to LOOKUP as the next instruction). If AL does contain 0 the JNZ will not take place and the RET instruction will execute instead.

IF-THEN-ELSE statements are very similar, with coding similar to this:

```
                  CALL    LOOKUP
                  CMP     AL,0
                  JZ      THENCODE
      ELSECODE:   ---
```

Other pseudocode structures include the REPEAT-UNTIL and WHILE-DO. The REPEAT-UNTIL structure looks like this:

```
          repeat
            <statements>
          until <condition>
```

Coding the REPEAT-UNTIL structure depends on the type of condition being tested. A sample structure and its associated code may look like this:

```
  initialize counter to 100        MOV     BX,100
  repeat
    GETDATA              AGAIN:     CALL    GETDATA
    PROCESSDATA                     CALL    PROCESSDATA
    decrement counter               DEC     BX
  until counter = 0                 JNZ     AGAIN
```

One important point about using loop counters is that the loop-count register (BX in this example) must not be altered during execution of the statements within the loop.

The WHILE-DO structure is slightly different, performing the condition test at the *beginning* of the loop instead of the end. One example of a WHILE-DO is:

```
          while char <> 'A' do
            <statements>
          end-while
```

The corresponding machine instructions for this loop might look like this:

```
      WHILE:    CMP     AL,'A'
                JZ      NEXT
                <loop instructions>
                JMP     WHILE
      NEXT:     ---
```

Here it is important to modify the loop variable (AL in this case) somewhere within the loop, to avoid getting stuck inside it.

Remember that there are no fixed methods for converting pseudocode into machine instructions. Use your imagination and you will undoubtedly come up with your own techniques.

6.3 DATA GATHERING

When a microprocessor is used in a control application, one of its most important tasks is to gather data from the external process. This data may be composed of inputs from different types of sensors, parallel or serial information transmitted to the system from a separate source, or simply keystrokes from the user's keyboard.

Usually a section of memory is set aside for the storage of the accumulated data, so the processor can alter or examine it at a later time. The rate at which new data arrives, as in keystrokes from a keyboard, may be very slow, with a new item arriving every few milliseconds or so. When the data rate is slow, the processor will waste valuable execution time waiting for the next new data item. Therefore, an efficient solution is to store the data as it arrives, and only process it when all items have been stored. We will examine two examples of gathering data in this section. The first one deals with keyboard buffering and the second with packing BCD numbers.

The Keyboard Buffer

One of the first things anyone involved with computers learns is that nothing happens until you hit Return. All keystrokes up to Return must be saved for processing after Return is hit. The subroutine presented here, KEYBUFF, is used to store these keystrokes in a buffer until Return is hit. The processor will then be free to examine the contents of the keyboard buffer at a later time. KEYBUFF makes use of an INT 21 function, which is used to get a keystroke from the keyboard. The ASCII code for the key is returned by INT 21 in the lower byte of AL. INT 21 takes care of echoing the key back to the user's display. An important point to keep in mind is that INT 21 will not return a value in AL until a key is struck.

The ASCII codes for the keys entered are saved in a buffer called KEYS, which is limited to 128 characters. No code is provided to prevent more than this number of keystrokes. Can you imagine what problems occur when the 129th key is entered?

```
        In the current data segment...
KEYS        DB      128 DUP(?)
        .
        .
        .
KEYBUFF     PROC    FAR
            LEA     DI,KEYS         ;DI points to start of buffer
NEXTKEY:    MOV     AH,1
            INT     21H             ;read keystroke and echo to screen
            MOV     [DI],AL         ;save key in buffer
```

```
            INC     DI              ;point to next buffer location
            CMP     AL,ODH          ;continue until return is seen
            JNZ     NEXTKEY
            RET
KEYBUFF     ENDP
```

An important feature missing in this example is the use of special codes for editing. No means are provided for editing mistaken keys entered by the user. At the very least, the user should be able to enter a backspace to correct a previous error. You are encouraged to solve this problem, and the other one dealing with limiting the number of keystrokes, yourself.

Packing BCD Numbers

Any program that deals with numbers must use one of two approaches to numeric processing. The program must either treat the numbers as binary values or as BCD values. The use of binary operations provides for large numbers with a small number of bits (integers over 16 million can be represented with only 24 bits), but is limited in accuracy when it comes to dealing with fractions. The use of BCD provides for greater accuracy but requires software to support the mathematical routines, and this software greatly increases the execution time required to get a result. Even so, BCD numbers have found many uses, especially in smaller computing systems. The example we will study here is used to accept a multidigit BCD number from a keyboard and store it in a buffer called BCDNUM. The trick is to take the ASCII codes that represent the numbers 0 through 9 and convert them into BCD numbers. Two BCD numbers at a time are packed into a byte. BCDNUM will be limited to 6 bytes, thus making 12-digit BCD numbers possible. The subroutine PACK-BCD will take care of packing the received BCD numbers into bytes and storing them in BCDNUM. No error checking is provided to ensure that no more than 12 digits are entered, or that the user has entered a valid digit. If the number entered is less than 12 digits long, the user enters Return to complete the entry. All numbers will be right justified when saved in BCDNUM. This means that numbers less than 12 digits long will be filled with leading zeros.

```
In current data segment...
BCDNUM      DB      6 DUP(?)
.
.
.

PACKBCD     PROC    FAR
            LEA     DI,BCDNUM       ;point to beginning of buffer
            MOV     CX,6            ;init loop counter
CLEARBUFF:  MOV     BYTE PTR [DI],0 ;clear all bytes in BCDNUM
            INC     DI              ;with this loop
            LOOP    CLEARBUFF
            DEC     DI              ;move to end of buffer
GETDIGIT:   MOV     AH,1            ;get a number from the user
            INT     21H
            CMP     AL,ODH          ;done?
            JZ      DONE
            SUB     AL,30H          ;remove ASCII bias
```

```
                    MOV     BL,AL           ;save first digit
                    MOV     AH,1            ;get another number
                    INT     21H
                    CMP     AL,0DH          ;done?
                    JZ      SAVEIT
                    SUB     AL,30H          ;remove ASCII bias
                    MOV     CL,4            ;prepare for 4-bit shift
                    SHL     BL,CL           ;move BCD digit into upper nibble
                    OR      AL,BL           ;pack both digits into AL
                    MOV     [DI],AL         ;save digits in buffer
                    DEC     DI              ;decrement pointer
                    JMP     GETDIGIT
        SAVEIT:     MOV     [DI],BL         ;save last digit in buffer
        DONE:       RET
        PACKBCD     ENDP
```

The loop at the beginning of PACKBCD writes zeros into all 6 bytes of BCDNUM. This is done to automatically place all leading zeros into the buffer before any digits are accepted. Notice also that DI has been advanced to the end of the buffer when the loop has finished. We need DI to start at the end of BCDNUM because we decrement it to store the digits as they are entered. INT 21 is used to get a BCD number from the user (assuming that no invalid digits are entered). Subtracting 30H from the ASCII values returned by INT 21 converts the ASCII character code (35H for "5") into the correct BCD value. The SHL and OR instructions perform the packing of two BCD digits into a single byte. Can you spot the changes made to the BCD number as it is stored?

6.4 SEARCHING DATA TABLES

In this section we will see a few examples of how a block of data may be searched for single or multibyte items. This technique is a valuable tool that has many applications. In a large database, information about many individuals may be stored. Their names, addresses, social security numbers, phone numbers, and many other items of importance may be saved. Finding out if a person is in the database by searching for any of the items just mentioned requires an extensive search of the database. In an operating system, information about users may be stored in a special access table. Their user names, account numbers, and passwords might be included in this table. When a user desires to gain access to the system, his or her entry in the table must be located by account number or name and the password checked and verified. Once on the system, the user will begin entering commands. The commands entered must be checked against an internal list to see if they exist before processing can take place. In a word processing program, a special feature might exist that allows a search of the entire document for a desired string. Every occurrence of this string must be replaced by a second string. For example, the author may notice that every occurrence of "apples" must be changed to "oranges." If only one or two of these strings exist, the author will edit them accordingly. But if "apples" occurs in 50 different places, it becomes very time consuming and inefficient to do this manually. Let us now look at a few examples of how a data table may be searched.

Searching for a Single Item

The first search technique we will examine involves searching for a single item. This item might be a byte or a word value. The following subroutine searches a 100-element data table for a particular byte value. Upon entry to the subroutine, the byte to be searched for is stored in ITEM. The item may or may not exist within the data table. To account for these two conditions, we will need to return an indication of the result of the search. The carry flag is used to do this. If the search is successful, we will return with the carry flag set. If the search fails, we return with the carry flag cleared.

```
        In current data segment...
        VALUES    DB      100 DUP(?)
        ITEM      DB      ?
        .
        .
        .
        FINDBYTE  PROC    FAR
                  LEA     SI,VALUES    ;init data pointer
                  MOV     CX,100       ;init loop counter
                  MOV     AL,ITEM      ;load AL with search item
        COMPARE:  CMP     AL,[SI]      ;compare item with data in table
                  JZ      FOUND
                  INC     SI           ;point to next item
                  LOOP    COMPARE      ;continue comparisons
                  CLC                  ;clear carry flag, search failed
                  RET
        FOUND:    STC                  ;set carry flag, item found
                  RET
```

Notice how STC and CLC have been used to directly modify the carry flag, depending on the results of the search. Using the carry flag in this manner allows the programmer to write much simpler code. For example, only two instructions are needed to determine the result of the search:

```
                  CALL    FINDBYTE
                  JC      SUCCESS
```

Of course, other techniques may be used to indicate the results. The nice thing about using the flags is that they require no external storage and can be used whenever a binary condition (true/false) is the result.

Searching for the Highest Integer

When working with data it often becomes necessary to find the largest value in a given set of numbers. This is useful for finding the range of the given set and also has an application in sorting. MAXVAL is a subroutine that will search an array called NUMBERS for the largest positive byte integer. No negative numbers are allowed at this time. The result of the search is passed back to the caller in the lower byte of BX.

```
          In current data segment...
          NUMBERS     DB      128 DUP(?)
          .
          .
          .
          MAXVAL      PROC    FAR
                      LEA     SI,NUMBERS    ;init data pointer
                      MOV     BL,0          ;assume 0 is largest to begin with
                      MOV     CX,128        ;init loop counter
          CHECKIT:    CMP     [SI],BL       ;compare current value with new data
                      JC      NOCHANGE      ;jump if new value is not larger
                      MOV     BL,[SI]       ;load new maximum value
          NOCHANGE:   INC     SI            ;point to next byte
                      LOOP    CHECKIT       ;continue until all bytes checked
                      RET
          MAXVAL      ENDP
```

Using JC after the compare operation treats all bytes as unsigned integers. Other forms of the conditional jump will allow signed numbers to be detected as well.

Comparing Strings

A very important part of any program that deals with input from a user involves recognizing the input data. Consider the password required by most users of large computing systems. The user must enter a correct password or be denied access to the system. Since the password may be thought of as a string of ASCII characters, some kind of string comparison operation is needed to see if the user's password matches the one expected by the system. The following subroutine compares two strings of 10 characters each, returning with the carry flag set if the strings are exactly the same. If you think of one string as the password entered by the user and the other as the password stored within the system, you will see how they are compared.

```
          In current data segment...
          STRINGA     DB      'alphabetic'
          STRINGB     DB      'alphabet  '
          .
          .
          .
          CHKSTRING   PROC    FAR
                      MOV     SI,0              ;init character pointer
                      MOV     CX,10             ;init loop counter
          CHECKCHAR:  MOV     AL,STRINGA[SI]    ;get character from STRINGA
                      CMP     AL,STRINGB[SI]    ;compare with STRINGB character
                      JNZ     NOMATCH           ;even one difference causes failure
                      INC     SI                ;point to next character
                      LOOP    CHECKCHAR         ;check all elements
                      STC                       ;strings match
                      RET
          NOMATCH:    CLC                       ;strings are different
                      RET
          CHKSTRING   ENDP
```

The two strings used in the example are not identical because the last two characters are different.

A Command Recognizer

Consider a small single-board computer system that allows you to do all of the following:

1. Examine/alter memory (EXAM)
2. Display memory (DUMP)
3. Execute a program (RUN)
4. Terminate program execution (STOP)
5. Load a program into memory (LOAD)

Each of the five example commands has a specific routine address within the memory map of the system. For example, the DUMP command is processed by the code beginning at address 04A2C. The **command recognizer** within the operating system of the small computer must recognize that the user has entered the DUMP command, and jump to address 04A2C. This requires that both a string-compare operation and a table lookup be performed. The following routine is one way this may be accomplished:

```
        In current data segment...
COMMANDS    DB      'EXAM'
            DB      'DUMP'
            DB      'RUN '
            DB      'STOP'
            DB      'LOAD'
JUMPTABLE   DW      DOEXAM
            DW      DODUMP
            DW      DORUN
            DW      DOSTOP
            DW      DOLOAD
COMBUFF     DB      4 DUP(?)
    .
    .
    .
RECOGNIZE   PROC    FAR
            LEA     BP,COMMANDS       ;point to command table
            MOV     BX,0              ;init index within JUMPTABLE
            MOV     CX,5              ;init loop counter
NEXTCOM:    PUSH    CX                ;save loop counter
            MOV     CX,4              ;prepare for command matching
            MOV     SI,0
CHKMATCH:   MOV     AL,[BP + SI]      ;get a table character
            CMP     COMBUFF[SI],AL    ;and compare it with command
            JNZ     NOMATCH
            INC     SI                ;point to next character
            LOOP    CHKMATCH          ;continue comparison
            POP     CX                ;match found, fix stack
            JMP     JUMPTABLE[BX]     ;jump to command routine
NOMATCH:    POP     CX                ;get loop counter back
            ADD     BP,4              ;point to next command text
            ADD     BX,2              ;and next routine address
            LOOP    NEXTCOM           ;go check next command
            JMP     COMERROR          ;command not found
RECOGNIZE   ENDP
```

The set of valid commands begins at COMMANDS. The addresses for each command routine begin at JUMPTABLE. The command entered by the user is saved in the 4 bytes beginning at COMBUFF. The purpose of RECOGNIZE is to compare entries in COMMANDS with COMBUFF. Every time a match is not found, a pointer (BX) is advanced to point to the next routine address in JUMPTABLE. When a match is found, BX will point to the start of the routine address saved in memory. This routine address is then used by JMP. If none of the commands match the user's, a jump is made to COMERROR (possibly a routine that will output an error message saying "Illegal command").

6.5   SORTING

It is often necessary to sort a group of data items into ascending (increasing) or descending order. On average, the search time for a sorted list of numbers is smaller than that of an unsorted list. Many different sorting algorithms exist, with some more efficient than others. The sorting algorithm covered here is called a **bubble sort.** A bubble sort consists of many passes over the elements being sorted, with comparisons and swaps of numbers being made during each pass. A short example should serve to introduce you to the technique of the bubble sort. Consider this group of numbers:

$$7 \quad 10 \quad 6 \quad 3 \quad 9$$

It is only necessary to perform four comparisons to determine the highest number in the group. We will repeatedly compare one element in the group with the next element, starting with the first. If the second element is larger than the first, the two numbers will be swapped. By this method we guarantee that after four comparisons, the largest number is at the end of the array. Check this for yourself. Initially, 7 and 10 are compared and not swapped. Then 10 and 6 are compared and swapped because 10 is greater than 6. The new array looks like this:

$$7 \quad 6 \quad 10 \quad 3 \quad 9$$

Next, 10 and 3 are compared and swapped. Then 10 and 9 are compared and swapped. At the end of the first pass, the array is:

$$7 \quad 6 \quad 3 \quad 9 \quad 10$$

It is not necessary now to ever compare any of the elements in the array with the last one, since we know it to be the largest. The next pass will only compare the first four numbers, giving this array at the end of the second pass:

$$6 \quad 3 \quad 7 \quad 9 \quad 10$$

The third pass will produce:

$$3 \quad 6 \quad 7 \quad 9 \quad 10$$

and you may notice now that the array is sorted. However, this is due to the original arrangement of the numbers; for completeness, a final pass must be performed on the first two numbers. It is interesting to note that the five numbers being sorted required four passes. In general, N numbers will require $N - 1$ passes. The subroutine SORT presented here implements a bubble sort. DX is used as the pass counter; registers AL and BL are used for swapping elements; and CX is used as a loop counter. The number of elements to be sorted is saved as a word count in NVAL. The appropriately sized DUP statement is needed for VALUES, with only 16 locations reserved in this example. Also, only positive integers may be sorted (because of the use of JNC in the comparison).

```
        In current data segment...
VALUES  DB      16 DUP(?)
NVALS   DW      ?
  .
  .
  .
SORT    PROC    FAR
        MOV     DX,NVALS            ;get number of data items
        DEC     DX                  ;subtract 1 to start
DOPASS: MOV     CX,DX               ;init loop counter
        MOV     SI,0                ;init data pointer
CHECK:  MOV     AL,VALUES[SI]       ;get first element
        CMP     VALUES[SI + 1],AL   ;compare with second element
        JNC     NOSWAP
        MOV     BL,VALUES[SI + 1]   ;swap elements
        MOV     VALUES[SI + 1],AL
        MOV     VALUES[SI],BL
NOSWAP: INC     SI                  ;point to next element
        LOOP    CHECK               ;continue with pass
        DEC     DX                  ;decrement pass counter
        JNZ     DOPASS              ;until finished
        RET
SORT    ENDP
```

By advancing SI in steps of one, memory references VALUES[SI] and VALUES[SI+1] always access the next two elements in the VALUES array. When it is necessary to swap them, temporary variable BL is used to hold the contents of the second location while it is being replaced by the contents of the first location. The stack may be used for this purpose also, at the expense of additional execution time. The use of different conditional jump instructions will allow for negative numbers to be sorted as well.

6.6   COMPUTATIONAL ROUTINES

This section covers examples of how the 8088 performs standard mathematical functions. Since the processor has specific instructions for both binary and

BCD operations, we will examine sample routines written around those instructions. Math processing is a major part of most high-level languages and the backbone of specialized application programs, such as spreadsheets and statistical analysis packages. Most processors, however, are limited in their ability to perform complicated math. When complex functions such as SIN(X) or LOG(Y) are needed, the programmer is faced with a very difficult task of writing the code to support them. Even after the code is written and judged to be correct, it will most likely be very lengthy and slow in execution speed. For this reason, some systems are designed with math coprocessor chips. These chips are actually microprocessors themselves whose instruction sets contain only mathematical instructions. Adding a coprocessor eliminates the need to write code to perform the math function. SIN(X) is now an instruction executed by the coprocessor. The main CPU simply reads the result from the coprocessor. The coprocessor available for the 8088 is the 8087 floating-point coprocessor, which we will examine in Chapter 10.

The examples we will see in this section deal only with addition, subtraction, multiplication, and division. We will, however, also look at a few ways these simple operations can be applied to simulate more complex ones.

Binary Addition

Binary addition is accomplished with ADD and ADC. Both perform addition on registers and/or memory locations. The example presented here is used to find the signed sum of a set of data. The data consists of signed 8-bit numbers. Since it is possible for the sum to exceed 127, we use 16 bits to represent the result.

```
        In current data segment...
        SCORES   DB      200 DUP(?)
        SUM      DW      ?
        .
        .
        .
        TOTAL    PROC    FAR
                 LEA     SI,SCORES    ;init pointer to data
                 MOV     CX,200       ;init loop counter
                 MOV     BX,0         ;clear result
        ADDEM:   MOV     AL,[SI]      ;load AL with value
                 CBW                  ;sign extend into 16-bits
                 ADD     BX,AX        ;add new value to result
                 INC     SI           ;point to next data item
                 LOOP    ADDEM        ;do all values
                 MOV     SUM,BX       ;save result in memory
                 RET
        TOTAL    ENDP
```

Even though the data consists of signed 8-bit numbers, we can perform 16-bit additions if we first use CBW to extend the signs of the input numbers (from 8 to 16 bits).

Binary Subtraction

Binary subtraction is implemented by SUB and SBB. Both instructions work with memory locations and/or registers. The example presented here shows how two blocks of memory may be subtracted from each other. One application in which this technique is useful involves digitally encoded waveforms. Suppose that two analog signals, sampled at an identical rate, must be compared. If the difference is computed by subtracting the binary representation of each waveform and the resultant waveform is displayed by sending the new data to a digital-to-analog converter, we will see a straight line at the output if the waveforms are identical. WAVE1 and WAVE2 are labels associated with the 2K word blocks of memory that must be subtracted. Because of the addressing mode used, the resulting data will overwrite the data saved in WAVE2's area.

```
In current data segment...
WAVE1       DW      2048 DUP(?)
WAVE2       DW      2048 DUP(?)
   .
   .
   .
SUBWAVE     PROC    FAR
            LEA     SI,WAVE1        ;init pointer to beginning of WAVE1
            LEA     DI,WAVE2        ;init pointer for WAVE2
            MOV     CX,2048         ;init loop counter
SUBEM:      MOV     AX,[SI]         ;get sample from WAVE1
            SUB     [DI],AX         ;subtract and replace WAVE2 sample
            ADD     SI,2            ;advance WAVE1 pointer
            ADD     DI,2            ;advance WAVE2 pointer
            LOOP    SUBEM           ;do all samples
            RET
SUBWAVE     ENDP
```

Binary Multiplication

Two instructions are available for performing binary multiplication. MUL (unsigned multiply) is used to multiply 8- or 16-bit operands, one of them contained in the accumulator. IMUL (signed multiply) generates a signed result using signed operands of 8- or 16-bits each. In both cases, the results are stored in AX or AX and DX. When 32-bit precision is not enough, we must turn to an alternate method to perform the math. One solution is to add a math coprocessor chip. The benefit of doing this is reflected in a decrease in time needed to perform the math. Also, many complex functions are available in the coprocessor. The disadvantage is in the added cost of the hardware. Coprocessors tend to be expensive.

If the hardware cost is excessive, the only other solution is to use software. The example presented here is used to perform 32- by 16-bit multiplication on unsigned integers. The 48-bit result represents a significant increase over the 32 bits the processor is limited to. The method used to perform the multiplication is diagrammed in Figure 6.1. The 32-bit operand is represented by two 16-bit halves, A and B. The 16-bit operand is represented by C. Multiplying B by C will yield a 32-bit result. The same is true for A and C, except that A is effectively shifted 16 bits to the left, making its actual value much larger. To accommodate this, 16 zeros are placed into the summing area in such a way that they shift the result of A times C the same number of positions to the left. This is analogous to writing down a zero during decimal multiplication by

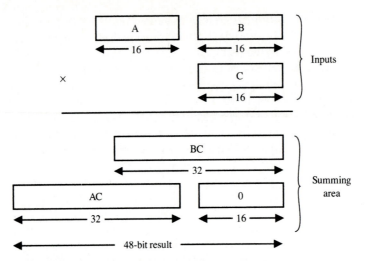

FIGURE 6.1 Diagram of 32- by 16-bit multiplication

hand. The lower 16 bits of the result are the same as the lower 16 bits of the BC product. The middle 16 bits of the result are found by adding the upper 16 bits of the BC product to the lower 16 bits of the AC product. The upper 16 bits of the result equal the upper 16 bits of the AC product, plus any carry out of the middle 16 bits. In the following routine, registers DX and AX contain the 32-bit value we know as AB (with DX holding the upper 16 bits). Register BX contains the 16-bit multiplier C.

```
        In current data segment...
        LOWER    DW    ?
        MIDDLE   DW    ?
        UPPER    DW    ?
         .
         .
         .
        MULTIPLY PROC  FAR
                 PUSH  DX           ;save a copy of DX (A) on stack
                 MUL   BX           ;do B times C
                 MOV   LOWER,AX     ;save partial results
                 MOV   MIDDLE,DX
                 POP   AX           ;pop stack (A) into AX
                 MUL   BX           ;do A times C
                 ADD   MIDDLE,AX    ;generate middle 16-bits of result
                 ADC   DX,0         ;increment DX if carry present
                 MOV   UPPER,DX     ;save upper 16-bits of result
                 RET
        MULTIPLY ENDP
```

It should be possible to relate the code of this example to Figure 6.1. Generating the individual AC and BC products is easily done via MUL. Adding the upper 16 bits of the BC product to the lower 16 bits of the AC product is accomplished by using the ADD instruction. Any overflow out of the middle 16 bits will be placed into the carry flag. This carry is then added to the upper

16 bits of the AC product to complete the operation. Test the routine with this product: 12345678 times ABCD equals 0C3789AB6618.

Binary Division

The 8088 microprocessor supports binary division with its DIV and IDIV (unsigned and signed division) instructions. Both instructions can divide a 32-bit quantity by a 16-bit quantity. The 32-bit result is composed of a 16-bit quotient and a 16-bit remainder. When division by zero is attempted, an interrupt will be generated on completion of the instruction. Many applications exist for the division operation. It can be used to find averages, probabilities, factors, and many other items that are useful when we are working with sets of data. The following subroutine is used to find a factor of a given number, when supplied with another factor. For example, FACTOR will return 50 as a factor, when 6 and 300 are supplied as input (because 300 divided by 6 equals 50 exactly). FACTOR will return 0 if no factor exists (for example, 300 divided by 7 gives 42.857143, which is not an integer; thus, the two numbers cannot be factors).

```
         In current data segment...
NUMBER        DD     ?            ;32-bit input number
FACTOR1       DW     ?            ;16-bit input factor
FACTOR2       DW     ?            ;16-bit output factor
         .
         .
         .
FACTOR        PROC   FAR
              LEA    SI,NUMBER    ;point to input number
              MOV    AX,[SI]      ;load input number into DX:AX
              MOV    DX,[SI + 2]
              DIV    FACTOR1      ;divide by input factor
              CMP    DX,0         ;was division even?
              JNZ    NOFACTOR
              MOV    FACTOR2,AX   ;save output factor
              RET
NOFACTOR:     MOV    FACTOR2,0    ;clear output factor
              RET
FACTOR        ENDP
```

Since the remainder appears in DX, we examine it for 0000 to see if the division was even.

BCD Addition

In the binary number system, we use 8 bits to represent integer numbers in the range 0 to 255 (00 to FF hexadecimal). When the same 8 bits are used to store a binary coded decimal (BCD) number, the range changes. Integers from 0 to 99 may now be represented, with the 10s and 1s digits using 4 bits each. If we expand this reasoning to 16 bits, we get a 0-to-65535 binary integer range, and a 0-to-9999 BCD range. Notice that the binary range has increased significantly. This is always the case and represents one of the major differences between binary and BCD numbers. Even so, we use BCD to solve a nasty

exponents in the calculations. A single byte gives a signed integer range from −128 to 127. This slightly changes the format of the BCD numbers represented, and requires **normalization** of the numbers before conversion. Normalization is necessary because we have no way of storing a decimal point within the binary data we use to represent a number. Through normalization, we end up with a standard representation by altering the mantissa and adjusting the exponent accordingly. For example, 576.4 and 5.764E2 are equal, as are 23497.28 and 2.349728E4. In these examples, both numbers have been normalized so that the first digit of the mantissa is always between 1 and 9. This method works for fractional numbers as well. Here we have 0.0035 equaling 3.5E−3. The addition of an exponent byte to our format, together with the new technique of normalization, will require that we now left justify our BCD numbers. Representing these numbers in our standard format gives

$$576.4: \quad 02 \quad 57 \quad 64 \quad 00 \quad 00$$
$$23497.28: \quad 04 \quad 23 \quad 49 \quad 72 \quad 80$$
$$0.0035: \quad FD \quad 35 \quad 00 \quad 00 \quad 00$$

where the first byte is used to represent the signed binary exponent.

Notice the 2's complement representation of the exponent −3 in the third set of data bytes.

Adding exponent capability to our BCD format complicates the routines we have already seen. The addition routine (as well as subtraction) will only give valid results when we are adding two numbers whose exponents are equal. Since this is rarely the case, we need to adjust the exponent of one number before doing the addition. For instance, if we wish to add 5027 and 394, we must first normalize both numbers:

$$5027: \quad 03 \quad 50 \quad 27 \quad 00 \quad 00$$
$$394: \quad 02 \quad 39 \quad 40 \quad 00 \quad 00$$

Because the exponents are different we have to adjust one of the numbers to correctly add them. If we adjust the number with the higher exponent, we may lose accuracy in our answer. It is much safer to adjust the smaller number. This gives us

$$5027: \quad 03 \quad 50 \quad 27 \quad 00 \quad 00$$
$$394: \quad 03 \quad 03 \quad 94 \quad 00 \quad 00$$

It is clear now that BCD addition of the four trailing bytes will give the correct answer. Notice that we have not changed the value of the second number, only its representation.

BCD multiplication and division also require the use of exponents for best results. Unfortunately, it is not a simple matter of adding exponents for multiplication and subtracting them for division. Special rules are invoked when we multiply or divide two negative numbers. In any case, we must take all rules into account when writing a routine that will handle exponents.

The BCD division routine presented here keeps track of exponents during its calculations. The subroutine ALIGN adjusts the dividend so that it is always 1 to 9 times greater than the divisor. ALIGN modifies the exponent of the dividend as well. Subroutine MSUB performs multiple subtractions. The number of times (0 to 9) the divisor is subtracted from the dividend is returned in the lower 4 bits of AL. Both routines utilize SI and DI as pointers to the memory locations containing the BCD representations of the dividend and divisor. Register BX accumulates the individual results from MSUB into a 4-digit BCD result. The exponent is generated by the EXPONENT subroutine, which uses the initial exponent values plus the results of ALIGN to calculate the final exponent, which is returned in the lower byte of AX.

```
        In current data segment...
        DIVIDEND  DB     5 DUP (?)          ;reserve 5 bytes (one for exponent)
        DIVISOR   DB     5 DUP (?)
          .
          .
          .
        BCDDIV    PROC   FAR
                  LEA    SI,DIVIDEND         ;init pointer to dividend
                  LEA    DI,DIVISOR          ;init pointer to divisor
                  MOV    AL,0                ;clear exponent accumulator
                  MOV    CX,4                ;init loop counter
        DIVIDE:   CALL   FAR PTR ALIGN       ;align numbers
                  CALL   FAR PTR MSUB        ;perform multiple subtractions
                  PUSH   CX                  ;save loop counter
                  MOV    CL,4
                  SHL    BX,CL               ;shift result one digit left
                  POP    CX                  ;get loop counter back
                  AND    AL,0FH              ;mask out result from MSUB
                  OR     BL,AL               ;save result in BL
                  LOOP   DIVIDE              ;continue for more precision
                  CALL   FAR PTR EXPONENT    ;generate final exponent
                  RET
        BCDDIV    ENDP
```

BCDDIV does not check for division by zero, but this test could be added easily with a few instructions.

Deriving Other Mathematical Functions

Once subroutines exist for performing the basic mathematical functions (addition, subtraction, multiplication, and division), they may be used to derive more complex functions. Though all forms of high-level math operations are available with the addition of a math coprocessor, there are times when we must get by without one. The examples presented here show how existing routines can be combined to simulate higher-level operations. All of the examples to be presented assume that the following multiprecision subroutines exist:

Routine	*Operation*
ADD	(BP) = (SI) + (DI)
SUBTRACT	(BP) = (SI) − (DI)
MULTIPLY	(BP) = (SI) * (DI)
DIVIDE	(BP) = (SI) / (DI)

In all cases, SI and DI point to the two input numbers upon entry to the subroutine and BP points to the result. Thus, (SI) means the number pointed to by SI, not the contents of SI. By defining the routines in this way, we can avoid discussion about whether the numbers are binary or BCD.

The first routine examined is used to raise a number to a specified power (for example, 5 raised to the 3rd power is 125). This routine uses the binary number in AL as the power. The number raised to this power is pointed to by SI. The final result is pointed to by BP.

```
POWER       PROC    FAR
            CALL    FAR PTR COPY        ;make a copy of the input number
MAKEPOW:    CALL    FAR PTR MULTIPLY    ;compute next power result
            XCHG    BP,SI               ;use result as next input
            DEC     AL                  ;continue until done
            JNZ     MAKEPOW
            XCHG    BP,SI               ;final result is pointed to by BP
            RET
POWER       ENDP
```

POWER is written such that the power must be 2 or more. Negative powers and powers equal to 0 or 1 are not implemented in this routine (they are left as an exercise). COPY is a subroutine that makes a copy of the input number pointed to by SI. The copied number is pointed to by DI.

The next routine is used to generate factorials. A factorial of a number (for example, 5! or 10! or 37!) is found by multiplying all integers up to and including the input number. For instance, 5! equals 1*2*3*4*5. This results in 5! equaling 120. Do a few factorial calculations yourself, and you will see that the result gets very large, very quickly! FACTORIAL will compute the factorial of the integer value stored in AL. The result is pointed to by BP.

```
FACTORIAL   PROC    FAR
            LEA     SI,ONE                ;init sequence counter
            LEA     DI,ONE                ;init first multiplier
NEXTNUM:    CALL    FAR PTR MULTIPLY      ;compute partial factorial
            XCHG    BP,DI                 ;use result as next input
            CALL    FAR PTR INCREMENT     ;increment sequence counter
            DEC     AL                    ;continue until done
            JNZ     NEXTNUM
            XCHG    BP,DI                 ;result pointed to by BP
            RET
FACTORIAL   ENDP
```

INCREMENT is a subroutine that performs a specific task: Add one to the number pointed to by SI. We use INCREMENT to generate the sequence of integers that get multiplied together. The symbol ONE refers to a predefined storage area in memory that contains the value 1 in standard format.

FIGURE 6.3 Finding square roots by iteration

$$\text{Estimate} = \frac{\dfrac{\text{number}}{\text{estimate}} + \text{estimate}}{2}$$

Example: Find square root of 42
Initial estimate: 21

Number of iterations	Estimate
0	21
1	11.5
2	7.57608
3	6.55992
4	6.48121
5	6.4807

$(6.4807)^2 = 41.999$

The next routine, ROOT, computes square roots. The formula, and an example of how it works, is presented in Figure 6.3. This type of formula is **iterative.** This means that we must run through the formula a number of times before getting the desired result. Notice in the figure how each new application of the square root formula brings the estimate of the answer closer to the correct value. After applying the formula only five times, we have a result that comes very close to the square root. A few more iterations will increase the accuracy of the result even more. Fewer iterations are needed when the initial estimate is close to the desired value. For instance, if the original estimate used in Figure 6.3 was 7 instead of 21, fewer iterations would have been needed to get to 6.4807. The routine presented here implements the formula of Figure 6.3.

```
In current data segment...
NUMBER      DB    5 DUP (?)
ESTIMATE    DB    5 DUP (?)
  .
  .
  .
ROOT        PROC  FAR
            LEA   SI,NUMBER           ;point to input number
            LEA   DI,TWO              ;predefined constant 2
            CALL  FAR PTR DIVIDE      ;calculate original estimate
            LEA   BX,ESTIMATE         ;save estimate
            CALL  FAR PTR SAVE
            MOV   CX,10               ;prepare for 10 iterations
ITERATE:    LEA   SI,NUMBER
            LEA   DI,ESTIMATE
            CALL  FAR PTR DIVIDE      ;number / estimate
            XCHG  BP,SI               ;use result in following addition
            CALL  FAR PTR ADD         ;(number / estimate) + estimate
```

```
                XCHG    BP,SI                ;use result in following division
                LEA     DI,TWO
                CALL    FAR PTR DIVIDE       ;entire formula implemented now
                LEA     BX,ESTIMATE          ;save new estimate
                CALL    FAR PTR SAVE
                LOOP    ITERATE
                RET
      ROOT      ENDP
```

The subroutine SAVE is used to make a copy of the number pointed to by BP. The copy is stored in memory starting at the location pointed to by BX. The XCHG instruction is used to swap pointers, thus making the results of ADD and DIVIDE available for the next operation.

The last example we will examine is used to computer powers of **base e.** From calculus, it can be shown that an infinite series of terms can be used to generate the result of raising e (2.7182818) to any power, as Figure 6.4 illustrates. Notice that only the first seven terms are needed to get a reasonable amount of accuracy. Many complex functions can be represented by an infinite series, which we can then implement in software using a loop operation. The following routine generates the first 10 terms of the exponential series, using the POWER and FACTORIAL routines already discussed. We assume, however, that POWER and FACTORIAL give valid results for all input values (including 0 and 1).

FIGURE 6.4 Generation of e^x by infinite series

$$e^x = \sum_{n-0}^{\infty} \frac{x^n}{n!}$$

$$= \frac{x^0}{0!} + \frac{x^1}{1!} + \frac{x^2}{2!} + \frac{x^3}{3!} + \frac{x^4}{4!} + \ldots$$

$$= 1 + x + \frac{x^2}{2} + \frac{x^3}{6} + \frac{x^4}{24} + \ldots$$

Example: Find e^1

Number of terms	Result
1	1
2	2
3	2.5
4	2.66666
5	2.70833
6	2.71666
7	2.71805

(e^1 = 2.7182818)

```
In current data segment...
X              DB      5 DUP (?)
TEMP           DB      5 DUP (?)
ETOX           DB      5 DUP (?)
 .
 .
 .
EPOWER         PROC    FAR
               LEA     SI,ZERO              ;predefined constant 0
               LEA     DI,ETOX
               CALL    FAR PTR COPY         ;clear result
               MOV     CX,10                ;init loop counter
NEXTERM:       LEA     SI,X                 ;compute numerator
               MOV     AL,CL
               CALL    FAR PTR POWER
               LEA     BX,TEMP              ;save numerator
               CALL    FAR PTR SAVE
               MOV     AL,CL                ;compute denominator
               CALL    FAR PTR FACTORIAL
               LEA     SI,TEMP              ;divide to generate term
               XCHG    BP,DI
               CALL    FAR PTR DIVIDE
               XCHG    BP,DI                ;add current term to result
               LEA     SI,ETOX
               CALL    FAR PTR ADD
               LEA     BX,ETOX              ;save result
               CALL    FAR PTR SAVE
               LOOP    NEXTERM
               RET
EPOWER         ENDP
```

Again, XCHG is used to redirect output results back into the math routines. XCHG is also used to swap pointers for storing results in memory. ETOX contains the final result when EPOWER finishes execution.

These examples should serve to illustrate the point that complex mathematical functions can be implemented with a small amount of software. Once a library of these routines has been defined and tested, even more complex equations and functions may be implemented. All that is needed is a CALL to the appropriate subroutine (or collection of subroutines).

6.7 CONTROL APPLICATIONS

In this section we will examine two examples of how the 8088 may be used in control applications. Control systems are designed in two different ways: open-loop and closed-loop systems. Figure 6.5 shows two simple block diagrams outlining the main difference between these two types of control systems. An open-loop control system uses its input data to effect changes in its outputs. A closed-loop system contains a feedback path, where data concerning the present output conditions is sampled and supplied along with the external inputs. A burglar alarm is an example of an open-loop control system. The system may be designed to monitor sensors at various windows and doors. It may also include circuitry to digitize readings from temperature sensors. When any of

FIGURE 6.5   Control system block diagram: (a) open-loop and (b) closed-loop

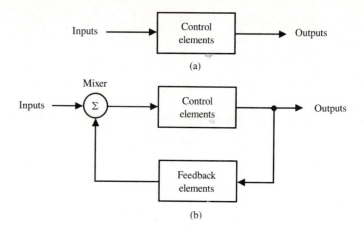

the sensors detects an abnormal condition (for example, a window opening), the computer may be directed to dial an emergency phone number and play a recorded help message.

A typical application of a closed-loop control system involves the operation of a motor. Suppose we want to control the speed of the motor by making adjustments to an input voltage to the system. The speed of the motor is proportional to the input voltage and increases as the input voltage increases. We cannot simply apply the input voltage to the motor's windings, for it may not be large enough to operate the motor. Usually an amplifier is involved that is capable of driving the motor. But a problem occurs when the motor encounters a load (for example, by connecting the motor shaft to a pump). The increased load on the motor will cause the motor speed to decrease. To maintain a constant speed in the motor at this point, we need an increase in the input voltage. We cannot hope or expect the operator to constantly watch the motor and adjust the input voltage accordingly. For this reason, we add a feedback loop, which is used to sample the motor speed and generate an equivalent voltage. An *error* voltage is generated by comparing the actual speed of the motor (the voltage generated by the feedback circuit) with the desired speed (set by the input voltage). The motor speed voltage may be generated by a tachometer connected to the output of the motor. The error voltage is used to increase or decrease the speed of the motor until it is operating at the proper speed.

Let us look at how the 8088 might be used to implement the two control systems just described.

A Computerized Burglar Alarm

In this section, we will use the 8088 to monitor activity on 100 windows and doors in a small office building. The office building consists of 4 floors, with 15 doors and 10 windows on each floor. The alarm console consists of an electronic display containing a labeled light-emitting diode for each window and door and a serial data terminal capable of displaying ASCII information. The operation of the system consists of two tasks: (1) illuminating the appropriate LED for all open doors and windows, and (2) sending a message to the terminal whenever a door or window opens or closes. It is necessary to continuously scan all of the windows and doors to detect any changes. The circuitry used to monitor the doors and windows and drive the LED display is connected to the processor's system bus so that all I/O can be done by reading and writing to ports. Figure 6.6 shows the assignments of all input and output devices for the first floor of the office building.

As the figure shows, 15 door and 10 window inputs are assigned for the first floor. Whenever a door or window is open, its associated bit will be low. To sample the bits, the processor must do an I/O read from the indicated port (7000 to 7003). Floors 2, 3, and 4 are assigned the same way, with the following port addresses:

> Floor 2: 7004–7007
> Floor 3: 7008–700B
> Floor 4: 700C–700F

The door and window LEDs for the first floor are illuminated when their respective bits are high. The processor must do an I/O write to ports 7800 through 7803 to activate LEDs for the first floor. The other-floor LEDs work the same way, with these port addresses assigned to them:

> Floor 2: 7804–7807
> Floor 3: 7808–780B
> Floor 4: 780C–780F

The serial device used by the system to communicate with the ASCII terminal is driven by a subroutine called CONSOLE. The 7-bit ASCII code in the lower byte of register AL is sent to the terminal when CONSOLE is called.

Knowing these definitions, we can design a system to constantly monitor all 100 doors and windows. The technique we will use is called **polling.** Each input port will be read and examined for any changes. If a door or window has changed state since the last time it was read, a message will be sent to the terminal, via CONSOLE, indicating the floor and door/window number. Since we need to remember the last state of each door and window, their states must be saved. A block of memory, called STATUS, will be used for this purpose. STATUS points to a 16-byte block of memory, which we will think of as 4 blocks of 4 bytes each. Each 4-byte block will store the bits for all doors and windows on a single floor.

When the program first begins operation, the state of each door and window is unknown. For this reason, we initialize STATUS by reading all system inputs when the program starts up. The code to perform the initialization is contained in a subroutine called INIT, and is as follows:

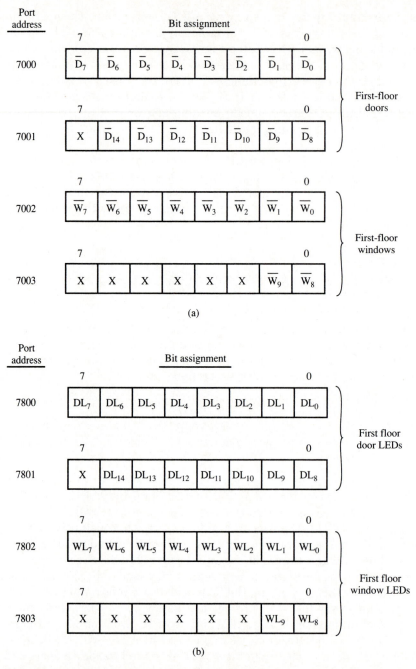

FIGURE 6.6 Burglar alarm I/O assignments: (a) system inputs and (b) system outputs

```
In current data segment...
STATUS      DB      16 DUP (?)
  .

  .

  .
INIT        PROC    FAR
            LEA     DI,STATUS       ;init pointer to STATUS
            MOV     DX,7000H        ;init pointer to first input port
            MOV     CX,16           ;init loop counter
SYSREAD:    IN      AL,DX           ;read system information
            MOV     [DI],AL         ;save it in memory
            NOT     AL              ;complement input data
            ADD     DX,800H         ;set up output port address
            OUT     DX,AL           ;update display
            SUB     DX,800H         ;generate next input port address
            INC     DX
            INC     DI              ;point to next STATUS location
            LOOP    SYSREAD
            RET
INIT        ENDP
```

When INIT completes execution, the display has been updated to show the state of all 100 doors and windows, and STATUS has been loaded with the same information.

Once the initial states are known, future changes can be detected by using an Exclusive OR operation. Remember that Exclusive OR only produces a 1 when both inputs are different. Figure 6.7 shows how state changes can be detected with Exclusive OR. To incorporate this into the program, XOR is used during updates to detect changes. Note that up to 16 changes at once can be detected by XORing entire words. It is then a matter of scanning the individual bits to determine if any state changes occurred. A subroutine called DETECT will do this for us. DETECT will sense any state changes and send the appropriate message (for example, first floor: door 12 opened) to the terminal. When DETECT is called, data registers AX, BX, and DX will be interpreted as follows:

FIGURE 6.7   Detecting state changes with XOR

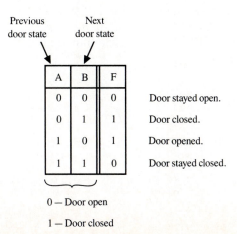

A	B	F	
0	0	0	Door stayed open.
0	1	1	Door closed.
1	0	1	Door opened.
1	1	0	Door stayed closed.

Previous door state
Next door state

0 — Door open

1 — Door closed

AX: Contains current door or window states.

BX: Contains door or window state changes.

DX: Bit 8 cleared means AX contains door information.
              Bit 8 set means AX contains window information.
              Bits 0 and 1 contain the floor number (0—first, 1—second, 2—third, 3—fourth)

We will not cover the code involved in getting DETECT to do its job. You are encouraged to write this routine yourself, preferably using a rotate or shift instruction to do the bit testing. Since DETECT will have to output ASCII text strings (for example, "First floor", "Second floor", "opened"), the following code may come in handy:

```
In current data segment...
MSG1    DB      'First floor $'
MSG2    DB      'Second floor $'
MSG3    DB      'Third floor $'
MSG4    DB      'Fourth floor $'
MSG5    DB      'door $'
MSG6    DB      'window $'
MSG7    DB      'opened $'
MSG8    DB      'closed $'
  .
  .
  .
SEND    PROC    FAR
        MOV     AL,[SI]         ;get a message character
        CMP     AL,'$'          ;end of message character?
        JZ      EXIT
        CALL    FAR PTR CONSOLE ;send character to terminal
        INC     SI              ;point to next character
        JMP     SEND
EXIT:   RET
SEND    ENDP
```

The SEND subroutine must be entered with register SI pointing to the address of the first character in the text string to be sent. SEND could be a subroutine called by DETECT during its analysis of the door and window states.

Using DETECT, the code to poll all doors and windows in the office building becomes:

```
          CALL FAR PTR INIT   ;get initial states and update display
BEGIN:    MOV  CX,0           ;start with first floor doors
          MOV  DX,7000H       ;point to first input port
          LEA  SI,STATUS      ;point to STATUS information
NEWFLOOR: IN   AL,DX          ;get door data
          NOT  AL
          ADD  DX,800H        ;update display
          OUT  DX,AL
          MOV  AH,AL          ;save first eight door states
          SUB  DX,800H        ;point to next door
          INC  DX
          IN   AL,DX          ;get remaining door data
          NOT  AL
          ADD  DX,800H        ;update display
```

```
        OUT   DX,AL
        XCHG  AL,AH              ;correct AX for DETECT
        NOT   AX
        MOV   BL,[SI]            ;get past door status
        MOV   BH,[SI + 1]
        ADD   SI,2              ;advance to next status group
        XOR   BX,AX             ;compute state changes
        XCHG  CX,DX             ;get floor number into DX
        CALL  FAR PTR DETECT    ;find doors that have changed
        XCHG  CX,DX             ;get port address back
        SUB   DX,800H           ;point to window data
        INC   DX
        IN    AL,DX             ;get window data
        NOT   AL
        ADD   DX,800H           ;update display
        OUT   DX,AL
        MOV   AH,AL             ;save first eight window states
        SUB   DX,800H           ;point to next window
        INC   DX
        IN    AL,DX             ;get remaining window data
        NOT   AL
        ADD   DX,800H           ;update display
        OUT   DX,AL
        XCHG  AL,AH             ;correct AX for DETECT
        NOT   AX
        MOV   BL,[SI]            ;get past window status
        MOV   BH,[SI + 1]
        ADD   SI,2              ;advance to next floor
        XOR   BX,AX             ;compute state changes
        OR    CX,100H           ;set bit-8 in CX
        XCHG  CX,DX             ;get floor number into DX
        CALL  FAR PTR DETECT    ;find windows that have changed
        XCHG  CX,DX             ;get port address back
        AND   CH,0             ;clear bit-8
        SUB   DX,800H           ;point to next floor
        INC   DX
        INC   CX               ;increment floor counter
        CMP   CX,4             ;done?
        JZ    REPEAT
        JMP   NEWFLOOR          ;both JMPs are needed since
REPEAT: JMP   BEGIN            ;relative range has been exceeded
```

While you write DETECT, do not forget that the main routine uses a number of
registers and that these registers should not be altered. The stack would be a
good place to store them for safekeeping.

A Constant-Speed Motor Controller

In this section we will see how the 8088 may be used in a closed-loop control
system to maintain constant speed in a motor. The schematic of the system is
shown in Figure 6.8. The speed control is a potentiometer whose output voltage
varies from 0 to some positive voltage. This voltage is digitized by an 8-bit
analog-to-digital converter, such that 0 volts is 00H and the most positive
voltage is FF. The processor reads this data from port 8000. For a purely digital
speed control system, this circuitry is eliminated and the speed set directly by
software.

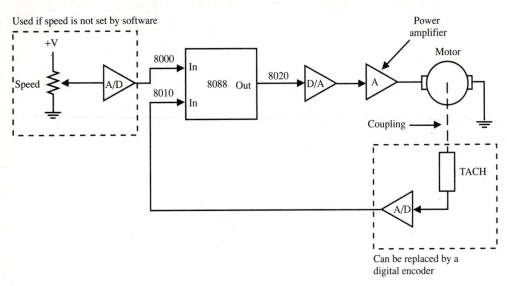

FIGURE 6.8 Constant speed motor controller

The motor speed is controlled by the output of an 8-bit digital-to-analog converter (with appropriate output amplifier, capable of driving the motor). The motor's minimum speed, 0 RPM, occurs when the computer outputs 00 to the D/A (by writing to port 8020). The motor's maximum speed occurs when FF is sent to the D/A. A tachometer is connected to the motor shaft through a mechanical coupling. The output of the tachometer is digitized also. Again, the minimum and maximum tachometer readings correspond to 00 and FF. A purely digital system would use a digital shaft encoder instead of a tachometer and A/D. The tach is read from input port 8010H.

Each converter is calibrated with respect to a common reference. In theory, a 17 from the SPEED A/D causes a 17 to be sent to the MOTOR D/A, which in turn causes the TACH A/D to read 17 when at the proper speed. In practice the relationship is not so linear, due to external effects of deadband, friction, and other losses in the motor.

The purpose of the program is to operate the motor at a constant speed, by comparing the SPEED data with the TACH data. When SPEED equals TACH the motor is turning at the desired speed. When SPEED is less than TACH, the motor is spinning too fast. When SPEED is greater than TACH, the motor is rotating too slow. The idea is to subtract the TACH value from the SPEED value. The difference determines how much the motor speed should be increased or decreased.

```
SERVO:      MOV   AL,0          ;initial motor speed is 0 RPM
            MOV   DX,8020H
            OUT   DX,AL
GETSPEED:   MOV   DX,8000H       ;read new speed value
            IN    AL,DX
            MOV   AH,AL          ;save speed here
```

```
              ADD    DX,10H              ;and new tachometer value
              IN     AL,DX
              CMP    AH,AL               ;SPEED minus TACH
              JG     INCREASE
              JZ     GETSPEED            ;no change
              XCHG   AL,AH
   INCREASE:  SUB    AH,AL               ;compute error value
              MOV    AL,AH
              CALL   FAR PTR GAIN
              MOV    DX,8020H            ;output new motor speed
              OUT    DX,AL
              JMP    GETSPEED
```

Since the motor's speed will not change instantly from very slow to very fast, or vice versa, the program will loop many times before the motor gets to the proper speed. For safety or functional reasons, it may not be desirable to try to change the motor speed from slow to fast instantly. Instead, the program should *ramp up* to speed gradually by limiting the size of the error voltage presented to the D/A during speed increases. Subroutine GAIN is used for this purpose, to alter the contents of AL, before AL is output to the motor D/A. The ramp up/down speed of the motor, and therefore the response of the closed-loop system, will be a function of the operation of GAIN.

6.8   INSTRUCTION EXECUTION TIMES

An important topic in the study of any microprocessor involves analysis of the execution time of programs, subroutines, or short sections of code. The most direct application of this study is in the design of programs that function under a time constraint. For example, high-resolution graphics operations, such as image rotation, filtering, and motion simulation, require all processing to be completed within a very short period of time (usually a few milliseconds or less). If analysis of the total instruction execution time for the graphics routine exceeds the allowed time of the system, a loss in image quality will most likely result. We will not get quite so involved with our analysis of the 8088's instruction times. Instead, we will look at one example subroutine and how its total execution time may be determined.

TOBIN is a subroutine that will convert a 4-digit BCD number in register BX into a binary number. The result is returned by TOBIN in AX. TOBIN is a good example to use for execution time determination because it contains two nested loops. The number of clock cycles for each instruction can be determined by referring to Appendix B. Table 6.1 is an example of how clock cycles are determined. The number of clock cycles an instruction takes to execute depends on a number of factors. Operand size is the first variable. Look at the clock cycles required by the MOV   CX instructions. The instruction itself takes four cycles, plus another four required by the 8088 to fetch a word operand from memory. The processor's 8-bit data bus requires two memory read cycles to obtain the word operand, resulting in the additional four clock cycles.

The addressing mode used by an instruction also affects the number of clock cycles required. Register addressing, as in the SUB   AX,AX and

TABLE 6.1   Required instruction execution clock cycles in a simple programming loop

	Instructions		Clock Cycles		
			Overhead Cycles	Outer-loop Cycles	Inner-loop Cycles
TOBIN	PROC	FAR			
	SUB	AX,AX	3		
	MOV	DX,AX	2		
	MOV	CX,4	4 + 4		
NEXTDIGIT:	PUSH	CX		11 + 4	
	SUB	BP,BP		3	
	MOV	CX,4		4 + 4	
GETNUM:	RCL	BX,1			2
	RCL	BP,1			2
	LOOP	GETNUM			17/5
	MOV	CX,10		4 + 4	
	MUL	CX		118–133	
	ADD	AX,BP		3	
	POP	CX		8 + 4	
	LOOP	NEXTDIGIT		17/5	
	RET		18 + 8		
TOBIN	ENDP				

ADD   AX,BP instructions, requires fewer clock cycles than an instruction that must access memory during its execution, such as PUSH and POP. The clock cycles required for each addressing mode are included in Appendix B. You must note that the clock cycles shown for each instruction assume that the instructions have already been fetched and placed in the instruction queue. This, in many cases, results in very few clock cycles for some instructions. An exception is the LOOP instruction, which has two times listed. The smaller time is used when the jump does *not* take place. This makes sense, since the instruction following LOOP can simply be fetched from the instruction queue. The larger time is required when the LOOP does take place, owing to the fact that the queue must be flushed and reloaded. Other instructions have a variable number of cycles as a function of the data they operate on. MUL is a good example of this, requiring anywhere from 118 to 133 cycles, depending on the number of 1s in the operands forming the product. It is best to use the **worst case** execution time. Then you will avoid nasty situations such as having to explain "Well. . . the routine may take longer than this time to execute because. . ."

The RET instruction requires an ample number of clock cycles to execute because it must pop the CS and IP return address off the stack. These operations require accesses to memory, which always increase the execution time.

Table 6.1 has three columns of clock cycles. The **overhead** column is for instructions that execute only once in the subroutine. They do not contribute significantly to the overall time, but cannot be ignored. The outer-loop and inner-loop cycles are repeated a number of times, and thus grow into a large number of clock cycles before the routine completes. Keep in mind that the overall execution time will only be an *estimate*, since other factors are normally present which affect execution time. These factors include the time required to initially load the instruction queue, or the time to reload it after a jump or loop instruction. Our estimate will be within 10 percent of the actual execution time, however.

To compute the execution time, we must first determine the total number of clock cycles needed. The inner-loop requires 21 cycles (worst case) for one pass. Since the inner-loop is designed to execute four times, this gives 84 cycles for one completion of the inner-loop instructions. But these instructions are contained within the outer-loop, which itself requires an additional 199 clock cycles (worst case). So, executing the outer-loop once uses 283 clock cycles. The outer-loop executes four times also, giving a total of 1132 cycles so far. Adding in 39 overhead cycles (do you see why overhead is not significant?) results in a grand total of 1171 clock cycles for the TOBIN subroutine.

How does this number translate into an execution time? Since each clock cycle has a period determined by its frequency, we need to know the clock frequency at which the processor is running. Suppose this frequency is 5 MHz. Each cycle will then have a period of 200 ns. Multiplying 200 ns by 1171 gives 234.2 μs! This is the execution time of TOBIN.

In conclusion, it is interesting to note that TOBIN can convert over 4200 BCD numbers to binary in one second.

6.9   INTERRUPT HANDLING

In Chapter 4, various kinds of interrupts supported by the 8088 were examined. In this section we will see two examples of how exceptions may be handled by the programmer. The first example deals with two exceptions that hopefully never occur: divide-by-zero and overflow. The purpose of the interrupt handler for these two routines will be to send an error message to the user's terminal, indicating that the error has occurred. Execution will then resume at the address following the instruction that caused the interrupt. Remember: All interrupts cause the 8088 to reference its interrupt vector table (located in memory from 00000 to 003FF). In this table, the processor will expect to find the address of the routine that will handle the designated interrupt. The following routines, DIV0 and OVERFLOW, are ORGed at 1000H and 2000H respectively. For the 8088 to find its way to them during interrupt processing, the starting addresses of these routines must be placed into the interrupt vector table at the proper addresses. Divide-error, a type-0 interrupt, requires its interrupt handler address to be stored in locations 00000 through 00003, with 00001 and 00002 containing the IP address, and locations 00002 and 00003 the CS address. Overflow is a type-4 interrupt, utilizing locations 00010H through 00013H in the interrupt vector table. Figure 6.9 shows how

FIGURE 6.9 Interrupt vector table address assignments for divide-error and overflow

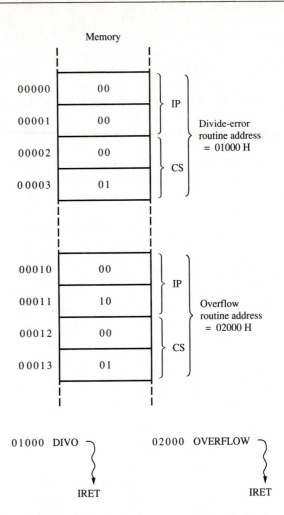

these locations should be loaded with the addresses of both interrupt service routines. Assume that both routines are located within the code segment beginning at 1000H. Then CS will contain 0100H, and the IP values needed for DIV0 and OVERFLOW are 0000 and 1000H, respectively.

Once the CPU has loaded the program counter and code segment register with the address of the interrupt service routine, it will begin executing instructions at a new location. The interrupt handlers, to be on the safe side, should save any registers they use on the stack, so that execution may resume with the proper information after interrupt processing has completed. Once this is done, DIV0 and OVERFLOW may perform their associated tasks. In this example, they will simply load the address of an ASCII error message that will be output to the display via INT 21. An interesting point in these routines is that the data segment is modified so that it occupies the same space as the code segment. This prevents us from having to define a separate data segment for the text messages. The original value of the data segment is saved on the stack and restored at the end of the routine.

```
            ORG     1000H
DIVO        PROC    FAR
            PUSH    DS              ;save registers on stack
            PUSH    DX
            PUSH    AX
            MOV     AX,CS           ;get CS address
            MOV     DS,AX           ;put it into DS
            LEA     DX,DIVMSG       ;point to error message
PINT:       MOV     AH,9            ;select display-message function
            INT     21H             ;output message to display
            POP     AX              ;restore registers
            POP     DX
            POP     DS
            IRET                    ;return from interrupt
DIVMSG      DB      ODH,OAH
            DB      'Divide-by-zero attempted!'
            DB      ODH,OAH,'$'
DIVO        ENDP
   .
   .
   .
            ORG     2000H
OVERFLOW    PROC    FAR
            PUSH    DS
            PUSH    DX
            PUSH    AX
            MOV     AX,CS
            MOV     DS,AX
            LEA     DX,OVMSG
            JMP     PINT            ;go use existing code
OVMSG       DB      ODH,OAH
            DB      'Overflow occurred, results questionable!'
            DB      ODH,OAH,'$'
OVERFLOW    ENDP
```

Note that we save some code in OVERFLOW's handler by using a portion of DIV0's routine. Also, the final instruction in any exception handler must be IRET (not RET). This is required to load the proper information from the stack when returning to the main routine (where the exception was initiated).

In addition to sending the error message, it may be desirable to output a list of register contents as well. The user would then be able to see the state of the processor registers at the instant the exception occurred. This requires a routine capable of converting the hexadecimal register contents into a corresponding string of ASCII characters to send to the user's terminal. This routine must be called *after* all registers have already been saved. Otherwise we end up destroying the contents of whatever registers we use in the conversion routine.

Our second example, a routine called TIMER, is used to keep accurate time. This example assumes that a stable 60-Hz clock is used to interrupt the processor 60 times a second, generating a type-31 interrupt each time. Again, the address of TIMER must be placed into the proper locations (00007C through 00007F) in the processor's interrupt vector table.

TIMER simply increments SECONDS, MINUTES, and HOURS (all byte locations) as necessary. These locations may be read by other routines that need to make use of timing functions. Why are the PUSH instructions absent from this interrupt handler?

```
In current data segment...
ICOUNT      DB     ?
SECONDS     DB     ?
MINUTES     DB     ?
HOURS       DB     ?
  .
  .
  .
TIMER       PROC   FAR
            ADD    ICOUNT,1      ;increment interrupt counter
            CMP    ICOUNT,60     ;has one second passed?
            JNZ    EXITIMER
            MOV    ICOUNT,0      ;reset interrupt counter
            ADD    SECONDS,1     ;increment seconds
            CMP    SECONDS,60    ;has one minute passed?
            JNZ    EXITIMER
            MOV    SECONDS,0     ;reset seconds
            ADD    MINUTES,1     ;increment minutes
            CMP    MINUTES,60    ;has one hour passed?
            JNZ    EXITIMER
            MOV    MINUTES,0     ;reset minutes
            ADD    HOURS,1       ;increment hours
            CMP    HOURS,24      ;has one day passed?
            JNZ    EXITIMER
            MOV    HOURS,0       ;reset hours
EXITIMER:   IRET
TIMER       ENDP
```

Can you think of a reason why this routine may not keep accurate time?

6.10 LINKED LISTS

A linked list is a collection of data elements called **nodes** that is created dynamically. Dynamic creation means that the size of the linked list is not fixed when it is first created. As a matter of fact, it is empty when first created. As an example, if we want to reserve enough room in memory for 100 integer bytes, we use

```
DATA    DB    100    DUP (?)
```

This assembler directive is utilized because we know beforehand how many numbers are going to be used. The beauty of a linked list is that its size can be changed as necessary, either increased or decreased, with a maximum size limited only by the amount of free memory available in the system. This method actually saves space in memory, since it does not dedicate entire blocks of RAM for storing numbers. Rather, a small piece of memory is allocated each time a node is added to the linked list. A node is most commonly represented by a pair of items. The first item is usually used for storing a piece of data. The second item is a pointer; it is used to point to the next node in the linked list. Figure 6.10 contains an example of a three-node linked list. Each node in the list stores a single ASCII character. The beginning of the linked list, the first node, is pointed to by P. The nodes are linked together via pointers from one node to another. The last node in the list, node 3, contains 0 in its pointer field.

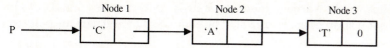

FIGURE 6.10   A sample linked list

We will interpret this as a pointer to nowhere (and thus the last node). The empty pointer is commonly called **nil.**

The actual representation of the node on a particular system can take many forms. Since the linked list must reside in memory, it makes sense to assign one or more locations for the data part (or data field), and two locations for the pointer part (also called the pointer field). Why two locations for the pointer field? Because all nodes reside in memory. To point to a certain node, we must know its address, and addresses in the 8088 occupy 16 bits.

For this discussion, assume that all nodes consist of four data bytes and two address bytes. Consider a subroutine called GETNODE that can be called every time a new node is added to the linked list. GETNODE must find 6 bytes of contiguous (sequential) memory to allocate the node. When it finds them, it will return the starting address of the 6-byte block in register SI. Let us take another look at our example linked list, only this time addresses have been added to each node. Figure 6.11 shows how the pointer field of each node contains the address of the next node in the list. The address in the pointer field of node 3 indicates the end of the list. The pointer P may be a register containing 10000, the address of the first node in the list. To generate this list, GETNODE has been called three times. GETNODE returned different addresses each time it was called. First came 10000, then 78000, and finally 20520. Linked lists do

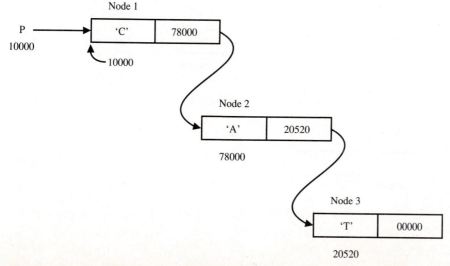

FIGURE 6.11   A linked list with address assignments

not have to occupy a single area of memory. Rather, they may be spread out all over the processor's address space and still be connected by the various pointer fields.

To add a node to the linked list, a simple procedure is followed. First, a new node is allocated by calling GETNODE. Register SI holds the address of this new node. The pointer field address of this new node, which will have to be modified to add it to the list, starts at SI plus 4 (because the data field occupies the first 4 bytes). To add the new node to the existing list, a copy of the pointer P is written into the pointer field of the new node. Then, to make the new node the first node in the list, P is changed to the address of the new node. Figure 6.12 shows this step-by-step process, assuming that register DI is used to store P. Once the new node has been inserted, its data field, now pointed to by DI, may be loaded with new data. Assume the new data comes from register

1. GETNODE returns new node.

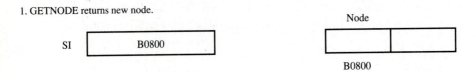

2. Pointer field of new node is loaded with P.

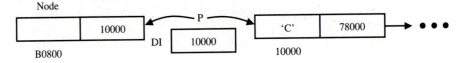

3. Pointer P to list is changed.

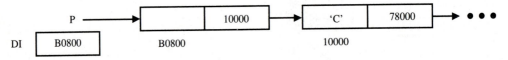

4. Data field of new node is loaded.

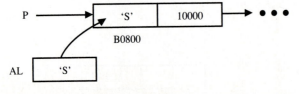

ASCII code for 'S' in lower byte of AX

FIGURE 6.12   Adding a node to a linked list

AL. Note from Figure 6.12 that insertion of the new node into the beginning of the linked list has changed its contents from 'CAT' to 'SCAT'. The code to perform the insertion described in Figure 6.12 is as follows:

```
INSERT   PROC    FAR
         CALL    FAR PTR GETNODE    ;get a new node from storage pool
         MOV     [SI + 4],DI        ;load pointer field with P
         MOV     DI,SI              ;update pointer P to new node
         MOV     [DI],AL            ;load data filed with AL
         MOV     [DI + 1],20H       ;pad rest of data field with blanks
         MOV     [DI + 2],20H
         MOV     [DI + 3],20H
         RET
INSERT   ENDP
```

ASCII blank codes (20H) are used to fill the remaining three e data bytes in the data field.

Linked lists are ordinarily used to represent arrays in memory. The data field may be used to store ASCII characters (as in this example), integers, Boolean data, and even pointers to other linked lists. Linked lists are very useful tools employed in the functions of operating systems. They are also supported by computer languages such as Pascal, Modula-2, and Ada.

6.11 MULTITASKING

In an ever-increasing effort to squeeze the most processing power out of the basic microprocessor, individuals have come up with ingenious techniques for getting a single CPU to do many wonderful things. Consider a standard, single-CPU microcomputing system. One user sits at a terminal entering commands, thinking, entering more commands, waiting for I/O from the system (as a file is loaded in from disk or tape), and so on and on. When computer specialists discovered that in this situation the CPU was wasting a great deal of time doing I/O, they thought of a way of getting more use out of the CPU. Suppose that circuitry could be added to the system to perform the I/O operations under the CPU's control. All the CPU would have to do is issue a command, such as "read the disk," and the disk controller would do the rest of the work. This would free up the processor for other things while the disk controller was busy reading the disk. What other things can the CPU do? The most obvious answer that came to mind was *service another user!* Thus, the age of multitasking was born. A microprocessor system capable of performing multitasking is able to communicate with several users, seemingly at once. Each user believes he or she is the only user on the system. What is actually happening is that one user gets a small slice of the processor's time, then another user gets another time slice, and the same goes for all other users. Figure 6.13 shows a simple diagram of this operation. It this figure we see that up to four users are executing their programs, seemingly at the same time. A single CPU can support more than one person at a time because of the high processing speed of the processor versus the slow thinking speed of the users. It is not

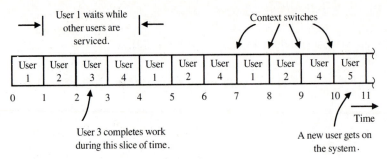

FIGURE 6.13   Multitasking with a single CPU

difficult to see that the user will spend long periods of time thinking about what to do next or waiting for I/O to appear on the terminal. The time slice allocated to each user is designed so that it is long enough to perform a significant number of instructions, without being so long as to be noticed by the user. For example, suppose that as many as 16 users may be on the system at once. If the CPU must service each user once every 10th of a second, the time slice required is 6.25 ms, possibly enough to complete a user's current program. So, even though all users are forced to wait while the CPU services the other users (as shown in Figure 6.13), the users probably do not even notice.

The software involved in supporting a multitasking system can become very involved, so we will only examine the basic details here. What exactly happens when one user's program is suspended so that the CPU can service a different user? Suppose that both users have written programs that use some of the same processor registers (for example, AX, BX, and SI are used by both programs). It becomes necessary to save one user's registers before letting the other user's program take over. This is referred to as a **context switch.** A context switch is used to save all registers for one user and load all registers used by the next user. Thus, a context switch is needed every time the CPU switches between users. The routine presented here, TSLICE, will handle context switches for four different users in a round-robin fashion. This means that user 1 will not execute again until all other users have had their chance. To get the processor to do a context switch, we have to inform it that the user's time slice has expired. The easiest way to do this is to periodically interrupt the processor (by connecting a timer circuit to the processor's interrupt input). TSLICE is then actually an interrupt handler that is executed every time a time slice is used up. TSLICE first saves all processor registers on the stack (the program counter and flags are already there thanks to the 8088 interrupt handling scheme), and then finds the next user that should execute. The registers for this user are then loaded from its stack area and execution resumes. This discussion assumes that all user programs remain in memory when not executing.

```
USER1      DW      64 DUP (?)      ;user stack areas
USER2      DW      64 DUP (?)
USER3      DW      64 DUP (?)
```

```
USER4        DW      64 DUP (?)
WHO          DB      ?                ;current user number (1-4)
STACK1       DW      ?                ;storage for user stack pointers
STACK2       DW      ?
STACK3       DW      ?
STACK4       DW      ?
  .
  .
  .
TSLICE:      PUSH    AX               ;save all registers
             PUSH    BX
             PUSH    CX
             PUSH    DX
             PUSH    SI
             PUSH    DI
             PUSH    BP
             PUSH    DS
             PUSH    ES
             MOV     AX,DATA          ;load system data segment
             MOV     DS,AX
             MOV     AL,WHO           ;get user number
             DEC     AL               ;need 0-3 user number for indexing
             CBW                      ;extend into 16 bits
             ADD     AX,AX            ;double accumulator
             MOV     DI,AX            ;load index
             LEA     BP,STACK1        ;point to stack pointer table
             MOV     [BP + DI],SP     ;save user stack pointer
             INC     WHO              ;increment user number
             ADD     DI,2             ;point to next stack pointer
             CMP     DI,8             ;wrap around to user 1?
             JNZ     GETSTACK
             MOV     WHO,1            ;reset user number
             MOV     DI,0            ;and index register
GETSTACK:    MOV     SP,[BP + DI]     ;load new stack pointer
             POP     ES               ;restore new user's registers
             POP     DS
             POP     BP
             POP     DI
             POP     SI
             POP     DX
             POP     CX
             POP     BX
             POP     AX
             IRET                     ;go service new user
```

One requirement of TSLICE is that all users use the same stack segment. This guarantees that all PUSHes, CALLs, and interrupts generated by any user will place data within memory governed by the system software. The complexity of this code results from the need to wrap around the buffer containing the stack pointers, when the context switch is from user 4 to user 1.

6.12   MEMORY MANAGEMENT

In the section on linked lists, we saw a routine called GETNODE, which was used to get a new node from the storage pool, the storage pool being the collection of all available memory locations that are not currently being used for something else (such as node, program, and stack storage). In this section we will see how entire blocks of memory can be assigned through the use of a **memory management** routine. This is a required feature in all operating systems that load multiple programs into memory for shared execution (as in multitasking). We can easily see why memory management is needed by examining Figure 6.14. In this figure, the memory space of a typical system is examined. Initially, three jobs are running (1). Since they were the first three to begin execution, all were assigned consecutive blocks of memory. In (2), we see that job B (or program B) terminates. The memory allocated to job B is returned to the storage pool. In (3), job D begins execution. Because the memory required by this job exceeded what was available in the area vacated by job B, this job is loaded into the first available space that is big enough. When job A ends in (4), its space is also returned to the storage pool. Job E quickly takes this space over in (5). Finally, job C terminates in (6).

The purpose of the memory manager is to keep track of all free blocks of memory. When the operating system needs to load a new job into memory, it will inform the memory manager of how much memory is needed by the new

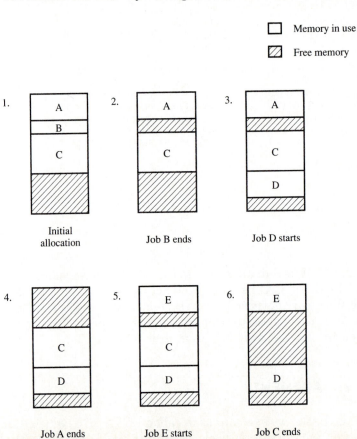

FIGURE 6.14 Memory allocation in an operating system

job. The memory manager will either find a big enough space and return the starting address of the block, or indicate that not enough memory is available for the job to execute at the present time. In this case, the job will have to wait until more memory becomes available.

The subroutine MANAGE, presented here, manages a 512KB block of RAM. Memory is assigned in 8KB blocks. Requests for memory are passed to MANAGE in register AL. So, if AL contains 7, MANAGE must try to find 56K of contiguous memory. If it can, it will return the starting address of the entire block in BP. The address returned in BP is then loaded into a segment register. If MANAGE cannot locate enough memory, it will return 0000 in BP. *Note:* MANAGE only allocates memory. Another routine is needed to return memory to the storage pool (and this is left as an exercise).

```
In current data segment...
UNITS     DB      64 DUP (?)        ;64 8K blocks are available, with
                                    ;each byte in UNITS representing an 8K
                                    ;block in the storage pool. If a byte
                                    ;contains 00, that 8K block is free. If
                                    ;a byte contains FF, that 8K block is
                                    ;not available.
POOL      EQU     2000H             ;segment address for beginning of
                                    ;storage pool
  .
  .
  .
MANAGE:   LEA     SI,UNITS          ;init pointer to UNITS
          MOV     BL,0              ;clear free-block counter
CHKPOOL:  CALL    FAR PTR FINDBLOCKS ;look for free memory in pool
          CMP     CL,AL             ;were enough blocks found?
          JNC     GETMEM            ;yes, go allocate
          CMP     CL,0              ;no free blocks at all?
          JNZ     CHKPOOL           ;maybe, keep checking
          MOV     BP,0              ;not enough memory available
          RET
GETMEM:   CALL    FAR PTR ALLOCATE  ;allocate blocks from UNITS
          MOV     AL,BL             ;calculate starting block address
          MOV     AH,0              ;AX contains block number
          MOV     BX,200H           ;segment size of 8K block
          MUL     BX                ;compute segment offset
          ADD     AX,POOL           ;actual free-block segment address
          MOV     BP,AX
          RET
```

The assembler directive **EQU** (Equate) is used to assign the value 2000H to the label POOL. This is the beginning address of the 512K block of RAM that is being managed. The FINDBLOCKS and ALLOCATE subroutines work as follows: FINDBLOCKS uses BL and SI as inputs. Each time it is called, it will look for the first contiguous block of free memory in the storage pool. This is done by examining the bytes in UNITS. Bytes equal to 00 represent a free 8K block. Bytes equal to FF represent allocated 8K blocks and are therefore not available. FINDBLOCKS will look for the first string of 00 bytes it can find. If memory is available, FINDBLOCKS will return the number of contiguous 8K blocks it found, in CL. The starting location of the free blocks (in UNITS) will be returned in SI, and the starting block number of the free blocks (in UNITS), in BL. If FINDBLOCKS cannot find any free memory, it will return with CL equal to 0.

ALLOCATE is used to convert free block bytes in UNITS (bytes that are 00s) into allocated block bytes (FFs). Its inputs are BL and AL. BL contains the block number (0 to 63) of the first byte to change. AL contains the number of bytes to change (the number of 8K blocks to allocate).

These routines are also left for you to design on your own. You may wish to experiment with a different system of keeping track of the free memory, possibly by using bit operations instead.

6.13 SUMMARY

In this chapter we examined a number of different applications the 8088 is capable of performing. These applications—control systems, multitasking, and memory management—find widespread use in industrial and commercial situations. In addition, we covered many different techniques, such as code conversion, table lookup, sorting, and mathematical processing with binary and BCD numbers. The overall idea is to get a sense of how the 8088's instructions can be combined to perform any task that we can imagine. Many more applications are possible, and we have not even scratched the surface here. But the routines presented in this chapter should serve as a foundation on which to build when you try to write an application of your own.

STUDY QUESTIONS

1. Modify the keyboard buffer routine KEYBUFF so that the user may not enter more than 128 keys. KEYBUFF should automatically return if 128 keys are entered.
2. Modify KEYBUFF to allow for two simple editing features. If a backspace key is entered (ASCII code 08H), the last key entered should be deleted. (What problem occurs, though, when backspace is the first key entered?) The second editing feature is used to cancel an entire line. If the user enters a Control-C (ASCII code 03H), the contents of the entire buffer are deleted.
3. Modify KEYBUFF to include a count of the number of keys entered, including the final return key. This number should be stored in COUNT on return from KEYBUFF.
4. Modify KEYBUFF so that all lowercase letters (a–z) are converted to uppercase (A–Z) before being placed in the buffer. All other ASCII codes should remain unchanged.
5. Modify KEYBUFF so that the contents of the buffer are displayed (using display-string from INT 21) if Control-R is entered, and the buffer is cleared if Control-C is entered.
6. Modify the PACKBCD routine so that a maximum of 12 digits may be entered. PACKBCD should automatically return after processing the 12th digit.
7. Write a subroutine called VALDIGIT, which will determine if the ASCII code contained in the lower byte of AL is a digit from 0 to 9. If so, simply return. If not, jump to ERROR.

8. Modify PACKBCD to include signed BCD numbers. If the first character entered by the user is a minus sign, place 80H into SIGN. If the first character is a number, or a plus sign, place 0 into SIGN.

9. How must the format for storing BCD digits be changed, to allow for fractional numbers like 0.783 or 457.05?

10. How might exponents be processed in numbers like 35E3 or 2.6E−7?

11. Write a subroutine that will convert the BCD number stored in BCDNUM into a binary number. Return the result in AX.

12. Modify the FINDBYTE data search subroutine so that the length, in bytes, of the data table is passed via LENGTH. The maximum length of the data is 1024 items.

13. Modify FINDBYTE so that the position of ITEM within VALUES is returned in POSITION, if the search is successful. For example, if ITEM is the first element, POSITION should be 0. If ITEM is the 11th element, POSITION should be 000A.

14. Write a subroutine called STRSIZE that returns the number of characters in a text string. The text string is terminated with an ASCII return character (0DH). The string begins at address TEXTLINE. Return the character count in BX.

15. Modify the MAXVAL subroutine so that negative numbers (represented in 2's complement notation) may be included in the data.

16. The CHECKSTR subroutine is limited for two reasons. First, the starting addresses of the two strings are set when the subroutine is entered. Second, the length of the two strings is fixed at 10 characters apiece. Modify CHECKSTR so that registers SI and DI are loaded from the addresses stored in locations STRING1 and STRING2 and the string length is loaded from LENGTH.

17. Using a modified version of CHECKSTR, write a routine that will count the number of occurrences of the word "the" in the block of text. The text block begins at address 3000 and ends at address 37FF.

18. The command recognizer RECOGNIZE only works with uppercase commands. Rewrite the code so that uppercase and lowercase commands may be recognized. For example, "DUMP" and "dump" should be identical in comparison.

19. Write a command recognizer that will recognize single-letter commands. The commands may be either uppercase or lowercase, and have the following addresses associated with them:

> A: 20BE
> B: 3000
> C: 589C
> D: 2900

20. Write a subroutine called BIGMUL that will compute the 64-bit result obtained by multiplying two 32-bit integers. The two input numbers should be in registers AX and BX on entry to BIGMUL. Use the MULTIPLY subroutine in your code to implement a process similar to that shown in Figure 6.1.

21. Write a subroutine to find the average of a block of words that starts at location SAMPLES and whose length, in words, is saved in SIZE. Place the average in AVERAGE.

22. Use the FACTOR subroutine to find all factors of the number saved in a new variable, INVALUE. Place the factors into a data array called FACTORS.

23. Does the code for Question 22 need to be changed if the input numbers (saved in INVALUE) are always even?

24. How are roundoff errors eliminated by using BCD?

25. Write a subroutine called JUSTIFY that will left justify any BCD number stored in the 4-byte array called BCDIN. For example, if BCDIN contains 00 05 37 19, JUSTIFY must replace BCDIN with 53 71 90 00.

26. Write a subroutine called TOBINARY that will convert the BCD number pointed to by DI into an unsigned binary number. The result should be returned in AX.

27. Write a subroutine called TOBCD that converts the unsigned 16-bit binary number in DX into a BCD number. The result should be returned in DX also.

28. Two sample routines for performing BCD multiplication were presented in this chapter. Both routines had limited precision. Build on these two routines by extending their precision. For example, BCDMUL2 was limited to multiplying two-digit numbers. Write a routine that will multiply four-digit BCD numbers, using BCDMUL2 as a subroutine.

29. Write a subroutine called BIGADD that will perform a BCD addition of all 16 bits in registers AX and BX. Place the result in CX.

30. Consider the normalization of two numbers, one positive and one negative. Are the exponents adjusted in the same way for each number?

31. In the treatment of BCD numbers, the proposed format contained no provision for representing negative numbers. How might the format be changed to include them?

32. Write a subroutine called EXPONENT that will return a signed 8-bit exponent in register BL. Inputs to EXPONENT are SI, DI, and AX. SI and DI both point to the exponent byte of the two numbers being divided (with DI pointing to the divisor exponent). AX initially contains an exponent adjustment value (in signed 8-bit format) that must always be added to the generated exponent value.

33. Write a subroutine called ZEROCHECK that examines the BCD number pointed to by register BP and returns with the zero flag set if the BCD number is equal to 0.

34. Write a subroutine that performs BCD division by first converting the BCD numbers to binary. DIV should be used to perform the division. The result should be converted back into BCD. Use TOBCD and TOBINARY in your subroutine.

35. Modify the POWER subroutine so that any integer power can be used, including negative powers and 0.

36. The 5-byte BCD format discussed in this chapter uses 1 byte for a signed exponent and 4 bytes for the mantissa. What is the largest positive integer that can be represented?

37. Change FACTORIAL so that factorials of 70 or more are not allowed. Return 0 as the result in these cases.

38. Write a subroutine called HYPOT that computes the hypotenuse of a triangle whose sides have lengths pointed to by SI and DI. Return the result address in BP. The lengths are stored as words.

39. Find the infinite series for SIN(X) in a calculus book and implement it in a subroutine called SIN. Use EPOWER as an example of how to do this.

40. Implement COS(X) via subroutine COS. Use the following formula as a guide and solve it for COS(X) before writing any code:

$$SIN^2(X) + COS^2(X) = 1$$

Make use of ROOT and SIN in your subroutine.

41. Write the DETECT subroutine used by the Computerized Burglar Alarm.

42. An office complex consisting of 64 offices and 16 hallways is to have its lighting controlled by a computer. Each office has one switch to control its light. Hallways

have a switch at each end. Each switch is assigned a bit position in a particular memory location that can be read by the computer, and a closed switch represents a zero. Each light (think of all lights in a hallway as a single light) is also assigned a certain bit in a memory location that the computer can write to. A logic 1 is needed to turn on any light. How many byte locations are needed for all I/O? Write a program that will constantly monitor all switches and adjust the complex lighting as necessary.

43. Consider the office complex of Question 42 and its associated definitions. Suppose for reasons of efficiency that no light may be on continuously for more than 30 minutes after 5 P.M. For example, if an office light is turned on at 6:17 the computer automatically shuts it off at 6:47. The system has a real-time clock whose time may be read from locations 6000 and 6001. Location 6000 contains the hour (0 to 23) and 6001 contains the minute (0 to 59). Rewrite the program of Question 42 so that any light on for 30 minutes is automatically turned off. *Note:* The light may be immediately turned on again (for another 30 minutes) if someone in the office hits the switch again. The automatic shutoff feature ends at 6 A.M.

44. What changes must be made to the program of Question 43 if hallway lights are exempted from the 30-minute timeout feature?

45. Modify the SERVO program so that the motor's speed will ramp up during periods where a large speed increase is needed.

46. Compute the execution time of this section of code. Assume an 8-MHz clock frequency.

```
            MOV     CX,1000H
NEXT:       ADD     AL,2
            MOV     [SI],AL
            LOOP    NEXT
```

47. Repeat Question 46, assuming that all memory references take an additional 2 clock cycles.

48. What must be done to support an interrupt handler for a type-30 interrupt, if the handler has a starting address of 3B150?

49. Modify the TIMER exception handler so that a 12-hour clock is implemented.

50. Write a subroutine called SEARCH that will search the data fields of a linked list for a certain piece of data. The data item to be located is saved in DL.

51. Modify the INSERT subroutine so that new nodes are placed at the end of the linked list instead of at the beginning.

52. Do the STACK and USER areas in TSLICE have to be loaded with initial information for proper execution? What information might this be?

53. Modify TSLICE so that up to eight users may be active at any time.

54. Does the UNITS data table need to be initialized before any memory can be allocated by MANAGE? If so, what should it be filled with? If it needs initialization, write a subroutine called MINIT that will do the job.

55. Write the FINDBLOCKS and ALLOCATE subroutines required by MANAGE.

56. Write a subroutine that will take care of returning freed memory back to the storage pool. Upon entry, AL will contain the number of 8K blocks being returned and ES the starting address of the entire block in the storage pool.

57. Modify the SORT routine so that signed and unsigned numbers are allowed.

58. Modify the SORT routine so that it exits as soon as an entire pass fails to produce a single swap.

Hardware Details of the 8088

Objectives

In this chapter you will learn about:

*   The general specifications of the 8088 microprocessor

*   The processor's control signal names and functions

*   General signal relationships and timing

*   Methods by which the 8088 can interface with external devices

*   The external interrupt signals and their operations

*   The 8088 bus controller

*   The method used to access an 8085 peripheral

7.1 INTRODUCTION

Before using any microprocessor, it is necessary to have an understanding of both its hardware requirements and its software functions. In this chapter we will examine all 40 pins of the 8088's package, learning what their use may be in a larger system employing the 8088 as its CPU. We will not concentrate on interfacing, since this important topic is covered in Chapters 8, 9, and 10. Upon completion of this chapter, we should, however, know about the various signals of the processor in order to begin interfacing it with support circuitry, which includes memories, I/O devices, and coprocessors.

Section 7.2 gives a quick overview of the capabilities of the 8088, its memory addressing capabilities, available clock speeds, and various other functions. Section 7.3 covers all 40 pins of the 8088 in detail. The pins are separated into eight functional groups, such as interrupt control, system control, processor status, and so on. Block diagrams and timing waveforms are given where applicable, except where they might apply to interfacing. Section 7.4 describes the operation of the 8284 clock generator, an essential integrated circuit used in 8088-based systems. A second essential component is the 8288 bus controller, which is covered in Section 7.5. Timing diagrams for certain processor operations are examined in Section 7.6. Section 7.7 covers the Personal Computer Bus Standard, which contains information needed to interface peripherals with the 8088-based motherboard found in many personal computers.

7.2   CPU SPECIFICATIONS

Although we have already covered some of the 8088's specifications in Chapter 2, it will be useful to cover them again, this time adding more detail.

The 8088 is a 16-bit microprocessor that communicates with the outside world via an 8-bit bidirectional data bus. This requires the 8088 to perform *two* read cycles to capture 16-bit chunks of data. This has the effect of increasing memory access time and program execution time. Though the increase in time is not significant, it is important to remember this feature of the 8088. The 8086, having a 16-bit data bus, only needs to perform *one* read cycle to fetch the same data and thus executes programs slightly faster than the 8088.

The 8088's 20-bit address bus can access over *one million* bytes of memory (1,048,576 bytes, to be exact). We commonly refer to this number as one **megabyte** of memory. Control signals are provided that enable external circuitry to take over the 8088's buses (a must for DMA operations), and two interrupt lines are included to provide maskable and nonmaskable interrupt capability. A number of status outputs are available, which may be used to decode any of eight internal CPU states, and other control signals are provided to allow interfacing with 8085 and 8088 peripherals.

The 8088 comes with maximum clock speeds of 5 or 8 MHz as of this writing, and has been on the market long enough to be purchased at a reasonable cost. But the power of the 8088 can only be tapped if we know how to use it. So let's begin examining the functional operation of the processor.

Minmode Operation

The 8088 has two functional modes of operation: minimum mode and maximum mode. Certain pins on the processor have been designed for dual purposes, one for minmode and the other for maxmode. Figure 7.1 shows a pinout diagram of the 8088. Notice how pins 24 through 31 and pin 34 have two sets of signal names. In minmode, these nine signals are $\overline{\text{INTA}}$, ALE, $\overline{\text{DEN}}$, DT/$\overline{\text{R}}$, IO/$\overline{\text{M}}$, $\overline{\text{WR}}$, HLDA, HOLD, and SS0. They correspond to control signals that are needed to operate memory and I/O devices connected to the 8088, and are compatible with signals used in older 8085-based systems. Because the 8088 generates these signals in minmode, fewer chips are needed in the overall system. However, some functions are unavailable when the 8088 operates in

FIGURE 7.1 8088 pin
assignments

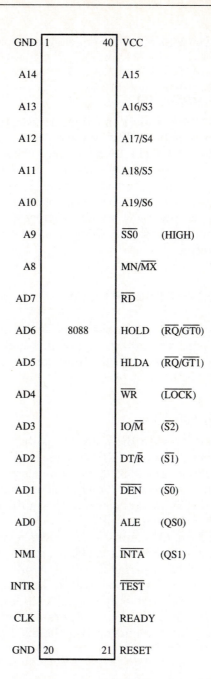

Note: ( ) denotes a MAX mode signal

minmode. These include bus request/grant operations and coprocessor capability.

Maxmode Operation

When the 8088 operates in maximum mode, the nine signals we just examined change their functions. The new signals become QS1, QS0, $\overline{S0}$, $\overline{S1}$, $\overline{S2}$, $\overline{LOCK}$, $\overline{RQ/GT1}$, $\overline{RQ/GT0}$, and HIGH. The lack of control signals (which exist only in minmode operation) now requires the use of the 8288 bus controller to generate memory and I/O read/write signals. Since an external chip is now generating these control signals, the processor is free to expand its functional capability. This allows the use of an 8087 coprocessor, and provides bus request/grant operation and queue status. All of these functions will be explained in detail in the next section.

7.3   CPU PIN DESCRIPTIONS

Refer to Figure 7.1 for another look at the 40 pins of the 8088's Dual In-line Package. There are eight groups of pins that we will examine in this section. Each group performs a specific function, necessary to the proper operation of the 8088.

V_{CC}, GND, and CLK

This group deals with the processor power and clock inputs. Note that there are two pins for ground (GND) and one for V_{CC}. Both grounds must be used for proper operation. The 8088 operates on a single, positive supply of 5 volts, plus or minus 10 percent (with some versions having a 5 percent tolerance), and will dissipate 2.5 watts of power at this voltage. The specified supply current is 340 mA at room temperature.

The CLK input requires a digital waveform with a 33 percent duty cycle. The minimum clock period is 200 ns, corresponding to a frequency of 5 MHz. The maximum clock period is 500 ns, resulting in a minimum clock speed of 2 MHz. Rise and fall times should be kept under 10 ns. The TTL-compatible clock signal is generated by the 8284 clock generator covered in Section 7.4. Even though the clock input is internally buffered, the clock signal should be kept at a *constant* frequency (via the 8284 and a crystal oscillator) for best operation.

MN/$\overline{MX}$

This pin is used to control the 8088's mode of operation. Remember from Section 7.2 that the 8088 may operate in minimum mode or maximum mode. The specific mode is selected with the MN/$\overline{MX}$ pin. Maxmode is enabled when MN/$\overline{MX}$ is connected to ground. Minmode is enabled when MN/$\overline{MX}$ is pulled high (through an appropriate pullup resistor). As we saw before, nine of the 8088's signals have two functions, with each function depending on the mode of processor operation.

$\overline{S}_0$, $\overline{S}_1$, and $\overline{S}_2$

These three signals are the 8088's status outputs and are only active when the processor is in maximum mode. They are used to indicate internal processor operations. The 8288 bus controller (covered in Section 7.5) uses the status outputs to generate memory and I/O read/write signals. Table 7.1 shows the eight different conditions that can be indicated by the status outputs. The *interrupt acknowledge* status can be used by external circuitry to manipulate the processor's interrupt mechanism. The *code access* status indicates when the processor is fetching instructions. When the 8088 has completed a bus cycle, the status outputs will indicate the passive state. An easy way to decode all eight processor states is to use a 3- to 8-line decoder such as the 74LS138; this is left for you to do as a homework problem. Normally in a small system we have no use for most of the decoded cycle states. In fact, an interrupt acknowledge signal ($\overline{INTA}$) is already provided for us when operating in minimum mode.

The status outputs are capable of tristating when the 8088 enters into hold acknowledge (see the description of HOLD and HLDA in the next section).

RESET, READY, HOLD, and HLDA

This group of signals is used for system control. RESET and READY operate the same way in both minimum and maximum modes. HOLD and HLDA *(hold acknowledge)* only work when the processor is in minimum mode.

RESET is the signal that really gets the processor running after a power-up. It is very important to RESET the 8088 when power is first applied, to guarantee that the 8088 begins doing intelligent things. A high logic level is needed to activate the RESET input, which must remain high for at least four clock cycles to ensure proper operation. RESET can be applied during program execution as well, as a sort of panic button used to start the program over from the beginning.

TABLE 7.1   8088 status signals

$\overline{S}_2$	$\overline{S}_1$	$\overline{S}_0$	Indicated Operation
0	0	0	Interrupt acknowledge
0	0	1	I/O read
0	1	0	I/O write
0	1	1	Halt
1	0	0	Code access
1	0	1	Memory read
1	1	0	Memory write
1	1	1	Passive

Issuing a RESET causes the 8088 to fetch the first instruction from memory, beginning at address FFFF0H. This requires some type of ROM data at that address to guarantee that the 8088 begins running correctly.

READY is an input that informs the processor that the selected memory or I/O device is ready to complete a data transfer. READY is often used to synchronize the fast processor with a slow memory or I/O device that may need an extended bus cycle to perform a read or write operation. A high logic level on READY indicates that the 8088 may go ahead and complete the bus cycle. A low logic level causes the processor to extend the bus cycle, with all signals frozen at their current logic levels. This means that the processor keeps the address lines, data bus, and control signals in their current states so that the external device may use them for a longer period of time.

HOLD is a minmode input that is used to place the processor into a **suspended** execution state. While the 8088 is in a hold state, it does not continue program execution. In fact, many of the processor's outputs are automatically tristated, to prevent conflict on the system bus. The most common use of HOLD is in a computer system having two or more processors. If the processors share memory (such as EPROM or RAM space), only one processor may access memory at a time. When a processor wishes to take control of the buses and access memory, it must first issue a HOLD request to the other processors in the system, which will suspend their processing and release the system bus. A high logic level is needed to activate HOLD. Furthermore, the 8088 will remain held only as long as the HOLD input remains high. The processor will resume program execution where it left off as soon as HOLD goes low.

HLDA (hold acknowledge) is a minmode output used to indicate to external devices that the 8088 has suspended execution (via HOLD). HLDA will go to a high logic level to show that the processor has actually stopped execution. Technically, another device should take over the system bus only *after* HLDA goes high. When execution resumes (i.e., HOLD has been taken low), HLDA will go low.

NMI, INTR, and $\overline{\text{INTA}}$

These three signals control the activity of external hardware interrupts. NMI and INTR are inputs and function identically in either processor mode. $\overline{\text{INTA}}$, an output, is only available in minimum mode.

External hardware interrupts are used to suspend current program execution and vector the processor to a special set of instructions called an **interrupt service routine (ISR)**. Interrupts are used to perform high priority tasks, without any effect on the main processor program (except for a loss of execution time). A very useful application of hardware interrupts is keeping track of time. It is not difficult to convert the 60 cycle powerline frequency into a digital signal (with the use of a Schmitt trigger). The resulting 60-Hz digital signal is then connected to NMI or INTR, generating 60 interrupts every second. The corresponding ISR that services the interrupt decrements a counter each time it runs. If the counter is initially set to 60, it is easy for the computer to know when one second has passed.

NMI *(nonmaskable interrupt)* requires a *rising edge* to be recognized. It cannot be internally disabled (masked) by software, hence its name. NMI generates a type-2 interrupt. We have seen (in Chapter 4) that there are 255 different types of interrupts. NMI is recognized by the 8088 at the end of the currently executing instruction. The address of the type-2 ISR is then read from a table containing all ISR addresses. This table is stored in memory and is called the **interrupt vector table.** The 8088 then jumps to the ISR address to process the interrupt code.

INTR (Interrupt Request) requires a *high* logic level to be recognized. Leaving INTR in a high state could cause repeated interrupts, so caution is advised. A bit in the processor's status register is used to enable/disable INTR. It is called the **interrupt enable flag (IF).** Using the IF to disable INTR can be done easily with software, and is referred to as *masking.* INTR operates in much the same way as NMI except for the way the interrupt type is generated. NMI automatically causes a type-2 interrupt. The interrupt type for INTR is actually read from the processor's data bus during an **interrupt acknowledge** cycle. The 8-bit interrupt vector read from the data bus is internally converted into the proper address for the interrupt vector table.

A priority is assigned to each interrupt, with NMI having the higher priority of the two. The priority is used to determine which interrupt is recognized first if both occur at the same time. The higher priority of NMI guarantees that it is recognized before INTR. A comparison of NMI and INTR is shown in Table 7.2.

INTA (interrupt acknowledge) is an active-low output that operates in minmode and is used to indicate that the 8088 has received an INTR and is beginning interrupt processing. The external circuitry connected to INTR should use INTA to control when the 8-bit interrupt vector is placed onto the data bus. The exact timing of INTA will be covered in Section 7.6.

RQ/GT0, RQ/GT1, and LOCK

These three maximum mode signals are used to interface the 8088 with other devices capable of taking over the system bus. In the description of the HOLD input we saw one way two 8088s could share a common system bus and memory. The three signals presented here offer a second technique. RQ/GT0 and RQ/GT1 are request/grant signals used by other devices called **bus masters** to take over the 8088's system bus. An example is the 8087 coprocessor, which periodically takes over the system bus to read data or write results into memory. Both RQ/GT signals are bidirectional, meaning that they act as inputs *and*

TABLE 7.2 Comparison of NMI and INTR

Interrupt	Logic Level Needed to Trigger	Disabled via Software	Priority
NMI	Rising edge	No	High
INTR	High	Yes	Low

outputs. $\overline{RQ/GT0}$ has priority over $\overline{RQ/GT1}$, and both have internal pullup resistors. The following discussion will concern $\overline{RQ/GT0}$ only, but applies to $\overline{RQ/GT1}$ as well.

When another bus master decides to take over the system bus, it will pull $\overline{RQ/GT0}$ low for one clock period. When the 8088 is ready to release the system bus it will use $\overline{RQ/GT0}$ as an output to inform the new bus master. A second low-level pulse of one clock period does this. The 8088 then enters a hold acknowledge state until the new bus master is ready to give the system bus back. This is done by a third low-level, one-clock-period pulse on $\overline{RQ/GT0}$ (from the new bus master back to the 8088). So, the normally high $\overline{RQ/GT0}$ signal went from being an input to an output and back to an input again.

$\overline{LOCK}$ is an active-low output used to inform other possible bus masters that the 8088's system bus is not available for takeover. A special instruction called a **LOCK prefix** activates the $\overline{LOCK}$ signal, which will go back to its inactive state after execution of the instruction following the LOCK prefix instruction. If an $\overline{RQ/GT}$ sequence is requested while the bus is $\overline{LOCK}$ed, it will not be acted on until the bus becomes un$\overline{LOCK}$ed.

ALE, $\overline{DEN}$, DT/$\overline{R}$, $\overline{WR}$, $\overline{RD}$, and IO/$\overline{M}$

Five of these signals operate in minmode. Only $\overline{RD}$ operates in both minmode and maxmode. Some of these signals are used to interface the 8088 with 8085 peripherals. All six signals are outputs, and all but ALE will be tristated during hold acknowledge.

ALE *(address latch enable)* is an output signal that is used to demultiplex the 8088's address/data bus. ALE is usually used to control an external latch capable of storing the lower 8 bits of the processor's address bus. ALE goes high to indicate that the 8088 is outputting address information. Take another look at Figure 7.1 and note the signals AD_0 through AD_7. These eight signals perform two functions. They operate as A_0 through A_7 during the beginning of a bus cycle, and as D_0 through D_7 for the rest of the bus cycle. So, AD_0 through

FIGURE 7.2 Demultiplexing the 8088's address/data bus

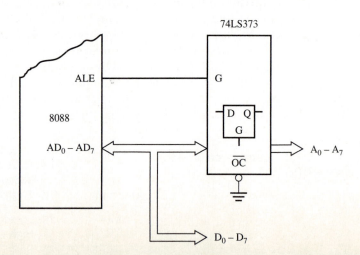

AD_7 are constantly switching back and forth between address bus mode and data bus mode. The processor uses ALE to indicate when AD_0 through AD_7 contain address information. Figure 7.2 shows one way the address/data lines may be demultiplexed. A 74LS373 octal D latch is used to capture A_0 through A_7 when enabled by ALE. We will see another example of how the address/data lines are demultiplexed when we cover the 8288 bus controller in Section 7.5.

$\overline{\text{DEN}}$ *(data enable)* is an active low output used in a minmode system to control a bidirectional buffer (also called a **transceiver**) connected to the processor's data bus. The bidirectional buffer is used to buffer data going both ways on the data bus (into the 8088 and out of the 8088). Since there may be times when we want to disconnect the data bus from the processor (e.g., when we are sharing memory with another processor), $\overline{\text{DEN}}$ gives us a way to turn the transceiver off. In Section 7.5 we will see how $\overline{\text{DEN}}$ is generated in a maxmode system.

$DT/\overline{R}$ *(data transmit/receive)* is an output used in a minmode system to control the direction of data flow in the bidirectional buffer used on the data bus. When $DT/\overline{R}$ is low, data should flow into the 8088. When $DT/\overline{R}$ is high, the 8088 is outputting data. We will see an example of how $DT/\overline{R}$ is used in Section 7.5.

$\overline{\text{WR}}$ (Write) is an active low output used to indicate when the processor is writing to a memory or I/O location.

$\overline{\text{RD}}$ (Read) is an active low output used to indicate when the processor is reading a memory or I/O location.

$IO/\overline{M}$ is an output that indicates whether the current bus cycle is a memory access or an I/O access. A memory access is indicated by a logic zero on $IO/\overline{M}$, and I/O access by a logic one. $IO/\overline{M}$ is used with $\overline{\text{RD}}$ and $\overline{\text{WR}}$ to generate separate read and write signals for memory and I/O devices. Figure 7.3 shows how OR gates can be used to decode different read/write operations. In Section 7.5 we will see that some of the signals generated by the 8288 Bus Controller are identical in operation to those generated in Figure 7.3.

FIGURE 7.3 Decoding 8088 memory and I/O read/write signals

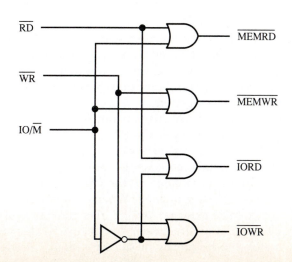

A_8 through A_{19}, AD_0 through AD_7

These signals constitute the 8088's 20-bit address bus and 8-bit data bus. AD_0 through AD_7 are the processor's multiplexed address/data bus. These signals can behave like A_0 through A_7 or D_0 through D_7 (depending on the state of ALE). Usually an external latch is used to store address information when it is present. The other address lines, A_8 through A_{19}, make up the rest of the 8088's address bus. These address lines do not have to be latched since their outputs are always valid. Together, the 20 address lines can access one megabyte of memory. The ability to directly address this many address locations provides the programmer with a very flexible programming environment. Older systems required that special software be used to manage memory in "pages" that were some portion of the system's main address space. This software is not even needed now, in some applications, because of the great increase in address lines and hence memory locations. The 8088 has special segment registers that are used to manage 64KB blocks of memory starting on any 16-byte boundary, so it is relatively easy to manage the system's addressing space.

A_0 through A_{15} have a dual role: They are also used to access I/O devices (depending on the state of $IO/\overline{M}$). Sixteen address lines provide for up to 65,536 I/O locations. We will see more about memory and I/O devices in Chapters 8 and 9.

Signal Summary

Table 7.3 summarizes all of the signals we have just covered. It shows whether a signal is an input or an output (or both), if it has tri-state capability, and what mode (min or max) it is active in. In the next two sections we will see how many of these signals are used in an actual system.

7.4   THE 8284 CLOCK GENERATOR

As we saw in the previous section, CLK, RESET, and READY are three of the most important signals in the overall operation of the processor. A small number of logic gates would be needed to implement the correct signals on CLK and RESET. Most of this circuitry is already provided for us in an 18-pin DIP called the 8284 clock generator. Figure 7.4 shows a pin diagram of the 8284. Two of the pins, X_1 and X_2, are meant to be directly connected to a crystal. The internal clock circuitry of the 8284 then generates the proper CLK signal for the 8088. Since the frequency of CLK will be one-third the crystal frequency (due to an internal frequency divider), the 8284 provides the OSC output, whose frequency is the same as the crystal's. When using a crystal, the 8284's $F/\overline{C}$ input must be grounded. When $F/\overline{C}$ is high, the 8284's EFI pin must be connected to an external oscillator, or some type of timing circuit that generates a TTL signal at the proper frequency. In this case, the frequency of OSC will match the frequency of the EFI input. In addition to $F/\overline{C}$, a second signal,

TABLE 7.3   8088 signal summary

Signal	Input	Output	Tri-state	Minmode	Maxmode
CLK	√			√	√
MN/$\overline{\text{MX}}$	√			√	√
$\overline{\text{S}}_0$, $\overline{\text{S}}_1$, $\overline{\text{S}}_2$		√	√		√
RESET	√			√	√
READY	√			√	√
HOLD	√			√	
HLDA		√		√	
NMI	√			√	√
INTR	√			√	√
$\overline{\text{INTA}}$		√		√	
$\overline{\text{RQ}/\text{GT0}}$	√	√			√
$\overline{\text{RQ}/\text{GT1}}$	√	√			√
$\overline{\text{LOCK}}$		√	√		√
ALE		√		√	
$\overline{\text{DEN}}$		√	√	√	
DT/$\overline{\text{R}}$		√	√	√	
$\overline{\text{WR}}$		√	√	√	
$\overline{\text{RD}}$		√	√	√	√
IO/$\overline{\text{M}}$		√	√	√	
AD$_0$–AD$_7$	√	√	√	√	√
A$_8$–A$_{19}$		√	√	√	√

CSYNC, is used to provide clock synchronization when EFI is used as the frequency source. When a crystal is used, CSYNC must be taken low.

Another signal, $\overline{\text{RES}}$, is the 8284's reset input. This input is normally connected to a simple resistor-capacitor network. When power is first applied, the RC network allows a logic zero to remain on the $\overline{\text{RES}}$ input for a short period of time. The internal circuitry of the 8284 uses $\overline{\text{RES}}$ to generate the processor's RESET signal. Together, the RC network and the 8284 provide a *power-on reset* signal to the 8088.

FIGURE 7.4 8284 clock generator

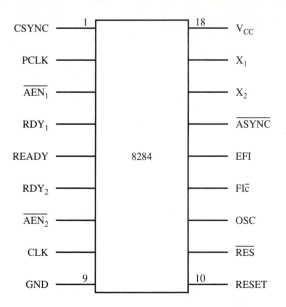

Two ready inputs are provided on the 8284, RDY_1 and RDY_2. Together with $\overline{AEN_1}$, and $\overline{AEN_2}$, the 8284 generates the processor's READY signal. In a system where memory and I/O devices are utilized, one RDY signal can be used with the memory circuitry and the other for the I/O circuitry. The $\overline{AEN}$ signals are used as *qualifiers* for the RDY inputs. For example, to use RDY_1, $\overline{AEN_1}$ must be low. It may be necessary to generate a **wait state** in the system, due to the use of slow memory or I/O devices. The RDY inputs are designed for this purpose. A fifth signal, $\overline{ASYNC}$, is used to select the number of stages of synchronization on READY. Only one stage is used when $\overline{ASYNC}$ is high.

Many of the devices in an 8088 system require a clock that is slower than the processor's (the UART is one example). The PCLK output of the 8284 has a frequency that is one-sixth that of the crystal (or EFI) frequency. Together with EFI, $F/\overline{C}$, and X_1 and X_2, we have a number of ways of controlling the timing of our system with the 8284. Figure 7.5 shows one way the 8284 can be connected to the 8088. Notice that a 10-MHz crystal is connected to X_1 and X_2, and that $F/\overline{C}$ is grounded. The 8284 will thus generate a CLK frequency just over 3.3 MHz! How fast would the processor run if a 12-MHz crystal was used?

The RC network on $\overline{RES}$ is used to provide the power-on reset signal. A pushbutton is connected across the capacitor to allow manual resets with power still applied. Figure 7.5 represents the timing circuitry used in the single board computer of Chapter 11.

7.5 THE 8288 BUS CONTROLLER

We have already seen a number of differences brought about by the 8088's minmode and maxmode operation. To get the maxmode signals, we sacrifice

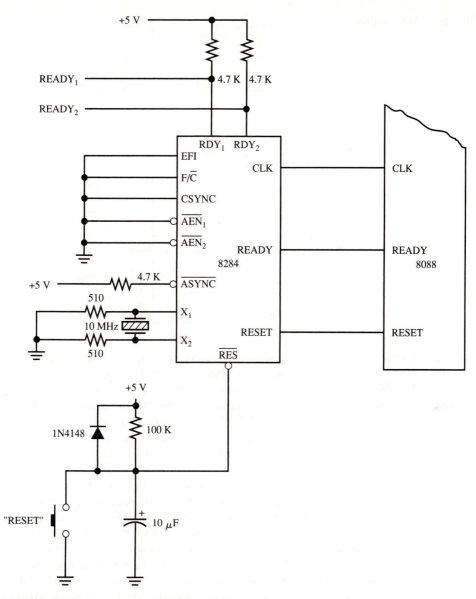

FIGURE 7.5   An actual 8284 timing circuit

other signals that have important uses. For example, in maxmode we get $\overline{RQ}/\overline{GT}$ signals but have to give up HOLD and HLDA. Other signals are replaced as well, leaving us with no ability to decode read/write accesses in maxmode *unless we use the status outputs.* Since $\overline{S}_0$, $\overline{S}_1$, $\overline{S}_2$ are available in maxmode, we use them as inputs to a special 8288 bus controller, which in turn, decodes the missing signals. Figure 7.6 shows a pin diagram of the 8288. Notice the three status inputs and also the three *outputs* ALE, DEN, and DT/$\overline{R}$. Three of the

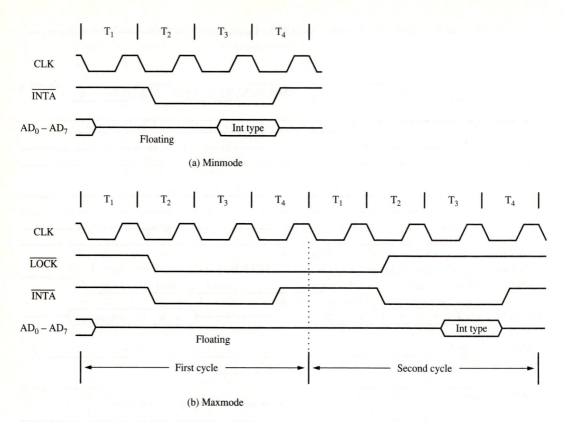

FIGURE 7.9   Interrupt acknowledge timing

In a maxmode system, two bus cycles are used for interrupt acknowledge. Figure 7.9(b) shows the events that occur in each cycle. In the first cycle the address bus is again placed into a high impedance state. In addition, $\overline{\text{LOCK}}$ is asserted to inform other devices on the system bus that they cannot take over the bus until completion of the second cycle. $\overline{\text{INTA}}$ is asserted twice, once during each cycle. Special interrupt peripherals exist that have been designed to respond to the interrupt acknowledge cycles. One example is the 8259 programmable interrupt controller, which we will examine in Chapter 10.

HOLD/HLDA Timing

From Section 7.3 we know that it is possible to place the 8088 into a HOLD state (the processor idles) by asserting HOLD. The processor will respond by placing its busses in the high impedance state and will acknowledge that it is in a HOLD state with HLDA. Figure 7.10 shows the corresponding timing relationship between HOLD and HLDA. The state of the HOLD input is sampled on every rising edge of CLK. If it is high, the processor will activate HLDA at the end of T_4 (or at the end of the current idle state). The processor

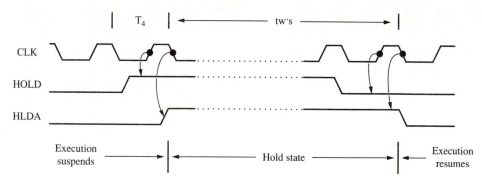

FIGURE 7.10 HOLD timing

may need a number of internal states to complete what it was doing (e.g., finishing a multiply instruction), but once HLDA is asserted it will no longer use its busses until it sees HOLD go low. While the 8088 is in the hold state, it will continue to sample HOLD on each rising edge of CLK. When HOLD does go low, the processor will reset HLDA at the beginning of the next T state and resume program execution. A technique that activates HOLD at the end of every instruction, so that the processor's busses can be examined, is called **single stepping.** So, a simple circuit could be used that would allow only one instruction to be executed by the 8088 each time a button was pressed. Think of how you might design such a single-step circuit (starting with a flip-flop might help).

7.7 THE PERSONAL COMPUTER BUS STANDARD

The relatively low expense and high power of the personal computer has made it a popular teaching machine. Software can be written, tested, and executed easily, and hardware interfacing is made simple by the use of a standard connection bus on the motherboard of the machine. If you were to make a list of which processor signals you might need in order to connect your computer to a disk drive, or a serial data terminal, or a video card, what signals would you choose? Certainly we would need data lines for the exchange of information, and address lines to select the device we wish to communicate with. Then, we would also need all the necessary control signals, such as memory and I/O read/write, ALE, and others.

The list we have been considering was made up many years ago and agreed upon by all people involved in the personal computer business. Figure 7.11 shows the pin assignments for a standard 62-pin connector found on all personal computer motherboards that allow expansion with the 8088 microprocessor. In addition to the signals already discussed, provisions for power and many levels of interrupts are also included. Do not confuse address lines A_0 through A_{19} with their respective connector pin names.

FIGURE 7.11   Personal computer
standard pin assignments

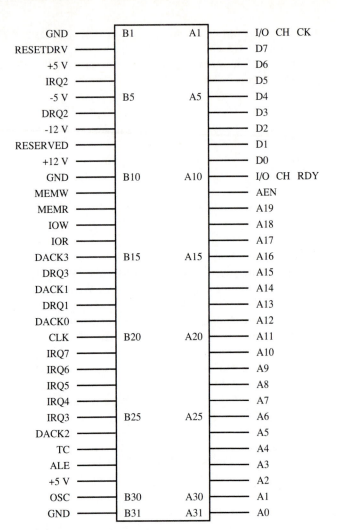

7.8   SUMMARY

In this chapter we examined the operation of the 8088's hardware signals. We
saw that there are actually two sets of processor signals, one for minmode
operation and the other for maxmode operation. Minmode signals can be directly decoded by memory and I/O circuits, resulting in a system with minimal
hardware requirements. Maxmode systems are generally more complicated,
resulting from the use of the 8288 bus controller and the new maxmode signals
that allow for bus grants.

We saw that the 8088 can access one megabyte of memory, and that it
contains two hardware interrupt mechanisms and uses a multiplexed address/
data bus. Hardware examples showing how the bus is demultiplexed, how
memory and I/O control signals are generated, and how the 8284 clock genera-

tor and 8288 bus controller are used were also given. The chapter finished with a short look at CPU timing diagrams and the interface connector for personal computers. In Chapters 8 through 11 we will draw on the information presented in this chapter, so use it as a handy reference.

STUDY QUESTIONS

1. What are some of the differences between minmode and maxmode operation?
2. How is the 8088 put into minmode operation?
3. Sketch four cycles of the 8088's CLK signal if its frequency is 3.125 MHz. Compute the time, in ns, of the low-portion and high-portion of each cycle.
4. If an instruction requires 20 states to complete, what is the instruction execution time if the CLK period is 250 ns?
5. What is the processor's CLK frequency if a 10-MHz crystal is used with the 8284?
6. Design a circuit that will turn a LED on when the status outputs $\overline{S}_0$ through $\overline{S}_2$ indicate the HALT state.
7. Show how a 3- to 8-line decoder (74LS138) can be used to decode the status assignments found in Table 7.1.
8. What address is used first after a RESET?
9. Why do 8088-based systems need EPROM at the high end of memory?
10. How is the 8088 slowed down enough to communicate with a slow memory device?
11. What signal(s) might a second 8088 use to take over the busses of another 8088?
12. What are the differences between NMI and INTR?
13. What would happen if INTR was stuck high?
14. What is so special about the operation of ALE?
15. What other types of data latches could be used in Figure 7.2 in place of the 74LS373?
16. If a minimal 8088 system uses only address lines A_0 through A_{17}, how many memory locations is it capable of accessing?
17. Show how the address 3A8C4 would be represented on the 20-bit address bus.
18. What is one advantage of a multiplexed address/data bus?
19. What is one disadvantage of a multiplexed address/data bus?
20. Show how NAND gates could be used to decode the signals in Figure 7.3.
21. Show the connections needed to feed a 12-MHz clock signal into the 8284 (note the lack of external crystal now).
22. In Figure 7.7, why does the data bus require a bidirectional driver?
23. During which state is ALE active?
24. Design a single-step circuit that allows only one instruction to execute each time a pushbutton is pressed.
25. When two or more 8088s share a common memory system, what do you expect happens to the overall bus activity of the system? What about the bus activity of each processor?
26. What are the states of IO/$\overline{\text{M}}$, $\overline{\text{RD}}$, and $\overline{\text{WR}}$ when the 8088 is:

    a) writing to memory
    b) reading from an I/O device

27. What is placed on D_0 through D_7 during an interrupt acknowledge cycle?

8

Memory System Design

Objectives

In this chapter you will learn about:

- The importance of bus buffering

- How the 8088 addresses (accesses) memory

- The design of custom memory address decoders

- The difference between full- and partial-address decoding

- How wait states may be inserted into memory read/write cycles

- The differences between static and dynamic RAMs

- How a dynamic RAM is addressed and what purpose refresh cycles serve

- DMA (direct memory access)

8.1 INTRODUCTION

The internal memory capacity of any microprocessor, with the exception of single-chip microprocessors, is severely limited. The 8088 itself has only a handful of 16-bit locations in which it can store numbers, and these locations are the actual data registers available to the programmer. The need for larger, external memories quickly becomes apparent, especially if an application involves number crunching or word processing. The purpose of this chapter is to explore ways of adding external memory to 8088-based systems. We will examine how the 8088's various control signals (ALE, DT/$\overline{R}$, $\overline{WR}$, $\overline{RD}$, and IO/$\overline{M}$) are used to supply memory read and write signals to read-only memories and both static and dynamic random access memories.

In addition we will see how an external device called a **bus master** takes over control of the 8088's memory system during a process called **direct memory access.**

The information provided in this chapter should enable you to design future memory systems from scratch.

Section 8.2 explains the 8088's address and data buses. The importance of bus buffering is discussed in Section 8.3. Section 8.4 shows how the 8088 accesses memory, Section 8.5 covers the design of a memory address decoder, and Section 8.6 introduces the partial-address decoder. Section 8.7 explores the use of a shift register to generate wait states. Section 8.8 contains a complete 8KB RAM/EPROM memory. In Section 8.9, we show how dynamic RAM can be used with the 8088. Section 8.10 explains how DMA works. Memory-mapped I/O is covered in Section 8.11.

8.2   THE 8088 ADDRESS AND DATA BUSES

As previously discussed, the 8088 microprocessor has an 8-bit data bus, and a 20-bit address bus that can access 1 megabyte of external memory. The lower eight address lines are multiplexed together with the eight data lines, resulting in signals AD_0 through AD_7. In maximum mode, this multiplexed bus is decoded by external hardware, specifically by the 8288 bus controller covered in Chapter 7, with the aid of the processor's status outputs. The 8288 takes care of latching the lower eight address lines and controlling the direction of a bidirectional buffer on the data bus. In minimum mode, the processor outputs the necessary control signals directly (via ALE, IO/$\overline{\text{M}}$, $\overline{\text{RD}}$, $\overline{\text{WR}}$, and others). Thus, we end up with data lines D_0 through D_7 and address lines A_0 through A_{19}. We will see that all of these signals are needed to communicate with the RAM and EPROM devices contained in the memory system.

8.3   BUS BUFFERING

Every microprocessor-based memory system, whether EPROM or RAM, will have standard buses connecting it to the microprocessor, whose functions are to direct the flow of information to and from the memory system. These buses

FIGURE 8.1   Memory bus structure

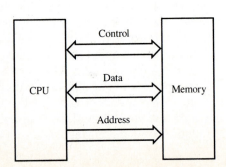

are generally called the **control** bus, the **data** bus, and the **address** bus. Figure 8.1 shows the relationship between the CPU, the buses, and the memory system. Note that the address bus is unidirectional, which means that data on the address bus goes one way, from the CPU to the memory system. The data and control buses, on the other hand, are bidirectional. Data may be written to or read from memory, hence the need for a bidirectional data bus. We will soon see why the control bus is also bidirectional.

Whether they are bidirectional or not, some care must be taken when the buses are connected to the memory section. It is possible to overload an address or data line by forcing it to drive too many loads. As always, it is important *not* to exceed the fanout of a digital output. If, for example, a certain output is capable of sinking 2 mA, how many 0.4 mA inputs can it drive? The answer is 5, which we get by dividing the output sink current by the required input current. If more than 5 inputs are connected, the output is overloaded and its ability to function properly is diminished. Clearly, the possibility of overloading the 8088's address or data buses exists when they are connected to external memory. For this reason, we will **buffer** the address and data buses.

Figure 8.2 shows how address lines A_8 through A_{15} are buffered by connecting them to a standard high-current buffer, the 74LS244 octal line driver/receiver. An address line on the 8088 is capable of sinking 2 mA all by itself. When the output of the 74LS244 is used instead, the address line has an effective sink current of 24 mA. This means that twelve times as many gates can be driven. Buffering the address lines allows the CPU to drive all the devices in our memory system, without the added worry of overloading the address line.

Buffering the data bus is a little trickier because the data bus is bidirectional. Data must now be buffered in both directions. Figure 8.3 shows how

FIGURE 8.2   Address bus buffering

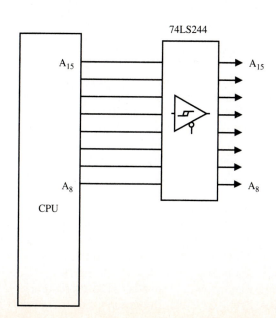

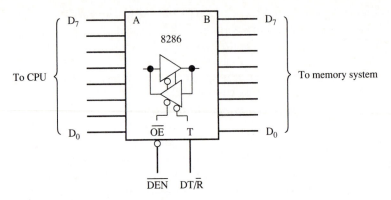

FIGURE 8.3 Data bus buffering

this bidirectional buffering is accomplished. The 8286 is an octal bus transceiver. Data flow through this device is controlled by the T (*transmit*) input, which tells the buffer to pass data from left to right, or from right to left. Left-to-right data is CPU output data. Right-to-left data is considered CPU input data. The natural choice for controlling the direction of the 8286 is the 8088's DT/$\overline{\text{R}}$ line, which always indicates the direction of data on the 8088 data bus. DT/$\overline{\text{R}}$ is directly generated by the 8088 in minimum mode, and by the 8288 in maximum mode. $\overline{\text{DEN}}$ is used to disable the 8286 when the bus is idle or contains address information.

In conclusion, then, remember that address and data buses should be buffered so that many gates can be connected to them instead of the few that can be directly driven by the unbuffered address or data line. All designs presented in this chapter will assume that the buses are already well buffered.

8.4 ACCESSING MEMORY

In addition to well-buffered address and data buses, a control bus must also be used to control the operation of the memory circuitry. The three operations we have to consider are the following:

1. Read data from memory

2. Write data to memory

3. Do not access memory

The first two cases represent data that gets transferred between the 8088 and memory. The third case occurs when the 8088 is performing some other duty (internal instruction execution, perhaps) and has no need for the memory system. Thus, it appears that the 8088 either accesses memory or does not access it. Does a processor signal (or group of signals) exist that tells external circuitry that the 8088 needs to use its memory? Yes, a number of signals indicate this need. In minimum mode, the processor will output a zero on IO/$\overline{\text{M}}$ to

FIGURE 8.4 Decoding memory read and write signals in minimum mode

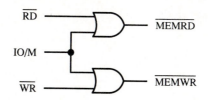

indicate that a memory reference is beginning. This signal is combined with $\overline{RD}$ and $\overline{WR}$ to form memory-read and memory-write signals for the memory system (as you can see in Figure 8.4). We use the active-low $\overline{MEMRD}$ and $\overline{MEMWR}$ signals to select and enable devices in the memory system.

In maximum mode, the 8288 bus controller decodes the processor status outputs and generates active-low $\overline{MRDC}$ (memory-read command) and $\overline{MWTC}$ (memory-write command) signals. The presence of a zero on either signal indicates a memory access.

Figure 8.5 shows a simplified timing diagram for a memory-read cycle. The cycle is composed of four T states, with each T state equivalent to one clock cycle. In T_1 the processor outputs a full 20-bit address on address lines A_8 through A_{19} and AD_0 through AD_7. ALE has also gone high, indicating that the multiplexed address/data bus contains address information. Since this is a memory access, the processor also has output a zero on $IO/\overline{M}$, which will remain low for the duration of the bus cycle.

In state T_2 the processor tristates the multiplexed address/data bus in preparation for the data read which will take place in T_3. Address lines A_{16} through A_{19} switch over to status outputs S_3 through S_6, and a zero is output on $\overline{RD}$ to specify a memory-read cycle to external hardware. It is the responsibility of the memory circuitry to utilize $IO/\overline{M}$, $\overline{RD}$, ALE, and the address lines in such a way that the data is placed onto the data bus only when $IO/\overline{M}$ *and* $\overline{RD}$ are both low.

Figure 8.6 shows the same basic timing for a memory-write cycle. The most noticeable difference (aside from the use of $\overline{WR}$ instead of $\overline{RD}$) is the

FIGURE 8.5 Memory read cycle timing

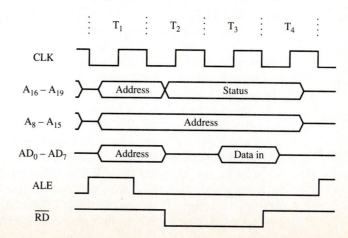

FIGURE 8.6 Memory write cycle timing

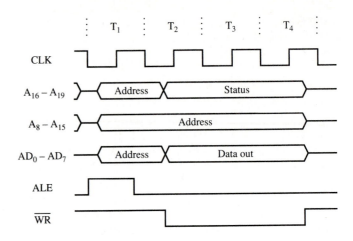

activity on the data bus. Unlike the read cycle, the data bus switches from address-out information to data-out information and keeps a valid copy of the output data on the bus for the remainder of the cycle. This should eliminate any setup times required by the memory chips.

In the next section we will see how a memory address decoder uses the address bus and the read/write signals to enable RAM and EPROM memories.

8.5 DESIGNING A MEMORY ADDRESS DECODER

The sole function of a memory address decoder is to monitor the state of the address bus and determine when the memory chips should be enabled. But what is meant by *memory chips?* These are the actual RAMs or EPROMs the designer wants to use in the computer. So, before the design begins, it must be decided how much memory is needed. If 8KB of EPROM is enough, then the designer knows that 13 address lines are needed to address a specific location inside the EPROM (because 2 raised to the 13th power is 8192). How many address lines are needed to select a specific location in a 32K memory? The answer is 15, because 2 to the 15th is 32768! The first step in designing a memory address decoder is determining how many address lines are needed just for the memory device itself. Any address lines remaining are used in the address decoder.

Figure 8.7(a) shows a block diagram of a memory address decoder connected to a memory chip. Figure 8.7(b) shows a simplified timing diagram representing the activity on the address bus and the IO/$\overline{\text{M}}$ output. The memory address decoder waits for a particular pattern on the address lines and a low on IO/$\overline{\text{M}}$ before making $\overline{\text{SEL}}$ low. When these conditions are satisfied, the low on $\overline{\text{SEL}}$ causes the $\overline{\text{CS}}$ (chip select) input on the memory chip to go low, which enables its internal circuitry, thus connecting the RAM or EPROM to the processor's data bus. When the address bus contains an address different from

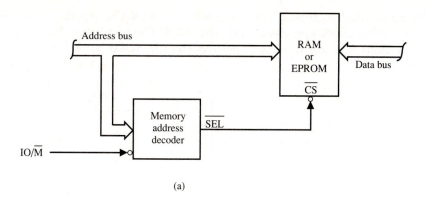

(a)

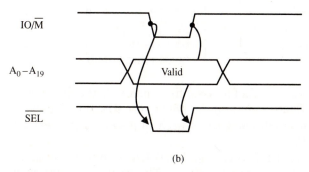

(b)

FIGURE 8.7   Simple memory address decoder: (a) block diagram and (b) timing

the one the address decoder expects to see, or if IO/$\overline{\text{M}}$ is high, the output of the decoder will remain high, disabling the memory chip and causing its internal buffers to tristate themselves. Thus, the RAM or EPROM is effectively disconnected from the data bus.

The challenge presented to us, the designers of the memory address decoder, is to chip-enable the memory device at the correct time. The following example illustrates the steps involved in the design of a memory address decoder.

Example 8.1:   A circuit containing 32KB of RAM is to be interfaced to an 8088-based system, so that the first address of the RAM (also called the **base** address) is at 48000H. What is the entire range of RAM addresses? How is the address bus used to enable the RAMs? What address lines should be used?

Solution: Figure 8.8 shows how the memory lines are assigned.

Since we are using a 32KB device, we need 15 address lines to select one of 32K possible addresses. We always use the lowest-numbered address lines first (the least significant ones). We start with A_0 and use the next 14 just for the

unnecessary waste of circuitry. If we instead look for a pattern, we see that address lines A_{19} and A_{18} are always low in the memory range 00000 to 3FFFF. In addition to this important piece of information, each RAM requires 15 address lines, A_0 through A_{14}, to select one of 32K locations within the RAM. This leaves us with address lines A_{15}, A_{16}, and A_{17} actually indicating a specific 32KB memory range. When these three address lines are all low, address range 00000 to 07FFF is selected. When A_{15} is high, and A_{16} and A_{17} low, address range 08000 to 0FFFF is selected. The last range, 38000 to 3FFFF, is selected when A_{15}, A_{16}, and A_{17} are all high. What we need then is a circuit that can decode these eight possible conditions by using only the three address lines. Figure 8.13 shows the required circuitry.

In this circuit, a 74LS138 3- to 8-line decoder is used to decode the different memory ranges. The 74LS138 has three select inputs and three control inputs. The select inputs are connected to address lines A_{15}, A_{16}, and A_{17}. The 3-bit binary number present on the select inputs will pull the selected output of the 74LS138 low (assuming that the 74LS138 is enabled), thus activating a spe-

FIGURE 8.13 Multibank address decoder

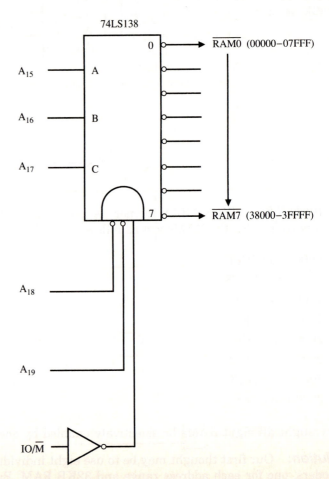

cific RAM bank. To enable the 74LS138, two lows and a high must be placed on its control inputs. The two lows are generated by A_{19} and A_{18}. The $IO/\overline{M}$ signal is inverted to generate the last control input.

By using special integrated circuits like the 74LS138 and a simple pattern recognition technique, we are able to greatly simplify the hardware required to generate all of our memory enables.

The last four examples have shown how we can decode a specific range of memory addresses using the full address bus of the 8088. In the next section, we will see how to further simplify our decoder, by using a technique called **partial address decoding.**

8.6 PARTIAL ADDRESS DECODING

Although the 8088 is capable of addressing over 1 million bytes of memory, it would be safe to assume that most applications would require much smaller memories. A good example might be an educational 8088 single-board computer, much like the one presented in Chapter 11, using only 8K words of EPROM and 8K words of RAM. This type of system needs only 14 address lines. The first 13, A_0 through A_{12}, go directly to the EPROM and RAM, and the last address line, A_{13}, is used to select either the EPROM or the RAM. Figure 8.14 details this example system.

In this figure, A_{13} is connected directly to the $\overline{CS}$ input of the RAM and is *inverted* before it gets to the $\overline{CS}$ input of the EPROM. So, whenever A_{13} is low, the RAM is enabled, and whenever A_{13} is high, the EPROM is enabled. We only have to use an inverter to do all the decoding in our memory section!

But what about the other address lines, A_{14} through A_{19}? They are ignored, and here is why: When the 8088 is powered up, a reset causes the processor to look first at memory location FFFF0. The 8088 is looking at memory location FFFF0 to get its initial instruction. We had better make sure good data is in that location at power-up. If we use an 8KB EPROM at FE000, we can be assured that the correct information will be present.

FIGURE 8.14 Partial address decoding for RAM/EPROM

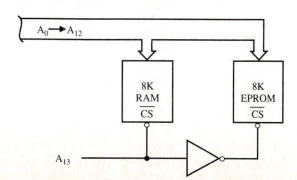

Going back to Figure 8.14, it is clear that the EPROM will be enabled at power-on, since A_{13} will be high when the processor tries to access location FFFF0.

But we still do not know why the other 6 upper address lines, A_{14} through A_{19} in this case, can be ignored. The answer lies in Figure 8.14. Do you see any address lines other than A_{13} being used to enable or disable the EPROM or RAM memories? No! Since we ignore these address lines, it does not matter if they are high or low. In this fashion we can read from memory locations FFFF0, 3BFF0, 07FF0, or C3FF0 and get the same data each time. The upper address bits have no effect on our memory circuitry, since we are only using the lower 14 address lines.

Partial-address decoding gives us a way to get the job done with a minimum of hardware. Since fewer address lines have to be decoded, less hardware is needed. This is its greatest advantage. A major disadvantage is that future expansion of memory is difficult, and usually requires a redesign of the memory address decoder. This may turn out to be a difficult, or even impossible, job. The difficulty lies in having to add hardware to the system. If a system manufactured by one company has been distributed to a number of users, making changes to all systems becomes a challenge. Furthermore, individuals wanting to make changes themselves may mistakenly place a new memory device into a partially decoded area. This will unfortunately result in two memories being accessed at the same time, probably resulting in invalid data during reads.

As long as these dangers and limitations are understood, partial-address decoding is a suitable compromise and acceptable in small systems.

Two more examples are presented to further show the simplicity of partial-address decoding.

Example 8.6:   A 16KB block of memory, composed of two 8KB EPROMs, is to have a starting address of 4000H. What is the address range for each EPROM? What circuitry is needed to implement a partial address decoder for a minmode system?

Solution: Figure 8.15(a) shows the address decoding table for the 16KB block of storage. The base address of 4000H is written down in binary, with the lower 13 bits associated with A_0 through A_{12}, the address lines needed to select locations within each 8KB EPROM. Note that A_{14} is high and A_{13} is low for all possible binary patterns of zeros and ones on A_0 through A_{12}. This sets the address range for the first EPROM, which is 4000 to 5FFF. An OR gate is used to recognize the 1 0 pattern on A_{14} and A_{13} (as shown in Figure 8.15(b)). Continuing with this technique, we see that A_{14} and A_{13} are both high when the second EPROM is being accessed. This translates into the address range 6000 to 7FFF, or a total address range of 4000 to 7FFF. Another OR gate is used to decode the 1 1 pattern on A_{14} and A_{13}. Since this memory is used in a minmode system, $IO/\overline{M}$ and $\overline{RD}$ are combined with a third OR gate and used to control the output-enable input of both EPROMs.

A_{19} A_{18} A_{17} A_{16}	A_{15} A_{14} A_{13} A_{12}	A_{11} A_{10} A_9 A_8	A_7 A_6 A_5 A_4	A_3 A_2 A_1 A_0
0 0 0 0	0 1 0 0	0 0 0 0	0 0 0 0	0 0 0 0
0 0 0 0	0 1 0 1	_____	_____	_____
0 0 0 0	0 1 1 0	_____	_____	_____
0 0 0 0	0 1 1 1	_____	_____	_____

For DECODER   To EPROM

(a)

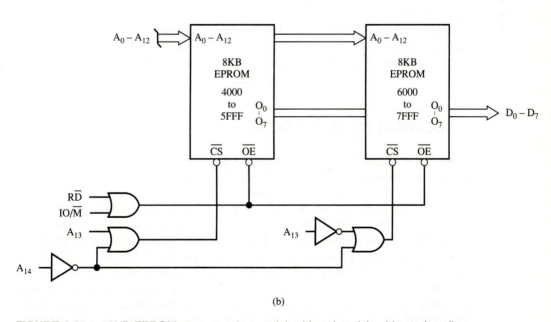

(b)

FIGURE 8.15 16KB EPROM storage using partial addressing: (a) address decoding table and (b) EPROM circuitry

You may want to practice by redesigning this circuit with two-input NAND gates.

Example 8.7: A 32KB EPROM needs a starting address of 30000, and a 32KB RAM needs a starting address of 20000. The circuitry in Figure 8.16 shows how these addresses are partially decoded. In this example, three-input NAND gates are used to do the decoding. All three inputs must be high for the

The delay time needed depends on the type of memory being used, the clock frequency, and the size (in stages) of the shift register. A one-shot (monostable multivibrator) could be used as well, but would not be as stable as the digital circuit due to the nature of the resistor/capacitor network needed.

We finish this section with an example of a delay circuit. In our next section we will see a complete schematic of an 8KB RAM/EPROM memory.

Example 8.8:   A delay circuit is composed of three D-type flip-flops connected as a 3-bit shift register driven by a 4-MHz clock. Compute the length of the delay generated by this circuit.

Solution: The length of delay is three times the period of the clock. A 4-MHz clock has a period of 250 ns; therefore the delay time is 750 ns.

Can the delay time in this circuit be doubled (to 1.5 μs) by adding only one more flip-flop? The answer is yes, and is left for you to prove as a homework problem.

8.8   A COMPLETE RAM/EPROM MEMORY

Now that we have covered all the required basics, a complete memory design is presented. Figure 8.19(a) shows the required hardware necessary for 8KB of EPROM (located at base address FE000) and 8KB of RAM (located at 00000). The control signals are associated with a minimum mode system. The addresses for each memory device are fully decoded. The 8-input NAND gate is used to enable the EPROM, and three 3-input NOR gates and a 3-input AND gate are used to enable the RAM. Different logic is required in each decoder, since the EPROM address requires recognition of seven 1s and the RAM decoder must recognize seven 0s. The 2764 is an 8KB EPROM, with an internal address range of 0000 to 1FFF, making its system address range FE000 to FFFFF. The 6264 is an 8KB static RAM with a system address range from 00000 to 01FFF. The memories were placed into the 8088's memory space in such a way that the EPROM is enabled upon reset, and the RAM is available for interrupt vector, program, and data storage.

Figure 8.19(b) shows an almost identical memory system, with a few changes made so that it can be placed into a maximum mode system. $\overline{RD}$ and $\overline{WR}$ now become $\overline{MRDC}$ and $\overline{MWTC}$ (generated by the 8288 bus controller). IO/$\overline{M}$ disappears, allllowing us to eliminate one of the NOR gates in the RAM section and requiring the addition of an inverter (the one that was previously used for IO/$\overline{M}$ in the EPROM section).

While 8KB of RAM is enough for small educational systems, other systems may require much more memory. In the next section, we will see how dynamic RAM can be interfaced to the 8088.

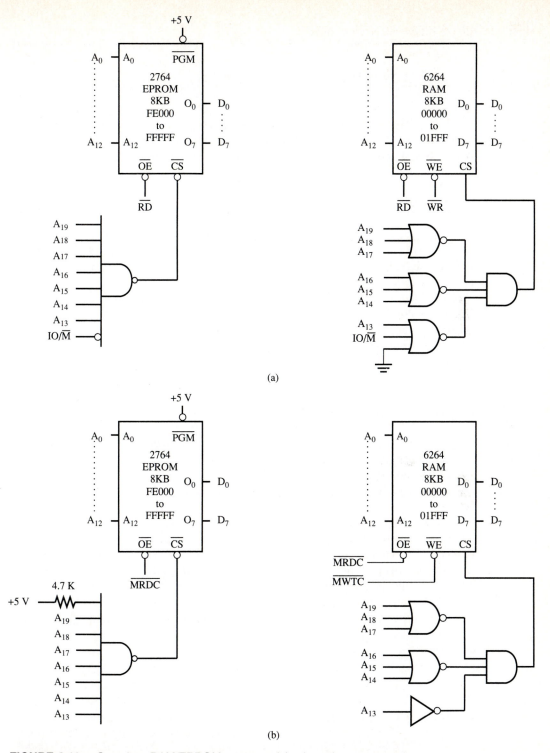

FIGURE 8.19 Complete RAM/EPROM memory: (a) minmode system and (b) maxmode system

8.9 DYNAMIC RAM INTERFACING

What Is Dynamic RAM?

Dynamic RAM is a special type of RAM memory that is currently the most popular form of memory used in large memory systems for microprocessors. It is important to discuss a few of the specific differences between static RAMs and dynamic RAMs. Static RAMs use digital flip-flops to store the required binary information, whereas dynamic RAMs use MOS capacitors. Because of the capacitive nature of the storage element, dynamic RAMs require less space per chip, per bit, and thus have larger densities. At the time of this writing, static RAMs are available in 28-pin packages in the 32K by 8-bit size, and dynamic RAMs are available in 16-pin packages, with 256K bit storage densities, at a much lower price!

In addition, static RAMs draw more power per bit. Dynamic RAMs employ MOS capacitors that retain their charges (stored information) for short periods of time, whereas static RAMs must saturate transistors within the flip-flop to retain the stored binary information, and saturated transistors dissipate maximum power.

A disadvantage of the dynamic RAM stems from the usage of the MOS capacitor as the storage element. Left alone, the capacitor will eventually discharge, thus losing the stored binary information. For this reason the dynamic RAM must be constantly **refreshed** to avoid data loss. During a refresh operation, all of the capacitors within the dynamic RAM (called DRAM from now on) are recharged.

This leads to a second disadvantage. The refresh operation takes time to complete, and the DRAM is unavailable for use by the processor during this time.

Older DRAMs required that all storage elements inside the chip be refreshed every 2 ms. Newer DRAMs have an extended 4-ms refresh time, but the overall refresh operation ties up an average of 3 percent of the total available DRAM time, which implies that the CPU has access to the DRAM only 97 percent of the time. Since static RAMs require no refresh, they are available to the CPU 100 percent of the time, a slight improvement over DRAMs.

In summary, we have static RAMs that are fast, require no refresh, and have low bit densities. DRAMs are slower and require extra logic for refresh and other timing controls, but are cheaper, consume less power, and have very large bit densities.

Accessing Dynamic RAM

A major difference in the usage of DRAMs lies in the way in which the DRAM is addressed. A 64K bit DRAM requires 16 address bits to select one of 65,536 possible bit locations, but its circuitry contains only 8 address lines. A study of Figure 8.20 will show how these 8 address lines are expanded into 16 address lines with the help of 2 additional control lines: $\overline{RAS}$ and $\overline{CAS}$.

The row address strobe and column address strob[e] ated within 100 ns of each other to avoid data loss. Th[e] ments for the DRAM depend on the manufacturer.

External logic is needed to generate the $\overline{RAS}$ and take care of presenting the right address bits to th[e] Figure 8.22 shows an example of the required logic.

The operation of this circuit is as follows: The add[ress] address bus for an address in the desired DRAM ran[ge] when it sees one. Normally the three Q outputs of [are] high. The first clock pulse will shift the logic 0 from t[he] output of the first flip-flop, causing $\overline{RAS}$ to go low. [The] second flip-flop is still high, the 74LS157s (quad 2-li[ne] are told to pass processor address lines A_0 through A_7 ROW address bits into the DRAM.

The second clock pulse will shift the logic 0 to the [which] is still low also), which causes the 74LS157s to sel[ect] lines A_8 through A_{15}. These address bits are recogn[ized] DRAM when the third clock pulse occurs, because th[e] to the third Q output, which causes $\overline{CAS}$ to go low. Th[e] with a full 16-bit address, and reading or writing may [be] the read or write cycle, IO/$\overline{M}$ will go high, presetting [the] preset line, and the shift register reverts back to it[s]

This sequence will repeat every time the addres[s] address.

Figure 8.23 shows a complete DRAM addressin[g] logic. When the 74LS138 detects a valid memory add[ress] puts will go low, removing the 74LS175 quad D flip-[flop] state. All four $\overline{Q}$ outputs are high at this time. As a [result] 74LS175 (connected as a 4-bit shift register), the $\overline{RA}$ will be generated. The resistors in the address and **damping** resistors, and are used to control the wave[forms] nals to the DRAMs. The damping resistors reduce rin[ging] would normally occur in a high-speed digital system[.] ing from Figure 8.23 is the required refresh logic, w[hich] next section.

Refreshing Dynamic RAM

Previously we learned that DRAMs need to be refre[shed] tors that retain the binary information will dischar[ge] Older DRAMs required that all cells (storage elemen[ts] ms. Although the process of reading or writing a D[RAM] fresh, it is possible that entire banks of DRAM remai[n] addresses other memories or I/O devices, so a safe d[esign] fresh circuit in the new DRAM system.

Newer DRAMs (such as the MCM6664) contain a[n] $\overline{REF}$ that automatically refreshes the DRAM when[ever]

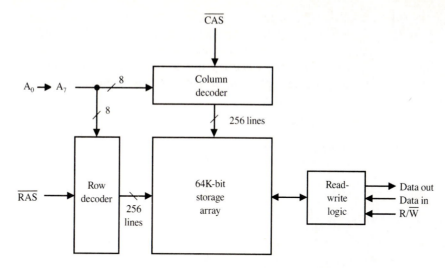

FIGURE 8.20 Internal block diagram of a 64K bit dynamic RAM

The 8 address lines are presented to row and column address buffers, and latched accordingly by the application of the $\overline{RAS}$ and $\overline{CAS}$ signals. To load a 16-bit address into the DRAM, 8 bits of the address are first latched by pulling $\overline{RAS}$ low. Then the other 8 address bits are presented to A_0 through A_7, and $\overline{CAS}$ is pulled low. By adding just one more address line to the DRAM, the addressing capability is increased by a factor of 4, since one extra address line signifies an extra row and column address bit. This explains why DRAMs tend to quadruple in size with each new release.

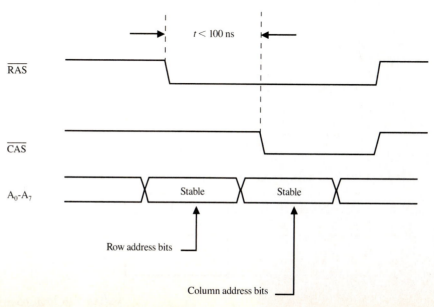

FIGURE 8.21 DRAM cycle timing

The actual method for addressin[...]
First the 8 row address bits are app[...]
low. Then A_0 through A_7 receive c[...]
pulled low. After a short delay, the [...]
coded the full 16-bit address, and re[...]

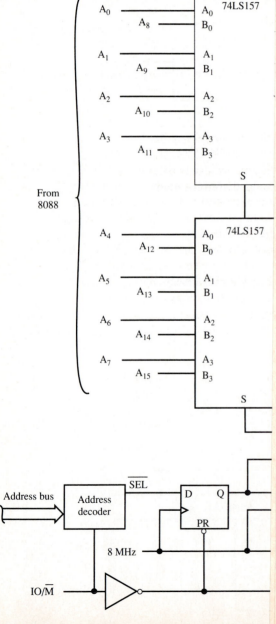

From 8088

FIGURE 8.22 Address bus selector for DRAM

the hard disk, place it in memory, increment a memory pointer, and then test for another byte to read. A DMA controller would be very handy in this example. It would merely take over the CPU's buses, write all the bytes into memory very quickly, and then return control to the CPU.

To perform DMA on the 8088, two signals may be used. They are $\overline{RQ}/\overline{GT}0$ *(request/grant)* and $\overline{RQ}/\overline{GT}1$. Both of these signals are bidirectional; they are both inputs and outputs. A logic zero must be placed on either signal to request the processor's bus, with $\overline{RQ}/\overline{GT}0$ having priority over $\overline{RQ}/\overline{GT}1$. The processor will acknowledge the takeover when the current bus cycle finishes and output a zero on the appropriate signal line. The low-level request signal must be at least one CLK period long for the 8088 to recognize it. The processor will output a zero for one CLK period during the next T_4 or T_1 state to acknowledge the takeover. It will then enter a "hold acknowledge" state until the new bus master sends another low-level pulse to $\overline{RQ}/\overline{GT}$. All bus takeovers must consist of this three-pulse sequence. It is important to note that the device performing the DMA is responsible for maintaining the DRAM refresh requirements, either by performing them itself, or by allowing them to happen normally with existing circuitry.

Still another way to transfer data to an external device is through a technique called **memory-mapped I/O,** which is slower than DMA but just as useful. It is even possible for a system to employ both DMA and memory-mapped I/O, using DMA for the high-speed transfers and memory-mapped I/O for the slow ones.

8.11   MEMORY-MAPPED I/O

Normally, a memory location, or group of locations, is used to store program data and other important information. Data is written into a particular memory location and read later for use. Through a process called memory-mapped I/O, we remove the storage capability of the memory location and instead use it to communicate with the outside world. Imagine that you have a keyboard that supplies an 8-bit ASCII code (complete with parity) whenever you press a key. Your job is to somehow get this parallel information into your computer. By using memory-mapped I/O, a memory *location* may be set aside that, when read, will contain the 8-bit code generated by the keyboard. Conversely, data may be sent to the outside world by writing to a memory-mapped output location. The 8088 CPU is capable of performing memory-mapped I/O in either byte or word lengths. All that is required is a memory address decoder, coupled with the appropriate bus circuitry. For a memory-mapped output location, the memory address decoder provides a clock pulse to an octal flip-flop capable of storing the output data. A memory-mapped input location would use the memory address decoder to enable a tri-state octal buffer, placing data from the outside world onto the CPU's data bus when active. Figure 8.27 shows the circuitry for an 8-bit memory-mapped I/O location, sometimes referred to as a memory-mapped I/O port. The memory address decoder may be used for both input and output.

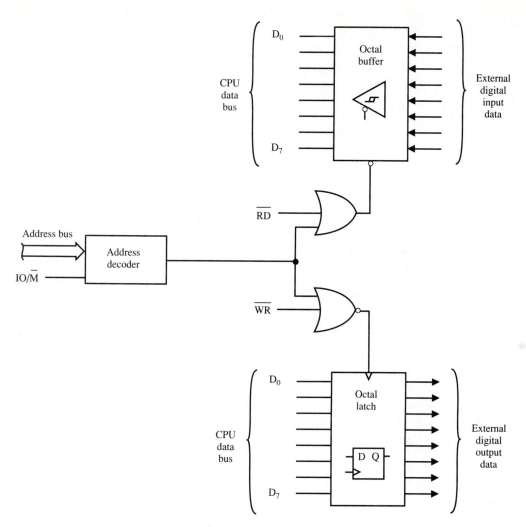

FIGURE 8.27 Memory-mapped I/O circuitry

8.12 SUMMARY

In this chapter we studied some of the most common methods used in the design of memory circuitry for microprocessor-based systems. Full- and partial-address decoding, memory-mapped I/O, direct memory access, and the logical requirements for static and dynamic RAMs were all covered. A good designer will employ many of these techniques in an effort to construct a new system that is logically simple and elegant but also functional and easy to troubleshoot. The end-of-chapter questions are designed to further test your knowledge of these topics. You are encouraged to work *all* of them to increase your ability to design memory address decoders, partial-address decoders, and complete memory systems.

STUDY QUESTIONS

1. Explain the different functions associated with processor signals AD_0 through AD_7.
2. How does external circuitry know when address information is present on the multiplexed address/data bus?
3. List the different control bus signals used in minimum mode and maximum mode.
4. How can the $\overline{RD}$, $\overline{WR}$, and IO/$\overline{M}$ outputs be used to detect *any* kind of access to memory? Design a circuit that will output a zero on $\overline{MEMORY}$ whenever a memory read or write occurs.
5. If a state time on an 8088-based system is 250 ns, what is the minimum time spent doing a memory read?
6. When (and why) are wait states inserted into memory accesses?
7. How many address lines are needed for a 128KB memory?
8. For the state time of Question 5, what is the time spent doing a memory read with two wait states?
9. Two 2KB EPROMs are used to make a 4KB memory. How many address lines are needed for the EPROMs? What upper address lines must be used for the decoder?
10. For the memory of Question 9, what is the address of the last memory location, if the starting address of the EPROM is E4000?

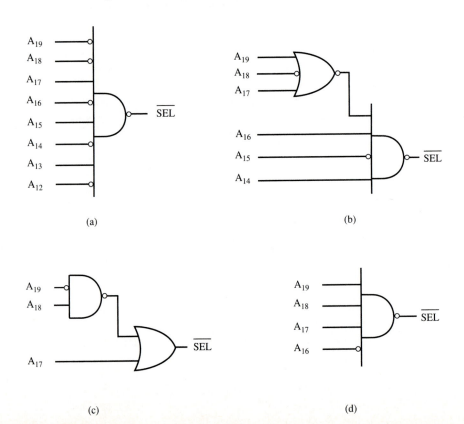

(a)

(b)

(c)

(d)

FIGURE 8.28

11. Design a memory address decoder for the EPROM memory of Question 10, using a circuit similar to that in Figure 8.9.
12. Repeat Questions 9 through 11 for these memory sizes and starting addresses:

   a) 8KB, base address of CC000
   b) 32KB, base address of 80000
   c) 256KB, base address of 00000

13. What are the decoded address ranges for the circuits in Figure 8.28.
14. What signal (or signals) is missing from the address decoder in Figure 8.28? Modify the decoders to include the missing signal (or signals).
15. What are the address range groups for the decoder in Figure 8.29?
16. Use a circuit similar to that of Figure 8.29 to decode these address ranges:

$$18000 \text{ to } 187FF$$
$$18800 \text{ to } 18FFF$$
$$19000 \text{ to } 197FF$$
$$19800 \text{ to } 19FFF$$
$$1A000 \text{ to } 1A7FF$$
$$1A800 \text{ to } 1AFFF$$
$$1B000 \text{ to } 1B7FF$$
$$1B800 \text{ to } 1BFFF$$

17. What are two main advantages gained in using partial-address decoding? Two disadvantages?
18. Give three possible address ranges for each decoder in Figure 8.30. Address lines A_0 through A_{13} are used by the memories.
19. Suppose that three different memory decoders have output signals $\overline{\text{RAMA}}$, $\overline{\text{RAMB}}$, and $\overline{\text{ROM}}$. Design a circuit to generate a READY delay of 200 ns using a 100-ns-period clock and a circuit similar to that of Figure 8.18. Any of the three signals going low triggers the generator.
20. Use an 8-bit parallel-out shift register to design a variable wait-state circuit. Assume that the shift register is clocked once every 125 ns, and that 0 to 7 125 ns wait states are allowed.
21. Design a 32KB memory using 8KB EPROMs. Show the address and data line connections to all EPROMs and the circuitry needed to switch between the four 8KB sections.

FIGURE 8.29

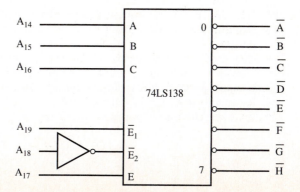

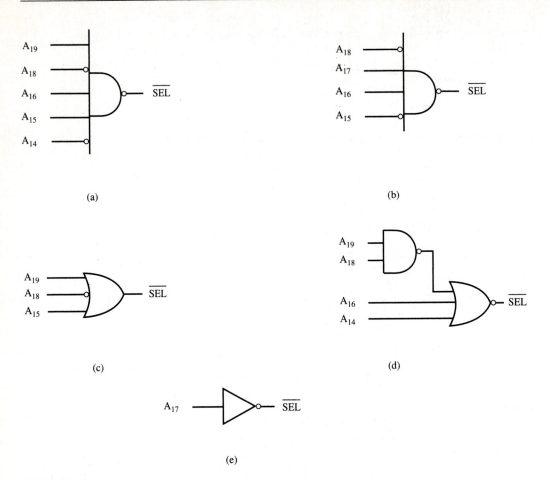

FIGURE 8.30

22. How do the $\overline{\text{RAS}}$ and $\overline{\text{CAS}}$ lines on a DRAM eliminate half of the required chip address lines?
23. Why does the size of a DRAM go up by a factor of 4 for each single address line that is added?
24. Why do DRAMs consume less power than static RAMs?
25. Explain how DRAM refreshing could be accomplished using an interrupt service routine.
26. How does program execution change on a system that supports DMA?
27. What is the 8088 doing while its external buses are involved in a DMA transfer?
28. Design a partial address decoder for a 64KB EPROM with a base address of 40000.
29. Redesign the circuit of Example 8.6 using NAND gates.
30. What are the ranges of addresses for the partial address decoders of Example 8.7?

CHAPTER

9

I/O System Design

Objectives

In this chapter you will learn about:

* I/O addressing space

* The design of full and partial I/O address decoders

* The operation of buffered input ports

* The operation of latched output ports

* Parallel I/O with the 8255 PPI

* Serial I/O with the 8251 UART

9.1 INTRODUCTION

In Chapter 8 we saw how the 8088 is connected to its memory system. Program data and instructions are stored in memory, and accessed over a system bus consisting of address, data, and control signals. Many times a microprocessor is used to control a process which requires an exchange of data between the processor and the hardware utilized by the process. For example, an 8088 controlling an assembly line may receive input data from switches or photocells that give the position of an assembly making its way down the line. The 8088 will be able to test the state of each sensor by reading its status with an input port. Indicator lights, solenoids, and video display terminals associated with the assembly line may be driven by a few of the 8088's output ports. In this chapter we will examine the design and operation of input and output ports, and see how they are used to communicate with the outside world.

Section 9.2 discusses the processor's I/O addressing space. Section 9.3 shows how a port address decoder is designed. The operation of input and output ports is covered in Sections 9.4 and 9.5, followed by binary counter and D/A conversion applications in Section 9.6. The 8255 PPI and 8251 UART are explained in Sections 9.7 and 9.8, including examples of serial data transmission, A/D conversion, and parallel I/O.

9.2 THE 8088 PORT ADDRESSING SPACE

Chapter 8 showed that the 8088 had a memory address space whose 1 megabyte size is determined by the processor's 20-bit address bus. Unique binary patterns on A_0 through A_{19} select one of the 1,048,576 locations within the processor's memory space. The 8088's **I/O addressing space** is smaller, containing just 65,536 possible input/output ports, accessed by A_0 through A_{15}. Data transfer between ports and the processor is over the CPU data bus, and may contain 8 or 16 bits of data. The accumulator (AL for 8-bit transfers and AX for 16-bit transfers) is the only processor register involved in an I/O operation with the single exception of the use of DX as the port address register. Figure 9.1 shows the organization of the 8088's I/O space. Ports 00 through FF may be addressed by one form of the IN and OUT instructions, and the entire I/O space (ports 0000 to FFFF) by another form of IN and OUT that utilizes register DX. In the first form, the port address may be used directly in the instruction, as in:

```
IN    AL,80H
IN    AX,6
OUT   3CH,AL
OUT   0A0H,AX
```

FIGURE 9.1   The 8088's I/O addressing space

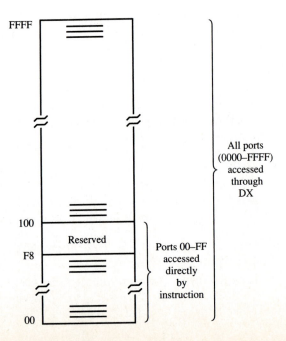

The port address in this form is limited to the range 00 to FF. Intel corporation reserves the right to use ports F8 through FF for their own needs, and programmers are urged to consider other addresses in their designs. Port addresses appear on address lines A_0 through A_7 when these instructions are executed.

The second way a port address may be specified is by placing it into register DX and using one of these instructions:

```
IN    AL,DX
IN    AX,DX
OUT   DX,AL
OUT   DX,AX
```

A good practice to follow is to use even port addresses for word transfers. This ensures the fastest 2-byte transfer the processor can perform. Word read or writes to odd I/O addresses require additional clock cycles.

When using DX as the port address register, the I/O addressing space becomes 0000 to FFFF, with the port address showing up on A_0 through A_{15}. This represents 65,536 8-bit ports (or 32K 16-bit ports). In the next section we will see how a port address is recognized and decoded.

9.3   DESIGNING A PORT ADDRESS DECODER

The port address decoder is a circuit designed to recognize the execution of an I/O instruction. In minimum mode, the processor uses the IO/$\overline{\text{M}}$ signal to indicate an I/O access by placing a high logic level on it, along with the port address on the address bus. In maximum mode, the 8288 bus controller decodes an I/O access and generates active $\overline{\text{IORC}}$ (*I/O read command*) and $\overline{\text{IOWC}}$ (*I/O write command*) signals. These control signals must be incorporated within the design of the port address decoder to distinguish port addresses from memory addresses.

Full Port Address Decoding

In this type of port address decoder, we include as many address lines as possible in the decoder. For example, Figure 9.2(a) shows the logic needed to do a full decode of port address 4F in a minmode system. Since the port address is between 00 and FF, it can be directly included in the I/O instruction (as in IN   AL,4FH) and we need only examine A_0 through A_7 for the required port address. We then combine the valid port address with IO/$\overline{\text{M}}$ to generate the $\overline{\text{RD4F}}$ and $\overline{\text{WR4F}}$ signals. These two outputs can also be generated with $\overline{\text{IORC}}$ and $\overline{\text{IOWC}}$, as shown in Figure 9.2(b).

When groups of ports are needed, a technique similar to the one used to map multiple RAMs or EPROMs is used. In Figure 9.3 we see how a 3-line to 8-line decoder is used to decode signals for eight different input ports. Address lines A_0 through A_2 are used by the 74LS138 to select one of its eight outputs

FIGURE 9.2   Port address decoder: (a) minmode system and (b) maxmode system

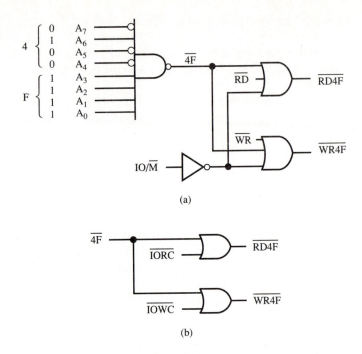

(a)

(b)

(output 0 when all three are low and output 7 when all three are high). Address lines A_3 through A_7 enable the 138 when the correct address is present. The correct port address is any address that matches 10011---. The *base* port address, when A_0 through A_2 are low, is 98H. The last port address is 9FH. So, IN   AL,98H will cause the $\overline{IN}_0$ signal to strobe low, IN   AL,99H will activate $\overline{IN}_1$, and so on. What needs to be changed to get this circuit to work for output ports in the same range? What must be done to decode port addresses 80 through 88?

If the port address has been placed in register DX, address lines A_0 through A_{15} must be utilized in the decoder. Figure 9.4 shows how port address A4C0 is decoded in a maxmode system. One 8-input NAND gate is used for each half of the address bus. One NAND gate recognizes A4 and the other C0.

FIGURE 9.3   Decoding multiple input ports

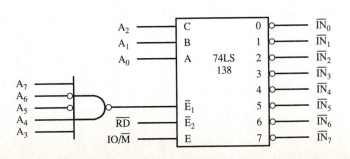

FIGURE 9.6   Partial address decoders

FIGURE 9.4   Decoding a 16-bit port address

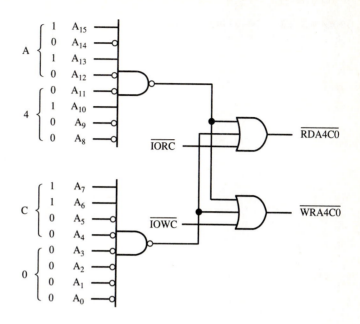

The outputs of each NAND gate are combined with $\overline{\text{IORC}}$ and $\overline{\text{IOWC}}$ to generate the required I/O signals.

An important point to remember when working with these kinds of address decoders is that they decode a *fixed* port address, or range of addresses. Manufacturers who design I/O boards for consumer use (within their personal computers) know that each user who buys their boards may have a different I/O address in mind, depending on how each system is configured with other hardware items. It would be much more convenient to design a port address decoder that allows selection of a port address through a DIP switch. In this case, some kind of binary **comparator** must be used, to compare the port address on the address bus with the desired port address represented by a DIP switch. Figure 9.5 shows how two 74LS85 4-bit magnitude comparators can be used to recognize an 8-bit port address. Each magnitude comparator determines if the address signals on the four A inputs are equal to the DIP switch information on the four B inputs. Each comparator has an A=B input and A=B output. To perform an 8-bit comparison, the 85s are cascaded by connecting the first A=B output to the second A=B input. The A=B output of the second comparator will only go high when there is an 8-bit address match. $\overline{\text{SEL}}$ will go low if the match exists when IO/$\overline{\text{M}}$ is high. $\overline{\text{RD}}$ and $\overline{\text{WR}}$ can be combined with $\overline{\text{SEL}}$ to get the required I/O read and write signals.

Partial Port Address Decoding

In a minimal system requiring only a handful of I/O ports, we can use **partial port address decoding** to reduce the hardware needed to produce I/O read

---

9.4   OPERATION OF A E

An input port is used to gate bus, where it is captured by not possible to simply place please, for this will surely i bytes constantly being read f priate time to do the I/O rea addition to the port address data onto the bus during the the bus when the processor is used for this purpose. Figure at the fully decoded port add device, meaning that its outp state, effectively disconnectii high-impedance state can be state of the 244. When a valid will be enabled by the OR ga data present on the eight inp only enabled when the proces

A 16-bit input port requir If port address 9C is to be used be enabled when port address use A_0 to enable each half of

9.5   OPERATION OF A LA

There is more to an output po data takes on the data bus. Da and is only placed onto the dat

FIGURE 9.5 Using cor
in an address decoder

FIGURE 9.7 An 8-bit input port

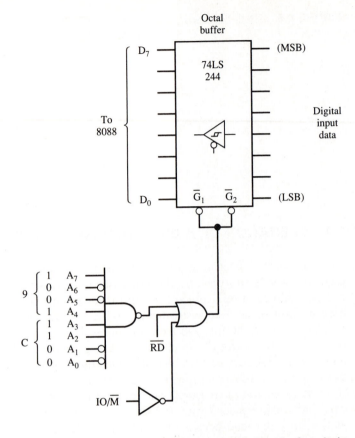

few hundred nanoseconds at the most to capture the output data before it is replaced by other data (an instruction read from memory perhaps). It is necessary to *store* a copy of the output data when it appears. This is why output ports must contain storage elements. The processor's control signals are used to tell the output port circuitry when to store what is on the data bus. The output port in Figure 9.8 is designed to have the same I/O address as the input port of the previous section. You are encouraged to redesign both ports so that they are contained in a single circuit.

The NOR gate is used to place a high level on the latch input (G) of the 74LS373. Whatever data is present on the CPU data bus when G is high will be stored when G goes back low. Thus, the 373 is used to take a snapshot of the contents of the data bus, and store the data until the next I/O write to port 9C. An edge-triggered storage device (such as the 74LS374) may be used in place of the 373.

9.6 SIMPLE I/O APPLICATIONS

In this section we will examine two applications of I/O ports. The first application involves a binary counter, whose 8-bit count is displayed with light emit-

and write s
tems, many
groups of a
ple, in Figu
with A_7 hi
reference to
gets to the
uses a 4-in
range 8000
cause SEL
eight port a
and 7F.

FIGURE 9.8 An 8-bit output port

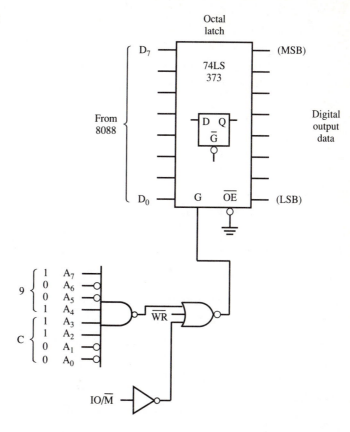

ting diodes connected to an output port. An input port wired to a set of switches is used to control the speed of the binary counter (all switches down is the fastest, all up is the slowest).

The second application shows how a data table containing sampled data from a sine wave can be output sequentially to a digital-to-analog converter to recreate the sine wave.

The Binary Counter

Figure 9.9 shows the logic needed to implement an input/output port with a base address of DE. Since A_0 is not used in the port address decoder, accesses to port DF will also work. The input port uses the 74LS244 octal buffer to read a set of DIP switches. An open switch makes a one. The information present on the DIP switches is read with IN   AL,0DEH and then moved into register CX. Register CX is used in a delay subroutine which is called between updates of the binary counter. Thus, the DIP switches have control over how fast or slow the binary counter counts. The count is displayed on a set of light emitting diodes by outputting the count to port DE with OUT   0DEH,AL, which stores the count in the 74LS373.

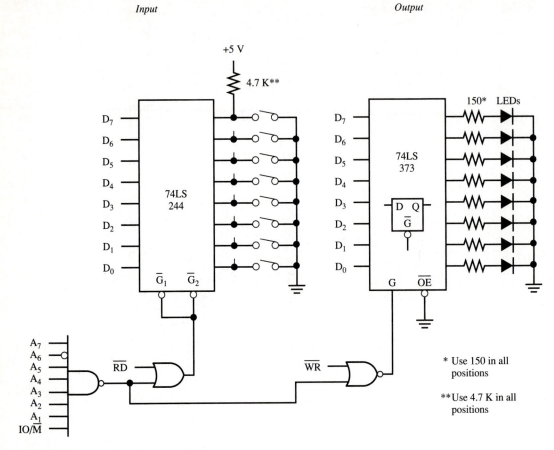

FIGURE 9.9 An input/output port

The software required for this application is as follows:

```
BINCNT:    MOV    AL,0              ;start count at 00
DISPCNT:   OUT    ODEH,AL          ;send count to LEDs
           CALL   FAR PTR DELAY    ;pause
           INC    AL               ;increment counter
           JMP    DISPCNT          ;repeat forever

DELAY      PROC   FAR
           MOV    BL,AL            ;save copy of counter
           IN     AL,ODEH          ;read DIP switches
           MOV    CH,AL            ;save speed byte
           MOV    CL,1             ;ensure at least one loop
WAIT:      NOP
           NOP
           LOOP   WAIT             ;waste a little time
           MOV    AL,BL            ;get counter value back
           RET
DELAY      ENDP
```

With the DIP switches all closed, a zero is read into the accumulator, giving CX an initial value of 0001. This will cause DELAY to execute the WAIT loop once before returning. The counter is updated at the fastest rate in this case. Opening all of the DIP switches causes FF to be read into AL, giving CX an initial value of FF01. This will cause over 65,000 WAIT loops to be executed, giving the longest possible delay between updates, and thus the slowest count.

A useful exercise to complete this application would be to determine the amount of time between outputs to the display port (the LEDs) for a particular setting of the input switches.

Sine Wave Generator

In this application, an 8-bit digital-to-analog converter is connected to an output port. The circuitry of Figure 9.10 shows how the 1408 DAC is wired to a 74LS373. The 1408 is designed to sink current at its output, the amount of current between 0 mA and some maximum value (not to exceed 2 mA), depending on the binary number present on its inputs. The output current is converted into voltage by the 741 op-amp so that a +/− range is generated. We will see that −2.5 V is created when 00 is at the DAC input, a value of 80 produces zero volts, and FF gives +2.5 V.

Square waves can be generated by sending out two alternating binary values. For example, outputting 00...FF...00...FF... produces a square

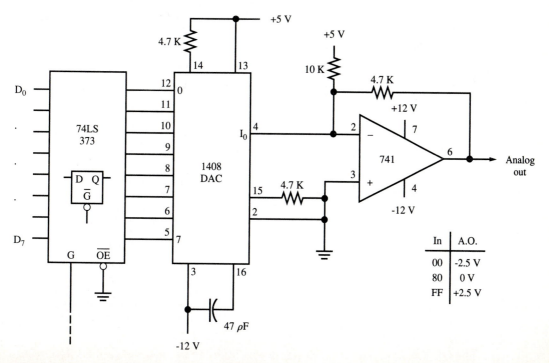

FIGURE 9.10   8-bit digital-to-analog converter

wave with a peak-to-peak voltage of 5 volts. Sending 20. . .60. . .20. . .60. . .
also produces a square wave, but with a different overall voltage. The software
shown here generates a sine wave by outputting each value from the SINE
data table. One pass through the table produces one cycle of a sine wave at the
DAC output. The information in the SINE data table was computed by breaking one cycle of a sine wave into 256 equal parts of 1.4 degrees. At each degree
increment (0, 1.4, 2.8, etc.) the value of sin(x) is computed and multiplied by
128. The resulting value is then converted into binary. Try a few conversions
for yourself and you should get the same pattern that appears in the table.

The frequency of the sine wave can be altered by playing with the DELAY
subroutine.

```
In current data segment. . .
SINE    DB      82H,85H,88H,8BH,8EH,91H,94H,97H
        DB      9BH,9EH,0A1H,0A4H,0A7H,0AAH,0ADH,0AFH
        DB      0B2H,0B5H,0B8H,0BBH,0BEH,0C0H,0C3H,0C6H
        DB      0C8H,0CBH,0CDH,0D0H,0D2H,0D4H,0D7H,0D9H
        DB      0DBH,0DDH,0DFH,0E1H,0E3H,0E5H,0E7H,0E9H
        DB      0EBH,0ECH,0EEH,0EFH,0F1H,0F2H,0F4H,0F5H
        DB      0F6H,0F7H,0F8H,0F9H,0FAH,0FBH,0FBH,0FCH
        DB      0FDH,0FDH,0FEH,0FEH,0FEH,0FEH,0FEH,0FFH
        DB      0FEH,0FEH,0FEH,0FEH,0FEH,0FDH,0FDH,0FCH
        DB      0FBH,0FBH,0FAH,0F9H,0F8H,0F7H,0F6H,0F5H
        DB      0F4H,0F2H,0F1H,0EFH,0EEH,0ECH,0EBH,0E9H
        DB      0E7H,0E5H,0E3H,0E1H,0DFH,0DDH,0DBH,0D9H
        DB      0D7H,0D4H,0D2H,0D0H,0CDH,0CBH,0C8H,0C6H
        DB      0C3H,0C0H,0BEH,0BBH,0B8H,0B5H,0B2H,0AFH
        DB      0ADH,0AAH,0A7H,0A4H,0A1H,9EH,9BH,97H
        DB      94H,91H,8EH,8BH,88H,85H,82H,7EH
        DB      7BH,78H,75H,72H,6FH,6CH,69H,66H
        DB      62H,5FH,5CH,59H,56H,53H,50H,4EH
        DB      4BH,48H,45H,42H,3FH,3DH,3AH,37H
        DB      35H,32H,30H,2DH,2BH,29H,26H,24H
        DB      22H,20H,1EH,1CH,1AH,18H,16H,14H
        DB      12H,11H,0FH,0EH,0CH,0BH,9,8
        DB      7,6,5,4,3,2,2,1,0,0,0,0,0,0,0,0
        DB      0,0,0,0,0,0,0,1,2,2,3,4,5,6,7,8
        DB      9,0BH,0CH,0EH,0FH,11H,12H,14H
        DB      16H,18H,1AH,1CH,1EH,20H,22H,24H
        DB      26H,29H,2BH,2DH,30H,32H,35H,37H
        DB      3AH,3DH,3FH,42H,45H,48H,4BH,4EH
        DB      50H,53H,56H,59H,5CH,5FH,62H,66H
        DB      69H,6CH,6FH,72H,75H,78H,7BH,7FH
        .
        .
        .
WAVER:  MOV     CX,256          ;init loop counter
        MOV     SI,0            ;and pointer to data
SINOUT: MOV     AL,SINE[SI]     ;read sine wave data
        OUT     0DEH,AL         ;send to 1408 DAC
        INC     SI              ;point to next item
        CALL    FAR PTR DELAY   ;pause between outputs
        LOOP    SINOUT          ;repeat forever
        JMP     WAVER
```

The OUT instruction uses the same port address as the one implemented in the
binary counter application. An analysis of the instruction cycles required for

one pass through the SINOUT loop, *not including* the CALL to DELAY, gives 17 cycles. Multiplying this by 256 gives 4352 CLK cycles used in the creation of one sine wave! If the processor is running at 5 MHz, this gives a sinewave frequency of over 1100 Hz. A DELAY subroutine requiring 50 additional cycles produces a sine wave with a frequency of only 290 Hz. These estimates should give you an indication as to the limits of the sine wave generator. High frequency waveforms will have to be created by other methods. Even so, this simple circuit can be used to create interesting audio effects by connecting the output of the 1408 to an amplifier. It is only a matter of sending the right data to the 1408.

9.7 PARALLEL DATA TRANSFER: THE 8255 PPI

In the previous section we interfaced switches, lights, and a digital-to-analog converter to an I/O port. The number of applications is endless, with each one performing a different function. Even so, they all have at least one thing in common: they all utilize *parallel* I/O. In parallel I/O, all data bits are sent or received at the same time, as a group. This is very necessary in many applications! What would the binary counter look like if each LED was not updated at the same time as every other LED?

Many applications require more than one I/O port to get the job done. Peripheral designers realized this years ago and came up with a parallel I/O peripheral containing three separate I/O ports, all of which are programmable. This device is the 8255 programmable peripheral interface. In this section we will see how the 8255 is interfaced to the 8088 and programmed.

Interfacing the 8255

Figure 9.11 shows a diagram of the 8255 and its I/O and control signals. Twenty-four of the 8255's 40 pins are dedicated to the three programmable ports A, B, and C. These three ports, and a fourth one called a control port, are accessed via $\overline{RD}$, $\overline{WR}$, $\overline{CS}$, and address lines A_0 and A_1. A RESET input is included to initialize the 8255 when power is first applied. Figure 9.11 shows how an 8-input NAND gate is used to decode port addresses A0 through A3. When the address bus contains one of these four port addresses during an I/O access, $\overline{CS}$ will be pulled low. The 8255 will internally decode the states of A_0 and A_1 and determine which port to access. In this example, Port A has port address A0. Ports B and C are accessed through ports A1 and A2, respectively, and the control port is at A3. It is very easy to determine the four port addresses by adding 0, 1, 2, and 3 to the base port address. The base port address is found by picking the upper 6 address lines (A_2 through A_7) to be what you need and assuming zeros for A_1 and A_0.

The nicest feature of the 8255 is that different hardware circuits can be connected to ports A, B, and C, with the direction (input or output) of each port configured with initial programming. This allows an 8088-based system with an 8255 in it to be used for many different purposes.

FIGURE 9.11 Interfacing the 8255 PPI

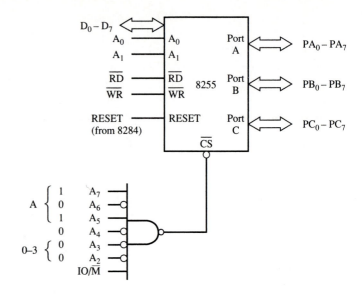

Programming the 8255

The 8255 has three modes of operation. The first is *mode 0: basic input/output.* In this mode, Ports A, B, and C can be individually programmed as input or output ports. Port C is divided into two 4-bit halves, directionally independent from each other. So, there are 16 combinations of input and output configurations available with this mode. A RESET automatically causes the 8255 to enter mode 0 with all ports programmed for input.

Input data is not latched. Data must be present when the port is being read by the processor. Output data is latched, as we would normally expect in an output port.

To program the 8255 for mode 0 operation and set the direction of each port, a mode word must be output to the control port. The definition of the mode word is shown in Figure 9.12. The MSB is the **mode-set flag,** which must be a one to program the 8255. Bits 5 and 6 are used to select the 8255's mode. 00 selects mode 0, 01 selects mode 1, and mode 2 is selected when bit 6 is high. Bit 2 is also used as a select bit for modes 0 and 1. The other four bits set the direction of ports A and B and both halves of C. A zero indicates an output port and a one indicates an input port. To configure the 8255 for mode 0, all ports programmed for input, the mode word must be 10011011 (9BH). This byte must be output to the control port to configure the 8255. The following two instructions will initialize the 8255 after a reset:

```
MOV    AL,9BH
OUT    0A3H,AL
```

Remember that the 8255 of Figure 9.11 has its control port at address A3.

Once the 8255 is programmed, the ports can be accessed with the appropriate IN instruction, such as IN   AL,0A0H (which reads port A). What mode

Control port

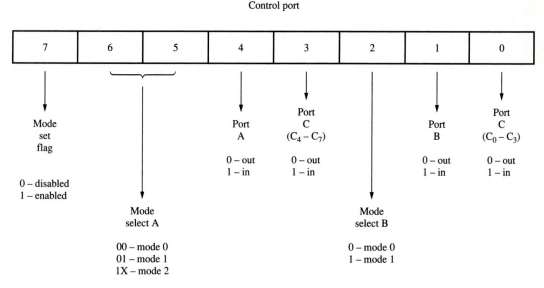

FIGURE 9.12 8255 mode word format

word is needed to program port A for input, port B for output, and both halves of port C for input? You should get 99H when using the mode word format of Figure 9.12.

Assume that the 8255 has a DIP switch wired to port A and a set of LEDs wired to port B. The following code can be used to repeatedly read the switches and send their state to the LEDs.

```
READEM:   MOV   AL,99H     ;configure 8255 for Ain, Bout, mode0
          OUT   0A3H,AL
GETSW:    IN    AL,0A0H    ;read switches
          OUT   0A1H,AL    ;send data to lights
          JMP   GETSW
```

In this case, a closed switch turns a LED off.

The next mode is *mode 1: strobed input/output*. In this mode, the 8255 uses port C as a *handshaking* port. Handshaking signals are commonly used in printers to sense the status of the paper-out sensor and the printer's readiness to accept new data. Ports A and B can be programmed for input or output. Data is latched in both directions. If port A is programmed for input, a strobe signal is needed on PC_4 to write data into port A. The 8255 will acknowledge the new input data by outputting a one on PC_5. These two signals on port C are defined as shown in Figure 9.13(a). PC_5 is IBF_a, input buffer A full. IBF is cleared when the processor reads port A. Port B operates in the same way, using PC_2 and PC_1 as handshaking signals. Both ports have the capability of causing an interrupt when data is strobed into them. The INTR output will go high when IBF goes high *and* the internal interrupt-enable bit is set. PC_4 and PC_2 make up the interrupt-enable bits for ports A and B. Setting PC_4 will cause $INTR_a$ to

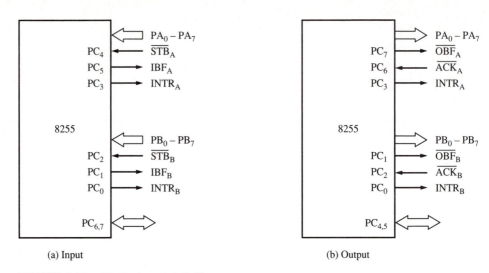

(a) Input   (b) Output

FIGURE 9.13   Mode 1 port definitions

go high when data is strobed into port A. Reading the input port will clear the interrupt request. This interrupt mechanism is a useful alternative to using software to constantly poll the input port. Polling wastes a lot of time waiting for input data that may not be there. Interrupting the processor only when new data has arrived results in more efficient program execution. This is one of the advantages of mode 1.

As Figure 9.13(a) shows, PC_6 and PC_7 are available for general purpose I/O when port A is programmed for input. The mode word needed to program the 8255 for mode 1, Ain, Bin, and PC_6 and PC_7 out is B6.

Figure 9.13(b) shows how the 8255 is configured for output in mode 1. Here we have *output buffer full* ($\overline{OBF}$) and *acknowledge* ($\overline{ACK}$) signals used to hand-shake with the output circuitry. $\overline{OBF}$ will go low when the processor writes to port A or B. This signal will remain low until a low pulse arrives on $\overline{ACK}$. $\overline{ACK}$ is used to indicate that the new output data was received. $\overline{ACK}$, together with interrupt-enable, can be used to generate an interrupt with INTR. This would interrupt the processor when the new output data has been read, and avoid the need to poll the $\overline{ACK}$ signal. To program the 8255 for mode 1, Aout, and Bout, use mode word A4.

You may notice that the port C bits are assigned differently in the output configuration. For example, PC_4 and PC_5 are now used for general purpose I/O. The type of hardware configuration must be decided on, and then connected to the appropriate bits in port C.

The last mode is *mode 2: strobed bidirectional I/O*. This mode allows port A to operate as an 8-bit bidirectional bus. This is needed to allow the 8255 to be interfaced with 8-bit peripherals such as UARTS, which require a bidirec-tional data bus. Bits in port C are again used for handshaking and general-purpose I/O, as indicated by Figure 9.14. Port B can operate as an input port or

FIGURE 9.14   Mode 2 operation

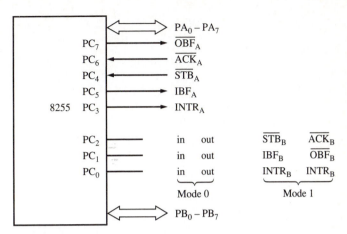

output port in mode 0 or mode 1. When operating port B in mode 0 (with port A in mode 2), PC_0 through PC_2 are available for general purpose I/O. The definitions for PC_0 through PC_2 in mode 1 apply when port B is operated in mode 1 with port A in mode 2.

As before, the INTR output can be used to interrupt the processor, for input or output operations. When the CPU writes data to port A, $\overline{OBF}$ will go low. To enable the output buffer on port A and read the data, $\overline{ACK}$ must be pulled low. Data is written into port A by pulling $\overline{STB}$ low. This will cause IBF to go high until the data is read by the processor.

An 8255 Application

The 8255 in Figure 9.15 is configured for mode 0, port A in, port B out, PC_0 through PC_3 in, and PC_4 through PC_7 out. The 8255 has a base address of 40H. An 8-bit analog-to-digital converter (ADC0804) is connected to ports A and C. Port C is used to control the $\overline{RD}$ and $\overline{WR}$ inputs on the 0804, and to read the end-of-conversion status. The 741 op-amp converts a $+/-$ input voltage swing into a 0-5 volt signal that can be digitized by the 0804. To start a conversion, the 0804's $\overline{WR}$ line must be pulled low. This will force the $\overline{INT}$ output high until the conversion is complete. When $\overline{INT}$ goes low, the 0804 can be read by pulling the $\overline{RD}$ input low and reading port A.

The following subroutine is called to perform a single conversion and return the results in AH:

```
VCON    PROC    FAR
        MOV     AL,80H    ;start a conversion by pulling
        OUT     42H,AL    ;WR low
        MOV     AL,90H    ;now pull WR high
        OUT     42H,AL
EOC:    IN      AL,42H    ;read port C
        AND     AL,1      ;test bit-0 (INT)
        JNZ     EOC       ;wait for end of conversion
        MOV     AL,10H    ;enable RD
```

```
            OUT    42H,AL
            IN     AL,40H      ;read port A (the 0804)
            OUT    41H,AL      ;echo data to port B
            MOV    AH,AL       ;return result in AH
            MOV    AL,90H      ;get RD back to normal
            OUT    42H,AL
            RET
    VCON    ENDP
```

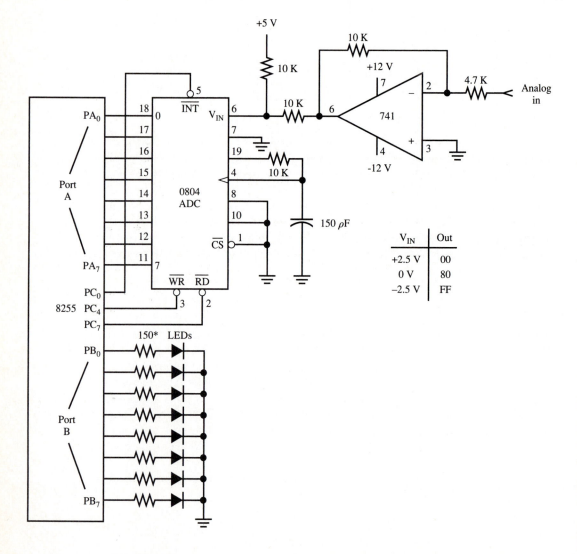

V_{IN}	Out
+2.5 V	00
0 V	80
−2.5 V	FF

* Use 150 in all positions

FIGURE 9.15   8-bit analog-to-digital converter

The data read from the 0804 is sent out to the LEDs on port B. This gives a visual indication that everything is working properly. Being able to split up port C makes the interface with the 0804 easy to accomplish.

The 8255 is configured and initialized in this way:

```
MOV    AL,91H    ;mode 0, Ain, Bout, CLin, CHout
OUT    43H,AL    ;send to control port
MOV    AL,90H    ;RD and WR both high
OUT    42H,AL    ;send to port C
```

A routine to digitize a waveform presented to the analog input would require successive CALLs to VCON, storing AH in a data table each time VCON returns. Once the waveform has been digitized, the data bytes that represent it can be altered and then output to a digital-to-analog converter for playback.

9.8   SERIAL DATA TRANSFER: THE 8251 UART

Serial data transmission offers the convenience of running a small number of wires between two points (three will do the job in most cases), while at the same time being very reliable. Though we must wait longer to receive our data, since it is transmitted only 1 bit at a time, we are able to place our communication devices (computers, terminals, and so on) far away from each other. Worldwide networks now exist, connected via satellites, based on serial data transmission. The peripheral covered in this section, the 8251 UART, implements serial data transmission in a variety of formats. The standard serial data transmission waveform for any UART is depicted in Figure 9.16.

The normal state of the line is a logic 1. This level indicates that no activity is present (that is, no data being transmitted). When the line level falls to a logic 0 (the start bit), the receiving UART knows that a new character is being transmitted. The data bits representing the character (or data) being transmitted are clocked out in the order shown, least significant to most signif-

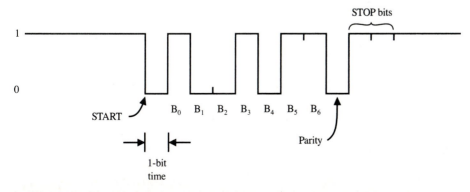

FIGURE 9.16   Standard TTL serial data waveform

icant. Following the data bits is the parity bit, which will be used by the receiving UART to determine the accuracy of the data it received. The parity bit in Figure 9.16 shows that the data has even parity. The last bits in any transmission are the stop bits, which are always high. This gets the line back into its inactive state. We are able to set the number of data bits, the type of parity used, the number of stop bits, and other parameters through software. Before we consider how to do this, let us examine the hardware operation of the 8251.

Interfacing the 8251

The 8251 was originally designed to be used with the 8080 and 8085 microprocessors, 8-bit machines that preceded the 8088. The 8088 interfaces with the 8251 easily, requiring the usual address decoder and a few control signals. Figure 9.17 shows a complete serial data circuit for the 8088. The 8251 is connected to the processor's data bus and $\overline{\text{IORC}}$ and $\overline{\text{IOWC}}$ signals. Since these signals are only active during I/O operations, the address decoder need only examine the state of the address bus. The NAND gate recognizes port addresses 78H and 79H. Address line A_0 is not used in the decoder. Instead, it is connected to the 8251's C/$\overline{\text{D}}$ input. This pin selects internal *control* or *data* registers. So, if A_0 is low (port 78H) and $\overline{\text{IORC}}$ is active, the UART's receive register will be read. If $\overline{\text{IOWC}}$ is active with A_0 low, the UART's transmitter register will be written to and a new transmission started.

The control functions are selected when A_0 is high (port 79H). Reading from port 79H gets one byte of status information; writing to it selects functions such as data size and parity. $\overline{\text{CTS}}$ (*clear to send*) and $\overline{\text{DSR}}$ (*data set ready*) are handshaking signals normally used when the 8251 is connected to a modem. They are grounded to keep them enabled. TxC and RxC are the transmitter and receiver clocks. The frequency of the TTL signal at these inputs determines the bit rate and time of the transmitter and receiver. It is common to run the UART at a clock speed 16 times greater than the baud rate. So, a 2400 baud transmission rate requires a 38.4 kHz clock (multiply 2400 by 16). This frequency and other standard baud rate frequencies are generated automatically by the 14411 baud rate generator. All that is needed is a 1.8432 MHz crystal.

Attempting to transmit a digital (0 to 5 volts) signal over a long length of wire causes distortion in the signal shape due to the line capacitance. It was discovered that making the signal switch from a positive voltage to a *negative* voltage helps to eliminate the distortion. Higher baud rates are possible using the $+/-$ swinging signal. A standard was developed for this type of signal, called the RS232C standard. Take another look at the waveform in Figure 9.16. This is the TTL waveform that comes out of the UART's transmitter. The RS232 waveform that gets transmitted over the wires is inverted and swings plus and minus. So, a high level on the TTL waveform creates a low (negative) level on the RS232C waveform. An integrated circuit capable of performing the RS232C-to-TTL conversions is the MAX232CPE. This chip is especially

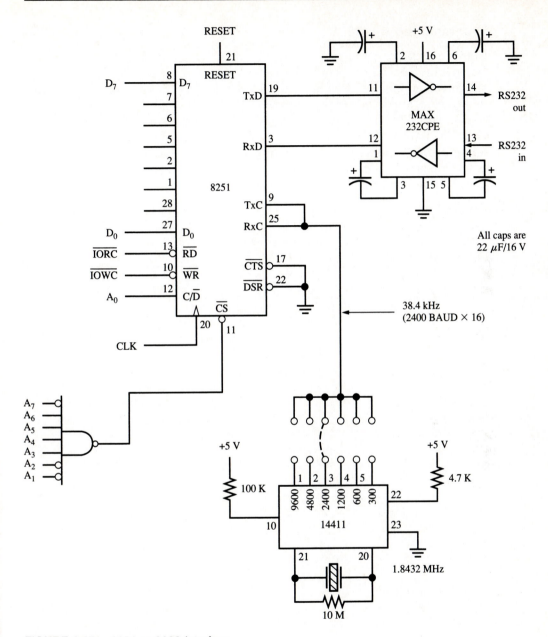

FIGURE 9.17 8251 to 8088 interface

useful because, by adding four 22 μF electrolytic capacitors, the MAX232 generates its own $+/-10$ volt supply while needing only the standard 5 volts. Older chips such as the 1488 line driver and 1489 line receiver required additional external power supplies. The MAX232 has two separate RS232C driver/receivers for systems requiring two serial data channels.

Programming the 8251

Since the 8251 is connected to RESET, we are assured that the 8251 is functional after a power on. It is still necessary to program the 8251, to ensure that the correct number of data bits will be used, that the parity will be generated as expected, and so on. To program the 8251, a series of bytes are output to the control port (79H from our example). The first byte is called the mode instruction. The format of this byte is shown in Figure 9.18. The 8251 can operate in **asynchronous mode** or **synchronous mode.** In asynchronous mode, the baud rate is determined by the lower two bits in the mode instruction. If these two bits are low, synchronous mode is selected.

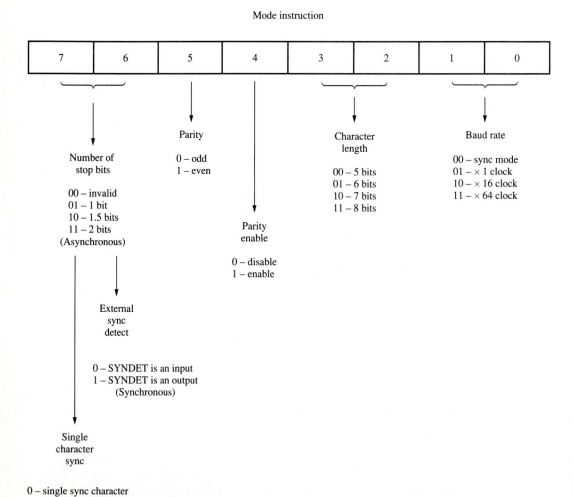

FIGURE 9.18   8251 mode instruction format

The number of data bits used in a transmission is selected by bits 2 and 3. To enable generation of a parity bit, bit 4 must be set. Odd or even parity is chosen by the setting of bit 5. Finally, the number of stop bits is chosen by the upper two bits in the mode instruction. The waveform of Figure 9.16 contained 7 data bits, an even parity bit, and two stop bits. The required mode instruction byte is FA. To program the 8251, use:

```
MOV   AL,OFAH
OUT   79H,AL
```

Since an X16 clock was selected, the 8251 will operate in asynchronous mode. Synchronous mode is used for high-speed data transmission (not usually needed for communication with a serial display terminal). Synchronous mode is selected by making the lower two mode instruction bits zero. In this case, the upper two mode instruction bits do not set the number of stop bits, but rather the number of sync characters transmitted and the function of the SYNDET pin.

A second byte must be output to the control port to complete the initialization of the 8251. This byte is called the *command* instruction. The bits are assigned as shown in Figure 9.19; they have the following meanings:

Bit 0: transmit enable. Enable transmitter when this bit is set.

Bit 1: data terminal ready. Setting this bit will force the $\overline{\text{DTR}}$ output low.

Bit 2: receive enable. Enable receiver when this bit is set.

Bit 3: send break character. Setting this bit forces TxD low.

Bit 4: error reset. Setting this bit clears the PE, OE, and FE error flags.

Bit 5: request to send. Setting this bit forces the $\overline{\text{CTS}}$ output low.

Bit 6: internal reset. To reset the 8251 and prepare for a new mode instruction, this bit must be set.

Bit 7: enter hunt mode. Setting this bit enables a search for SYNC characters (in synchronous mode only).

The command instruction needed to enable the transmitter and receiver and ignore all other functions is 05H. This byte must be output to the control port after the mode instruction. So, to totally initialize the 8251 for operation in the circuit of Figure 9.17, we need these instructions:

Command instruction

7	6	5	4	3	2	1	0
EH	IR	RTS	ER	SBRK	RxE	DTR	TxE

FIGURE 9.19   8251 command instruction format

```
MOV    AL,OFAH        ;mode instruction
OUT    79H,AL
MOV    AL,5           ;command instruction
OUT    79H,AL
```

Once the UART has been programmed we have no need for the control port. Instead, we utilize the 8251's *status* port to help control the way data is transmitted and received. Figure 9.20 shows the bit assignments in the 8251's status port. Particularly important are the TxRDY (*transmitter ready*) and RxRDY (*receiver ready*) flags. They tell us when the transmitter is ready to transmit a new character and when the receiver has received a complete character. A number of error bits are included to show what may have gone wrong with the last reception. PE is parity error, and will go high if the parity of the received character is wrong. OE is overrun error, and will be set if a new character is received before the processor read the last one. FE stands for framing error, and goes high when stop bits are not detected. SYNDET (*sync character detected*) will go high when a sync byte is received in synchronous mode. DSR (*data set ready*) will go high whenever $\overline{\text{DSR}}$ is low.

The programmer must utilize the 8251's status bits in order to ensure proper serial data communication. Figure 9.21 shows how the first two bits are used to implement a simple serial input/output procedure.

Both flowcharts indicate that repeated testing of the RxRDY/TxRDY bits may be necessary. For example, to show the importance of this repeated testing, consider the following case. Suppose that an 8251 is configured to transmit and receive data at 1200 baud, with 7 data bits, odd parity, and 1 stop bit. How long does it take to fully transmit or receive a character? At 1200 baud, the bit time is just over 833 μs, and the selected word length of 10 bits makes the total time to receive or transmit a single character roughly 8.3 ms.

It is not difficult to imagine how many instructions the 8088 might be able to execute in 8.3 ms. Would a few thousand be unreasonable? Probably not. Therefore, we use the status bits to actually slow down the 8088, so that it does not try to send or receive data from the 8251 faster than the 8251 can handle.

The two short routines that follow show how a character input and a character output routine might be written in 8088 code.

Character Input

The character input routine is used to read a character from the receiver, returning it in AL. It is necessary to check the state of RxRDY before reading the receiver.

Status byte

7	6	5	4	3	2	1	0
DSR	SYNDET	FE	OE	PE	TxEMPTY	RxRDY	TxRDY

FIGURE 9.20   8251 status byte

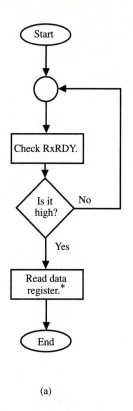

(a)

* This clears RxRDY.

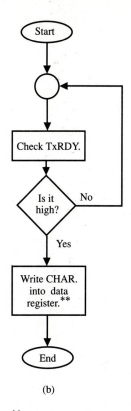

(b)

** This clears TxRDY.

FIGURE 9.21   I/O flowcharts

```
CHARIN      PROC    FAR
RSTAT:      IN      AL,79H      ;read UART status
            AND     AL,02H      ;examine RxRDY
            JNZ     RSTAT       ;wait until receiver is ready
            IN      AL,78H      ;read receiver
            AND     AL,7FH      ;ensure 7-bit ASCII code
            RET
CHARIN      ENDP
```

The data byte received is ANDed with 7F to clear the MSB. Since the UART is being used for character transmission, only a 7-bit ASCII code is required.

Character Output

This routine checks to see if the transmitter is ready for a new character. If it is, the ASCII character stored in AL is output to the transmitter.

```
CHAROUT     PROC    FAR
            MOV     AH,AL       ;save character
TSTAT:      IN      AL,79H      ;read UART status
            AND     AL,1        ;examine TxRDY
```

```
                    JNZ     TSTAT      ;wait until transmitter is ready
                    MOV     AL,AH      ;get character back
                    OUT     78H,AL     ;output to transmitter
                    RET
        CHAROUT     ENDP
```

An 8251 Application

Once the routines to communicate with the UART are in place we can begin using them in applications. A video typewriter requires that a serial display terminal be connected to the UART that is controlled by CHARIN and CHAROUT. The simple programming loop that follows is used to echo every character received (presumably from the keyboard) to the screen. Linefeed characters are inserted when a carriage return is seen.

```
    TVT:    CALL    FAR PTR CHARIN      ;get keyboard character
            CALL    FAR PTR CHAROUT     ;send it to screen
            CMP     AL,0DH              ;carriage return?
            JNZ     TVT
            MOV     AL,0AH              ;output a linefeed character
            CALL    FAR PTR CHAROUT
            JMP     TVT
```

This simple routine can be modified to allow editing and other features, and is left for you to think about on your own.

9.9   SUMMARY

In this chapter we examined the design and operation of input and output ports. We saw that the 8088 has a smaller port addressing space than memory space. Two types of port addresses (and associated I/O instructions) may be used. One set of port addresses are one byte wide, from 00 to FF. The second set of port addresses, which are two bytes in length, range from 0000 to FFFF, and must be placed into register DX before use.

The hardware details of full and partial port address decoders were covered, with examples of actual input and output ports given. These ports were expanded into applications dealing with controlled time delays and waveform generation through a digital-to-analog converter. The programming and interfacing requirements of two I/O-based peripherals, the 8255 PPI and 8251 UART were also covered. Additional peripherals for the 8088 will be covered in the next chapter.

STUDY QUESTIONS

1. Show two ways of reading input port 40H. What instructions are required?
2. Explain the processor bus activity when OUT   20,AL executes. Assume a min-mode system.

3. Design a minmode <u>full port</u> address decoder for input/output port B0. You must generate active-low $\overline{RDB0}$ and $\overline{WRB0}$ signals.

4. Design a minmode full port address decoder for input ports B0 through B7. Eight individual port select outputs should be generated.

5. What changes must be made to the designs of Questions 3 and 4 for a maxmode system?

6. Design a minmode partial address decoder for an output port whose binary address is 10X01X1X11111111, where X is a *don't care* bit. What are all possible port address ranges for this decoder?

7. Use the magnitude comparators of Figure 9.5 to design a partial address decoder with selectable port ranges. The base port address is 1011CCCCCCCC0100, where C represents the 8-bit number matched by the comparators.

8. What is the first selectable port address in Question 7? What is the last? How far apart is each port address (in locations)?

9. What are the decoded port address ranges for each circuit in Figure 9.22?

10. Why are input ports buffered rather than latched?

11. Modify the design of Figure 9.7 so that the port address is 409C.

12. Modify the design of Figure 9.7 so that the port is 16-bits wide (lower 8 at port 9C and upper 8 at 9D).

13. Repeat Questions 11 and 12 for the output port in Figure 9.8.

14. Modify the BINCNT program so that the lower 7 bits of the input port adjust the counting speed, while the most significant bit controls the direction, up or down, of the count.

15. Write a program called KATERPILAR, which will output a sequence of rotating bit patterns to the LEDs of Figure 9.9. The sequence might look like this:

```
XXX-----
-XXX----
--XXX---
---XXX--
----XXX-
-----XXX
```

The sequence should change direction when all LEDs on the right are lit. Use the input port to control the speed of the display.

16. Modify BINCNT and the design of Figure 9.9 to allow a 16-bit counter to be displayed.

17. The data table in the WAVER routine does not have to be 256 bytes long to get decent looking waveforms. What frequency is possible if only 10 bytes are used to generate a waveform? What about 50 or 100 bytes?

18. Write a subroutine called TONES that generates two different frequency square waves and alternates them. TONES should output 100 cycles of the low frequency signal and 50 cycles of the high frequency signal. This should be repeated 10 times before TONES returns. The high frequency signal should have four times the frequency of the low frequency one.

19. Redesign the port address decoder of Figure 9.11 so that port A is at address 8A. What are the other three port addresses?

20. Determine the mode words for each 8255 configuration:

   a) Mode 0, Ain, Bout, Cin
   b) Mode 1, Aout, Bin
   c) Mode 2, Bin (Mode 0)

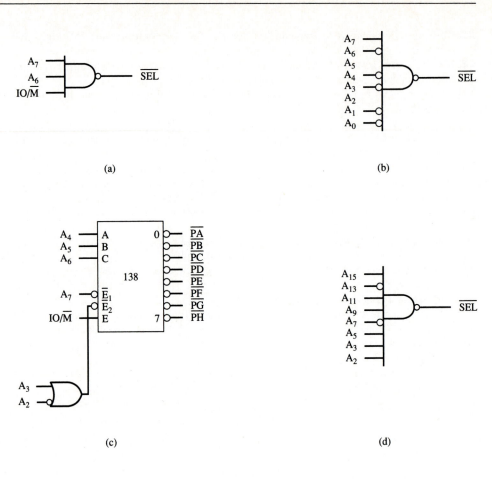

(a)

(b)

(c)

(d)

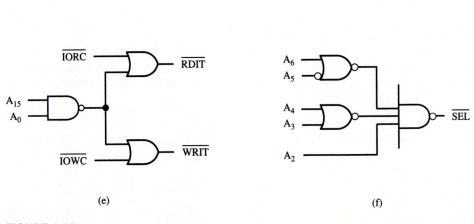

(e)

(f)

FIGURE 9.22

21. Redo the BINCNT program by adapting it for use with an 8255 with a base address of 48H. Assign ports A, B, or C as you like. Draw a schematic of your design.

22. Use the VCON procedure to assist you in writing a subroutine called ONEWAVE, which will do the following:

a) Wait for the analog signal to cross 0 (80H).

b) Read and store samples from VCON until the signal crosses zero twice.

The signal samples should be stored in a data table pointed to by register DI. Do not write more than 1024 samples into the table.

23. Rewrite VCON so that the $\overline{RD}$ input of the 0804 is always zero, and the $\overline{INT}$ output is fed back to the $\overline{WR}$ input. Note that only a software connection will exist between $\overline{INT}$ and $\overline{WR}$.

24. Sketch the 11-bit transmission code for an ASCII "K". Use even parity and two stop bits.

25. How long does the character in Question 24 take to transmit if the BAUD rate is 1200?

26. Use partial address decoding to put the 8251 of Figure 9.17 into port space at address 40H.

27. Show the instructions needed to program the 8251 for:

a) Asynchronous mode, 7 data bits, odd parity, X16 clock, 2 stop bits.

b) Asynchronous mode, 8 data bits, no parity, X1 clock, 1 stop bit.

c) Synchronous mode, 7 data bits per character.

28. Modify the CHARIN and CHAROUT routines so that bit shift/rotate instructions are used in place of AND to check the status.

29. Modify the CHAROUT routine so that any ASCII code between 01 and 1A will be displayed as a two-character sequence. The first character will always be "^". The second character is found by adding 40H to the original character byte. For example, if the character to display is 03H, CHAROUT should output "^C". All other codes should be directly output.

30. Modify the TVT program so that all characters including the carriage return are stored in a buffer pointed to by register BP. The length of the buffer (not to exceed 255 characters) is returned in CL. When carriage return is hit, or when the buffer is full, call the far routine SCANBUFF.

31. Modify the buffered TVT program so that it detects special control characters. The first is the backspace character (ASCII 08H). If a backspace is received, back up one position in the buffer. Next is Control-C (03H). Reset BP to the beginning of the buffer when this character is received. Last is Control-R (12H). This code causes the entire contents of the current buffer to be displayed on a new line.

10

Programming with 8088 Peripherals

Objectives

In this chapter you will learn about:

- Hardware interrupt handling

- Programmable time delays using an interval counter

- Floating-point coprocessor functions

10.1 INTRODUCTION

The power of a microprocessor can be increased by the use of peripherals designed to implement special functions, functions that may be very difficult to implement via software. A good example of this principle would be in the use of a coprocessor. The coprocessor comes equipped with the ability to perform complex mathematical tasks, such as logarithms, exponentials, and trigonometry. The 8088, though powerful, would require extensive programming to implement these functions, and even then would not compute the results with the same speed. Thus, we see that there are times when we have to make a hardware/software trade-off. In this chapter we will concentrate on applications that employ the use of standard peripherals, designed specifically for the 8088. In each case, we will examine the interfacing requirements of the peripheral, and then see how software is used to control it.

You are encouraged to refer to Appendix C as you read the chapter in order to get a more detailed look at each peripheral. Section 10.2 covers the 8259 programmable interrupt controller. Section 10.3 shows how accurate time delays can be generated with the 8254 programmable interval timer. Finally, Section 10.4 explains the operation of the 8087 floating-point coprocessor.

10.2 THE 8259 PROGRAMMABLE INTERRUPT CONTROLLER

We saw in the previous chapter that a microprocessor must be interfaced with an I/O device in order to communicate with the outside world. Software support is required for each I/O device to ensure its proper operation. For example, the receiver status of a UART must be frequently examined to ensure that no received characters are lost. If a loop is used to test the receiver status, the processor may end up spending a great deal of time waiting for the chance to send the next character. While it is doing this it cannot do anything else! An efficient solution to this situation is accomplished by adding an interrupt signal to the processor. Whenever a character is received by the UART, the UART will interrupt the processor. A special interrupt service routine will be used to read the UART and process the new character. When the UART is interfaced in this way, the processor is free to execute other code during the times when the UART has not yet received a character. In this interrupt-driven I/O scheme, the processor only accesses the UART when it has to. This example illustrates the basic differences between **polled** I/O and **interrupt-driven** I/O. For some systems, polling is a good solution. This is especially true when the system is dedicated to doing one task over and over again. When a system is used in a more general way, the processor cannot afford to spend its time constantly polling each I/O device. In this case, interrupts provide a simple way to service all peripherals only when they need the processor's attention.

If we expand the idea of interrupt-driven I/O to an entire system, the number of interrupts required quickly adds up. Separate interrupts may be used for real-time clock/calendars, floppy and hard disk drives, the computer's keyboard, serial and parallel interfaces, video displays, and many other devices. Each device will require its own interrupt handler. The interrupts may also be assigned individual priorities, to ensure that they get serviced in a manner desired by the programmer. How is it possible to utilize this many interrupts on the 8088, which has only two external hardware interrupt inputs (NMI and INTR)? The answer is the 8259 programmable interrupt controller, a special peripheral designed to support 8 levels of prioritized hardware interrupts. The 8259 is considered an I/O device on the system bus, and can be written and read like an I/O port. For systems requiring more than 8 levels of prioritized interrupts, it is possible to cascade 8259s to obtain up to 64 levels of interrupts. The 8259 is configured after power-on through software, and may be reconfigured at any time. The 8259 is designed to interface with the early 8-bit machines (the 8080 and 8085) and also the 16-bit 8088 and 8086. We will only examine its operation with respect to the 8088.

Figure 10.1 shows a simplified block diagram of the 8259. Eight levels of hardware interrupts are provided by inputs IR_0 through IR_7. These eight inputs go directly to the *interrupt request register* (IRR). This register keeps track of what interrupts have requested service. The 8259 can be programmed to allow level-sensitive or edge-sensitive interrupt inputs.

The output of the IRR feeds the *priority resolver,* which selects the highest priority interrupt from those requesting service. For example, if IR_2 and IR_5

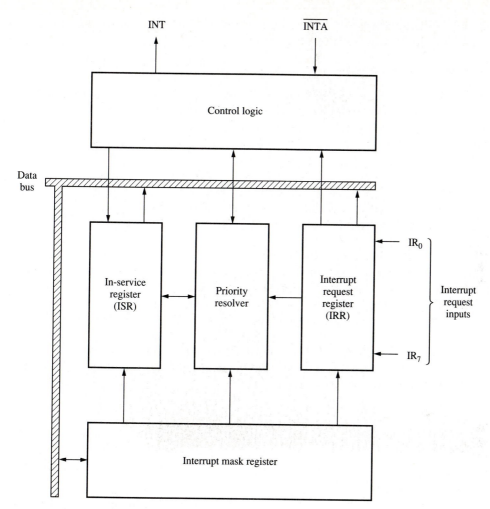

FIGURE 10.1 8259 block diagram

both request service simultaneously, IR_5 will be selected first by the priority resolver.

The output of the priority resolver is used by the *in-service register* (ISR). The ISR indicates which interrupts are being serviced.

All three of these registers communicate with the control logic section, which performs the handshaking with the processor's INTR and $\overline{\text{INTA}}$ signals.

Individual interrupts may be disabled by data written to the *interrupt mask register*. Any combination of interrupts can be disabled (or *masked*) without affecting the priority of the remaining interrupts.

The 8259 can be programmed by writing the appropriate data values to a set of internal registers that are used to control the operation of each of the

8259's functional blocks. Before we see how this is done, let us examine how the 8259 interfaces with the processor.

Interfacing the 8259

The 8259 connects to the system bus like an ordinary I/O device. Figure 10.2 shows an example of the 8259 mapped to I/O ports F8 and F9 in a minmode system. A port-address decoder utilizing an 8-input NAND gate is used to detect port addresses F8 and F9. The processor's A_0 address line connects directly to the 8259 to select internal registers, along with $\overline{RD}$ and $\overline{WR}$. The 8259 takes over the use of the processor's INTR input, which it activates during an interrupt request. Up to eight devices may request an interrupt from the 8259, via interrupt inputs IR_0 through IR_7. These eight lines may be programmed for edge-sensitive or level-sensitive operation, and are prioritized, with IR_7 having the highest priority.

Three cascade lines, CAS_0 through CAS_2, are used to expand the 8259 in a system requiring more than eight levels of interrupts. These signals may be left unconnected when there is a single 8259 in a system. Multiple 8259s require CAS_0 through CAS_2 to be connected in parallel.

Lastly, the $\overline{SP/EN}$ line is used to select master/slave operation in the 8259. When a single 8259 is utilized, it must be operated as a master. This can be selected by placing a 1 on $\overline{SP/EN}$. When two or more 8259s are used, only one 8259 may be a master. The remaining 8259s must be operated as slaves (with $\overline{SP/EN}$ grounded).

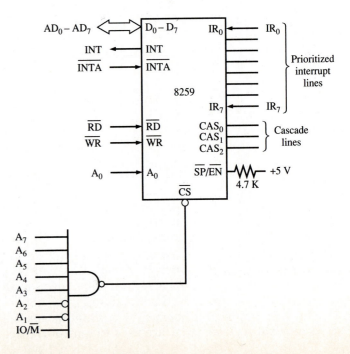

FIGURE 10.2 8259 interfaced to the 8088 in minimum mode

The operation of a properly programmed 8259 is as follows:

1. One or more of the interrupting devices connected to the 8259 request an interrupt by activating the appropriate IR input. The corresponding bit in the IRR is set.
2. The 8259 examines the interrupts requested, and issues an INTR signal to the 8088 for the highest-priority active interrupt input.
3. The processor responds with a pulse on $\overline{\text{INTA}}$.
4. The 8259 sets the bit for the highest priority active interrupt in the in-service register and clears the corresponding bit in the interrupt request register (to remove the request).
5. The 8088 outputs a second pulse on $\overline{\text{INTA}}$ (as it usually does with *any* interrupt caused by INTR).
6. The 8259 outputs an 8-bit interrupt vector number on the data bus. This number is captured by the processor and used to select the corresponding interrupt service routine address from the vector table.

This process illustrates the usefulness of the 8259. Individual vector numbers are assigned to each of the IR inputs connected to a device. When a particular device issues an interrupt request to the 8259, the 8259 sends the corresponding vector number to the processor.

In the next section we will see how a single 8259 is programmed to provide these vector numbers to the CPU.

Programming the 8259

The port-address decoder shown in Figure 10.2 maps the 8259 to ports F8 and F9. These port addresses must be used to access the 8259 during initialization and also during normal operation. It is important to note that the 8259 can be reconfigured whenever necessary by issuing initialization commands to it. This may be useful to some designers who may wish to modify the interrupt mechanism of their system as necessary.

When a single 8259 is used in a system, operating in master mode, it requires two types of control information from the CPU: **initialization command words (ICW)** and **operation command words (OCW)**. Once these words are written to the 8259 it is capable of servicing its eight levels of prioritized interrupts. If more than one 8259 is used, each must be programmed individually.

Initialization is accomplished by sending a sequence of two to four bytes (ICWs) to the 8259. Figure 10.3 shows the makeup of the first ICW. Zeros are inserted in bit positions that control the 8259's operation in an 8085 system (bits 2 and 5-7). For the purposes of this discussion, only the bits that directly affect the operation of the 8259 in an 8088 system are explained.

IC4 (bit 0), when set, indicates that ICW4 must be read during initialization.

7							0
0	0	0	1	LTIM	0	SNGL	IC4

FIGURE 10.3   Initialization command word 1

SNGL (bit 1), when set, indicates that only one 8259 is being used in a system. To allow cascaded 8259s, this bit must be cleared (and ICW3 issued).

LTIM (bit 3), when set, indicates that the 8259 should operate the IR inputs in level-sensitive mode. When LTIM is cleared, the eight IR inputs will be edge-sensitive.

Example 10.1:   What is the interpretation of ICW1 when it contains 1AH?

Solution: The bit pattern produced by 1AH is 00011010. This indicates that both LTIM and SNGL are set, and IC4 is cleared. This will select level-sensitive inputs, inform the 8259 that it is the only interrupt controller in the system, and that ICW4 is not required.

Using the circuit of Figure 10.2 as an example, ICW1 must be output to port F8 (A_0 equals 0) to be properly received. The 8259 recognizes ICW1 by the 1 seen in bit position 4. Reception of this control word also causes the 8259 to perform some internal housekeeping.

Once ICW1 is processed, the 8259 awaits ICW2, which must be output to port F9 (A_0 equals 1). This control word is shown in Figure 10.4, and is used to program the eight interrupt vector numbers that will be associated with the IR inputs. T_3 through T_7 become the five most-significant bits of the vector number supplied by the 8259 during an interrupt acknowledge cycle. The lower three bits are generated by the IR input that has been selected for service. Figure 10.5 shows the makeup of the interrupt vector number. Do you see the relationship between bits 0-2 and the corresponding IR signal? If IR_0 requests service, the vector number generated will contain three 0s in the lower bits. Suppose that ICW2 is issued with the data byte 68. This indicates that T_7 through T_3 are assigned the values 01101. What are the eight possible interrupt vector numbers, using the information from Figure 10.5? IR_7 will create vector number 6F. IR_0 will create vector number 68. Vector numbers 69 through 6E are generated by IR_1 through IR_6, respectively.

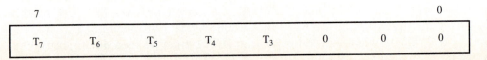

7							0
T_7	T_6	T_5	T_4	T_3	0	0	0

FIGURE 10.4   Initialization command word 2

FIGURE 10.5 Generating the interrupt vector number

Interrupt	Vector number							
	D_7							D_0
IR_7	T_7	T_6	T_5	T_4	T_3	1	1	1
IR_6						1	1	0
IR_5						1	0	1
IR_4						1	0	0
IR_3						0	1	1
IR_2						0	1	0
IR_1						0	0	1
IR_0	T_7	T_6	T_5	T_4	T_3	0	0	0

If a single 8259 is utilized in a system, ICW3 is not needed. For multiple 8259s, ICW3 serves two functions. When an 8259 is used as a master, each bit in ICW3 is used to indicate a slave connected to an IR input. When the 8259 is used as a slave, only the lower three bits of ICW3 are used, and they set the slave's cascade number (0 to 7). Figure 10.6 shows two 8259s connected as master and slave. The INT output on the slave device connects to the IR_6 input on the master device. Thus, any requests on interrupt lines INT_7 through INT_{14} will cause IR_6 to be activated on the master. The master will then examine bit 6 in ICW3 to see if it is set (indicating that a slave is connected to IR_6). If so, it will output the cascade number of the slave (110 in this case) on CAS_0 through CAS_2. These cascade bits are received by the slave device, which examines its ICW3 to see if there is a match. The programmer must have previously programmed 110 into the slave's ICW3. If there is a match between the cascade number and ICW3, the slave device will output the appropriate vector number during the second $\overline{INTA}$ pulse.

To get this scheme to work, the first 8259 must have bit 6 set in its ICW3, and the second 8259 must have the bit pattern 110 in the lower three bits of its ICW3. Both forms of ICW3 are shown in Figure 10.7.

Example 10.2: How many slave devices are required if ICW3 in a master 8259 contains 10010010? What IR inputs are connected to each slave device?

Solution: Since ICW3 contains three 1s, three slave devices are being used. The INT outputs on each slave connect to IR inputs IR_7, IR_4, and IR_1 on the master. Each of the three slaves must have its own ICW3 programmed with a unique cascade code. The three codes are 111 (for IR_7), 100, and 001. All of the slave devices will receive the same cascade code from the master, so using unique codes for each slave will guarantee that only one slave responds during the interrupt acknowledge cycle.

ICW3 must be output to port F9 (A_0 equals 1) to be properly received.

The last initialization command word is ICW4 (also output to port F9). Remember that this word is only needed when bit 0 of ICW1 is set. The format of ICW4 is shown in Figure 10.8. The operation of each bit is as follows:

FIGURE 10.6   Two 8259s
cascaded

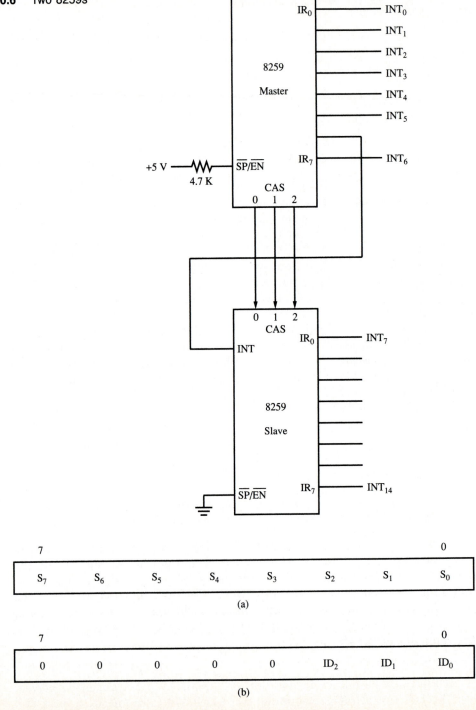

FIGURE 10.7   ICW3 format: (a) master mode, and (b) slave mode

7							0
0	0	0	SFNM	BUF	M/S	AEOI	1

FIGURE 10.8   Format of ICW4

AEOI (bit 1) is used to program automatic end-of-interrupt mode when high. When AEOI mode is set, the 8259 automatically clears the selected bit in the in-service register. When not operated in AEOI mode, the in-service bit must be cleared manually through software.

M/S (bit 2) is used to set the function of the 8259 when operated in buffered mode. If M/S is set, the 8259 will function as a master. If M/S is cleared, the 8259 will function as a slave.

BUF (bit 3), when set, selects buffered mode. When the 8259 operates in buffered mode, the SP/EN pin becomes an output which can be used to control data buffers connected to the 8259's data bus. When BUF is cleared, SP/EN is used as an input to determine the function (master/slave) of the 8259.

SFNM (bit 4), when set, causes the 8259 to operate in special fully-nested mode. This mode is used when multiple 8259s are cascaded. The master must operate in special fully-nested mode to support prioritized interrupts in each of its slave 8259s.

Let us look at an example of how a single 8259 can be programmed.

Example 10.3:   What instructions are needed to program a single 8259 to operate as a master and provide the following features:

1. Edge-sensitive interrupts
2. ICW4 needed
3. A base interrupt vector number of 40H
4. No special fully-nested mode
5. No buffered mode
6. AEOI mode enabled

Solution: First, the data values for each ICW must be determined. To set SNGL and IC4 and clear LTIM, ICW1 must contain 13H. This takes care of conditions 1 and 2. Placing 40H into ICW2 will program the desired base-interrupt vector of condition 3. This will allow generation of interrupt vectors 40H through 47H. Since SNGL will be set in ICW1, there is no need to write to ICW3 during initialization. The remaining three conditions are met by placing 03H into ICW4.

Initialization can be performed by the instructions shown here:

```
MOV    AL,13H
OUT    0F8H,AL      ;output ICW1
```

```
MOV     AL,40H
OUT     0F9H,AL      ;output ICW2
MOV     AL,03H
OUT     0F9H,AL      ;output ICW4
```

A system designed with flexibility in mind may require that the initialization bytes come from a data table placed somewhere in memory. In this case, ICW1's byte could be tested by the initialization routine to see if it needs to output ICW4 (and similar reasoning applies to ICW3).

Once the 8259 has received all of its ICWs, it is ready to begin processing interrupt requests. The exact way the 8259 handles each interrupt is programmed with three OCWs. This information must be output to the 8259 after initialization.

The first OCW is used to mask off selected interrupts by altering the bit pattern in the interrupt mask register. Any of the eight inputs can be disabled by setting its corresponding bit in OCW1.

Example 10.4: What interrupts are disabled by writing 10100001 into OCW1?

Solution: Interrupts IR_7, IR_5, and IR_0 are masked out by this control word. Interrupt requests on these inputs will be ignored until a different pattern is output to OCW1.

The second OCW is illustrated in Figure 10.9. We saw earlier that the AEOI bit in ICW4 is used to enable/disable *AEOI mode*. AEOI mode supports repetitive interrupts of the same priority by automatically resetting bits in the in-service register. It may be desirable for an interrupt service routine to complete before allowing a second interrupt of the same type or level. In this case, AEOI will be set to zero, and the interrupt service routine is responsible for resetting the in-service register bit for a particular interrupt. This can be done by outputting a *specific EOI command* to OCW2. The level of the interrupt being reset must be placed in the lower three bits of OCW2. Other features, such as automatic rotation of the interrupt priorities, can also be selected. When many devices in a system have equal priority, rotating interrupt priorities ensures that all devices get serviced in a round-robin fashion.

The third OCW is used to enable/disable *special mask mode*. Remember that OCW1 allows us to mask off individual interrupts. Normally, when an interrupt of a certain priority is processed by the 8259, the in-service register bit for that interrupt is set. This automatically disables additional interrupts of the same and lower level. For example, an IR_3 request will disable further IR_3 through IR_0 requests. In special mask mode, setting a bit in OCW1 will only disable the associated IR input, leaving the lower priority interrupts enabled.

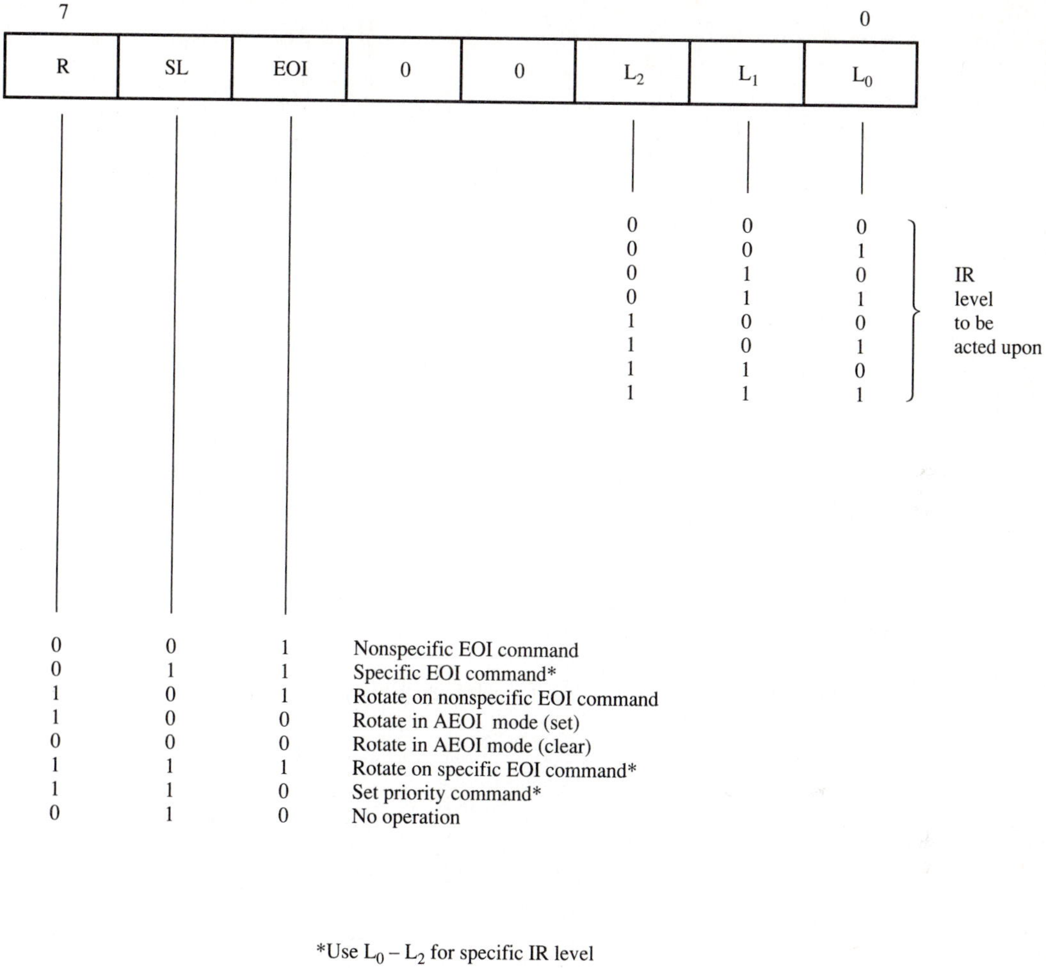

7							0
R	SL	EOI	0	0	L_2	L_1	L_0

0	0	0	
0	0	1	
0	1	0	IR
0	1	1	level
1	0	0	to be
1	0	1	acted upon
1	1	0	
1	1	1	

0	0	1	Nonspecific EOI command
0	1	1	Specific EOI command*
1	0	1	Rotate on nonspecific EOI command
1	0	0	Rotate in AEOI mode (set)
0	0	0	Rotate in AEOI mode (clear)
1	1	1	Rotate on specific EOI command*
1	1	0	Set priority command*
0	1	0	No operation

*Use $L_0 - L_2$ for specific IR level

FIGURE 10.9 Format of OCW2

OCW3 is also used to allow the interrupt request and in-service registers to be read by the processor. This is accomplished by writing the necessary pattern into the lower two bits of OCW3 and then reading port F8 (A_0 equals 0).

A final function of OCW3 is to enable/disable *poll mode*. In this mode the 8259 does not generate interrupt requests on INT. When read, the 8259 will output the level of the highest priority device requesting service on the lower three bits of the data bus.

The format of OCW3 is shown in Figure 10.10.

There are times when many of the special features provided by the 8259 will not be needed. However, the introduction to this device should show you that a very complex interrupt system, expandable to 64 inputs, is possible with a handful of 8259s and port-select logic.

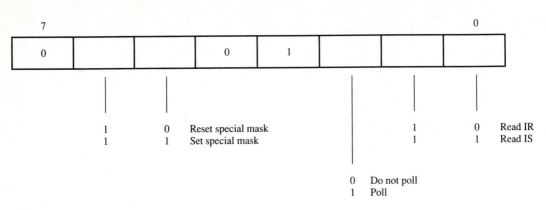

FIGURE 10.10 Format of OCW3

10.3 THE 8254 PROGRAMMABLE INTERVAL TIMER

Many applications require the processor to perform an accurate time delay between a set of operations. For example, a microprocessor might be dedicated to reading a custom keypad or driving a multiplexed display. Both applications require a small time delay between repeated input or output operations. A programmer may decide to use a software delay loop, such as:

```
DELAY:    MOV   CX,4000    ;init delay counter
  WAIT:   LOOP  WAIT       ;LOOP until CX=0
```

The total amount of delay involves 4000 executions of the LOOP instruction. This time can be estimated by multiplying the processor's clock period by the total number of states required to execute the LOOP instructions. This type of delay loop has two main disadvantages. While the loop is executing, the processor is not able to do anything else, such as execute instructions not related to the loop. Also, the time delay becomes inaccurate if the processor is interrupted. For these reasons some designers (and programmers) prefer to do their timing with hardware. Software is used to program the hardware for a specific time delay. At the end of the time delay the processor is interrupted. This frees up the processor for other kinds of execution while the hardware is performing the time delay.

A peripheral designed to implement the type of time delay just described (and many others) is the 8254 programmable interval timer. Figure 10.11 shows the signal groups of the 8254. The 8254 is interfaced through a group of I/O ports. Three internal counters can be programmed in a variety of formats, including, 4-digit BCD or 16-bit binary counting, square-wave generation, and one-shot operation. These formats allow the 8254 to be used for a number of different timing purposes. A short list of these applications includes real-time clocks (and/or calendars), specific time delay generation, frequency synthesis, frequency measurement, and pulse-width modulation.

First let us see how the 8254 is interfaced to the 8088.

FIGURE 10.11   The 8254 programmable interval timer

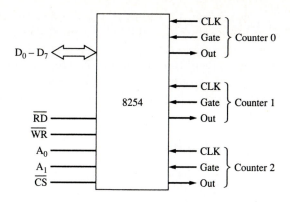

Interfacing the 8254

The port-address decoder needed to connect the 8254 to the processor's address bus is shown in Figure 10.12. Here the 8254 is interfaced with an 8088 operating in maximum mode (indicated by the $\overline{IORC}$ and $\overline{IOWC}$ command signals).

FIGURE 10.12   8254 interfaced to the 8088

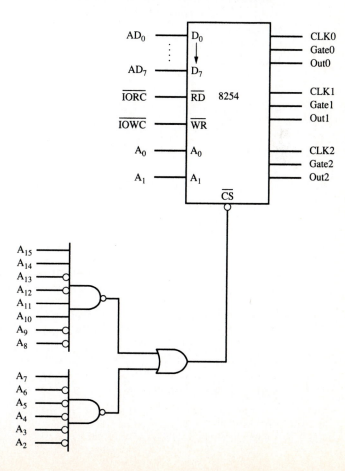

The two 8-input NAND gates in the port-address decoder map the 8254 into four I/O locations, CC80H through CC83. The first port (CC80H) is used to read and write counter 0. The second two ports (CC81H and CC82H) access counters 1 and 2, respectively. The fourth port (CC83H) is used to control the 8254. Each counter contains CLK and GATE inputs, and one output, OUT. Counters may be cascaded by connecting the OUTput of one to the GATE of the other.

Programming the 8254

Each of the 8254's three counters can be programmed and operated independently of the others. This discussion will concentrate on programming and using counter 0 only.

Counter 0 is a 16-bit synchronous down counter that can be preset to a specific count, and decremented to 0 by pulses on the CLK0 input. Counter 0 may operate in any of six different modes (selected with the use of a control word). Each mode supports 4-digit BCD and 16-bit binary counting. Thus, counts may range from 9999 to 0000 BCD or FFFF to 0000 hexadecimal. Programming the counter requires outputting a control word and an initial count to the 8254.

Figure 10.13 shows the bit assignments in the 8254's control word. Two bits (7 and 6) are used to select the counter being programmed. Another two bits (5 and 4) are used to control the way the counter is loaded with a new count. Bits 3, 2, and 1 are used to select one of six modes of operation. The least significant bit is used to select BCD or binary counting.

To begin a counting operation, the control word must be output, followed by the one- or two-byte initial count. The initial count value output to the 8254 goes into a *count register*. The count register is cleared when the counter is programmed (upon reception of the control word), and transferred to the actual down counter after it gets loaded with the one- or two-byte initial count. The counter may be loaded with a new count at any time, without the need for a new control word.

Example 10.5: What instructions are needed to program counter 0 for BCD counting in mode 4. The initial count is 4788.

Solution: Using the port addresses assigned by the hardware in Figure 10.12, it is necessary to output the control word to port CC83H and the initial count to port CC80H. The control word needed to program counter 0 for BCD counting in mode 4 and a 16-bit initial count is 00111001 (39H). This value must be output to the control port. The initial count is represented by hex-pairs 47H and 88H.

The counter is initialized by the following instructions:

```
MOV     DX,0CC83H
MOV     AL,39H
```

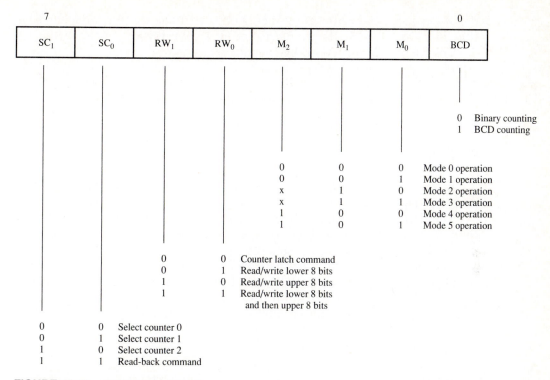

SC₁	SC₀	RW₁	RW₀	M₂	M₁	M₀	BCD

						0	Binary counting
						1	BCD counting

		M₂	M₁	M₀	
		0	0	0	Mode 0 operation
		0	0	1	Mode 1 operation
		x	1	0	Mode 2 operation
		x	1	1	Mode 3 operation
		1	0	0	Mode 4 operation
		1	0	1	Mode 5 operation

RW₁	RW₀	
0	0	Counter latch command
0	1	Read/write lower 8 bits
1	0	Read/write upper 8 bits
1	1	Read/write lower 8 bits and then upper 8 bits

SC₁	SC₀	
0	0	Select counter 0
0	1	Select counter 1
1	0	Select counter 2
1	1	Read-back command

FIGURE 10.13   8254 control word

```
OUT   DX,AL          ;output control word
MOV   DX,0CC80H
MOV   AL,88H
OUT   DX,AL          ;output lower 8 bits
MOV   AL,47H
OUT   DX,AL          ;output upper 8 bits
```

To load a new BCD count at any time, the last five instructions must be repeated.

Some time delays may be very short, but still require the use of the 8254. If the counter value is less than 256 for binary counting (or 100 for BCD counting), then the counter may be programmed by outputting the lower 8 bits only.

Example 10.6:   What control word is needed to program counter 2 for binary counting in mode 1, with an initial count of A0H?

Solution: The control word required is 10010010 (92H). Since the count register is cleared when the counter is programmed, writing A0H to the lower half results in an initial count of 00A0H. Notice that the control word indicates that only the lower 8 bits are needed to load the counter.

The counter is initialized by the following instructions:

```
MOV   DX,0CC83H
MOV   AL,92H
OUT   DX,AL          ;output control word
MOV   DX,0CC82H
MOV   AL,0A0H
OUT   DX,AL          ;output initial count
```

It may be necessary to read the state of a counter while counting is in progress. The 8254 allows this to be done in three different ways.

The first method employs a read from the input port associated with the counter. This technique will not be accurate unless the counter is temporarily paused by stopping the CLK signal or placing a zero on the GATE input.

The second technique uses the 8254's *counter latch command*. This command is selected by clearing bits 5 and 4 in the control word for a particular counter. This causes the 8254 to transfer a copy of the selected count register into an output latch. The output latch can then be read at any time by reading the desired 8254 port.

Example 10.7:   What instructions are needed to latch the count in counter 1 and save it in register BX?

Solution: The control word necessary to latch counter 1 is 01000000 (40H). This must be output to the control port (CC83H). The latched count may then be read from port CC81H.

These instructions will read the count and save it in register BX:

```
MOV   DX,0CC83H
MOV   AL,40H
OUT   DX,AL          ;latch counter 1
MOV   DX,0CC81H
IN    AL,DX          ;read lower byte
MOV   BL,AL          ;save lower byte
IN    AL,DX          ;read upper byte
MOV   BH,AL          ;save upper byte
```

Note that if the software fails to read the latched counter value before a new counter latch command is issued for the same counter, no new latching takes place. The count will remain latched and unchanged until it is read.

The third technique uses a *read-back command* to read the state of a counter. The read-back command is issued by setting bits 7 and 6 in the control word. The remaining bits take on new meanings, as shown in Figure 10.14. Bits 1, 2, and 3 are used to select any combination of counters (from none to all three). Bit 4, $\overline{\text{STATUS}}$, causes the status to be latched for any selected counter.

7							0
1	1	$\overline{\text{COUNT}}$	$\overline{\text{STATUS}}$	CNT_2	CNT_1	CNT_0	0

FIGURE 10.14   8254 read-back command word

Bit 5, $\overline{\text{COUNT}}$, causes the count to be latched in the same fashion. $\overline{\text{STATUS}}$ and $\overline{\text{COUNT}}$ are active low control bits.

Example 10.8:   What control word is needed to latch the count of counters 0 and 2?

Solution: $\overline{\text{COUNT}}$ must be low to latch the count of any counter. CNT0 and CNT2 must be high to select counters 0 and 2. The required control word is 11011010 (DAH). Once this control word is output, counter 0 and counter 2 may be read from ports CC80H and CC82H.

Do you see how a single read-back command can be used to eliminate multiple counter latch commands?

When the read-back command is used to read status information, a one-byte status word is generated for the selected counter. The format of the status word is shown in Figure 10.15. The lower 6 bits indicate the mode and counting scheme currently being used by the counter. NULL COUNT (bit 6) goes low when the new count written to a counter is actually loaded into the counter. This will occur at different times depending on the mode selected. OUTPUT (bit 7) reflects the current state of the OUT signal for the counter. When counters are assigned and programmed dynamically, it is useful to be able to read the operating parameters by latching the status.

Example 10.9:   What instructions are necessary to latch the count and status of counter 1? The status must be returned in AH and the count in BX. If the status byte indicates that BCD counting is being used, return 01 in CL, otherwise return with CL = 00.

Solution: The command word needed to latch the count and status for Counter 1 is 11000100 (C4H). After this byte is output to the control port, the status of counter 1 may be read (from counter 1's input port). Then the two-byte count may be read.

These instructions will read Counter 1's status and count and test for BCD counting:

```
        MOV   DX,0CC83H
        MOV   AL,0C4H
```

7							0
OUTPUT	NULL COUNT	RW_1	RW_0	M_2	M_1	M_0	BCD

FIGURE 10.15   Status word format

```
OUT   DX,AL          ;latch counter 1 data
MOV   DX,0CC81H
IN    AL,DX          ;read status
MOV   AH,AL
IN    AL,DX          ;read lower byte of count
MOV   BL,AL
IN    AL,DX          ;read upper byte of count
MOV   BH,AL
MOV   CL,AH          ;get status back
AND   CL,01H         ;test BCD bit
```

The AND instruction is used to test the BCD bit in the status byte. Other bits may be tested in a similar way, using different bit patterns in the immediate byte of the AND instruction.

The remaining discussion is devoted to an explanation of the six modes of operation possible with the 8254.

Mode 0: Interrupt on Terminal Count   This mode can be used to interrupt the processor after a certain time period has elapsed, or after a number of events have occurred. Its operation is as follows: Initially, the programmer writes the control word specifying mode 0 to the control port of the 8254. This forces the selected counter's OUT signal to go low. Next, the programmer outputs the initial count, which is loaded into the counter during the next falling edge of CLK. Each successive falling edge of CLK will decrement the counter. When the counter gets to 0, OUT will go high. OUT can be used to interrupt the processor (possibly via the 8259 programmable interrupt controller). OUT remains high until a new count (or control word) is issued.

The count can be paused at any time by placing a zero on the GATE input. Bringing GATE high again resumes counting. If a new count value is output while GATE is low, the next falling edge of CLK will still load it into the counter. When a two-byte count is output, the first byte output causes the count to terminate and OUT to immediately go low. The second byte output enables the counter to be loaded on the next falling edge of CLK.

Example 10.10:   Show how the 8254 can be used to generate a time delay of 5 milliseconds. A 1-MHz clock is connected to the CLK input of counter 1.

Solution: Figure 10.16 shows the connections to counter 1's input and output signals. GATE is tied high to enable counting all the time. OUT is con-

FIGURE 10.16 Generating a 5 millisecond delay with the 8254

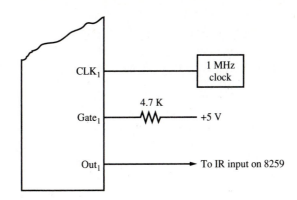

nected to an IR input on the 8259 programmable interrupt controller. Assuming the IR inputs are edge sensitive, when OUT goes high at the end of the count, an interrupt will be generated. The trick is to get OUT to go high 5 milliseconds after we start the counter. The period of the 1-MHz clock is 1 μs. Dividing 5 ms by 1 μs gives 5000, the number of CLK pulses required to get a 5-ms delay. Since one of these CLK pulses will be used to load the counter, the initial counter value must be 4999. Thus, the counter can operate in binary or BCD mode.

These instructions can be used to implement the 5-ms time delay in mode 0, with BCD counting:

```
MOV     DX,0CC83H
MOV     AL,71H
OUT     DX,AL           ;counter 1, mode 0, BCD
MOV     DX,0CC81H
MOV     AL,99H
OUT     DX,AL           ;lower byte of count
MOV     AL,49H
OUT     DX,AL           ;upper byte of count
```

In general, a count of N requires N + 1 CLK pulses to complete. One CLK pulse is used to load the counter and N are used to count it down to zero. Also note that an initial BCD count of 0000 will require 10,000 CLK pulses to count down to 0000, and an initial binary count of 0000 will require 65,536!

Mode 1: Hardware Retriggerable One-shot In this mode, the 8254 is programmed to output a low-level pulse on OUT for a predetermined length of time. The length of the pulse is obtained by multiplying the CLK period by the initial count value. OUT goes high when the control word is written.

The 8254 is triggered by transitions on GATE, and may be retriggered during counting by a high-going pulse on GATE. Triggering the counter causes OUT to go low while the counter decrements to 0.

Example 10.11: Counter 2 is to be programmed to generate a 63 μs pulse when triggered. A 1-MHz clock is connected to CLK. What instructions are needed to use counter 2 as a one-shot?

Solution: The control word for counter 2 must select mode 1, BCD or binary counting, and a load method. Since only 63 CLK pulses will be required for the one-shot pulse, we can get by without having to output a two-byte count. Only the lower byte value (63 for binary counting, 63H for BCD counting) need be output.

The required instructions are:

```
MOV    DX,0CC83H
MOV    AL,92H
OUT    DX,AL          ;counter 2, mode 1, binary counting
MOV    DX,0CC82H
MOV    AL,63
OUT    DX,AL          ;output lower byte of count
```

Mode 2: Rate Generator   This mode of operation is designed to be *periodic*. Instead of generating a single pulse on OUT, this mode generates a pulse on OUT every N CLK cycles. Thus, the *rate* of output pulses depends on the CLK frequency and the initial count value N. Mode 2 really simulates a modulo-N counter. A zero on the GATE input can be used to suspend counting.

OUT goes high when the control word is written and remains high until the counter decrements to 1. OUT then goes low for one CLK pulse and the counter is reloaded with the initial count. OUT goes high again at the beginning of the next counting cycle.

Example 10.12:   A programmer needs to generate a waveform that goes high once every 7 CLK0 cycles. What instructions are required? What does the timing diagram for CLK0 and OUT0 look like? How is the waveform generated?

Solution: Counter 0 must be programmed for mode 2 counting in either binary or BCD. If binary counting is used, these instructions will create the required pulses on OUT0:

```
MOV    DX,0CC83H
MOV    AL,14H
OUT    DX,AL          ;counter 0, mode 2, binary counting
MOV    DX,0CC80H
MOV    AL,7
OUT    DX,AL          ;lower byte of count
```

Mode 2 operation will cause OUT0 to go low once every 7 CLK pulses. An inverter must be used to get the desired output waveform. Figure 10.17 shows the circuit diagram and waveforms for the modulo-7 counter.

FIGURE 10.17   Modulo-7
counter: (a) circuit diagram, and
(b) timing diagram

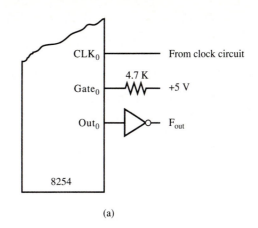

(a)

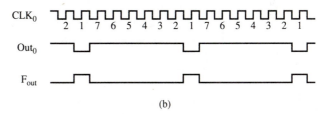

(b)

Since the counters are limited to 16-bit values (either FFFFH or 9999 BCD), what options are available to the programmer that needs to divide by 250,000, or count groups of 10,000 pulses? These kinds of numbers require counters with more bits than those available in the 8254. One simple way to solve this problem is to *cascade two or more counters*. Cascading two counters can result in binary counts of over 4 billion (and BCD counts of up to 100 million). Cascading counters that are operating in different modes can lead to the creation of some interesting and complex waveforms.

Example 10.13:   A 2-MHz clock is available for timing in a system that needs to be interrupted once every 4 seconds. How can two counters be cascaded to obtain this interrupt rate?

Solution: Figure 10.18 shows how counters 0 and 1 are connected to implement the 0.25-Hz interrupt clock. The 2-MHz clock connected to CLK0 will create output pulses on OUT0 when counter 0 is programmed in mode 2. These output pulses serve as the clock for counter 1 (also programmed in mode 2). Dividing 2-MHz by 0.25-Hz gives 8,000,000! This is the count that must be simulated by both counters. Many different counting schemes are possible. Once scheme requires that counter 0 be loaded with 50,000 and counter 1 with

FIGURE 10.18 Cascading two 8254 counters

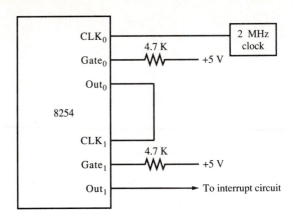

160. Note that the product of these two numbers is 8,000,000. Counter 0 will output one pulse for every 50,000 CLK0 pulses. Counter 1 will output one pulse for every 160 CLK1 pulses.

The instructions needed for this interrupt timing circuit are:

```
        MOV     DX,0CC83H
        MOV     AL,34H
        OUT     DX,AL          ;counter 0, mode 2, binary counting
        MOV     AL,54H
        OUT     DX,AL          ;counter 1, mode 2, binary counting
        MOV     DX,0CC80H
        MOV     AX,50000
        OUT     DX,AL          ;output lower byte of count-0
        MOV     AL,AH
        OUT     DX,AL          ;output upper byte of count-0
        INC     DX             ;point to counter 1
        MOV     AL,160
        OUT     DX,AL          ;output lower byte of count-1
```

Note the order of the OUT instructions. It is possible to output all control words before sending any counter values. This leads to simpler code and some reuse of registers.

Mode 3: Square Wave Mode   When a 50 percent duty cycle is required in a timing circuit, mode 3 can be used. The operation of mode 3 is similar to mode 2's rate generation in that it is also periodic. The difference lies in the use of the counter.

When the counter is loaded, the 8254 operating in this mode will decrement it by two every CLK pulse. When the counter gets to zero, OUT will change state and the counter will be reloaded. The counter will decrement by two again for each CLK pulse. When it reaches zero a second time, OUT will go back to its original high state. Thus, one complete cycle at OUT requires N clock pulses: N/2 pulses for the first countdown and N/2 pulses for the second.

When N is an odd number, OUT will be high for (N + 1)/2 CLK pulses and low for (N − 1)/2 CLK pulses.

As always, a low on GATE will disable counting.

Example 10.14:   The CLK2 input of the 8254 is connected to a 2.4576-MHz clock (a standard baud-rate generation frequency). OUT2 will be used to drive the transmitter and receiver clock inputs of a UART operating at 2400 baud with an X16 clock. How must counter 2 be programmed to operate the UART correctly?

Solution: A UART operating at 2400 baud with an X16 clock requires transmitter and receiver clocks of 38.4-kHz. Dividing 2.4576-MHz by 38.4-kHz gives 64. If counter 2 is programmed for mode 3 with an initial count of 64 the correct frequency will be generated.

The instructions for this application are:

```
MOV   DX,0CC83H
MOV   AL,97H
OUT   DX,AL      ;counter 2, mode 3, BCD counting
DEC   DX         ;point to counter 2
MOV   AL,64H
OUT   DX,AL      ;output lower byte of count
```

Mode 4: Software Triggered Strobe   In this mode of operation, the 8254 generates a low-going pulse on OUT (lasting one CLK pulse) when the counter has decremented to zero. OUT will go low N + 1 CLK pulses after the initial count has been written. The extra CLK pulse is needed to load the counter. Only one pulse will be generated on OUT. To get additional pulses, the counter must be reloaded by outputting the initial count value again.

Example 10.15:   A 500-kHz clock is connected to CLK1. The initial count written to counter 1 is 40. How much time expires before OUT1 goes low? How long does OUT1 remain low?

Solution: Counter 1 will be loaded with 40 on the first CLK pulse and decremented to zero over the next 40 pulses. It will take a total of 41 CLK pulses of time before OUT1 goes low. This corresponds to 82 μs of time. Since OUT1 will remain low for only one CLK period, its duration is 2 μs.

Mode 5: Hardware Triggered Strobe   This final mode provides the ability for a hardware generated timing pulse. After writing the control word and initial count, OUT will go high. A rising edge on GATE will trigger the 8254 and begin the countdown sequence (after one CLK pulse has been used to load the initial count into the counter). When the counter gets to zero (after N + 1 CLK pulses) OUT will go low for one CLK pulse.

A rising edge on GATE during counting will cause the 8254 to retrigger and begin a new counting sequence (that requires an additional N + 1 pulses to complete).

Example 10.16: An 8254 will be used to generate a strobe pulse on OUT0 50 CLK cycles after it is triggered by GATE. What instructions are needed to implement this timing need?

Solution: Counter 0 in the 8254 must be programmed for mode 5, and either BCD or binary counting. Since the strobe cannot be issued for 50 CLK cycles, it is necessary to use 49 as the initial count.

These instructions will program counter 0:

```
MOV    DX,0CC83H
MOV    AL,1AH
OUT    DX,AL        ;counter 0, mode 5, binary counting
MOV    DX,0CC80H
MOV    AL,49
OUT    DX,AL        ;output lower byte of count
```

These six modes of operation provide the programmer (or system designer) with many ways of generating timing pulses, delays, and waveforms. Spend a few moments writing down additional timing applications for the 8254. What modes are needed to implement your applications? What is possible with two or more 8254s?

10.4   THE 8087 FLOATING-POINT COPROCESSOR

Coprocessors have been mentioned numerous times throughout this text. A coprocessor is used to enhance the power of its host processor, which, by design, does not include an extensive set of instructions capable of handling floating-point numbers. A floating-point number (defined by the **IEEE Standard for Floating Point Arithmetic,** and utilized by the 8087), consists of up to 64 bits of mantissa, a sign bit, and a 15-bit exponent. This 80-bit number does not fit into any of the 8088's registers (which are only 16 bits wide). For this reason the 8087 contains a set of eight internal floating-point registers. The registers are organized into a stack, with ST(0) referring to the register on top of the stack, and ST(7) to the register on the bottom. Figure 10.19 shows this organization. When data is read in from memory it is *pushed* onto the register stack. Thus, ST(7) becomes ST(6), ST(6) becomes ST(5), and so on, with ST(0) getting replaced by the data from memory. Data written to memory is *popped* off the register stack.

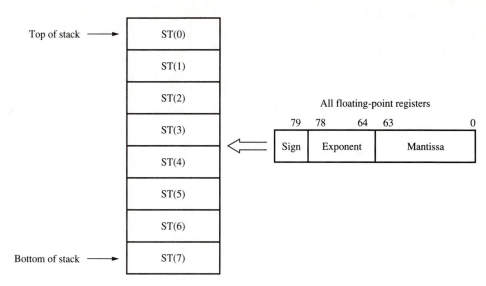

FIGURE 10.19   Floating-point register and stack organization in the 8087

The 8087 contains many instructions for manipulating data on the stack. These instructions include the standard add, subtract, multiply, and divide operations (but now with 80-bit precision), as well as logarithms, power functions, square root, loading useful constants such as pi, and others. The sheer size of the floating-point registers gives the 8087 a much higher degree of computational ability over the 8088. Computations are performed quickly, since the 8087 was specifically designed for floating-point number crunching.

We will examine the instruction set of the 8087, and a few programming examples, after we look at how the 8087 communicates with the 8088.

Interfacing the 8087

The 8087 is not interfaced the same as the other peripherals we have examined in this (and earlier) chapters. No port-address decoder is used to enable the 8087. Instead, the 8087 operates in parallel with the 8088, sharing access to the address and data busses, and using a handful of signals for control purposes.

Figure 10.20 shows the connections between the 8088 and the 8087. Note that the 8088 must be operated in maximum mode. This allows the 8087 to use $\overline{RQ/GT0}$ to initiate a DMA operation. DMA is needed to enable the 8087 to access system memory.

When coprocessor instructions are encountered on the data bus, the 8087 will capture them and initiate processing. Since they are not part of the 8088's instruction set, the processor will ignore them, and proceed with a fetch of the next instruction from memory. If it is necessary to pause the 8088 while the 8087 performs a computation, an FWAIT instruction (floating-point WAIT)

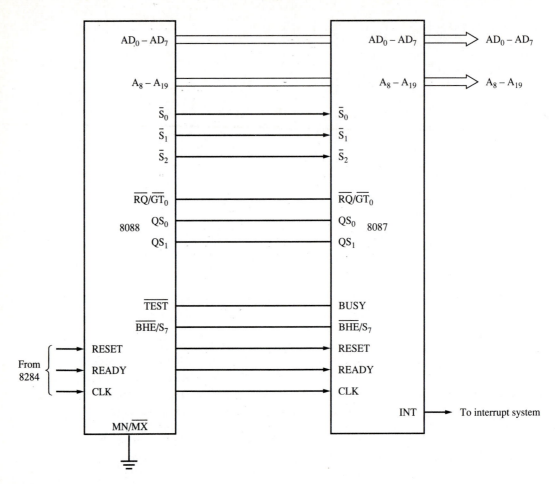

FIGURE 10.20   Connecting the 8087 to the 8088

must be used. This instruction causes the processor to examine the level of its TEST input. The 8088 will enter a wait state if TEST is high and remain there until TEST goes low. TEST is controlled by the BUSY output of the 8087. If the 8087 is in the middle of a computation, BUSY will be high, which makes TEST high. An FWAIT instruction will then force the processor into a wait state until the 8087 completes execution.

The 8087 may encounter an unexpected result during computation (such as divide by zero, overflow, or precision errors) and generate an interrupt. The INT output must be connected to the systems interrupt circuitry (or directly to INTR if available).

With its shared address and data busses, the 8087 is capable of directly accessing memory to read and write floating-point operands. All that is needed is a set of coprocessor instructions.

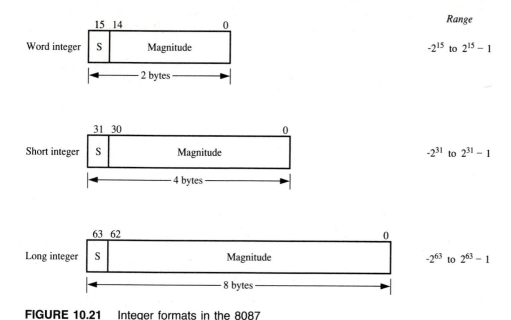

FIGURE 10.21   Integer formats in the 8087

8087 Data Types

The 8087 implements over 70 different types of floating-point operations on a wide variety of data types. Let us first examine the 8087's data organization, and then proceed to coverage of the instruction set.

Seven different data types are available with the 8087. Three of these deal exclusively with positive and negative integers. An integer may be coded as a *word* integer, a *short* integer, or a *long* integer. Word integers are 16 bits long, with the MSB acting as a sign bit. Two's complement notation is used for storage of negative integers.

Short integers are 32 bits long (with the MSB as sign bit) and long integers occupy 64 bits. All bits except the MSB are used to represent the magnitude of the integer. This leads to three different ranges of integers. Figure 10.21 shows the format of the three integer data types, and their ranges. Integers can be defined within a source file by using certain assembler directives. The assembler will code numbers in the operand field into the format used by the 8087.

Example 10.17:   The six source lines shown here indicate how the assembler converts decimal numbers into the three integer formats used by the 8087.

```
                              .8087
    03 E8                  WORDINT     DW     1000
    FC 18                              DW     −1000
    C0 CF 6A 00            SHORTINT    DD     7000000
```

```
40 30 95 FF                            DD    −7000000
00 2E 88 DE 6A 00 00 00   LONGINT      DQ    459000000000
00 D2 77 21 95 FF FF FF                DQ    −459000000000
```

The DW directive is used for word integers, and generates 2 bytes. The DD (define double) and DQ (define quad) directives generate 4 and 8 bytes, respectively. Note the change in the last byte for each group of numbers when the "−" sign is used.

The .8087 assembler directive instructs the assembler to use the IEEE Standard for Floating-Point Numbers when doing a conversion. Without the .8087, the assembler will convert the numbers into a different binary format, which is incompatible with the 8087 coprocessor.

The next data type is *packed BCD*. In this format 10 bytes are used to represent a BCD number. Nine bytes are used to store the magnitude, with each byte holding two BCD digits. The last byte contains only the sign bit. Figure 10.22 shows the organization of this data type. The packed BCD number really represents an integer, with a range roughly equivalent to that of the long integer format.

Example 10.18:   The packed decimal numbers shown here were created by the assembler in response to the DT (define tens) directive.

```
                                 .8087
90 78 56 34 12 00 00 00 00 00    PACKBCD   DT    1234567890
90 78 56 34 12 00 00 00 00 80              DT    −1234567890
```

The effect of the minus sign in the second number is easy to spot by examining the most significant byte of both numbers. Also, the packed decimal numbers are left justified within the 10-byte data area. Familiarity with the format of any data type aids in interpreting its value.

Two data types are devoted to the use of *real* numbers. *Short* real format uses a 32-bit data block composed of 23 magnitude bits, 8 exponent bits, and one sign bit. *Long* real numbers use a 64-bit format composed of 52 magnitude bits, 11 exponent bits, and one sign bit. Both formats are shown in Figure

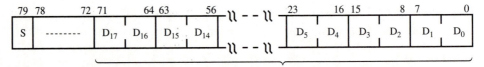

An 18-digit integer

FIGURE 10.22   Packed BCD format

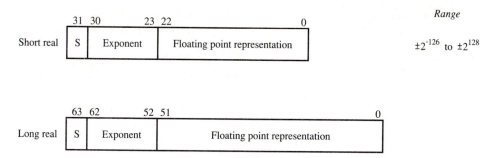

FIGURE 10.23 Short- and long-real formats

10.23. A brief introduction to floating-point numbers is needed to fully understand these two new formats.

Figure 10.24 gives a general equation for the definition and representation of a short-real binary number. The first part of the equation generates the sign of the number. A positive number is generated when the sign bit is zero. Negative numbers require the sign bit to be set.

The exponent part of the number is used as a multiplier for the fractional part. The E-127 term moves the decimal point in the fraction to the left (making the number smaller) or to the right (making the number larger) a certain number of places. The E variable is controlled by the 8 exponent bits, which are interpreted as an unsigned number in the range 0 to 255. This gives an exponent range for the short-real format of -126 to $+128$.

The fraction represents the *normalized* binary equivalent of the decimal number. Normalization is a process that converts any binary number into standard format by adjusting the exponent of the number until the mantissa is in the form 1.F. For example, 1010.1111 becomes 1.0101111 with a power-of-2 exponent of 3. Similarly, 0.000011011 becomes 1.1011 with an exponent of -5. Since every number will begin with 1, it is only necessary to store the F part of the number. In the short-real format, F is 23-bits wide. Thus, a 24-bit number is actually represented via normalization.

FIGURE 10.24 Equation for short-real format representation

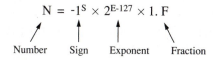

$$N = -1^S \times 2^{E-127} \times 1.\,F$$

Number Sign Exponent Fraction

Example 10.19: What are the steps involved in converting 209.8125 into the normalized short-real format?

Solution: The first step is to convert 209.8125 into binary. This gives a result of 11010001.1101.

Next, the binary result is normalized by shifting the decimal point 7 places to the left. This gives a normalized result of 1.10100011101, with an exponent of +7. Since 23 bits are used to represent the fraction, we end up with a fraction of 10100011101000000000000. Note that the leading 1 (which is always there) is not stored.

The third step creates the required exponent bits by adding 127 to the exponent obtained during normalization (+7). The result is 134, or 10000110.

The final step clears the sign bit so that it represents a positive number. Putting all 32 bits together gives 01000011 01010001 11010000 00000000, or 43 51 D0 00. Checking our conversion with the assembler gives:

```
                        .8087
    00 D0 51 43    SHORTREAL    DD    209.8125
```

You will notice that the assembler swaps the order of the bytes.

The same technique that was used in Example 10.19 will work on long-real formats, the only differences being the number of bits used to represent the exponent (11) and the fraction (52). Exponents are generated by adding 1023 to the exponent found during normalization.

A number stored in short- or long-real format can be converted back into decimal by reversing the steps outlined in Example 10.19. This can be done without much difficulty in software, and you are encouraged to think about how the conversion could be accomplished. Example 10.20 may give you some ideas.

Example 10.20: Convert the DD short-real result 00 57 5A C5 into its decimal equivalent.

Solution: First, reverse the four data bytes so that they are in MSB to LSB order. This gives C5 5A 57 00. In binary, we have 11000101 01011010 01010111 00000000.

Grouping the data bits into sign, exponent, and fraction bits gives 1 10001010 10110100101011100000000. The 1 in the sign bit indicates a negative result. The 8-bit pattern in the exponent evaluates to 138. To get the exponent of the normalized fraction, we subtract 127. This gives a normalized exponent of 11. The decimal point in the fraction must be moved 11 places to the right.

The fraction (with the leading 1 added) is 1.10110100101011100000000. Multiplying by the normalized exponent results in 110110100101.0111 (with trailing 0s left off). Converting the integer and fractional parts into decimal (and multiplying by −1) gives −3493.4375.

None of the above steps require an extensive amount of software, with rotate or shift instructions most likely implementing the conversion within the fraction.

The final data type is called *temporary real;* it is not a data type that can be specified by the programmer. However, all numbers within the 8087 are converted to temporary real format to provide accuracy during computations. The temporary real format allows 15 bits for the exponent and 64 bits for the mantissa (including the leading 1). Including the sign bit results in an 80-bit storage format. The 8087 converts from temporary real to one of the other specific data types when storing results in memory.

The instruction set of the 8087 consists of a number of functional groups. These groups are comprised of the data transfer, arithmetic, compare, transcendental, constant, and processor control instructions. Each group will be introduced briefly. You are encouraged to refer to the peripheral data sheets of the 8087 for more details.

8087 Instructions

A wide variety of instructions are available with the 8087. When interfaced to the 8088, a powerful instruction set is created, eliminating the need for extensive software subroutines. Let us take a brief look at the different groups of instructions utilized by the 8087.

Data Transfer Instructions   These instructions are used to move data around inside the 8087, and between the 8087 and system memory.

Source and destination operands are not required on many of the 8087's instructions. When no operands are explicitly included in an instruction, the 8087 will use the number (or numbers) located on the top of its floating-point stack. Results are written back onto the stack, or into memory. Calculations involving repeated loops are best written in a way that uses the stack, to avoid endless delays due to the access time of the system memory.

Source and destination operands are indicated by <src> and <dst>, respectively.

The data transfer instructions are:

```
FLD      <src>      ;load real
FILD     <src>      ;load integer
FBLD     <src>      ;load BCD
FST      <dst>      ;store real
FIST     <dst>      ;store integer
FBSTP    <dst>      ;store BCD and pop
FSTP     <dst>      ;store real and pop
FISTP    <dst>      ;store integer and pop
FXCH     <dst>      ;exchange registers
```

Note that all floating-point instructions begin with F. This helps to differentiate them from processor (8088) instructions.

Arithmetic Instructions   The arithmetic instructions are designed to perform a wide variety of computations on all of the data types supported by the 8087. The hardware performing the operations produces results much faster than an

8088 program could. This computation speed-up is a great advantage for an 8088 interfaced with the 8087.

The arithmetic instructions are:

```
FADD     <dst>,<src>      ;add real
FADDP    <dst>,<src>      ;add real and pop
FIADD    <src>            ;add integer
FSUB     <dst>,<src>      ;subtract real
FSUBP    <dst>,<src>      ;subtract real and pop
FSUBR    <dst>,<src>      ;subtract real reversed
FSUBRP   <dst>,<src>      ;subtract real reversed and pop
FISUB    <src>            ;subtract integer
FISUBR   <src>            ;subtract integer reversed
FMUL     <dst>,<src>      ;multiply real
FMULP    <dst>,<src>      ;multiply real and pop
FIMUL    <src>            ;multiply integer
FDIV     <dst>,<src>      ;divide real
FDIVP    <dst>,<src>      ;divide real and pop
FDIVR    <dst>,<src>      ;divide real reversed
FDIVRP   <dst>,<src>      ;divide real reversed and pop
FIDIV    <src>            ;divide integer
FIDIVR   <src>            ;divide integer reversed
FABS                      ;absolute value
FCHS                      ;change sign
FPREM                     ;partial remainder
FRNDINT                   ;round to integer
FSCALE                    ;scale
FSQRT                     ;square root
FXTRACT                   ;extract exponent and fraction
```

Some instructions (like FSQRT and FABS) require no operands, and will perform their indicated operation on the number stored on top of the stack. The programming applications that follow will utilize some of these mathematical operations, and show their various operand forms.

Compare Instructions   It is useful during a computation to be able to check the results before continuing on to a new set of calculations. The compare instructions allow the programmer to examine the value of the number stored on top of the stack. The compare instructions affect flags stored in the 8087's *status register*. The status register is 16 bits wide, and contains a number of flags and status indicators. One bit indicates that division by zero has occurred. Another is set when an exponent overflow is detected. A programmer can look for these conditions by testing specific bits within the status register.

The compare instructions are:

```
FCOM     <src>      ;compare real
FCOMP    <src>      ;compare real and pop
FCOMPP              ;compare real and pop twice
FICOM    <src>      ;compare integer
FICOMP   <src>      ;compare integer and pop
FTST               ;test top of stack (compare with 0.0)
FXAM               ;examine top of stack
```

Transcendental Instructions   The transcendental instructions use the two numbers stored on top of the stack (the first and second stack elements) and write their results back onto the stack. These instructions can be combined with the arithmetic instructions to form other functions that are not implemented on the 8087.

The transcendental instructions are:

```
F2XM1      ;calculate 2^X - 1
FPATAN     ;partial arctangent
FPTAN      ;partial tangent
FYL2X      ;calculate Y * log2(X)
FYL2XP1    ;calculate Y * log2(X + 1)
```

The "partial" term in FPATAN and FPTAN indicates that the tangent only operates over the range of angles from 0 to 45 degrees.

Constant Instructions   The constant instructions are used to load the top of the stack with a commonly used number. This helps to speed up execution of routines that would otherwise have to store the constants in memory. All constants are stored with the temporary real format.

The constant instructions are:

```
FLDZ       ;load 0.0
FLD1       ;load 1.0
FLDPI      ;load PI (3.14159...)
FLDL2E     ;load log2(E) where E=2.7182818...
FLDL2T     ;load log2(10)
FLDLG2     ;load log10(2)
FLDLN2     ;load logE(2)
```

Note that some constants are useful for conversion between base-10 and base-2, and also between base-E and base 2.

Processor Control Instructions   These instructions are useful for controlling the operation of the 8087. Access to the status and control register is provided, and programmer control of interrupts, error flags, and the 8087's internal environment is also available.

The processor control instructions are:

```
FINIT                ;reset the 8087
FDISI                ;disable interrupts
FENI                 ;enable interrupts
FCLEX                ;clear error flags
FINCSTP              ;increment stack pointer
FDECSTP              ;decrement stack pointer
FSTSW    <dst>       ;store status register
FSTCW    <dst>       ;store control register
FLDCW    <src>       ;load control register
FSTENV   <dst>       ;store environment
FLDENV   <src>       ;load environment
FSAVE    <dst>       ;save state
FRSTOR   <src>       ;restore state
FFREE    <dst>       ;free register
FNOP                 ;no operation
```

8087 Programming Applications

The brief introduction to the 8087's instruction set should not prevent us from examining some simple programming applications. The two applications that follow will show the usage and form of a number of different coprocessor instructions. Remember that these floating-point instructions would need to be implemented in software, through time-consuming subroutines, if the 8087 were not available.

Example 10.21: The floating-point instructions in this example are used to calculate the standard deviation of a group of samples. There are n samples in the group, and they are saved in memory beginning at SAMPLES. The following equation will be used to compute the standard deviation (assuming that n is larger than 10):

$$\text{S.D.} = \sqrt{\frac{1}{n}\sum_{i=1}^{n} (X_i - \overline{X})^2}$$

where n = the number of samples
$\overline{X}$ = the average of the samples

First the average ($\overline{X}$) will be computed, since this is needed during the calculations. The final result (the standard deviation) is found in SDRES.

```
        SAMPLES   DD      ?               ;samples are stored in short-real
                                          ;format (4-byte numbers)

                  .
                  .
                  DD      ?
        N         DB      ?               ;the number of samples goes here
        XAVE      DD      ?               ;floating-point average
        TEMP1     DD      ?
        TEMP2     DD      ?
        SDRES     DD      ?               ;floating-point result
                  .
                  .
        FINDSD:   LEA     BP,SAMPLES      ;init pointer to data
                  MOV     SI,0
                  MOV     BL,N            ;init loop counter
                  FINIT                   ;reset 8087
                  FLDZ                    ;clear top of stack
        SRADD:    FADD    [BP][SI]        ;add sample to total
                  ADD     SI,4            ;point to next sample
                  DEC     BL              ;repeat for all samples
                  JNZ     SRADD
                  FDIV    N               ;compute average
                  FST     XAVE            ;save average
                  MOV     SI,0            ;clear index to sample data
                  MOV     BL,N            ;init loop counter
                  FLDZ
                  FST     TEMP1           ;clear temporary result
        SQRSUM:   FLD     [BP][SI]        ;load a sample
```

```
FSUB    XAVE         ;subtract average
FST     TEMP2        ;save difference
FMUL    TEMP2        ;find square of difference
FADD    TEMP1        ;accumulate result
FST     TEMP1        ;replace result
ADD     SI,4         ;point to next sample
DEC     BL           ;repeat for all samples
JNZ     SQRSUM
FLD     TEMP1        ;get sum of squares
FDIV    N            ;divide by N
FSQRT                ;compute standard deviation
FST     SDRES        ;store result
```

Example 10.22:   A resistor-capacitor circuit is shown in Figure 10.25(a). It consists of a resistor, a capacitor, and a DC voltage source, E. At time t equal to 0, the switch is closed and the capacitor begins to charge. The time constant for the circuit, which determines how fast the capacitor charges, is found by the product of R and C (and is 1 ms in this example). Figure 10.25(b) shows a sketch of the charging curve for the capacitor. Notice that V_C reaches the applied voltage E in five time constants.

FIGURE 10.25   Exponential charging in a capacitor

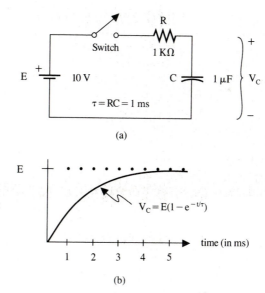

(a)

(b)

The equation that governs the capacitor's charging rate is also shown in Figure 10.25(b). This is the equation implemented by CHARGE, the 8087 routine listed here, which is used to compute the capacitor's voltage at any time T. The result is returned in VOLTAGE.

```
R    DD    1000.0        ;resistance equals 1000 ohms
C    DD    0.000001      ;capacitance equals 1 μF
E    DD    10.0          ;voltage equals 10 volts
T    DD    ?             ;time
```

```
          VOLTAGE   DD      ?                     ;voltage at time T
     .
     .
          CHARGE:   FINIT                         ;reset 8087
                    FLD     R                     ;load resistance
                    FMUL    C                     ;find time constant
                    FDIVR   T                     ;divide T by RC
                    FCHS                          ;change sign (for -T/RC)
                    FLDL2E                         ;load log2(E)
                    FMUL                          ;calculate e-to-x (2^N - 1)
                    F2XM1
                    FLD1                          ;add 1 to correct result
                    FADD                          ;now we have E^(-T/RC)
                    FCHS                          ;subtract this term from one
                    FLD1
                    FADD                          ;now we have 1-E^(-T/RC)
                    FMUL    E                     ;multiply by E
                    FST     VOLTAGE               ;store result
```

10.5   SUMMARY

In this chapter we examined the operation of three peripherals designed to complement the operation of the 8088. The first peripheral, the 8259 programmable interrupt controller, exhibited many useful features. A range of interrupt vectors can be programmed and then issued via level- or edge-sensitive inputs that are prioritized. Eight levels of prioritized interrupts are available with a single 8259 operating as a master. The 8259 can be cascaded to provide up to 64 levels of interrupts.

The second peripheral examined was the 8254 programmable interval timer. This device contains three independent 16-bit down counters, that can be programmed to count in binary or BCD. Six modes of operation are possible, allowing generation of square and pulse waveforms, programmed time delays, and other time-related functions.

Lastly, we covered the 8087 floating-point coprocessor, a device which extends the instruction set of the 8088 to include operations on a number of different data types, from 32-bit integers to 80-bit real numbers. The 8087 provides quick execution of complex mathematical operations, eliminating the need for slower—and possibly less accurate—software routines.

STUDY QUESTIONS

1. What are the main differences between polled I/O and interrupt-driven I/O?
2. Redesign the port-address decoder of Figure 10.2 so that the 8259 is mapped to a base port address of 70H. What are all of the port addresses the 8259 will respond to with the new design?

3. What ICWs are needed to program a single 8259 with edge-sensitive inputs and a base interrupt vector of C0H? (ICW4 is not needed.)

4. How many slaves are required if ICW3 in a master 8259 contains 01100101? What devices are connected to each IR input?

5. Draw a schematic of the cascaded 8259 circuit needed in Question 4. Label all interrupt signals in order from lowest to highest priority.

6. A master 8259 has slaves connected to IR2 and IR5. What are the cascade numbers that must be written to each slave?

7. Write the instructions needed to program the 8259 described in Question 2 with the parameters of Question 3.

8. What OCW1 is needed to disable interrupts on IR3 through IR6?

9. A new computer system has five devices that generate interrupts. The devices, in order of highest-to-lowest priority, generate the following signals: DISK, KEYBOARD, TIMER, VIDEO, and IODEV. Show how these signals could be connected to an 8259. What exactly happens if DISK, KEYBOARD, and IODEV interrupts are requested simultaneously?

10. Why does a delay loop become inaccurate if the processor is interrupted? How is this avoided by using the 8254?

11. What instructions are needed to program counter 2 in an 8254 for binary counting in mode 0? The initial count is 3000H. Assume the base port address is B0H.

12. What two ways can be used to load a counter with an initial count of 9F00H?

13. Write a routine that will latch the count of counter 0, store it in register DX, and call TIMEOUT if the count is less than 7.

14. What mode-0 counter value is needed to get a 25-ms time delay? A 1-MHz clock is connected to CLK.

15. What is the longest delay possible with a BCD counter and a 250-kHz clock?

16. Repeat Question 15 for a binary counter.

17. Show how counters 0 and 2 can be cascaded to provide 32-bit counting.

18. Refer to Example 10.13. Name three additional pairs of counts that will produce the 8,000,000 count division.

19. Write a routine to generate a square wave whose frequency, in kHz, is specified in BL. BL can take on the values 1 to 99. A 2-MHz clock is available for your use. The 8254 has a base port address of 38H.

20. What are the decimal ranges for each of the 8087's integer formats?

21. Show how the number 1020.6 is converted into a normalized, short-real format.

22. What decimal number is represented by these four assembler-created short-real bytes: C3 E5 A9 2B?

23. Show the 8087 instructions needed to find the square root of the number stored at LEVEL. Replace LEVEL with the new value.

24. Rewrite the code for the standard deviation routine so that it makes better use of the stack (i.e., reduce the number of accesses to memory).

25. Write an 8087 routine to convert degrees to radians. The input is stored in DEG. Save the result in RAD.

26. Write an 8087 routine to compute the area of a circle whose radius is stored in RADIUS. Save the result in AREA.

27. Name five applications that could make good use of the speed advantage provided by the 8087.

28. Write an 8088 routine that will convert a short-real number stored at RESULT into an integer part and a fractional part. For example, 80.29 is split into 80 and 0.29.

Store the integer part in register AX and the fractional part in BX. Do not use any 8087 instructions in your routine.

29. Write the 8087 instructions needed to evaluate the expression $X = A^2 - 5*A*B + B^2$.

30. What expression is evaluated by the following section of 8087 code?

```
FINIT
FLD     W
FDIV    X
FCHS
FMUL    Y
FLD1
FADD
FSQRT
FST     Z
```

CHAPTER

11

Building a Working 8088 System

Objectives

In this chapter you will learn about

- The main parts of a single-board computer

- The design of custom circuitry for the major sections of the microcomputer system

- How to generate and answer the necessary questions for the design or modification of a single-board computer

- The operation of a software monitor program

- How to modify an existing monitor program by writing additional routines

11.1   INTRODUCTION

This final chapter deals exclusively with the design of a custom 8088-based microcomputer system. The system is an ideal project for students wishing to get some hands-on experience, and is also a very educational way of utilizing all of the concepts we have studied so far.

Ideally, we wish to design a system that is easy to build, has a minimal cost, and yet gives the most for the money. The very least we expect the system to do is execute programs written in 8088 code. It is therefore necessary to have some kind of software monitor that will provide us with the ability to enter 8088 code into memory, execute programs, and even aid in debugging. This chapter, then, will consist of two parts. The first deals with the design of the minimal system, and the second with the design of a software monitor and the use of its commands.

Pay close attention to the trade-offs that we will be making during the design process. A difficult hardware task can often be performed by cleverly written machine code, and the same goes for the reverse. Do not forget our main goal: to design a *minimal* 8088-based system suitable for custom programming.

Section 11.2 covers the minimum requirements of the system we will design. Section 11.3 describes the design of the system hardware. Section 11.4 contains the parts list for the system. Section 11.5 gives hints on how the system may be constructed. Section 11.6 deals with the design of the software monitor program for the system. Section 11.7 explains a sample session with the single-board computer.

11.2 MINIMAL SYSTEM REQUIREMENTS

The requirements of our minimal system are the same as those of any computer system, and consist of four main sections: timing, CPU, memory, and input/output. Since we are the designers, building this system for our personal use, it is up to us to answer the following questions:

1. How fast should the CPU clock speed be?
2. How much EPROM memory is needed?
3. How much RAM memory is needed?
4. Should we use static or dynamic RAMs?
5. What kind of I/O should be used—parallel, serial, or both?
6. Do we want interrupt capability?
7. Will future expansion (of memory, I/O, and so on) be required?
8. What kind of software is required?

It should be clear that we have a big task ahead of us. During the design, all of these questions will be answered and the reasons for choosing one answer over another explained. Make sure you understand each step before proceeding to the next one. In this fashion, you should be able to design your *own* computer system, from scratch, and without any outside help.

11.3 DESIGNING THE HARDWARE

In this section, the four main functional components of the system will be designed. In each case, there will be questions to answer regarding specific choices that must be made. You may want to make a list of all important questions as you go.

The Timing Section

The timing section has the main responsibility of providing the CPU with a nicely functioning stable clock. Any type of digital oscillator will work in many cases. It is then necessary to decide on a frequency for the oscillator. Many times this frequency is the operating frequency of the CPU being used. Micro-processors are commonly available with different clock speeds.

One important factor limiting the clock speed is the speed of the memories being used in the system. A 12-MHz CPU might require RAMs or EPROMs with access times less than 100 ns! In our design, we will use a 10-MHz crystal, together with the 8284 clock generator. This is fast enough to provide very quick execution of programs, while at the same time allowing for use of less expensive RAMs with longer access times (200 ns).

The circuit of Figure 11.1 shows a 10-MHz crystal connected to the 8284 clock generator. The output of the 8284 drives two buffers. This is done so that any external loading on the CLK signal will not affect its operation. One of the

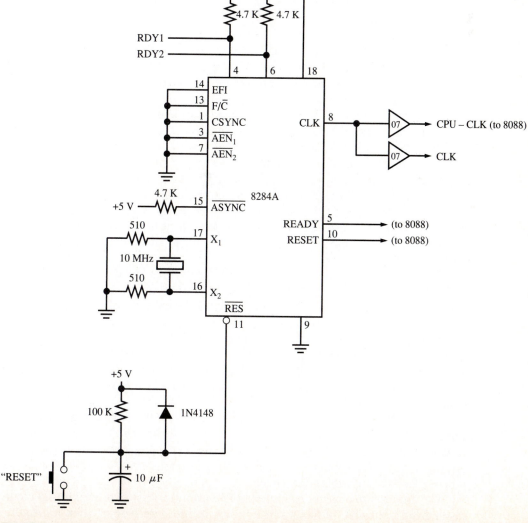

FIGURE 11.1   Clock generator for single-board computer

outputs, CPU-CLK, is the master CPU clock signal. Since many other circuits might also require the use of this master clock, we make the CLK signal available too. The CPU therefore gets its own clock signal. It is desirable to separate the clock in this fashion, to aid in any digital troubleshooting that may need to be done. By making multiple clocks available, it is easier to trace the cause of a missing clock, should that problem occur.

In addition to the clock, the CPU must be provided with a reset pulse upon application of power. It is very important to properly reset the CPU at power-up, to ensure that it begins executing its main program correctly. The 8284 has built-in reset circuitry that uses an external R-C network to generate the power-on reset pulse. The values shown in Figure 11.1 (100K ohms and 10 μF) produce a reset pulse of about 1 ms in duration, long enough to satisfy the hardware reset requirement of the CPU and other system devices.

The CPU Section

Once we have a working timing section, we must design the CPU portion of our system. It is during the design of this section that we answer our question about interrupts, and pose a few more important questions. For instance, do we need to buffer the address and data lines? Do we want to give bus-granting capability to an external device? Should the system operate in maximum mode or minimum mode? Take a good look at Figure 11.2 before continuing with the reading.

The figure details the connections we must make to the CPU for it to function in our minimal system. On the right side of the CPU we see the data and address lines. These signals are used in both the memory and I/O sections. The CPU is capable of driving only a few devices by itself (one RAM and one EPROM safely). Since the system we are designing will contain RAM, EPROM, serial *and* parallel I/O, it is best to buffer the address and data lines. As Figure 11.2 shows, a 74LS244 octal buffer is used to drive address lines A_8 through A_{15}. Address lines A_0 through A_7 are multiplexed together with the eight data lines, requiring an 8282 octal latch (together with the ALE signal from the 8288) to demultiplex and drive the lower byte of the address bus. These 16 address lines will allow for 64KB of system memory in our design.

The upper four address lines are not used in this system, since we will not be expanding the system memory requirements past 64KB.

The data bus is buffered in two directions by the 8286 bidirectional line driver/receiver. The direction of data in this device is controlled by the DT/$\overline{\text{R}}$ output of the 8288.

The schematic of the CPU section shows the 8088's MN/$\overline{\text{MX}}$ pin wired to ground. This selects maximum mode operation within the CPU and requires that we use the 8288 bus controller to generate memory and I/O control signals. Do not confuse the description of our system (a *minimal* system) with its mode of operation (*maximum* mode).

The decision to operate the processor in minimum mode or maximum mode depends on a number of factors. If low chip count is necessary, then minimum mode can be used and the 8288 eliminated. If coprocessor support will be

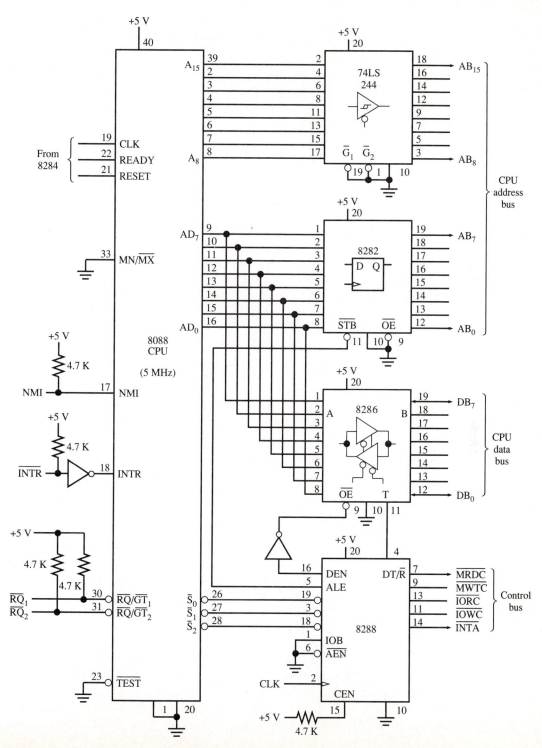

FIGURE 11.2 CPU section of single-board computer

needed in a future expansion of the system, it is best to operate in maximum mode from the beginning. The 8288 may also eliminate the need for additional decoding logic in a minimum mode system.m. Furthermore, bus-granting capability is only available in maximum mode. Since no devices in the minimal system utilize this feature, both $\overline{RQ/GT}$ inputs are pulled high. The pullup resistors will not prevent us from connecting a DMA device to either input, at a future time.

Since our goal is to design a system with a minimum of hardware, extensive interrupt support logic will not be necessary. The processor's two external hardware interrupt inputs should serve our needs adequately.

An inverter is used to make the 8088's high-level INTR interrupt respond to a low-level signal. This technique keeps the INTR input in the inactive state if no devices are connected to $\overline{INTR}$. NMI is also pulled up to a high level. Remember that NMI is edge-sensitive. When no interrupting device is connected, NMI will remain in the high state, and no interrupt will be requested. If we connect a device to NMI in the future, the pullup resistor will not have an adverse effect on any rising-edge NMI signal that is generated.

Technically, though there are five integrated circuits in the CPU section, a *bare-bones* system could get by with only the 8088 running in minimum mode. But this would most likely require the addition of hardware in the future (to drive the busses and/or possibly switch to maximum mode). Any unexpected expansion of hardware is a costly, and sometimes impossible, venture. So, though the minimal system already contains a handful of integrated circuits, choosing maximum mode for our project leaves the door open for easy expansion in the future.

The Memory Section

A number of questions must be answered before we get involved in the design of our memory section. For instance, how much EPROM memory is needed? How much RAM? Should we use static or dynamic RAM? Should we use full or partial address decoding? Will we allow DMA operations?

The answer to each one of these questions will help to specify the required hardware for the memory section. If we first consider what *applications* we will be using our computer for, the previous questions will almost answer themselves. Our application at this time is educational. We desire an 8088-based system that will run short machine language programs. Keeping this point in mind, we will now proceed to find answers to our design questions.

A programmer, through experience, can estimate the required amount of machine code needed to perform a desired task. The software monitor that we will need to control our system will have to be placed in the EPROMs of our memory section. One standard 2764 EPROM will provide us with 8192 bytes of programmable memory. This is more than enough EPROM to implement our software monitor. We will still have space left over in the EPROM in case we want to add more functions to the monitor in the future.

The amount of RAM required also depends on our application. Since we will only be using our system to test short, educational programs, we can get by with a few hundred bytes or so. Since dynamic RAMs are generally used in very large memory systems (64K, 256K, and more), we will not use them because most of the memory would go to waste. Other reasons exist for not choosing dynamic RAMs at this time. They require complex timing and refresh logic, and will also need to be wired very carefully to prevent messy noise problems from occurring. Even if we use a DRAM controller, we will need some external logic to support the controller, which itself could be a very costly item.

For these reasons, we decide to use static RAM. Even though a few hundred bytes will cover our needs, we will use one 6264 static RAM, thus making our RAM memory 8192 bytes long also. The 6264 is a low-power static RAM, with a pinout almost exactly identical to the 2764 we are using for our EPROM memory. So, by adding only two more integrated circuits (plus a few for control), our memory needs are taken care of.

Figure 11.3 shows how we use a 74LS138 3- to 8-line decoder to perform partial-address decoding for us. Since we are not concerned with future expansion on a large scale, partial-address decoding becomes the cheapest way to generate our addressing signals. Address lines A_{13} through A_{15} are used because they break up the 8088's memory space into convenient ranges (8KB blocks in this case). We completely ignore the state of the upper four address lines (A_{16} through A_{19}). If future expansion beyond the 64KB range is necessary, the upper four address lines must be used to enable the 74LS138.

With A_{13} through A_{15} all low, the 74LS138 decoder will output a zero on the output connected to the RAM's chip-enable input. With A_0 through A_{12} selecting individual locations within the 6264 RAM, we get an address range of 00000H to 01FFFH. Thus, any time the processor accesses memory in the range 00000H to 01FFFH, the RAM will be enabled. This is a good place for system RAM, since the interrupt vector table must be stored in locations 00000H through 003FFH.

When A_{13} through A_{15} are all high (as they are after a reset causes the initial instruction fetch from FFFF0H), the chip-enable of the 2764 8KB EPROM is pulled low (by the 74LS138). Together with information on the thirteen lower address lines, this maps the EPROM into locations FE000H to FFFFFH. Since partial-address decoding is being used, we can imagine the upper four address lines to be anything we want. This is why we conveniently made them low for the RAM range and high for the EPROM range. Other acceptable RAM ranges are 10000H through 11FFFH, 50000H through 51FFFH, and C0000H through C1FFFH. These are only three more of the 16 possible RAM address ranges, all of which look identical to the processor. EPROM ranges can be found in a similar manner.

In addition to the RAM and EPROM chip-select signals, the 74LS138 also decodes six additional blocks of addresses. Table 11.1 shows the address range associated with each output of the 74LS138. If additional 8KB RAMs or EPROMs need to be added at a later date, the FREE decode signals can be used to map them into the desired range.

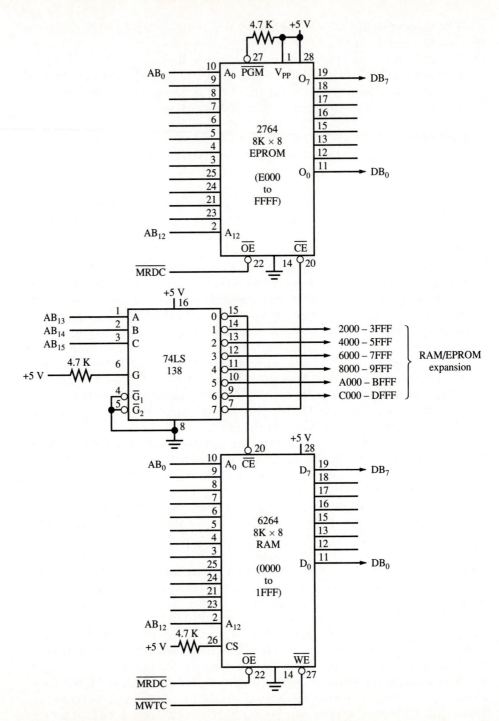

FIGURE 11.3 Memory circuitry for the single-board computer

TABLE 11.1   Partially-decoded address ranges in the minimal system

74LS138 OUTPUT	Decoded Address Range	Use
0	×0000 to ×1FFF	Main RAM
1	×2000 to ×3FFF	Free
2	×4000 to ×5FFF	Free
3	×6000 to ×7FFF	Free
4	×8000 to ×9FFF	Free
5	×A000 to ×BFFF	Free
6	×C000 to ×DFFF	Free
7	×E000 to ×FFFF	Main EPROM

× = don't care (can be anything from 0 to F)

If we were allowing DMA operations, we might not want the 74LS138 to operate in the same way. The enable inputs of the 74LS138 provide us with a way to disable it (all outputs remain high) during a DMA operation, so that an external device may take over the system.

The $\overline{MRDC}$ and $\overline{MWTC}$ signals generated in the CPU section are used to control the transfer of data between the processor and memory.

The Serial Section

The serial section of our computer will contain all hardware required to communicate with the outside world (via an EIA-compatible data terminal). One question that must be answered concerns the baud rate at which we will be transmitting and receiving. A very acceptable speed is 2400 baud. Speeds higher than this will be too fast to read on the screen, and slower speeds will take too long to read.

Figure 11.4 shows the schematic of the serial section, where an 8251 is used to provide serial communications. The chip-enable input of the 8251 is controlled by output 2 of the 74LS138 port-address decoder. Address lines A_5 through A_7 are used by the 74LS138 to decode eight port-address ranges. The 8251 responds to any I/O accesses to ports 40H through 5FH. The remaining seven groups of port-addresses are available for expansion. One of these groups will be used to access an 8255 to provide parallel I/O (as shown in the next section).

The MC14411, together with a 1.8432 MHz crystal, generates the required transmitter and receiver clock frequencies for standard baud rates from 300 to 9600. A DIP switch or jumper can be used to select one of these rates.

The 8251 communicates with the processor via the 8-bit data bus. $\overline{IORC}$ and $\overline{IOWC}$, together with A_0, control read and write operations in the 8251. CLK is provided to take care of the 8251's internal activities, and RESET is used to initialize the 8251 at power-up.

Since no modem is connected, the 8251's $\overline{DSR}$ and $\overline{CTS}$ inputs can be grounded. This ensures that the 8251 is always ready to communicate.

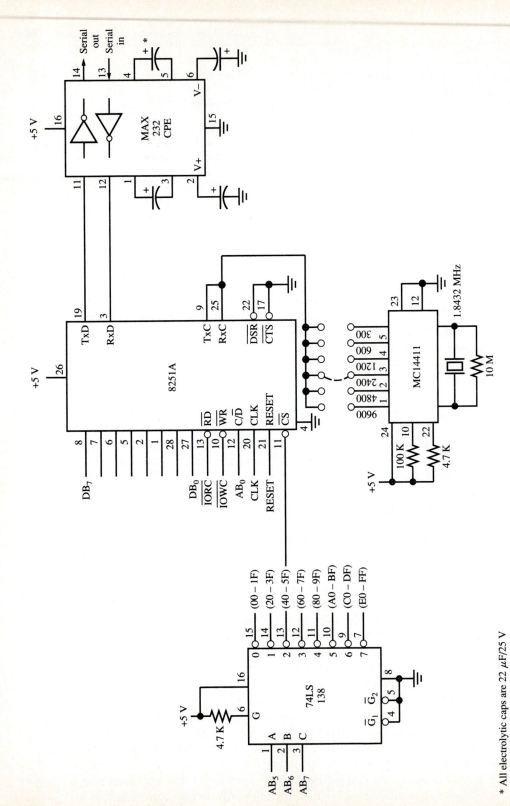

FIGURE 11.4 Serial I/O circuitry for minimal system

* All electrolytic caps are 22 μF/25 V

Serial data enters and leaves the 8251 on RxD and TxD. These signals are connected to a MAX232CPE, which converts the 8251's TTL signal levels into RS232-compatible voltage levels, and vice versa. Four 22 μF electrolytic capacitors are used to create a $+/-10$ volt swing on the output of the MAX232. This eliminates the need for an external power supply for these two voltages. The serial-in and serial-out signals from the MAX232 can be wired to a DB25 connector or other suitable connector.

Though any port address in the range 40H through 5FH will activate the 8251, the software (via A_0) uses only ports 40H and 41H. Port 40H is the 8251's *data* port, and is used to read and write to the receiver and transmitter. Port 41H is the 8251's *status* port, which is used by the software to determine when it is safe to access the receiver or transmitter.

If one serial channel is not sufficient for your needs, a second one can be added by interfacing a second 8251. One of the free port-address ranges should be used to enable the second 8251. Its baud rate clock will be supplied by the MC14411, and the other half of the MAX232 can be used to drive the second set of serial data lines. A second serial channel is useful for down-loading machine code into the minimal system's memory (although this can also be done with a single channel), or for echoing data to a printer.

The Parallel Section

If parallel I/O is needed, simple latching and buffering circuitry can be used to add a single I/O port, utilizing one of the free port-address decoder ranges. If more than one port is needed, it is best to use a multi-port device such as the 8255. The 8255 provides three programmable I/O ports and is easily interfaced with the processor.

Figure 11.5 shows how an 8255 is connected in the minimal system. All of the usual data and I/O signals are connected. Since there are four internal ports in the 8255 (three for data and one for control), two address lines are required to select one of the four internal ports. A_0 and A_1 are used for this purpose. With the chip-enable input of the 8255 wired to the first output of the 74LS138 port-address decoder, port addresses 00H through 03H can be used to select the 8255.

Figure 11.5 also shows how the 8255 is used to provide the minimal system with analog I/O capability. This additional circuitry may not be needed in many applications. In that case, the 8255 merely provides 24-bits of parallel I/O. When analog I/O is a requirement, the circuit of Figure 11.5 provides an acceptable range of analog input and output voltages. A 1408 8-bit digital-to-analog converter is connected to port A of the 8255 (which must be programmed for output operation). The current output of the 1408 is converted into a $+/-2.5$ volt swing by a 741 op-amp.

Port B of the 8255 is used to read the output of an 0804 8-bit analog-to-digital converter (which must be programmed for input operation). A second 741 is used to adjust the input voltage range of $+/-2.5$ volts to the 0 to 5 volt swing needed by the 0804. The 0804 is controlled by 2 bits in the 8255's C port.

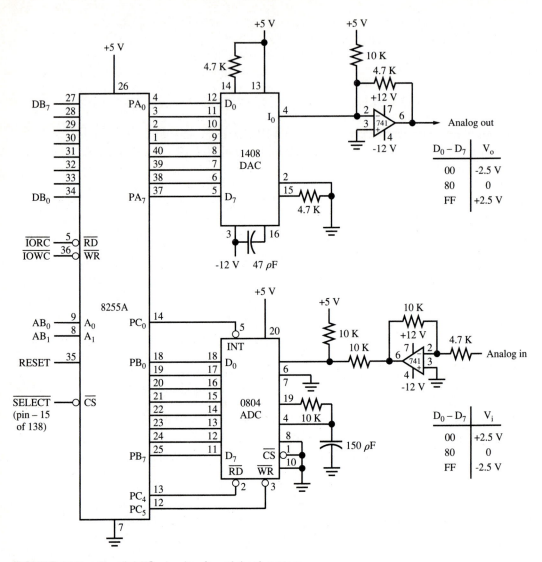

FIGURE 11.5   Parallel I/O circuitry for minimal system

With the 0804 connected in this way, it is possible to digitize over 8000 analog samples in one second (one sample every 125 microseconds).

Control of the analog circuitry is provided by instructions in the monitor program.

11.4   THE MINIMAL SYSTEM PARTS LIST

Now that we have finished designing the minimal system, we can look back on all the figures and decide how many ICs we will need to build it. The whole idea behind the design was to build a working maxmode system with a minimum of parts. The following list summarizes all the ICs that are needed (excluding the analog I/O circuitry). Pullup resistors, discrete components, and sockets are not included.

one 8284A clock generator

one 74LS07 buffer

one 74LS04 hex inverter

one 8088 microprocessor

one 74LS244 octal buffer

one 8282 octal latch

one 8286 bidirectional bus driver

one 8288 bus controller

two 74LS138 3- to 8-line decoders

one 2764 8K by 8 EPROM

one 6264 8K by 8 RAM

one 8251 UART

one MC14411 baud rate generator

one MAX232CPE TTL to RS232 converter

one 10-MHz crystal

one 1.8432-MHz crystal

In short, only 15 integrated circuits are needed to build a working 8088 maxmode system.

11.5 CONSTRUCTION TIPS

The easiest way to build the minimum system is to wire-wrap it. A printed circuit board may be used, but it would be very complex and most likely double sided.

The minimum system will work the first time power is applied, if the following points are kept in mind:

1. Keep all wires as short as possible. Long wires pick up noise.
2. Connect 0.1-μF bypass capacitors across +5 volts and GND on all ICs.
3. Trim all excess component leads to avoid short circuits.
4. Connect power and ground to all ICs before wiring anything else.
5. Pull all unused TTL inputs to +5 volts with 4.7K ohm resistors.
6. Mark off connections on a copy of the schematic, as they are made.
7. Make sure no ICs are plugged in backward before applying power.

8. Use an ohmmeter to check each connection as it is made.

9. Plug in only the clock ICs first. If the clock does not work, neither will the rest of the system.

10. Check that each IC has proper power before beginning any major trouble-shooting.

Experience, of course, is the best teacher, but these hints should be enough to get you started. There is nothing like the feeling of building a circuit that works the first time! If it fails to operate properly, do not get discouraged. With your knowledge of TTL, you should be able to track down the source of the problem in no time. You might be surprised that most problems will be due to wrong wiring. Always check your wiring very carefully!

11.6 WRITING THE SOFTWARE MONITOR

Now that we have the system hardware designed, we must tackle the job of writing the system software. Since our goal is to use the system for the testing of custom 8088 programs, the monitor program must be capable of performing every step that is needed for us to get the new program into memory, edit it if necessary, display it in hexadecimal format, and execute it. This will require the use of a number of monitor commands. The commands available with the monitor program are:

B—set breakpoint

C—clear breakpoint

D—dump memory contents

E—enter new register data

G—go execute a user program

H—display help message

I—input data from port

L—downline load a program

M—move memory

O—output data to port

R—display registers

S—stop processor

T—test analog I/O

X—examine memory

To implement the required monitor commands, we have to write machine language subroutines that perform each function. Many of these routines will perform identical tasks (such as reading an address from the keyboard, con-

TABLE 11.2   Auxiliary routines

Name	Function
IN_IT	Initialize I/O devices and system tables
BLANK	Send ASCII blank to the display
CRLF	Send ASCII CR (carriage-return),
	LF (line feed) to display
HTOA	Convert hex to ASCII
A_BIAS	Add ASCII bias to hex value
H_OUT	Output 4-digit hex number to display
C_OUT	Output ASCII character to display
CH_CASE	Convert ASCII to upper-case
ERROR	Display error message
C_IN	Read ASCII character from keyboard
CHK_SUM	Check sum during downline load
GET_BYT	Read byte value from keyboard
GET_WRD	Read word value from keyboard
CON_V	Convert ASCII to hex
GET_NUM	Read number from keyboard
S_END	Output ASCII message to display
ENVIR	Save system environment
D_ENV	Display system environment
D_FLG	Display processor flag states
DPR	Display processor registers

verting from hex to ASCII, and outputting data to the display terminal); therefore, we will also need a collection of smaller routines to perform these chores. These routines are called **auxiliary** subroutines, and are summarized in Table 11.2. We will study the operation of each auxiliary subroutine first, and then see how they are used within the command routines.

Keep in mind that the monitor program has been written using simple instructions and addressing modes. It is very possible that many of the routines presented can be simplified. You are encouraged to rewrite them, once the computer has been built and the basic monitor program is up and running.

The Auxiliary Routines

Each auxiliary routine is designed to perform a specific function. Enough detail will be provided for you to grasp the overall operation of each routine. Pay attention to the methods used to pass information to/from each routine. It will also be useful for you to make a table showing (for each routine) what registers are used for input, which ones are used for output, and which registers are simply used during computations.

IN_IT   This routine initializes the 8251 serial I/O device so that it will be capable of generating waveforms containing 8 data bits, no parity, and 2 stop bits. A x16 clock is also selected. IN_IT also programs the 8255 for port A out and port B in, with port C used for handshaking with the ADC. The DAC is initialized to output 0 volts. The monitor's breakpoint flag is reset. The receiver of the 8251 is read to clear any stray character that may be present at power-on. The 8251 is accessed through data port 40H and control/status port 41H. The 8255 is accessed through ports 0 through 3. Equate statements are included in the monitor program to associate these port addresses with labels. For example, the data port of the 8251 is defined like this:

```
                S_DATA      EQU      40H
```

The label is used in an instruction to aid in understanding what port is being accessed. The routine looks like this:

```
        IN_IT   PROC    NEAR
                MOV     AL,0CEH
                OUT     S_CTRL,AL     ;output 8251 mode word
                MOV     AL,5
                OUT     S_CTRL,AL     ;output 8251 command word
                MOV     AL,83H
                OUT     AD_CTRL,AL    ;init 8255
                MOV     AL,80H
                OUT     D_AC,AL       ;zero DAC
                MOV     AL,10H
                OUT     AD_STAT,AL
                MOV     AL,30H
                OUT     AD_STAT,AL    ;reset ADC
                MOV     ES:[BR_STAT + RTOP],0   ;clear breakpoint flag
                IN      AL,S_DATA     ;clear 8251 receiver
                RET
        IN_IT   ENDP
```

Blank   This routine outputs an ASCII blank character to the display. It may first appear that a routine dedicated to this simple function is a waste of time (and code). But consider that there may be many routines that need to output blanks during their execution. It is much more convenient for the programmer to simply CALL BLANK than to duplicate the instructions each time.

```
        BLANK   PROC    NEAR
                MOV     AL,20H    ;code for ASCII blank
                CALL    C_OUT
                RET
        BLANK   ENDP
```

CRLF   This routine is used to make the display scroll up one line. The codes for carriage-return and linefeed are output to the display. This routine, like BLANK, is needed often.

```
        CRLF    PROC    NEAR
                MOV     AL,13    ;ASCII CR
                CALL    C_OUT
                MOV     AL,10    ;ASCII LF
                CALL    C_OUT
                RET
        CRLF    ENDP
```

HTOA   This routine performs hex-to-ASCII conversion. The data byte contained in register AL is converted into a 2-character sequence of ASCII characters and output to the display. For example, if AL contains 3FH, an ASCII "3" and an ASCII "F" are output to the display.

```
HTOA    PROC    NEAR
        PUSH    AX
        SHR     AL,1        ;get upper nibble
        SHR     AL,1
        SHR     AL,1
        SHR     AL,1
        CALL    A_BIAS      ;convert to ASCII and output
        POP     AX          ;get lower nibble
        CALL    A_BIAS      ;convert and output again
        RET
HTOA    ENDP
```

A_BIAS   This routine converts the lower 4 bits of register AL into a printable ASCII equivalent character. For example, ----0011 becomes 33H, which is "3". ----1011 becomes 42H, which is "B". The character is then output to the display.

```
A_BIAS    PROC    NEAR
          AND     AL,0FH      ;clear upper 4 bits
          ADD     AL,30H      ;add ASCII bias
          CMP     AL,3AH      ;is it A through F?
          JC      NO_7        ;no
          ADD     AL,7        ;yes, correct to alphabetic
NO_7:     CALL    C_OUT       ;output to display
          RET
A_BIAS    ENDP
```

H_OUT   This routine outputs the 4-character ASCII equivalent of the number stored in register DX. For example, if DX contains 3E7CH, the ASCII characters "3", "E", "7", and "C" are output to the display. Notice how HTOA is used to simplify this routine.

```
H_OUT    PROC    NEAR
         MOV     AL,DH       ;do upper byte first
         CALL    HTOA
         MOV     AL,DL       ;then lower byte
         CALL    HTOA
         RET
H_OUT    ENDP
```

C_OUT   This routine examines the level of the 8251's transmitter-ready flag, and, when it is ready, outputs the character in AL to the transmitter (for viewing on the display).

```
C_OUT    PROC    NEAR
         PUSH    AX
         MOV     AH,AL
CO_S:    IN      AL,S_CTRL    ;get 8251 status
         AND     AL,01H       ;test TRDY
```

```
                    JZ      CO_S            ;loop until not busy
                    MOV     AL,AH
                    OUT     S_DATA,AL       ;output character
                    POP     AX
                    RET
        C_OUT       ENDP
```

CH_CASE This routine examines the ASCII character in register AL. If the character is lower-case ("a" through "z") it is converted into upper-case ("A" through "Z").

```
        CH_CASE     PROC    NEAR
                    CMP     AL,'a'          ;test for 'a'...'z' range
                    JC      UN_ALPH
                    CMP     AL,'z' + 1
                    JNC     UN_ALPH
                    AND     AL,0DFH         ;convert into upper-case
        UN_ALPH:    RET
        CH_CASE     ENDP
```

ERROR This routine gives an audible beep when an error is detected. A "?" is also displayed on the screen to indicate an error.

```
        ERROR       PROC    NEAR
                    MOV     AL,'?'          ;output '?'
                    CALL    C_OUT
                    MOV     AL,7            ;beep terminal (control-G)
                    CALL    C_OUT
                    RET
        ERROR       ENDP
```

C_IN This routine examines the level of the 8251's receiver-ready flag, and, when ready, reads a character from the receiver. The MSB of the byte returned in register AL is always cleared.

```
        C_IN        PROC    NEAR
        CI_S:       IN      AL,S_CTRL       ;read 8251 status
                    AND     AL,02H          ;test RRDY
                    JZ      CI_S            ;loop until ready
                    IN      AL,S_DATA       ;read new character
                    AND     AL,7FH          ;clear MSB
                    RET
        C_IN        ENDP
```

CHK_SUM This routine checks the C_SUM location in the monitor's data table and returns an error message if it is not zero. A nonzero C_SUM means that a program was downline-loaded incorrectly.

```
        CHK_SUM     PROC    NEAR
                    CMP     ES:[C_SUM + RTOP],0   ;test C_SUM
                    JZ      GD_LD           ;OK if zero
                    LEA     SI,CSE          ;load address of error message
                    CALL    S_END           ;output message
                    JMP     GET_COM         ;get a new command
        GD_LD:      RET
        CHK_SUM     ENDP
```

The error message is stored in the monitor's data area, like this:

```
                CSE        DB        '<-Checksum error->$'
```

with the "$" serving as the end-of-string character.

GET_BYT   This routine is used to read two successive characters from the serial port and convert them into their 8-bit equivalent. For example, if "5" and "C" are received, register AL will contain 5CH upon return.

```
GET_BYT     PROC    NEAR
            CALL    C_IN        ;get a character
            CALL    C_OUT       ;echo it to display
            CALL    CON_V       ;convert into binary
            SHL     AL,1        ;move result into upper 4 bits
            SHL     AL,1
            SHL     AL,1
            SHL     AL,1
            MOV     BL,AL       ;save upper half of result
            CALL    C_IN        ;get second character
            CALL    C_OUT       ;echo it
            CALL    CON_V       ;convert to binary
            OR      AL,BL       ;combine with upper half
            ADD     ES:[C_SUM + RTOP],AL   ;add new value to C_SUM
            RET
GET_BYT     ENDP
```

Notice that the received byte is added to C_SUM. This allows GET_BYT to be used in the downline-loading command.

GET_WRD   This routine calls GET_BYT twice to read a 4-character number from the serial port. The number is returned in register AX.

```
GET_WRD     PROC    NEAR
            CALL    GET_BYT     ;get first byte
            MOV     BH,AL       ;save it
            CALL    GET_BYT     ;get second byte
            MOV     AH,BH       ;return result in AX
            RET
GET_WRD     ENDP
```

CON_V   This routine converts an ASCII character in the range "0" to "9" or "A" to "F" into its corresponding 4-bit binary equivalent. The result is returned in the lower half of register AL.

```
CON_V       PROC    NEAR
            SUB     AL,'0'      ;remove ASCII bias
            CMP     AL,10       ;test 'A' to 'F' range
            JC      NO_SUB7     ;not a letter
            SUB     AL,7        ;remove alpha bias
NO_SUB7:    RET
CON_V       ENDP
```

GET_NUM   This routine accepts a multidigit hexadecimal number from the keyboard and stores it in register DX. If more than four characters are entered, only the last four will be used in the conversion. A CR or blank will terminate the input. If no characters are entered prior to the CR or blank, register BH will contain "0", otherwise it will contain "1". Any illegal character causes exit to ERROR.

This short table gives a few examples of GET_NUM at work:

Input	Outputs
'3','A','7' \<cr\>	DX=03A7 BH='1'
'1','2','3','4','5' \<cr\>	DX=2345 BH='1'
\<cr\>	DX=0000 BH='0'

This is the actual routine:

```
GET_NUM  PROC    NEAR
TOP_N:   MOV     BH,'0'        ;init BH
         MOV     DX,0          ;clear DX
GT_NM:   CALL    C_IN          ;get a character
         CMP     AL,13         ;is it CR?
         JZ      GT_BYE        ;yes
         CALL    C_OUT         ;no, echo it
         CMP     AL,20H        ;is it a blank?
         JZ      GT_BYE        ;yes
         MOV     BH,'1'        ;no, adjust BH
         CALL    CH_CASE       ;convert to upper-case
         CMP     AL,'0'        ;test '0' to '9' range
         JC      BAD_NM
         CMP     AL,'9' + 1
         JC      OK_SUB
         CMP     AL,'A'        ;test 'A' to 'F' range
         JC      BAD_NM
         CMP     AL,'F' + 1
         JNC     BAD_NM
         SUB     AL,7          ;remove alpha bias
OK_SUB:  SUB     AL,30H        ;remove ASCII bias
         SHL     DX,1          ;make room for new nibble
         SHL     DX,1
         SHL     DX,1
         SHL     DX,1
         ADD     DL,AL         ;adjust result
         JMP     GT_NM         ;repeat as necessary
GT_BYE:  CLC
         RET
BAD_NM:  CALL    ERROR
         JMP     TOP_N
GET_NUM  ENDP
```

SEND   This routine reads ASCII characters from memory and outputs them to the display. The characters are pointed to by register SI. All character strings must terminate with "$". Upon entry, SI must point to the first character in the string.

```
S_END    PROC    NEAR
S_NXT:   MOV     AL,[SI]       ;get a character
         CMP     AL,'$'        ;end of string?
         JZ      S_QWT         ;yes
         CALL    C_OUT         ;no, output to display
         INC     SI            ;point to next character
         JMP     S_NXT         ;repeat
S_QWT:   RET
S_END    ENDP
```

ENVIR   This routine saves the monitor's environment (all registers and flags) when the monitor is reentered from an external source. The usual reentry technique requires an INT 95H instruction at the end of the user routine (see Section 11.7). You may think of ENVIR as the interrupt service routine for INT 95H. ENVIR also reestablishes the monitor's segment registers, which may have been altered by the external software. All registers are stored in memory as 2-byte words (low byte first) beginning at location R_DATA[RTOP] (location 1F80 in the system RAM). The registers are stored in the following order: AX, BX, CX, DX, BP, SI, DI, SP, DS, SS, ES. The flags are stored in locations 1FA1 and 1FA2.

When ENVIR completes execution it *falls into* D_ENV to display the system environment.

```
ENVIR   PROC   NEAR
        PUSHF                   ;save flags on stack
        PUSH   AX               ;save AX on stack
        MOV    AX,DS
        PUSH   AX               ;save DS on stack
        MOV    AX,DATA
        ADD    AX,0E00H
        MOV    DS,AX            ;reload monitor DS
        MOV    AX,ES
        PUSH   AX               ;save ES on stack
        MOV    AX,0
        MOV    ES,AX            ;reload monitor ES
        POP    AX               ;pop and save old ES
        MOV    ES:R_DATA[RTOP + 20],AX
        POP    AX               ;pop and save old DS
        MOV    ES:R_DATA[RTOP + 16],AX
        POP    AX               ;pop and save old AX
        MOV    ES:R_DATA[RTOP + 0],AX
        MOV    ES:R_DATA[RTOP + 2],BX    ;save all other registers
        MOV    ES:R_DATA[RTOP + 4],CX
        MOV    ES:R_DATA[RTOP + 6],DX
        MOV    ES:R_DATA[RTOP + 8],BP
        MOV    ES:R_DATA[RTOP + 10],SI
        MOV    ES:R_DATA[RTOP + 12],DI
        POP    AX
        POP    BX
        MOV    ES:R_DATA[RTOP + 14],SP   ;save SP
        PUSH   BX
        PUSH   AX
        MOV    ES:R_DATA[RTOP + 18],SS   ;save SS
        POP    AX
        MOV    ES:[F_LAGS + RTOP],AX     ;save flags
```

This routine physically appears just before the code for D_ENV. The instruction following the last MOV in ENVIR is the first instruction of D_ENV.

The data table containing the stored register values is defined like this:

```
R_DATA   DW   11 DUP(?)
```

where memory space for 11 words (one for each register saved) is reserved. When INT 95H is used at the end of a user routine, it causes ENVIR to execute, which in turn saves the final state of each register at the completion of the user routine.

D_ENV This routine displays the contents of all CPU registers stored in the R_DATA table by ENVIR. The display format (with sample register values) is as follows:

```
AX:1111  BX:2222  CX:3333  DX:4444
BP:5555  SI:6666  DI:7777  SP:8888
DS:9999  SS:AAAA  ES:BBBB
```

After outputting the value of ES, the routine falls into D_FLG to display the state of the flags.

```
D_ENV:    MOV    SI,0                    ;init pointer to register data
          MOV    CX,11                   ;init loop counter
          CALL   CRLF
T_DR:     MOV    AL,R_LETS[SI]           ;output register name
          CALL   C_OUT
          MOV    AL,R_LETS[SI + 1]
          CALL   C_OUT
          MOV    AL,':'                  ;and a ':'
          CALL   C_OUT
          MOV    DX,ES:R_DATA[RTOP + SI] ;get register data
          CALL   H_OUT                   ;and output it
          CALL   BLANK                   ;2 blanks for spacing
          CALL   BLANK
          ADD    SI,2                    ;point to next register
          MOV    AX,SI                   ;do display formatting
          AND    AL,7
          JNZ    ADJST
          CALL   CRLF
ADJST:    LOOP   T_DR                    ;repeat for all registers
```

D_ENV requires a predefined data table of register names. The table looks like this:

```
R_LETS    DB        'AXBXCXDXBPSIDISPDSSSES'
```

D_FLG This routine displays the state of each of the five arithmetic flags: sign, zero, auxiliary carry, parity, and carry, in the following format:

```
Flags: S=1  Z=0  A=0  P=1  C=1
```

Together with the register display of D_ENV, D_FLG provides a method for determining exactly what a user routine has done to the registers and flags during execution.

```
D_FLG:    LEA    SI,FL_MSG        ;output flag message
          CALL   S_END
          MOV    SI,0             ;init pointer to tables
          MOV    CX,5             ;init loop counter
N_FLG:    MOV    AL,F_SYM[SI]     ;get a flag name
          CALL   C_OUT            ;display it
          MOV    AL,'='
          CALL   C_OUT            ;display '='
          MOV    AX,ES:[F_LAGS + RTOP]  ;get flag byte
          AND    AL,F_MASK[SI]    ;mask out specific flag
          MOV    AL,'0'           ;adjust AL according to flag state
          JZ     NOT_1
          INC    AL
```

```
NOT_1:   CALL   C_OUT       ;display flag state
         CALL   BLANK       ;and output spacing blanks
         CALL   BLANK
         INC    SI          ;point to next flag
         LOOP   N_FLG       ;repeat
         RET
ENVIR    ENDP
```

D_FLG requires three predefined data tables, which are:

```
FL_MSG   DB     13,10,'Flags: $'
F_SYM    DB     'SZAPC'
F_MASK   DB     80H,40H,10H,4,1
```

Note the use of the ENDP statement in the routine. ENVIR, D_ENV, and D_FLG are all contained within the same procedure block.

DPR   This final auxiliary routine is used to enter D_ENV and display the flags, *assuming they have already been previously saved.*

```
DPR      PROC   NEAR
         JMP    D_ENV
DPR      ENDP
```

This code is used to display the environment without having to encounter an INT 95H in the user code.

As you study the command routines in the next section, watch how the auxiliary routines are used to simplify the code required to execute a monitor command.

The Monitor Commands

The monitor commands are really the heart of the software monitor. Through the use of the monitor commands, the job of creating new and useful software becomes much easier. We will now examine just how these commands are implemented. Study the methods used to perform I/O with the user, and how decisions are made within the routines. You should be able to gain a very good understanding of the structure of a command routine, and be able to use that knowledge to write *your own* command routine to perform a job that the basic monitor cannot.

The Command Recognizer

In order to use a command routine, we must be able to get to its starting address in memory (to fetch the first instruction of the command routine). It is much easier and more convenient to enter a single letter command, such as D, G, or R, than to enter a multidigit hexadecimal starting address. The purpose of the command recognizer is to determine which of the monitor commands has been entered by the user, and jump to the command routine for execution. The command recognizer accepts upper- and lower-case command letters.

Once the command is recognized, the address of the selected command routine is read from a data table, and the routine is jumped to. For this reason, the command routines must jump back to the beginning of the monitor program (GET_COM), and not return as a subroutine would.

The command recognizer is written so that new commands may be easily added with a minimum of change in its code.

```
GET_COM:    MOV     SP,2000H      ;init stack pointer
            CALL    CRLF          ;newline
            MOV     AL,'>'        ;output command prompt
            CALL    C_OUT
            CALL    C_IN          ;get command letter
            CALL    C_OUT         ;echo it
            CALL    CH_CASE       ;convert to upper-case
            CMP     AL,13         ;if CR, start again
            JZ      GET_COM
            MOV     CX,NUM_COM    ;init loop counter
            MOV     SI,0          ;init table pointer
C_TEST:     CMP     AL,COMS[SI]   ;compare user command with table item
            JZ      CHK_SN        ;match
            ADD     SI,2          ;no match, point to next item
            LOOP    C_TEST        ;repeat test
            CALL    ERROR         ;no match at all
            JMP     GET_COM
CHK_SN:     CALL    C_IN          ;command must be followed by CR
            CMP     AL,13         ;or blank
            JZ      DO_JMP
            CALL    C_OUT
            CMP     AL,20H
            JZ      DO_JMP
            CALL    ERROR
            JMP     GET_COM
DO_JMP:     JMP     J_UMPS[SI]    ;fetch command routine address and jump
```

GET_COM uses the COMS data table (shown below) during the search for a matching command letter. The individual command letters are all followed by a blank, so that when SI is incremented by 2 it will always access the next command letter. This lets GET_COM use SI to point to the correct location within the command routine address table J_UMPS as well.

The data tables utilized by GET_COM are:

```
NUM_COM    DW    14
COMS       DB    'B C D E G H I L M O R S T X '
J_UMPS     DW    B_RKP, C_BRP, D_UMP, I_NIT
           DW    E_XEC, H_ELP, P_IN, L_OAD
           DW    M_OVE, P_OUT, D_REG, S_TOP
           DW    T_EST, E_XAM
```

The Command Routines

The command routines are designed to provide the features necessary to load a new program into memory, debug it (find/fix errors), and execute it. Some routines perform operations on the system itself, rather than on the user program. Examples of these types of commands are M (move memory), S (stop processor), and I (input data from port). Study the command routines carefully. Look for ways to improve them once your personal system is up and running.

The B Command: Set Breakpoint   This command is used to specify the address where the user program should break away from its execution and return to the monitor. All registers are saved and displayed upon return.

Breakpoints are very useful when debugging code. To use a breakpoint, select an instruction (and its associated address in memory). The instruction located at the breakpoint address is saved and then replaced by an INT 3 instruction (opcode byte CCH). When the processor gets to the INT 3 instruction (during execution of the user program), a special monitor reentry procedure will be executed, which saves and displays the registers and flags. Then the original instruction is restored and the breakpoint cleared.

If a breakpoint is already set, additional B commands will produce an error message and the breakpoint will not be changed.

The format of the command is B <address>. An example of the B command is:

```
                         B 110C
```

which will cause a breakpoint at address 110C of the user program.

```
B_RKP:  CALL    GET_NUM                     ;get breakpoint address
        MOV     AL,ES:[BR_STAT + RTOP]      ;check breakpoint status
        CMP     AL,0
        JZ      DO_BP                       ;no breakpoint saved yet
        LEA     SI,BP_AS                    ;breakpoint already saved
        CALL    S_END
        JMP     GET_COM
DO_BP:  MOV     ES:[B_MMA + RTOP],DX        ;save breakpoint address
        MOV     SI,DX
        MOV     AL,ES:[SI]                  ;fetch byte at breakpoint
        MOV     ES:[OP_KODE + RTOP],AL      ;and save it
        MOV     AL,0CCH                     ;insert breakpoint code
        MOV     ES:[SI],AL
        MOV     ES:[BR_STAT + RTOP],1       ;adjust breakpoint status
        LEA     SI,BP_SA                    ;inform user about breakpoint
        CALL    S_END
        JMP     GET_COM
```

B_RKP uses two messages to inform the user of what it has done:

```
        BP_AS   DB      'Breakpoint already saved...$'
        BP_SA   DB      'Breakpoint saved.$'
```

B_RKP determines which message to send based on the user's actions.

The C Command: Clear Breakpoint   This command clears the saved breakpoint address. The breakpoint status is adjusted and the user instruction restored. This command must be used before attempting to set a new breakpoint.

The C command has no parameters.

```
C_BRP:  MOV     AL,ES:[BR_STAT + RTOP]      ;check breakpoint status
        CMP     AL,1
        JZ      OP_LD                       ;breakpoint exists
        LEA     SI,BR_ALC                   ;no breakpoint, inform user
        CALL    S_END
        JMP     GET_COM
```

```
OP_LD:  LEA   SI,BR_CLR                      ;tell user breakpoint cleared
        CALL  S_END
        MOV   SI,ES:[B_MMA + RTOP]    ;load breakpoint address
        MOV   AL,ES:[OP_KODE + RTOP]  ;load user instruction byte
        MOV   ES:[SI],AL              ;restore user byte
        MOV   ES:[BR_STAT + RTOP],0   ;clear breakpoint status
        JMP   GET_COM
```

C_BRP uses two pre-defined messages to inform the user about what it has done:

```
        BR_ALC  DB    'Breakpoint already cleared.$'
        BR_CLR  DB    'Breakpoint cleared.$'
```

The D Command: Display Memory Contents   This command displays the contents of memory in hexadecimal format. Each line of the display contains the starting address, followed by 16 bytes of code. A sample line of the display looks like this:

```
    1000   F3 1A 29 B3 02 CA 33 F7 88 34 CD 02 10 2A BB C9
```

The first byte (F3H) was read out of memory location 1000, the second one (1AH) from location 1001, and so on. The last byte on the line (C9H) is read out of location 100F.

The format of the command is: D <starting address> <ending address>. An example of the D command is:

```
                        D 1000 100F
```

which results in the sample output shown just earlier.

The routine takes this form:

```
D_UMP:    CALL  GET_NUM      ;get starting address
          PUSH  DX           ;save it on stack
          CALL  BLANK
          CALL  GET_NUM      ;get ending address
          POP   SI           ;retrieve starting address
          SUB   DX,SI        ;compute length of block
          MOV   CX,DX        ;init loop counter
          INC   CX
          MOV   DX,SI        ;go start dump
          JMP   DO_DMP
CHK_ADR:  MOV   DX,SI        ;check for address wrap-around
          MOV   AL,DL
          AND   AL,0FH       ;is least-significant digit zero?
          JNZ   NO_ADR       ;no
DO_DMP:   CALL  CRLF         ;yes, output newline and address
          CALL  H_OUT
          CALL  BLANK
NO_ADR:   CALL  BLANK
          MOV   AL,ES:[SI]   ;get a byte from memory
          CALL  HTOA         ;display it
          INC   SI           ;point to next location
          LOOP  CHK_ADR      ;repeat
          JMP   GET_COM
```

The E Command: Enter New Register Data   This command allows the stored register data (in R_DATA) to be changed. All processor registers may be altered. The routine displays the name of each register, its current value, and then gives the user the option of entering a new value. If no new value is entered, the current value is not changed. For example:

```
                    AX - 1A23?200
```

represents the first line of output from the E command. Register AX currently contains 1A23, but the user has changed this value to 0200. To skip over a register and not change its current value, simply hit the Return key.

The E command has no parameters.

```
I_NIT:  MOV   SI,0                    ;init pointer
        MOV   CX,11                   ;init loop counter
I_NEX:  CALL  CRLF                    ;output register name
        MOV   AL,R_LETS[SI]
        CALL  C_OUT
        MOV   AL,R_LETS[SI + 1]
        CALL  C_OUT
        CALL  BLANK
        MOV   AL,'-'                  ;and a dash
        CALL  C_OUT
        CALL  BLANK
        MOV   DX,ES:R_DATA[RTOP + SI]   ;and the saved value
        CALL  H_OUT
        MOV   AL,'?'                  ;ask for a new value
        CALL  C_OUT
        CALL  GET_NUM                 ;read new value
        CMP   BH,'0'                  ;change?
        JZ    NUN                     ;no
        MOV   ES:R_DATA[RTOP + SI],DX   ;yes, save new value
NUN:    ADD   SI,2                    ;point to next register
        LOOP  I_NEX                   ;repeat
        JMP   GET_COM
```

The G Command: Go Execute a User Program   This command loads registers AX, BX, CX, DX, BP, SI, and DI from the monitor's register storage area (R_DATA) and then jumps to the user-supplied address to execute the user routine. Since system RAM is from 00000H to 01FFFH, the user program must be located within the first 8KB of memory. It is suggested that user programs have an ORG of at least 400H so that they do not interfere with the interrupt vector table located in locations 00000H through 003FFH. Also, the monitor reserves a block of system RAM at the high end of free memory (for its internal stack and storage tables). This block begins at address 1F80H. User programs should not utilize RAM above this address either.

The jump to the user program is actually accomplished by pushing the starting address onto the stack and "RETurning" to it.

The format of the command is: G <execution address>. An example of the G command is:

```
        G 1000
```

which causes the user program beginning at address 1000H to be executed.

```
E_XEC:   CALL   GET_NUM                      ;get starting address
         SUB    AX,AX                        ;clear AX
         PUSH   AX                           ;let CS=0000 on stack
         PUSH   DX                           ;let IP=DX on stack
         CALL   CRLF
         MOV    AX,ES:R_DATA[RTOP + 0]       ;load data registers
         MOV    BX,ES:R_DATA[RTOP + 2]
         MOV    CX,ES:R_DATA[RTOP + 4]
         MOV    DX,ES:R_DATA[RTOP + 6]
         MOV    BP,ES:R_DATA[RTOP + 8]
         MOV    SI,ES:R_DATA[RTOP + 10]
         MOV    DI,ES:R_DATA[RTOP + 12]
         RET                                 ;pop stack to execute user code
```

The H Command: Display Help Message   This command displays a help message showing the syntax of each monitor command. The help message is stored as a long text string (terminated by "$") beginning at H_MSG.

The H command has no parameters. Its routine is:

```
H_ELP:   LEA    SI,H_MSG    ;init pointer to help message
         CALL   S_END       ;display message
         JMP    GET_COM
```

The I Command: Input Data from Port   This command is used to read and display the byte present at a specific input port. The byte read from the specified input port is displayed in square brackets, as in [34].

The format of the command is: I <port address>. An example of the I command is:

I 2F

which displays the byte seen at input port 2FH.

```
P_IN:    CALL   GET_NUM     ;get input port address
         CALL   CRLF
         MOV    AL,'['      ;display left bracket
         CALL   C_OUT
         IN     AL,DX       ;read input port
         CALL   HTOA        ;display byte
         MOV    AL,']'      ;display right bracket
         CALL   C_OUT
         JMP    GET_COM
```

The L Command: Downline Load a User Program   This command is used to downline load a standard Intel-format HEX file into system RAM. The HEX file is created by the 8088 assembler and linker. A sample line from the HEX file might look like this:

:11307A00627920746865204153534C4D424C4552212A

All lines begin with a ":". Embedded within the line of text is a length byte (11), a load address (307A), a record type (00), data bytes (6279...), and a final byte called a **checksum** byte (2A). A downline loader routine must retrieve the information present in the HEX file and use it to load the embedded information into memory. The L command always loads a program into memory beginning at address 00400H and supports four record types:

00—Data record

01—End-of file record

02—Extended-address record

03—Starting-address record

The HEX file is received by the serial input of the single-board (as if someone were quickly entering it through the keyboard). The routine checks the sum of each line as it is received and gives an error message if the checksum is incorrect.

The L command has no parameters.

```
L_OAD:      CALL    CRLF
            MOV     BP,400H    ;program always loads at 400H
NXT_REC:    MOV     ES:[C_SUM + RTOP],0 ;clear checksum
KOLON:      CALL    C_IN       ;wait for ':'
            CALL    C_OUT
            CMP     AL,':'
            JNZ     KOLON
            CALL    GET_BYT    ;get record length
            MOV     CL,AL      ;init loop counter
            MOV     CH,0
            CALL    GET_WRD    ;get load address
            MOV     DI,AX
            CALL    GET_BYT    ;get record type
            CMP     AL,0
            JZ      D_REC      ;record 00
            CMP     AL,1
            JZ      EOF_REC    ;record 01
            CMP     AL,2
            JZ      EA_REC     ;record 02
            CMP     AL,3
            JZ      SA_REC     ;record 03
            LEA     SI,URT     ;record type not valid
            CALL    S_END
            JMP     GET_COM
D_REC:      CALL    GET_BYT             ;now get all data bytes
            MOV     ES:[BP][DI],AL   ;one by one and store them
            INC     DI                  ;in memory
            LOOP    D_REC
            CALL    GET_BYT    ;read checksum
            CALL    CHK_SUM    ;check for correct sum
            JMP     NXT_REC
EOF_REC:    CALL    GET_BYT    ;read checksum
            CALL    CHK_SUM    ;check for correct sum
            JMP     GET_COM
EA_REC:     CALL    GET_WRD    ;get new segment address
            SHL     AX,1       ;shift left 4 bits
            SHL     AX,1
            SHL     AX,1
            SHL     AX,1
            MOV     BP,AX      ;load memory pointer
            CALL    GET_BYT    ;read and check sum
            CALL    CHK_SUM
            JMP     NXT_REC
```

```
SA_REC:   CALL   GET_WRD    ;load starting address
          CALL   GET_WRD    ;even though it is ignored
          CALL   GET_BYT
          CALL   CHK_SUM
          JMP    NXT_REC
```

L_OAD requires a predefined error message for acknowledging invalid record types:

```
URT       DB         '<-Unidentified record type->$'
```

The M Command: Move Memory   This command routine is useful for moving blocks of memory data from one location to another. The data included in the input range is not actually moved anywhere, it is *copied* instead. The starting and ending addresses of the block to be moved (copied) must be specified, along with the starting address of the destination. This command can be used after a downline load to move the user program to a different location in system RAM (or to copy monitor code from EPROM into RAM).

The format of the command is: M <starting address> <ending address> <destination address>. An example of the M command is:

M 1200 12FF 1600

which copies 256 bytes of RAM from addresses 1200H through 12FFH to memory beginning at address 1600H.

```
M_OVE:    CALL   GET_NUM    ;get starting address
          MOV    SI,DX
          CALL   GET_NUM    ;get ending address
          SUB    DX,SI      ;compute length of block
          MOV    CX,DX      ;init loop counter
          INC    CX
          CALL   GET_NUM    ;get destination address
          MOV    DI,DX
MVIT:     MOV    AL,ES:[SI] ;read a byte
          MOV    ES:[DI],AL ;write it at new location
          INC    SI         ;advance pointers
          INC    DI
          LOOP   MVIT       ;repeat
          JMP    GET_COM
```

The O Command: Output Data to Port   This routine is used to output a data byte to a specific port. The byte and port addresses are specified in the command. This command is useful for testing output-port hardware (such as the serial and parallel I/O sections).

The format of the command is O <output port address> <data>. An example of the O command is:

0 7 33

which outputs the data byte 33H to port 07H.

```
P_OUT:    CALL   GET_NUM    ;get port address
          PUSH   DX
          MOV    AL,' '
```

```
            CALL    C_OUT
            CALL    GET_NUM     ;get output data
            MOV     AL,DL
            POP     DX
            OUT     DX,AL       ;output data to port
            JMP     GET_COM
```

The R Command: Display Registers   This command is used to display the contents of all processor registers (and flags) saved in the R_DATA storage area. It utilizes code already contained in the auxiliary routine DPR.

The R command has no parameters.

```
    D_REG:      CALL    DPR
                JMP     GET_COM
```

The S Command: Stop the Processor   This command halts the processor. It may be useful to examine the level of the 8088's signals when it is halted (or to escape from the halt state with an interrupt).

```
    S_TOP:      LEA     SI,S_MSG
                CALL    S_END
                HLT
```

S_TOP uses a predefined message to indicate that the machine has halted.

```
    S_MSG       DB      'Placing 8088 in HALT state.$'
```

The T Command: Test Analog I/O Ports   This command is used to test the operation of the analog I/O circuitry (as depicted in Figure 11.5). The user is provided with a choice of two operations. The first test option exercises the digital-to-analog converter by outputting values from a data table that generates a sine wave at the analog output. The system must be RESET to get out of the sine wave routine.

The second test option reads the analog-to-digital converter and echos the data to the digital-to-analog. The echo test is also terminated by RESET.

The T command has no parameters.

```
    T_EST:      LEA     SI,TST_MSG      ;output choice message
                CALL    S_END
    GET_RP:     CALL    C_IN            ;get user choice
                CALL    C_OUT           ;echo it
                CMP     AL,'1'          ;must be '1' or '2'
                JZ      WAVER
                CMP     AL,'2'
                JZ      EK_O
                CALL    ERROR           ;give an error beep
                JMP     GET_RP
    WAVER:      MOV     CX,256          ;init loop counter
                MOV     SI,0            ;init pointer to data
    P_IE:       MOV     AL,SINE[SI]     ;get a sine wave sample
                OUT     D_AC,AL         ;output to D/A
                ADD     SI,1            ;point to next data sample
                LOOP    P_IE            ;repeat
                JMP     WAVER           ;go generate another cycle
```

```
EK_0:   IN    AL,AD_STAT    ;check for end-of-conversion signal
        AND   AL,01H
        JNZ   EK_0
        MOV   AL,AD_RD       ;do handshaking for A/D read
        OUT   AD_STAT,AL
        IN    AL,A_DC        ;read A/D
        NOT   AL             ;maintain phase relationship
        OUT   D_AC,AL        ;echo data to D/A
        MOV   AL,AD_WR       ;start a new conversion
        OUT   AD_STAT,AL
        MOV   AL,AD_NOM
        OUT   AD_STAT,AL
        JMP   EK_0           ;repeat
```

WAVER makes use of a 256-byte data table containing the digitized samples of a one-cycle sine wave. The table is as follows:

```
SINE  DB   82H,85H,88H,8BH,8EH,91H,94H,97H
      DB   9BH,9EH,0A1H,0A4H,0A7H,0AAH,0ADH,0AFH
      DB   0B2H,0B5H,0B8H,0BBH,0BEH,0C0H,0C3H,0C6H
      DB   0C8H,0CBH,0CDH,0D0H,0D2H,0D4H,0D7H,0D9H
      DB   0DBH,0DDH,0DFH,0E1H,0E3H,0E5H,0E7H,0E9H
      DB   0EBH,0ECH,0EEH,0EFH,0F1H,0F2H,0F4H,0F5H
      DB   0F6H,0F7H,0F8H,0F9H,0FAH,0FBH,0FBH,0FCH
      DB   0FDH,0FDH,0FEH,0FEH,0FEH,0FEH,0FEH,0FFH
      DB   0FEH,0FEH,0FEH,0FEH,0FEH,0FDH,0FDH,0FCH
      DB   0FBH,0FBH,0FAH,0F9H,0F8H,0F7H,0F6H,0F5H
      DB   0F4H,0F2H,0F1H,0EFH,0EEH,0ECH,0EBH,0F9H
      DB   0E7H,0E5H,0E3H,0E1H,0DFH,0DDH,0DBH,0D9H
      DB   0D7H,0D4H,0D2H,0D0H,0CDH,0CBH,0C8H,0C6H
      DB   0C3H,0C0H,0BEH,0BBH,0B8H,0B5H,0B2H,0AFH
      DB   0ADH,0AAH,0A7H,0A4H,0A1H,9EH,9BH,97H
      DB   94H,91H,8EH,8BH,88H,85H,82H,7EH
      DB   7BH,78H,75H,72H,6FH,6CH,69H,66H
      DB   62H,5FH,5CH,59H,56H,53H,50H,4EH
      DB   4BH,48H,45H,42H,3FH,3DH,3AH,37H
      DB   35H,32H,30H,2DH,2BH,29H,26H,24H
      DB   22H,20H,1EH,1CH,1AH,18H,16H,14H
      DB   12H,11H,0FH,0EH,0CH,0BH,9,8
      DB   7,6,5,4,3,2,2,1,0,0,0,0,0,0,0,0
      DB   0,0,0,0,0,0,0,1,2,2,3,4,5,6,7,8
      DB   9,0BH,0CH,0EH,0FH,11H,12H,14H
      DB   16H,18H,1AH,1CH,1EH,20H,22H,24H
      DB   26H,29H,2BH,2DH,30H,32H,35H,37H
      DB   3AH,3DH,3FH,42H,45H,48H,4BH,4EH
      DB   50H,53H,56H,59H,5CH,5FH,62H,66H
      DB   69H,6CH,6FH,72H,75H,78H,7BH,7FH
```

A predefined message is also required to provide the test choices:

```
TST_MSG  DB   13,10,'1) Send sinewave to D/A converter, or'
         DB   13,10,'2) Echo A/D to D/A'
         DB   13,10,'Choice ?$'
```

The X Command: Examine Memory   This command is used to manually enter a program by hand, or to examine the contents of selected memory locations. The user supplies the starting address in memory. The X command routine displays the address and the contents of each memory location. The user is given the chance to enter a new value, or to leave the data unchanged. The format of the X command is: X <starting address>. An example of the X command is:

X 1000

which generates the following string of addresses:

```
1000    3A?<sp>
1001    29?07<cr>
1002    B6?<cr>
```

The 3A at address 1000 remained unchanged, since a space was entered at the '?' prompt. The 29 at address 1001 was changed to 07 and the <cr> on the third line terminated the X command.

```
E_XAM:    CALL    GET_NUM     ;get starting address
          MOV     SI,DX
DO_LYN:   CALL    CRLF        ;display starting address
          MOV     DX,SI
          CALL    H_OUT
          CALL    BLANK
          CALL    BLANK
          MOV     AL,ES:[SI]  ;read memory
          CALL    HTOA        ;display byte
          MOV     AL,'?'      ;ask for new data
          CALL    C_OUT
          CALL    GET_NUM
          CMP     BH,'0'      ;change?
          JZ      E_MIP       ;no (must have been CR or SP)
          MOV     ES:[SI],DL  ;yes, replace data
EX_GNA:   INC     SI          ;point to next location
          JMP     DO_LYN      ;repeat
E_MIP:    CMP     AL,20H      ;skip over data?
          JZ      EX_GNA      ;yes
          JMP     GET_COM     ;no, exit
```

The Body of the Monitor

At this point we have covered the creation of all routines (command and auxiliary) that we need inside our monitor. The last step we need to perform is to collect all the routines together, and organize them into a source file. The source file must provide an interrupt vector for the INT 3 instruction used by the breakpoint routine. It must also contain code to initialize the stack pointer, and handle breakpoint and reentry (INT 95H) procedures.

The following source code must reside at the beginning of the source file. It is followed by the code of the command and auxiliary routines.

```
CODE    SEGMENT    PARA 'CODE'
MAIN    PROC       FAR
        ASSUME     CS:CODE,DS:DATA,ES:DATA2
;segment usage is as follows:
;       CS for machine code
;       DS for EPROM-based data tables
;       ES for user RAM operations
;       SS for RAM-stack operations
```

```
            ORG      100H
    RTOP    EQU      1F80H              ;starting address of reserved RAM
            LEA      BX,RE_STRT
            MOV      CX,0E00H           ;segment address of monitor
            MOV      AX,0
            MOV      SI,0
            MOV      DS,AX
            MOV      [SI + 254H],BX     ;init restart address (INT 95H)
            MOV      [SI + 256H],CX
            LEA      BX,BR_ENTR         ;init breakpoint address (INT 3)
            MOV      [SI + 0CH],BX
            MOV      [SI + 0EH],CX
            MOV      AX,CS              ;init all segment registers
            ADD      AX,DATA
            MOV      DS,AX
            SUB      AX,AX
            MOV      ES,AX
            MOV      SS,AX
            MOV      SP,2000H           ;init stack pointer
            CALL     IN_IT              ;init I/O devices
            LEA      SI,HELLO           ;send monitor greeting
            CALL     S_END
            JMP      GET_COM            ;go get first command

;entry point during a breakpoint (via INT 3)
BR_ENTR:
            CALL     ENVIR                    ;save/display environment
            LEA      SI,BR_BAK                ;display breakpoint message
            CALL     S_END
            POP      AX                       ;get breakpoint address from stack
            MOV      ES:[BR_IP + RTOP],AX
            POP      AX
            MOV      ES:[BR_CS + RTOP],AX
            POP      AX
            MOV      DX,ES:[BR_CS + RTOP]     ;display address of breakpoint
            CALL     H_OUT                    ;in CS:IP format
            MOV      AL,':'
            CALL     C_OUT
            MOV      DX,ES:[BR_IP + RTOP]
            DEC      DX
            CALL     H_OUT
            MOV      AL,']'
            CALL     C_OUT
            MOV      SI,ES:[B_MMA + RTOP]     ;restore user code
            MOV      AL,ES:[OP_KODE + RTOP]
            MOV      ES:[SI],AL
            MOV      ES:[BR_STAT + RTOP],0    ;clear breakpoint status
            JMP      GET_COM

;normal entry point (via INT 95H)
;this routine falls into GET_COM
RE_STRT:
            CALL     ENVIR                    ;save/display environment
            LEA      SI,RENTER                ;display re-entry message
            CALL     S_END
            POP      AX                       ;get exit address from stack
            MOV      ES:[BR_IP + RTOP],AX
            POP      AX
            MOV      ES:[BR_CS + RTOP],AX
            POP      AX
            MOV      DX,ES:[BR_CS + RTOP]     ;display exit address
            CALL     H_OUT
```

```
          MOV      AL,':'
          CALL     C_OUT
          MOV      DX,ES:[BR_IP + RTOP]
          SUB      DX,2
          CALL     H_OUT
          MOV      AL,']'
          CALL     C_OUT
GET_COM:  <now include command recognizer code>
```

Two data segments are also used by the monitor software. The first segment, DATA, contains all of the text messages used by the system, other types of data tables (including the sine wave table), and the system equates (for definition of I/O ports).

The second data segment, DATA2, contains all of the reserved storage locations for the monitor.

```
DATA     SEGMENT  PARA   'DATA'
HELLO    DB       13,10,'8088 Monitor, Ver:1.0$'
WR_BY    DB       13,10,'C1987 James L. Antonakos$'
RENTER   DB       13,10,'Re-entry by external program at [$'
BR_BAK   DB       13,10,'Breakpoint encountered at [$'

;messages from auxiliary and command routines go here also

D_AC     EQU      0
A_DC     EQU      1
AD_STAT  EQU      2
AD_CTRL  EQU      3
AD_RD    EQU      20H
AD_WR    EQU      10H
AD_NOM   EQU      30H
C8255    EQU      83H   ;Aout, Bin, CLin, CHout
S_DATA   EQU      40H
S_STAT   EQU      41H
S_CTRL   EQU      41H
M8251    EQU      0CEH  ;2 stop, no parity, 8 data, *16 clock
C8251    EQU      05H   ;R and T enable only
TRDY     EQU      01H
RRDY     EQU      02H
DATA     ENDS

DATA2    SEGMENT  PARA 'DATA'
R_DATA   DW       11 DUP(?)
GO_ADR   DW       ?
BR_STAT  DB       ?
B_MMA    DW       ?     ;breakpoint main-memory address
OP_KODE  DB       ?     ;opcode byte
BR_CS    DW       ?     ;breakpoint CS
BR_IP    DW       ?     ;breakpoint IP
F_LAGS   DW       ?     ;system flags
C_SUM    DB       ?     ;checksum storage
DATA2    ENDS
```

The entire source file must be assembled and burned into an EPROM. Your instructor should have a copy of the entire source file (SBC-MON.ASM) for your use.

To get the monitor program to start up correctly, a far jump instruction is placed into the EPROM at the location corresponding to address FFFF0H. The code for the jump instruction is EA 00 01 00 0E, which jumps to the first instruction of the monitor program located at CS:IP = 0E00:0100.

You may already have ideas for improving the design of the monitor program (by rewriting existing commands or adding new ones). *But if you plan to build the minimal system, make sure the basic monitor works before you begin changing it!*

11.7 A SAMPLE SESSION WITH THE SINGLE-BOARD COMPUTER

Once you have constructed the minimal system and burned the monitor program into EPROM, you will be ready to test the system. The following sample session illustrates many of the 8088 single-board computer's features. You may wish to try to duplicate the session on your computer. Keep in mind that all user inputs are in **boldface**:

1. Turn computer on. A greeting should appear:

```
8088 Monitor, Ver1.0
```

2. Consider the following test program:

```
1000   03 D8   ADD     BX,AX
1002   03 D1   ADD     DX,CX
1004   CD 95   INT     95H
```

3. To load the test program into memory, use the X command:

```
>X 1000
1000   C7?03
1001   06?D8
1002   74?03
1003   50?D1
1004   CD?<SP>
1005   00?95
1006   B2?<CR>
>
```

Note: The <sp> skips over the data in location 1004 (which is already correct) and the <cr> terminates the command.

4. Display the program now stored in memory:

```
>D 1000 1005
1000   03 D8 03 D1 CD 95
>
```

5. Load AX through DX with initial data to be passed to the program:

```
>E
AX - FF20?1111
BX - 7E36?2222
CX - 3352?3333
DX - A5E8?4444
       etc.
```

6. Check the register contents:

```
>R
AX:1111   BX:2222   CX:3333   DX:4444
                etc.
```

7. Execute the program:

```
>G 1000
AX:1111   BX:3333   CX:3333   DX:7777
                etc.
Re-entry by external program at [0000:1004]
```

Note: BX now equals BX+AX and DX now equals DX+CX. Also, the INT 95H instruction caused the registers to be saved and displayed upon re-entry to the monitor.

8. Place a breakpoint at the beginning of the second instruction:

```
>B 1002
Breakpoint saved.
```

9. Check the user code again:

```
>D 1000 1005
1000   03 D8 CC D1 CD 95
```

Note: The "CC" opcode is the breakpoint interrupt. The user code "03" is now saved in system RAM, to be replaced after the breakpoint is encountered during execution.

10. Execute the program again:

```
>G 1000
AX:1111   BX:4444   CX:3333   DX:7777
                etc.
Breakpoint encountered at [0000:1002]
```

Note: By examining the register contents we see that BX has been changed (by another addition with AX) but CX and DX remain unchanged. This was the intent of placing the breakpoint at address 1002.

11. Check the user code again:

```
>D 1000 1005
1000   03 D8 03 D1 CD 95
```

Note: The breakpoint service routine has restored the original instruction byte at address 1002.

11.8 SUMMARY

This chapter dealt with the hardware and software design of a minimal 8088-maxmode single-board computer. The system uses 8K of EPROM, 8KB of RAM, and has a 2400-baud serial I/O section. In addition, a parallel device is included to provide analog I/O capability.

Many design ideas were suggested, and reasons for choosing one idea over another were given.

The software monitor program is composed of many auxiliary routines, each of which performs one task. The monitor command routines selectively call the auxiliary routines, resulting in shorter, more logical code.

The software monitor is by no means complete, and may be improved by adding commands or features after the basic system is up and running.

STUDY QUESTIONS

1. Modify the circuitry of Figure 11.2 so that the entire address bus can be tristated by a zero placed on a control signal called $\overline{\text{UNBUS}}$.
2. What changes must be made to the memory section (see Figure 11.3) to allow the use of 16KB 27128 EPROMs? Assume that a total of four 27128s will be used.
3. What then will be the address range for each memory in Question 2?
4. How can the 74LS138 memory-address decoder be disabled?
5. Design a selector circuit that will allow a single switch to select either 300 or 2400 baud operation in the serial device.
6. Redesign the port-address decoder in Figure 11.4 so that the 74LS138 is only enabled when $\overline{\text{IORC}}$ or $\overline{\text{IOWC}}$ is low.
7. Redesign the port-address decoder to decode port addresses in the range 00?? only (i.e., the upper byte of the address must be zero).
8. Design a parallel circuit (using an 8255) that has LEDs on port B, switches on port A, and a common-cathode 7-segment display on port C. Each LED must turn on when its associated bit is high. An open switch indicates a logic 1 level. The LSB of port C drives segment A of the display. Each successive bit drives the next segment. The base port address is E0.
9. Write the software necessary to initialize the parallel circuit of Question 8. All LEDs should be off and the 7-segment display should be showing a U (for "up and running").
10. Write an auxiliary routine that will display the decimal equivalent (0 to 255) of the contents of register AL.
11. Repeat Question 10 for the value contained in DX. The decimal range is now 0-65,535.
12. Modify C_OUT so that it automatically calls CRLF if register AL contains 0DH on entry.
13. Using the auxiliary routines, complete the following table:

Command	Inputs	Outputs	Registers Used
GET_WRD	–	AX	AX, BH, [GET_BYT]

The routine name GET_BYT in square brackets means that it is called by GET_WRD. Show a table entry for each auxiliary routine.
14. Write an auxiliary routine to accept a multidigit decimal number from the keyboard and place its binary equivalent into register AX. Give an error message if the number is greater than 65,535.
15. What changes must be made to allow the command recognizer to recognize entire

names for commands? For example, instead of D, use DUMP or DISP. For G, use EXEC or GO.

16. Show the changes needed to add the command V to the monitor program. The V command needs no inputs. The command routine associated with V is V_ERIFY.

17. Write a command routine called V_ERIFY that will test all available RAM locations. It will display the address, data written, and data read for any locations that fail the test.

18. Write a command routine that will calculate the checksum of RAM and EPROM and display the results in hexadecimal. The checksum is obtained by adding up all bytes in the desired memory range, ignoring carries.

19. Write a command routine to add and subtract two supplied hexadecimal numbers.

20. How can the breakpoint routine be modified to allow for more than one breakpoint at a time?

21. What other formats for displaying memory contents might be useful?

22. Modify the D_UMP routine so that the display is paused if Control-S is entered from the keyboard. A paused display is restarted by pressing any key.

23. Rewrite the I_NIT routine so that a single register may be changed by naming it in the command. For example, E CX will only allow register CX to be updated.

24. What instructions must be added to the E_XEC command routine so that any address outside the range 400H to 1F00H causes an error message?

25. Modify the port-input routine so that the data at the input port is continuously updated until <cr> is entered.

26. Write an interrupt service routine for INT 80H. Modify the monitor's start-up code to initialize the INT 80H vector table entry to point to the D_ISPAT routine. The D_ISPAT interrupt service routine uses the number in register AL to call a specific auxiliary command, according to the following table:

AL Value	Routine Called
00	C_IN
01	C_OUT
02	S_END
10	BLANK
11	CRLF
20	GET_BYT
28	GET_WRD
2F	GET_NUM
40	CH_CASE
80	DPR

27. Compute the approximate frequency of the sinewave output during the analog test procedure.

28. Assemble this code fragment using DEBUG. Execute it with the monitor commands. What are the final results?

```
MOV     AX,1234H
MOV     BX,5678H
ADD     AL,BL
XOR     AH,BH
```

29. What monitor commands would you deem nonessential? Explain your reasons for doing so.

30. What monitor commands have not been discussed at all (or mentioned in the study questions)? What are the requirements of any additional commands you can think of? Is there enough room in the 2764 EPROM to include them?

APPENDIX

A

8088 Data Sheets

8088
8-BIT HMOS MICROPROCESSOR
8088/8088-2

- 8-Bit Data Bus Interface
- 16-Bit Internal Architecture
- Direct Addressing Capability to 1 Mbyte of Memory
- Direct Software Compatibility with 8086 CPU
- 14-Word by 16-Bit Register Set with Symmetrical Operations
- 24 Operand Addressing Modes

- Byte, Word, and Block Operations
- 8-Bit and 16-Bit Signed and Unsigned Arithmetic in Binary or Decimal, Including Multiply and Divide
- Two Clock Rates:
  — 5 MHz for 8088
  — 8 MHz for 8088-2
- Available in EXPRESS
  — Standard Temperature Range
  — Extended Temperature Range

The Intel® 8088 is a high performance microprocessor implemented in N-channel, depletion load, silicon gate technology (HMOS-II), and packaged in a 40-pin CERDIP package. The processor has attributes of both 8- and 16-bit microprocessors. It is directly compatible with 8086 software and 8080/8085 hardware and peripherals.

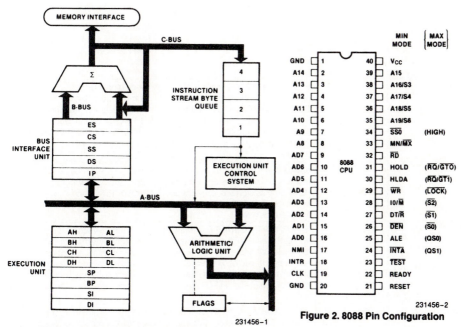

Figure 1. 8088 CPU Functional Block Diagram

Figure 2. 8088 Pin Configuration

231456–1

231456–2

Table 1. Pin Description

The following pin function descriptions are for 8088 systems in either minimum or maximum mode. The "local bus" in these descriptions is the direct multiplexed bus interface connection to the 8088 (without regard to additional bus buffers).

Symbol	Pin No.	Type	Name and Function
AD7–AD0	9–16	I/O	**ADDRESS DATA BUS:** These lines constitute the time multiplexed memory/IO address (T1) and data (T2, T3, Tw, T4) bus. These lines are active HIGH and float to 3-state OFF during interrupt acknowledge and local bus "hold acknowledge".
A15–A8	2–8, 39	O	**ADDRESS BUS:** These lines provide address bits 8 through 15 for the entire bus cycle (T1–T4). These lines do not have to be latched by ALE to remain valid. A15–A8 are active HIGH and float to 3-state OFF during interrupt acknowledge and local bus "hold acknowledge".
A19/S6, A18/S5, A17/S4, A16/S3	35–38	O	**ADDRESS/STATUS:** During T1, these are the four most significant address lines for memory operations. During I/O operations, these lines are LOW. During memory and I/O operations, status information is available on these lines during T2, T3, Tw, and T4. S6 is always low. The status of the interrupt enable flag bit (S5) is updated at the beginning of each clock cycle. S4 and S3 are encoded as shown. This information indicates which segment register is presently being used for data accessing. These lines float to 3-state OFF during local bus "hold acknowledge".

	S4	S3	Characteristics
	0 (LOW)	0	Alternate Data
	0	1	Stack
	1 (HIGH)	0	Code or None
	1	1	Data
	S6 is 0 (LOW)		

Symbol	Pin No.	Type	Name and Function
$\overline{RD}$	32	O	**READ:** Read strobe indicates that the processor is performing a memory or I/O read cycle, depending on the state of the IO/$\overline{M}$ pin or S2. This signal is used to read devices which reside on the 8088 local bus. $\overline{RD}$ is active LOW during T2, T3 and Tw of any read cycle, and is guaranteed to remain HIGH in T2 until the 8088 local bus has floated. This signal floats to 3-state OFF in "hold acknowledge".
READY	22	I	**READY:** is the acknowledgement from the addressed memory or I/O device that it will complete the data transfer. The RDY signal from memory or I/O is synchronized by the 8284 clock generator to form READY. This signal is active HIGH. The 8088 READY input is not synchronized. Correct operation is not guaranteed if the set up and hold times are not met.
INTR	18	I	**INTERRUPT REQUEST:** is a level triggered input which is sampled during the last clock cycle of each instruction to determine if the processor should enter into an interrupt acknowledge operation. A subroutine is vectored to via an interrupt vector lookup table located in system memory. It can be internally masked by software resetting the interrupt enable bit. INTR is internally synchronized. This signal is active HIGH.
$\overline{TEST}$	23	I	**TEST:** input is examined by the "wait for test" instruction. If the $\overline{TEST}$ input is LOW, execution continues, otherwise the processor waits in an "idle" state. This input is synchronized internally during each clock cycle on the leading edge of CLK.

Table 1. Pin Description (Continued)

Symbol	Pin No.	Type	Name and Function
NMI	17	I	**NON-MASKABLE INTERRUPT:** is an edge triggered input which causes a type 2 interrupt. A subroutine is vectored to via an interrupt vector lookup table located in system memory. NMI is not maskable internally by software. A transition from a LOW to HIGH initiates the interrupt at the end of the current instruction. This input is internally synchronized.
RESET	21	I	**RESET:** causes the processor to immediately terminate its present activity. The signal must be active HIGH for at least four clock cycles. It restarts execution, as described in the instruction set description, when RESET returns LOW. RESET is internally synchronized.
CLK	19	I	**CLOCK:** provides the basic timing for the processor and bus controller. It is asymmetric with a 33% duty cycle to provide optimized internal timing.
V$_{CC}$	40		**V$_{CC}$:** is the + 5V ± 10% power supply pin.
GND	1, 20		**GND:** are the ground pins.
MN/$\overline{MX}$	33	I	**MINIMUM/MAXIMUM:** indicates what mode the processor is to operate in. The two modes are discussed in the following sections.

The following pin function descriptions are for the 8088 minimum mode (i.e., MN/$\overline{MX}$ = V$_{CC}$). Only the pin functions which are unique to minimum mode are described; all other pin functions are as described above.

Symbol	Pin No.	Type	Name and Function
IO/$\overline{M}$	28	O	**STATUS LINE:** is an inverted maximum mode $\overline{S2}$. It is used to distinguish a memory access from an I/O access. IO/$\overline{M}$ becomes valid in the T4 preceding a bus cycle and remains valid until the final T4 of the cycle (I/O = HIGH, M = LOW). IO/$\overline{M}$ floats to 3-state OFF in local bus "hold acknowledge".
$\overline{WR}$	29	O	**WRITE:** strobe indicates that the processor is performing a write memory or write I/O cycle, depending on the state of the IO/$\overline{M}$ signal. WR is active for T2, T3, and Tw of any write cycle. It is active LOW, and floats to 3-state OFF in local bus "hold acknowledge".
$\overline{INTA}$	24	O	**INTA:** is used as a read strobe for interrupt acknowledge cycles. It is active LOW during T2, T3, and Tw of each interrupt acknowledge cycle.
ALE	25	O	**ADDRESS LATCH ENABLE:** is provided by the processor to latch the address into an address latch. It is a HIGH pulse active during clock low of T1 of any bus cycle. Note that ALE is never floated.
DT/$\overline{R}$	27	O	**DATA TRANSMIT/RECEIVE:** is needed in a minimum system that desires to use a data bus transceiver. It is used to control the direction of data flow through the transceiver. Logically, DT/$\overline{R}$ is equivalent to $\overline{S1}$ in the maximum mode, and its timing is the same as for IO/$\overline{M}$ (T = HIGH, R = LOW). This signal floats to 3-state OFF in local "hold acknowledge".
$\overline{DEN}$	26	O	**DATA ENABLE:** is provided as an output enable for the data bus transceiver in a minimum system which uses the transceiver. $\overline{DEN}$ is active LOW during each memory and I/O access, and for $\overline{INTA}$ cycles. For a read or $\overline{INTA}$ cycle, it is active from the middle of T2 until the middle of T4, while for a write cycle, it is active from the beginning of T2 until the middle of T4. $\overline{DEN}$ floats to 3-state OFF during local bus "hold acknowledge".

Table 1. Pin Description (Continued)

Symbol	Pin No.	Type	Name and Function
HOLD, HLDA	31, 30	I, O	**HOLD:** indicates that another master is requesting a local bus "hold". To be acknowledged, HOLD must be active HIGH. The processor receiving the "hold" request will issue HLDA (HIGH) as an acknowledgement, in the middle of a T4 or Ti clock cycle. Simultaneous with the issuance of HLDA the processor will float the local bus and control lines. After HOLD is detected as being LOW, the processor lowers HLDA, and when the processor needs to run another cycle, it will again drive the local bus and control lines. HOLD and HLDA have internal pull-up resistors. Hold is not an asynchronous input. External synchronization should be provided if the system cannot otherwise guarantee the set up time.
$\overline{SSO}$	34	O	**STATUS LINE:** is logically equivalent to $\overline{SO}$ in the maximum mode. The combination of $\overline{SSO}$, IO/$\overline{M}$ and DT/$\overline{R}$ allows the system to completely decode the current bus cycle status.

IO/$\overline{M}$	DT/$\overline{R}$	$\overline{SSO}$	Characteristics
1(HIGH)	0	0	Interrupt Acknowledge
1	0	1	Read I/O Port
1	1	0	Write I/O Port
1	1	1	Halt
0(LOW)	0	0	Code Access
0	0	1	Read Memory
0	1	0	Write Memory
0	1	1	Passive

The following pin function descriptions are for the 8088/8288 system in maximum mode (i.e., MN/$\overline{MX}$ = GND). Only the pin functions which are unique to maximum mode are described; all other pin functions are as described above.

Symbol	Pin No.	Type	Name and Function
$\overline{S2}$, $\overline{S1}$, $\overline{S0}$	26–28	O	**STATUS:** is active during clock high of T4, T1, and T2, and is returned to the passive state (1,1,1) during T3 or during Tw when READY is HIGH. This status is used by the 8288 bus controller to generate all memory and I/O access control signals. Any change by $\overline{S2}$, $\overline{S1}$, or $\overline{S0}$ during T4 is used to indicate the beginning of a bus cycle, and the return to the passive state in T3 and Tw is used to indicate the end of a bus cycle. These signals float to 3-state OFF during "hold acknowledge". During the first clock cycle after RESET becomes active, these signals are active HIGH. After this first clock, they float to 3-state OFF.

$\overline{S2}$	$\overline{S1}$	$\overline{S0}$	Characteristics
0(LOW)	0	0	Interrupt Acknowledge
0	0	1	Read I/O Port
0	1	0	Write I/O Port
0	1	1	Halt
1(HIGH)	0	0	Code Access
1	0	1	Read Memory
1	1	0	Write Memory
1	1	1	Passive

Table 1. Pin Description (Continued)

Symbol	Pin No.	Type	Name and Function
$\overline{RQ}/\overline{GT0}$, $\overline{RQ}/\overline{GT1}$	30, 31	I/O	**REQUEST/GRANT:** pins are used by other local bus masters to force the processor to release the local bus at the end of the processor's current bus cycle. Each pin is bidirectional with $\overline{RQ}/\overline{GT0}$ having higher priority than $\overline{RQ}/\overline{GT1}$. $\overline{RQ}/\overline{GT}$ has an internal pull-up resistor, so may be left unconnected. The request/grant sequence is as follows (See Figure 8): 1. A pulse of one CLK wide from another local bus master indicates a local bus request ("hold") to the 8088 (pulse 1). 2. During a T4 or TI clock cycle, a pulse one clock wide from the 8088 to the requesting master (pulse 2), indicates that the 8088 has allowed the local bus to float and that it will enter the "hold acknowledge" state at the next CLK. The CPU's bus interface unit is disconnected logically from the local bus during "hold acknowledge". The same rules as for HOLD/HOLDA apply as for when the bus is released. 3. A pulse one CLK wide from the requesting master indicates to the 8088 (pulse 3) that the "hold" request is about to end and that the 8088 can reclaim the local bus at the next CLK. The CPU then enters T4. Each master-master exchange of the local bus is a sequence of three pulses. There must be one idle CLK cycle after each bus exchange. Pulses are active LOW. If the request is made while the CPU is performing a memory cycle, it will release the local bus during T4 of the cycle when all the following conditions are met: 1. Request occurs on or before T2. 2. Current cycle is not the low bit of a word. 3. Current cycle is not the first acknowledge of an interrupt acknowledge sequence. 4. A locked instruction is not currently executing. If the local bus is idle when the request is made the two possible events will follow: 1. Local bus will be released during the next clock. 2. A memory cycle will start within 3 clocks. Now the four rules for a currently active memory cycle apply with condition number 1 already satisfied.
$\overline{LOCK}$	29	O	**LOCK:** indicates that other system bus masters are not to gain control of the system bus while $\overline{LOCK}$ is active (LOW). The $\overline{LOCK}$ signal is activated by the "LOCK" prefix instruction and remains active until the completion of the next instruction. This signal is active LOW, and floats to 3-state off in "hold acknowledge".
QS1, QS0	24, 25	O	**QUEUE STATUS:** provide status to allow external tracking of the internal 8088 instruction queue. The queue status is valid during the CLK cycle after which the queue operation is performed.

QS1	QS0	Characteristics
0(LOW)	0	No Operation
0	1	First Byte of Opcode from Queue
1(HIGH)	0	Empty the Queue
1	1	Subsequent Byte from Queue

Symbol	Pin No.	Type	Name and Function
—	34	O	Pin 34 is always high in the maximum mode.

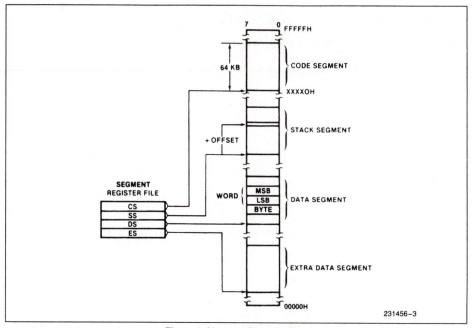

Figure 3. Memory Organization

FUNCTIONAL DESCRIPTION

Memory Organization

The processor provides a 20-bit address to memory which locates the byte being referenced. The memory is organized as a linear array of up to 1 million bytes, addressed as 00000(H) to FFFFF(H). The memory is logically divided into code, data, extra data, and stack segments of up to 64K bytes each, with each segment falling on 16-byte boundaries (See Figure 3).

All memory references are made relative to base addresses contained in high speed segment registers. The segment types were chosen based on the ad-

dressing needs of programs. The segment register to be selected is automatically chosen according to the rules of the following table. All information in one segment type share the same logical attributes (e.g. code or data). By structuring memory into relocatable areas of similar characteristics and by automatically selecting segment registers, programs are shorter, faster, and more structured.

Word (16-bit) operands can be located on even or odd address boundaries. For address and data operands, the least significant byte of the word is stored in the lower valued address location and the most significant byte in the next higher address location. The BIU will automatically execute two fetch or write cycles for 16-bit operands.

Memory Reference Used	Segment Register Used	Segment Selection Rule
Instructions	CODE (CS)	Automatic with all instruction prefetch.
Stack	STACK (SS)	All stack pushes and pops. Memory references relative to BP base register except data references.
Local Data	DATA (DS)	Data references when: relative to stack, destination of string operation, or explicity overridden.
External (Global) Data	EXTRA (ES)	Destination of string operations: Explicitly selected using a segment override.

Certain locations in memory are reserved for specific CPU operations (See Figure 4). Locations from addresses FFFF0H through FFFFFH are reserved for operations including a jump to the initial system initialization routine. Following RESET, the CPU will always begin execution at location FFFF0H where the jump must be located. Locations 00000H through 003FFH are reserved for interrupt operations. Four-byte pointers consisting of a 16-bit segment address and a 16-bit offset address direct program flow to one of the 256 possible interrupt service routines. The pointer elements are assumed to have been stored at their respective places in reserved memory prior to the occurrence of interrupts.

Minimum and Maximum Modes

The requirements for supporting minimum and maximum 8088 systems are sufficiently different that they cannot be done efficiently with 40 uniquely defined pins. Consequently, the 8088 is equipped with a strap pin (MN/$\overline{\text{MX}}$) which defines the system con-

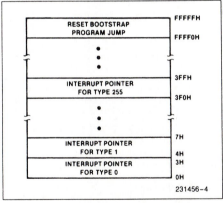

Figure 4. Reserved Memory Locations

figuration. The definition of a certain subset of the pins changes, dependent on the condition of the strap pin. When the MN/$\overline{\text{MX}}$ pin is strapped to GND, the 8088 defines pins 24 through 31 and 34 in maximum mode. When the MN/$\overline{\text{MX}}$ pin is strapped to V_{CC}, the 8088 generates bus control signals itself on pins 24 through 31 and 34.

The minimum mode 8088 can be used with either a multiplexed or demultiplexed bus. The multiplexed bus configuration is compatible with the MCS-85™ multiplexed bus peripherals. This configuration (See Figure 5) provides the user with a minimum chip count system. This architecture provides the 8088 processing power in a highly integrated form.

The demultiplexed mode requires one latch (for 64K addressability) or two latches (for a full megabyte of addressing). A third latch can be used for buffering if the address bus loading requires it. A transceiver can also be used if data bus buffering is required (See Figure 6). The 8088 provides $\overline{\text{DEN}}$ and DT/$\overline{\text{R}}$ to control the transceiver, and ALE to latch the addresses. This configuration of the minimum mode provides the standard demultiplexed bus structure with heavy bus buffering and relaxed bus timing requirements.

The maximum mode employs the 8288 bus controller (See Figure 7). The 8288 decodes status lines $\overline{\text{S0}}$, $\overline{\text{S1}}$, and $\overline{\text{S2}}$, and provides the system with all bus control signals. Moving the bus control to the 8288 provides better source and sink current capability to the control lines, and frees the 8088 pins for extended large system features. Hardware lock, queue status, and two request/grant interfaces are provided by the 8088 in maximum mode. These features allow co-processors in local bus and remote bus configurations.

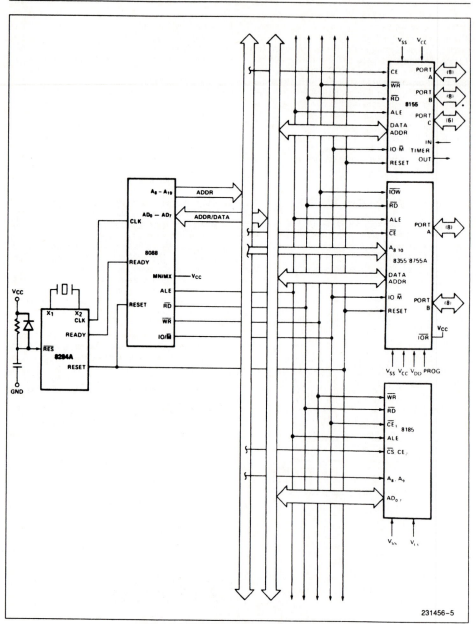

Figure 5. Multiplexed Bus Configuration

231456-5

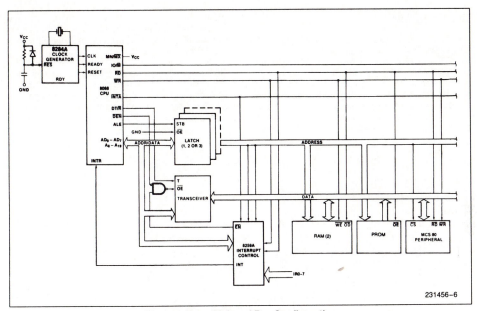

Figure 6. Demultiplexed Bus Configuration

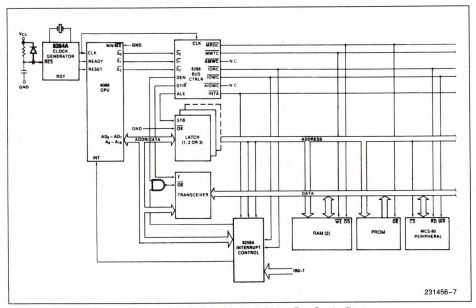

Figure 7. Fully Buffered System Using Bus Controller

387

8088

Bus Operation

The 8088 address/data bus is broken into three parts—the lower eight address/data bits (AD0–AD7), the middle eight address bits (A8–A15), and the upper four address bits (A16–A19). The address/data bits and the highest four address bits are time multiplexed. This technique provides the most efficient use of pins on the processor, permitting the use of a standard 40 lead package. The middle eight address bits are not multiplexed, i.e. they remain val-

id throughout each bus cycle. In addition, the bus can be demultiplexed at the processor with a single address latch if a standard, non-multiplexed bus is desired for the system.

Each processor bus cycle consists of at least four CLK cycles. These are referred to as T1, T2, T3, and T4 (See Figure 8). The address is emitted from the processor during T1 and data transfer occurs on the bus during T3 and T4. T2 is used primarily for chang-

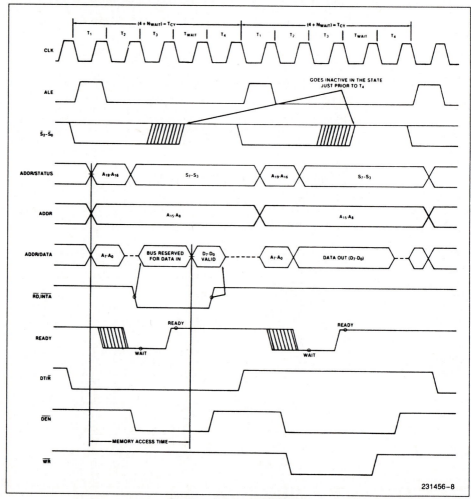

Figure 8. Basic System Timing

231456–8

ing the direction of the bus during read operations. In the event that a "NOT READY" indication is given by the addressed device, "wait" states (Tw) are inserted between T3 and T4. Each inserted "wait" state is of the same duration as a CLK cycle. Periods can occur between 8088 driven bus cycles. These are referred to as "idle" states (Ti), or inactive CLK cycles. The processor uses these cycles for internal housekeeping.

During T1 of any bus cycle, the ALE (address latch enable) signal is emitted (by either the processor or the 8288 bus controller, depending on the MN/$\overline{\text{MX}}$ strap). At the trailing edge of this pulse, a valid address and certain status information for the cycle may be latched.

Status bits $\overline{S0}$, $\overline{S1}$, and $\overline{S2}$ are used by the bus controller, in maximum mode, to identify the type of bus transaction according to the following table:

$\overline{S2}$	$\overline{S1}$	$\overline{S0}$	Characteristics
0(LOW)	0	0	Interrupt Acknowledge
0	0	1	Read I/O
0	1	0	Write I/O
0	1	1	Halt
1(HIGH)	0	0	Instruction Fetch
1	0	1	Read Data from Memory
1	1	0	Write Data to Memory
1	1	1	Passive (No Bus Cycle)

Status bits S3 through S6 are multiplexed with high order address bits and are therefore valid during T2 through T4. S3 and S4 indicate which segment register was used for this bus cycle in forming the address according to the following table:

S_4	S_3	Characteristics
0(LOW)	0	Alternate Data (Extra Segment)
0	1	Stack
1(HIGH)	0	Code or None
1	1	Data

S5 is a reflection of the PSW interrupt enable bit. S6 is always equal to 0.

I/O Addressing

In the 8088, I/O operations can address up to a maximum of 64K I/O registers. The I/O address appears in the same format as the memory address on bus lines A15–A0. The address lines A19–A16 are zero in I/O operations. The variable I/O instructions, which use register DX as a pointer, have full address capability, while the direct I/O instructions directly address one or two of the 256 I/O byte locations in page 0 of the I/O address space. I/O ports are addressed in the same manner as memory locations.

Designers familiar with the 8085 or upgrading an 8085 design should note that the 8085 addresses I/O with an 8-bit address on both halves of the 16-bit address bus. The 8088 uses a full 16-bit address on its lower 16 address lines.

EXTERNAL INTERFACE

Processor Reset and Initialization

Processor initialization or start up is accomplished with activation (HIGH) of the RESET pin. The 8088 RESET is required to be HIGH for greater than four clock cycles. The 8088 will terminate operations on the high-going edge of RESET and will remain dormant as long as RESET is HIGH. The low-going transition of RESET triggers an internal reset sequence for approximately 7 clock cycles. After this interval the 8088 operates normally, beginning with the instruction in absolute locations FFFF0H (See Figure 4). The RESET input is internally synchronized to the processor clock. At initialization, the HIGH to LOW transition of RESET must occur no sooner than 50 μs after power up, to allow complete initialization of the 8088.

NMI asserted prior to the 2nd clock after the end of RESET will not be honored. If NMI is asserted after that point and during the internal reset sequence, the processor may execute one instruction before responding to the interrupt. A hold request active immediately after RESET will be honored before the first instruction fetch.

All 3-state outputs float to 3-state OFF during RESET. Status is active in the idle state for the first clock after RESET becomes active and then floats to 3-state OFF. ALE and HLDA are driven low.

Interrupt Operations

Interrupt operations fall into two classes: software or hardware initiated. The software initiated interrupts and software aspects of hardware interrupts are specified in the instruction set description in the iAPX 88 book or the iAPX 86,88 User's Manual. Hardware interrupts can be classified as nonmaskable or maskable.

Interrupts result in a transfer of control to a new program location. A 256 element table containing address pointers to the interrupt service program locations resides in absolute locations 0 through 3FFH (See Figure 4), which are reserved for this purpose. Each element in the table is 4 bytes in size and corresponds to an interrupt "type." An interrupting device supplies an 8-bit type number, during the interrupt acknowledge sequence, which is used to vector through the appropriate element to the new interrupt service program location.

Non-Maskable Interrupt (NMI)

The processor provides a single non-maskable interrupt (NMI) pin which has higher priority than the maskable interrupt request (INTR) pin. A typical use would be to activate a power failure routine. The NMI is edge-triggered on a LOW to HIGH transition. The activation of this pin causes a type 2 interrupt.

NMI is required to have a duration in the HIGH state of greater than two clock cycles, but is not required to be synchronized to the clock. Any higher going transition of NMI is latched on-chip and will be serviced at the end of the current instruction or between whole moves (2 bytes in the case of word moves) of a block type instruction. Worst case response to NMI would be for multiply, divide, and variable shift instructions. There is no specification on the occurrence of the low-going edge; it may occur before, during, or after the servicing of NMI. Another high-going edge triggers another response if it occurs after the start of the NMI procedure. The signal must be free of logical spikes in general and be free of bounces on the low-going edge to avoid triggering extraneous responses.

Maskable Interrupt (INTR)

The 8088 provides a single interrupt request input (INTR) which can be masked internally by software with the resetting of the interrupt enable (IF) flag bit. The interrupt request signal is level triggered. It is internally synchronized during each clock cycle on the high-going edge of CLK. To be responded to, INTR must be present (HIGH) during the clock period preceding the end of the current instruction or the end of a whole move for a block type instruction. During interrupt response sequence, further interrupts are disabled. The enable bit is reset as part of the response to any interrupt (INTR, NMI, software interrupt, or single step), although the FLAGS register which is automatically pushed onto the stack reflects the state of the processor prior to the interrupt. Until the old FLAGS register is restored, the

enable bit will be zero unless specifically set by an instruction.

During the response sequence (See Figure 9), the processor executes two successive (back to back) interrupt acknowledge cycles. The 8088 emits the LOCK signal (maximum mode only) from T2 of the first bus cycle until T2 of the second. A local bus "hold" request will not be honored until the end of the second bus cycle. In the second bus cycle, a byte is fetched from the external interrupt system (e.g., 8259A PIC) which identifies the source (type) of the interrupt. This byte is multiplied by four and used as a pointer into the interrupt vector lookup table. An INTR signal left HIGH will be continually responded to within the limitations of the enable bit and sample period. The interrupt return instruction includes a flags pop which returns the status of the original interrupt enable bit when it restores the flags.

HALT

When a software HALT instruction is executed, the processor indicates that it is entering the HALT state in one of two ways, depending upon which mode is strapped. In minimum mode, the processor issues ALE, delayed by one clock cycle, to allow the system to latch the halt status. Halt status is available on IO/$\overline{M}$, DT/$\overline{R}$, and $\overline{SSO}$. In maximum mode, the processor issues appropriate HALT status on $\overline{S2}$, $\overline{S1}$, and $\overline{S0}$, and the 8288 bus controller issues one ALE. The 8088 will not leave the HALT state when a local bus hold is entered while in HALT. In this case, the processor reissues the HALT indicator at the end of the local bus hold. An interrupt request or RESET will force the 8088 out of the HALT state.

Read/Modify/Write (Semaphore) Operations via LOCK

The LOCK status information is provided by the processor when consecutive bus cycles are required during the execution of an instruction. This allows the processor to perform read/modify/write operations on memory (via the "exchange register with memory" instruction), without another system bus master receiving intervening memory cycles. This is useful in multiprocessor system configurations to accomplish "test and set lock" operations. The $\overline{LOCK}$ signal is activated (LOW) in the clock cycle following decoding of the LOCK prefix instruction. It is deactivated at the end of the last bus cycle of the instruction following the LOCK prefix. While $\overline{LOCK}$ is active, a request on a $\overline{RQ}/\overline{GT}$ pin will be recorded, and then honored at the end of the LOCK.

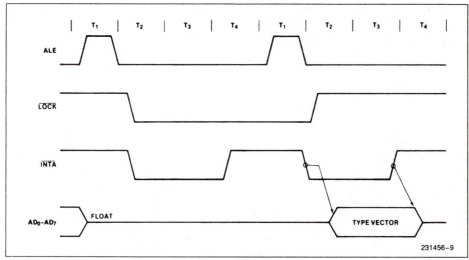

Figure 9. Interrupt Acknowledge Sequence

External Synchronization via $\overline{\text{TEST}}$

As an alternative to interrupts, the 8088 provides a single software-testable input pin ($\overline{\text{TEST}}$). This input is utilized by executing a WAIT instruction. The single WAIT instruction is repeatedly executed until the $\overline{\text{TEST}}$ input goes active (LOW). The execution of WAIT does not consume bus cycles once the queue is full.

If a local bus request occurs during WAIT execution, the 8088 3-states all output drivers. If interrupts are enabled, the 8088 will recognize interrupts and process them. The WAIT instruction is then refetched, and reexecuted.

Basic System Timing

In minimum mode, the MN/$\overline{\text{MX}}$ pin is strapped to V_{CC} and the processor emits bus control signals compatible with the 8085 bus structure. In maximum mode, the MN/$\overline{\text{MX}}$ pin is strapped to GND and the processor emits coded status information which the 8288 bus controller uses to generate MULTIBUS compatible bus control signals.

System Timing—Minimum System

(See Figure 8)

The read cycle begins in T1 with the assertion of the address latch enable (ALE) signal. The trailing (low

going) edge of this signal is used to latch the address information, which is valid on the address/data bus (AD0–AD7) at this time, into the 8282/8283 latch. Address lines A8 through A15 do not need to be latched because they remain valid throughout the bus cycle. From T1 to T4 the IO/$\overline{\text{M}}$ signal indicates a memory or I/O operation. At T2 the address is removed from the address/data bus and the bus goes to a high impedance state. The read control signal is also asserted at T2. The read ($\overline{\text{RD}}$) signal causes the addressed device to enable its data bus drivers to the local bus. Some time later, valid data will be available on the bus and the addressed device will drive the READY line HIGH. When the processor returns the read signal to a HIGH level, the addressed device will again 3-state its bus drivers. If a transceiver is required to buffer the 8088 local bus, signals DT/$\overline{\text{R}}$ and $\overline{\text{DEN}}$ are provided by the 8088.

A write cycle also begins with the assertion of ALE and the emission of the address. The IO/$\overline{\text{M}}$ signal is again asserted to indicate a memory or I/O write operation. In T2, immediately following the address emission, the processor emits the data to be written into the addressed location. This data remains valid until at least the middle of T4. During T2, T3, and Tw, the processor asserts the write control signal. The write ($\overline{\text{WR}}$) signal becomes active at the beginning of T2, as opposed to the read, which is delayed somewhat into T2 to provide time for the bus to float.

The basic difference between the interrupt acknowledge cycle and a read cycle is that the interrupt acknowledge ($\overline{\text{INTA}}$) signal is asserted in place of the read ($\overline{\text{RD}}$) signal and the address bus is floated. (See Figure 9) In the second of two successive $\overline{\text{INTA}}$ cycles, a byte of information is read from the data bus, as supplied by the interrupt system logic (i.e. 8259A priority interrupt controller). This byte identifies the source (type) of the interrupt. It is multiplied by four and used as a pointer into the interrupt vector lookup table, as described earlier.

Bus Timing—Medium Complexity Systems

(See Figure 10)

For medium complexity systems, the MN/$\overline{\text{MX}}$ pin is connected to GND and the 8288 bus controller is added to the system, as well as a latch for latching the system address, and a transceiver to allow for bus loading greater than the 8088 is capable of handling. Signals ALE, $\overline{\text{DEN}}$, and DT/$\overline{\text{R}}$ are generated by the 8288 instead of the processor in this configuration, although their timing remains relatively the same. The 8088 status outputs ($\overline{\text{S2}}$, $\overline{\text{S1}}$, and $\overline{\text{S0}}$) provide type of cycle information and become 8288 inputs. This bus cycle information specifies read (code, data, or I/O), write (data or I/O), interrupt acknowledge, or software halt. The 8288 thus issues control signals specifying memory read or write, I/O read or write, or interrupt acknowledge. The 8288 provides two types of write strobes, normal and advanced, to be applied as required. The normal write strobes have data valid at the leading edge of write. The advanced write strobes have the same timing as read strobes, and hence, data is not valid at the leading edge of write. The transceiver receives the usual T and $\overline{\text{OE}}$ inputs from the 8288's DT/$\overline{\text{R}}$ and $\overline{\text{DEN}}$ outputs.

The pointer into the interrupt vector table, which is passed during the second $\overline{\text{INTA}}$ cycle, can derive from an 8259A located on either the local bus or the system bus. If the master 8289A priority interrupt controller is positioned on the local bus, a TTL gate is required to disable the transceiver when reading from the master 8259A during the interrupt acknowledge sequence and software "poll".

The 8088 Compared to the 8086

The 8088 CPU is an 8-bit processor designed around the 8086 internal structure. Most internal functions of the 8088 are identical to the equivalent 8086 functions. The 8088 handles the external bus the same way the 8086 does with the distinction of handling only 8 bits at a time. Sixteen-bit operands are fetched or written in two consecutive bus cycles. Both processors will appear identical to the software engineer, with the exception of execution time. The internal register structure is identical and all instructions have the same end result. The differences between the 8088 and 8086 are outlined below. The engineer who is unfamiliar with the 8086 is referred to the iAPX 86, 88 User's Manual, Chapters 2 and 4, for function description and instruction set information. Internally, there are three differences between the 8088 and the 8086. All changes are related to the 8-bit bus interface.

- The queue length is 4 bytes in the 8088, whereas the 8086 queue contains 6 bytes, or three words. The queue was shortened to prevent overuse of the bus by the BIU when prefetching instructions. This was required because of the additional time necessary to fetch instructions 8 bits at a time.

- To further optimize the queue, the prefetching algorithm was changed. The 8088 BIU will fetch a new instruction to load into the queue each time there is a 1 byte hole (space available) in the queue. The 8086 waits until a 2-byte space is available.

- The internal execution time of the instruction set is affected by the 8-bit interface. All 16-bit fetches and writes from/to memory take an additional four clock cycles. The CPU is also limited by the speed of instruction fetches. This latter problem only occurs when a series of simple operations occur. When the more sophisticated instructions of the 8088 are being used, the queue has time to fill and the execution proceeds as fast as the execution unit will allow.

The 8088 and 8086 are completely software compatible by virtue of their identical execution units. Software that is system dependent may not be completely transferable, but software that is not system dependent will operate equally as well on an 8088 and an 8086.

The hardware interface of the 8088 contains the major differences between the two CPUs. The pin assignments are nearly identical, however, with the following functional changes:

- A8–A15—These pins are only address outputs on the 8088. These address lines are latched internally and remain valid throughout a bus cycle in a manner similar to the 8085 upper address lines.

- $\overline{\text{BHE}}$ has no meaning on the 8088 and has been eliminated.

- $\overline{SSO}$ provides the $\overline{SO}$ status information in the minimum mode. This output occurs on pin 34 in minimum mode only. DT/$\overline{R}$, IO/$\overline{M}$, and $\overline{SSO}$ provide the complete bus status in minimum mode.

- IO/$\overline{M}$ has been inverted to be compatible with the MCS-85 bus structure.
- ALE is delayed by one clock cycle in the minimum mode when entering HALT, to allow the status to be latched with ALE.

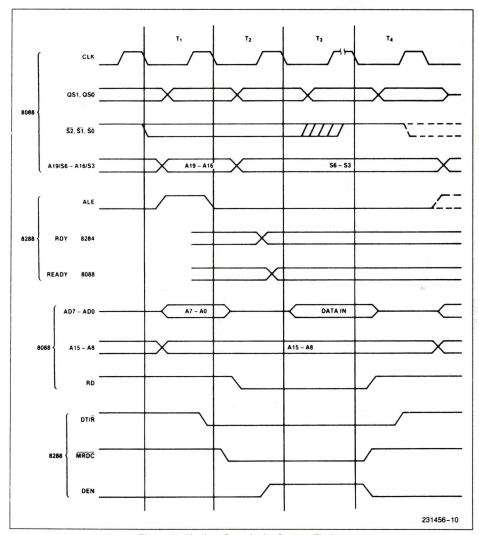

Figure 10. Medium Complexity System Timing

231456–10

B

Instruction Set and Execution Times

8086/8088 Instruction Set Summary

Mnemonic and Description	Instruction Code			
DATA TRANSFER				
MOV = Move:	7 6 5 4 3 2 1 0	7 6 5 4 3 2 1 0	7 6 5 4 3 2 1 0	7 6 5 4 3 2 1 0
Register/Memory to/from Register	1 0 0 0 1 0 d w	mod reg r/m		
Immediate to Register/Memory	1 1 0 0 0 1 1 w	mod 0 0 0 r/m	data	data if w = 1
Immediate to Register	1 0 1 1 w reg	data	data if w = 1	
Memory to Accumulator	1 0 1 0 0 0 0 w	addr-low	addr-high	
Accumulator to Memory	1 0 1 0 0 0 1 w	addr-low	addr-high	
Register/Memory to Segment Register	1 0 0 0 1 1 1 0	mod 0 reg r/m		
Segment Register to Register/Memory	1 0 0 0 1 1 0 0	mod 0 reg r/m		
PUSH = Push:				
Register/Memory	1 1 1 1 1 1 1 1	mod 1 1 0 r/m		
Register	0 1 0 1 0 reg			
Segment Register	0 0 0 reg 1 1 0			
POP = Pop:				
Register/Memory	1 0 0 0 1 1 1 1	mod 0 0 0 r/m		
Register	0 1 0 1 1 reg			
Segment Register	0 0 0 reg 1 1 1			
XCHG = Exchange:				
Register/Memory with Register	1 0 0 0 0 1 1 w	mod reg r/m		
Register with Accumulator	1 0 0 1 0 reg			
IN = Input from:				
Fixed Port	1 1 1 0 0 1 0 w	port		
Variable Port	1 1 1 0 1 1 0 w			
OUT = Output to:				
Fixed Port	1 1 1 0 0 1 1 w	port		
Variable Port	1 1 1 0 1 1 1 w			
XLAT = Translate Byte to AL	1 1 0 1 0 1 1 1			
LEA = Load EA to Register	1 0 0 0 1 1 0 1	mod reg r/m		
LDS = Load Pointer to DS	1 1 0 0 0 1 0 1	mod reg r/m		
LES = Load Pointer to ES	1 1 0 0 0 1 0 0	mod reg r/m		
LAHF = Load AH with Flags	1 0 0 1 1 1 1 1			
SAHF = Store AH into Flags	1 0 0 1 1 1 1 0			
PUSHF = Push Flags	1 0 0 1 1 1 0 0			
POPF = Pop Flags	1 0 0 1 1 1 0 1			

8086/8088 Instruction Set Summary (Continued)

Mnemonic and Description	Instruction Code			
ARITHMETIC	7 6 5 4 3 2 1 0	7 6 5 4 3 2 1 0	7 6 5 4 3 2 1 0	7 6 5 4 3 2 1 0
ADD = Add:				
Reg./Memory with Register to Either	0 0 0 0 0 0 d w	mod reg r/m		
Immediate to Register/Memory	1 0 0 0 0 0 s w	mod 0 0 0 r/m	data	data if s:w = 01
Immediate to Accumulator	0 0 0 0 0 1 0 w	data	data if w = 1	
ADC = Add with Carry:				
Reg./Memory with Register to Either	0 0 0 1 0 0 d w	mod reg r/m		
Immediate to Register/Memory	1 0 0 0 0 0 s w	mod 0 1 0 r/m	data	data if s:w = 01
Immediate to Accumulator	0 0 0 1 0 1 0 w	data	data if w = 1	
INC = Increment:				
Register/Memory	1 1 1 1 1 1 1 w	mod 0 0 0 r/m		
Register	0 1 0 0 0 reg			
AAA = ASCII Adjust for Add	0 0 1 1 0 1 1 1			
BAA = Decimal Adjust for Add	0 0 1 0 0 1 1 1			
SUB = Subtract:				
Reg./Memory and Register to Either	0 0 1 0 1 0 d w	mod reg r/m		
Immediate from Register/Memory	1 0 0 0 0 0 s w	mod 1 0 1 r/m	data	data if s:w = 01
Immediate from Accumulator	0 0 1 0 1 1 0 w	data	data if w = 1	
SSB = Subtract with Borrow				
Reg./Memory and Register to Either	0 0 0 1 1 0 d w	mod reg r/m		
Immediate from Register/Memory	1 0 0 0 0 0 s w	mod 0 1 1 r/m	data	data if s:w = 01
Immediate from Accumulator	0 0 0 1 1 1 w	data	data if w = 1	
DEC = Decrement:				
Register/memory	1 1 1 1 1 1 1 w	mod 0 0 1 r/m		
Register	0 1 0 0 1 reg			
NEG = Change sign	1 1 1 1 0 1 1 w	mod 0 1 1 r/m		
CMP = Compare:				
Register/Memory and Register	0 0 1 1 1 0 d w	mod reg r/m		
Immediate with Register/Memory	1 0 0 0 0 0 s w	mod 1 1 1 r/m	data	data if s:w = 01
Immediate with Accumulator	0 0 1 1 1 1 0 w	data	data if w = 1	
AAS = ASCII Adjust for Subtract	0 0 1 1 1 1 1 1			
DAS = Decimal Adjust for Subtract	0 0 1 0 1 1 1 1			
MUL = Multiply (Unsigned)	1 1 1 1 0 1 1 w	mod 1 0 0 r/m		
IMUL = Integer Multiply (Signed)	1 1 1 1 0 1 1 w	mod 1 0 1 r/m		
AAM = ASCII Adjust for Multiply	1 1 0 1 0 1 0 0	0 0 0 0 1 0 1 0		
DIV = Divide (Unsigned)	1 1 1 1 0 1 1 w	mod 1 1 0 r/m		
IDIV = Integer Divide (Signed)	1 1 1 1 0 1 1 w	mod 1 1 1 r/m		
AAD = ASCII Adjust for Divide	1 1 0 1 0 1 0 1	0 0 0 0 1 0 1 0		
CBW = Convert Byte to Word	1 0 0 1 1 0 0 0			
CWD = Convert Word to Double Word	1 0 0 1 1 0 0 1			

8086/8088 Instruction Set Summary (Continued)

Mnemonic and Description	Instruction Code			
LOGIC	7 6 5 4 3 2 1 0	7 6 5 4 3 2 1 0	7 6 5 4 3 2 1 0	7 6 5 4 3 2 1 0
NOT = Invert	1 1 1 1 0 1 1 w	mod 0 1 0 r/m		
SHL/SAL = Shift Logical/Arithmetic Left	1 1 0 1 0 0 v w	mod 1 0 0 r/m		
SHR = Shift Logical Right	1 1 0 1 0 0 v w	mod 1 0 1 r/m		
SAR = Shift Arithmetic Right	1 1 0 1 0 0 v w	mod 1 1 1 r/m		
ROL = Rotate Left	1 1 0 1 0 0 v w	mod 0 0 0 r/m		
ROR = Rotate Right	1 1 0 1 0 0 v w	mod 0 0 1 r/m		
RCL = Rotate Through Carry Flag Left	1 1 0 1 0 0 v w	mod 0 1 0 r/m		
RCR = Rotate Through Carry Right	1 1 0 1 0 0 v w	mod 0 1 1 r/m		
AND = **And:**				
Reg./Memory and Register to Either	0 0 1 0 0 0 d w	mod reg r/m		
Immediate to Register/Memory	1 0 0 0 0 0 0 w	mod 1 0 0 r/m	data	data if w = 1
Immediate to Accumulator	0 0 1 0 0 1 0 w	data	data if w = 1	
TEST = **And Function to Flags. No Result:**				
Register/Memory and Register	1 0 0 0 0 1 0 w	mod reg r/m		
Immediate Data and Register/Memory	1 1 1 1 0 1 1 w	mod 0 0 0 r/m	data	data if w = 1
Immediate Data and Accumulator	1 0 1 0 1 0 0 w	data	data if w = 1	
OR = **Or:**				
Reg./Memory and Register to Either	0 0 0 0 1 0 d w	mod reg r/m		
Immediate to Register/Memory	1 0 0 0 0 0 0 w	mod 0 0 1 r/m	data	data if w = 1
Immediate to Accumulator	0 0 0 0 1 1 0 w	data	data if w = 1	
XOR = **Exclusive or:**				
Reg./Memory and Register to Either	0 0 1 1 0 0 d w	mod reg r/m		
Immediate to Register/Memory	1 0 0 0 0 0 0 w	mod 1 1 0 r/m	data	data if w = 1
Immediate to Accumulator	0 0 1 1 0 1 0 w	data	data if w = 1	
STRING MANIPULATION				
REP = Repeat	1 1 1 1 0 0 1 z			
MOVS = Move Byte/Word	1 0 1 0 0 1 0 w			
CMPS = Compare Byte/Word	1 0 1 0 0 1 1 w			
SCAS = Scan Byte/Word	1 0 1 0 1 1 1 w			
LODS = Load Byte/Wd to AL/AX	1 0 1 0 1 1 0 w			
STOS = Stor Byte/Wd from AL/A	1 0 1 0 1 0 1 w			
CONTROL TRANSFER				
CALL = **Call:**				
Direct Within Segment	1 1 1 0 1 0 0 0	disp-low	disp-high	
Indirect Within Segment	1 1 1 1 1 1 1 1	mod 0 1 0 r/m		
Direct Intersegment	1 0 0 1 1 0 1 0	offset-low	offset-high	
		seg-low	seg-high	
Indirect Intersegment	1 1 1 1 1 1 1 1	mod 0 1 1 r/m		

8086/8088 Instruction Set Summary (Continued)

Mnemonic and Description	Instruction Code		
JMP = Unconditional Jump:	7 6 5 4 3 2 1 0	7 6 5 4 3 2 1 0	7 6 5 4 3 2 1 0
Direct Within Segment	1 1 1 0 1 0 0 1	disp-low	disp-high
Direct Within Segment-Short	1 1 1 0 1 0 1 1	disp	
Indirect Within Segment	1 1 1 1 1 1 1 1	mod 1 0 0 r/m	
Direct Intersegment	1 1 1 0 1 0 1 0	offset-low	offset-high
		seg-low	seg-high
Indirect Intersegment	1 1 1 1 1 1 1 1	mod 1 0 1 r/m	
RET = Return from CALL:			
Within Segment	1 1 0 0 0 0 1 1		
Within Seg Adding Immed to SP	1 1 0 0 0 0 1 0	data-low	data-high
Intersegment	1 1 0 0 1 0 1 1		
Intersegment Adding Immediate to SP	1 1 0 0 1 0 1 0	data-low	data-high
JE/JZ = Jump on Equal/Zero	0 1 1 1 0 1 0 0	disp	
JL/JNGE = Jump on Less/Not Greater or Equal	0 1 1 1 1 1 0 0	disp	
JLE/JNG = Jump on Less or Equal/ Not Greater	0 1 1 1 1 1 1 0	disp	
JB/JNAE = Jump on Below/Not Above or Equal	0 1 1 1 0 0 1 0	disp	
JBE/JNA = Jump on Below or Equal/ Not Above	0 1 1 1 0 1 1 0	disp	
JP/JPE = Jump on Parity/Parity Even	0 1 1 1 1 0 1 0	disp	
JO = Jump on Overflow	0 1 1 1 0 0 0 0	disp	
JS = Jump on Sign	0 1 1 1 1 0 0 0	disp	
JNE/JNZ = Jump on Not Equal/Not Zero	0 1 1 1 0 1 0 1	disp	
JNL/JGE = Jump on Not Less/Greater or Equal	0 1 1 1 1 1 0 1	disp	
JNLE/JG = Jump on Not Less or Equal/ Greater	0 1 1 1 1 1 1 1	disp	
JNB/JAE = Jump on Not Below/Above or Equal	0 1 1 1 0 0 1 1	disp	
JNBE/JA = Jump on Not Below or Equal/Above	0 1 1 1 0 1 1 1	disp	
JNP/JPO = Jump on Not Par/Par Odd	0 1 1 1 1 0 1 1	disp	
JNO = Jump on Not Overflow	0 1 1 1 0 0 0 1	disp	
JNS = Jump on Not Sign	0 1 1 1 1 0 0 1	disp	
LOOP = Loop CX Times	1 1 1 0 0 0 1 0	disp	
LOOPZ/LOOPE = Loop While Zero/Equal	1 1 1 0 0 0 0 1	disp	
LOOPNZ/LOOPNE = Loop While Not Zero/Equal	1 1 1 0 0 0 0 0	disp	
JCXZ = Jump on CX Zero	1 1 1 0 0 0 1 1	disp	
INT = **Interrupt**			
Type Specified	1 1 0 0 1 1 0 1	type	
Type 3	1 1 0 0 1 1 0 0		
INTO = Interrupt on Overflow	1 1 0 0 1 1 1 0		
IRET = Interrupt Return	1 1 0 0 1 1 1 1		

8086/8088 Instruction Set Summary (Continued)

Mnemonic and Description	Instruction Code	
	76543210	76543210
PROCESSOR CONTROL		
CLC = Clear Carry	11111000	
CMC = Complement Carry	11110101	
STC = Set Carry	11111001	
CLD = Clear Direction	11111100	
STD = Set Direction	11111101	
CLI = Clear Interrupt	11111010	
STI = Set Interrupt	11111011	
HLT = Halt	11110100	
WAIT = Wait	10011011	
ESC = Escape (to External Device)	11011xxx	mod x x x r/m
LOCK = Bus Lock Prefix	11110000	

NOTES:
AL = 8-bit accumulator
AX = 16-bit accumulator
CX = Count register
DS = Data segment
ES = Extra segment
Above/below refers to unsigned value
Greater = more positive:
Less = less positive (more negative) signed values
if d = 1 then "to" reg; if d = 0 then "from" reg
if w = 1 then word instruction; if w = 0 then byte
    instruction
if mod = 11 then r/m is treated as a REG field
if mod = 00 then DISP = 0*, disp-low and disp-high are
    absent
if mod = 01 then DISP = disp-low sign-extended to
    16 bits, disp-high is absent
if mod = 10 then DISP = disp-high; disp-low
if r/m = 000 then EA = (BX) + (SI) + DISP
if r/m = 001 then EA = (BX) + (DI) + DISP
if r/m = 010 then EA = (BP) + (SI) + DISP
if r/m = 011 then EA = (BP) + (DI) + DISP
if r/m = 100 then EA = (SI) + DISP
if r/m = 101 then EA = (DI) + DISP
if r/m = 110 then EA = (BP) + DISP*
if r/m = 111 then EA = (BX) + DISP
DISP follows 2nd byte of instruction (before data if required)
*except if mod = 00 and r/m = then EA = disp-high:
    disp-low.
if s:w = 01 then 16 bits of immediate data form the operand
if s:w = 11 then an immediate data byte is sign extended
    to form the 16-bit operand
if v = 0 then "count" = 1; if v = 1 then "count" in (CL)
    register
x = don't care
z is used for string primitives for comparison with ZF FLAG
SEGMENT OVERRIDE PREFIX

0 0 1 reg 1 1 0

REG is assigned according to the following table:

16-Bit (w = 1)		8-Bit (w = 0)		Segment	
000	AX	000	AL	00	ES
001	CX	001	CL	01	CS
010	DX	010	DL	10	SS
011	BX	011	BL	11	DS
100	SP	100	AH		
101	BP	101	CH		
110	SI	110	DH		
111	DI	111	BH		

Instructions which reference the flag register file as a 16-bit
object use the symbol FLAGS to represent the file:
FLAGS =
X:X:X:X:(OF):(DF):(IF):(TF):(SF):(ZF):X:(AF):X:(PF):X:(CF)

Mnemonics © Intel, 1978

DATA SHEET REVISION REVIEW

The following list represents key differences between this and the -005 data sheet. Please review this summary carefully.

1. The Intel® 8088 implementation technology (HMOS) has been changed to (HMOS-II).

INSTRUCTION EXECUTION TIMES

The following addressing-mode abbreviations are used throughout this section:

Reg - Register   **Mem** - Memory
Imm - Immediate   **Acc** - Accumulator

Arithmetic Instructions

Instruction	Clock Cycles	Transfers
AAA	4	
AAD	60	
AAM	83	
AAS	4	
ADC		
Reg to Reg	3	
Mem to Reg	9 + EA	1
Reg to Mem	16 + EA	2
Imm to Reg	4	
Imm to Mem	17 + EA	2
Imm to Acc	4	
ADD		
Reg to Reg	3	
Mem to Reg	9 + EA	1
Reg to Mem	16 + EA	2
Imm to Reg	4	
Imm to Mem	17 + EA	2
Imm to Acc	4	
CBW	2	
CWD	5	
DAA	4	
DAS	4	
DEC		
8-bit	3	
16-bit	2	
Mem	15 + EA	2
DIV		
8-bit Reg	80−90	
16-bit Reg	144−162	
8-bit Mem	86−96 + EA	1
16-bit Mem	150−168 + EA	1
IDIV		
8-bit Reg	101−112	
16-bit Reg	165−184	
8-bit Mem	107−118 + EA	1
16-bit Mem	171−190 + EA	1

Arithmetic Instructions (continued)

Instruction	Clock Cycles	Transfers
IMUL		
8-bit Reg	80−98	
16-bit Reg	128−154	
8-bit Mem	86−104 + EA	1
16-bit Mem	134−160 + EA	1
INC		
8-bit	3	
16-bit	2	
Mem	15 + EA	2
MUL		
8-bit Reg	70−77	
16-bit Reg	118−133	
8-bit Mem	76−83 + EA	1
16-bit Mem	124−139 + EA	1
NEG		
Reg	3	
Mem	16 + EA	2
SBB		
Reg from Reg	3	
Mem from Reg	9 + EA	1
Reg from Mem	16 + EA	2
Imm from Reg	4	
Imm from Mem	17 + EA	2
Imm from Acc	4	
SUB		
Reg from Reg	3	
Mem from Reg	9 + EA	1
Reg from Mem	16 + EA	2
Imm from Reg	4	
Imm from Mem	17 + EA	2
Imm from Acc	4	

Logical Instructions

Instruction	Clock Cycles	Transfers
AND		
Reg to Reg	3	
Mem to Reg	9 + EA	1
Reg to Mem	16 + EA	2
Imm to Reg	4	
Imm to Mem	17 + EA	2
Imm to Acc	4	
CMP		
Reg to Reg	3	
Mem to Reg	9 + EA	1
Reg to Mem	9 + EA	1
Imm to Reg	4	
Imm to Mem	10 + EA	1
Imm to Acc	4	
NOT		
Reg	3	
Mem	16 + EA	2
OR		
Reg to Reg	3	
Mem to Reg	9 + EA	1
Reg to Mem	16 + EA	2
Imm to Reg	4	
Imm to Mem	17 + EA	2
Imm to Acc	4	
RCL		
1-bit Reg	2	
Multi-bit Reg	8 + 4/bit	
1-bit Mem	15 + EA	2
Multi-bit Mem	20 + EA + 4/bit	2
RCR		
1-bit Reg	2	
Multi-bit Reg	8 + 4/bit	
1-bit Mem	15 + EA	2
Multi-bit Mem	20 + EA + 4/bit	2
ROL		
1-bit Reg	2	
Multi-bit Reg	8 + 4/bit	
1-bit Mem	15 + EA	2
Multi-bit Mem	20 + EA + 4/bit	2
ROR		
1-bit Reg	2	
Multi-bit Reg	8 + 4/bit	
1-bit Mem	15 + EA	2
Multi-bit Mem	20 + EA + 4/bit	2

Logical Instructions (continued)

Instruction	Clock Cycles	Transfers
SAL/SHL		
1-bit Reg	2	
Multi-bit Reg	8 + 4/bit	
1-bit Mem	15 + EA	2
Multi-bit Mem	20 + EA + 4/bit	2
SAR		
1-bit Reg	2	
Multi-bit Reg	8 + 4/bit	
1-bit Mem	15 + EA	2
Multi-bit Mem	20 + EA + 4/bit	2
SHR		
1-bit Reg	2	
Multi-bit Reg	8 + 4/bit	
1-bit Mem	15 + EA	2
Multi-bit Mem	20 + EA + 4/bit	2
XOR		
Reg to Reg	3	
Mem to Reg	9 + EA	1
Reg to Mem	16 + EA	2
Imm to Reg	4	
Imm to Mem	17 + EA	2
Imm to Acc	4	

String Instructions

Instruction	Clock Cycles	Transfers
CMPS/CMPSB/CMPSW		
Not Repeated	22	2
Repeated	9 + 22/rep	2/rep
LDS	16 + EA	2
LEA	2 + EA	
LES	16 + EA	2
LODS/LODSB/LODSW		
Not Repeated	12	1
Repeated	9 + 13/rep	1/rep
MOVS/MOVSB/MOVSW		
Not Repeated	18	2
Repeated	9 + 17/rep	2/rep
SCAS/SCASB/SCASW		
Not Repeated	15	1
Repeated	9 + 15/rep	1/rep
STOS/STOSB/STOSW		
Not Repeated	11	1
Repeated	9 + 10/rep	1/rep

Loop and Jump Instructions

Instruction	Clock Cycles	Transfers
JA/JNBE	16/4	
JAE/JNB/JNC	16/4	
JB/JNAE/JC	16/4	
JBE/JNA	16/4	
JCXZ	18/6	
JE/JZ	16/4	
JG/JNLE	16/4	
JGE/JNL	16/4	
JL/JNGE	16/4	
JLE/JNG	16/4	
JMP		
Intrasegment direct short	15	
Intrasegment direct	15	
Intersegment direct	15	
Intrasegment Mem-indirect	18 + EA	1
Intrasegment Reg-indirect	11	
Intersegment indirect	24 + EA	2
JNE/JNZ	16/4	
JNO	16/4	
JNP/JPO	16/4	
JNS	16/4	
JO	16/4	
JP/JPE	16/4	
JS	16/4	
LOOP	17/5	
LOOPE/LOOPZ	18/6	
LOOPNE/LOOPNZ	19/5	

x/y − **x** cycles when jump is not taken
    y cycles when jump is taken

Data Transfer Instructions

Instruction	Clock Cycles	Transfers
IN		
Fixed-port	10	1
Variable-port	8	1
LAHF	4	
MOV		
Acc to Mem	10	1
Mem to Acc	10	1
Reg to Reg	2	
Mem to Reg	8 + EA	1
Reg to Mem	9 + EA	1
Imm to Reg	4	
Imm to Mem	10 + EA	1
Reg to SS, DS, or ES	2	
Mem to SS, DS, or ES	8 + EA	1
Segment Reg to Reg	2	
Segment Reg to Mem	9 + EA	1
OUT		
Fixed-port	10	1
Variable-port	8	1
POP		
Reg	8	1
SS, DS, or ES	8	1
Mem	16 + EA	2
POPF	8	1
PUSH		
Reg	11	1
Segment Reg	10	1
Mem	16 + EA	2
PUSHF	10	1
SAHF	4	
XCHG		
Reg with Acc	3	
Reg with Mem	17 + EA	2
Reg with Reg	4	
XLAT/XLATB	11	1

Subroutine and Interrupt Instructions

Instruction	Clock Cycles	Transfers
CALL		
Intrasegment direct	19	1
Intersegment direct	28	2
Intrasegment Mem-indirect	21 + EA	2
Intrasegment Reg-indirect	16	1
Intersegment indirect	37 + EA	4
INT		
Type-3	52	5
Not Type-3	51	5
INTO		
Taken	53	5
Not Taken	4	
INTR	61	7
IRET	24	3
NMI	50	5
RET		
Intrasegment	8	1
Intrasegment with pop	12	1
Intersegment	18	2
Intersegment with pop	17	2

Note: INTR and NMI are included for timing purposes only.

Processor Control Instructions

Instruction	Clock Cycles	Transfers
CLC	2	
CLD	2	
CLI	2	
CMC	2	
ESC		
Reg	2	
Mem	8 + EA	1
HLT	2	
LOCK	2	
NOP	3	
REP	2	
REPE/REPZ	2	
REPNE/REPNZ	2	
STC	2	
STD	2	
STI	2	
TEST		
Reg with Reg	3	
Mem with Reg	9 + EA	1
Imm with Acc	4	
Imm with Reg	5	
Imm with Mem	11 + EA	
WAIT	3 + 5n	

EFFECTIVE ADDRESS (EA) CALCULATION TIMES

Addressing-mode	Clock Cycles
Displacement	6
Base or Index	5
Disp + Base or Index	9
Base + Index	
BP + DI, BX + SI	7
BP + SI, BX + DI	8
Disp + Base + Index	
BP + DI + Disp	11
BX + SI + Disp	11
BP + SI + Disp	12
BX + DI + Disp	12

Notes:
1. Add 2 clock cycles for segment override (e.g., MOV AL,**ES:**[100])
2. Add 4 clock cycles for each word transfer to/from memory

C

8088 Peripheral Data Sheets

8259A
PROGRAMMABLE INTERRUPT CONTROLLER
(8259A/8259A-2)

- **8086, 8088 Compatible**
- **MCS-80®, MCS-85® Compatible**
- **Eight-Level Priority Controller**
- **Expandable to 64 Levels**
- **Programmable Interrupt Modes**
- **Individual Request Mask Capability**

- **Single +5V Supply (No Clocks)**
- **Available in 28-Pin DIP and 28-Lead PLCC Package**
  (See Packaging Spec., Order #231369)
- **Available in EXPRESS**
  — **Standard Temperature Range**
  — **Extended Temperature Range**

The Intel 8259A Programmable Interrupt Controller handles up to eight vectored priority interrupts for the CPU. It is cascadable for up to 64 vectored priority interrupts without additional circuitry. It is packaged in a 28-pin DIP, uses NMOS technology and requires a single +5V supply. Circuitry is static, requiring no clock input.

The 8259A is designed to minimize the software and real time overhead in handling multi-level priority interrupts. It has several modes, permitting optimization for a variety of system requirements.

The 8259A is fully upward compatible with the Intel 8259. Software originally written for the 8259 will operate the 8259A in all 8259 equivalent modes (MCS-80/85, Non-Buffered, Edge Triggered).

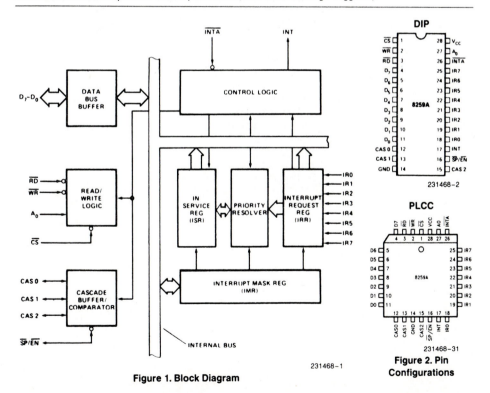

Figure 1. Block Diagram

231468-1

Figure 2. Pin Configurations

231468-31

Table 1. Pin Description

Symbol	Pin No.	Type	Name and Function
V$_{CC}$	28	I	**SUPPLY:** +5V Supply.
GND	14	I	**GROUND**
$\overline{CS}$	1	I	**CHIP SELECT:** A low on this pin enables $\overline{RD}$ and $\overline{WR}$ communication between the CPU and the 8259A. INTA functions are independent of CS.
$\overline{WR}$	2	I	**WRITE:** A low on this pin when CS is low enables the 8259A to accept command words from the CPU.
$\overline{RD}$	3	I	**READ:** A low on this pin when CS is low enables the 8259A to release status onto the data bus for the CPU.
D$_7$–D$_0$	4–11	I/O	**BIDIRECTIONAL DATA BUS:** Control, status and interrupt-vector information is transferred via this bus.
CAS$_0$–CAS$_2$	12, 13, 15	I/O	**CASCADE LINES:** The CAS lines form a private 8259A bus to control a multiple 8259A structure. These pins are outputs for a master 8259A and inputs for a slave 8259A.
$\overline{SP}$/$\overline{EN}$	16	I/O	**SLAVE PROGRAM/ENABLE BUFFER:** This is a dual function pin. When in the Buffered Mode it can be used as an output to control buffer transceivers (EN). When not in the buffered mode it is used as an input to designate a master (SP = 1) or slave (SP = 0).
INT	17	O	**INTERRUPT:** This pin goes high whenever a valid interrupt request is asserted. It is used to interrupt the CPU, thus it is connected to the CPU's interrupt pin.
IR$_0$–IR$_7$	18–25	I	**INTERRUPT REQUESTS:** Asynchronous inputs. An interrupt request is executed by raising an IR input (low to high), and holding it high until it is acknowledged (Edge Triggered Mode), or just by a high level on an IR input (Level Triggered Mode).
$\overline{INTA}$	26	I	**INTERRUPT ACKNOWLEDGE:** This pin is used to enable 8259A interrupt-vector data onto the data bus by a sequence of interrupt acknowledge pulses issued by the CPU.
A$_0$	27	I	**AO ADDRESS LINE:** This pin acts in conjunction with the $\overline{CS}$, $\overline{WR}$, and $\overline{RD}$ pins. It is used by the 8259A to decipher various Command Words the CPU writes and status the CPU wishes to read. It is typically connected to the CPU A0 address line (A1 for 8086, 8088).

FUNCTIONAL DESCRIPTION

Interrupts in Microcomputer Systems

Microcomputer system design requires that I.O devices such as keyboards, displays, sensors and other components receive servicing in a an efficient manner so that large amounts of the total system tasks can be assumed by the microcomputer with little or no effect on throughput.

The most common method of servicing such devices is the *Polled* approach. This is where the processor must test each device in sequence and in effect "ask" each one if it needs servicing. It is easy to see that a large portion of the main program is looping through this continuous polling cycle and that such a method would have a serious detrimental effect on system throughput, thus limiting the tasks that could be assumed by the microcomputer and reducing the cost effectiveness of using such devices.

A more desirable method would be one that would allow the microprocessor to be executing its main program and only stop to service peripheral devices when it is told to do so by the device itself. In effect, the method would provide an external asynchronous input that would inform the processor that it should complete whatever instruction that is currently being executed and fetch a new routine that will service the requesting device. Once this servicing is complete, however, the processor would resume exactly where it left off.

This method is called *Interrupt*. It is easy to see that system throughput would drastically increase, and thus more tasks could be assumed by the microcomputer to further enhance its cost effectiveness.

The Programmable Interrupt Controller (PIC) functions as an overall manager in an Interrupt-Driven system environment. It accepts requests from the peripheral equipment, determines which of the incoming requests is of the highest importance (priority), ascertains whether the incoming request has a higher priority value than the level currently being serviced, and issues an interrupt to the CPU based on this determination.

Each peripheral device or structure usually has a special program or "routine" that is associated with its specific functional or operational requirements; this is referred to as a "service routine". The PIC, after issuing an Interrupt to the CPU, must somehow input information into the CPU that can "point" the Program Counter to the service routine associated with the requesting device. This "pointer" is an address in a vectoring table and will often be referred to, in this document, as vectoring data.

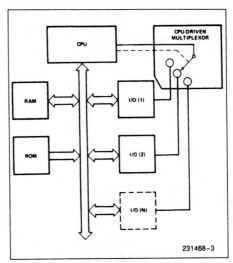

231468-3

Figure 3a. Polled Method

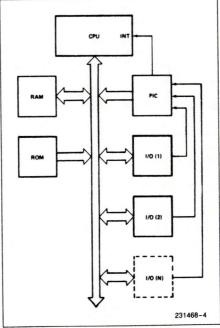

231468-4

Figure 3b. Interrupt Method

The 8259A is a device specifically designed for use in real time, interrupt driven microcomputer systems. It manages eight levels or requests and has built-in features for expandability to other 8259A's (up to 64 levels). It is programmed by the system's software as an I/O peripheral. A selection of priority modes is available to the programmer so that the manner in which the requests are processed by the 8259A can be configured to match his system requirements. The priority modes can be changed or reconfigured dynamically at any time during the main program. This means that the complete interrupt structure can be defined as required, based on the total system environment.

INTERRUPT REQUEST REGISTER (IRR) AND IN-SERVICE REGISTER (ISR)

The interrupts at the IR input lines are handled by two registers in cascade, the Interrupt Request Register (IRR) and the In-Service (ISR). The IRR is used to store all the interrupt levels which are requesting service; and the ISR is used to store all the interrupt levels which are being serviced.

PRIORITY RESOLVER

This logic block determines the priorites of the bits set in the IRR. The highest priority is selected and strobed into the corresponding bit of the ISR during $\overline{INTA}$ pulse.

INTERRUPT MASK REGISTER (IMR)

The IMR stores the bits which mask the interrupt lines to be masked. The IMR operates on the IRR. Masking of a higher priority input will not affect the interrupt request lines of lower quality.

INT (INTERRUPT)

This output goes directly to the CPU interrupt input. The V_{OH} level on this line is designed to be fully compatible with the 8080A, 8085A and 8086 input levels.

$\overline{INTA}$ (INTERRUPT ACKNOWLEDGE)

$\overline{INTA}$ pulses will cause the 8259A to release vectoring information onto the data bus. The format of this data depends on the system mode (μPM) of the 8259A.

DATA BUS BUFFER

This 3-state, bidirectional 8-bit buffer is used to interface the 8259A to the system Data Bus. Control words and status information are transferred through the Data Bus Buffer.

READ/WRITE CONTROL LOGIC

The function of this block is to accept OUTput commands from the CPU. It contains the Initialization Command Word (ICW) registers and Operation Command Word (OCW) registers which store the various control formats for device operation. This function block also allows the status of the 8259A to be transferred onto the Data Bus.

$\overline{CS}$ (CHIP SELECT)

A LOW on this input enables the 8259A. No reading or writing of the chip will occur unless the device is selected.

$\overline{WR}$ (WRITE)

A LOW on this input enables the CPU to write control words (ICWs and OCWs) to the 8259A.

$\overline{RD}$ (READ)

A LOW on this input enables the 8259A to send the status of the Interrupt Request Register (IRR), In Service Register (ISR), the Interrupt Mask Register (IMR), or the Interrupt level onto the Data Bus.

A_0

This input signal is used in conjunction with $\overline{WR}$ and $\overline{RD}$ signals to write commands into the various command registers, as well as reading the various status registers of the chip. This line can be tied directly to one of the address lines.

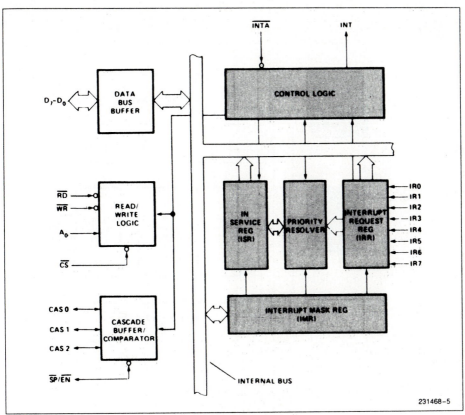

Figure 4a. 8259A Block Diagram

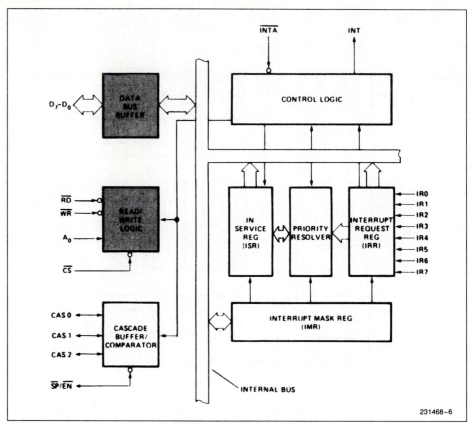

Figure 4b. 8259A Block Diagram

THE CASCADE BUFFER/COMPARATOR

This function block stores and compares the IDs of all 8259A's used in the system. The associated three I/O pins (CAS0-2) are outputs when the 8259A is used as a master and are inputs when the 8259A is used as a slave. As a master, the 8259A sends the ID of the interrupting slave device onto the CAS0-2 lines. The slave thus selected will send its preprogrammed subroutine address onto the Data Bus during the next one or two consecutive $\overline{\text{INTA}}$ pulses. (See section "Cascading the 8259A".)

INTERRUPT SEQUENCE

The powerful features of the 8259A in a microcomputer system are its programmability and the interrupt routine addressing capability. The latter allows direct or indirect jumping to the specific interrupt routine requested without any polling of the interrupting devices. The normal sequence of events during an interrupt depends on the type of CPU being used.

The events occur as follows in an MCS-80/85 system:

1. One or more of the INTERRUPT REQUEST lines (IR7–0) are raised high, setting the corresponding IRR bit(s).

2. The 8259A evaluates these requests, and sends an INT to the CPU, if appropriate.

3. The CPU acknowledges the INT and responds with an $\overline{\text{INTA}}$ pulse.

4. Upon receiving an $\overline{\text{INTA}}$ from the CPU group, the highest priority ISR bit is set, and the corresponding IRR bit is reset. The 8259A will also release a CALL instruction code (11001101) onto the 8-bit Data Bus through its D7–0 pins.

5. This CALL instruction will initiate two more $\overline{\text{INTA}}$ pulses to be sent to the 8259A from the CPU group.

6. These two $\overline{\text{INTA}}$ pulses allow the 8259A to release its preprogrammed subroutine address onto the Data Bus. The lower 8-bit address is re-

leased at the first $\overline{\text{INTA}}$ pulse and the higher 8-bit address is released at the second $\overline{\text{INTA}}$ pulse.

7. This completes the 3-byte CALL instruction released by the 8259A. In the AEOI mode the ISR bit is reset at the end of the third $\overline{\text{INTA}}$ pulse. Otherwise, the ISR bit remains set until an appropriate EOI command is issued at the end of the interrupt sequence.

The events occuring in an 8086 system are the same until step 4.

4. Upon receiving an $\overline{\text{INTA}}$ from the CPU group, the highest priority ISR bit is set and the corresponding IRR bit is reset. The 8259A does not drive the Data Bus during this cycle.

5. The 8086 will initiate a second $\overline{\text{INTA}}$ pulse. During this pulse, the 8259A releases an 8-bit pointer onto the Data Bus where it is read by the CPU.

6. This completes the interrupt cycle. In the AEOI mode the ISR bit is reset at the end of the second $\overline{\text{INTA}}$ pulse. Otherwise, the ISR bit remains set until an appropriate EOI command is issued at the end of the interrupt subroutine.

If no interrupt request is present at step 4 of either sequence (i.e., the request was too short in duration) the 8259A will issue an interrupt level 7. Both the vectoring bytes and the CAS lines will look like an interrupt level 7 was requested.

When the 8259A PIC receives an interrupt, INT becomes active and an interrupt acknowledge cycle is started. If a higher priority interrupt occurs between the two INTA pulses, the INT line goes inactive immediately after the second INTA pulse. After an unspecified amount of time the INT line is activated again to signify the higher priority interrupt waiting for service. This inactive time is not specified and can vary between parts. The designer should be aware of this consideration when designing a system which uses the 8259A. It is recommended that proper asynchronous design techniques be followed.

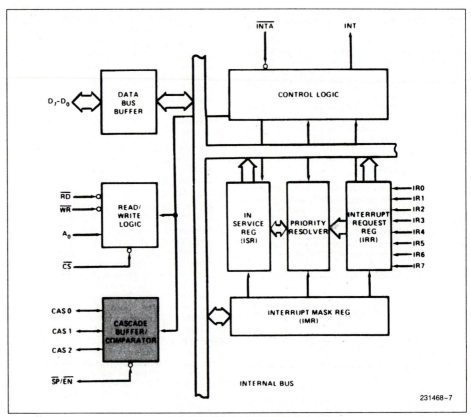

Figure 4c. 8259A Block Diagram

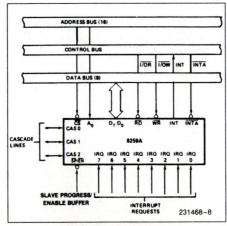

**Figure 5. 8259A Interface to
Standard System Bus**

INTERRUPT SEQUENCE OUTPUTS

MCS-80®, MCS-85®

This sequence is timed by three $\overline{\text{INTA}}$ pulses. During the first $\overline{\text{INTA}}$ pulse the CALL opcode is enabled onto the data bus.

Content of First Interrupt Vector Byte

	D7	D6	D5	D4	D3	D2	D1	D0
CALL CODE	1	1	0	0	1	1	0	1

During the second $\overline{\text{INTA}}$ pulse the lower address of the appropriate service routine is enabled onto the data bus. When Interval = 4 bits A_5–A_7 are programmed, while A_0–A_4 are automatically inserted by the 8259A. When Interval = 8 only A_6 and A_7 are programmed, while A_0–A_5 are automatically inserted.

Content of Second Interrupt Vector Byte

IR	Interval = 4							
	D7	D6	D5	D4	D3	D2	D1	D0
7	A7	A6	A5	1	1	1	0	0
6	A7	A6	A5	1	1	0	0	0
5	A7	A6	A5	1	0	1	0	0
4	A7	A6	A5	1	0	0	0	0
3	A7	A6	A5	0	1	1	0	0
2	A7	A6	A5	0	1	0	0	0
1	A7	A6	A5	0	0	1	0	0
0	A7	A6	A5	0	0	0	0	0

IR	Interval = 8							
	D7	D6	D5	D4	D3	D2	D1	D0
7	A7	A6	1	1	1	0	0	0
6	A7	A6	1	1	0	0	0	0
5	A7	A6	1	0	1	0	0	0
4	A7	A6	1	0	0	0	0	0
3	A7	A6	0	1	1	0	0	0
2	A7	A6	0	1	0	0	0	0
1	A7	A6	0	0	1	0	0	0
0	A7	A6	0	0	0	0	0	0

During the third $\overline{INTA}$ pulse the higher address of the appropriate service routine, which was programmed as byte 2 of the initialization sequence (A_8–A_{15}), is enabled onto the bus.

Content of Third Interrupt Vector Byte

D7	D6	D5	D4	D3	D2	D1	D0
A15	A14	A13	A12	A11	A10	A9	A8

8086, 8088

8086 mode is similar to MCS-80 mode except that only two Interrupt Acknowledge cycles are issued by the processor and no CALL opcode is sent to the processor. The first interrupt acknowledge cycle is similar to that of MCS-80, 85 systems in that the 8259A uses it to internally freeze the state of the interrupts for priority resolution and as a master it issues the interrupt code on the cascade lines at the end of the $\overline{INTA}$ pulse. On this first cycle it does not issue any data to the processor and leaves its data bus buffers disabled. On the second interrupt acknowledge cycle in 8086 mode the master (or slave if so programmed) will send a byte of data to the processor with the acknowledged interrupt code

composed as follows (note the state of the ADI mode control is ignored and A_5–A_{11} are unused in 8086 mode):

Content of Interrupt Vector Byte for 8086 System Mode

	D7	D6	D5	D4	D3	D2	D1	D0
IR7	T7	T6	T5	T4	T3	1	1	1
IR6	T7	T6	T5	T4	T3	1	1	0
IR5	T7	T6	T5	T4	T3	1	0	1
IR4	T7	T6	T5	T4	T3	1	0	0
IR3	T7	T6	T5	T4	T3	0	1	1
IR2	T7	T6	T5	T4	T3	0	1	0
IR1	T7	T6	T5	T4	T3	0	0	1
IR0	T7	T6	T5	T4	T3	0	0	0

PROGRAMMING THE 8259A

The 8259A accepts two types of command words generated by the CPU:

1. *Initialization Command Words (ICWs):* Before normal operation can begin, each 8259A in the system must be brought to a starting point—by a sequence of 2 to 4 bytes timed by $\overline{WR}$ pulses.

2. *Operation Command Words (OCWs):* These are the command words which command the 8259A to operate in various interrupt modes. These modes are:

   a. Fully nested mode

   b. Rotating priority mode

   c. Special mask mode

   d. Polled mode

The OCWs can be written into the 8259A anytime after initialization.

INITIALIZATION COMMAND WORDS (ICWS)

General

Whenever a command is issued with A0 = 0 and D4 = 1, this is interpreted as Initialization Command Word 1 (ICW1). ICW1 starts the intiitalization sequence during which the following automatically occur.

a. The edge sense circuit is reset, which means that following initialization, an interrupt request (IR) input must make a low-to-high transistion to generate an interrupt.

b. The Interrupt Mask Register is cleared.

c. IR7 input is assigned priority 7.

d. The slave mode address is set to 7.

e. Special Mask Mode is cleared and Status Read is set to IRR.

f. If IC4 = 0, then all functions selected in ICW4 are set to zero. (Non-Buffered mode*, no Auto-EOI, MCS-80, 85 system).

*NOTE:
Master/Slave in ICW4 is only used in the buffered mode.

Initialization Command Words 1 and 2 (ICW1, ICW2)

A_5-A_{15}: *Page starting address of service routines.* In an MCS 80/85 system, the 8 request levels will generate CALLs to 8 locations equally spaced in memory. These can be programmed to be spaced at intervals of 4 or 8 memory locations, thus the 8 routines will occupy a page of 32 or 64 bytes, respectively.

The address format is 2 bytes long (A_0-A_{15}). When the routine interval is 4, A_0-A_4 are automatically inserted by the 8259A, while A_5-A_{15} are programmed externally. When the routine interval is 8, A_0-A_5 are automatically inserted by the 8259A, while A_6-A_{15} are programmed externally.

The 8-byte interval will maintain compatibility with current software, while the 4-byte interval is best for a compact jump table.

In an 8086 system $A_{15}-A_{11}$ are inserted in the five most significant bits of the vectoring byte and the 8259A sets the three least significant bits according to the interrupt level. $A_{10}-A_5$ are ignored and ADI (Address interval) has no effect.

LTIM: If LTIM = 1, then the 8259A will operate in the level interrupt mode. Edge detect logic on the interrupt inputs will be disabled.

ADI: CALL address interval. ADI = 1 then interval = 4; ADI = 0 then interval = 8.

SNGL: Single. Means that this is the only 8259A in the system. If SNGL = 1 no ICW3 will be issued.

IC4: If this bit is set—ICW4 has to be read. If ICW4 is not needed, set IC4 = 0.

Initialization Command Word 3 (ICW3)

This word is read only when there is more than one 8259A in the system and cascading is used, in which

case SNGL = 0. It will load the 8-bit slave register. The functions of this register are:

a. In the master mode (either when SP = 1, or in buffered mode when M/S = 1 in ICW4) a "1" is set for each slave in the system. The master then will release byte 1 of the call sequence (for MCS-80/85 system) and will enable the corresponding slave to release bytes 2 and 3 (for 8086 only byte 2) through the cascade lines.

b. In the slave mode (either when $\overline{SP}$ = 0, or if BUF = 1 and M/S = 0 in ICW4) bits 2–0 identify the slave. The slave compares its cascade input with these bits and, if they are equal, bytes 2 and 3 of the call sequence (or just byte 2 for 8086) are released by it on the Data Bus.

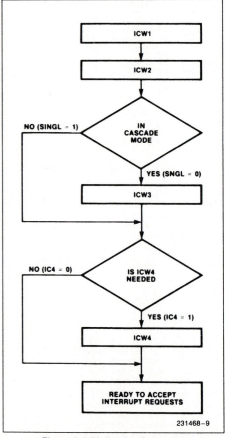

Figure 6. Initialization Sequence

Initialization Command Word 4 (ICW4)

SFNM: If SFNM = 1 the special fully nested mode is programmed.

BUF: If BUF = 1 the buffered mode is programmed. In buffered mode $\overline{SP}/\overline{EN}$ becomes an enable output and the master/slave determination is by M/S.

M/S: If buffered mode is selected: M/S = 1 means the 8259A is programmed to be a master, M/S = 0 means the 8259A is programmed to be a slave. If BUF = 0, M/S has no function.

AEOI: If AEOI = 1 the automatic end of interrupt mode is programmed.

μPM: Microprocessor mode: μPM = 0 sets the 8259A for MCS-80, 85 system operation, μPM = 1 sets the 8259A for 8086 system operation.

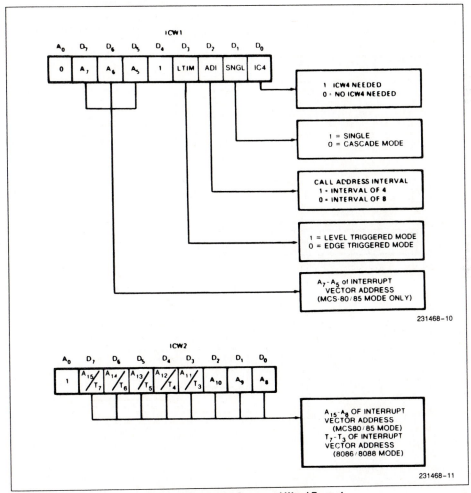

Figure 7. Initialization Command Word Format

231468-10

231468-11

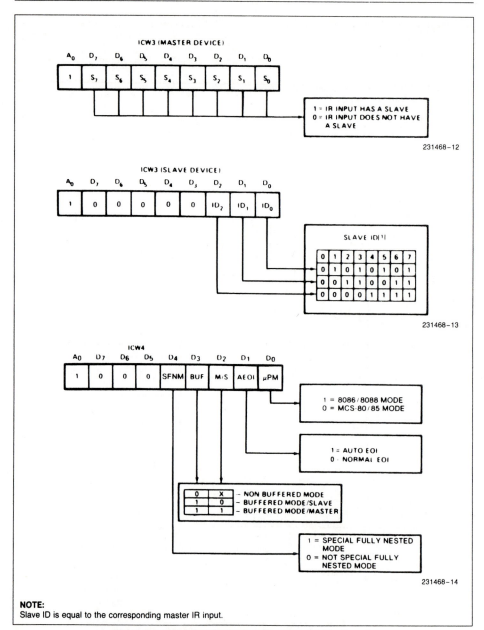

Figure 7. Initialization Command Word Format (Continued)

NOTE:
Slave ID is equal to the corresponding master IR input.

OPERATION COMMAND WORDS (OCWS)

After the Initialization Command Words (ICWs) are programmed into the 8259A, the chip is ready to accept interrupt requests at its input lines. However, during the 8259A operation, a selection of algorithms can command the 8259A to operate in various modes through the Operation Command Words (OCWs).

Operation Control Words (OCWs)

OCW1

A0	D7	D6	D5	D4	D3	D2	D1	D0
1	M7	M6	M5	M4	M3	M2	M1	M0

OCW2

A0	D7	D6	D5	D4	D3	D2	D1	D0
0	R	SL	EOI	0	0	L2	L1	L0

OCW3

A0	D7	D6	D5	D4	D3	D2	D1	D0
0	0	ESMM	SMM	0	1	P	RR	RIS

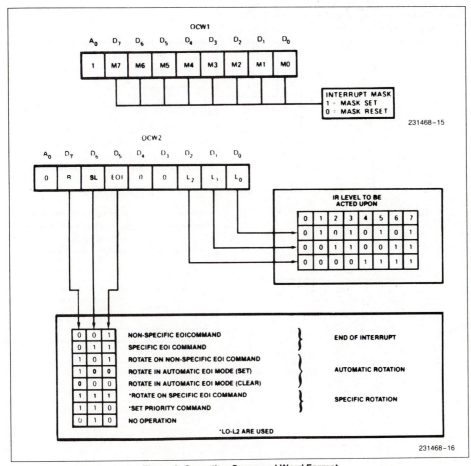

Figure 8. Operation Command Word Format

Operation Control Word 1 (OCW1)

OCW1 sets and clears the mask bits in the interrupt Mask Register (IMR). M_7–M_0 represent the eight mask bits. M = 1 indicates the channel is masked (inhibited), M = 0 indicates the channel is enabled.

Operation Control Word 2 (OCW2)

R, SL, EOI—These three bits control the Rotate and End of Interrupt modes and combinations of the two. A chart of these combinations can be found on the Operation Command Word Format.

L_2, L_1, L_0—These bits determine the interrupt level acted upon when the SL bit is active.

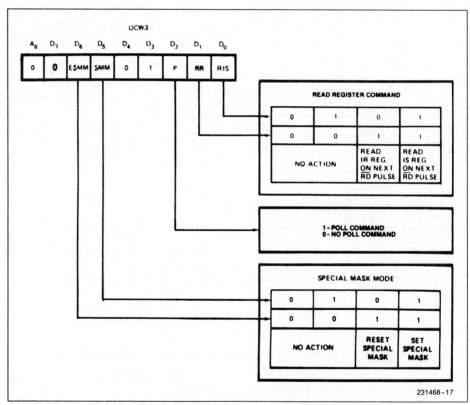

231468–17

Figure 8. Operation Command Word Format (Continued)

Operation Control Word 3 (OCW3)

ESMM—Enable Special Mask Mode. When this bit is set to 1 it enables the SMM bit to set or reset the Special Mask Mode. When ESMM = 0 the SMM bit becomes a "don't care".

SMM—Special Mask Mode. If ESMM = 1 and SMM = 1 the 8259A will enter Special Mask Mode. If ESMM = 1 and SMM = 0 the 8259A will revert to normal mask mode. When ESMM = 0, SMM has no effect.

Fully Nested Mode

This mode is entered after initialization unless another mode is programmed. The interrupt requests are ordered in priority from 0 through 7 (0 highest). When an interrupt is acknowledged the highest priority request is determined and its vector placed on the bus. Additionally, a bit of the Interrupt Service register (ISO-7) is set. This bit remains set until the microprocessor issues an End of Interrupt (EOI) command immediately before returning from the service routine, or if AEOI (Automatic End of Interrupt) bit is set, until the trailing edge of the last INTA. While the IS bit is set, all further interrupts of the same or lower priority are inhibited, while higher levels will generate an interrupt (which will be acknowledged only if the microprocessor internal Interrupt enable flip-flop has been re-enabled through software).

After the initialization sequence, IR0 has the highest prioirity and IR7 the lowest. Priorities can be changed, as will be explained, in the rotating priority mode.

End of Interrupt (EOI)

The In Service (IS) bit can be reset either automatically following the trailing edge of the last in sequence INTA pulse (when AEOI bit in ICW1 is set) or by a command word that must be issued to the 8259A before returning from a service routine (EOI command). An EOI command must be issued twice if in the Cascade mode, once for the master and once for the corresponding slave.

There are two forms of EOI command: Specific and Non-Specific. When the 8259A is operated in modes which perserve the fully nested structure, it can determine which IS bit to reset on EOI. When a Non-Specific EOI command is issued the 8259A will automatically reset the highest IS bit of those that are set, since in the fully nested mode the highest IS level was necessarily the last level acknowledged and serviced. A non-specific EOI can be issued with OCW2 (EOI = 1, SL = 0, R = 0).

When a mode is used which may disturb the fully nested structure, the 8259A may no longer be able to determine the last level acknowledged. In this case a Specific End of Interrupt must be issued which includes as part of the command the IS level to be reset. A specific EOI can be issued with OCW2 (EOI = 1, SL = 1, R = 0, and L0–L2 is the binary level of the IS bit to be reset).

It should be noted that an IS bit that is masked by an IMR bit will not be cleared by a non-specific EOI if the 8259A is in the Special Mask Mode.

Automatic End of Interrupt (AEOI) Mode

If AEOI = 1 in ICW4, then the 8259A will operate in AEOI mode continuously until reprogrammed by ICW4. in this mode the 8259A will automatically perform a non-specific EOI operation at the trailing edge of the last interrupt acknowledge pulse (third pulse in MCS-80/85, second in 8086). Note that from a system standpoint, this mode should be used only when a nested multilevel interrupt structure is not required within a single 8259A.

The AEOI mode can only be used in a master 8259A and not a slave. 8259As with a copyright date of 1985 or later will operate in the AEOI mode as a master or a slave.

Automatic Rotation (Equal Priority Devices)

In some applications there are a number of interrupting devices of equal priority. In this mode a device, after being serviced, receives the lowest priority, so a device requesting an interrupt will have to wait, in the worst case until each of 7 other devices are serviced at most *once*. For example, if the priority and "in service" status is:

Before Rotate (IR4 the highest prioirity requiring service)

"IS" Status   231468–18

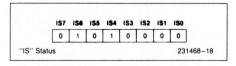

Priority Status   231468–19

After Rotate (IR4 was serviced, all other priorities rotated correspondingly)

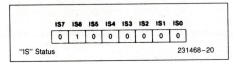

"IS" Status   231468-20

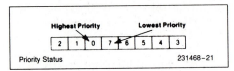

Priority Status   231468-21

There are two ways to accomplish Automatic Rotation using OCW2, the Rotation on Non-Specific EOI Command (R = 1, SL = 0, EOI = 1) and the Rotate in Automatic EOI Mode which is set by (R = 1, SL = 0, EOI = 0) and cleared by (R = 0, SL = 0, EOI = 0).

Specific Rotation
(Specific Priority)

The programmer can change priorities by programming the bottom priority and thus fixing all other priorities; i.e., if IR5 is programmed as the bottom priority device, then IR6 will have the highest one.

The Set Priority command is issued in OCW2 where: R = 1, SL = 1, L0–L2 is the binary priority level code of the bottom priority device.

Observe that in this mode internal status is updated by software control during OCW2. However, it is independent of the End of Interrupt (EOI) command (also executed by OCW2). Priority changes can be executed during an EOI command by using the Rotate on Specific EOI command in OCW2 (R = 1, SL = 1, EOI = 1 and LO–L2 = IR level to receive bottom priority).

Interrupt Masks

Each Interrupt Request input can bem masked individually by the Interrupt Mask Register (IMR) programmed through OCW1. Each bit in the IMR masks one interrupt channel if it is set (1). Bit 0 masks IR0, Bit 1 masks IR1 and so forth. Masking an IR channel does not affect the other channels operation.

Special Mask Mode

Some applications may require an interrupt service routine to dynamically alter the system priority structure during its execution under software control. For example, the routine may wish to inhibit lower priority requests for a portion of its execution but enable some of them for another portion.

The difficulty here is that if an Interrupt Request is acknowledged and an End of Interrupt command did not reset its IS bit (i.e., while executing a service routine), the 8259A would have inhibited all lower priority requests with no easy way for the routine to enable them.

That is where the Special Mask Mode comes in. In the special Mask Mode, when a mask bit is set in OCW1, it inhibits further interrupts at that level *and* enables interrupts from *all other* levels (lower as well as higher) that are not masked.

Thus, any interrupts may be selectively enabled by loading the mask register.

The special Mask Mode is set by OWC3 where: SSMM = 1, SMM = 1, and cleared where SSMM = 1, SMM = 0.

Poll Command

In Poll mode the INT output functions as it normally does. The microprocessor should ignore this output. This can be accomplished either by not connecting the INT output or by masking interrupts within the microprocessor, thereby disabling its interrupt input. Service to devices is achieved by software using a Poll command.

The Poll command is issued by setting P = '1" in OCW3. The 8259A treats the next $\overline{RD}$ pulse to the 8259A (i.e., $\overline{RD}$ = 0, $\overline{CS}$ = 0) as an interrupt acknowledge, sets the appropriate IS bit if there is a request, and reads the priority level. Interrupt is frozen from $\overline{WR}$ to $\overline{RD}$.

The word enabled onto the data bus during $\overline{RD}$ is:

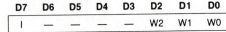

D7	D6	D5	D4	D3	D2	D1	D0
I	—	—	—	—	W2	W1	W0

W0–W2: Binary code of the highest priority level requesting service.

    I: Equal to "1" if there is an interrupt.

This mode is useful if there is a routine command common to several levels so that the $\overline{INTA}$ sequence is not needed (saves ROM space). Another application is to use the poll mode to expand the number of priority levels to more than 64.

Reading the 8259A Status

The input status of several internal registers can be read to update the user information on the system.

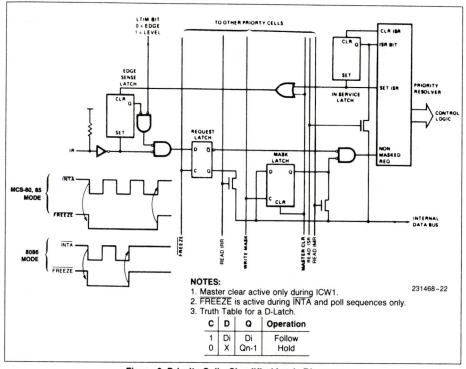

NOTES:
1. Master clear active only during ICW1.
2. FREEZE is active during INTA and poll sequences only.
3. Truth Table for a D-Latch.

C	D	Q	Operation
1	Di	Di	Follow
0	X	Qn-1	Hold

231468–22

Figure 9. Priority Cell—Simplified Logic Diagram

The following registers can be read via OCW3 (IRR and ISR or OCW1 [IMR]).

Interrupt Request Register (IRR): 8-bit register which contains the levels requesting an interrupt to be acknowledged. The highest request level is reset from the IRR when an interrupt is acknowledged. (Not affected by IMR.)

In-Service Register (ISR): 8-bit register which contains the priority levels that are being serviced. The ISR is updated when an End of Interrupt Command is issued.

Interrupt Mask Register: 8-bit register which contains the interrupt request lines which are masked.

The IRR can be read when, prior to the RD pulse, a Read Register Command is issued with OCW3 (RR = 1, RIS = 0.)

The ISR can be read, when, prior to the RD pulse, a Read Register Command is issued with OCW3 (RR = 1, RIS = 1).

There is no need to write an OCW3 before every status read operation, as long as the status read corresponds with the previous one; i.e., the 8259A "remembers" whether the IRR or ISR has been previously selected by the OCW3. This is not true when poll is used.

After initialization the 8259A is set to IRR.

For reading the IMR, no OCW3 is needed. The output data bus will contain the IMR whenever RD is active and A0 = 1 (OCW1).

Polling overrides status read when P = 1, RR = 1 in OCW3.

Edge and Level Triggered Modes

This mode is programmed using bit 3 in ICW1.

If LTIM = '0', an interrupt request will be recognized by a low to high transition on an IR input. The IR input can remain high without generating another interrupt.

425

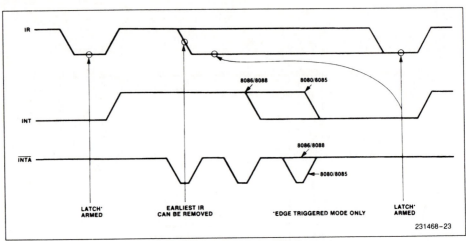

Figure 10. IR Triggering Timing Requirements

If LTIM = '1', an interrupt request will be recognized by a 'high' level on IR Input, and there is no need for an edge detection. The interrupt request must be removed before the EOI command is issued or the CPU interrupts is enabled to prevent a second interrupt from occurring.

The priority cell diagram shows a conceptual circuit of the level sensitive and edge sensitive input circuitry of the 8259A. Be sure to note that the request latch is a transparent D type latch.

In both the edge and level triggered modes the IR inputs must remain high until after the falling edge of the first INTA. If the IR input goes low before this time a DEFAULT IR7 will occur when the CPU acknowledges the interrupt. This can be a useful safeguard for detecting interrupts caused by spurious noise glitches on the IR inputs. To implement this feature the IR7 routine is used for "clean up" simply executing a return instruction, thus ignoring the interrupt. If IR7 is needed for other purposes a default IR7 can still be detected by reading the ISR. A normal IR7 interrupt will set the corresponding ISR bit, a default IR7 won't. If a default IR7 routine occurs during a normal IR7 routine, however, the ISR will remain set. In this case it is necessary to keep track of whether or not the IR7 routine was previously entered. If another IR7 occurs it is a default.

The Special Fully Nest Mode

This mode will be used in the case of a big system where cascading is used, and the priority has to be conserved within each slave. In this case the fully nested mode will be programmed to the master (us-

ing ICW4). This mode is similar to the normal nested mode with the following exceptions:

a. When an interrupt request from a certain slave is in service this slave is not locked out from the master's priority logic and further interrupt requests from higher priority IR's within the slave will be recognized by the master and will initiate interrupts to the processor. (In the normal nested mode a slave is masked out when its request is in service and no higher requests from the same slave can be serviced.)

b. When exiting the Interrupt Service routine the software has to check whether the interrupt serviced was the only one from that slave. This is done by sending a non-specific End of Interrupt (EOI) command to the slave and then reading its In-Service register and checking for zero. If it is empty, a non-specific EOI can be sent to the master too. If not, no EOI should be sent.

Buffered Mode

When the 8259A is used in a large system where bus driving buffers are required on the data bus and the cascading mode is used, there exists the problem of enabling buffers.

The buffered mode will structure the 8259A to send an enable signal on SP/EN to enable the buffers. In this mode, whenever the 8259A's data bus outputs are enabled, the SP/EN output becomes active.

This modification forces the use of software programming to determine whether the 8259A is a master or a slave. Bit 3 in ICW4 programs the buffered mode, and bit 2 in ICW4 determines whether it is a master or a slave.

CASCADE MODE

The 8259A can be easily interconnected in a system of one master with up to eight slaves to handle up to 64 priority levels.

The master controls the slaves through the 3 line cascade bus. The cascade bus acts like chip selects to the slaves during the $\overline{INTA}$ sequence.

In a cascade configuration, the slave interrupt outputs are connected to the master interrupt request inputs. When a slave request line is activated and afterwards acknowledged, the master will enable the corresponding slave to release the device routine address during bytes 2 and 3 of $\overline{INTA}$. (Byte 2 only for 8086/8088).

The cascade bus lines are normally low and will contain the slave address code from the trailing edge of the first $\overline{INTA}$ pulse to the trailing edge of the third pulse. Each 8259A in the system must follow a separate initialization sequence and can be programmed to work in a different mode. An EOI command must be issued twice: once for the master and once for the corresponding slave. An address decoder is required to activate the Chip Select (CS) input of each 8259A.

The cascade lines of the Master 8259A are activated only for slave inputs, non-slave inputs leave the cascade line inactive (low).

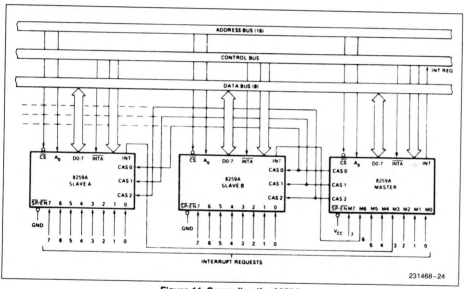

Figure 11. Cascading the 8259A

231468–24

8254
PROGRAMMABLE INTERVAL TIMER

- ■ Compatible with All Intel and Most Other Microprocessors
- ■ Handles Inputs from DC to 10 MHz
  - — 5 MHz 8254-5
  - — 8 MHz 8254
  - — 10 MHz 8254-2
- ■ Status Read-Back Command

- ■ Six Programmable Counter Modes
- ■ Three Independent 16-Bit Counters
- ■ Binary or BCD Counting
- ■ Single +5V Supply
- ■ Available in EXPRESS
  - — Standard Temperature Range

The Intel® 8254 is a counter/timer device designed to solve the common timing control problems in microcomputer system design. It provides three independent 16-bit counters, each capable of handling clock inputs up to 10 MHz. All modes are software programmable. The 8254 is a superset of the 8253.

The 8254 uses HMOS technology and comes in a 24-pin plastic or CERDIP package.

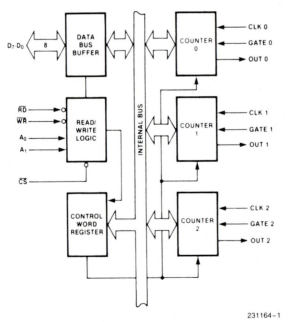

231164–1

Figure 1. 8254 Block Diagram

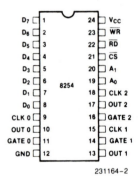

231164–2

Figure 2. Pin Configuration

Table 1. Pin Description

Symbol	Pin No.	Type	Name and Function		
D_7–D_0	1–8	I/O	**DATA:** Bi-directional three state data bus lines, connected to system data bus.		
CLK 0	9	I	**CLOCK 0:** Clock input of Counter 0.		
OUT 0	10	O	**OUTPUT 0:** Output of Counter 0.		
GATE 0	11	I	**GATE 0:** Gate input of Counter 0.		
GND	12		**GROUND:** Power supply connection.		
V_{CC}	24		**POWER:** + 5V power supply connection.		
$\overline{WR}$	23	I	**WRITE CONTROL:** This input is low during CPU write operations.		
$\overline{RD}$	22	I	**READ CONTROL:** This input is low during CPU read operations.		
$\overline{CS}$	21	I	**CHIP SELECT:** A low on this input enables the 8254 to respond to $\overline{RD}$ and $\overline{WR}$ signals. $\overline{RD}$ and $\overline{WR}$ are ignored otherwise.		
A_1, A_0	20–19	I	**ADDRESS:** Used to select one of the three Counters or the Control Word Register for read or write operations. Normally connected to the system address bus.		
			A_1	A_0	Selects
			0	0	Counter 0
			0	1	Counter 1
			1	0	Counter 2
			1	1	Control Word Register
CLK 2	18	I	**CLOCK 2:** Clock input of Counter 2.		
OUT 2	17	O	**OUT 2:** Output of Counter 2.		
GATE 2	16	I	**GATE 2:** Gate input of Counter 2.		
CLK 1	15	I	**CLOCK 1:** Clock input of Counter 1.		
GATE 1	14	I	**GATE 1:** Gate input of Counter 1.		
OUT 1	13	O	**OUT 1:** Output of Counter 1.		

FUNCTIONAL DESCRIPTION

General

The 8254 is a programmable interval timer/counter designed for use with Intel microcomputer systems. It is a general purpose, multi-timing element that can be treated as an array of I/O ports in the system software.

The 8254 solves one of the most common problems in any microcomputer system, the generation of accurate time delays under software control. Instead of setting up timing loops in software, the programmer configures the 8254 to match his requirements and programs one of the counters for the desired delay. After the desired delay, the 8254 will interrupt the CPU. Software overhead is minimal and variable length delays can easily be accommodated.

Some of the other counter/timer functions common to microcomputers which can be implemented with the 8254 are:

- Real time clock
- Event-counter
- Digital one-shot
- Programmable rate generator
- Square wave generator
- Binary rate multiplier
- Complex waveform generator
- Complex motor controller

Block Diagram

DATA BUS BUFFER

This 3-state, bi-directional, 8-bit buffer is used to interface the 8254 to the system bus (see Figure 3).

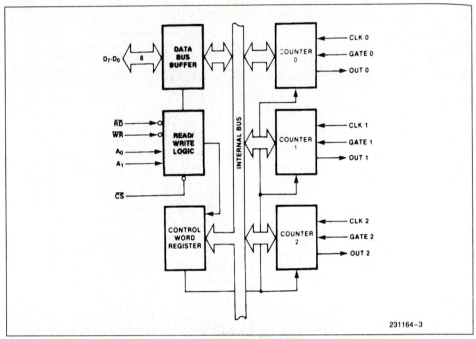

Figure 3. Block Diagram Showing Data Bus Buffer and Read/Write Logic Functions

READ/WRITE LOGIC

The Read/Write Logic accepts inputs from the system bus and generates control signals for the other functional blocks of the 8254. A_1 and A_0 select one of the three counters or the Control Word Register to be read from/written into. A "low" on the $\overline{RD}$ input tells the 8254 that the CPU is reading one of the counters. A "low" on the $\overline{WR}$ input tells the 8254 that the CPU is writing either a Control Word or an initial count. Both $\overline{RD}$ and $\overline{WR}$ are qualified by $\overline{CS}$; $\overline{RD}$ and $\overline{WR}$ are ignored unless the 8254 has been selected by holding $\overline{CS}$ low.

CONTROL WORD REGISTER

The Control Word Register (see Figure 4) is selected by the Read/Write Logic when $A_1, A_0 = 11$. If the CPU then does a write operation to the 8254, the data is stored in the Control Word Register and is interpreted as a Control Word used to define the operation of the Counters.

The Control Word Register can only be written to; status information is available with the Read-Back Command.

COUNTER 0, COUNTER 1, COUNTER 2

These three functional blocks are identical in operation, so only a single Counter will be described. The internal block diagram of a single counter is shown in Figure 5.

The Counters are fully independent. Each Counter may operate in a different Mode.

The Control Word Register is shown in the figure; it is not part of the Counter itself, but its contents determine how the Counter operates.

The status register, shown in Figure 5, when latched, contains the current contents of the Control Word Register and status of the output and null count flag. (See detailed explanation of the Read-Back command.)

The actual counter is labelled CE (for "Counting Element"). It is a 16-bit presettable synchronous down counter.

OL_M and OL_L are two 8-bit latches. OL stands for "Output Latch"; the subscripts M and L stand for "Most significant byte" and "Least significant byte"

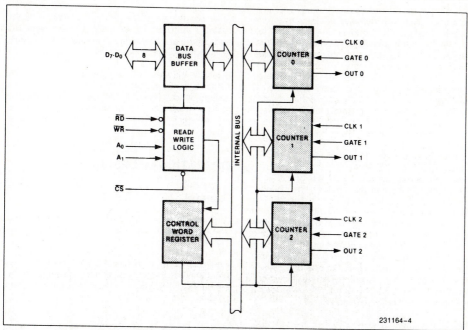

Figure 4. Block Diagram Showing Control Word Register and Counter Functions

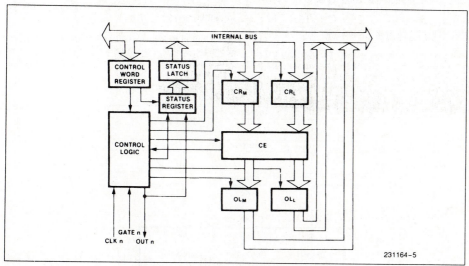

Figure 5. Internal Block Diagram of a Counter

respectively. Both are normally referred to as one unit and called just OL. These latches normally "follow" the CE, but if a suitable Counter Latch Command is sent to the 8254, the latches "latch" the present count until read by the CPU and then return to "following" the CE. One latch at a time is enabled by the counter's Control Logic to drive the internal bus. This is how the 16-bit Counter communicates over the 8-bit internal bus. Note that the CE itself cannot be read; whenever you read the count, it is the OL that is being read.

Similarly, there are two 8-bit registers called CR_M and CR_L (for "Count Register"). Both are normally referred to as one unit and called just CR. When a new count is written to the Counter, the count is stored in the CR and later transferred to the CE. The Control Logic allows one register at a time to be loaded from the internal bus. Both bytes are transferred to the CE simultaneously. CR_M and CR_L are cleared when the Counter is programmed. In this way, if the Counter has been programmed for one byte counts (either most significant byte only or least significant byte only) the other byte will be zero. Note that the CE cannot be written into; whenever a count is written, it is written into the CR.

The Control Logic is also shown in the diagram. CLK n, GATE n, and OUT n are all connected to the outside world through the Control Logic.

8254 SYSTEM INTERFACE

The 8254 is a component of the Intel Microcomputer Systems and interfaces in the same manner as all other peripherals of the family. It is treated by the system's software as an array of peripheral I/O ports; three are counters and the fourth is a control register for MODE programming.

Basically, the select inputs A_0,A_1 connect to the A_0, A_1 address bus signals of the CPU. The CS can be derived directly from the address bus using a linear select method. Or it can be connected to the output of a decoder, such as an Intel 8205 for larger systems.

OPERATIONAL DESCRIPTION

General

After power-up, the state of the 8254 is undefined. The Mode, count value, and output of all Counters are undefined.

How each Counter operates is determined when it is programmed. Each Counter must be programmed before it can be used. Unused counters need not be programmed.

Programming the 8254

Counters are programmed by writing a Control Word and then an initial count.

The Control Words are written into the Control Word Register, which is selected when A_1,A_0 = 11. The Control Word itself specifies which Counter is being programmed.

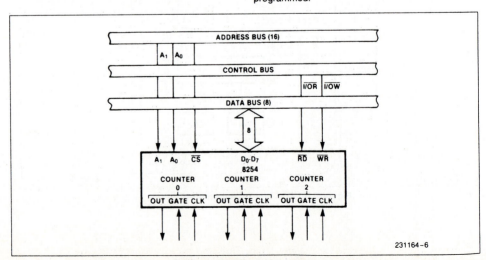

Figure 6. 8254 System Interface

Control Word Format

$A_1, A_0 = 11 \quad \overline{CS} = 0 \quad \overline{RD} = 1 \quad \overline{WR} = 0$

D7	D6	D5	D4	D3	D2	D1	D0
SC1	SC0	RW1	RW0	M2	M1	M0	BCD

SC—Select Counter

SC1	SC0	
0	0	Select Counter 0
0	1	Select Counter 1
1	0	Select Counter 2
1	1	Read-Back Command (see Read Operations)

M—Mode

M2	M1	M0	
0	0	0	Mode 0
0	0	1	Mode 1
X	1	0	Mode 2
X	1	1	Mode 3
1	0	0	Mode 4
1	0	1	Mode 5

RW—Read/Write

RW1	RW0	
0	0	Counter Latch Command (see Read Operations)
0	1	Read/Write least significant byte only
1	0	Read/Write most significant byte only
1	1	Read/Write least significant byte first, then most significant byte

BCD

0	Binary Counter 16-bits
1	Binary Coded Decimal (BCD) Counter (4 Decades)

NOTE:
Don't care bits (X) should be 0 to insure compatibility with future Intel products.

Figure 7. Control Word Format

By contrast, initial counts are written into the Counters, not the Control Word Register. The A_1, A_0 inputs are used to select the Counter to be written into. The format of the initial count is determined by the Control Word used.

Write Operations

The programming procedure for the 8254 is very flexible. Only two conventions need to be remembered:

1) For each Counter, the Control Word must be written before the initial count is written.

2) The initial count must follow the count format specified in the Control Word (least significant byte only, most significant byte only, or least significant byte and then most significant byte).

Since the Control Word Register and the three Counters have separate addresses (selected by the A_1, A_0 inputs), and each Control Word specifies the Counter it applies to (SC0, SC1 bits), no special instruction sequence is required. Any programming sequence that follows the conventions in Figure 7 is acceptable.

A new initial count may be written to a Counter at any time without affecting the Counter's programmed Mode in any way. Counting will be affected as described in the Mode definitions. The new count must follow the programmed count format.

If a Counter is programmed to read/write two-byte counts, the following precaution applies: A program must not transfer control between writing the first and second byte to another routine which also writes into that same Counter. Otherwise, the Counter will be loaded with an incorrect count.

	A_1	A_0		A_1	A_0
Control Word—Counter 0	1	1	Control Word—Counter 2	1	1
LSB of count—Counter 0	0	0	Control Word—Counter 1	1	1
MSB of count—Counter 0	0	0	Control Word—Counter 0	1	1
Control Word—Counter 1	1	1	LSB of count—Counter 2	1	0
LSB of count—Counter 1	0	1	MSB of count—Counter 2	1	0
MSB of count—Counter 1	0	1	LSB of count—Counter 1	0	1
Control Word—Counter 2	1	1	MSB of count—Counter 1	0	1
LSB of count—Counter 2	1	0	LSB of count—Counter 0	0	0
MSB of count—Counter 2	1	0	MSB of count—Counter 0	0	0

	A_1	A_0		A_1	A_0
Control Word—Counter 0	1	1	Control Word—Counter 1	1	1
Control Word—Counter 1	1	1	Control Word—Counter 0	1	1
Control Word—Counter 2	1	1	LSB of count—Counter 1	0	1
LSB of count—Counter 2	1	0	Control Word—Counter 2	1	1
LSB of count—Counter 1	0	1	LSB of count—Counter 0	0	0
LSB of count—Counter 0	0	0	MSB of count—Counter 1	0	1
MSB of count—Counter 0	0	0	LSB of count—Counter 2	1	0
MSB of count—Counter 1	0	1	MSB of count—Counter 0	0	0
MSB of count—Counter 2	1	0	MSB of count—Counter 2	1	0

NOTE:
In all four examples, all Counters are programmed to read/write two-byte counts. These are only four of many possible programming sequences.

Figure 8. A Few Possible Programming Sequences

Read Operations

It is often desirable to read the value of a Counter without disturbing the count in progress. This is easily done in the 8254.

There are three possible methods for reading the counters: a simple read operation, the Counter Latch Command, and the Read-Back Command. Each is explained below. The first method is to perform a simple read operation. To read the Counter, which is selected with the A1, A0 inputs, the CLK input of the selected Counter must be inhibited by using either the GATE input or external logic. Otherwise, the count may be in the process of changing when it is read, giving an undefined result.

COUNTER LATCH COMMAND

The second method uses the "Counter Latch Command". Like a Control Word, this command is written to the Control Word Register, which is selected when $A_1,A_0 = 11$. Also like a Control Word, the SC0, SC1 bits select one of the three Counters, but two other bits, D5 and D4, distinguish this command from a Control Word.

$A_1,A_0 = 11$; CS = 0; RD = 1; WR = 0

D_7	D_6	D_5	D_4	D_3	D_2	D_1	D_0
SC1	SC0	0	0	X	X	X	X

SC1,SC0—specify counter to be latched

SC1	SC0	Counter
0	0	0
0	1	1
1	0	2
1	1	Read-Back Command

D5,D4—00 designates Counter Latch Command

X—don't care

NOTE:
Don't care bits (X) should be 0 to insure compatibility with future Intel products.

Figure 9. Counter Latching Command Format

The selected Counter's output latch (OL) latches the count at the time the Counter Latch Command is received. This count is held in the latch until it is read by the CPU (or until the Counter is reprogrammed). The count is then unlatched automatically and the OL returns to "following" the counting element (CE). This allows reading the contents of the Counters "on the fly" without affecting counting in progress. Multiple Counter Latch Commands may be used to latch more than one Counter. Each latched Counter's OL holds its count until it is read. Counter Latch Commands do not affect the programmed Mode of the Counter in any way.

If a Counter is latched and then, some time later, latched again before the count is read, the second Counter Latch Command is ignored. The count read will be the count at the time the first Counter Latch Command was issued.

With either method, the count must be read according to the programmed format; specifically, if the Counter is programmed for two byte counts, two bytes must be read. The two bytes do not have to be read one right after the other; read or write or programming operations of other Counters may be inserted between them.

Another feature of the 8254 is that reads and writes of the same Counter may be interleaved; for example, if the Counter is programmed for two byte counts, the following sequence is valid.

1) Read least significant byte.
2) Write new least significant byte.
3) Read most significant byte.
4) Write new most significant byte.

If a Counter is programmed to read/write two-byte counts, the following precaution applies: A program must not transfer control between reading the first and second byte to another routine which also reads from that same Counter. Otherwise, an incorrect count will be read.

READ-BACK COMMAND

The third method uses the Read-Back Command. This command allows the user to check the count value, programmed Mode, and current states of the OUT pin and Null Count flag of the selected counter(s).

The command is written into the Control Word Register and has the format shown in Figure 10. The command applies to the counters selected by setting their corresponding bits D3, D2, D1 = 1.

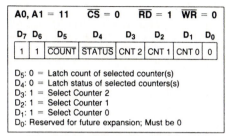

A0, A1 = 11 $\overline{CS}$ = 0 $\overline{RD}$ = 1 $\overline{WR}$ = 0

D7	D6	D5	D4	D3	D2	D1	D0
1	1	COUNT	STATUS	CNT 2	CNT 1	CNT 0	0

D_5: 0 = Latch count of selected counter(s)
D_4: 0 = Latch status of selected counter(s)
D_3: 1 = Select Counter 2
D_2: 1 = Select Counter 1
D_1: 1 = Select Counter 0
D_0: Reserved for future expansion; Must be 0

Figure 10. Read-Back Command Format

The read-back command may be used to latch multiple counter output latches (OL) by setting the COUNT bit D5 = 0 and selecting the desired counter(s). This single command is functionally equivalent to several counter latch commands, one for each counter latched. Each counter's latched count is held until it is read (or the counter is reprogrammed). The counter is automatically unlatched when read, but other counters remain latched until they are read. If multiple count read-back commands are issued to the same counter without reading the count, all but the first are ignored; i.e., the count which will be read is the count at the time the first read-back command was issued.

The read-back command may also be used to latch status information of selected counter(s) by setting STATUS bit D4 = 0. Status must be latched to be read; status of a counter is accessed by a read from that counter.

The counter status format is shown in Figure 11. Bits D5 through D0 contain the counter's programmed Mode exactly as written in the last Mode Control Word. OUTPUT bit D7 contains the current state of the OUT pin. This allows the user to monitor the counter's output via software, possibly eliminating some hardware from a system.

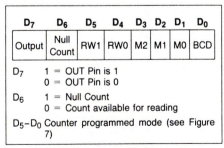

D7	D6	D5	D4	D3	D2	D1	D0
Output	Null Count	RW1	RW0	M2	M1	M0	BCD

D_7 1 = OUT Pin is 1
      0 = OUT Pin is 0

D_6 1 = Null Count
      0 = Count available for reading

D_5–D_0 Counter programmed mode (see Figure 7)

Figure 11. Status Byte

NULL COUNT bit D6 indicates when the last count written to the counter register (CR) has been loaded into the counting element (CE). The exact time this happens depends on the Mode of the counter and is described in the Mode Definitions, but until the count is loaded into the counting element (CE), it can't be read from the counter. If the count is latched or read before this time, the count value will not reflect the new count just written. The operation of Null Count is shown in Figure 12.

COUNT and STATUS bits D5,D4 = 0. This is functionally the same as issuing two separate read-back commands at once, and the above discussions apply here also. Specifically, if multiple count and/or status read-back commands are issued to the same counter(s) without any intervening reads, all but the first are ignored. This is illustrated in Figure 13.

If both count and status of a counter are latched, the first read operation of that counter will return latched status, regardless of which was latched first. The next one or two reads (depending on whether the counter is programmed for one or two type counts) return latched count. Subsequent reads return unlatched count.

This Action	Causes
A. Write to the control word register;[1]	Null Count = 1
B. Write to the count register (CR);[2]	Null Count = 1
C. New Count is loaded into CE (CR → CE);	Null Count = 0

NOTE:
1. Only the counter specified by the control word will have its Null Count set to 1. Null count bits of other counters are unaffected.
2. If the counter is programmed for two-byte counts (least significant byte then most significant byte) Null Count goes to 1 when the second byte is written.

Figure 12. Null Count Operation

If multiple status latch operations of the counter(s) are performed without reading the status, all but the first are ignored; i.e., the status that will be read is the status of the counter at the time the first status read-back command was issued.

Both count and status of the selected counter(s) may be latched simultaneously by setting both

CS	RD	WR	A1	A0	
0	1	0	0	0	Write into Counter 0
0	1	0	0	1	Write into Counter 1
0	1	0	1	0	Write into Counter 2
0	1	0	1	1	Write Control Word
0	0	1	0	0	Read from Counter 0
0	0	1	0	1	Read from Counter 1
0	0	1	1	0	Read from Counter 2
0	0	1	1	1	No-Operation (3-State)
1	X	X	X	X	No-Operation (3-State)
0	1	1	X	X	No-Operation (3-State)

Figure 14. Read/Write Operations Summary

Command								Description	Result
D7	D6	D5	D4	D3	D2	D1	D0		
1	1	0	0	0	0	1	0	Read back count and status of Counter 0	Count and status latched for Counter 0
1	1	1	0	0	1	0	0	Read back status of Counter 1	Status latched for Counter 1
1	1	1	0	1	1	0	0	Read back status of Counters 2, 1	Status latched for Counter 2, but not Counter 1
1	1	0	1	1	0	0	0	Read back count of Counter 2	Count latched for Counter 2
1	1	0	0	0	1	0	0	Read back count and status of Counter 1	Count latched for Counter 1, but not status
1	1	1	0	0	0	1	0	Read back status of Counter 1	Command ignored, status already latched for Counter 1

Figure 13. Read-Back Command Example

Mode Definitions

The following are defined for use in describing the operation of the 8254.

CLK Pulse: a rising edge, then a falling edge, in that order, of a Counter's CLK input.

Trigger: a rising edge of a Counter's GATE input.

Counter loading: the transfer of a count from the CR to the CE (refer to the "Functional Description")

MODE 0: INTERRUPT ON TERMINAL COUNT

Mode 0 is typically used for event counting. After the Control Word is written, OUT is initially low, and will remain low until the Counter reaches zero. OUT then goes high and remains high until a new count or a new Mode 0 Control Word is written into the Counter.

GATE = 1 enables counting; GATE = 0 disables counting. GATE has no effect on OUT.

After the Control Word and initial count are written to a Counter, the initial count will be loaded on the next CLK pulse. This CLK pulse does not decrement the count, so for an initial count of N, OUT does not go high until N + 1 CLK pulses after the initial count is written.

If a new count is written to the Counter, it will be loaded on the next CLK pulse and counting will continue from the new count. If a two-byte count is written, the following happens:

1) Writing the first byte disables counting. OUT is set low immediately (no clock pulse required)

2) Writing the second byte allows the new count to be loaded on the next CLK pulse.

This allows the counting sequence to be synchronized by software. Again, OUT does not go high until N + 1 CLK pulses after the new count of N is written.

If an initial count is written while GATE = 0, it will still be loaded on the next CLK pulse. When GATE goes high, OUT will go high N CLK pulses later; no CLK pulse is needed to load the Counter as this has already been done.

MODE 1: HARDWARE RETRIGGERABLE ONE-SHOT

OUT will be initially high. OUT will go low on the CLK pulse following a trigger to begin the one-shot pulse, and will remain low until the Counter reaches zero.

OUT will then go high and remain high until the CLK pulse after the next trigger.

After writing the Control Word and initial count, the Counter is armed. A trigger results in loading the Counter and setting OUT low on the next CLK pulse, thus starting the one-shot pulse. An initial count of N will result in a one-shot pulse N CLK cycles in duration. The one-shot is retriggerable, hence OUT will remain low for N CLK pulses after any trigger. The one-shot pulse can be repeated without rewriting the same count into the counter. GATE has no effect on OUT.

If a new count is written to the Counter during a one-shot pulse, the current one-shot is not affected unless the counter is retriggered. In that case, the Counter is loaded with the new count and the one-shot pulse continues until the new count expires.

MODE 2: RATE GENERATOR

This Mode functions like a divide-by-N counter. It is typically used to generate a Real Time Clock interrupt. OUT will initially be high. When the initial count has decremented to 1, OUT goes low for one CLK pulse. OUT then goes high again, the Counter reloads the initial count and the process is repeated. Mode 2 is periodic; the same sequence is repeated indefinitely. For an initial count of N, the sequence repeats every N CLK cycles.

GATE = 1 enables counting; GATE = 0 disables counting. If GATE goes low during an output pulse, OUT is set high immediately. A trigger reloads the Counter with the initial count on the next CLK pulse; OUT goes low N CLK pulses after the trigger. Thus the GATE input can be used to synchronize the Counter.

After writing a Control Word and initial count, the Counter will be loaded on the next CLK pulse. OUT goes low N CLK Pulses after the initial count is written. This allows the Counter to be synchronized by software also.

Writing a new count while counting does not affect the current counting sequence. If a trigger is received after writing a new count but before the end of the current period, the Counter will be loaded with the new count on the next CLK pulse and counting will continue from the new count. Otherwise, the new count will be loaded at the end of the current counting cycle. In mode 2, a COUNT of 1 is illegal.

MODE 3: SQUARE WAVE MODE

Mode 3 is typically used for Baud rate generation. Mode 3 is similar to Mode 2 except for the duty cycle of OUT. OUT will initially be high. When half the

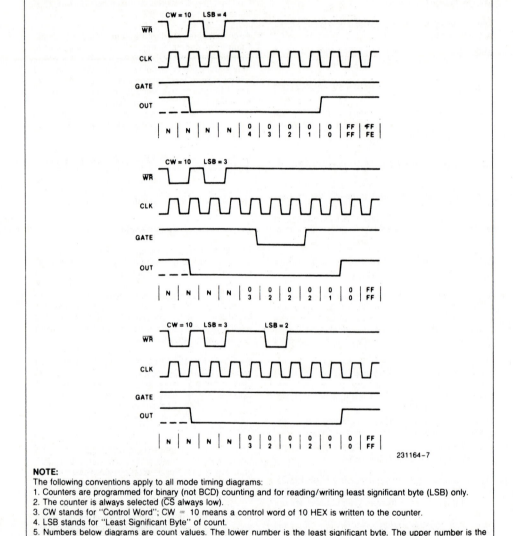

231164-7

NOTE:
The following conventions apply to all mode timing diagrams:
1. Counters are programmed for binary (not BCD) counting and for reading/writing least significant byte (LSB) only.
2. The counter is always selected (CS always low).
3. CW stands for "Control Word"; CW = 10 means a control word of 10 HEX is written to the counter.
4. LSB stands for "Least Significant Byte" of count.
5. Numbers below diagrams are count values. The lower number is the least significant byte. The upper number is the most significant byte. Since the counter is programmed to read/write LSB only, the most significant byte cannot be read.
  N stands for an undefined count.
  Vertical lines show transitions between count values.

Figure 15. Mode 0

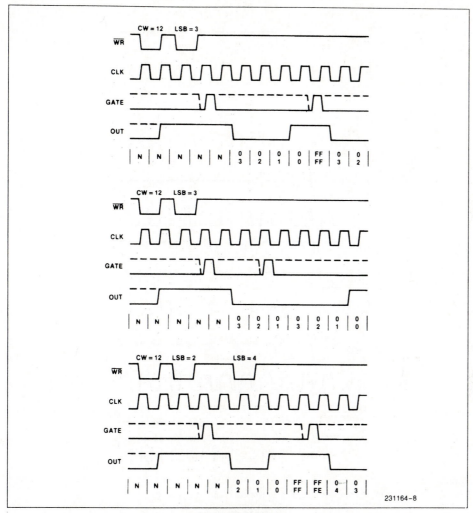

Figure 16. Mode 1

initial count has expired, OUT goes low for the remainder of the count. Mode 3 is periodic; the sequence above is repeated indefinitely. An initial count of N results in a square wave with a period of N CLK cycles.

GATE = 1 enables counting; GATE = 0 disables counting. If GATE goes low while OUT is low, OUT is set high immediately; no CLK pulse is required. A trigger reloads the Counter with the initial count on the next CLK pulse. Thus the GATE input can be used to synchronize the Counter.

After writing a Control Word and initial count, the Counter will be loaded on the next CLK pulse. This allows the Counter to be synchronized by software also.

Writing a new count while counting does not affect the current counting sequence. If a trigger is received after writing a new count but before the end of the current half-cycle of the square wave, the Counter will be loaded with the new count on the next CLK pulse and counting will continue from the

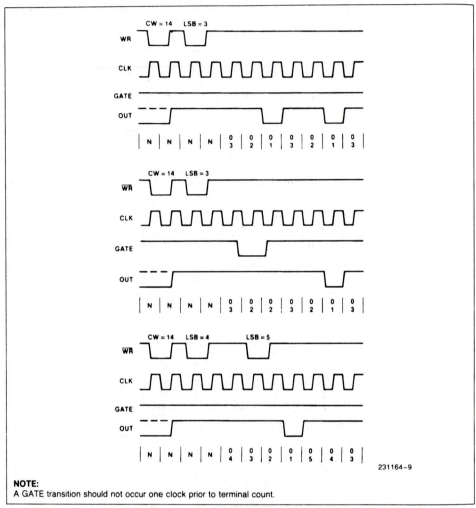

NOTE:
A GATE transition should not occur one clock prior to terminal count.

Figure 17. Mode 2

new count. Otherwise, the new count will be loaded at the end of the current half-cycle.

Mode 3 is implemented as follows:

Even counts: OUT is initially high. The initial count is loaded on one CLK pulse and then is decremented by two on succeeding CLK pulses. When the count expires OUT changes value and the Counter is reloaded with the initial count. The above process is repeated indefinitely.

Odd counts: OUT is initially high. The initial count minus one (an even number) is loaded on one CLK pulse and then is decremented by two on succeeding CLK pulses. One CLK pulse *after* the count expires, OUT goes low and the Counter is reloaded with the initial count minus one. Succeeding CLK pulses decrement the count by two. When the count expires, OUT goes high again and the Counter is reloaded with the initial count minus one. The above process is repeated indefinitely. So for odd counts, OUT will be high for $(N + 1)/2$ counts and low for $(N - 1)/2$ counts.

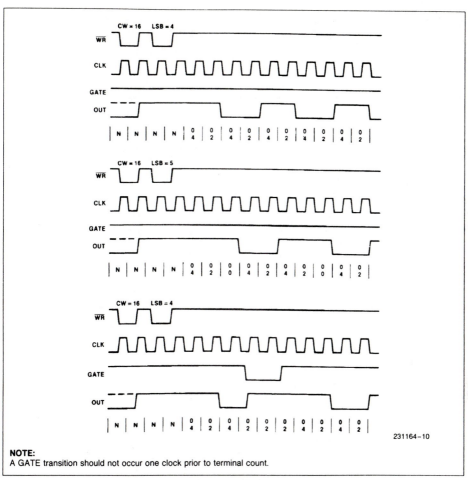

NOTE:
A GATE transition should not occur one clock prior to terminal count.

231164-10

Figure 18. Mode 3

MODE 4: SOFTWARE TRIGGERED STROBE

OUT will be initially high. When the initial count expires, OUT will go low for one CLK pulse and then go high again. The counting sequence is "triggered" by writing the initial count.

GATE = 1 enables counting; GATE = 0 disables counting. GATE has no effect on OUT.

After writing a Control Word and initial count, the Counter will be loaded on the next CLK pulse. This CLK pulse does not decrement the count, so for an

initial count of N, OUT does not strobe low until N + 1 CLK pulses after the initial count is written.

If a new count is written during counting, it will be loaded on the next CLK pulse and counting will continue from the new count. If a two-byte count is written, the following happens:

1) Writing the first byte has no effect on counting.

2) Writing the second byte allows the new count to be loaded on the next CLK pulse.

This allows the sequence to be "retriggered" by software. OUT strobes low N + 1 CLK pulses after the new count of N is written.

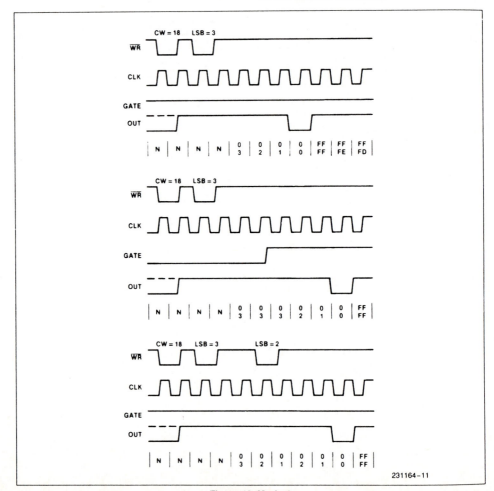

Figure 19. Mode 4

MODE 5: HARDWARE TRIGGERED STROBE (RETRIGGERABLE)

OUT will initially be high. Counting is triggered by a rising edge of GATE. When the initial count has expired, OUT will go low for one CLK pulse and then go high again.

After writing the Control Word and initial count, the counter will not be loaded until the CLK pulse after a trigger. This CLK pulse does not decrement the count, so for an initial count of N, OUT does not strobe low until N + 1 CLK pulses after a trigger.

A trigger results in the Counter being loaded with the initial count on the next CLK pulse. The counting sequence is retriggerable. OUT will not strobe low for N + 1 CLK pulses after any trigger. GATE has no effect on OUT.

If a new count is written during counting, the current counting sequence will not be affected. If a trigger occurs after the new count is written but before the current count expires, the Counter will be loaded with the new count on the next CLK pulse and counting will continue from there.

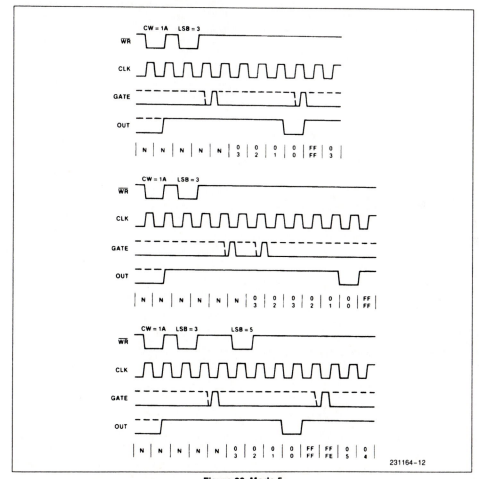

Figure 20. Mode 5

231164–12

Signal Status Modes	Low Or Going Low	Rising	High
0	Disables Counting	— —	Enables Counting
1	— —	1) Initiates Counting 2) Resets Output after Next Clock	— —
2	1) Disables Counting 2) Sets Output Immediately High	Initiates Counting	Enables Counting
3	1) Disables Counting 2) Sets Output Immediately High	Initiates Counting	Enables Counting
4	Disables Counting	— —	Enables Counting
5	— —	Initiates Counting	— —

Figure 21. Gate Pin Operations Summary

Mode	Min Count	Max Count
0	1	0
1	1	0
2	2	0
3	2	0
4	1	0
5	1	0

NOTE:
0 is equivalent to 2^{16} for binary counting and 10^4 for BCD counting.

Figure 22. Minimum and Maximum Initial Counts

Operation Common to All Modes

PROGRAMMING

When a Control Word is written to a Counter, all Control Logic is immediately reset and OUT goes to a known initial state; no CLK pulses are required for this.

GATE

The GATE input is always sampled on the rising edge of CLK. In Modes 0, 2, 3, and 4 the GATE input is level sensitive, and the logic level is sampled on the rising edge of CLK. In Modes 1, 2, 3, and 5 the GATE input is rising-edge sensitive. In these Modes, a rising edge of GATE (trigger) sets an edge-sensitive flip-flop in the Counter. This flip-flop is then sampled on the next rising edge of CLK; the flip-flop is reset immediately after it is sampled. In this way, a trigger will be detected no matter when it occurs—a high logic level does not have to be maintained until the next rising edge of CLK. Note that in Modes 2 and 3, the GATE input is both edge- and level-sensitive. In Modes 2 and 3, if a CLK source other than the system clock is used, GATE should be pulsed immediately following $\overline{WR}$ of a new count value.

COUNTER

New counts are loaded and Counters are decremented on the falling edge of CLK.

The largest possible initial count is 0; this is equivalent to 2^{16} for binary counting and 10^4 for BCD counting.

The Counter does not stop when it reaches zero. In Modes 0, 1, 4, and 5 the Counter "wraps around" to the highest count, either FFFF hex for binary counting or 9999 for BCD counting, and continues counting. Modes 2 and 3 are periodic; the Counter reloads itself with the initial count and continues counting from there.

ABSOLUTE MAXIMUM RATINGS*

Ambient Temperature Under Bias ......0°C to 70°C
Storage Temperature .... − 65°C to + 150°C
Voltage on Any Pin with
   Respect to Ground.............. − 0.5V to + 7V
Power Dissipation 1W

NOTICE: This is a production data sheet. The specifications are subject to change without notice.

*WARNING: Stressing the device beyond the "Absolute
Maximum Ratings" may cause permanent damage.
These are stress ratings only. Operation beyond the
"Operating Conditions" is not recommended and ex-
tended exposure beyond the "Operating Conditions"
may affect device reliability.

D.C. CHARACTERISTICS T_A = 0°C to 70°C, V_{CC} = 5V ± 10%

Symbol	Parameter	Min	Max	Units	Test Conditions
V_{IL}	Input Low Voltage	− 0.5	0.8	V	
V_{IH}	Input High Voltage	2.0	V_{CC} + 0.5V	V	
V_{OL}	Output Low Voltage		0.45	V	I_{OL} = 2.0 mA
V_{OH}	Output High Voltage	2.4		V	I_{OH} = − 400 μA
I_{IL}	Input Load Current		± 10	μA	V_{IN} = V_{CC} to 0V
I_{OFL}	Output Float Leakage		± 10	μA	V_{OUT} = V_{CC} to 0.45V
I_{CC}	V_{CC} Supply Current		170	mA	
C_{IN}	Input Capacitance		10	pF	f_c = 1 MHz
$C_{I/0}$	I/O Capacitance		20	pF	Unmeasured pins returned to V_{SS}[4]

A.C. CHARACTERISTICS T_A = 0°C to 70°C, V_{CC} = 5V ± 10%, GND = 0V

Bus Parameters[1]

READ CYCLE

Symbol	Parameter	8254-5 Min	8254-5 Max	8254 Min	8254 Max	8254-2 Min	8254-2 Max	Unit
t_{AR}	Address Stable Before $\overline{RD}$ ↓	45		45		30		ns
t_{SR}	$\overline{CS}$ Stable Before $\overline{RD}$ ↓	0		0		0		ns
t_{RA}	Address Hold Time After $\overline{RD}$ ↑	0		0		0		ns
t_{RR}	$\overline{RD}$ Pulse Width	150		150		95		ns
t_{RD}	Data Delay from $\overline{RD}$ ↓		120		120		85	ns
t_{AD}	Data Delay from Address		220		220		185	ns
t_{DF}	$\overline{RD}$ ↑ to Data Floating	5	90	5	90	5	65	ns
t_{RV}	Command Recovery Time	200		200		165		ns

NOTE:
1. AC timings measured at V_{OH} = 2.0V, V_{OL} = 0.8V.

A.C. CHARACTERISTICS T_A = 0°C to 70°C, V_{CC} = 5V ± 10%, GND = 0V (Continued)

WRITE CYCLE

Symbol	Parameter	8254-5		8254		8254-2		Unit
		Min	Max	Min	Max	Min	Max	
t_{AW}	Address Stable Before $\overline{WR}$ ↓	0		0		0		ns
t_{SW}	$\overline{CS}$ Stable Before $\overline{WR}$ ↓	0		0		0		ns
$t_{\overline{WA}}$	Address Hold Time After $\overline{WR}$ ↓	0		0		0		ns
t_{WW}	$\overline{WR}$ Pulse Width	150		150		95		ns
t_{DW}	Data Setup Time Before $\overline{WR}$ ↑	120		120		95		ns
t_{WD}	Data Hold Time After $\overline{WR}$ ↑	0		0		0		ns
t_{RV}	Command Recovery Time	200		200		165		ns

CLOCK AND GATE

Symbol	Parameter	8254-5		8254		8254-2		Unit
		Min	Max	Min	Max	Min	Max	
t_{CLK}	Clock Period	200	DC	125	DC	100	DC	ns
t_{PWH}	High Pulse Width	60[3]		60[3]		30[3]		ns
t_{PWL}	Low Pulse Width	60[3]		60[3]		50[3]		ns
t_R	Clock Rise Time		25		25		25	ns
t_F	Clock Fall Time		25		25		25	ns
t_{GW}	Gate Width High	50		50		50		ns
t_{GL}	Gate Width Low	50		50		50		ns
t_{GS}	Gate Setup Time to CLK ↑	50		50		40		ns
t_{GH}	Gate Setup Time After CLK ↑	50[2]		50[2]		50[2]		ns
t_{OD}	Output Delay from CLK ↓		150		150		100	ns
t_{ODG}	Output Delay from Gate ↓		120		120		100	ns
t_{WC}	CLK Delay for Loading ↓	0	55	0	55	0	55	ns
t_{WG}	Gate Delay for Sampling	−5	50	−5	50	−5	40	ns
t_{WO}	OUT Delay from Mode Write		260		260		240	ns
t_{CL}	CLK Set Up for Count Latch	−40	45	−40	45	−40	40	ns

NOTES:
2. In Modes 1 and 5 triggers are sampled on each rising clock edge. A second trigger within 120 ns (70 ns for the 8254-2) of the rising clock edge may not be detected.
3. Low-going glitches that violate t_{PWH}, t_{PWL} may cause errors requiring counter reprogramming.
4. Sampled, not 100% tested. T_A = 25°C.
5. If CLK present at TWC min then Count equals N + 2 CLK pulses, TWC max equals Count N + 1 CLK pulse. TWC min to TWC max, count will be either N + 1 or N + 2 CLK pulses.
6. In Modes 1 and 5, if GATE is present when writing a new Count value, at TWG min Counter will not be triggered, at TWG max Counter will be triggered.
7. If CLK present when writing a Counter Latch or ReadBack Command, at TCL min CLK will be reflected in count value latched, at TCL max CLK will not be reflected in the count value latched.

8087
MATH COPROCESSOR

- Adds Arithmetic, Trigonometric, Exponential, and Logarithmic Instructions to the Standard 8086/8088 and 80186/80188 Instruction Set for All Data Types

- CPU/8087 Supports 7 Data Types: 16-, 32-, 64-Bit Integers, 32-, 64-, 80-Bit Floating Point, and 18-Digit BCD Operands

- Compatible with IEEE Floating Point Standard 754

- Available in 5 MHz (8087), 8 MHz (8087-2) and 10 MHz (8087-1): 8 MHz 80186/80188 System Operation Supported with the 8087-1

- Adds 8 x 80-Bit Individually Addressable Register Stack to the 8086/8088 and 80186/80188 Architecture

- 7 Built-In Exception Handling Functions

- MULTIBUS® System Compatible Interface

The Intel 8087 Math CoProcessor is an extension to the Intel 8086/8088 microprocessor architecture. When combined with the 8086/8088 microprocessor, the 8087 dramatically increases the processing speed of computer applications which utilize mathematical operations such as CAM, numeric controllers, CAD or graphics.

The 8087 Math CoProcessor adds 68 mnemonics to the 8086 microprocessor instruction set. Specific 8087 math operations include logarithmic, arithmetic, exponential, and trigonometric functions. The 8087 supports integer, floating point and BCD data formats, and fully conforms to the ANSI/IEEE floating point standard.

The 8087 is fabricated with HMOS III technology and packaged in a 40-pin cerdip package.

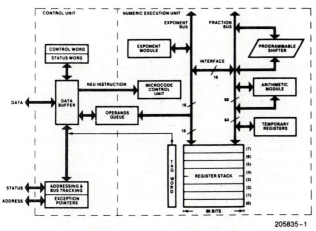

205835–1

Figure 1. 8087 Block Diagram

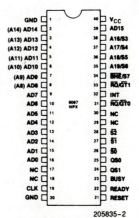

205835–2

Figure 2. 8087 Pin Configuration

Table 1. 8087 Pin Description

Symbol	Type	Name and Function
AD15–AD0	I/O	**ADDRESS DATA:** These lines constitute the time multiplexed memory address (T_1) and data (T_2, T_3, T_W, T_4) bus. A0 is analogous to the $\overline{BHE}$ for the lower byte of the data bus, pins D7–D0. It is LOW during T_1 when a byte is to be transferred on the lower portion of the bus in memory operations. Eight-bit oriented devices tied to the lower half of the bus would normally use A0 to condition chip select functions. These lines are active HIGH. They are input/output lines for 8087-driven bus cycles and are inputs which the 8087 monitors when the CPU is in control of the bus. A15–A8 do not require an address latch in an 8088/8087 or 80188/8087. The 8087 will supply an address for the T_1–T_4 period.
A19/S6, A18/S5, A17/S4, A16/S3	I/O	**ADDRESS MEMORY:** During T_1 these are the four most significant address lines for memory operations. During memory operations, status information is available on these lines during T_2, T_3, T_W, and T_4. For 8087-controlled bus cycles, S6, S4, and S3 are reserved and currently one (HIGH), while S5 is always LOW. These lines are inputs which the 8087 monitors when the CPU is in control of the bus.
BHE/S7	I/O	**BUS HIGH ENABLE:** During T_1 the bus high enable signed ($\overline{BHE}$) should be used to enable data onto the most significant half of the data bus, pins D15–D8. Eight-bit-oriented devices tied to the upper half of the bus would normally use $\overline{BHE}$ to condition chip select functions. $\overline{BHE}$ is LOW during T_1 for read and write cycles when a byte is to be transferred on the high portion of the bus. The S7 status information is available during T_2, T_3, T_W, and T_4. The signal is active LOW. S7 is an input which the 8087 monitors during the CPU-controlled bus cycles.
$\overline{S2}$, $\overline{S1}$, $\overline{S0}$	I/O	**STATUS:** For 8087-driven, these status lines are encoded as follows: $\overline{S2}$ $\overline{S1}$ $\overline{S0}$ 0 (LOW) X X Unused 1 (HIGH) 0 0 Unused 1 0 1 Read Memory 1 1 0 Write Memory 1 1 1 Passive Status is driven active during T_4, remains valid during T_1 and T_2, and is returned to the passive state (1, 1, 1) during T_3 or during T_W when READY is HIGH. This status is used by the 8288 Bus Controller (or the 82188 Integrated Bus Controller with an 80186/ . 80188 CPU) to generate all memory access control signals. Any change in $\overline{S2}$, $\overline{S1}$, or $\overline{S0}$ during T_4 is used to indicate the beginning of a bus cycle, and the return to the passive state in T_3 or T_W is used to indicate the end of a bus cycle. These signals are monitored by the 8087 when the CPU is in control of the bus.
$\overline{RQ}/\overline{GT0}$	I/O	**REQUEST/GRANT:** This request/grant pin is used by the 8087 to gain control of the local bus from the CPU for operand transfers or on behalf of another bus master. It must be connected to one of the two processor request/grant pins. The request/grant sequence on this pin is as follows: 1. A pulse one clock wide is passed to the CPU to indicate a local bus request by either the 8087 or the master connected to the 8087 $\overline{RQ}/\overline{GT1}$ pin. 2. The 8087 waits for the grant pulse and when it is received will either initiate bus transfer activity in the clock cycle following the grant or pass the grant out on the $\overline{RQ}/\overline{GT1}$ pin in this clock if the initial request was for another bus master. 3. The 8087 will generate a release pulse to the CPU one clock cycle after the completion of the last 8087 bus cycle or on receipt of the release pulse from the bus master on $\overline{RQ}/\overline{GT1}$. For 80186/80188 systems the same sequence applies except $\overline{RQ}/\overline{GT}$ signals are converted to appropriate HOLD, HLDA signals by the 82188 Integrated Bus Controller. This is to conform with 80186/80188's HOLD, HLDA bus exchange protocol. Refer to the 82188 data sheet for further information.

Table 1. 8087 Pin Description (Continued)

Symbol	Type	Name and Function
$\overline{RQ}/\overline{GT}1$	I/O	**REQUEST/GRANT:** This request/grant pin is used by another local bus master to force the 8087 to request the local bus. If the 8087 is not in control of the bus when the request is made the request/grant sequence is passed through the 8087 on the $\overline{RQ}/\overline{GT}0$ pin one cycle later. Subsequent grant and release pulses are also passed through the 8087 with a two and one clock delay, respectively, for resynchronization. $\overline{RQ}/\overline{GT}1$ has an internal pullup resistor, and so may be left unconnected. If the 8087 has control of the bus the request/grant sequence is as follows: 1. A pulse 1 CLK wide from another local bus master indicates a local bus request to the 8087 (pulse 1). 2. During the 8087's next T_4 or T_1 a pulse 1 CLK wide from the 8087 to the requesting master (pulse 2) indicates that the 8087 has allowed the local bus to float and that it will enter the "RQ/GT acknowledge" state at the next CLK. The 8087's control unit is disconnected logically from the local bus during "RQ/GT acknowledge." 3. A pulse 1 CLK wide from the requesting master indicates to the 8087 (pulse 3) that the "RQ/GT" request is about to end and that the 8087 can reclaim the local bus at the next CLK. Each master-master exchange of the local bus is a sequence of 3 pulses. There must be one dead CLK cycle after each bus exchange. Pulses are active LOW. For 80186/80188 system, the $\overline{RQ}/\overline{GT}1$ line may be connected to the 82188 Integrated Bus Controller. In this case, a third processor with a HOLD, HLDA bus exchange system may acquire the bus from the 8087. For this configuration, $\overline{RQ}/\overline{GT}1$ will only be used if the 8087 is the bus master. Refer to 82188 data sheet for further information.
QS1, QS0	I	**QS1, QS0:** QS1 and QS0 provide the 8087 with status to allow tracking of the CPU instruction queue. QS1 QS0 0 (LOW) 0 No Operation 0 1 First Byte of Op Code from Queue 1 (HIGH) 0 Empty the Queue 1 1 Subsequent Byte from Queue
INT	O	**INTERRUPT:** This line is used to indicate that an unmasked exception has occurred during numeric instruction execution when 8087 interrupts are enabled. This signal is typically routed to an 8259A for 8086/8088 systems and to INT0 for 80186/80188 systems. INT is active HIGH.
BUSY	O	**BUSY:** This signal indicates that the 8087 NEU is executing a numeric instruction. It is connected to the CPU's $\overline{TEST}$ pin to provide synchronization. In the case of an unmasked exception BUSY remains active until the exception is cleared. BUSY is active HIGH.
READY	I	**READY:** READY is the acknowledgement from the addressed memory device that it will complete the data transfer. The RDY signal from memory is synchronized by the 8284A Clock Generator to form READY for 8086 systems. For 80186/80188 systems, RDY is synchronized by the 82188 Integrated Bus Controller to form READY. This signal is active HIGH.
RESET	I	**RESET:** RESET causes the processor to immediately terminate its present activity. The signal must be active HIGH for at least four clock cycles. RESET is internally synchronized.
CLK	I	**CLOCK:** The clock provides the basic timing for the processor and bus controller. It is asymmetric with a 33% duty cycle to provide optimized internal timing.
V_{CC}		**POWER:** V_{CC} is the +5V power supply pin.
GND		**GROUND:** GND are the ground pins.

NOTE:
For the pin descriptions of the 8086, 8088, 80186 and 80188 CPUs, reference the respective data sheets (8086, 8088, 80186, 80188).

APPLICATION AREAS

The 8087 provides functions meant specifically for high performance numeric processing requirements. Trigonometric, logarithmic, and exponential functions are built into the coprocessor hardware. These functions are essential in scientific, engineering, navigational, or military applications.

The 8087 also has capabilities meant for business or commercial computing. An 8087 can process Binary Coded Decimal (BCD) numbers up to 18 digits without roundoff errors. It can also perform arithmetic on integers as large as 64 bits $\pm 10^{18}$).

PROGRAMMING LANGUAGE SUPPORT

Programs for the 8087 can be written in Intel's high-level languages for 8086/8088 and 80186/80188 Systems; ASM-86 (the 8086, 8088 assembly language), PL/M-86, FORTRAN-86, and PASCAL-86.

RELATED INFORMATION

For 8086, 8088, 80186 or 80188 details, refer to the respective data sheets. For 80186 or 80188 systems, also refer to the 82188 Integrated Bus Controller data sheet.

FUNCTIONAL DESCRIPTION

The 8087 Math CoProcessor's architecture is designed for high performance numeric computing in conjunction with general purpose processing.

The 8087 is a numeric processor extension that provides arithmetic and logical instruction support for a variety of numeric data types. It also executes numerous built-in transcendental functions (e.g., tangent and log functions). The 8087 executes instructions as a coprocessor to a maximum mode CPU. It effectively extends the register and instruction set of the system and adds several new data types as well. Figure 3 presents the registers of the CPU + 8087. Table 2 shows the range of data types supported by the 8087. The 8087 is treated as an extension to the CPU, providing register, data types, control, and instruction capabilities at the hardware level. At the programmer's level the CPU and the 8087 are viewed as a single unified processor.

System Configuration

As a coprocessor to an 8086 or 8088, the 8087 is wired in parallel with the CPU as shown in Figure 4. Figure 5 shows the 80186/80188 system configuration. The CPU's status (S0–S2) and queue status lines (QS0–QS1) enable the 8087 to monitor and decode instructions in synchronization with the CPU and without any CPU overhead. For 80186/80188 systems, the queue status signals of the 80186/80188 are synchronized to 8087 requirements by the 8288 Integrated Bus Controller. Once started, the 8087 can process in parallel with, and independent of, the host CPU. For resynchronization, the 8087's BUSY signal informs the CPU that the 8087 is executing an instruction and the CPU WAIT instruction tests this signal to insure that the 8087 is ready to execute subsequent instructions. The 8087 can interrupt the CPU when it detects an error or exception. The 8087's interrupt request line is typically routed to the CPU through an 8259A Programmable Interrupt Controller for 8086, 8088 systems and INT0 for 80186/80188.

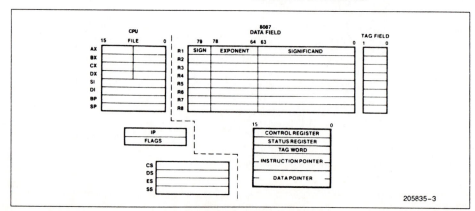

Figure 3. CPU + 8087 Architecture

The 8087 uses one of the request/grant lines of the 8086/8088 architecture (typically $\overline{RQ}/\overline{GT}0$) to obtain control of the local bus for data transfers. The other request/grant line is available for general system use (for instance by an I/O processor in LOCAL mode). A bus master can also be connected to the 8087's $\overline{RQ}/\overline{GT}1$ line. In this configuration the 8087 will pass the request/grant handshake signals between the CPU and the attached master when the 8087 is not in control of the bus and will relinquish the bus to the master directly when the 8087 is in control. In this way two additional masters can be configured in an 8086/8088 system; one will share the 8086/8088 bus with the 8087 on a first-come first-served basis, and the second will be guaranteed to be higher in priority than the 8087.

For 80186/80188 systems, $\overline{RQ}/\overline{GT}0$ and $\overline{RQ}/\overline{GT}1$ are connected to the corresponding inputs of the 82188 Integrated Bus Controller. Because the 80186/80188 has a HOLD, HLDA bus exchange protocol, an interface is needed which will translate $\overline{RQ}/\overline{GT}$ signals to corresponding HOLD, HLDA signals and vice versa. One of the functions of the 82188 IBC is to provide this translation. $\overline{RQ}/\overline{GT}0$ is translated to HOLD, HLDA signals which are then directly connected to the 80186/80188. The $\overline{RQ}/\overline{GT}1$ line is also translated into HOLD, HLDA signals (referred to as SYSHOLD, SYSHLDA signals) by the 82188 IBC. This allows a third processor (using a HOLD, HLDA bus exchange protocol) to gain control of the bus.

Unlike an 8086/8087 system, $\overline{RQ}/\overline{GT}$ is only used when the 8087 has bus control. If the third processor requests the bus when the current bus master is the 80186/80188, the 82188 IBC will directly pass the request onto the 80186/80188 without going through the 8087. The third processor has the highest bus priority in the system. If the 8087 requests the bus while the third processor has bus control, the grant pulse will not be issued until the third processor releases the bus (using SYSHOLD). In this configuration, the third processor has the highest priority, the 8087 has the next highest, and the 80186/80188 has the lowest bus priority.

Bus Operation

The 8087 bus structure, operation and timing are identical to all other processors in the 8086/8088 series (maximum mode configuration). The address is time multiplexed with the data on the first 16/8 lines of the address/data bus. A16 through A19 are time multiplexed with four status lines S3–S6. S3, S4 and S6 are always one (HIGH) for 8087-driven bus cycles while S5 is always zero (LOW). When the 8087 is monitoring CPU bus cycles (passive mode) S6 is also monitored by the 8087 to differentiate 8086/8088 activity from that of a local I/O processor or any other local bus master. (The 8086/8088 must be the only processor on the local bus to drive S6 LOW). S7 is multiplexed with and has the same value as $\overline{BHE}$ for all 8087 bus cycles.

Table 2. 8087 Data Types

Data Formats	Range	Precision	Most Significant Byte								
			7 0	7 0	7 0	7 0	7 0	7 0	7 0	7 0	7 0
Word Integer	10^4	16 Bits	I_{15} $\qquad$ I_0 Two's Complement								
Short Integer	10^9	32 Bits	I_{31} $\qquad$ I_0 Two's Complement								
Long Integer	10^{18}	64 Bits	I_{63} $\qquad$ I_0 Two's Complement								
Packed BCD	10^{18}	18 Digits	S — $D_{17}D_{16}$ $\qquad$ D_1 D_0								
Short Real	$10^{\pm38}$	24 Bits	S E_7 $\quad$ E_0 F_1 $\quad$ F_{23} F_0 Implicit								
Long Real	$10^{\pm308}$	53 Bits	S E_{10} $\quad$ E_0 F_1 $\qquad$ F_{52} F_0 Implicit								
Temporary Real	$10^{\pm4932}$	64 Bits	S E_{14} $\quad$ E_0 F_0 $\qquad$ F_{63}								

Integer: I
Packed BCD: $(-1)^S(D_{17}...D_0)$
Real: $(-1)^S(2^{E-Bias})(F_0 \bullet F_1...)$
bias = 127 for Short Real
       1023 for Long Real
       16383 for Temp Real

The first three status lines, $\overline{S0}-\overline{S2}$, are used with an 8288 bus controller or 82188 Integrated Bus Controller to determine the type of bus cycle being run:

$\overline{S2}$	$\overline{S1}$	$\overline{S0}$	
0	X	X	Unused
1	0	0	Unused
1	0	1	Memory Data Read
1	1	0	Memory Data Write
1	1	1	Passive (no bus cycle)

Programming Interface

The 8087 includes the standard 8086, 8088 instruction set for general data manipulation and program control. It also includes 68 numeric instructions for extended precision integer, floating point, trigonometric, logarithmic, and exponential functions. Sample execution times for several 8087 functions are shown in Table 3. Overall performance is up to 100 times that of an 8086 processor for numeric instructions.

Any instruction executed by the 8087 is the combined result of the CPU and 8087 activity. The CPU and the 8087 have specialized functions and registers providing fast concurrent operation. The CPU controls overall program execution while the 8087 uses the coprocessor interface to recognize and perform numeric operations.

Table 2 lists the seven data types the 8087 supports and presents the format for each type. Internally, the 8087 holds all numbers in the temporary real format. Load and store instructions automatically convert operands represented in memory as 16-, 32-, or 64-bit integers, 32- or 64-bit floating point numbers or 18-digit packed BCD numbers into temporary real format and vice versa. The 8087 also provides the capability to control round off, underflow, and overflow errors in each calculation.

Computations in the 8087 use the processor's register stack. These eight 80-bit registers provide the equivalent capacity of 20 32-bit registers. The 8087 register set can be accessed as a stack, with instructions operating on the top one or two stack elements, or as a fixed register set, with instructions operating on explicitly designated registers.

Table 5 lists the 8087's instructions by class. All appear as ESCAPE instructions to the host. Assembly language programs are written in ASM-86, the 8086, 8088 assembly language.

Table 3. Execution Times for Selected 8086/8087 Numeric Instructions and Corresponding 8086 Emulation

Floating Point Instruction	Approximate Execution Time (μs)	
	8086/8087 (8 MHz Clock)	8086 Emulation
Add/Subtract	10.6	1000
Multiply (Single Precision)	11.9	1000
Multiply (Extended Precision)	16.9	1312
Divide	24.4	2000
Compare	~5.6	812
Load (Double Precision)	~6.3	1062
Store (Double Precision)	13.1	750
Square Root	22.5	12250
Tangent	56.3	8125
Exponentiation	62.5	10687

NUMERIC PROCESSOR EXTENSION ARCHITECTURE

As shown in Figure 1, the 8087 is internally divided into two processing elements, the control unit (CU) and the numeric execution unit (NEU). The NEU executes all numeric instructions, while the CU receives and decodes instructions, reads and writes memory operands and executes 8087 control instructions. The two elements are able to operate independently of one another, allowing the CU to maintain synchronization with the CPU while the NEU is busy processing a numeric instruction.

Control Unit

The CU keeps the 8087 operating in synchronization with its host CPU. 8087 instructions are intermixed with CPU instructions in a single instruction stream. The CPU fetches all instructions from memory; by monitoring the status ($\overline{S0}-\overline{S2}$, S6) emitted by the CPU, the control unit determines when an instruction is being fetched. The CPU monitors the data bus in parallel with the CPU to obtain instructions that pertain to the 8087.

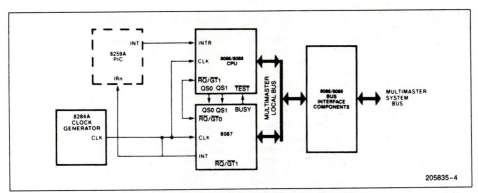

Figure 4. 8086/8087, 8088/8087 System Configuration

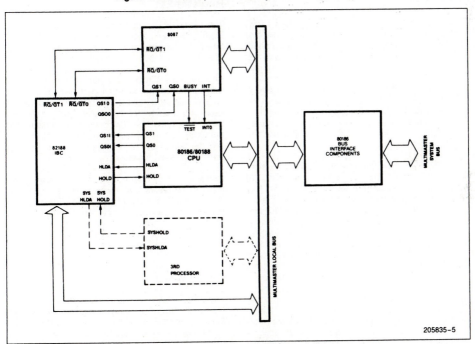

Figure 5. 80186/8087, 80188/8087 System Configuration

The CU maintains an instruction queue that is identical to the queue in the host CPU. The CU automatically determines if the CPU is an 8086/80186 or an 8088/80188 immediately after reset (by monitoring the BHE/S7 line) and matches its queue length accordingly. By monitoring the CPU's queue status lines (QS0, QS1), the CU obtains and decodes instructions from the queue in synchronization with the CPU.

A numeric instruction appears as an ESCAPE instruction to the CPU. Both the CPU and 8087 decode and execute the ESCAPE instruction together. The 8087 only recognizes the numeric instructions shown in Table 5. The start of a numeric operation is accomplished when the CPU executes the ESCAPE instruction. The instruction may or may not identify a memory operand.

The CPU does, however, distinguish between ESC instructions that reference memory and those that do not. If the instruction refers to a memory operand, the CPU calculates the operand's address using any one of its available addressing modes, and then performs a "dummy read" of the word at that location. (Any location within the 1M byte address space is allowed.) This is a normal read cycle except that the CPU ignores the data it receives. If the ESC instruction does not contain a memory reference (e.g. an 8087 stack operation), the CPU simply proceeds to the next instruction.

An 8087 instruction can have one of three memory reference options: (1) not reference memory; (2) load an operand word from memory into the 8087; or (3) store an operand word from the 8087 into memory. If no memory reference is required, the 8087 simply executes its instruction. If a memory reference is required, the CU uses a "dummy read" cycle initiated by the CPU to capture and save the address that the CPU places on the bus. If the instruction is a load, the CU additionally captures the data word when it becomes available on the local data bus. If data required is longer than one word, the CU immediately obtains the bus from the CPU using the request/grant protocol and reads the rest of the information in consecutive bus cycles. In a store operation, the CU captures and saves the store address as in a load, and ignores the data word that follows in the "dummy read" cycle. When the 8087 is ready to perform the store, the CU obtains the bus from the CPU and writes the operand starting at the specified address.

Numeric Execution Unit

The NEU executes all instructions that involve the register stack; these include arithmetic, logical, transcendental, constant and data transfer instructions. The data path in the NEU is 84 bits wide (68 fractions bits, 15 exponent bits and a sign bit) which allows internal operand transfers to be performed at very high speeds.

When the NEU begins executing an instruction, it activates the 8087 BUSY signal. This signal can be used in conjunction with the CPU WAIT instruction to resynchronize both processors when the NEU has completed its current instruction.

Register Set

The CPU + 8087 register set is shown in Figure 3. Each of the eight data registers in the 8087's register stack is 80 bits and is divided into "fields" corresponding to the 8087's temporary real data type.

At a given point in time the TOP field in the control word identifies the current top-of-stack register. A "push" operation decrements TOP by 1 and loads a value into the new top register. A "pop" operation stores the value from the current top register and then increments TOP by 1. Like CPU stacks in memory, the 8087 register stack grows "down" toward lower-addressed registers.

Instructions may address the data registers either implicitly or explicitly. Many instructions operate on the register at the top of the stack. These instructions implicitly address the register pointed to by the TOP. Other instructions allow the programmer to explicitly specify the register which is to be used. Explicit register addressing is "top-relative."

Status Word

The status word shown in Figure 6 reflects the overall state of the 8087; it may be stored in memory and then inspected by CPU code. The status word is a 16-bit register divided into fields as shown in Figure 6. The busy bit (bit 15) indicates whether the NEU is either executing an instruction or has an interrupt request pending (B = 1), or is idle (B = 0). Several instructions which store and manipulate the status word are executed exclusively by the CU, and these do not set the busy bit themselves.

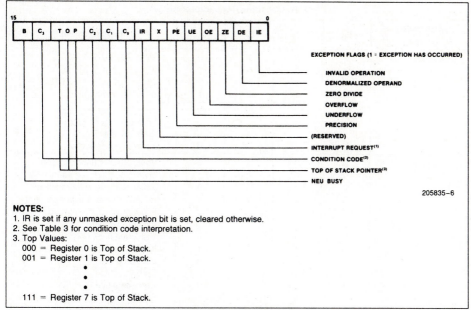

NOTES:
1. IR is set if any unmasked exception bit is set, cleared otherwise.
2. See Table 3 for condition code interpretation.
3. Top Values:
    000 = Register 0 is Top of Stack.
    001 = Register 1 is Top of Stack.
           •
           •
    111 = Register 7 is Top of Stack.

Figure 6. 8087 Status Word

The four numeric condition code bits (C_0–C_3) are similar to flags in a CPU: various instructions update these bits to reflect the outcome of the 8087 operations. The effect of these instructions on the condition code bits is summarized in Table 4.

Bits 14–12 of the status word point to the 8087 register that is the current top-of-stack (TOP) as described above.

Bit 7 is the interrupt request bit. This bit is set if any unmasked exception bit is set and cleared otherwise.

Bits 5–0 are set to indicate that the NEU has detected an exception while executing an instruction.

Tag Word

The tag word marks the content of each register as shown in Figure 7. The principal function of the tag word is to optimize the 8087's performance. The tag word can be used, however, to interpret the contents of 8087 registers.

Instruction and Data Pointers

The instruction and data pointers (see Figure 8) are provided for user-written error handlers. Whenever the 8087 executes a math instruction, the CU saves the instruction address, the operand address (if present) and the instruction opcode. 8087 instructions can store this data into memory.

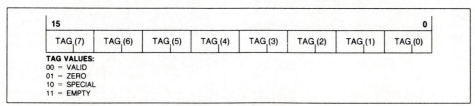

Figure 7. 8087 Tag Word

Table 4a. Condition Code Interpretation

Instruction Type	C_3	C_2	C_1	C_0	Interpretation
Compare, Test	0	0	X	0	ST > Source or 0 (FTST)
	0	0	X	1	ST < Source or 0 (FTST)
	1	0	X	0	ST = Source or 0 (FTST)
	1	1	X	1	ST is not comparable
Remainder	Q_1	0	Q_0	Q_2	Complete reduction with three low bits of quotient (See Table 4b)
	U	1	U	U	Incomplete Reduction
Examine	0	0	0	0	Valid, positive unnormalized
	0	0	0	1	Invalid, positive, exponent = 0
	0	0	1	0	Valid, negative, unnormalized
	0	0	1	1	Invalid, negative, exponent = 0
	0	1	0	0	Valid, positive, normalized
	0	1	0	1	Infinity, positive
	0	1	1	0	Valid, negative, normalized
	0	1	1	1	Infinity, negative
	1	0	0	0	Zero, positive
	1	0	0	1	Empty
	1	0	1	0	Zero, negative
	1	0	1	1	Empty
	1	1	0	0	Invalid, positive, exponent = 0
	1	1	0	1	Empty
	1	1	1	0	Invalid, negative, exponent = 0
	1	1	1	1	Empty

NOTES:
1. ST = Top of stack
2. X = value is not affected by instruction
3. U = value is undefined following instruction
4. Q_n = Quotient bit n

Table 4b. Condition Code Interpretation after FPREM Instruction As a Function of Divided Value

Dividend Range	Q_2	Q_1	Q_0
Dividend < 2 * Modulus	C_3[1]	C_1[1]	Q_0
Dividend < 4 * Modulus	C_3[1]	Q_1	Q_0
Dividend ≥ 4 * Modulus	Q_2	Q_1	Q_0

NOTE:
1. Previous value of indicated bit, not affected by FPREM instruction execution.

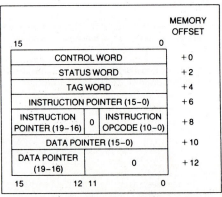

Figure 8. 8087 Instruction and Data Pointer Image in Memory

Control Word

The 8087 provides several processing options which are selected by loading a word from memory into the control word. Figure 9 shows the format and encoding of the fields in the control word.

The low order byte of this control word configures 8087 interrupts and exception masking. Bits 5–0 of the control word contain individual masks for each of the six exceptions that the 8087 recognizes and bit 7 contains a general mask bit for all 8087 interrupts. The high order byte of the control word configures the 8087 operating mode including precision, rounding, and infinity controls. The precision control bits (bits 9–8) can be used to set the 8087 internal operating precision at less than the default of temporary real precision. This can be useful in providing compatibility with earlier generation arithmetic processors of smaller precision than the 8087. The rounding control bits (bits 11–10) provide for directed rounding and true chop as well as the unbiased round to nearest mode specified in the proposed IEEE standard. Control over closure of the number space at infinity is also provided (either affine closure, $\pm\infty$, or projective closure, ∞, is treated as unsigned, may be specified).

Exception Handling

The 8087 detects six different exception conditions that can occur during instruction execution. Any or all exceptions will cause an interrupt if unmasked and interrupts are enabled.

If interrupts are disabled the 8087 will simply continue execution regardless of whether the host clears the exception. If a specific exception class is masked and that exception occurs, however, the 8087 will post the exception in the status register and perform an on-chip default exception handling procedure, thereby allowing processing to continue. The exceptions that the 8087 detects are the following:

1. INVALID OPERATION: Stack overflow, stack underflow, indeterminate form (0/0, $\infty - \infty$, etc.) or the use of a Non-Number (NAN) as an operand. An exponent value is reserved and any bit pattern with this value in the exponent field is termed a Non-Number and causes this exception. If this exception is masked, the 8087's default response is to generate a specific NAN called IN-DEFINITE, or to propagate already existing NANs as the calculation result.

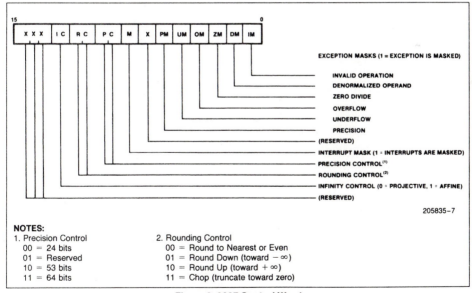

NOTES:

1. Precision Control	2. Rounding Control
00 = 24 bits	00 = Round to Nearest or Even
01 = Reserved	01 = Round Down (toward $-\infty$)
10 = 53 bits	10 = Round Up (toward $+\infty$)
11 = 64 bits	11 = Chop (truncate toward zero)

Figure 9. 8087 Control Word

2. OVERFLOW: The result is too large in magnitude to fit the specified format. The 8087 will generate an encoding for infinity if this exception is masked.

3. ZERO DIVISOR: The divisor is zero while the dividend is a non-infinite, non-zero number. Again, the 8087 will generate an encoding for infinity if this exception is masked.

4. UNDERFLOW: The result is non-zero but too small in magnitude to fit in the specified format. If this exception is masked the 8087 will denormal-ize (shift right) the fraction until the exponent is in range. This process is called gradual underflow.

5. DENORMALIZED OPERAND: At least one of the operands or the result is denormalized; it has the smallest exponent but a non-zero significand. Normal processing continues if this exception is masked off.

6. INEXACT RESULT: If the true result is not exactly representable in the specified format, the result is rounded according to the rounding mode, and this flag is set. If this exception is masked, processing will simply continue.

ABSOLUTE MAXIMUM RATINGS*

Ambient Temperature Under Bias . . . . . . 0°C to 70°C

Storage Temperature . . . . -65°C to $+150$°C

Voltage on Any Pin with
Respect to Ground . . . . -1.0V to $+7$V

Power Dissipation . . . . 3.0 Watt

NOTICE: This is a production data sheet. The specifi-cations are subject to change without notice.

*WARNING: Stressing the device beyond the "Absolute Maximum Ratings" may cause permanent damage. These are stress ratings only. Operation beyond the "Operating Conditions" is not recommended and ex-tended exposure beyond the "Operating Conditions" may affect device reliability.

D.C. CHARACTERISTICS T_A = 0°C to 70°C, V_{CC} = 5V ±5%

Symbol	Parameter	Min	Max	Units	Test Conditions
V_{IL}	Input Low Voltage	-0.5	0.8	V	
V_{IH}	Input High Voltage	2.0	$V_{CC} + 0.5$	V	
V_{OL}	Output Low Voltage (Note 8)		0.45	V	I_{OL} = 2.5 mA
V_{OH}	Output High Voltage	2.4		V	I_{OH} = $-400\,\mu$A
I_{CC}	Power Supply Current		475	mA	T_A = 25°C
I_{LI}	Input Leakage Current		± 10	μA	$0V \leq V_{IN} \leq V_{CC}$
I_{LO}	Output Leakage Current		± 10	μA	T_A = 25°C
V_{CL}	Clock Input Low Voltage	-0.5	0.6	V	
V_{CH}	Clock Input High Voltage	3.9	$V_{CC} + 1.0$	V	
C_{IN}	Capacitance of Inputs		10	pF	fc = 1 MHz
C_{IO}	Capacitance of I/O Buffer (AD0–15, A_{16}–A_{19}, BHE, S2–S0, RQ/GT) and CLK		15	pF	fc = 1 MHz
C_{OUT}	Capacitance of Outputs BUSY INT		10	pF	fc = 1 MHz

A.C. CHARACTERISTICS T_A = 0°C to 70°C, V_{CC} = 5V ±5%

TIMING REQUIREMENTS

Symbol	Parameter	8087		8087-2		8087-1 (See Note 7)		Units	Test Conditions
		Min	Max	Min	Max	Min	Max		
TCLCL	CLK Cycle Period	200	500	125	500	100	500	ns	
TCLCH	CLK Low Time	118		68		53		ns	
TCHCL	CLK High Time	69		44		39		ns	
TCH1CH2	CLK Rise Time		10		10		15	ns	From 1.0V to 3.5V
TCL2CL2	CLK Fall Time		10		10		15	ns	From 3.5V to 1.0V
TDVCL	Data In Setup Time	30		20		15		ns	
TCLDX	Data In Hold Time	10		10		10		ns	
TRYHCH	READY Setup Time	118		68		53		ns	
TCHRYX	READY Hold Time	30		20		5		ns	
TRYLCL	READY Inactive to CLK (Note 6)	−8		−8		−10		ns	
TGVCH	RQ/GT Setup Time (Note 8)	30		15		15		ns	
TCHGX	RQ/GT Hold Time	40		30		20		ns	
TQVCL	QS0−1 Setup Time (Note 8)	30		30		30		ns	
TCLQX	QS0−1 Hold Time	10		10		5		ns	
TSACH	Status Active Setup Time	30		30		30		ns	
TSNCL	Status Inactive Setup Time	30		30		30		ns	
TILIH	Input Rise Time (Except CLK)		20		20		20	ns	From 0.8V to 2.0V
TIHIL	Input Fall Time (Except CLK)		12		12		15	ns	From 2.0V to 0.8V

TIMING RESPONSES

Symbol	Parameter	8087		8087-2		8087-1 (See Note 7)		Units	Test Conditions
		Min	Max	Min	Max	Min	Max		
TCLML	Command Active Delay (Notes 1, 2)	10/0	35/70	10/0	35/70	10/0	35/70	ns	C_L = 20–100 pF for all 8087 Outputs (in addition to 8087 self-load)
TCLMH	Command Inactive Delay (Notes 1, 2)	10/0	35/55	10/0	35/55	10/0	35/70	ns	
TRYHSH	Ready Active to Status Passive (Note 5)		110		65		45	ns	
TCHSV	Status Active Delay	10	110	10	60	10	45	ns	
TCLSH	Status Inactive Delay	10	130	10	70	10	55	ns	
TCLAV	Address Valid Delay	10	110	10	60	10	55	ns	
TCLAX	Address Hold Time	10		10		10		ns	

A.C. CHARACTERISTICS $T_A = 0°C$ to $70°C$, $V_{CC} = 5V \pm 5\%$ (Continued)

TIMING RESPONSES (Continued)

Symbol	Parameter	8087		8087-2		8087-1 (See Note 7)		Units	Test Conditions
		Min	Max	Min	Max	Min	Max		
TCLAZ	Address Float Delay	TCLAX	80	TCLAX	50	TCLAX	45	ns	$C_L = 20-100$ pF for all 8087 Outputs (in addition to 8087 self-load)
TSVLH	Status Valid to ALE High (Notes 1, 2)		15/30		15/30		15/30	ns	
TCLLH	CLK Low to ALE Valid (Notes 1, 2)		15/30		15/30		15/30	ns	
TCHLL	ALE Inactive Delay (Notes 1, 2)		15/30		15/30		15/30	ns	
TCLDV	Data Valid Delay	10	110	10	60	10	50	ns	
TCHDX	Status Hold Time	10		10		10	45	ns	
TCLDOX	Data Hold Time	10		10		10		ns	
TCVNV	Control Active Delay (Notes 1, 3)	5	45	5	45	5	45	ns	
TCVNX	Control Inactive Delay (Notes 1, 3)	10	45	10	45	10	45	ns	
TCHBV	BUSY and INT Valid Delay	10	150	10	85	10	65	ns	
TCHDTL	Direction Control Active Delay (Notes 1, 3)		50		50		50	ns	
TCHDTH	Direction Control Inactive Delay (Notes 1, 3)		30		30		30	ns	
TSVDTV	STATUS to DT/$\overline{R}$ Delay (Notes 1, 4)	0	30	0	30	0	30	ns	
TCLDTV	DT/$\overline{R}$ Active Delay (Notes 1, 4)	0	55	0	55	0	55	ns	
TCHDNV	$\overline{DEN}$ Active Delay (Notes 1, 4)	0	55	0	55	0	55	ns	
TCHDNX	$\overline{DEN}$ Inactive Delay (Notes 1, 4)	5	55	5	55	5	55	ns	
TCLGL	RQ/GT Active Delay (Note 8)	0	85	0	50	0	38	ns	$C_L = 40$ pF (in addition to 8087 self-load)
TCLGH	RQ/GT Inactive Delay	0	85	0	50	0	45	ns	
TOLOH	Output Rise Time		20		20		15	ns	From 0.8V to 2.0V
TOHOL	Output Fall Time		12		12		12	ns	From 2.0V to 0.8V

NOTES:
1. Signal at 8284A, 8288, or 82188 shown for reference only.
2. 8288 timing/82188 timing.
3. 8288 timing.
4. 82188 timing.
5. Applies only to T_3 and wait states.
6. Applies only to T_2 state (8 ns into T_3).
7. IMPORTANT SYSTEM CONSIDERATION: Some 8087-1 timing parameters are constrained relative to the corresponding 8086-1 specifications. Therefore, 8086-1 systems incorporating the 8087-1 should be designed with the 8087-1 specifications.
8. Changes since last revision.

A.C. TESTING INPUT, OUTPUT WAVEFORM

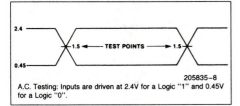

205835-8

A.C. Testing: Inputs are driven at 2.4V for a Logic "1" and 0.45V for a Logic "0".

A.C. TESTING LOAD CIRCUIT

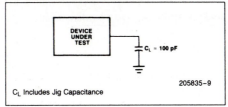

205835-9

C_L Includes Jig Capacitance

WAVEFORMS

MASTER MODE (with 8288 references)

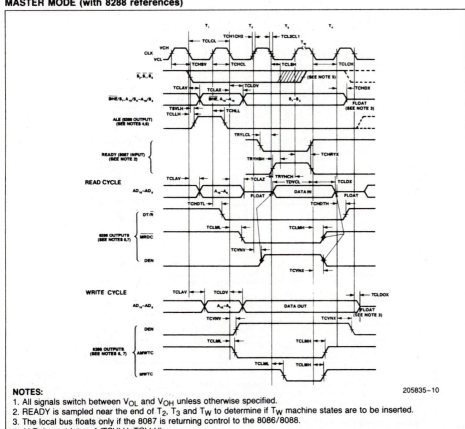

205835-10

NOTES:
1. All signals switch between V_{OL} and V_{OH} unless otherwise specified.
2. READY is sampled near the end of T_2, T_3 and T_W to determine if T_W machine states are to be inserted.
3. The local bus floats only if the 8087 is returning control to the 8086/8088.
4. ALE rises at later of (TSVLH, TCLLH).
5. Status inactive in state just prior to T_4.
6. Signals at 8284A or 8288 are shown for reference only.
7. The issuance of 8288 command and control signals ($\overline{MRDC}$, ($\overline{MWTC}$, $\overline{AMWC}$, and DEN) lags the active high 8288 CEN.
8. All timing measurements are made at 1.5V unless otherwise noted.

461

WAVEFORMS (Continued)

MASTER MODE (with 82188 references)

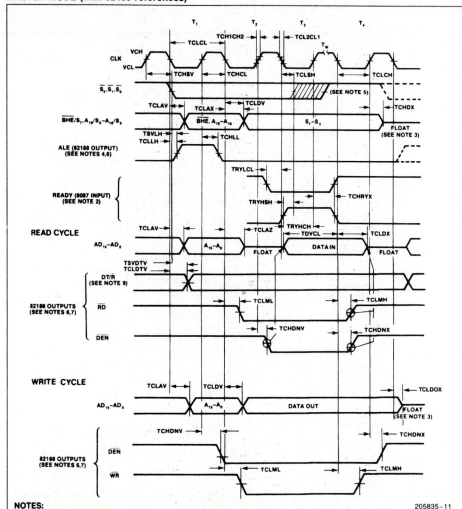

205835-11

NOTES:
1. All signals switch between V_{OL} and V_{OH} unless otherwise specified.
2. READY is sampled near the end of T_2, T_3 and T_W to determine if T_W machine states are to be inserted.
3. The local bus floats only if the 8087 is returning control to the 80186/80188.
4. ALE rises at later of (TSVLH, TCLLH).
5. Status inactive in state just prior to T_4.
6. Signals at 8284A or 82188 are shown for reference only.
7. The issuance of 8288 command and control signals ($\overline{MRDC}$, ($\overline{MWTC}$, $\overline{AMWC}$, and DEN) lags the active high 8288 CEN.
8. All timing measurements are made at 1.5V unless otherwise noted.
9. DT/$\overline{R}$ becomes valid at the later of (TSVDTV, TCLDTV).

WAVEFORMS (Continued)

PASSIVE MODE

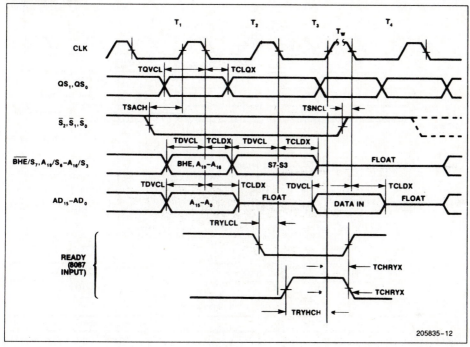

205835–12

RESET TIMING

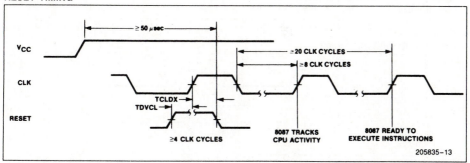

205835–13

WAVEFORMS (Continued)

REQUEST/GRANT₀ TIMING

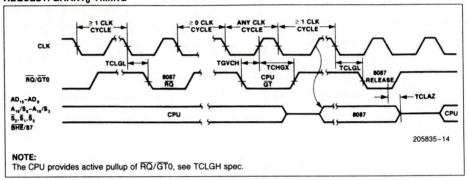

205835–14

NOTE:
The CPU provides active pullup of RQ/GT0, see TCLGH spec.

REQUEST/GRANT₁ TIMING

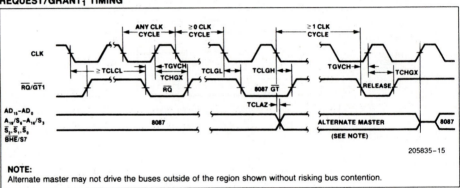

205835–15

NOTE:
Alternate master may not drive the buses outside of the region shown without risking bus contention.

BUSY AND INTERRUPT TIMING

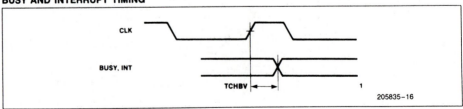

205835–16

Table 5. 8087 Extensions to the 86/186 Instructions Sets

Data Transfer		Optional 8,16 Bit Displacement	Clock Count Range 32 Bit Real	32 Bit Integer	64 Bit Real	16 Bit Integer
FLD = LOAD	MF =		00	01	10	11
Integer/Real Memory to ST(0)	ESCAPE MF 1 | MOD 0 0 0 R/M	DISP	38–56 +EA	52–60 +EA	40–60 +EA	46–54 +EA
Long Integer Memory to ST(0)	ESCAPE 1 1 1 | MOD 1 0 1 R/M	DISP	60–68 + EA			
Temporary Real Memory to ST(0)	ESCAPE 0 1 1 | MOD 1 0 1 R/M	DISP	53–65 + EA			
BCD Memory to ST(0)	ESCAPE 1 1 1 | MOD 1 0 0 R/M	DISP	290–310 + EA			
ST(i) to ST(0)	ESCAPE 0 0 1 | 1 1 0 0 0 ST(i)		17–22			
FST = STORE						
ST(0) to Integer/Real Memory	ESCAPE MF 1 | MOD 0 1 0 R/M	DISP	84–90 +EA	82–92 +EA	96–104 +EA	80–90 +EA
ST(0) to ST(i)	ESCAPE 1 0 1 | 1 1 0 1 0 ST(i)		15–22			
FSTP = STORE AND POP						
ST(0) to Integer/Real Memory	ESCAPE MF 1 | MOD 0 1 1 R/M	DISP	86–92 +EA	84–94 +EA	98–106 +EA	82–92 +EA
ST(0) to Long Integer Memory	ESCAPE 1 1 1 | MOD 1 1 1 R/M	DISP	94–105 + EA			
ST(0) to Temporary Real Memory	ESCAPE 0 1 1 | MOD 1 1 1 R/M	DISP	52–58 + EA			
ST(0) to BCD Memory	ESCAPE 1 1 1 | MOD 1 1 0 R/M	DISP	520–540 + EA			
ST(0) to ST(i)	ESCAPE 1 0 1 | 1 1 0 1 1 ST(i)		17–24			
FXCH = Exchange ST(i) and ST(0)	ESCAPE 0 0 1 | 1 1 0 0 1 ST(i)		10–15			
Comparison						
FCOM = Compare						
Integer/Real Memory to ST(0)	ESCAPE MF 0 | MOD 0 1 0 R/M	DISP	60–70 +EA	78–91 +EA	65–75 +EA	72–86 +EA
ST(i) to ST(0)	ESCAPE 0 0 0 | 1 1 0 1 0 ST(i)		40–50			
FCOMP = Compare and Pop						
Integer/Real Memory to ST(0)	ESCAPE MF 0 | MOD 0 1 1 R/M	DISP	63–73 +EA	80–93 +EA	67–77 +EA	74–88 +EA
ST(i) to ST(0)	ESCAPE 0 0 0 | 1 1 0 1 1 ST(i)		45–52			
FCOMPP = Compare ST(1) to ST(0) and Pop Twice	ESCAPE 1 1 0 | 1 1 0 1 1 0 0 1		45–55			
FTST = Test ST(0)	ESCAPE 0 0 1 | 1 1 1 0 0 1 0 0		38–48			
FXAM = Examine ST(0)	ESCAPE 0 0 1 | 1 1 1 0 0 1 0 1		12–23			

205835–17

465

Table 5. 8087 Extensions to the 86/186 Instructions Sets (Continued)

Constants			Optional 8,16 Bit Displacement	Clock Count Range			
				32 Bit Real	32 Bit Integer	64 Bit Real	16 Bit Integer
	MF	=		00	01	10	11
FLDZ = LOAD + 0.0 into ST(0)	ESCAPE 0 0 1	1 1 1 0 1 1 1 0		11–17			
FLD1 = LOAD + 1.0 into ST(0)	ESCAPE 0 0 1	1 1 1 0 1 0 0 0		15–21			
FLDPI = LOAD π into ST(0)	ESCAPE 0 0 1	1 1 1 0 1 0 1 1		16–22			
FLDL2T = LOAD $\log_2 10$ into ST(0)	ESCAPE 0 0 1	1 1 1 0 1 0 0 1		16–22			
FLDL2E = LOAD $\log_2 e$ into ST(0)	ESCAPE 0 0 1	1 1 1 0 1 0 1 0		15–21			
FLDLG2 = LOAD $\log_{10} 2$ into ST(0)	ESCAPE 0 0 1	1 1 1 0 1 1 0 0		18–24			
FLDLN2 = LOAD $\log_e 2$ into ST(0)	ESCAPE 0 0 1	1 1 1 0 1 1 0 1		17–23			

Arithmetic

FADD = Addition

Integer/Real Memory with ST(0)	ESCAPE MF 0	MOD 0 0 0 R/M	DISP	90–120 + EA	108–143 + EA	95–125 + EA	102–137 + EA
ST(i) and ST(0)	ESCAPE d P 0	1 1 0 0 0 ST(i)		70–100 (Note 1)			

FSUB = Subtraction

Integer/Real Memory with ST(0)	ESCAPE MF 0	MOD 1 0 R R/M	DISP	90–120 + EA	108–143 + EA	95–125 + EA	102–137 + EA
ST(i) and ST(0)	ESCAPE d P 0	1 1 1 0 R R/M		70–100 (Note 1)			

FMUL = Multiplication

Integer/Real Memory with ST(0)	ESCAPE MF 0	MOD 0 0 1 R/M	DISP	110–125 + EA	130–144 + EA	112–168 + EA	124–138 + EA
ST(i) and ST(0)	ESCAPE d P 0	1 1 0 0 1 R/M		90–145 (Note 1)			

FDIV = Division

Integer/Real Memory with ST(0)	ESCAPE MF 0	MOD 1 1 R R/M	DISP	215–225 + EA	230–243 + EA	220–230 + EA	224–238 + EA
ST(i) and ST(0)	ESCAPE d P 0	1 1 1 1 R R/M		193–203 (Note 1)			

FSQRT = Square Root of ST(0)	ESCAPE 0 0 1	1 1 1 1 1 0 1 0		180–186			
FSCALE = Scale ST(0) by ST(1)	ESCAPE 0 0 1	1 1 1 1 1 1 0 1		32–38			
FPREM = Partial Remainder of ST(0) ÷ ST(1)	ESCAPE 0 0 1	1 1 1 1 1 0 0 0		15–190			
FRNDINT = Round ST(0) to Integer	ESCAPE 0 0 1	1 1 1 1 1 1 0 0		16–50			

205835–18

NOTE:
1. If P = 1 then add 5 clocks.

8087

Table 5. 8087 Extensions to the 86/186 Instructions Sets (Continued)

Instruction	Encoding	Optional 8,16 Bit Displacement	Clock Count Range
FXTRACT – Extract Components of St(0)	ESCAPE 0 0 1 | 1 1 1 1 0 1 0 0		27–55
FABS = Absolute Value of ST(0)	ESCAPE 0 0 1 | 1 1 1 0 0 0 0 1		10–17
FCHS = Change Sign of ST(0)	ESCAPE 0 0 1 | 1 1 1 0 0 0 0 0		10–17

Transcendental

Instruction	Encoding	Optional 8,16 Bit Displacement	Clock Count Range
FPTAN = Partial Tangent of ST(0)	ESCAPE 0 0 1 | 1 1 1 1 0 0 1 0		30–540
FPATAN = Partial Arctangent of ST(0) ÷ ST(1)	ESCAPE 0 0 1 | 1 1 1 1 0 0 1 1		250–800
F2XM1 = $2^{ST(0)}$ – 1	ESCAPE 0 0 1 | 1 1 1 1 0 0 0 0		310–630
FYL2X = $ST(1) \cdot Log_2$ |ST(0)|	ESCAPE 0 0 1 | 1 1 1 1 0 0 0 1		900–1100
FYL2XP1 = $ST(1) \cdot Log_2$ [ST(0) +1]	ESCAPE 0 0 1 | 1 1 1 1 1 0 0 1		700–1000

Processor Control

Instruction	Encoding	Optional 8,16 Bit Displacement	Clock Count Range
FINIT = Initialized 8087	ESCAPE 0 1 1 | 1 1 1 0 0 0 1 1		2–8
FENI = Enable Interrupts	ESCAPE 0 1 1 | 1 1 1 0 0 0 0 0		2–8
FDISI = Disable Interrupts	ESCAPE 0 1 1 | 1 1 1 0 0 0 0 1		2–8
FLDCW = Load Control Word	ESCAPE 0 0 1 | MOD 1 0 1 R/M	DISP	7–14 + EA
FSTCW = Store Control Word	ESCAPE 0 0 1 | MOD 1 1 1 R/M	DISP	12–18 + EA
FSTSW = Store Status Word	ESCAPE 1 0 1 | MOD 1 1 1 R/M	DISP	12–18 + EA
FCLEX = Clear Exceptions	ESCAPE 0 1 1 | 1 1 1 0 0 0 1 0		2–8
FSTENV = Store Environment	ESCAPE 0 0 1 | MOD 1 1 0 R/M	DISP	40–50 + EA
FLDENV = Load Environment	ESCAPE 0 0 1 | MOD 1 0 0 R/M	DISP	35–45 + EA
FSAVE = Save State	ESCAPE 1 0 1 | MOD 1 1 0 R/M	DISP	197–207 + EA
FRSTOR = Restore State	ESCAPE 1 0 1 | MOD 1 0 0 R/M	DISP	197–207 + EA
FINCSTP = Increment Stack Pointer	ESCAPE 0 0 1 | 1 1 1 1 0 1 1 1		6–12
FDECSTP = Decrement Stack Pointer	ESCAPE 0 0 1 | 1 1 1 1 0 1 1 0		6–12

205835–19

Table 5. 8087 Extensions to the 86/186 Instructions Sets (Continued)

		Clock Count Range
FFREE = Free ST(i)	ESCAPE 1 0 1 1 1 0 0 0 ST(i)	9–16
FNOP = No Operation	ESCAPE 0 0 1 1 1 0 1 0 0 0 0	10–16
FWAIT = CPU Wait for 8087	1 0 0 1 1 0 1 1	3 + 5n*
		205835–20

*n = number of times CPU examines TEST line before 8087 lowers BUSY.

NOTES:
1. if mod = 00 then DISP = 0*, disp-low and disp-high are absent
   if mod = 01 then DISP = disp-low sign-extended to 16-bits, disp-high is absent
   if mod = 10 then DISP = disp-high; disp-low
   if mod = 11 then r/m is treated as an ST(i) field
2. if r/m = 000 then EA = (BX) + (SI) + DISP
   if r/m = 001 then EA = (BX) + (DI) + DISP
   if r/m = 010 then EA = (BP) + (SI) + DISP
   if r/m = 011 then EA = (BP) + (DI) + DISP
   if r/m = 100 then EA = (SI) + DISP
   if r/m = 101 then EA = (DI) + DISP
   if r/m = 110 then EA = (BP) + DISP
   if r/m = 111 then EA = (BX) + DISP
   *except if mod = 000 and r/m = 110 then EA = disp-high; disp-low.
3. MF = Memory Format
       00–32-bit Real
       01–32-bit Integer
       10–64-bit Real
       11–16-bit Integer
4. ST(0) = Current stack top
   ST(i) = i^{th} register below stack top
5. d = Destination
       0—Destination is ST(0)
       1—Destination is ST(i)
6. P = Pop
       0—No pop
       1—Pop ST(0)
7. R = Reverse: When d = 1 reverse the sense of R
       0—Destination (op) Source
       1—Source (op) Destination
8. For **FSQRT:** $-0 \leq ST(0) \leq +\infty$
   For **FSCALE:** $-2^{15} \leq ST(1) < +2^{15}$ and ST(1) integer
   For **F2XM1:** $0 \leq ST(0) \leq 2^{-1}$
   For **FYL2X:** $0 < ST(0) < \infty$
                       $-\infty < ST(1) < +\infty$
   For **FYL2XP1:** $0 \leq |ST(0)| < (2 - \sqrt{2})/2$
                       $-\infty < ST(1) < \infty$
   For **FPTAN:** $0 \leq ST(0) \leq \pi/4$
   For **FPATAN:** $0 \leq ST(0) < ST(1) < +\infty$

D

The 8085 Microprocessor:
A Historical Perspective

D.1 INTRODUCTION

Discussion of an older 8-bit machine like the 8085 is important so as to maintain a historical perspective about the evolution of microprocessors. Intel introduced the 8085 about the same time that other 8-bit CPUs, such as Motorola's 6800, became available. The ease of use and large peripheral support of the 8085 made it an ideal teaching CPU, and many colleges adopted it for use in the classroom. This appendix is not intended to be a detailed reference on the 8085, but merely a review of its functions for those already familiar with it, and a source of information for those unfamiliar with it. Whoever the reader, the ultimate goal is to compare the features of the 8085 with those of the 8088.

D.2 THE SOFTWARE MODEL OF THE 8085

Figure D.1 shows the internal register structure of the 8085 microprocessor. Six general purpose registers (B, C, D, E, H, and L) and an accumulator (A) are available for use by the programmer. The accumulator is a special 8-bit register used by many of the 8085's arithmetic and logical instructions. The other six registers are also 8 bits in length. Some instructions are designed to use pairs of registers, making some 16-bit operations possible. When this is done, we have a choice of using the BC register pair, the DE pair, or the HL pair. B, D, and H are the most significant byte of each register pair. As an example, suppose that the hexadecimal value 3FA8 must be stored for use by our program. A convenient place to put this value is into one of the register pairs. If 3FA8 was stored in register pair BC, register B would contain 3F (the upper 8 bits) and register C would contain A8.

The use of many internal registers in the 8085 is very helpful when writing complicated programs.

FIGURE D.1 Software model of the 8085

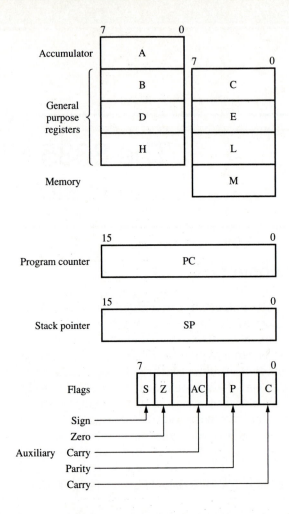

The 8085 also contains two 16-bit registers. Each 16-bit register serves a specific purpose. The *program counter* (PC) contains the address of the memory location where the next instruction will be fetched from. Since the program counter is 16 bits wide, its range of addresses goes from 0000 to FFFF. This corresponds to 65,536 (2 raised to the 16th power) different addresses. Thus, the 8085 is capable of accessing 64KB of memory. Any single one of these memory locations can be thought of as the contents of register M (for *memory*). The 8085 automatically updates the contents of the program counter to ensure proper program execution.

The other 16-bit register is the *stack pointer* (SP). The stack pointer is used to maintain the address of the area in memory commonly called a stack. The stack is used to store temporary data values such as subroutine return addresses. The 8085 uses the stack pointer to go to the correct memory locations when it needs to read or write stack information As it does in the 8088, the stack builds towards zero. As new items get stored on the stack the address in the stack pointer gets smaller. To prevent a stack from overwriting a program, the program is usually loaded into memory at a low starting address (usually the beginning of usable RAM), with the stack pointer initialized to a much higher address (near the end of RAM).

One other register is available for limited use and testing by the programmer: the *flag* register. Flags are 1-bit status indicators that show how conditions inside the 8085 have changed as a result of previous instruction execution. For example, if a decrement instruction (such as DCR B) reduces the number in a register (B) to zero, the *zero flag* is set. The flags are tested by certain instructions called **conditional** instructions.

D.3   A FUNCTIONAL DESCRIPTION OF THE 8085

Before we examine the instruction set of the 8085 it would be wise to review the operation of all its input and output signals. Indeed, we often grasp the theory behind an instruction by knowing how it affects one of the processor's signals. In this section we will briefly survey the hardware operation of the 8085.

AD_0-AD_7, A_8-A_{15}

Figure D.2 shows a diagram containing all input and output signals utilized by the 8085. The 16-bit address bus is contained in two groups of signals. The

FIGURE D.2   8085 input/output signals

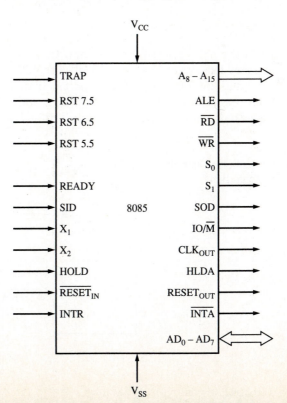

upper half of the address bus is output by the processor as A_8 through A_{15}. The other half of the address bus is mixed with the 8-bit bidirectional data bus. The resulting combination is called AD_0 through AD_7. We commonly refer to this type of architecture as a multiplexed *address/data bus*. During execution of a program there are times when AD_0 through AD_7 represent A_0 through A_7 (the lower half of the address bus), and times when they represent D_0 through D_7 (the bidirectional data bus). The use of the multiplexed bus reduces the number of connections that need to be made to the chip, but also unfortunately slows down program execution slightly, since address and data information cannot exist on the multiplexed bus at the same time.

ALE

How does the external circuitry connected to the 8085 know when AD_0-AD_7 is an address bus? How does it know when AD_0-AD_7 is a data bus? An additional signal, ALE, meaning *address latch enable*, is also output by the processor. When ALE becomes active it is an indication to external circuitry that the lower address byte must be captured from AD_0-AD_7. Usually an 8-bit latch is used to store the lower half of the address bus. When ALE is not active (when it is low), it is assumed that AD_0-AD_7 represent D_0-D_7. An example of how A_0-A_7 may be captured can be seen in Figure D.3, where a 74LS373 is used to capture and hold the lower half of the address bus.

IO/$\overline{\text{M}}$

From the previous section we know that the 8085 is capable of accessing 64K memory locations. More specifically, the 8085 can access 65,536 memory locations and 256 I/O ports. An I/O port is little different from a memory location, from the standpoint of simply reading and writing to it. However, the hardware that makes an I/O port work is different from the devices used to make a

FIGURE D.3 Demultiplexing the 8085's address/data bus

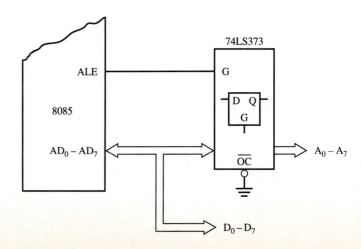

memory. Input ports require buffers to gate input data onto the data bus. Output ports require latches to store output data from the data bus.

The range of allowable memory addresses is 0000 to FFFF. The range of allowable port addresses is 00 to FF. Memory address 0078 is not the same as port address 78, even though the processor uses A_0 through A_7 to point to each of them. The 8085 has an unusual way of using its signals to do a couple of different things. In order for us to distinguish between memory and port addresses that appear on A_0-A_7, the 8085 supplies the IO/$\overline{\text{M}}$ signal. The name is short for *input-output/memory* and the operation is very simple. If the 8085 is accessing a memory location, IO/$\overline{\text{M}}$ will be low. If the 8085 is accessing an I/O port, IO/$\overline{\text{M}}$ will be high. This is a way of telling external circuitry to use A_0-A_7 differently when IO/$\overline{\text{M}}$ is high.

This type of architecture (which we see used on the 8088 microprocessor as well) is nothing more than a clever way of getting the processor to do as many things as possible with as few IC pins as possible.

$\overline{\text{RD}}$ and $\overline{\text{WR}}$

Now that we can access a memory or I/O location, how do we read its data, or write new data to it? The 8085 provides two additional signals for this purpose. $\overline{\text{RD}}$ (read) is used to read data into the processor. $\overline{\text{WR}}$ (write) is used to store the contents of the data bus in the selected location. Both signals are active when they are low. Normally, $\overline{\text{RD}}$ and $\overline{\text{WR}}$ are high, indicating that the 8085 is neither reading nor writing. Figure D.4 shows how IO/$\overline{\text{M}}$, $\overline{\text{RD}}$, and $\overline{\text{WR}}$ are combined to generate memory and I/O read and write signals.

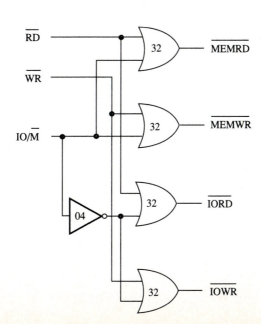

FIGURE D.4 Decoding memory and I/O read/write signals

S$_0$ and S$_1$

Two status signals are output to let external circuitry know what the 8085 is doing. S$_0$ and S$_1$ are used for this purpose. When S$_0$ and S$_1$ are both low, the processor is indicating that it has halted. Can you imagine why we might want to know something like this if the 8085 is being used to control the engine speed in our car? S$_0$ and S$_1$ have three other states that signify *write*, *read*, and *fetch* operations. Most of the time we can do without the status signals.

SOD

A neat feature of the 8085 is its SOD line. SOD stands for *serial output data* and is really a 1-bit output port. Do you need to control a relay or flash a light? Would you like to stimulate speech or complex sounds through an amplifier? Having a 1-bit output port built right into the chip eliminates the need for external circuitry to do the same thing. It is not uncommon, when the 8085 is used in a control application, for only one thing to be controlled. Turning a relay on and off, or flashing a LED can be easily accomplished with SOD. An early video game used SOD to generate game sounds via multifrequency square waves. How interesting!

CLKout, X$_1$, and X$_2$

CLKout is provided to assist in operating the external circuitry at the same speed as the processor. This is important when UARTs are used for serial data communication. The frequency of CLKout is exactly one-half of the frequency generated by a crystal connected to X$_1$ and X$_2$. For example, if a 4-MHz crystal is connected to X$_1$ and X$_2$, CLKout will be 2-MHz. It is important to use a crystal to control the timing in any microprocessor. In the case of the 8085, the internal rate at which the processor performs its functions is also one-half of the crystal frequency.

RESET-IN and RESET-OUT

It is very important to start the processor off at the right point after a power-on sequence. The RESET-IN input is used for this purpose. RESET-IN must be pulled low for a certain number of clock cycles to initialize the processor. The processor's interrupt and hold circuitry will be cleared and the program counter set to 0000. Thus, after a reset operation, the first instruction will be fetched from address 0000. This is a very important point and the reason why machines based on the 8085 usually have EPROM in the beginning of the 8085's address space. There must be intelligence (a valid instruction) at address 0000 because that is where the processor looks first!

RESET-OUT will be active while the CPU is being reset and can be used to initialize external circuitry in the system.

HOLD and HLDA

If execution must be suspended temporarily, the HOLD input is used to place the 8085 into a wait state. While the 8085 is waiting it will tristate its address and data busses and other control signals, such as $\overline{RD}$, $\overline{WR}$, ALE, and IO/$\overline{M}$. HLDA (*hold acknowledge*) is active when the CPU is in a wait state as a result of HOLD. This signal may be used to notify external circuitry that the 8085 is suspended.

READY

It is sometimes necessary to slow the processor down, without tristating its busses and control signals. This is the case when a slow memory device is interfaced with the processor. The read or write time of the memory may be so long that the processor's memory cycle must be extended. The READY input is used for this purpose. A low input on READY tells the 8085 to extend its read or write cycle until READY goes high. The external memory system controls the state of the READY line.

SID

Since SOD was used to send serial data out of the processor, SID (*serial input data*) can be used to bring it in. The state of a single pushbutton or switch can be easily sampled by connecting it to SID. A rather exotic use of SID and SOD is a software application that turns the 8085 into a UART, a device capable of transmitting and receiving serial information from a data terminal or modem.

RST5.5, RST6.5, RST7.5, TRAP, INTR, and $\overline{INTA}$

The remaining signals all deal with the interrupt mechanism of the 8085. Five external hardware interrupts are provided. Four of them may be internally disabled by software under the programmer's control. They are RST5.5, RST6.5, RST7.5, and INTR. The fifth one, TRAP, is a nonmaskable interrupt. It cannot be disabled by software and always causes the 8085 to respond when it is activated.

Both TRAP and RST7.5 are edge-sensitive inputs, whereas the others are level-sensitive.

The five interrupts each cause the 8085 to jump to a designated location in memory to begin interrupt processing. Table D.1 shows how these addresses are assigned and the priority associated with each interrupt. In the case of INTR, the address is not fixed and may be controlled by hardware. Usually a specific type of instruction is used in conjunction with INTR, resulting in a fixed address for interrupt processing. When INTR is the active interrupt, $\overline{INTA}$ (interrupt acknowledge) will go low, indicating to external circuitry that the 8085 has entered into interrupt processing.

TABLE D.1: 8085 interrupt priorities and addresses

Name	Priority	Interrupt Address
TRAP	1*	0024H
RST7.5	2	003CH
RST6.5	3	0034H
RST5.5	4	002CH
INTR	5	?

*The lowest number has the highest priority

We see how the operation of a microprocessor-based system is a complex process, totally controlled by the input and output signals of the processor.

Example D.1: Interfacing the 8085 to an EPROM

Now that we have covered the operation of the 8085's hardware signals, we can put some of them to use. We saw before that it is important to have startup intelligence (legitimate instructions stored in EPROM) located at the beginning of the 8085's address space, since the processor fetches its first instruction from 0000 after a reset. In this interfacing example a 2764 8KB EPROM is used. Since the EPROM contains 8192 locations, the processor will use address lines A_0 through A_{12} to point to a single location within the EPROM. Thirteen address lines are needed to produce the required number of binary combinations to represent all 8192 addresses. Since we want the EPROM to have its

FIGURE D.5 Interfacing a 2764 EPROM to the 8085

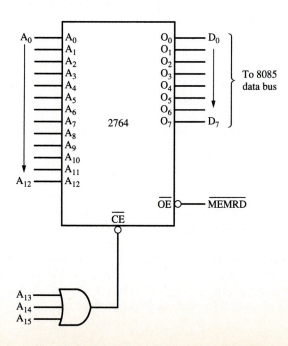

first location read when the 8085 reads address 0000, the EPROM must be enabled when address lines A_{13}, A_{14}, and A_{15} are all low. Anytime these three upper address lines are low, the EPROM will be enabled. This allows us to determine that the address range for the EPROM is from 0000 to 1FFF. Notice that this range represents 2000 hexadecimal addresses, which is exactly 8192 locations. Figure D.5 shows how the interfacing is accomplished. The lower thirteen address lines connect directly to the 2764's A_0-A_{12} inputs. The eight outputs of the 2764 connect to the 8085's data bus. The $\overline{CE}$ (*chip enable*) input of the EPROM is used to activate the EPROM whenever an address in the proper range of addresses is detected on the 8085's address bus. A three-input OR gate is used to control the EPROM, activating it only when A_{13}, A_{14}, and A_{15} are all low. To read the EPROM data, $\overline{OE}$ (*output enable*) must also be low. This input is controlled by the memory read signal $\overline{MEMRD}$ we generated in Figure D.4. Since $\overline{MEMRD}$ is used as the final activating signal we need not worry that an I/O port is being accessed—$\overline{MEMRD}$ would not be active in that case.

D.4   THE 8085 INSTRUCTION SET

In Section D.2 we examined the software model of the 8085 and learned that it contains a number of general purpose 8-bit registers (B, C, D, E, H, L, A), a flag register, and two 16-bit registers (PC and SP). In this section we will review the numerous instructions that compose the 8085's instruction set, and see how they are used to move data around, perform mathematical and logical operations, and control program behavior.

Arithmetic Instructions

The arithmetic instructions provide a simple way of adding or subtracting quantities present in registers or memory. Both 8-bit binary and BCD arithmetic is available, and some limited 16-bit operations on register pairs are allowed too. Many of the instructions affect the flags (also called **condition codes**), allowing a clever programmer to implement 9-bit arithmetic via use of the carry flag.

As you examine the different instructions it will be helpful for you to remember that "r" in an instruction operand can be *any* single register: A, B, C, D, E, H, L, or M. When M is used, the processor accesses the memory location pointed to by the HL register pair. HL is thus used in this fashion as an index register. Also, some operands are referred to as d8 or d16, which stand for 8- and 16-bit data values. Register pairs BC, DF, HL, and SP are referred to as "rp". A special register pair is called the PSW (*program status word*) and consists of the accumulator and flags. Some instructions allow a memory address to be specified in their operand fields. The symbol "adr" is used for this purpose.

The arithmetic instructions consist of the following:

ADD	r	Add register to accumulator
ADC	r	Add register plus carry to accumulator
ADI	d8	Add a byte of immediate data to accumulator
ACI	d8	Add a byte of immediate data plus carry to accumulator
SUB	r	Subtract register from accumulator
SBB	r	Subtract register and borrow from accumulator
SUI	d8	Subtract a byte of immediate data from accumulator
SBI	d8	Subtract a byte of immediate data and borrow from accumulator
INR	r	Increment register
DCR	r	Decrement register
INX	rp	Increment register pair
DCX	rp	Decrement register pair
DAD	rp	Double add register pair to HL
DAA		Decimal adjust accumulator

Examples of arithmetic instructions are:

```
ADD   B       SUB   C       INR   A
ADC   M       SBB   E       DCR   D
ADI   20H     SUI   4       INX   B
ACI   17      SBI   0A5H    DCX   H
                            DAD   D
```

Notice that register pairs in the INX, DCX, and DAD instructions are referred to by one letter only. This may cause some confusion for the beginning programmer and may take some getting used to.

Logical Instructions

The logical instructions are included to perform binary and Boolean operations on various data types. AND, OR, Exclusive OR, complements, and other operations can be performed with the logical operations. One drawback to the 8085 is that the operations always involve an entire 8-bit quantity. Newer microprocessors allow for single bits to be adjusted within a register.

The logical instructions consist of the following:

ANA	r	AND accumulator with register
ANI	d8	AND accumulator with a byte of immediate data
XRA	r	Exclusive-OR accumulator with register
XRI	d8	Exclusive-OR accumulator with a byte of immediate data
ORA	r	OR accumulator with register
ORI	d8	OR accumulator with a byte of immediate data

CMP	r	Compare register with accumulator
CPI	d8	Compare accumulator with a byte of immediate data
RLC		Rotate accumulator left
RRC		Rotate accumulator right
RAL		Rotate accumulator left through carry
RAR		Rotate accumulator right through carry
CMA		Complement accumulator
CMC		Complement carry flag
STC		Set carry flag

Examples of logical instructions are:

```
ANA   H      XRA   L      ORA   A
ANI   OFH    XRI   80H    CMP   B
                          CPI   10
```

Data Transfer Instructions

This group of instructions lets the programmer move data around inside the 8085, between registers, and also between the 8085 and its memory. There are instructions for loading registers with 8- and 16-bit data values, instructions for swapping data between registers, and many that work specifically with the accumulator. Since many arithmetic and logical instructions place their results into the accumulator, it is nice to have many ways to move the contents of the accumulator around.

Some of the data transfer instructions use two operands. In these instructions the first operand is the destination and the second operand is the source (e.g., *to, from*).

The data transfer instructions consist of the following:

MOV	r1,r2	Move data from register 2 to register 1
MVI	r,d8	Move a byte of immediate data into register
LXI	rp,d16	Move two bytes of immediate data into a register pair
LDA	adr	Load accumulator from memory location
STA	adr	Store accumulator into memory location
LHLD	adr	Load HL register pair from memory
SHLD	adr	Store register pair HL in memory
LDAX	rp	Load accumulator from memory via register pair
STAX	rp	Store accumulator in memory via register pair
XCHG		Swap contents of DE and HL

In the case of LDAX and STAX, only the BC and DE register pairs may be used to point to memory.

Examples of data transfer instructions are:

```
MOV  A,C     LXI  H,3000H    LHLD  1000
MOV  M,E     LDA  8C00H      SHLD  2000H
MVI  A,33H   STA  2400H      LDAX  B
MVI  M,0                     STAX  D
```

Conditional Instructions

The conditional instructions test the state of the flags and may or may not perform the desired operation. For example: JNZ TOP means to "jump if not zero to TOP." The thing that "is not zero" is the zero flag. If the last instruction to change the zero flag cleared the zero flag, a "not zero" condition results. In this case the jump will take place and execution will resume at TOP. If, however, the zero flag was set by the last instruction (possibly a DCR instruction making a register go to zero), then a "zero" condition is true, and JNZ TOP will not take place.

The conditional instructions test for eight conditions, which are:

NZ	Not zero (Z=0)	PO	Parity odd (P=0)
Z	Zero (Z=1)	PE	Parity even (P=1)
NC	No carry (C=0)	P	Plus (S=0)
C	Carry (C=1)	M	Minus (S=1)

Examples of conditional instructions are:

```
JZ   TOP    CC   SKIP   JPO  BEGIN
CNZ  TEST   JNC  OVER   RPE
RNZ                     RM
```

Conditional instructions are usually placed after instructions that modify the flags.

Machine Control Instructions

This last group of instructions contains a wide variety of operations. Unconditional calls and jumps, port input and output, operations that manipulate the stack, and others for controlling interrupts are all available.

The machine control instructions consist of the following:

JMP	adr	Unconditional jump to address
CALL	adr	Call subroutine at address
RET		Return from subroutine
RST	n	Restart. The range of n is from 0 to 7.
PCHL		Load HL into program counter (an indirect jump)
PUSH	rp	Push register pair onto stack
POP	rp	Pop register pair off stack

XTHL		Exchange top of stack with HL
SPHL		Load stack pointer with HL
IN	port	Read input port into accumulator
OUT	port	Write accumulator to output port
EI		Enable interrupts
DI		Disable interrupts
HLT		Halt processor
NOP		No operation
RIM		Read interrupt mask
SIM		Set interrupt mask

The RIM and SIM instructions are also used to read and write the data present on the SID and SOD lines. Bit 7 of the accumulator is loaded with SID data during execution of RIM, and with output to SOD during execution of SIM. The IN and OUT instructions require a port address in their operand fields. The address must be from 00 to FF hexadecimal, since only 256 ports are available. The RST instruction provides a way to call a subroutine at a fixed address. Table D.2 shows how the eight RST instructions have been assigned to specific addresses. The beauty of using a RST instruction is that only one byte is needed to store the instruction (RST   7 for example), while a CALL instruction (CALL 0038H) requires three bytes. A clever programmer will make good use of the RST instructions when many CALLs are needed, in order to cut down the size of the program.

In the next section we will see how the 8085 instructions can be used to write simple control programs.

D.5   8085 PROGRAMMING EXAMPLES

In this section we will look at three sample programs, each designed to illustrate the use of the 8085 in a simple control/testing application. The examples are kept short and simple, but still contain a good mix of instructions from all of the instruction groups covered in Section D.4.

TABLE D.2   Assigned restart addresses

Restart	Call Address
RST 0	0000H
RST 1	0008H
RST 2	0010H
RST 3	0018H
RST 4	0020H
RST 5	0028H
RST 6	0030H
RST 7	0038H

Performing EPROM Checksums

It is often important to check the entire contents of an EPROM, to ensure the correctness of its data. Checking each and every byte would unfortunately slow things down and make the test more complex. An easier method, which yields good results, is to perform a *checksum* of the EPROM. This involves adding up the data from each location (ignoring the overflow), to come up with a sum representative of the entire EPROM contents. The idea is that if a single bit changes in any location, the sum will be different and the bad EPROM recognized.

In this example, the last location in the EPROM will be used to store the 2s complement of the checksum. When the EPROM is then checked and all locations are added up, the result should be zero! Any nonzero answer means the EPROM data has changed. The routine CHKSUM will be employed to perform the test, using the carry flag upon return to indicate success or failure.

```
CHKSUM   MVI    B,0      ;initialize sum to zero
         LHLD   LAST     ;get ending EPROM address
         XCHG            ;swap ending address into DE
         LHLD   FIRST    ;get starting EPROM address
NEXT     MOV    A,B      ;move temporary sum into accumulator
         ADD    M        ;add EPROM data to accumulator
         MOV    B,A      ;save result
         INX    H        ;point to next EPROM location
         MOV    A,L      ;get lower half of EPROM address
         CMP    E        ;match with last location?
         JNZ    NEXT     ;no, continue adding
         MOV    A,H      ;get upper half of EPROM address
         CMP    D        ;match?
         JNZ    NEXT
         MOV    A,B      ;get checksum back
         ORA    A        ;set flags (Z=1 means good EPROM)
         RET
```

FIRST and LAST are reserved memory locations that must be loaded with the starting and ending EPROM locations, prior to calling CHKSUM. Using these data areas allows for testing of different size EPROMs without modifying the program.

Monitoring Temperature Levels

In this example the 8085 will be used to monitor the temperature of an industrial process. When the temperature exceeds a predetermined threshold value, a warning light will be turned on, The temperature will be monitored by the use of a thermistor, a resistor whose value changes with temperature. This change in resistance will cause a similar change in voltage, which will be converted into an 8-bit binary value via an analog-to-digital converter. This value is obtained by reading memory location 8C00. The warning indicator is a LED that can be turned on by writing a logic 1 to bit 5 of memory location 8D00. Figure D.6 shows a simple block diagram of the entire control process. The threshold value used for comparisons is stored in location THRESH.

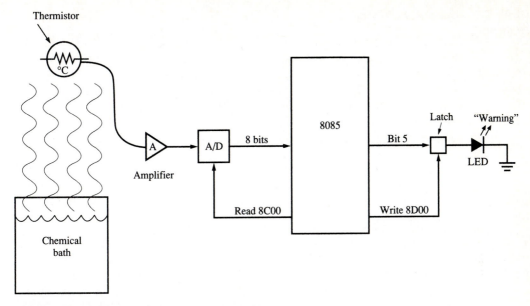

FIGURE D.6   Monitoring temperature in an industrial process

TEMPMON is designed as a continuous loop, constantly monitoring the temperature as long as the microprocessor is running.

```
TEMPMON    XRA    A         ;clear accumulator
           STA    8D00H     ;make sure LED is off
           LDA    THRESH    ;get threshold value
           MOV    C,A       ;save it in C
GETAD      LDA    8C00H     ;get A/D data (temperature reading)
           CMP    C         ;compare with threshold value
           JC     GETAD     ;if C=1 temp. is lower than threshold
           MVI    A,20H     ;bit pattern to turn on LED
           STA    8D00H     ;turn on warning LED
OVER       LDA    8C00H     ;now monitor temperature
           CMP    C         ;until it drops below threshold
           JNC    OVER
           JMP    TEMPMON
```

Keeping Time with Interrupts

In this example, we will use the 60-Hz powerline frequency as a reference for our program. The task before us is to write a routine that will issue an RST 4 once every second. One obvious application of this would be in a software clock. But dedicating the computer to the mundane chore of keeping time would be inefficient, since most of the computer's time would be spent looking for transitions on the slowly changing 60-cycle waveform. A better solution is to let the powerline frequency interrupt the computer 60 times a second, freeing up the processor for other things during times when it is not being interrupted. The interrupt service routine will keep track of the number of interrupts received

FIGURE D.7 Creating a 60-cycle reference

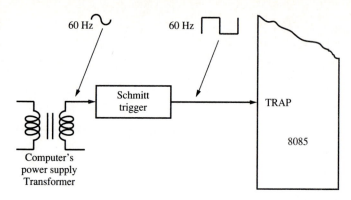

and issue the RST 4 when 60 have occurred. Figure D.7 shows a Schmitt trigger converting the sinusoidal powerline frequency into a 60-Hz square wave, which is used to trigger TRAP. The reference waveform is available on the low-voltage secondary of the transformer in the computer's power supply. The routine NMITIME uses the value contained in COUNT to keep track of the number of interrupts received. The instruction at location 0024H (see Table D.1) must jump (JMP) to the address of NMITIME. In addition, start-up software must take care of initializing COUNT to 60, for proper timekeeping.

```
NMITIME   PUSH    PSW       ;save accumulator and flags
          LDA     COUNT     ;get interrupt count
          DCR     A         ;subtract 1 from count
          JZ      ONESEC    ;have 60 occurred?
          STA     COUNT     ;no, save count
EXIT      EI                ;enable interrupts
          POP     PSW       ;restore accumulator and flags
          RET               ;resume current program
ONESEC    MVI     A,60      ;reset interrupt counter
          STA     COUNT
          RST     4         ;issue one-per-second call
          JMP     EXIT      ;and go back properly
```

D.6   THE 8085 VERSUS THE 8088

Though the 8088 is a more advanced microprocessor than the 8085, some similarities still exist between the two machines. Like the 8085, the 8088 has both a memory space and a port space, a multiplexed address/data bus, and a seemingly reversed way of writing the operands down in instructions. Even so, the 8088 is still radically different. A simple crystal cannot be used to provide a clock for the 8088. An entire integrated circuit is used for this purpose (called a clock generator). The port and memory spaces are also larger on the 8088. Up to 64K I/O-ports may be used, and up to 1024KB of memory (one *megabyte*). So, the memory space is 16 times larger than that of the 8085.

SID and SOD are no longer available in the 8088's architecture, but the processor utilizes much more powerful bus controlling circuitry, which is capable of *prefetching* instructions before they are ready to be executed (and as others are in the process of executing).

The 8088 also contains a larger instruction set, providing multiply and divide instructions among others, and a much larger set of registers, which are now 16-bits wide instead of 8 (although they can be split up into 8-bit halves). The 8088 uses an entirely different scheme of addressing than that of the 8085, requiring the use of *segment registers* and a little more work from the programmer. Where the 8085 had only five levels of interrupts, the 8088 has 256! Some are special and generated by the processor itself, such as the divide-by-zero interrupt. Unfortunately, none of the programs written for the 8085 will run on the 8088. Fortunately, the 8088 became such a popular processor after it was introduced that many thousands of programs are now available for it!